Jason Beres

SAMS Teach Yourself

Visual Studio .NET 2003 in 21 Days

SAMS
800 East 96th Street, Indianapolis, Indiana 46240 USA

Sams Teach Yourself Visual Studio .NET 2003 in 21 Days

International Standard Book Number: 0-672-32421-0

Library of Congress Catalog Card Number: 2002102792

Printed in the United States of America

First Printing: January 2003

05 5

Trademarks

Warning and Disclaimer

Associate Publisher
Michael Stephens

Acquisitions Editor
Neil Rowe

Development Editor
Mark Renfrow

Managing Editor
Charlotte Clapp

Project Editor
George Nedeff

Copy Editor
Mike Henry

Indexer
Johnna Dinse

Proofreader
Jessica McCarty

Technical Editor
Jason McCarthy

Team Coordinator
Lynne Williams

Interior Designer
Gary Adair

Cover Designer
Aren Howell

Page Layout
Juli Cook
Stacey Richwine-DeRome

Contents at a Glance

Contents

About the Author

Jason Beres is a Microsoft Certified Trainer, Microsoft Certified Solutions Developer, and a Microsoft Certified Database Administrator. He's also the Chief Technology Evangelist for Computer Ways, Inc., a Microsoft Gold Certified Partner located in Deerfield Beach, Florida.

Jason has been writing code since he was 18 years old. Starting out on IBM mainframes writing COBOL 74 code and then DEC Micro-VAX systems writing DCL and VAX-BASIC, Jason had the fortunate opportunity to be exposed to a variety of computer systems, programming languages, and business issues before dedicating his career to using and implementing solutions using Microsoft technologies.

Jason is the coauthor of *The Visual Basic .NET Bible* and *The C# Bible*, both from John Wiley and Sons. He's the technical editor of and a contributing author to *SQL 2000: The Complete Reference*, from Osborne McGraw-Hill. He's a contributing author to *ASP .NET @ Work: 10 Enterprise Applications* and *Building Components in Visual Basic .NET*, both from John Wiley and Sons.

Jason is very active in the .NET community. He started the Florida .NET Users Groups, and is a frequent speaker at .NET user group events around the country. Jason also started Non-Profit Ways, an organization that helps not-for-profit organizations get great .NET Web sites developed by user groups around the country.

In his spare time, Jason likes to read technology and sci-fi books, test out all cool software products, and he tries to never miss an episode of *Star Trek*.

About the Technical Editor

Jason McCarthy is a senior consultant specializing in Web-based and mobile applications for i3solutions in Sterling, Virginia. He has experience in both architecting and building applications using technologies such as C#, Visual Basic, .NET, Smart Device Extensions, eMbedded Visual Tools, COM/DCOM, and C++.

Acknowledgments

This book would not be a reality if it were not for the help of many patient people.

First and foremost, I would like to thank the Sams Publishing team for giving me this opportunity and for giving me the flexibility to do what I thought you needed to know about Visual Studio .NET. I would like to thank Neil Rowe for getting this project started and give special thanks to Mark Renfrow for keeping it on track and for all of his excellent help and suggestions as the book moved along. I would also like to thank Jason McCarthy who did an A+ job checking the facts of the book and making valuable suggestions along the way. George Nedeff and Mike Henry from Sams made the pages of this book sound like I understand how to write. Being a developer is a lot different from being a writer, and without their help, corrections, and changes, this book would have never made it to print.

From Computer Ways in Florida, I really want to thank Dave Noderer, Shervin Shakibi, Dave Archuleta, and Marshal Ebright, who helped me out on some key chapters. Without their assistance, this could have never happened.

I would especially like to thank Sheri Nawrocki from Computer Ways who kept me on track, read and checked every chapter, and helped me get through the time it took to get all of this done.

Last but not least, I want to thank you, the reader, for letting me try to help you out in your exploration of Visual Studio .NET. In my mind, it's the most exciting development tool on earth, and I hope that by getting through this book, you'll learn something valuable that will help you out when working and playing! Thanks for giving me your time to make that happen.

We Want to Hear from You!

As the reader of this book, *you* are our most important critic and commentator. We value your opinion and want to know what we're doing right, what we could do better, what areas you'd like to see us publish in, and any other words of wisdom you're willing to pass our way.

As an Associate Publisher for Sams, I welcome your comments. You can email or write me directly to let me know what you did or didn't like about this book—as well as what we can do to make our books better.

Please note that I cannot help you with technical problems related to the *topic* of this book. We do have a User Services group, however, where I will forward specific technical questions related to the book.

When you write, please be sure to include this book's title and author as well as your name, email address, and phone number. I will carefully review your comments and share them with the author and editors who worked on the book.

Email: `feedback@samspublishing.com`

Mail: Michael Stephens
Associate Publisher
Sams Publishing
800 East 96th Street
Indianapolis, IN 46240 USA

For more information about this book or another Sams title, visit our Web site at `www.samspublishing.com`. Type the ISBN (excluding hyphens) or the title of a book in the Search field to find the page you're looking for.

We Want to Hear from You!

Introduction

Welcome to *Sams Teach Yourself Visual Studio .NET 2003 in 21 Days*! By going through the lessons over the next 21 days, you'll learn about the key components that make up Visual Studio .NET and the .NET Framework. The .NET Framework is a colossal technology, but over the next 21 days, you'll learn how to effectively use what you need to start writing applications immediately. Throughout the book, all the code examples are in both Visual Basic .NET and C#, so if you have a preference for one language, you can implement any of the code immediately.

How This Book Is Organized

Starting with the Visual Studio .NET IDE and writing Windows and Web applications, you'll dive right into Visual Studio .NET in the first 7 days of your 21-day journey. All the concepts that you learn in Week 1 are critical to writing applications using .NET. By the end of the week, you'll understand the ins and outs of writing, testing, debugging, and deploying Windows Forms and ASP.NET applications.

In Week 2, you get into the meat of .NET and learn how to access data, work with XML, and write components. By going through the lessons in Week 2, you'll be able to write data- and component-driven applications that can be accessed from the desktop, the Web, or through XML Web services.

Week 3 introduces you to some supporting tools that ship with Visual Studio .NET, but are less well known than topics such as data access and Web services. You'll learn how to automate the Visual Studio .NET IDE with the new automation capabilities in .NET, how to write data-driven reports using Crystal Reports, and how to use Visual SourceSafe from within the Visual Studio .NET IDE. You'll also learn about some lesser known but very powerful tools that ship with Visual Studio .NET, such as the Application Center Test tool that enables you to stress test your applications. You'll also get an introduction to object role modeling using Visio, which is a conceptual data-modeling platform that integrates with Visual Studio .NET and ODBC-compliant data sources.

Each day is designed to give you the information you need to start using Visual Studio .NET right away. I can't cover every aspect of the .NET Framework, but you don't need a book like that when you're just learning the tool. Everything I've written is geared toward what you need *now*, and each day I give you links to further information online that will supplement what you learned.

Speaking of online support, the popularity and acceptance of Visual Studio .NET and the .NET Framework have created an enormous online community of informational Web sites containing tons of great articles, code samples, and complete sample applications of every aspect of .NET development that you can think of. The best online resources I've found are

- `http://www.dotnet247.com`—This site is unreal. It's a summary site that catalogs all the .NET sites on the Web, including Microsoft. Just type in a topic or keyword you're interested in, and I can almost guarantee you that all the articles on the Web related to that topic will come up in its Google search engine.
- `http://www.123aspx.com`—This site is just like the dotnet247 site, except that it relates to ASP.NET-specific information. It's a hugely important resource to have at your fingertips when you need to get information fast.
- `http://msdn.microsoft.com`—The million-page developer heaven. This site has not only thousands of .NET samples and articles, but it also covers all technologies from Microsoft, not just .NET. This should be your browser's home page, just to see what's fun and new every day for developers using Microsoft technologies.
- `http://www.angrycoder.com`—This is not a sample Web site, but rather a .NET e-zine. It's not a site you'll go to every day, but you should check it out once a month to read some of the editorial pieces and personal anecdotes of other .NET developers. At a minimum, you'll get a good laugh reading some of the pieces, which is sometimes necessary when learning new technologies.
- `http://www.gotdotnet.com`—This is Microsoft's .NET community portal. It has message boards, code uploads, and tons of samples. The best thing about this site is the .NET QuickStart tutorials are online and working, so you always have a reference place to go if you need access to the QuickStarts.
- `http://www.asp.net`—This is Microsoft's ASP.NET community Web site. This site has great links to other sites, great downloads for server controls for ASP.NET, and an extremely active message board. This is a good place to get ASP.NET questions answered.
- `www.windowsforms.net`—This is Microsoft's Windows Forms community site. I personally love Windows Forms because they provide a richer development environment for the applications than the browser does, and they can be run just like browser-based applications. So, make sure that you check out this site to get hardcore Windows Forms information.

I've been working with .NET since the alpha version. Since then, I've started a .NET user group in Florida that has grown from 30 people to more than 1,000, with monthly meetings in three different cities. So, as you start down the path of .NET, know that there is a lot of support and information out there to help you learn. You should find a user group in your area and get involved—there are many developers out there just like you. You can check out these resources for user groups in your area:

- `http://www.ineta.org`—The International .NET User Group Association was founded to help user groups around the world get the resources and information they need to spread the word about .NET. You can go to this site and search by country, region, and state to find a user group in your area.
- `http://www.fladotnet.net`—This is the user group I helped found in Florida. We have monthly meetings in Boca Raton, Miami, and Tampa, so if you're in Florida, you can go to the site and get info about the next meeting.
- `http://www.nonprofitways.net`—I helped found this organization, which enables developers to write applications for not-for-profit organizations. A lot of developers aren't using .NET at work, but they're involved with user groups and other online communities. So, a couple of friends and I decided that we could funnel some of that excitement and energy to give something back to the world. This started as something for our local user group to work on, but has grown into a worldwide community. If you want to write some .NET code in real-life applications, check out the site and get involved!

My own site will have the code samples, fixes, errors and omissions, additional stuff I forgot about, and other goodies for this book at `http://www.vbasp.net`.

About This Book

This book covers all of the important aspects of using Visual Studio .NET to write VB.NET and C# applications. Visual Studio .NET is a vast product, with many features that are not obvious. By working through each day's lesson, you will be exposed to the important information you need to use Visual Studio .NET to develop great .NET applications. To learn each feature of Visual Studio .NET, the weeks are broken up in a logical fashion, which progressively leads you from the simpler aspects of the tool to the more complicated features. By the time you have completed the three weeks, you will have all of the ammunition you need to tackle any .NET project that you need to develop.

Who Should Read This Book

This book is broken down into three groups:

- Novices

  If you are new to .NET and programming in general, nothing is taken for granted in any of the days. The programming terms used are clear and concise, and the step-by-step approach to each day's work will help you complete each code sample and exercise in the book.

- People who have used .NET

  If you have been using .NET, you will be amazed at what Visual Studio .NET can offer to rapidly develop your applications. There are many features of VS.NET that most developers do not know about, especially when it comes to using XML and the data access tools. By going through each day's lesson, you will learn about the important features that the IDE offers to help you develop applications.

- Experienced developers in other languages

  If you are a seasoned developer coming from another language or development tool, this book will give you the facts about using Visual Studio .NET to write applications. Understanding Visual Studio .NET is paramount to efficiently developing .NET applications. Each day is organized to help you learn the tools and languages that you need to start writing .NET applications today.

How This Book Is Structured

This book is most effective when read over the course of three weeks. During each week, you will read seven chapters that present concepts related to Visual Studio .NET. Each day you will learn something new and interesting about using Visual Studio .NET. Though there are many topics covered, each day is designed to help you get up to speed quickly using the most important aspects of Visual Studio .NET. Along the way you will learn VB.NET and C#, and you will be doing hands-on exercises designed to give you real world implementations of the topics covered.

Conventions

Note

> A Note presents interesting, sometimes technical, pieces of information related to the surrounding discussion.

VB.NET

The VB.NET icon flags VB.NET code.

C#

The C# icon flags code written in C#.

Text that you type and text that should appear on your screen is presented in **`bold monospace`** type: **`It will look like this`**.

This font mimics the way text looks on your screen. Placeholders for variables and expressions appear in monospace *italic*.

The end of each lesson offers commonly asked questions about that day's subject matter with answers from the authors, a chapter-ending quiz to test your knowledge of the material, and two exercises that you can try on your own.

You can email me anytime with any issues about the book or code you're running into trouble with at `jasonberes@msn.com`.

WEEK 1

At a Glance

Week 1 gets you on the ground and running with an introduction to the .NET Framework and Visual Studio .NET. You'll learn about the inner workings of the common language runtime and Visual Studio .NET. During week 1, you'll learn how to write and deploy Windows Forms applications and ASP.NET applications. You'll discover how to effectively use the debugging features in Visual Studio .NET to understand how to avoid errors and why and where your applications might be going wrong.

Week 1 covers the following:

- Day 1 gets you up to speed on the .NET Framework, the common language runtime, and how XML Web services are positioned to give you a fully distributed platform for developing enterprise applications with Visual Studio .NET. Understanding the concepts introduced in Day 1 is critical in understanding what .NET is all about and how it will dramatically improve the way you write your applications using Visual Studio .NET.
- Day 2 gives you a tour of Visual Studio .NET and its features. You will learn about the windows, toolboxes, and options that will help you learn and customize your environment. The concepts you learn in Day 2 will make your transition to using Visual Studio .NET as your development environment easy.
- Day 3 introduces you to Windows Forms. You'll learn about how Windows Forms applications are developed and how to respond to events from Windows Forms controls.

- Day 4 teaches you how to use the new deployment applications in Visual Studio .NET. Using Windows Installer technology and the built-in templates for deployment projects, you'll learn how to create customized and robust deployment packages for Windows Forms applications.
- Day 5 introduces you to ASP.NET applications. You'll learn how ASP differs from ASP.NET, how to use the new code-behind features in ASP.NET, and the different ways to manage session state in ASP.NET.
- Day 6 takes the deployment options that you learned about in Day 4 to the Web. You'll learn about the new XCopy deployment capabilities in .NET, and you'll learn how to customize Windows Installer deployment projects for Web-based applications.
- Day 7 teaches you how to use structured exception handling in Visual Basic .NET and C#, and how to use Visual Studio .NET to debug your applications. Writing error-free applications is always necessary, and understanding how to use the built-in tools in Visual Studio .NET to debug and handle errors sets you on your way to writing error-free applications.

WEEK 1

DAY 1

Introduction to the Microsoft .NET Framework

This week you learn about the tools that Visual Studio .NET offers. You'll get a good understanding of what types of applications you can create using Visual Studio .NET. But before we get to that point, you must have a solid understanding of what the .NET Framework is and what it can do for you. Understanding the internals of the .NET Framework helps you better understand what's happening when Visual Studio .NET is helping you create applications. By the end of the day, you'll have better insight into the technologies that make up the .NET Framework, how the .NET Framework fits into Microsoft's vision of the future of computing, and how things are much different from the past.

What Is .NET?

When .NET was announced in late 1999, Microsoft positioned the technology as a platform for building and consuming Extensible Markup Language (XML) Web services. XML Web services allow any type of application, be it a Windows- or browser-based application running on any type of computer system, to consume data from any type of server over the Internet. The reason this idea is so great is the way in which the XML messages are transferred: over established standard protocols that exist today. Using protocols such as SOAP, HTTP, and SMTP, XML Web services make it possible to expose data over the wire with little or no modifications to your existing code.

Figure 1.1 presents a high-level overview of the .NET Framework and how XML Web services are positioned.

FIGURE 1.1
Stateless XML Web services model.

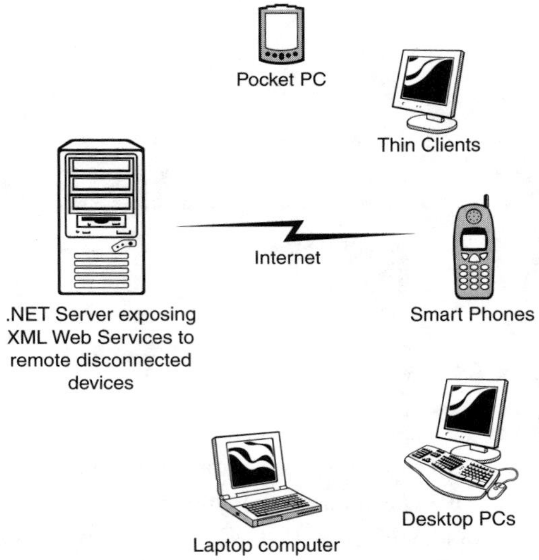

Since the initial announcement of the .NET Framework, it's taken on many new and different meanings to different people. To a developer, .NET means a great environment for creating robust distributed applications. To an IT manager, .NET means simpler deployment of applications to end users, tighter security, and simpler management. To a CTO or CIO, .NET means happier developers using state-of-the-art development technologies and a smaller bottom line. To understand why all these statements are true, you need to get a grip on what the .NET Framework consists of, and how it's truly a revolutionary step forward for application architecture, development, and deployment.

Windows of the Past

In the past, millions of applications were developed for Windows-based systems using a variety of development tools and languages. Visual Basic, C++, Delphi, Java, and Access provided a great toolset that enabled you to write applications for Windows. The problem that crept up again and again was how these applications communicated with each other and how they could communicate with data beyond the departmental server. Because each language has its own runtime environment, they all run essentially inside their own box, using their own way to communicate with core system services. There was no way to get outside the box. When a new feature to a language had to be added, it would be bolted somewhere on to the runtime environment through a new set of API calls. If you wanted to access the new features, each language had its own way of doing so. And, as was the case with Visual Basic, many features were simply not available because the runtime environment of Visual Basic couldn't support them. This problem seemed to have been solved with the Windows Distributed Internet Applications (DNA) architecture, which was based on Component Object Model (COM) components moving data between different types of distributed applications.

Windows DNA and COM

Writing distributed Internet applications became easier as the model of COM services that Windows servers could provide became more stable and widespread. You could write an Active Server Pages (ASP) application and access methods, properties, and events through the object model of components running inside of COM+ services on remote machines. Figure 1.2 shows the flow of a DNA/COM application.

FIGURE 1.2
DNA and COM in action.

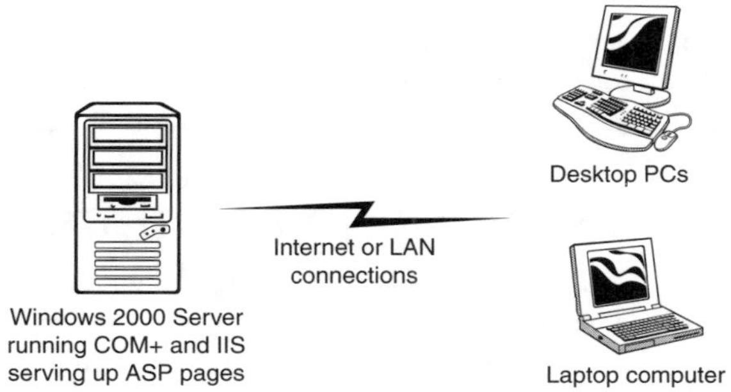

Windows DNA became more accepted because of the ease with which a Visual Basic 6 developer could write components that could be accessed from any other type of application, as long as he had access to the Windows 2000 server that the COM+ services were running on. This is where the problems begin.

If you provide data to outside vendors in an application, you must write the user interface and code to allow them access to what they need. There's no simple way to expose methods, or allow other applications to call methods, on your servers. You have to open up security and give them the keys to the farm, which isn't what IT managers are likely to do. If you want to maintain multiple versions of a component, you are in a very bad way with COM. Because COM makes heavy use of the Registry and doesn't allow for a simple versioning policy, you're essentially maintaining the same component forever. You're constantly adding new features to it, but leaving the old stuff in. This is one of the big rules of COM: Thou shall not change any interfaces to your components. Doing so makes for a huge headache in deployment. If you change an in or out parameter on a method, you've broken the functionality of the component. That means all the components must be recompiled to restore the correct interfaces that the caller expects. After a component is deployed, how do you easily scale it across machines while maintaining any state data that the code expects? This isn't a trivial problem, and companies have spent millions of dollars writing state machines to handle the scalability problems that come with COM.

All these issues are solved with the .NET Framework. The services provided by the .NET Framework enable us to expose methods over HTTP and SOAP through XML Web services. The Windows Registry is *not* used in .NET, which eliminates the DLL Hell of the past and gives us a strong versioning policy. There are many ways to maintain state data, so we can scale applications across processors and across servers with no worry about crashing the applications running on those servers. This all starts with the common language runtime and the base class libraries.

Note

> On Day 13, "XML Web Services in .NET," you learn more about the different protocols and messaging standards that make up an XML Web service.

The Common Language Runtime

At the heart of the .NET Framework is the common language runtime. The common language runtime is responsible for providing the execution environment that code written in a .NET language runs under. The common language runtime can be compared to the Visual Basic 6 runtime, except that the common language runtime is designed to handle all .NET languages, not just one, as the Visual Basic 6 runtime did for Visual Basic 6. The following list describes some of the benefits the common language runtime gives you:

- Automatic memory management
- Cross-language debugging
- Cross-language exception handling
- Full support for component versioning
- Access to legacy COM components
- XCOPY deployment
- Robust security model

You might expect all those features, but this has never been possible using Microsoft development tools. Figure 1.3 shows where the common language runtime fits into the .NET Framework.

FIGURE 1.3

The common language runtime and the .NET Framework.

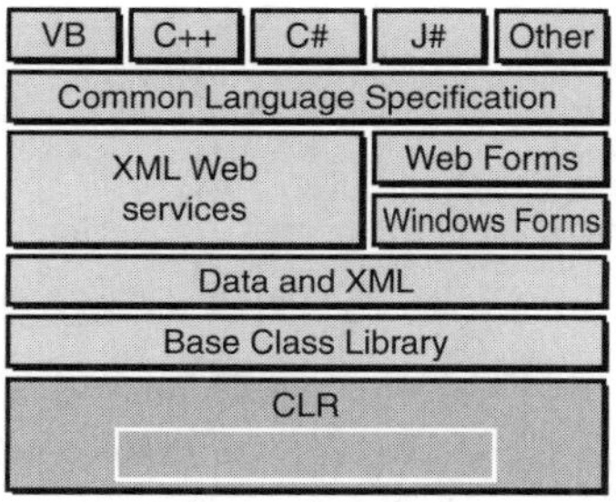

Note

Code written using a .NET language is known as *managed code*. Code that uses anything but the common language runtime is known as *unmanaged code*. The common language runtime provides a managed execution environment for .NET code, whereas the individual runtimes of non-.NET languages provide an unmanaged execution environment.

Inside the Common Language Runtime

The commonlanguage runtime enables code running in its execution environment to have features such as security, versioning, memory management, and exception handling because of the way .NET code actually executes. When you compiled Visual Basic 6 forms applications, you had the ability to compile down to native node or p-code. Figure 1.4 should refresh your memory of what the Visual Basic 6 options dialog looked like.

When you compile your applications in .NET, you aren't creating anything in native code. When you compile in .NET, you're converting your code—no matter what .NET language you're using—into an assembly made up of an intermediate language called

Microsoft Intermediate Language (MSIL or just IL, for short). The IL contains all the information about your application, including methods, properties, events, types, exceptions, security objects, and so on, and it also includes metadata about what types in your code can or cannot be exposed to other applications. This was called a *type library* in Visual Basic 6 or an IDL (interface definition language) file in C++. In .NET, it's simply the metadata that the IL contains about your assembly.

FIGURE 1.4
Visual Basic 6 compiler options dialog.

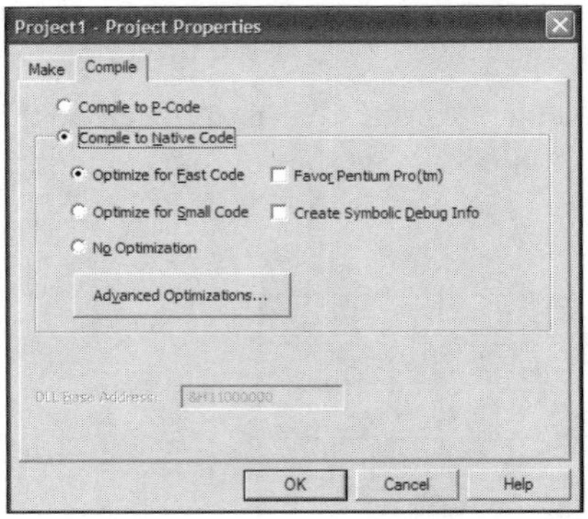

Note

The file format for the IL is known as PE (portable executable) format, which is a standard format for processor-specific execution.

When a user or another component executes your code, a process occurs called just-in-time (JIT) compilation, and it's at this point that the IL is converted into the specific machine language of the processor it's executing on. This makes it very easy to port a .NET application to any type of operating system on any type of processor because the IL is simply waiting to be consumed by a JIT compiler.

Note

The first time an assembly is called in .NET, the JIT process occurs. Subsequent calls don't re-JIT the IL; the previously JITted IL remains in cache and is used over and over again. On Day 5, "Writing ASP.NET Applications," you learn more about the JITting process and how it can affect your ASP.NET applications. On Day 19, "Understanding Microsoft Application Center Test," when you learn about Application Center Test, you also see how the warm-up time of the JIT process can affect application performance.

Understanding the process of compilation in .NET is very important because it makes clear how features such as cross-language debugging and exception handling are possible. You're not actually compiling to any machine-specific code—you're simply compiling down to an intermediate language that's the same for all .NET languages. The IL produced by J# .NET and C# looks just like the IL created by the Visual Basic .NET compiler. These instructions are the same, only how you type them in Visual Studio .NET is different, and the power of the common language runtime is apparent.

When the IL code is JITted into machine-specific language, it does so on an as-needed basis. If your assembly is 10MB and the user is only using a fraction of that 10MB, only the required IL and its dependencies are compiled to machine language. This makes for a very efficient execution process. But during this execution, how does the common language runtime make sure that the IL is correct? Because the compiler for each language creates its own IL, there must be a process that makes sure what's compiling won't corrupt the system. The process that validates the IL is known as *verification*. Figure 1.5 demonstrates the process the IL goes through before the code actually executes.

FIGURE 1.5

The JIT process and verification.

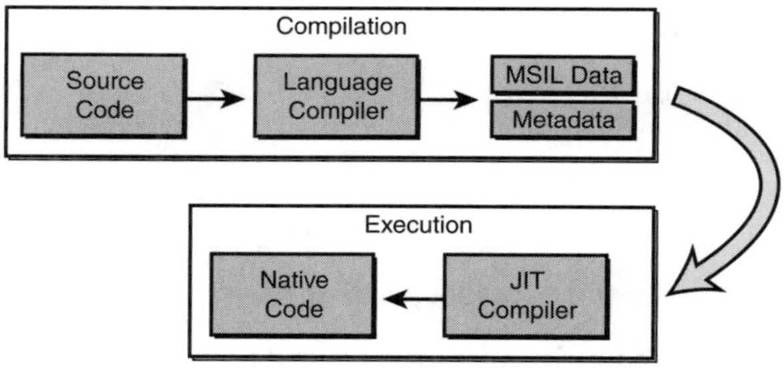

When code is JIT compiled, the common language runtime checks to make sure that the IL is correct. The rules that the common language runtime uses for verification are set forth in the Common Language Specification (CLS) and the Common Type System (CTS).

Understanding the Common Language Specification

The CLS describes the concrete guidelines that make a .NET language compliant with the common language runtime. That doesn't mean a .NET language can't have language-specific features, but it does indicate that to be considered a .NET language, the language must comply with the set of requirements set forth in the CLS. All features added to a .NET language and that aren't part of the CLS won't be exposed to other .NET languages at runtime.

If your code is fully CLS compliant, it's guaranteed to interoperate with all other components written in any .NET language. Certain languages, such as C#, attempt to accommodate developers moving from C and C++ with the similarity of their syntaxes. Because C# attracts such developers, it includes functionality familiar from their native languages, such as pointers and code access to unsafe memory blocks. This functionality is not CLS compliant and won't be accessible by other .NET languages, but it's allowed by the common language runtime and the language-specific compilers. To make sure that your code is CLS compliant, compilers such as C# include checks for non-CLS-compliant code through the use of attributes. If you apply the `CLSCompliantAttribute` attribute to a class or method in your code and the code isn't CLS compliant, an error occurs and the compile fails. The following code demonstrates how to apply the `CLSCompliantAttribute` attribute in your code:

```
using System;
[assembly: CLSCompliantAttribute(true)]
[CLSCompliantAttribute(true)]
public class Class1
{
   public void x(UInt32 x){}
   public static void Main( )
  {
  }
}
```

In this case, the code won't compile because unsigned integers aren't part of the CLS.

The second part of the verification process that the JIT compiler goes through to make sure that your code executes correctly is the verification of types. All types used in .NET must conform to the CTS.

Understanding the Common Type System

The CTS sets forth the guidelines for data type safety in .NET.

> In the past, there were no rules for type safety across execution runtimes, hence the general protection fault (GPF) and blue screen of death errors that could occur when running applications. The culprit behind those meltdowns was the overlapping of memory by data types. This was a common occurrence in Windows 3.1, Windows 95, and Windows 98. When a Visual Basic developer deployed a new application, fingers had to be crossed to make sure that the data types and memory access between the newly installed DLLs and the existing ones on the system mingled happily. Most of the time they did, but when they didn't, errors occurred.

In .NET, the CTS defines types and how they can act within the bounds of the common language runtime. There are two type classifications in .NET: value types and reference types.

Value Types

Value types directly contain the data you assign them. They're built into the common language runtime and derive directly from the base `System.Object` type. Examples of value types are primitive types, structures, and enumerations. Primitive types can be further broken down into numbers, such as Boolean, byte, short, integer, long, single, double, decimal, date, and char.

Reference Types

Reference types don't directly contain any data; rather, they point to a memory location that contains the actual data. Reference types are built into the common language runtime and derive directly from the base `System.Object` type. Some examples of reference types are strings, classes, arrays, delegates, and modules (see Figure 1.6).

FIGURE 1.6

The common type system defined.

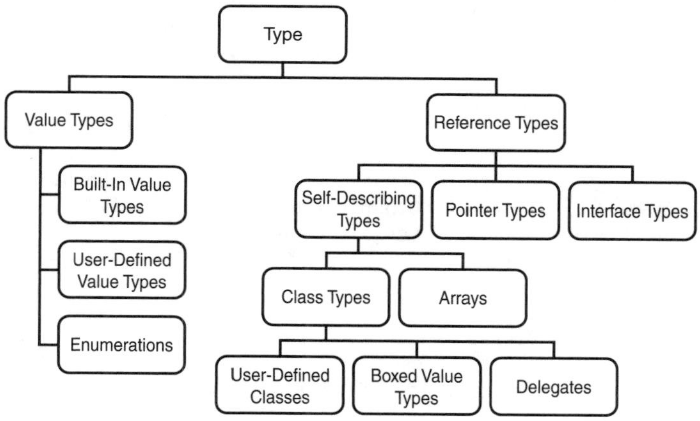

To make the difference between Value types and Reference types clearer, consider the following code. It accesses a primitive type (which is a value type) and a class (which is a reference type), and attempts to assign values to them.

C#

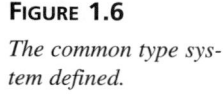

```
using System;
namespace cSharp_ValueReference
{
```

```
        class Class1
        {
                static public int x;
                 [STAThread]
                static void Main(string[] args)
                {
                        x=4;
                        int y;
                        y = x;
                        x=0;
                        // Since each Value type contains its own data,
                        // modifying the variable X after setting Y to the value
                        // of X does not affect either variable
                        Console.WriteLine(x);
                        Console.WriteLine(y);

                        // Create an instance of Class2
                        Class2 ref1 = new Class2();
                        // Set the refValue of this instance to 5
                        ref1.refValue=5;

                        // Create an object reference to the ref1 class
                        Class2 ref2 = ref1;
                        // Set the refValue of the object
                        ref2.refValue=10;

                        // Notice how the results are the same, even
                        // though you set re1.refValue to 5, the reference
                        // to this memory was overridden by the value of 10
                        Console.WriteLine(ref1.refValue);
                        Console.WriteLine(ref2.refValue);
                        Console.ReadLine();
                }
        }

        class Class2
        {
                public int refValue;
        }
}
```

VB.NET

```
Module Module1

    Sub Main()

        Dim X As Integer = 4
        Dim Y As Integer
```

```
        intY = X
        intX = 0
        Console.WriteLine(X)
        Console.WriteLine(Y)

        Dim ref1 As Class2 = New Class2()
        ref1.refValue = 5

        Dim ref2 As Class2 = ref1
        ref2.refValue = 10

        Console.WriteLine(ref1.refValue)
        Console.WriteLine(ref2.refValue)
        Console.ReadLine()
    End Sub

End Module

Class Class2
    Public refValue As Integer
End Class
```

In both examples, the values of the value type variables `X` and `Y` are `0` and `4`, whereas the values of the reference types `ref1` and `ref2` are both `10`. Because the reference type points to the same memory allocation for the initial object `ref1`, the value for all variables set to an instance of that object is always the last value assigned. Figure 1.7 shows the console output of the code.

FIGURE 1.7

Value and reference type test output.

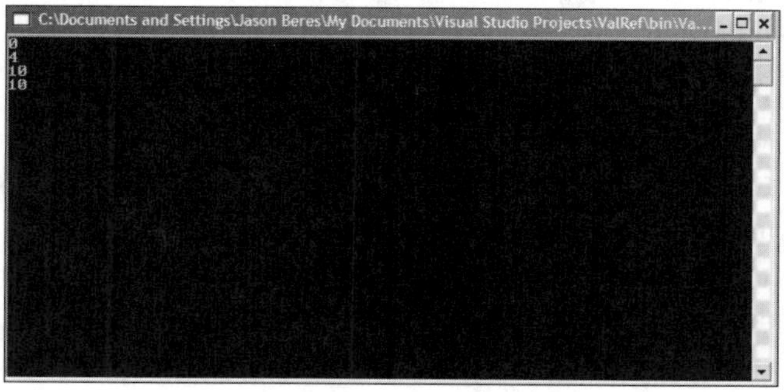

Tip

> You don't normally get into much trouble when dealing with reference types and value types like the example describes. When you're creating instances of classes, always derive from a new instance of the object, not a previously set instance.

Now that you have an understanding of what the CTS is and how it works, you need to see how the types are removed from memory. Removing types that are no longer referenced in your applications is known as *garbage collection*.

Handling Memory and Garbage

The common language runtime handles all memory allocation and management that your application requires. This includes the initial allocation that occurs when you declare an object and store data in it, and the release of memory back to the operating system when the object is no longer in use. The automatic garbage collection of unused objects solves all the inherent problems of Win32-based applications when it comes to the mysterious resource losses that Windows would succumb to after running applications.

Memory management is improved with each new version of the Windows operating system, but the fault is not completely that of the operating system. If you're writing C++ applications, it's very easy to forget to destroy object handles and memory blocks after they've been used. When this happens, there's no way for Windows to recover that memory until the machine is rebooted. In Visual Basic 6, you had to set all your object instances to `Nothing` to guarantee that memory would be freed after an object was used. The limitations for the runtime environments of all languages lead to the problems of resource loss in Windows. So, in the end, it isn't really the fault of Windows—it's the fault of the developers writing the code that runs in Windows.

The garbage collection mechanism used in .NET is very simple and can be summed up in the following steps:

1. The garbage collector (GC) allocates memory resources on the managed heap when a process starts and sets a pointer to that memory allocation.
2. Each object created for the allocated resource is given the next address space in the managed heap when it's created.
3. The GC continuously scans the managed heap for objects that are out of scope and no longer in use.
4. The GC reclaims stack heaps that it determines are out of scope and compacts the managed heap for the running process.

This four-step process occurs over and over during the execution lifetime of your application. Under the hood, the GC divides the managed heap running your processes into three generations. Each generation is examined separately by the GC based on when the objects on the heap were created and their dependency to each other. This mechanism improves the overall performance of garbage collection because constantly scanning the entire managed heap for unused resources would be processor-intensive and time-consuming. By splitting apart when and where objects are created, the process of garbage collection can effectively determine what objects are in use and what objects are out of scope.

Although the GC can handle the destruction of most objects on the managed heap, objects such as file handles, network handles, database connections, and window handles are unmanaged resources that are created on the managed heap. These resources can be given the correct memory allocation, and the GC knows when they are out of scope, but it doesn't know when to destroy those objects to reclaim the memory on the stack. To reclaim memory from unmanaged resources, you must explicitly destroy the objects by creating the necessary cleanup code to implement the `IDisposable` interface and override the `Dispose` method of the object. This isn't always necessary, and should be used only if you know that a resource must be freed when your component is no longer being used.

If you're using an object and you know it's a CTS-compliant managed type, the automatic garbage collection handles reclaiming the resource. Haphazardly calling the `Dispose` method on objects consumes resources and forces garbage collection. When writing components that use unmanaged resources, you can close file handles and network handles in the `Dispose` method, and the normal process of garbage collection destroys the object and reclaims the memory allocation.

Note

Because the common language runtime determines when garbage collection takes place, it's referred to as *nondeterministic finalization*. In other words, you have no idea when the `finalize` method, which marks an object for collection, will occur.

The reason that understanding the existence of `Dispose` method is important is because of an unlikely worst-case scenario in which object resources aren't freed and a component attempts to create them again. This situation could occur if the system running a component is depleting its resources and garbage collection isn't occurring on a regular basis. The following code demonstrates how to implement the `Dispose` method when creating a Windows User Control and implementing a database connection.

VB.NET

```
Imports System.Data.SqlClient

Public Class UserControl1
    Inherits System.Windows.Forms.UserControl
    Private cn As New SqlConnection()
    Public Sub New()
```

```
        MyBase.New()
        cn.ConnectionString = "uid=sa;pwd=;database=pubs;server=."
        cn.Open()
        InitializeComponent()
    End Sub

    Protected Overloads Overrides Sub Dispose(ByVal disposing As Boolean)
        If disposing Then
            If Not (components Is Nothing) Then
                components.Dispose()
                cn.Close()
                cn = Nothing
            End If
        End If
        MyBase.Dispose(disposing)
    End Sub

    Private components As System.ComponentModel.IContainer

    Private Sub InitializeComponent()
        Me.Name = "UserControl1"
    End Sub
End Class
```

C#

```
using System;
using System.Collections;
using System.ComponentModel;
using System.Drawing;
using System.Data;
using System.Windows.Forms;
using System.Data.SqlClient;

namespace cSharpDispose
{
        public class UserControl1 : System.Windows.Forms.UserControl
        {
                private System.ComponentModel.Container components = null;
                private SqlConnection cn;
                public UserControl1()
                {
                        InitializeComponent();
                        cn.ConnectionString=
                           "database=pubs;server=localhost;uid=sa;pwd=;";
                        cn.Open();
                }
                protected override void Dispose( bool disposing )
                {
                        if( disposing )
```

```
                {
                        if( components != null )
                                components.Dispose();
                                cn.Close();
                                cn=null;
                }
                base.Dispose( disposing );
        }

        private void InitializeComponent()
        {
                this.Name = "UserControl1";
                this.Load += new
                   System.EventHandler(this.UserControl1_Load);
        }
    }
}
```

As you can see, implementing `Dispose` is a simple task. By default, any class that derives from `System.ComponentModel.Component` has a `Dispose` method that you can override. If you're writing a component that doesn't derive from `System.ComponentModel.Component`, you can implement the `IDisposable` interface and create your own `Dispose` method.

The .NET Framework Class Library

The second most important piece of the .NET Framework is the .NET Framework class library (FCL). As you've seen, the common language runtime handles the dirty work of actually running the code you write. But to write the code, you need a foundation of available classes to access the resources of the operating system, database server, or file server. The FCL is made up of a hierarchy of namespaces that expose classes, structures, interfaces, enumerations, and delegates that give you access to these resources.

The namespaces are logically defined by functionality. For example, the `System.Data` namespace contains all the functionality available to accessing databases. This namespace is further broken down into `System.Data.SqlClient`, which exposes functionality specific to SQL Server, and `System.Data.OleDb`, which exposes specific functionality for accessing OLEDB data sources. The bounds of a namespace aren't necessarily defined by specific assemblies within the FCL; rather, they're focused on functionality and logical grouping. In total, there are more than 20,000 classes in the FCL, all logically grouped in a hierarchical manner. Figure 1.8 shows where the FCL fits into the .NET Framework and the logical grouping of namespaces.

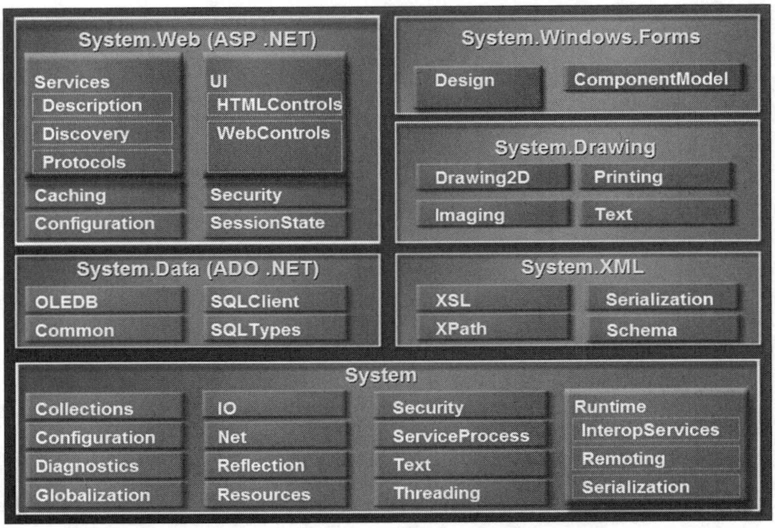

FIGURE 1.8
The .NET Framework class library.

To use an FCL class in your application, you use the `Imports` statement in Visual Basic .NET or the `using` statement in C#. When you reference a namespace in Visual Basic .NET or C#, you also get the convenience of auto-complete and auto-list members when you access the objects' types using Visual Studio .NET. This makes it very easy to determine what types are available for each class in the namespace you're using. As you'll see over the next several weeks, it's very easy to start coding in Visual Studio .NET. The following code adds a reference to the data classes in both Visual Basic .NET and C#.

VB.NET

```
Imports System
Imports System.Data.SqlClient
Imports System.Data.OleDb
```

C#

```
using System;
using System.Data.SqlClient;
using System.Data.OleDb;
```

On Day 10, "Accessing Data with ADO.NET," you learn more about the common FCL namespaces and assemblies, and how to write applications using them. For now, you can see that without the FCL, the common language runtime and Visual Studio .NET wouldn't be very easy tools to use. The key idea to grasp is that the FCL is 100% available to all .NET languages, so the FCL namespace that implements file I/O capability in C# is the same FCL namespace that's used in Visual Basic .NET, J# .NET, and COBOL .NET.

What about C++?

With the introduction of Visual Studio .NET and great new languages like C# and Visual Basic .NET, Microsoft has also improved the C++ language. By providing Managed Extensions for C++, an application written in C++ can take advantage of the core features of .NET and the common language runtime. Garbage collection, cross-language debugging and code access security are all fundamental aspects of .NET, and are the foundation of the Visual Basic .NET and C# languages. Using Managed Extensions for C++, a traditional C++ developer can take advantage of the features of the .NET Framework directly from Visual Studio .NET, writing applications that contain both managed and unmanaged code. New project templates for C++ are built into VS.NET, and improved compiler options allow C++ applications written using VS.NET to live in the managed environment of the .NET Framework. All of the power and flexibility that has made C++ a great language is still there, the Managed Extensions take the language to the next level with the power and flexibility of the .NET Framework. Using Managed Extensions for C++ will allow you to create .NET classes that are callable from managed C++ or unmanaged C++ applications.

In this book, to reach the broadest audience possible, all of the code is written in either Visual Basic .NET or C#. If you are a C++ developer, and new to .NET, the syntax of C# will be familiar to you, and you will be able to write applications immediately using C#. Using Visual Studio .NET as your development tool will allow you to create applications faster and easier than ever, so you can look at this book as a reference on the tool, not the language. No matter what language you develop in, using VS.NET will allow you create better applications faster.

.NET Servers and the Future of .NET

The designers of the .NET Framework put much thought into how distributed computing should work. It seems that .NET is the next killer app, but to make the .NET Framework a widespread success, actual servers must be built using the .NET Framework. Currently, there are no true .NET servers. There are servers that take advantage of the common language runtime and its managed execution environment, but most servers from Microsoft today still run under COM and unmanaged code.

Commerce Server 2002 is positioned as a .NET server for e-commerce, and applications you design with it can be completely written using Visual Basic .NET or C#, but the underlying infrastructure of Commerce Server is still based on COM. Because rewriting server applications is a truly monumental task, the move to completely .NET servers could take several years. Along the way, there'll be servers such as Commerce Server 2002 that are half managed code and half unmanaged code. From a developer's viewpoint that's fine, because you don't want to write ASP and Visual Basic 6 code for server products while the rest of your distributed application development is in a .NET language.

Currently, Microsoft seems to be positioning server products as .NET Enterprise Servers if they can integrate XML Web services into their existing infrastructure. For example, SQL Server 2000 certainly isn't written in managed code, but there are add-ons to SQL Server 2000 that enable you to expose stored procedures as XML Web services. The SQL Server Notification Service is a .NET add-on that allows notification to .NET applications if certain events trigger in SQL. BizTalk server's purpose in life is the orchestration and automation of complex business processes, and it's positioned as a .NET server because of its capability to consume XML Web services. The following Microsoft server products are considered .NET Enterprise Servers because of their capability to at least interact with a distributed environment such as the Internet and have some relationship with the .NET Framework concepts:

- Internet Security and Acceleration Server
- Application Center 2000
- Commerce Server 2000 and Commerce Server 2002
- BizTalk Server 2000 and BizTalk Server 2002
- SQL Server 2000
- Exchange Server 2000
- Host Integration Server 2000

In my opinion, the fact that a .NET server is truly running under the common language runtime is not a deal breaker. For .NET to get to the next step, it must run on other operating systems, not just the Windows family of desktop and server operating systems. Currently, the Mono project is a grass-roots move to port the .NET Framework class library to the Linux operating system. That means the code you're writing now for Windows will also eventually run under Linux and, hopefully, Unix as well. You can learn more about the Mono project and where it currently is in the development process at `http://www.go-mono.org`. It would be a huge step forward if .NET were ported to the Macintosh operating system also. Although the Mac is still a small percentage of the overall market in desktop PCs, its incompatibility with Windows creates headaches for application developers. There needs to be consistency across platforms eventually.

Moving into the future with .NET, the sky seems to be the limit. This isn't necessarily because Microsoft is going to think of some great new thing to add to the .NET Framework, even though it most likely will, but it has to do with computing in general and the general infrastructure of our daily lives. As every household and business installs high-speed data access, and as computers become faster and cheaper, the applications you write will have a greater influence on how people look at what computer programs can do. You aren't bound to single servers anymore. Writing truly distributed and scalable applications is very easy because of the groundwork laid out by the .NET Framework. You can begin to look at the code you write not as blocks of modules running on a Windows 2000 Server, but as distributed objects that you can reuse in multiple applications across an enterprise simply by plugging them into an XML Web service. The future of .NET is the concept of a true distributed environment.

Summary

Today you learned about the core concepts of the .NET Framework and how it fits into the vision of .NET. The common language runtime, in conjunction with the .NET Framework class library, gives you the foundation in which to write distributed, scalable, and robust applications. Technologies such as the common type system, garbage collection, and the Common Language Specification make up the core infrastructure that help the common language runtime and the .NET Framework make your applications run better. Starting tomorrow, you'll learn the essentials of writing applications using the tools provided in Visual Studio .NET.

Q&A

Q I'm confused. What's the difference between the .NET Framework and Visual Studio .NET?

A The .NET Framework provides the execution environment in which code written using Visual Studio .NET runs. Visual Studio .NET is simply the tool to write the code, whereas the .NET Framework actually provides the runtime environment for the code. You could use Notepad to write your applications, but tools such as Visual Studio .NET help you create distributed applications very quickly.

Q Should I write all my code in C# because it runs more efficiently than Visual Basic .NET or COBOL .NET?

A Each .NET compiler produces the MSIL that the common language runtime converts to machine-specific code at runtime. Although one compiler might produce more efficient MSIL, there's really no difference in the performance at runtime among C#, Visual Basic .NET, COBOL .NET, or any other .NET language.

Quiz

1. How can you prevent compile errors in your C# applications when using types that aren't compliant with the CLS?
2. The garbage collector takes care of managing memory for managed applications, but under what circumstances doesn't the garbage collector know when to release objects from memory?
3. True or False: Because Windows .NET Server is out now, all the server products that Microsoft offers should be considered .NET Servers because they all use the managed execution environment of the .NET Framework.

Quiz Answers

1. By adding the `CLSCompliantAttribute(true)` to either an assembly or a class
2. Unmanaged resources that are created on the managed heap
3. False. Only future server products that are written in managed code can be considered true .NET servers.

Exercises

Not a whole lot of code was written today. To prepare yourself for Day 10 when we talk about assemblies and namespaces, spend about 10 or 20 minutes looking at the namespaces in the .NET Framework software development kit (SDK). Try to develop a good understanding of how the hierarchy works and how the namespaces seem to be grouped together.

WEEK 1

DAY 2

Introduction to Visual Studio .NET

Yesterday you learned about the .NET Framework and what it means to you as a developer. For the next 20 days, you're going to learn how to write applications using the .NET Framework and how to use the tools to achieve rapid application development (RAD). All of that starts with having a solid understanding of the development tool that you'll be using: Visual Studio .NET. Visual Studio .NET includes everything you need to rapidly develop and debug all aspects of any type of application that you can think of. It's somewhat overshadowed by the whole concept of .NET. The bottom line to you is that anything and everything was thought of when the development environment was designed. In fact, most of it was written using .NET. So, from the .NET Framework to the tool you use to write .NET Framework applications, .NET was used. Many of the items you learn about today might seem to be stating the obvious, if you're a seasoned Visual Basic 6 or Visual Studio 6 developer, and most of the IDE might seem familiar, or at least can be figured out by clicking around for a few hours. I still recommend reading through this chapter because there are some nice features in .NET that might pleasantly surprise you. Today you learn about

- The many windows and menu options available in Visual Studio .NET
- Generating help pages for your applications
- How to use Dynamic Help
- The different project types and what types of applications you can write
- Creating code libraries using the .NET Toolbox
- Customizing your development environment

Introducing the Start Page

Visual Studio .NET and its tools are located in the Microsoft Visual Studio .NET folder of the Program Files folder. The shortcut to Visual Studio .NET is located in the Visual Studio .NET folder on the Start menu in Windows. To get through today, open Visual Studio .NET from the Program Files, Visual Studio .NET folder. The first time the integrated development environment (hereafter referred to simply as *IDE*) is opened, you're presented with the Start Page, as Figure 2.1 demonstrates.

FIGURE 2.1
The Start Page.

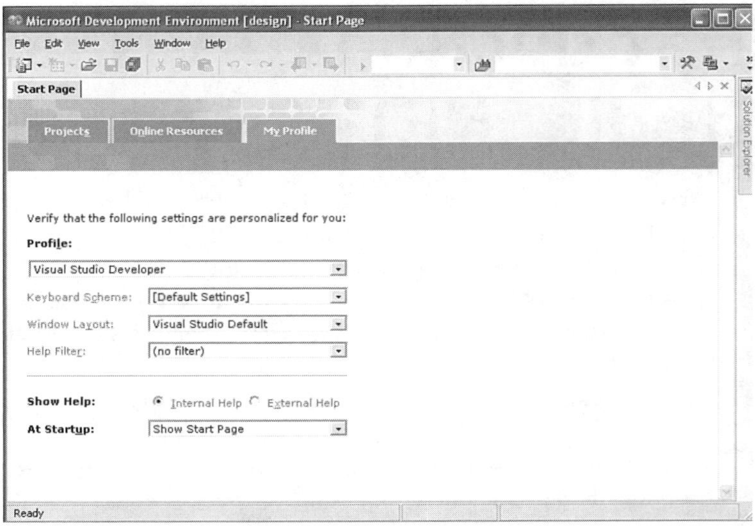

The Start Page is a tabbed HTML page with three main navigation options across the top, Projects, Online Resources and My Profile. We will look at each of the options that each page represents throughout today, but first, examine the My Profile tab, which is the first page that opens if you have never run Visual Studio .NET before.

Tip

> If you're running Windows XP or Windows .NET Server, take advantage of the Pin To Start Menu ability. Because you'll use Visual Studio .NET all the time, you should right-click on the shortcut in the Start Menu, Program Files, Visual Studio .NET folder and select Pin To Start Menu from the contextual menu. Now the shortcut is a simple click, instead of navigating the Start menu tree each time you need to start Visual Studio .NET. Another useful shortcut is the Visual Studio .NET Command Line shortcut in the Visual Studio .NET Tools subfolder. You should pin that shortcut to the Start menu also.

The My Profile page enables you to set up the general settings for your IDE. By selecting a profile, you can dictate the initial settings of the toolbars and menus. For example, if you're an Active Server Pages (ASP) developer who has always used Visual InterDev, you can select Visual Studio Developer as the default profile. If you're a Visual Basic 6 developer, you should select Visual Basic 6 Developer as the default profile. When you choose a profile, you're telling Visual Studio .NET how you want windows arranged, what type of help topics you want displayed, and what the keyboard shortcuts should be set to. In Visual InterDev, the F11 key stepped through code in debug mode, but in Visual Basic 6, F8 was the Step Into shortcut. So, these types of options are set based on your profile.

Later today, you'll see how to override specific IDE settings using the Options dialog. If you're not happy with your choice or just want to see the difference, you can modify the settings by returning back to the My Profile page on the Start Page, or you can alter the settings in more detail in the Options dialog.

We'll go through the remaining items on the Start Page navigation menu from the bottom up.

Getting a Web Hosting Provider

If you click the Online Resources tab, you are brought to a page with a left navigation menu that gives you access to online resources. The last option on the left navigation menu is the Web Hosting option, which gives you easy access to the Microsoft-approved Web hosting providers for ASP.NET applications. This seems like marketing at first, but the tab does more than simply list Web hosting providers. From this tab, you can sign up for a new account with a hosting provider and easily upload files to the hosting provider.

To test this out, I selected the Signup with iNNERHOST hyperlink on the Web Hosting tab, as Figure 2.2 shows.

After I selected iNNERHOST, I was taken directly to a hosting options page on its corporate Web site.

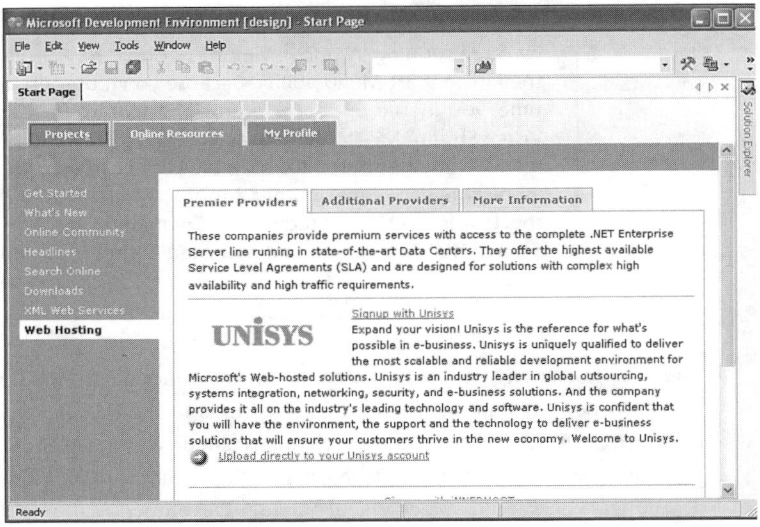

FIGURE 2.2

Selecting a Web hosting provider.

iNNERHOST happens to have a bunch of options for Web hosting, but it also offers a free 90-day ASP.NET account to Visual Studio .NET users. After I filled out my information, such as email address, username, and password options, I was directed to the Thank You page shown in Figure 2.3, and within seconds I had an email confirmation with my activated iNNERHOST account information.

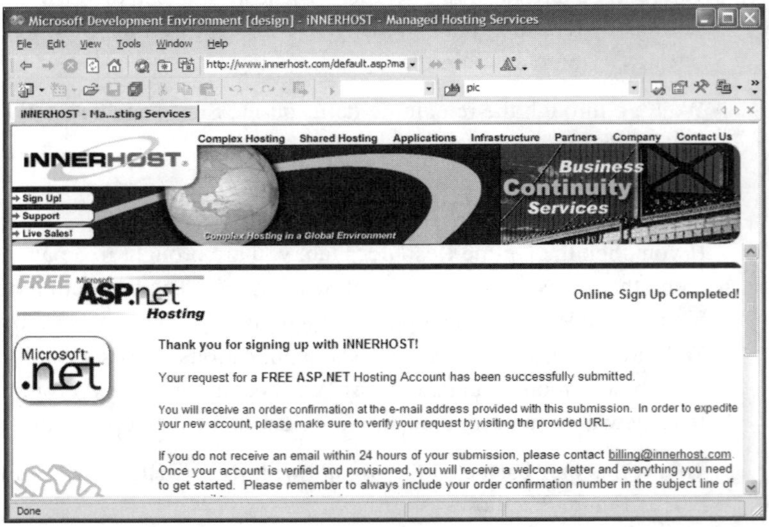

FIGURE 2.3

Registering with iNNERHOST through Visual Studio .NET.

As you can see, I never had to leave the Visual Studio .NET IDE, and within literally two minutes I had a live Web account with a premiere ASP.NET Web hosting provider. Now, directly from Visual Studio .NET, I can log in to my iNNERHOST account and upload my ASP.NET Web applications, as Figure 2.4 demonstrates.

FIGURE 2.4

Logging into my iNNERHOST account from Visual Studio .NET.

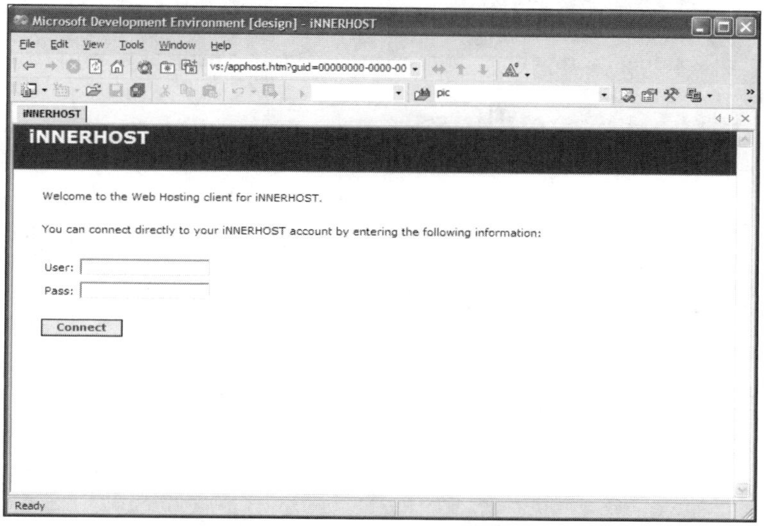

So, you can immediately test applications you write using Visual Studio .NET on a remote server—you aren't limited to running the application only on your local machine.

XML Web Services

The XML Web Services menu item gives you a link to available extensible markup language (XML) Web services on the Web. You learn about XML Web services on Day 13, "XML Web Services in .NET," and you'll realize how useful this menu option is when learning about XML Web services that are in use and live on the Web. The UDDI.org Web site is the worldwide central repository for XML Web services. (UDDI stands for Universal Description, Discovery, and Integration.) From that page, you can search the UDDI directory for Web services broken down by category. You can even upload your own Web services to UDDI.org from this link.

Downloads

The Downloads menu item lists free downloads and updates from `download.microsoft.com`. If you're a Microsoft Developers Network (MSDN) subscriber, you can also log in to your account from this page and access all MSDN subscriber downloads. The Downloads page gives you only the downloads relevant to .NET and developing applications, so it's a one-stop shop for all the latest goodies from Microsoft.

Searching Online

The Search Online menu item enables you to directly link into the millions of pages at `http://msdn.microsoft.com` for help and support. Using the Search Online tool gets you the information you need fast, without having to remember where to look.

MSDN Headlines

The Headlines menu item takes you directly to the MSDN home page's recent headlines. If you're new to Microsoft development tools, you'll find that MSDN is the ultimate resource for getting the latest information, samples, demos, chats, links, seminars and articles on all Microsoft development tools. This link always takes you to the most recent articles list available at MSDN.

Online Community

The Online Community menu item takes you to the most recent list of available community sites for .NET. This includes newsgroups hosted by Microsoft and third-party sites that have many useful sample code and how-tos about .NET. With the release of .NET, the online community for .NET has grown by about 10,000%. So, there's always an answer somewhere if you get in a bind, and this link is a good place to get familiar with the most popular resources online.

The What's New Page

The What's New page summarizes the new product updates for .NET and lists useful links to training partners, books, and tips for using .NET. Figure 2.5 gives you an idea of what's available on the What's New page.

The Get Started Page

The Get Started page gives you links to samples in the MSDN library that is installed as part of VS.NET. You have the option of selecting the language you are working in, and a filter by keyword or type. Once you select your filter options, the Get Started page offers you a list of links to the help file that gives you the information you need to accomplish the task you searched for.

FIGURE 2.5
The What's New link on the Online Resources tab.

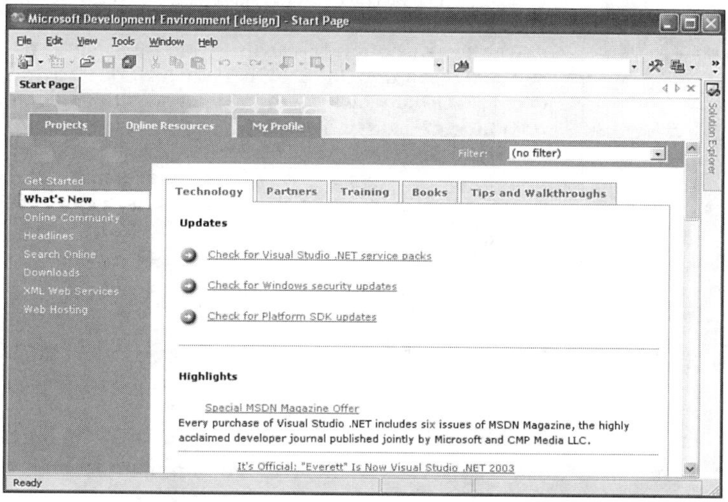

The Projects Tab

The Projects tab is the default page that starts when you start Visual Studio .NET after the initial setup of your profile. From the Getting Started page, you can create a new Visual Studio .NET project or select from a list of recently created projects. Figure 2.6 shows you what the Getting Started page would look like after before creating any new projects. The number of projects listed in the Recent Projects list is 10 by default. You can change this number to as high as 24 in the Options dialog. Depending on your screen resolution, you can vary what's displayed. On my computer, I have the last 24 items displayed because my screen resolution makes that easy to see.

FIGURE 2.6
The Projects tab.

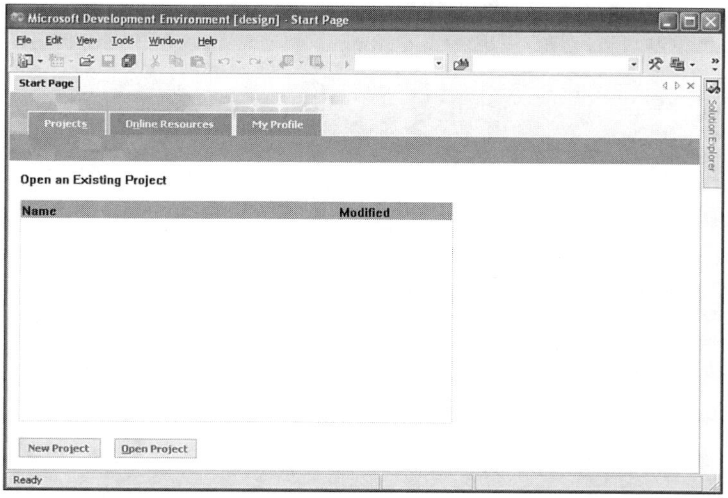

Note

All the screenshots in this chapter and throughout the book are taken at 800×600 resolution. In real life, I use 1600×1200 on my Sony laptop's 16" screen, which enables me to have many windows open and appreciate the full range of tools and windows you'll learn about today. I bought the laptop specifically because of Visual Studio .NET. You'll realize after you get used to the IDE that so many tools are available, it's nice to have them all open. But if you're using 1024×768 resolution, the window model in .NET works nicely, and that would be the minimum screen resolution for getting things effectively done in the Visual Studio .NET IDE.

Using Dynamic Help

You've just seen the Start Page and all great things it offers you. The next best thing about the Visual Studio .NET IDE is a new feature to Microsoft products called Dynamic Help. Dynamic Help literally gives you the help file information about whatever item in the IDE has the current focus. When Visual Studio .NET starts, the focus is the Start Page. To start Dynamic Help, press the Ctrl+F1 keys. The Help contents window appears on the screen, and the current help file for the Start Page shows up, as Figure 2.7 demonstrates.

FIGURE 2.7

Dynamic Help for the Start Page.

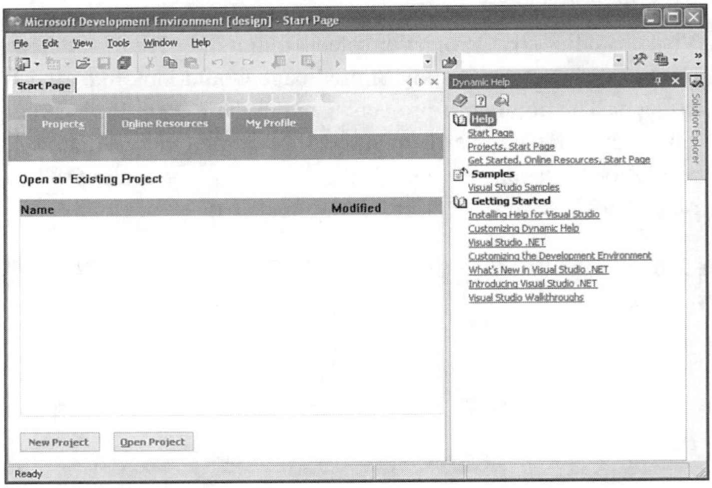

From this point, you can click the available hyperlinks in the Dynamic Help window to learn more about the IDE and customizing your environment. The Dynamic Help window also has three buttons on its toolbar: Contents, Index, and Search. If you click the Contents button, the window changes to the contents of the software development kit (SDK) help file. If you click the Search button, you have the ability to search for items. Clicking the Index button gives you the searchable index of the help file. Figure 2.8

demonstrates the Search capability. Notice how the Results window appears at the bottom of the screen. From this point, you can click on items in the results, and the help screen changes to that particular topic. You can also change the default filter of the help search. My default was Visual Basic and Related, but you can simply change the Filtered By drop-down list and select another language.

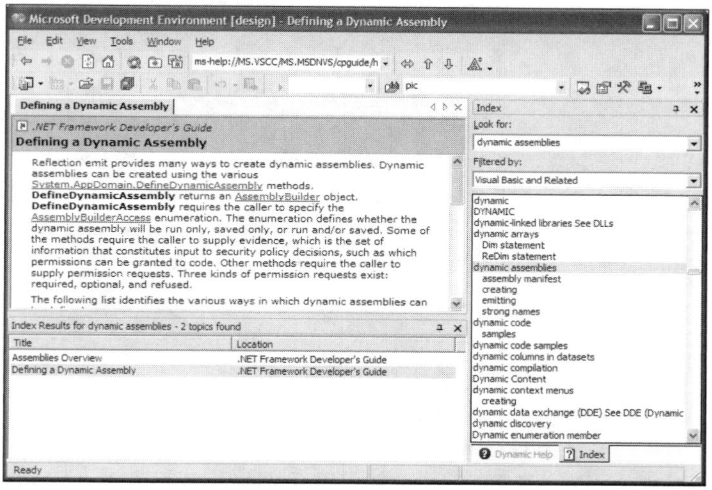

FIGURE 2.8

Using Search in Dynamic Help.

The predefined filters for Dynamic Help can be modified by selecting Help, Edit Filters from the Help main menu. You won't normally need to modify the filters or add new filters, but the capability is there to do so.

From the Help screen, you can get back to the Start Page by selecting Show Start Page from the Help menu or by clicking the Home button on the main toolbar.

The New Projects Dialog

From the Getting Started page on the Start Page, click the New Project button. The New Project dialog pops up, as shown in Figure 2.9.

The New Project dialog lists all the possible project types that Visual Studio .NET can create. All the different project types are predefined templates that include different classes, namespaces, and designers to make working with the specific project type easier. As you go through the next 20 days, you'll learn how to use the key project templates that are offered.

You should also notice the project types are broken down by language and language-agnostic types. The types of projects that you can create in Visual Basic and C# are identical. There are no special project differences between them, except for the default language settings. Project types for C++ are specific to the C++ Active Template Library tools that come with .NET.

FIGURE 2.9
The New Project dialog box.

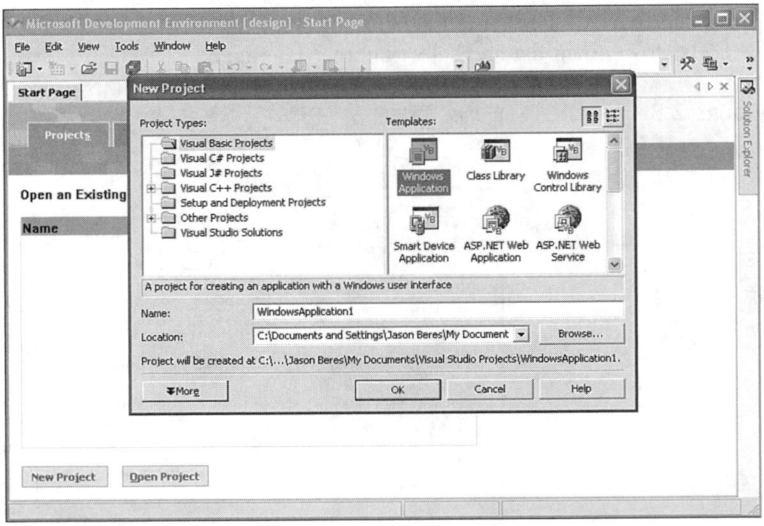

When you create a project, you can specify the name and location of the project source files. The default directory for all created projects is the Visual Studio Projects folder in your My Documents folder.

For Web-based projects, the actual source files are created in the `Inetpub\wwwroot` directory of your local Web server, and the project solution file is saved in the Visual Studio Projects folder in a folder named after the project name. For all non-Web projects, all the project source files are created in a new folder using the name you enter in the Name box of the Visual Studio Project folder in My Documents. From the New Project dialog, you can change the default path of any new projects being created by clicking the Browse button and navigating to a folder on your local machine.

Tip

> By default, when you create a new ASP.NET Web application or ASP.NET Web service application, the virtual Web directory in Internet Information Server (IIS) is created for you, so you don't need to do anything special with the Internet Information Server tools. The default path for all Web projects is `\Inetpub\wwwroot` on your system drive.

To get started working with the IDE, change the name of the project to ExploringVSNET as Figure 2.10 demonstrates and click the OK button.

FIGURE 2.10

Creating the ExploringVSNET project.

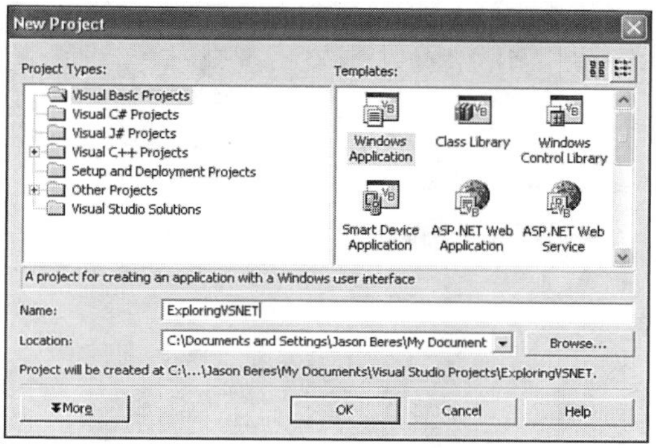

Note

> The IDE tour and configuration settings you'll learn about for the rest of the day are shown using the ExploringVSNET project you just created in Visual Basic .NET. The screenshots and tools shown throughout the day are the same for both C# projects and Visual Basic projects. So, if you're a C# developer, you have the same IDE options as a Visual Basic developer.

Exploring the Visual Studio .NET IDE

After the ExploringVSNET project is open, you're given the default Form1 in the main window. Figure 2.11 shows you not only the new project, but it also highlights some of the main features of Visual Studio .NET.

To maximize your development environment, the main windows in the IDE slide in and out if you hover the mouse over the tab on the right or left side of the screen.

If you want a window to be visible all the time, you can click the pushpin on the window's toolbar to pin it to the screen, and from that point on, it remains open. The horizontal or vertical position of the pushpin indicates whether the window will slide in or out. A vertical pin appears when the window is pinned; otherwise, a horizontal pin is visible.

There are two main window options in Visual Studio .NET: tabbed windows or multiple document interface (MDI) windows. The tabbed theme is new to Visual Studio .NET, and as Figure 2.11 shows, the Form1.vb [Design] caption is on the only visible tab. If you open more windows, more tabs are added to the screen. You can close the current window by clicking the X in the upper-right corner of the active window. If you prefer the

MDI environment that was used in Visual Basic 6 and Visual InterDev, you can change the window setup in the Tools, Options dialog screen. You'll get used to tabbed windows very quickly; they're a nice feature.

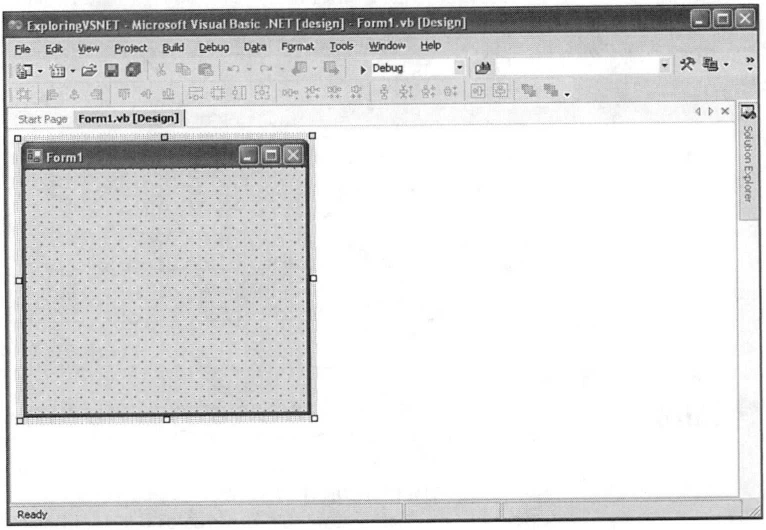

FIGURE 2.11
The ExploringVSNET project.

If you pin all the hovering windows and then close the project, the settings are saved from the previous open instance, so you don't have to reset the windows each time you open Visual Studio .NET. As in previous Microsoft development environments, you can drag and drop windows wherever you want, and the default profile that you set up on the My Profile page defaults the windows to the environment you selected at that time.

I prefer the tabbed windows to be always pinned, so my IDE looks like Figure 2.12. It gets very difficult to work fast with windows constantly popping in and out of the screen, so by pinning everything, I have my Solution Explorer, Properties window, Toolbox, Server Explorer, and Dynamic Help always available.

Using the Solution Explorer

As you can see by Figure 2.12, the Solution Explorer has the hierarchical structure of your current project. The toolbar on the Solution Explorer window enables you to switch between Design view and Code view, refresh the files list in the Solution Explorer, and show or hide files that aren't part of your solution.

When Visual Studio .NET creates a project, the `.SLN` file contains the path to the actual location of the solution files. The files listed in the Solution Explorer are all the pertinent files in the directory of the solution. So, files that aren't pertinent to the project, such as the `Bin` and `Obj` directory, aren't included in the project—they're hidden. To include a file in the project, you can right-click on a file that's dimmed in the Solution Explorer and select Include in Project from the contextual menu. If you don't see the `Bin` and `Obj` folders, click the Show All Files button on the Solution Explorer toolbar.

FIGURE 2.12

Tabbed windows that are pinned.

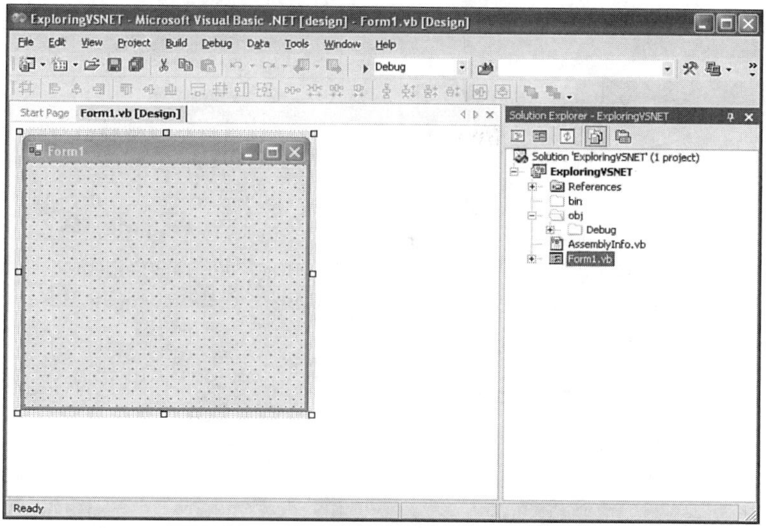

Here are some tips for using the Solution Explorer:

- The Solution Explorer is a representation of the solution's folder on the file system. If you add items to the folder outside of Visual Studio .NET, click the Refresh button, make sure that you're showing hidden files, and you'll see the files you added to the file system.
- You can drag items from the Desktop, Windows Explorer, Web folders, or anywhere else, directly to the Solution Explorer. When working with Visual Basic .NET and C# projects, the files dragged into the Solution Explorer are physically copied to the source directory; they aren't shortcuts to the files added.
- There is full cut, copy, and paste capability between files and folders in the Solution Explorer, and files and folders from the file system to the Solution Explorer.
- You can right-click on a file or folder in the Solution Explorer and select Exclude From Project to make the file hidden to the solution, which means it won't be included in the compile.

- Deleting a file from the Solution Explorer physically deletes the file from the file system and places the file in the Recycle Bin, so be careful when you delete. If you want to get rid of a file and not delete it, either remove or exclude the file.
- The Solution Explorer can manage multiple projects. From the right-click contextual menu on the Solution Explorer, you can add new items such as forms or files to the project, or add new projects to the solution. The number of projects a solution can contain is unlimited, and the number or individual files that a project can contain is also unlimited.

Using the Properties Window

The Properties window enables you to set properties on items that you select on forms in the IDE. You can also right-click on items in the Solution Explorer and select Properties from the contextual menu to see the properties for the files, such as file location. You'll learn more about the Properties window over the next few days when you begin building applications.

Using the Toolbox

The Toolbox contains visual and nonvisual controls that can be added to Web Forms or Windows Forms in Design mode. By dragging items from the Toolbox to a form, you can set properties and write code that responds to events for the control you have added.

In Visual Studio .NET, the Toolbox is slightly different from Visual Basic 6, but similar to Visual InterDev. The Toolbox has multiple tabs that group items based on functionality. You can customize the tabs that are visible and create new tabs by right-clicking on the Toolbox and selecting Show All Tabs or Add New Tab, respectively. Figure 2.13 shows the Toolbox with the Show All Tabs option selected. You can see by the number of tabs that there are many new controls you can add to the designers and forms in your projects.

Another huge addition to the Toolbox is the ability to drag items from the Code Editor to the Toolbox. This feature enables you to save code items for later use. Every item added to the Toolbox is persisted with the IDE, so it remains there for all instances that you open. To use it effectively, you should create new tabs in the Toolbox to differentiate your code snippets from the controls. You can then drag items from the code window to the Toolbox, and right-click on the item to rename it to something meaningful.

The Clipboard Ring tabtab keeps track of all things copied to the Clipboard in Windows. So, if you're copying items from outside of the IDE, they'll appear in the Clipboard Ring tab. You can then either drag the items to a new tab or drag them directly to the Code Editor.

FIGURE 2.13

The Toolbox showing all tabs.

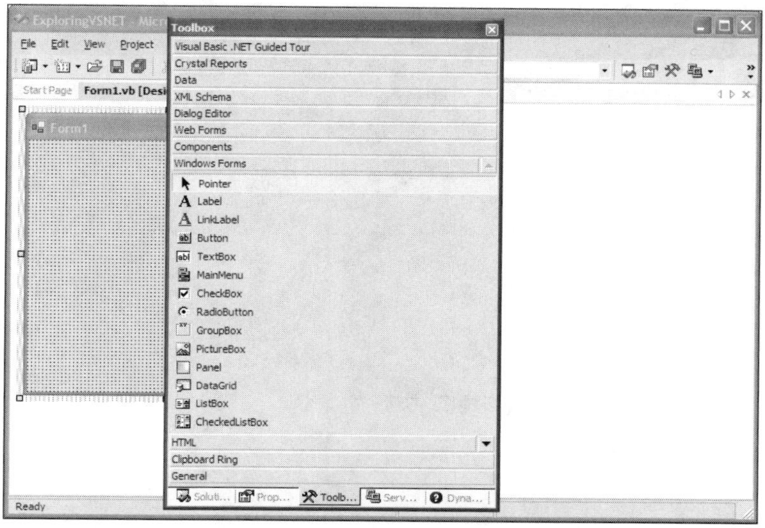

Caution

Visual Studio .NET saves the state of the last instance of Visual Studio .NET that you had open. So, if you have five instances of Visual Studio .NET open, and you're dragging items to new tabs and setting up your development environment, make sure that you close the "good" copy last. If you close it first, all your customization is lost.

Using the Server Explorer

The Server Explorer is a window into the server resources on your computer or other computers on your network. From the Server Explorer, you can view OLE DB database connections, which can also be created in a number of ways using either the Server Explorer or tools from the Data tab in the Toolbox. You can also view event logs, message queues, performance counters, services, and SQL Servers installed on your computer. Figure 2.14 demonstrates some of the features available in the Server Explorer.

To add new servers to the Server Explorer, you can right-click on the Servers node or click the Add Server button on the Server Explorer toolbar. You're prompted for the name of the server to connect to, and you can modify the security context under which you're logging in to the server.

On Day 11, "Understanding Visual Database Tools," you make heavy use of the Server Explorer data access features.

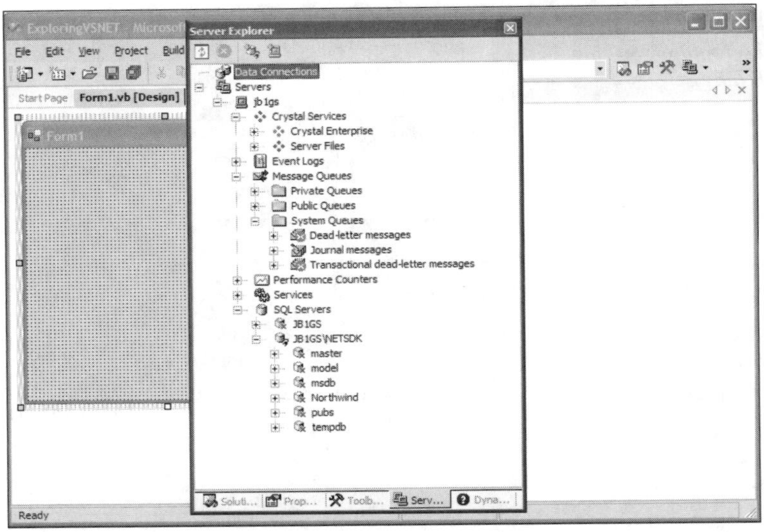

FIGURE 2.14
The Server Explorer.

Tip

> There are many times when you need access to tables, views, and stored procedures in a SQL Server database, but don't have access to the Enterprise Manager for SQL Server or don't have the correct permissions to log in to the SQL Server through the SQL Servers node of the Server Explorer. To get around this, you can click the Connect to a Database button on the Server Explorer and create an OLE DB connection to the database using your credentials. This gives you almost the same functionality as using the SQL Servers node of the Server Explorer without the hassle of getting the correct permissions set up on the server that SQL Server is running on. After you have a database connection, you can create and alter tables, create and alter stored procedures, create and alter views, and create and alter functions as if you were using SQL Server's Enterprise Manager or the SQL Server node in the Solution Explorer. Best of all, this functionality is available to any OLE DB connection, such as Microsoft Access databases and Oracle databases.

Getting to the Other Windows

The Solution Explorer, Properties window, Toolbox, and Server Explorer are the most common windows that you'll use, but Visual Studio .NET has dozens of other useful windows that integrate directly with the IDE.

On the Standard toolbar, there are buttons to gain access to each window available in Visual Studio .NET, and they're also accessible by selecting the View option from the main menu.

Figure 2.15 shows the full list of windows available by selecting View from the main menu.

FIGURE 2.15

Selecting other windows from the View menu.

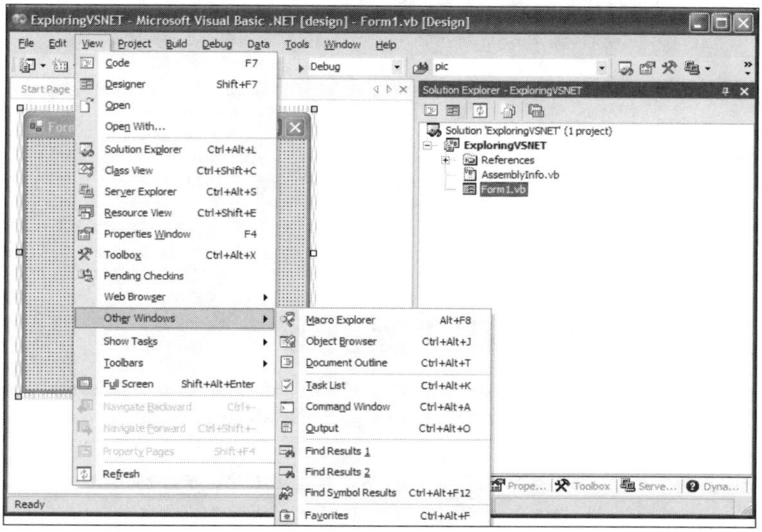

Depending on the menu item you select, the window could be pinned to the right, left, or bottom of your screen. Each window that opens in Visual Studio .NET has the ability to be pinned, docked, floating, or sliding.

Over the next three weeks, you'll learn about each of the windows in Figure 2.15 and the context in which each one is used.

Using the Project Menu

The Project menu gives you the ability to add new items to your current project. You can also access this menu by right-clicking your project name in the Solution Explorer. From this menu, you can also add assembly references, COM references, Web services references, and existing items from other projects or the file system to your application. Figure 2.16 shows the Add New Item dialog box that you can access from the Project menu.

By default, the items listed in the Project menu are specific to the type of project template you're using. The current project is a Windows Forms application, so the available default items are Forms based. If you were working with an ASP.NET application, the project items would be specific to Web projects. Using the Add New Item dialog box, you have access to all available item types for all project types.

FIGURE 2.16
The Add New Item dialog box.

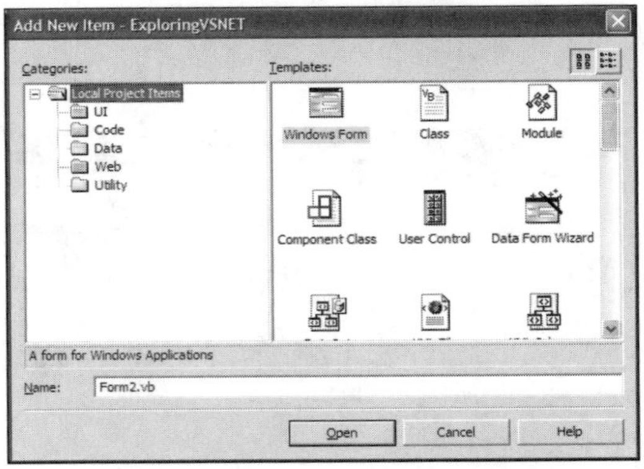

Using the Build Menu

The Build menu gives you options for compiling, or building, your project or group of projects in a solution. The options for building items are demonstrated in Figure 2.17.

FIGURE 2.17
Build options in Visual Studio .NET.

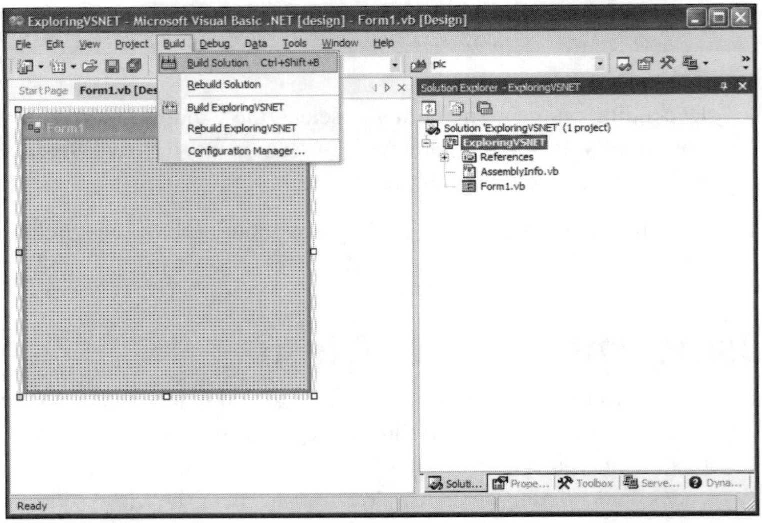

When you build a solution, you're doing a full build on all items in the solution. A rebuild only builds items that have changed since the last build or rebuild. The Configuration Manager shown in Figure 2.18 enables you to specify the type of build you're performing. If the build is a debug build, a PDB file is created with your output assembly that contains debug information that can be used by the Visual Studio .NET debugger or external debuggers. If you select Release for the build, the debug information won't be created.

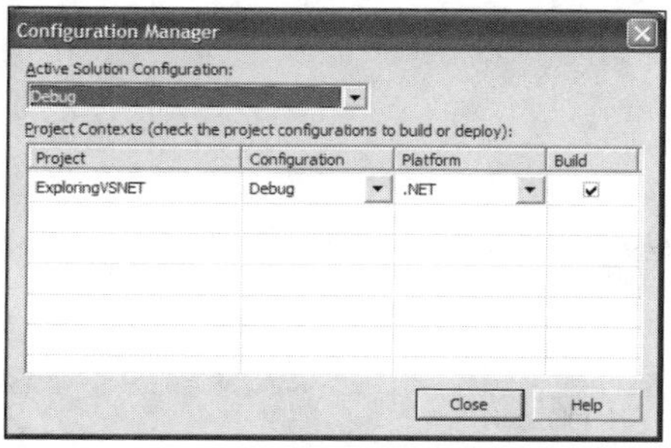

FIGURE 2.18
The Configuration Manager.

You can create new build configurations from the Configuration Manager dialogConfiguration Manager dialog box.

> **Tip**
>
> On the Main toolbar, you can switch between the build configurations. A drop-down list has the available build options. Selecting this via the toolbar is quicker than going through the Build Configuration dialog box.

Using the Debug Menu

On Day 7, "Exceptions, Debugging, and Tracing," you learn all about the various debugging capabilities in Visual Studio .NET. From the Debug menu, you can get to the multitude of debugging windows, you can start your project with or without debugging, and you can step into and over breakpoints in your project. As in Visual Basic 6, the F5 key runs your applications, and the Ctrl+F5 shortcut runs your application without debugging, meaning the syntax checks are skipped. Figure 2.19 demonstrates the Debug menu and the Breakpoints window pinned to the bottom of the IDE.

Using the Format Menu

The Format menu was introduced to Visual Basic developers with Visual Basic 5. It was always a standard item in Microsoft Access. In Visual Studio .NET, the Format menu has every option you could ever want for formatting controls on your forms. You can set sizing, spacing, tab order, and alignment from the Format menu. This menu is also available from the Format toolbar. Figure 2.20 demonstrates the Format menu and some of the Make Same Size options.

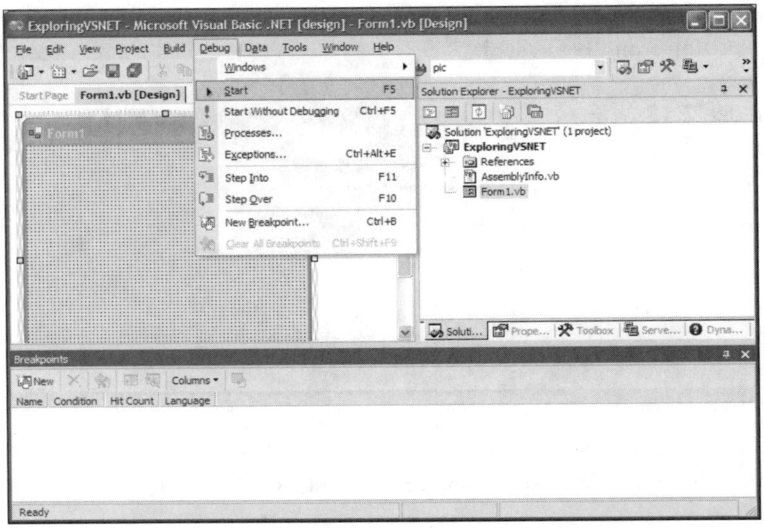

FIGURE 2.19

The Debug menu and Breakpoints window.

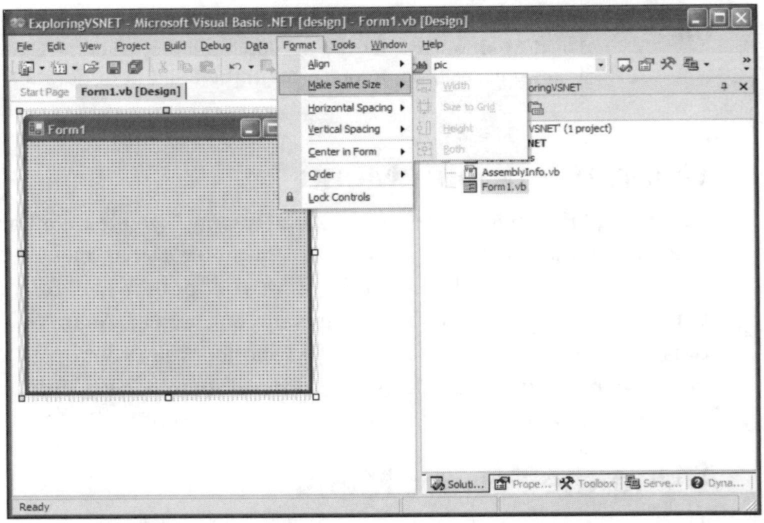

FIGURE 2.20

Setting size and alignment with the Format menu.

Using the Tools Menu

The Tools menu has the remainder of the vast array of tools available in Visual Studio .NET. From the Tools menu, you can do everything from debugging processes to running external applications such as Spy++, which comes with the Enterprise Architect version of Visual Studio .NET. Instead of listing all the available items, take a look at Figure 2.21 to get an idea of the options offered by the Tools menu.

In Figure 2.21, you'll notice that Build Comment Web Pages is selected. This is a cool feature that generates HTML pages on the structure of classes, methods, properties, and events in your solution.

FIGURE 2.21

Options from the Tools menu.

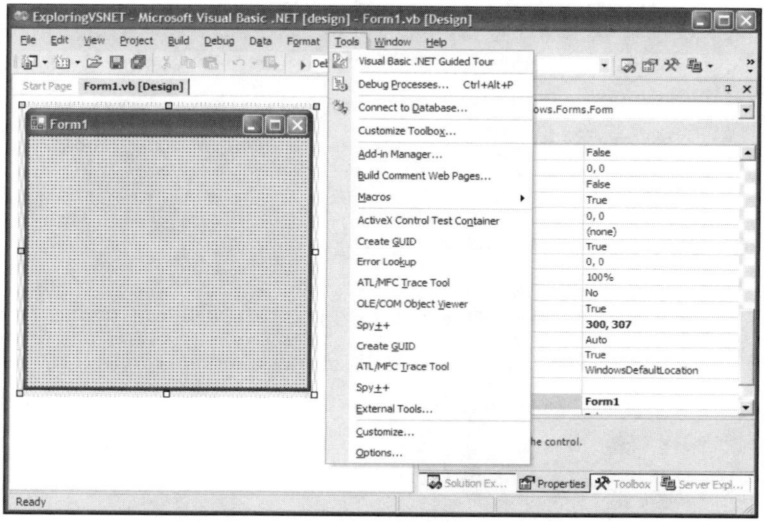

To test this feature, click the Build Comment Web Pages menu item. When the dialog pops up, simply click the OK button. The comment pages are generated, and should look something like Figure 2.22.

FIGURE 2.22

Build Comment Web Pages results.

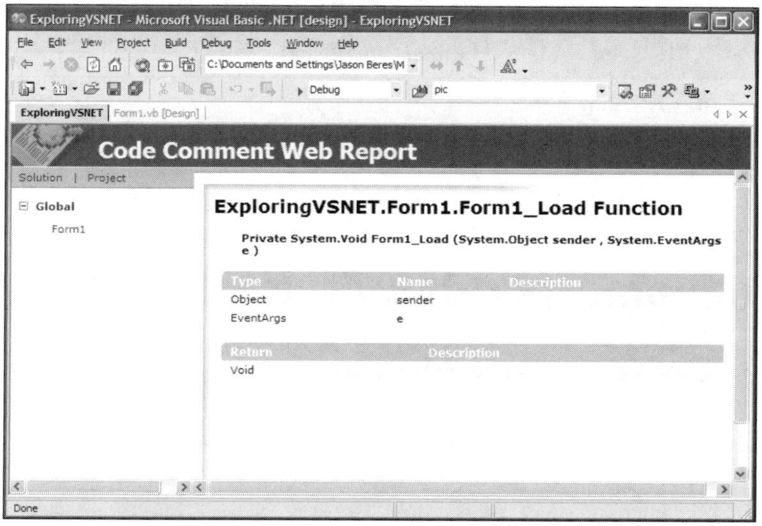

After the HTML reports are built, you can view the hierarchy of the types in your solution. The files are saved to your hard disk, so they can be distributed to team members who need to know what's going on with a project. This will become a useful tool for both the one-man consultant and the large teams of developers working on projects. You can get a bird's-eye view of your whole project simply by building these comment pages.

If you're a C# developer, you can embed custom comments in your code with an XML-like syntax as the following code snippet demonstrates:

```
///<summary>
/// summary description of any item
///</summary>
///<remarks>
/// Relevant remarks on an object
///</remarks>
```

The complete list of tags that C# supports for building comment Web pages is as follows:

- `<summary></summary>`—Describes a member for a type
- `<remarks></remarks>`—Specifies overview information for a class or other type
- `<param></param>`—Used in the comment for a method declaration to describe one of the parameters for the method
- `<returns></returns>`—Used in the comment for a method declaration to describe the return value
- `<newpara></newpara>`—Starts a new paragraph in the comments

As long as you prefix the code comment tags with `///`, comments are generated in the resulting Build Comment HTML pages. Unfortunately, the built-in functionality for XML comments isn't supported in Visual Basic .NET, but you can find some third-party XML documentation builders for Visual Basic .NET at

`http://www.gotdotnet.com/team/vb/`

and

`http://www.fesersoft.com/products/VBXmlComments/default.asp`

Managing Code Windows and Designers

When you're writing code, it's always nice to see the form you're working on and the code window at the same time, or even the help file and the code window at the same time. With a tabbed document interface, this might not seem possible. But if you click the Windows menu, you'll notice several options for splitting the screen and creating new tab groups. To view as much information at once as possible, you can select New Horizontal Tab Group or New Vertical Tab Group from the Window menu. This splits the main window either vertically or horizontally, giving you a better view of what you're working on.

Figure 2.23 shows the Forms Designer and the Code Editor split into two separate windows. Of course, the screen resolution at 800×600 makes this unusable to a degree, but at a higher resolution, you can have all your forms, code editors, and help files open at once and still have plenty of room to work.

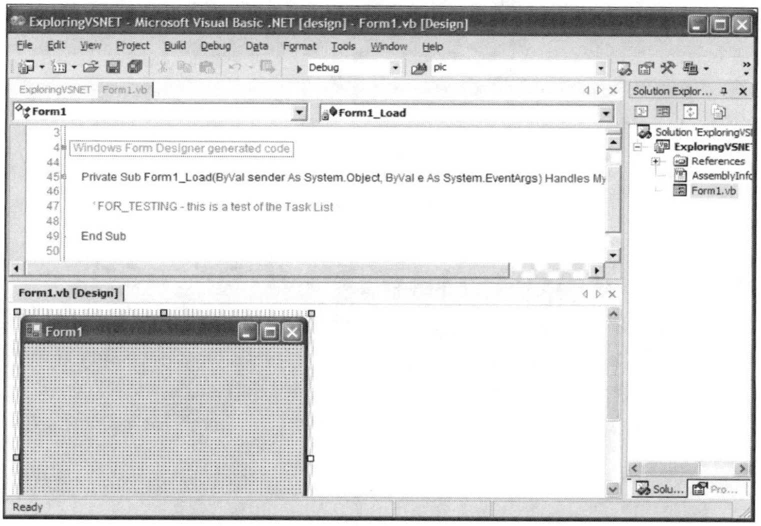

FIGURE 2.23

Horizontally split windows.

If there were controls on Form1 in design mode, the Code Editor would dynamically change based on the items you select.

Getting the Right Toolbars

Until now, you've seen the different IDE features and how to access them from the various menu items on the main Visual Studio .NET menu.

Each item you've seen so far also has its own toolbar. To view a list of available toolbars, you can right-click the main toolbar on the top of the IDE and a checked list of toolbars pops up. To view a toolbar, simply select it from the list. If you select a toolbar that isn't specific to the item you're working on in the IDE, the toolbar buttons are disabled. Figure 2.24 lists the available toolbars for the Visual Studio .NET IDE.

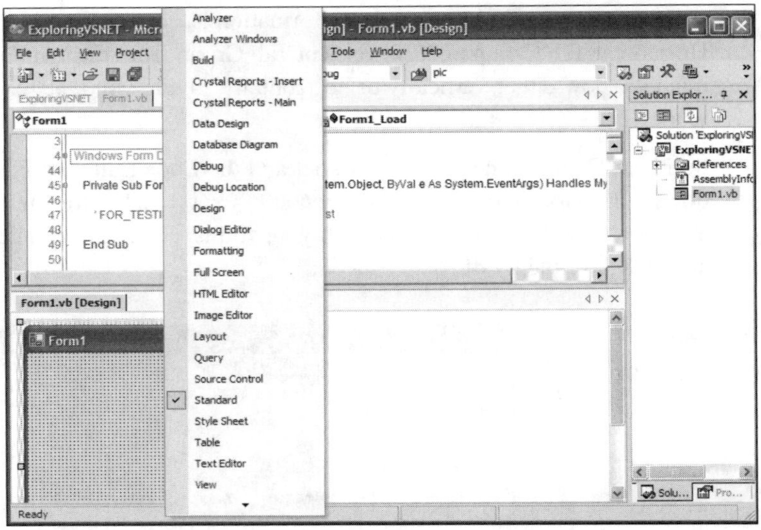

FIGURE 2.24

The Visual Studio .NET toolbars.

Customizing Your Environment

Being able to customize your IDE will make your life easier in the long run. Because you've just started using Visual Studio .NET, you probably don't know what customizations would be useful. In this section, I discuss the most useful customization options based on what I've learned using Visual Studio .NET over the last two years.

To get to the Options dialog, select Tools, Options from the main menu. You're presented with the Options dialog box shown in Figure 2.25.

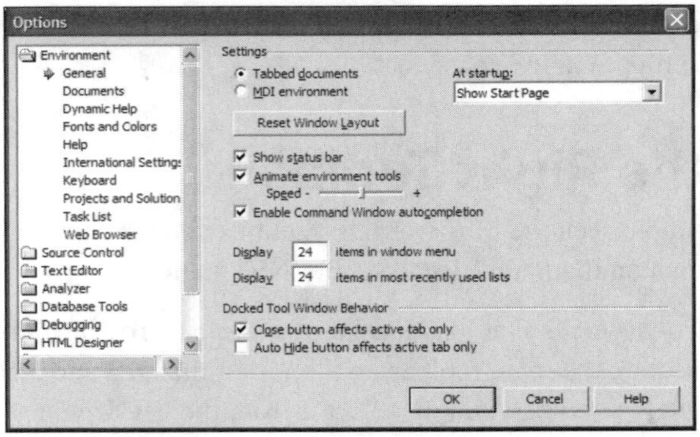

FIGURE 2.25

The Options dialog box.

The Options dialog is broken down by tree nodes displayed on the left side of the dialog box. The right side of the dialog changes based on what you select from the left nodes.

The Environment, General node enables you to modify general IDE settings, such as the number of items to display on the Start Page, tabbed or MDI documents, auto-complete, and the docking behavior of the windows. Depending on your screen resolution, I'd bump up the number of display items in the Items window menu and the Most Recently Used List to somewhere between 15 and 24.

Changing Fonts and Colors

The Fonts and Colors item under Environment changes the default font of the Code Editors. I can't stand Times New Roman or Courier, so I always use Arial and I set my font to 14 point. The higher resolution makes reading easier on the eyes. If you prefer other colors or even want to change the background and foreground colors of the Code Editors, you can do so here.

Customizing Help Location

The Help node shown in Figure 2.26 is also a useful option to change based on your preferences. It's nice to have the Dynamic Help show everything inside of the IDE, but you might be short on screen space and want to display it outside the IDE. Choosing External Help opens all F1 requests outside the Visual Studio .NET IDE.

FIGURE 2.26

The Help Options dialog box.

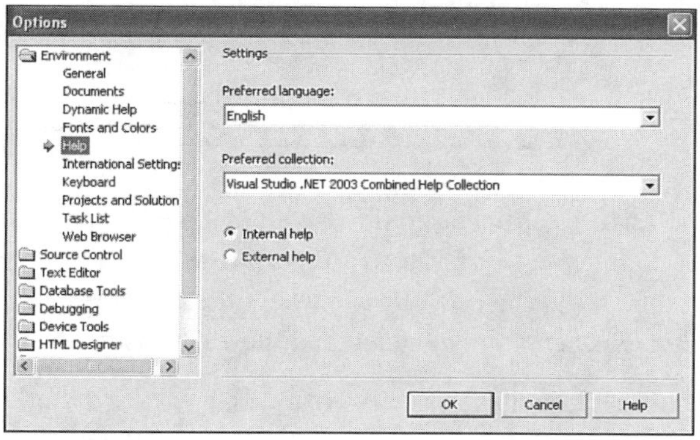

Modifying the Keyboard Layout

The Keyboard node enables you to modify or add new shortcut keys for quicker access to frequently used items. Modifying the default keyboard mapping scheme is useful if you're used to multiple environments and want the best of all worlds inside .NET.

Saving Files in Projects and Solutions

By default, Visual Studio .NET automatically saves any changes in open documents when you run the application. This was a bad thing in Visual Basic 6 because you always had a way to revert back to the old code if your results weren't what you expected at design time. This was possible because Visual Basic 6 was interpreted, not compiled. In .NET, all code must be compiled before it can be run, so it must be saved. Leaving the default option to Save Changed to Open Documents on Build and Run is a good idea.

Task List and Comments

The Task List is a major feature in the Visual Studio .NET IDE that mimics the Tasks in Outlook. When you compile your application, any errors show up in the Task List. You can also add comments throughout your applications with special predefined tokens or custom tokens that you add. Figure 2.27 shows the Comment Tokens section. I added the `FOR_TESTING` comment token to my Task List.

FIGURE 2.27

Adding custom comment tokens to the Task List.

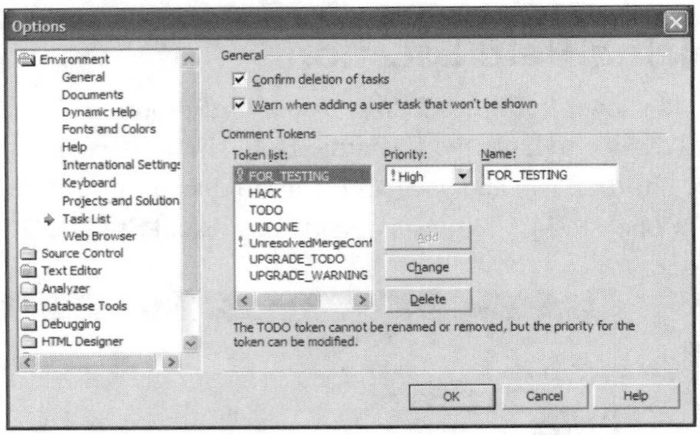

Now, any time I add a comment prefixed with `FOR_TESTING`, it shows up in my Task List with the other comment information. From the Task List, I can double-click on task items and get directly to the line of code where the comment was placed. Figure 2.28 shows an example of a comment added and the Task List displaying my current tasks.

By default, the Task List displays only errors. To see everything, you must right-click on the Task List and select Show Tasks, All from the contextual menu.

If you go back to the Tools, Options dialog, you can peruse the remaining items that you can customize. Altogether, there are approximately 500 different customization options. You'll really only use a few because the defaults are based on what most developers use. The few items I have shown you are the most important. Depending on the tools you use the most and your language preference, there are options for just about everything in the Options dialog.

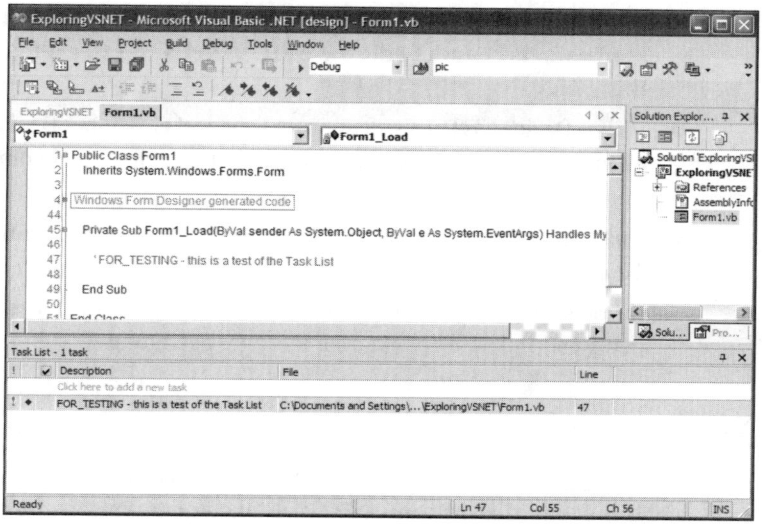

FIGURE 2.28
The Task List with custom comment tokens added.

Summary

Today you learned about the Visual Studio .NET IDE and all the great things it offers. As you go through the next three weeks, you'll learn more about the IDE every day, and you'll begin to realize its true power. Just remember that in Visual Studio .NET, everything is a right-click away and there are toolbars for every possible option, so you don't have to look far for what you need to get your job done.

Q&A

Q I'm having trouble managing my windows. They keep flying all over the place, and I just want them back to the way they were when I first installed Visual Studio .NET. What can I do?

A The easiest way to change your window scheme is to return to the My Profile page on the Start Page. If you test a few of the configuration options, you'll probably find one you like. Dragging and positioning windows always seems to be the hardest thing for new developers to figure out. If you're having problems docking windows, try double-clicking the window's toolbar. The window will dock to its last location.

Q I've been playing with some Visual Basic .NET code, and when I break in my application, I cannot edit the code. Why? I did this all the time in Visual Basic 6!

A Visual Basic .NET doesn't support Edit and Continue. Because the code is compiled, you can't modify code on-the-fly by setting breakpoints and setting the next statement.

Q I use some external editors for various reasons. How can I add them to the Tools menu?

A If you select the External Tools option from the Tools menu, you can add menu items and links to any external tool you need to use.

Quiz

1. The ________________ dialog box gives you complete control over the look and feel of the Visual Studio .NET IDE, including font size for the text editor window and the type of Dynamic Help files you want to use.
2. Using the ________________ menu item, you can quickly generate HTML-based summaries of your applications.
3. True or False: When adding XML comments in Visual Basic .NET, you must import the `Microsoft.VisualBasic.CodeComments` namespace.

Quiz Answers

1. Options
2. Build Comment Web Pages
3. False. Visual Basic .NET doesn't support XML comments, and there's no such namespace as `Microsoft.VisualBasic.CodeComments`.

Exercises

1. Understanding the different types of projects and the file structures are extremely important. To see what each project type offers and how each one looks, select a few different types of applications from the New Project dialog. Look to see what files are added to your solution and where the files are located.
2. Using Dynamic Help, do a search for `.sln`, as Figure 2.29 demonstrates. From this help link, read about the different file types and extensions that make up solutions, and read the related topics that link in this file.

FIGURE 2.29

Searching for .SLN *in Dynamic Help.*

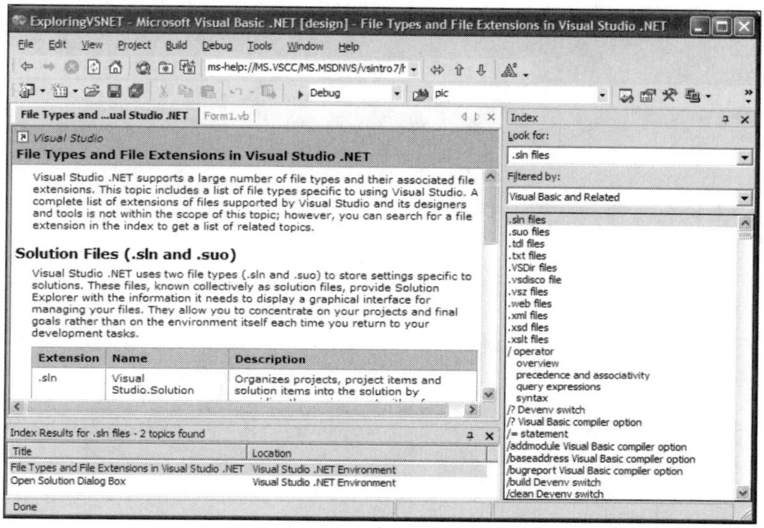

WEEK 1

DAY 3

Writing Windows Forms Applications

The ability to rapidly develop and deploy forms-based applications is what led to the phenomenal success of Visual Basic. Visual Basic enables you to build enterprise-level applications at lightning speed without requiring you to fully understand what the underlying infrastructure of the operating system is doing. With .NET, this ability is taken to the next level. The Windows Forms model for .NET is fully integrated into the .NET Framework. The development model is fully object oriented, enabling you to create better applications faster using Visual Studio .NET. The *rapid* in Rapid Application Development (RAD) has never been truer when developing with Windows Forms. Today, you learn about

- Using forms and controls
- How to handle events in Windows Forms
- Adding controls to forms
- Dynamically adding controls to Forms
- Creating MDI applications with Windows Forms
- Inheriting Windows Forms
- Using common dialogs in Windows Forms

Hello .NET!

Every introduction to writing applications needs to start with the Hello World type application. This isn't because it's such a cool cliché. It's to get you familiar with the environment you're working in and to better explain what's going on when you're running the application. To get you started with Visual Studio .NET development, you're going to create the HelloNET application.

To begin, start Visual Studio .NET. On the Getting Started page, click the New Project button. You're prompted with the New Project dialog you learned about yesterday. Figure 3.1 demonstrates the New Project dialog.

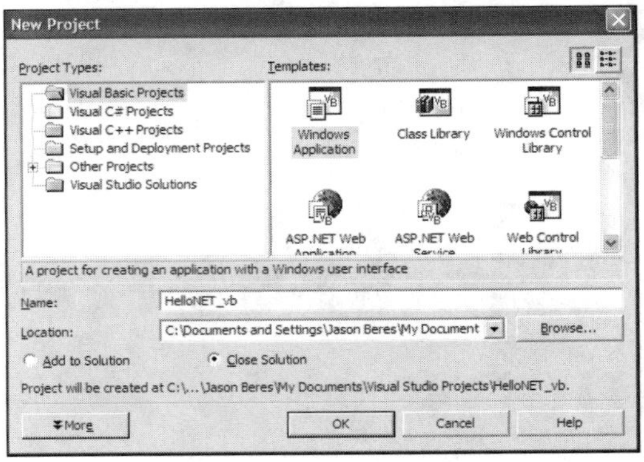

FIGURE 3.1
The New Project dialog box.

Select the Windows Application template from either the C# or Visual Basic folder, and change the Name to HelloNET. Click the OK button to create the application.

After the project has been created, you should be looking at something like Figure 3.2.

Note

Throughout this book, there are code examples for Visual Basic .NET and C# for everything you learn. When I ask you to create a new application, most of the time I say to call it *something_vb* or *something_cs*, depending on the language you're writing your code in. To differentiate the code in the downloads for the book and to enable you to write the same application in both languages, you can't have the same project name. So, if there are screenshots that look like a project name is different from what I ask you to create, that's the reason. By the end of the book, you'll see there's very little difference between C# and Visual Basic .NET, and you'll be bilingual!

FIGURE 3.2
The HelloNET application.

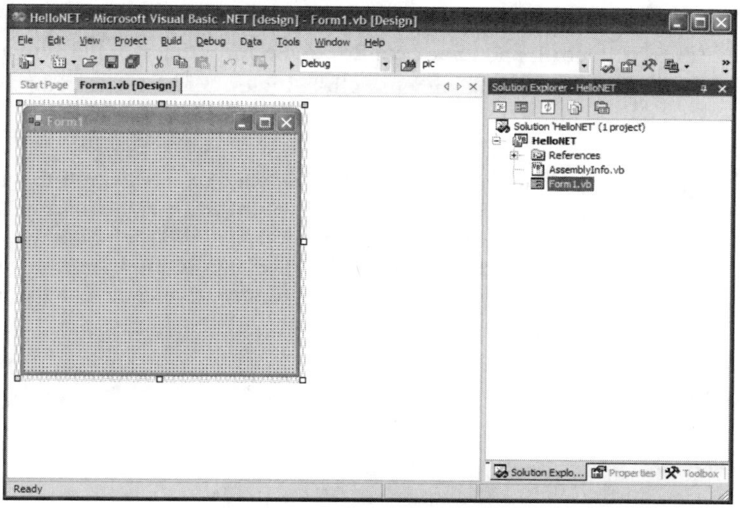

As you learned yesterday, there are many useful windows when developing applications. The key items you'll use when creating Windows Forms applications are the Solution Explorer, the Properties window, and the Toolbox. If you don't see these windows on your screen, you can get to them in the ways shown in Table 3.1.

TABLE 3.1 Shortcuts to Main Windows When Designing Forms

Window	*Shortcut Options*
Properties	F4 key
	View, Properties from the View menu
	The Properties button on the standard toolbar
Toolbox	Ctrl+Alt+X shortcut keys
	View, Toolbox from the View menu
	The Toolbox button on the standard toolbar
Solution Explorer	Ctrl+Alt+L shortcut keys
	View, Solution Explorer from the View menu
	The Solution Explorer button on the standard toolbar

The key to rapid development with Windows Forms is the ability to easily drag items from the Toolbox onto the forms, set properties on the controls that you add using the Properties window, and write code that responds to the controls and form events. That's why the three windows in Table 3.1 are so important.

Next, you must add some controls to the form. From the Toolbox, drag a `Button` control, `Textbox` control, and `Label` control to the form that's in the Windows Forms designer. Your form should look something like Figure 3.3 after the controls are added.

Tip

> There are a couple of other ways to add controls to a form. First, you can double-click Toolbox controls to add them to a form. They are added on top of the last control added to the form. The second way is to select a control from the Toolbox and "draw" it onto the form with your mouse. This will let you position and size the control as you add it to the form.

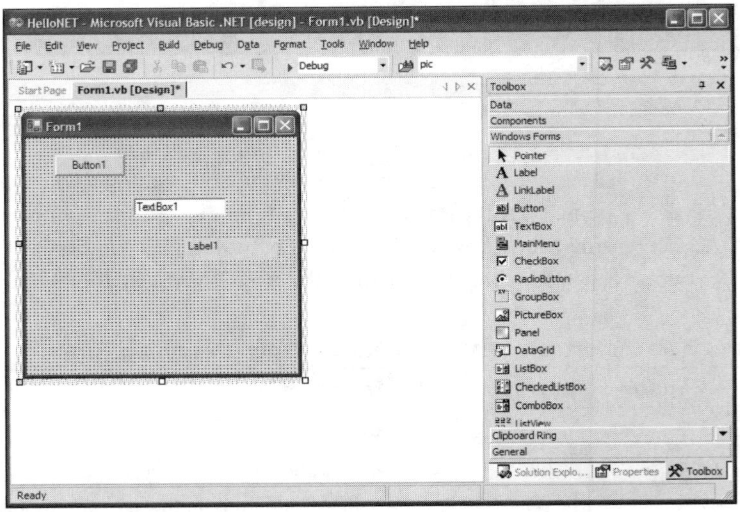

FIGURE 3.3
Adding controls to the default form.

Next, single-click the form and press the F4 key to view its properties. Change the following properties on the form:

- `StartPosition`: CenterScreen
- `MaximumSize`: 400, 400
- `MinimumSize`: 200, 200
- `Font`: Tahoma, 14pt

After you set the `Font` property, notice that the font sizes of the controls on the form change to the form's font properties. This is a new feature in Windows Forms; the controls inherit the font properties of the form. You can easily override these properties by setting properties on the individual controls. You learn more about the different controls a little later.

Next, double-click `Button1` to get to the Code Editor window. This works like Visual Basic 6 did: You double-click controls and you're taken to their default event.

You're now looking at the `Form_Load` event. Notice that the load event accepts two arguments—`System.Object` and `System.EventArgs`—as the following code snippet demonstrates:

VB.NET

```
Private Sub Form1_Load(ByVal sender As System.Object, _
                ByVal e As System.EventArgs) Handles MyBase.Load

End Sub
```

C#

```
        private void Form1_Load(object sender, System.EventArgs e)
        {

        }
```

Every control that you add to a form (and the form itself) always has to accept the object that's passing it the data and then the event arguments for that object. Depending on the control and the event, it won't always be `System.EventArgs`, but there will always be an event arguments parameter.

In the `Form_Load` event, add the code in Listing 3.1, which displays a message box welcoming you to Visual Studio .NET.

LISTING 3.1 The `Form_Load` Event Code for HelloNET

VB.NET

```
Private Sub Form1_Load(ByVal sender As System.Object, _
                ByVal e As System.EventArgs) Handles MyBase.Load

    MessageBox.Show("Welcome to .NET!")

End Sub
```

C#

```
private void Form1_Load(object sender, System.EventArgs e)
{
    MessageBox.Show("Welcome to .NET!");
}
```

You'll notice that the `MessageBox` class is used to prompt information back to the user. The functionality of the `MessageBox` class is very similar to that of the `MsgBox` function in Visual Basic 6. You can pass a prompt, respond to button events, and set the title for the message box that's displayed.

Next, you need to add code for the click event of the `Button` you added to the form earlier. There are several ways to write code that responds to events in Windows Forms. The easiest way to write code for an event is to double-click a control on the Forms Designer and you're taken to the default event for that control in the Code Editor.

If you're writing in Visual Basic, you can select the control from the Class Name drop-down list in the upper-left corner of the Code Editor. After you select the control you want to write an event for, you can select the correct method from the Method Name drop-down list, which is next to the Class Name drop-down list. Figure 3.4 demonstrates the Method Name drop-down list for some of the `Button1` events. Notice that `Button1` was selected from the Class Name list.

FIGURE 3.4

The `Button1` *Method Name options.*

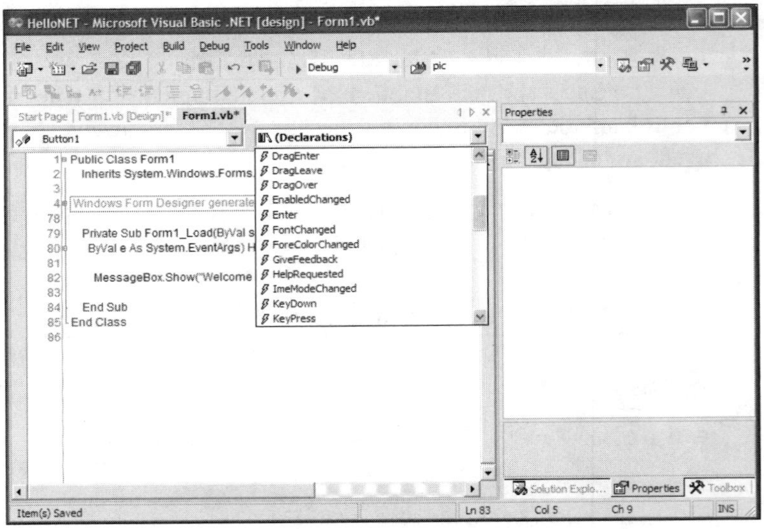

You'll also notice the (Overrides) and (Base Class Events) options in the Class Name drop-down. The (Overrides) option gives you all the methods, properties, and events that you can programmatically override for the form. The (Base Class Events) option gives you the methods for the `Form` class. A little later today you'll better understand how classes work and what they'll mean to you as you develop not only in Windows Forms, but also in .NET as a whole.

If you're a C# developer, you don't have the Class Name and Method Name drop-down lists in the Code Editor for events that haven't been added to the form. To add new events for the form and for controls on the form, you must select the control on the form while you're in the Forms Designer. Then, on the toolbar of the Properties window for the selected control, click the lightning bolt button, which gives you the list of events for the selected control. When you find the event you want to write code for, you can double-click the event name in the list, and you're taken to the Code Editor for that event. Figure 3.5 demonstrates the `button1_Click` event selected in the Properties window.

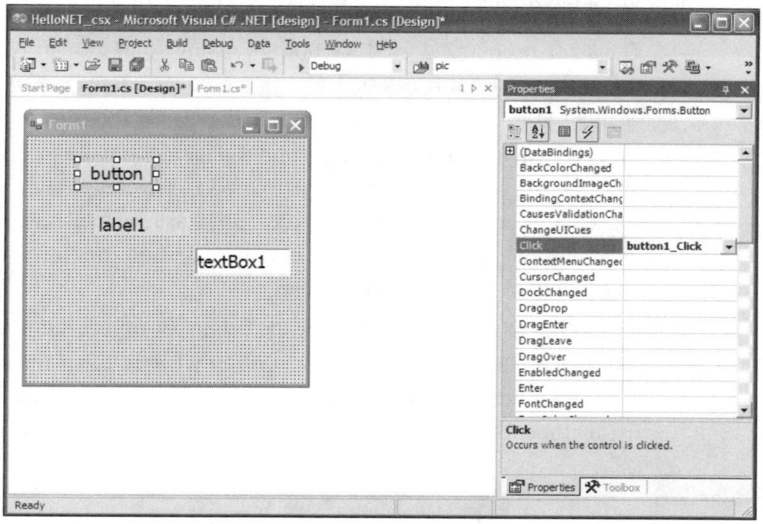

FIGURE 3.5
The `button1_Click` *event of the Properties window for a C# application.*

Now that you know how to add events with the IDE, add the code in Listing 3.2 to the `button1_Click` event.

LISTING 3.2 `button1_Click` Event for the HelloNET Application

VB.NET

```
Private Sub Button1_Click(ByVal sender As Object, _
            ByVal e As System.EventArgs) Handles Button1.Click

    Label1.Text = TextBox1.Text

End Sub
```

LISTING 3.2 continued

C#

```
private void button1_Click(object sender, System.EventArgs e)
{
    label1.Text = textBox1.Text;
}
```

There are a few items to note on the code you just wrote:

- The `Text` property is used for both the `Label` and the `TextBox` control. This is different from Visual Basic 6. There is no longer a `Caption` property for labels, forms, or other controls—it's replaced with the `Text` property.
- C# is a case-sensitive language, and the casing defaults to *camel casing*, meaning that the first character of an object name is lowercase and the first letters of any subsequent concatenated words are uppercase. Visual Basic uses *Pascal casing*, meaning that the first character is uppercase and the first letters of any subsequent concatenated words are uppercase.
- Visual Basic automatically fixes the casing of object names, but C# does not. This also means the auto-list members do not work in C# if the casing isn't correct. Figure 3.6 demonstrates auto-list members in C# when the casing is correct. Auto-list members works in Visual Basic even if the casing is incorrect.

FIGURE 3.6

Auto-list members in the C# Code Editor.

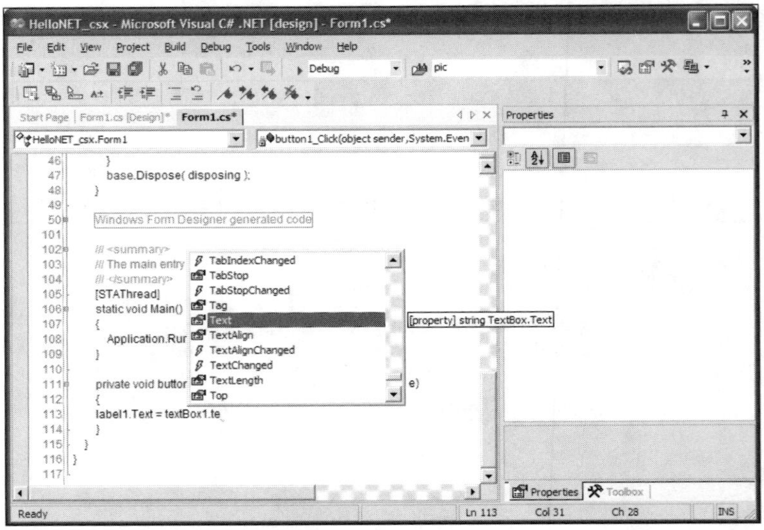

Now that the code has been added and you're getting an idea of how to work with the IDE, press the F5 button to run the application. Pressing F5 has the same effect as selecting Start from the Debug menu or clicking the Start button on the Standard toolbar.

When the application starts, you're prompted with `Welcome to .NET!` that you added in the `Form_Load` event. After the form is active, type **`Hello .NET`** into the `TextBox` and click the `Button` on the form. The `Label` control is filled with the contents of the `TextBox`.

You also set some properties in the form, such as `MinimumSize`, `MaximumSize`, `AutoScroll`, and `StartPosition`. When the application starts, the form shows up in the middle of the screen. If you now resize the form, you'll see that it can only grow to a certain size and shrink to a certain size. This is a cool feature that wasn't in Visual Basic 6. The bigger-than-life feature is `AutoScroll`. If you resize the form and the controls can't remain visible, scrollbars appear automatically. Figure 3.7 demonstrates `AutoScroll` in action.

FIGURE 3.7

The `AutoScroll` *property for a form in action.*

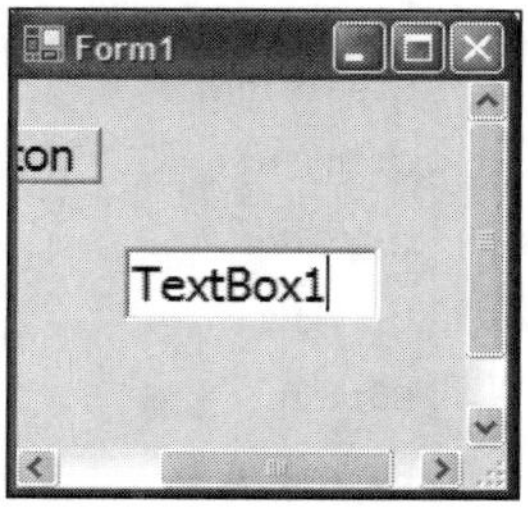

You can click the X in the upper-right of the form to close the form and get back to the designer.

Note

When you're in the integrated development environment (IDE) and press the F5 key to run the application, you're in Debug mode. In Debug mode, the application is running and you have access to all the debugging features in Visual Studio .NET that you learn about on Day 7, "Exceptions, Debugging, and Tracing." When you stop debugging, by closing the main form that is running or clicking the Stop button on the Debug toolbar, you go back to Design time. So, when you're writing an application in the Visual Studio .NET IDE, you're either in Debug mode or Design time mode. When the application is compiled and you run it from the file system, it's called *runtime*.

The `AutoScroll` property is one of many cool properties that forms and controls have in .NET. To see some of the new properties, follow Table 3.2 and change the corresponding properties.

TABLE 3.2 Properties to Change on the `Form1` Controls

Control	*Property*	*Value*
`Form1`	`Name`	`frmMain`
	`Opacity`	`80%`
	`FormBorderStyle`	`SizeableToolWindow`
	`SizeGripStyle`	`Auto`
	`Text`	`Wow This Is Great!`
	`TopMost`	`True`
`Button1`	`Anchor`	`Top, Left, Right`
	`Cursor`	`Hand`
	`FlatStyle`	`Flat`
	`BackColor`	`SteelBlue`
	`Text`	`Click Me!`
	`ForeColor`	`LightGray`
	`Name`	`ClickMe`
`Label1`	`Dock`	`Bottom`
	`TextAlign`	`BottomRight`
`Textbox1`	`CharacterCasing`	`Upper`
	`MultiLine`	`True`
	`AcceptsReturn`	`300,300`
	`Anchor`	`Top, Bottom, Left, Right`
	`Size`	`292, 140`
	`Location`	`28, 68`
	`TextAlign`	`Right`
	`Cursor`	`Cross`

After you've changed the properties for the controls, press the F5 key to run the application. Figure 3.8 shows the form after typing some text in the box and resizing the form.

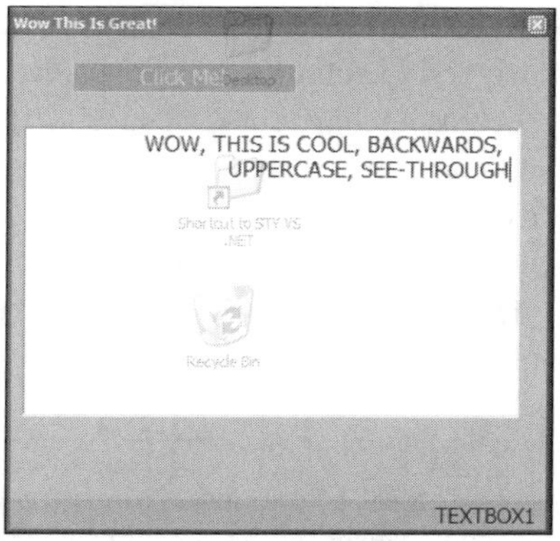

FIGURE 3.8
Running the HelloNET application after changing object properties.

You'll notice some very cool things happening with this form:

- It is almost invisible. The `Opacity` property can be set anywhere from 0% to 100%, which makes the forms see-through. When the `TransparencyKey` property on the form is set, all controls that contain the color set in the `TransparencyKey` are 100% transparent. Try it out!
- Setting the `Dock` property on the `Label` control glues it to the bottom of the form. All controls can be docked in Windows Forms.
- Setting the `Anchor` property automatically resizes the control when the form is resized. This is automatic, and every control in Windows Forms can be anchored. No more resize code!
- The `ScrollBars` are no longer there. Because the `Anchor` and `Dock` properties are set on the form, there's no need to scroll—the controls always resize within the bound of the form.
- The `Cursor` property is easily changed for all controls in Windows Forms. This enables you to customize the look and feel for each control when the mouse hovers over it.
- The text in the `Textbox` is UPPERCASE, and the words display from right to left. You can use the Enter key inside the Textbox. Setting the `CharacterCasing`, `AcceptsReturn`, and `TextAlign` properties allow complete customization of the `Textbox` control.
- The form stays on top of all other open applications. Using this property in conjunction with the `Opacity` property can give you some great options for always-open, nonintrusive applications.

Besides making a form that has no real use, the goal of setting the properties for the controls on the form was to introduce you to some of the cooler features of Windows Forms. When you changed properties such as `Anchor`, `Dock`, `Cursor`, and `TextAlign`, you learned that the Properties window options are visual and easy to use. In addition to the many new properties coming from a Visual Basic 6 environment, using the Properties window is easier than ever. As usual, the description for each property is still visible on the lower portion of the Properties window, so you don't need to press the F1 key for help when you're not sure about a property's functionality.

Tip

> Hopefully, you see the power of Windows Forms. The `Opacity` property used in conjunction with the `TransparencyKey` property has a great use if you're a consultant or a company providing demo software. You can literally make the form, or controls on the form, disappear before the viewer's eyes by using the properties correctly.
>
> Let's say you have 20-day demo software and after the 30 days, the user must purchase the full version. Each day, starting with day 1, you could reduce the `Opacity` property by 5%. By the 20th day, the application would be literally invisible, so the user has to pay the money for the full version. If you're a consultant and you're worried about getting paid, just randomly change the `Backcolor` of controls to the same `TransparencyKey` color. When you do so, the controls become transparent, making it appear that data is disappearing. After the customer pays up, you can modify the code to be more user-friendly!

Now that you have your feet wet with the IDE, you can learn about how the applications you write using Windows Forms actually work.

Note

> When working with controls on a form, you can select multiple controls with the Ctrl+click combination. After you've selected multiple controls, you can set properties on all the selected controls at the same time. You can also use Shift+click to select multiple controls, just like you would in Windows Explorer to select multiple files.

Understanding Windows Forms

Each form you add to a Windows Forms application is simply a class file. In fact, every single object that exists in the .NET Framework is a class file. What differentiates each class file is the base class that it inherits. Visual Basic .NET and C# are object-oriented programming languages, and as you learned on Day 1, "Introduction to the Microsoft .NET Framework," all languages in .NET are on an equal standing with each other. This is because they all share the same base classes in the framework class library. A Windows Form is a Windows Form because it inherits its functionality from the `System.Windows.Forms` namespace. This namespace is used across all .NET languages that must implement Windows Forms applications. If you double-click `Form1` of the HelloNET application, you'll see the following code, which tells the class file it's a Windows Form:

VB.NET

```
Public Class frmMain
    Inherits System.Windows.Forms.Form
```

C#

```
public class frmMain : System.Windows.Forms.Form
```

The class name in this case is `frmMain`, which is the `Name` property of the form you set in the Properties window. The class file is inheriting the `System.Windows.Forms.Form` class. By inheriting this class, the `frmMain` class now has all the base class events that you saw earlier when you learned how to add events to the `frmMain` form. Anytime you inherit a class, you're exposing its functionality to your class.

When working with classes, an object lifetime is predefined by events that are part of all objects. Because a form is a class, it has predefined events that dictate its lifetime. The difference between a Windows Form and a class in a DLL is that a user decides when to close a form. In a DLL, a class instance is created, some code is run, and the class instance is destroyed. To understand this better and to get an understanding of the lifetime of a Windows Form, lets examine the lifecycle of an object.

The Life Cycle of an Object

Every object has a constructor that fires when an object is instantiated and a destructor that fires before it's destroyed.

An object's life begins when an instance of a class is created using the `New` keyword. New objects often require initialization tasks to be performed before they're used for the first time. Some common initialization tasks include connecting to a database, opening files, or checking configuration settings. In Windows Forms, this initialization occurs in the constructor for the form, which is the `Sub New` event in VB.NET and the Main event in C#. In VB.NET, when the `Sub New` event is fired, the `InitializeComponent` method is called, which handles the initialization of the form's controls. In the `InitializeComponent` event, controls you added at design time are created and the properties of those controls are set. In C#, the Main method creates the class instance by calling the Application.Run method, which passes a new instance of the class being created. This is the form that will load first in a C# application.

When an object is destroyed, the memory it was consuming is given back to the operating system. In Windows Forms, the `Closed` event calls the destructor for forms that aren't shown modally. If you're showing a form modally, you'll need to call the `Dispose` method of the form to release the form's memory back to the operating system.

> **Note** Calling `Dispose` on a nonmodal form doesn't call the `Closing` and `Closed` events, so use caution when calling `Dispose`—you might miss your cleanup code!

To see this happening in your application, drill into the Windows Form Designer generated code region in `frmMain`. You'll see `New` and `Dispose` events shown in Listing 3.3. Notice the `New` method calls the `InitializeComponent` method.

LISTING 3.3 Examining `Sub New` and `Sub Dispose` in Windows Forms

VB.NET

```
Public Sub New()
    MyBase.New()

    'This call is required by the Windows Form Designer.
    InitializeComponent()

    'Add any initialization after the InitializeComponent() call
End Sub

'Form overrides dispose to clean up the component list.
Protected Overloads Overrides Sub Dispose(ByVal disposing As Boolean)
    If disposing Then
        If Not (components Is Nothing) Then
            components.Dispose()
        End If
    End If
    MyBase.Dispose(disposing)
End Sub
```

Listing 3.3 continued

C#

```
public frmMain()
{
        //
        // Required for Windows Form Designer support
        //
        InitializeComponent();

        //
        // TODO: Add any constructor code after InitializeComponent call
        //
}

/// <summary>
/// Clean up any resources being used.
/// </summary>
protected override void Dispose( bool disposing )
{
        if( disposing )
        {
        if (components != null)
                {
                        components.Dispose();
                }
        }
        base.Dispose( disposing );
}
```


Note

Regions are a way of separating code in class files. Using the `#Region` and `#End Region` syntax, you can create a tree-like structure of your code in the Code Editor. In Windows Forms and ASP.NET, regions are used to differentiate the code generated by the designer and the code you're writing. You can create your own regions to further define a structure for your code.

The Life Cycle of a Windows Form

To get a handle on the events that occur when you're working with forms, you'll write some code that fires at each stage of a form's lifetime.

To start, add two new forms to your HelloNET application. To do so, right-click on the HelloNET project name in the Solution Explorer and select Add, Add Windows Form from the contextual menu. You're now prompted with the Add New Item dialog shown in Figure 3.9.

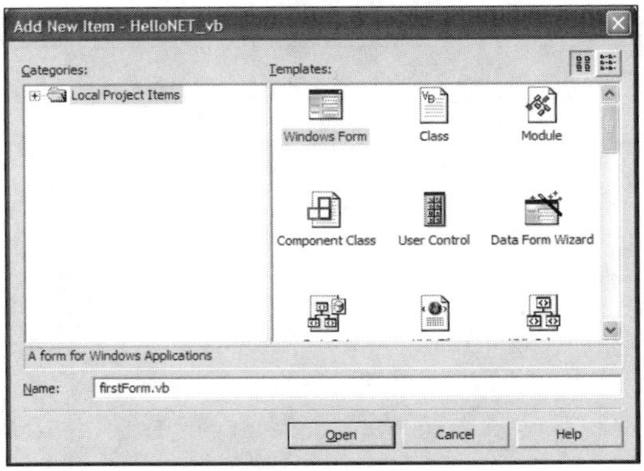

FIGURE 3.9
Adding a new form to the HelloNET application.

Change the `Name` to `firstForm` and click the OK button. You should see `firstForm` in the Solution Explorer. Next, add another form and name it `secondForm`.

In the Windows Forms Designer, `secondForm` is now visible. Your IDE should look something like Figure 3.10.

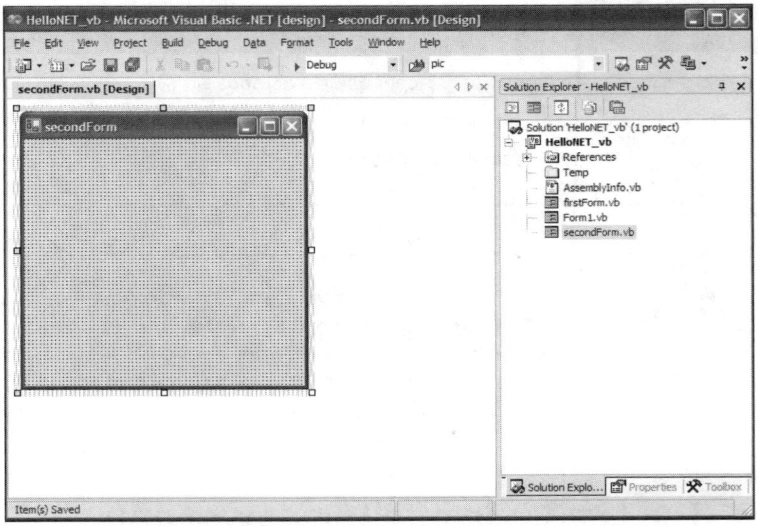

FIGURE 3.10
The HelloNET application after adding two new forms.

Follow these steps to set up the application:

- Double-click `firstForm` in the Solution Explorer to make it the active form in the designer.
- Drag a `Button` control from the `Toolbox` onto the form. Change its `Name` property to `showSecondForm` and its `Text` property to `Show Second Form`.

- Double-click the showSecondForm button and add the following code to the `showSecondForm_click` event:

VB.NET

```
MessageBox.Show("Attempting to Load Second Form")
Dim f As New secondForm()
MessageBox.Show("Second Form Created")
f.Show()
MessageBox.Show("Second Form Loaded")
```

C#

```
MessageBox.Show("Attempting to Load Second Form");
secondForm f = new secondForm();
MessageBox.Show("Second Form Created");
f.Show();
MessageBox.Show("Second Form Loaded");
```


- Double-click the `secondForm` file in the Solution Explorer to make it active in the designer. Double-click the form to get to the code-behind class file.
- Locate the method call to `InitializeComponent` in the `secondForm` class file. In Visual Basic .NET, this would be the `Sub New` event; in C#, syntax does not use a `New` keyword, it's just the instance declaration of the form. Add the following code to the `New` event, directly above the call to the `InitializeComponent`.

VB.NET

```
MessageBox.Show("Initializing from Second Form")
```

C#

```
MessageBox.Show("Initializing from Second Form");
```

- Add the event handler for the `Activated` event to the `secondForm` class file. In Visual Basic .NET, you can click the Class Name drop-down box and select (Base Class Events) and then click the Method Name drop-down box and select Activated. In C#, switch to the Form view, press F4 to get the Properties window, and click the Events button to add the `Activated` event procedure. In the `secondForm_Activated` event, enter the following code:

VB.NET

```
Me.Text = "Activated from Second Form"
```

C#

```
this.Text = "Activated from Second Form";
```

- Add an event handler for the `Load` event of the `secondForm` class file and add the following code:

VB.NET

```
MessageBox.Show("Load from Second Form")
```

C#

```
MessageBox.Show("Load from Second Form");
```

- Add an event handler for the `Deactivate` event of the `secondForm` class file and add the following code:

VB.NET

```
Me.Text = "Deactivate from Second Form"
```

C#

```
this.Text = "Deactivate from Second Form";
```

- Add an event handler for the `Closing` event of the `secondForm` class file and add the following code:

VB.NET

```
If MessageBox.Show("Are you sure you want to close?", "HelloNET!", _
    MessageBoxButtons.YesNo, MessageBoxIcon.Question) = _
    DialogResult.No Then

    e.Cancel = True
    MessageBox.Show("Canceled Closing from Second Form")

Else
    MessageBox.Show("Closing from Second Form")
End If
```

C#

```
if (MessageBox.Show ("Are you sure you want to close?", "HelloNET!",
        MessageBoxButtons.YesNo, MessageBoxIcon.Question) == DialogResult.No)
{
    e.Cancel = true;
    MessageBox.Show("Canceled Closing from Second Form");
}
else
{
    MessageBox.Show("Closing from Second Form");
}
```

- Add an event handler for the `Closed` event of the `secondForm` class file and add the following code:

VB.NET

```
MessageBox.Show("Closed from Second Form")
```

C#

```
MessageBox.Show("Closed from Second Form");
```

- Set the `StartUp` object for this application to `firstForm`. You can do this in Visual Basic .NET by right-clicking on the HelloNET project name in the Solution Explorer and selecting Properties from the contextual menu. In the Properties dialog, select `firstForm` from the StartUp object drop-down list.

  In C#, change the code in the `Sub Main` routine of `frmMain` to look like this:

```
[STAThread]
static void Main()
{
   Application.Run(new firstForm());
}
```


You can finally press the F5 key to run the application. After `firstForm` is loaded, click the Show Second Form button. You are prompted for each stage of the form's creation. After `secondForm` in loaded, click back on `firstForm`. Notice the `Text` property of the `secondForm` has changed to `Deactivated`. Next, click the `x` on `secondForm` to close the form. You're prompted with a `MessageBox` asking whether you want to close the form. This is the same as the `QueryUnload` event in Visual Basic 6, except that in .NET you're reacting to the `CancelEventArgs` event. If you click Yes, you'll notice the `Closing` and `Closed` events firing. If you click No, the `Closing` and `Closed` events don't fire.

Remembering that forms are just classes, click the Show Second Form button again. After the `secondForm` loads, click the Show Second Form button again. You now should have two instances of `secondForm` running. As you click between the forms, observe that the `Text` property of the form changes if the form is or is not active. Because each form is a class, each time you declare a new instance of `secondForm`, a new copy of the form is made in memory, and the form events occur independent of each other.

To use the events in a real-life scenario, if you need to perform a task every time a form gets the focus, you must put your code in the `Activated` event. If you want to set some default properties for your controls, you might do it in the form `Load` event or, if you want to set values for global variables, you could do it in the constructor for the class.

Note

> In Visual Basic 6, the `Activate` event occurred when a form was activated within the Visual Basic 6 application it was running in. In Windows Forms, the `Activate` event is independent of the application. For example, if you maximize Outlook or Word over your form, the `Deactivate` event occurs. When the form gets the focus again, the `Activate` event fires.

In the exercise you just completed, `secondForm` was shown nonmodally. In Visual Basic 6, you passed the `vbModal` constant to the `Show` method to display a modal form. In .NET, you simply call `ShowDialog` instead of the `Show` method. In this way, messages can be passed back to the form that called the `ShowModal`. For example, to retrieve a message back from a form shown with `ShowDialog`, you could use the following code:

```
If f.ShowDialog() = DialogResult.Cancel Then
```

The `DialogResult` property of a `Button` control determines what value is passed back to the calling form.

Working with Controls Dynamically in Code

Each control in the Toolbox is a member of the `Control` class in the `System.Windows.Forms` namespace. Because each control in the Toolbox is a class, similar to a Window Forms class, you can dynamically create controls in code at runtime. Earlier you looked at the `InitializeComponent` method, which created the controls on the form. You can do the same type of dynamic code creation when writing applications. Doing so gives you flexibility in the user interface and enables you to create complete forms based on user settings that might be stored in a database or configuration file.

To find out how to create controls dynamically at runtime, add the code in Listing 3.4 to the `Form_Load` event of `firstForm`.

LISTING 3.4 Creating Controls Dynamically at Runtime

VB.NET

```
Private Sub firstForm_Load(ByVal sender As System.Object, _
             ByVal e As System.EventArgs) Handles MyBase.Load

      ' Declare new instances of the RadioButton control class
      Dim Rd1 As RadioButton = New RadioButton()
      Dim Rd2 As RadioButton = New RadioButton()
      Dim Rd3 As RadioButton = New RadioButton()
```

LISTING 3.4 continued

```
        ' Position the controls
                Rd1.Location = New System.Drawing.Point(15, 90)
                Rd2.Location = New System.Drawing.Point(15, 120)
                Rd3.Location = New System.Drawing.Point(15, 150)

                ' Assign a text value for these controls
        Rd1.Text = "Red"
        Rd2.Text = "White"
        Rd3.Text = "Blue"

                ' Add to the forms controls collection
        Me.Controls.AddRange(New Control() {Rd1, Rd2, Rd3})

                ' Add event handlers for the controls
        AddHandler Rd1.Click, AddressOf GenericClick
        AddHandler Rd2.Click, AddressOf GenericClick
        AddHandler Rd3.Click, AddressOf GenericClick

    End Sub

        Public Sub GenericClick(ByVal sender As System.Object, _
           ByVal e As System.EventArgs)

                Select Case sender.text
                        Case "Red"
                                Me.BackColor = Color.Red
                        Case "White"
                                Me.BackColor = Color.White
                        Case "Blue"
                                Me.BackColor = Color.Blue
                End Select

        End Sub
```

C#

```
private void firstForm_Load(object sender, System.EventArgs e)
{
    // Declare new instances of the RadioButton control class
    RadioButton rd1 = new RadioButton();
    RadioButton rd2 = new RadioButton();
    RadioButton rd3 = new RadioButton();

    // Position the controls
    rd1.Location = new System.Drawing.Point(15, 90);
    rd2.Location = new System.Drawing.Point(15, 120);
    rd2.Location = new System.Drawing.Point(15, 150);
```

3

LISTING 3.4 continued

```
        //  Assign a text value for these controls
        rd1.Text = "Red";
        rd2.Text = "White";
        rd3.Text = "Blue";
        //  Add to the forms controls collection
        this.Controls.AddRange(new Control[]  {rd1, rd2, rd3});

        // Add the generic event handler
        rd1.Click += new System.EventHandler(genericClick);
        rd2.Click += new System.EventHandler(genericClick);
        rd3.Click  += new System.EventHandler(genericClick);
    }

    private void genericClick(object sender, System.EventArgs e)
    {
        RadioButton rdb;
        rdb = (RadioButton)sender;
        this.BackColor = Color.FromName(rdb.Text);
    }
```

After the code is in, press F5 to run the application. You'll see that the three `RadioButton` controls appear on your form. Just like any other object, declaring a new instance of a control gives you the properties, methods, and events for that control. In Visual Basic 6, you could dynamically create controls with the `New` keyword, and then set the `Right`, `Left`, and `Top` properties to position them, but you needed to set the `Visible` property to `True` for them to show up on the form. In .NET, you set the X and Y screen coordinates of the newly created controls, and then add the controls to the form's `Controls` collection with the `AddRange` method.

The `AddRange` method takes an array of controls and adds them to the `Controls` collection. After the controls are added to the `Controls` collection, you add an event handler delegate to tell the control what event should fire and what method should handle the event. Inside the `genericClick` event, you accept the `System.Object` and `System.EventArgs` parameters. By accepting the `System.Object` parameter, the object that's associated with the event handler is passed to the event handler. So, you can convert the `System.Object` to the correct type (in this case, the type is `RadioButton`), and have available its properties, methods, and events. This is an immensely efficient way of handling multiple events with a single event handler. In the `genericClick` event, the `Text` property of the `RadioButton` is converted to a `Color` type, which has a `FromName` method to convert a common color name to the actual `System.Drawing.Color` type.

In the Visual Basic .NET code, I used the `Select Case` statement as an example of another great feature in .NET. When you typed in `Select Case sender.Text` and pressed the Enter key, the `End Select` was automatically added. This same behavior occurs in `If...Then` statements and `With...End With` statements, to name a few. On Day 8, "Core Language Concepts in Visual Basic .NET and C#," you learn about the language features of both Visual Basic .NET and C#, and you'll see the advantages of the Code Editor in more detail when you're using all the language features.

Using Menus and MDI Forms

One of the worst interfaces ever created was the Menu Editor in Visual Basic 6 and earlier. It was a top complaint of developers; Microsoft heard their screams and provided an amazing, easy-to-use Menu Editor in Windows Forms. In addition to the editor being great, because items added to a menu are derived from a `Menu` class, you can easily create menu items dynamically at runtime, which was almost possible in Visual Basic 6. To test the new Menu Editor's features, you're going to create a Multiple Document Interface (MDI) application. The flexibility of MDI applications in .NET has also improved dramatically, as you'll see when you're done with the following exercise.

Note

> The HelloNET application has been a SDI (single document interface) application until now. That means each form in the application is its own container. An MDI application has a parent form that contains children, and the child forms can't leave the screen boundary of the parent. MDI applications used to be the most popular type of UI, but in recent years SDI applications and Explorer-style applications have become more popular. Microsoft drives the UI trends with each new release of any product. Consider Microsoft Outlook: The Outlook Bar–style spread like wildfire when it was introduced, and it can be seen in hundreds of third-party applications today.

To get started, add three new forms to the HelloNET application by right-clicking the HelloNET project name in the Solution Explorer and selecting Add, New Windows Form. Name the new forms as follows:

- `parentForm`
- `child1`
- `child2`

You'll notice that there is no MDI form template. This is now just a property on a form. After the three new forms are added, your Solution Explorer should look something like Figure 3.11.

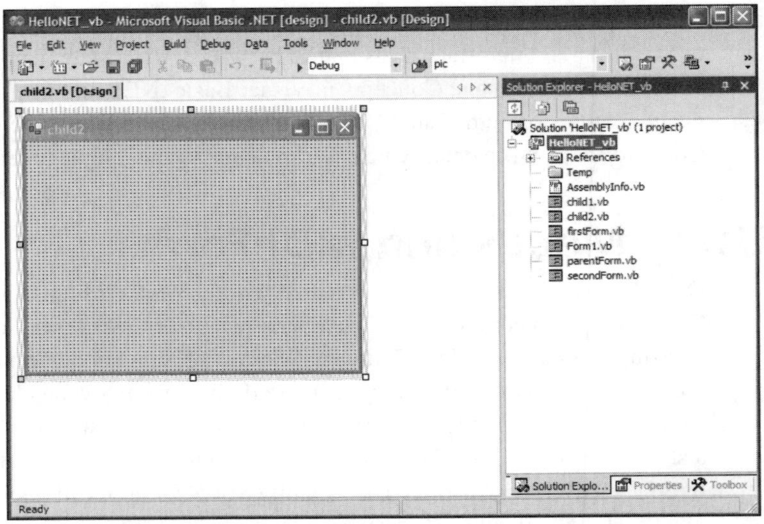

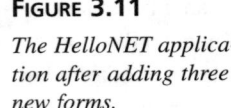

FIGURE 3.11
The HelloNET application after adding three new forms.

From the Solution Explorer, double-click the `parentForm` form so that it's in the Forms Designer. In the Properties window, change the `IsMdiContainer` property to `True`. You'll notice that the form now has a dark gray background color, which is the indication that it's a MDI parent form.

Next, drag a `MainMenu` control from the Toolbox to the form. The `MainMenu` control is a nonvisual control, which means it doesn't appear as part of the form. When nonvisual controls are added to a form, the screen splits and the controls are added to the bottom portion of the Forms Designer. This makes it very easy to see what nonvisual controls have been added to a form. At this point, your application should look something like Figure 3.12.

Adding menu items to the `MainMenu` is very intuitive: You simply type the name that you want the menu to display, and it shows up. Notice that you can go as many levels deep into a menu as you want—you just keep typing where the arrow is in the editor, and that's where the menu item appears. Use the up-, down-, right-, and left-arrow keys on your keyboard to navigate the menu levels. Figure 3.13 demonstrates the addition of items to a `MainMenu`.

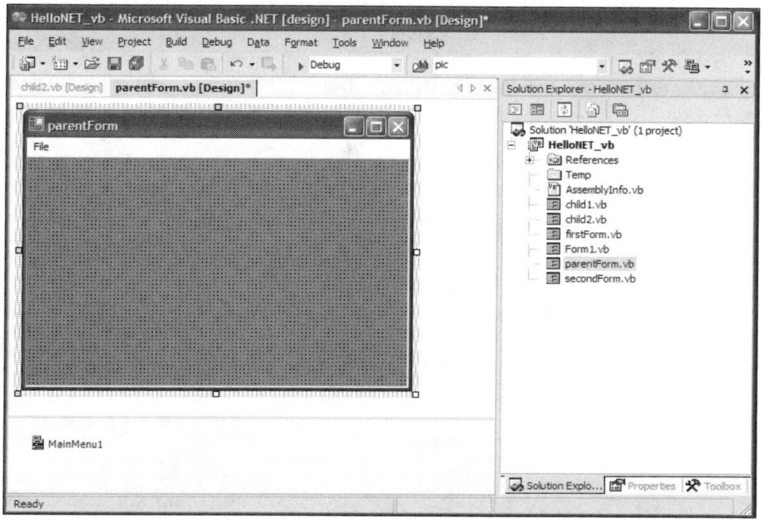

FIGURE 3.12

The `parentForm` *after adding a* `MainMenu` *control.*

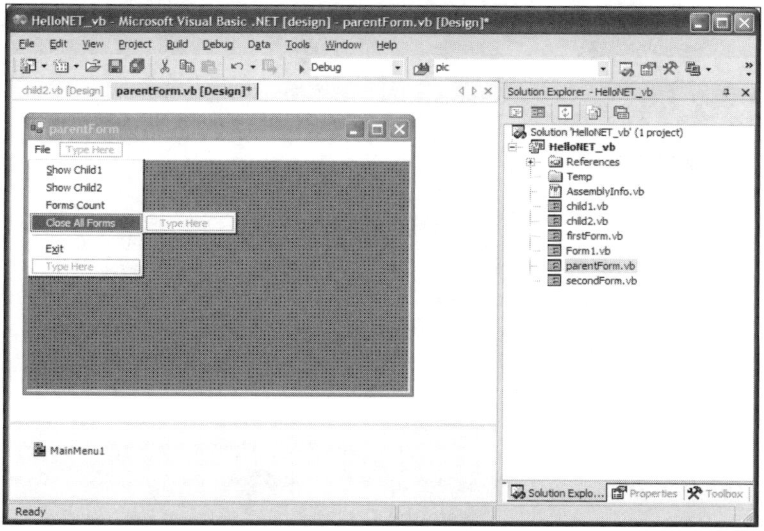

FIGURE 3.13

Adding items to a `MainMenu`.

Add the following five menu items to the `MainMenu` control:

- Top Level Menu—&File
- Sub Level 1—&Show child1, Name = `showChild1`
- Sub Level 2—&Show child2, Name = `showChild2`
- Sub Level 3—&Forms Count, Name = `formsCount`
- Sub Level 4—&Close All Forms, Name = `exitApplication`

While adding items to the menu, you can right-click on the menu itself to get the contextual menu with available options for the `MainMenu` control. One of the most useful items is the EditNames toggle. If you click EditNames, you can change the name of the menu item directly from the Menu Editor. You can also do this via the Properties window. From the Properties window, some of the individual properties that can be set are the `Shortcut`, `RadioCheck`, and `Visible` properties.

Note

> In the code you just added to create the menu items, an ampersand was placed in front of each of the menu item captions. The ampersand will place an underscore underneath the character it prefixes in the menu, and will allow the end user to use the ALT key in combination with the underlined character as a shortcut to the menu item.

After you've added the new menu items, you'll add some code that brings up the `child1` and `child2` forms, gets a count of open forms, and exits the application.

To do this, add the code in Listing 3.5 to the click events for their corresponding controls.

LISTING 3.5 The Code-Behind for the MDI Application

VB.NET

```
Private Sub MenuItem2_Click(ByVal sender As System.Object, _
    ByVal e As System.EventArgs) Handles showChild1.Click

      Dim f As New child1()
      f.MdiParent = Me
      f.Show()

   End Sub

Private Sub showChild2_Click(ByVal sender As System.Object, _
    ByVal e As System.EventArgs) Handles showChild2.Click

      Dim f As New child2()
      f.MdiParent = Me
      f.Show()

   End Sub

Private Sub formsCount_Click(ByVal sender As System.Object, _
    ByVal e As System.EventArgs) Handles formsCount.Click

      ' Get the number of children
      MessageBox.Show(Me.MdiChildren.Length)
```

LISTING 3.5 continued

```
        ' Declare a Form object to get object properties
        Dim f As Form
        For Each f In Me.MdiChildren
           MessageBox.Show(f.Name.ToString)
        Next

    End Sub

    Private Sub closeAllForms_Click(ByVal sender As System.Object, _
         ByVal e As System.EventArgs) Handles closeAllForms.Click

        ' Declare a Form object and call the Close event
        Dim f As Form
        For Each f In Me.MdiChildren
           f.Close()
        Next

    End Sub

    Private Sub exitApplication_Click(ByVal sender As System.Object, _
         ByVal e As System.EventArgs) Handles exitApplication.Click

        ' Exit the Application
        Application.Exit()

    End Sub
```

C#

```
private void showChild2_Click(object sender, System.EventArgs e)
{
   Form f = new child1();
   f.MdiParent = this;
   f.Show();
}

private void showChild1_Click(object sender, System.EventArgs e)
{
   Form f = new child2();
   f.MdiParent = this;
   f.Show();
}

private void formsCount_Click(object sender, System.EventArgs e)
{
   MessageBox.Show(this.MdiChildren.Length.ToString());
   foreach (Form f in this.MdiChildren)
   {
      MessageBox.Show(f.Name.ToString());
   }
}
```

LISTING 3.5 continued

```
private void closeAllForms_Click(object sender, System.EventArgs e)
{
   foreach (Form f in this.MdiChildren)
   {
      f.Close();
   }
}

private void exitApplication_Click(object sender, System.EventArgs e)
{
   Application.Exit();
}
}
```

Now press the F5 key to run the application. You should change the `StartUp` form in the parent form before starting. When the application is running, click the Show Child1 and Show Child2 menu items a few times each. You should see something like Figure 3.14.

FIGURE 3.14
Multiple `MDIChildren` *open in an* `MDIParent` *form.*

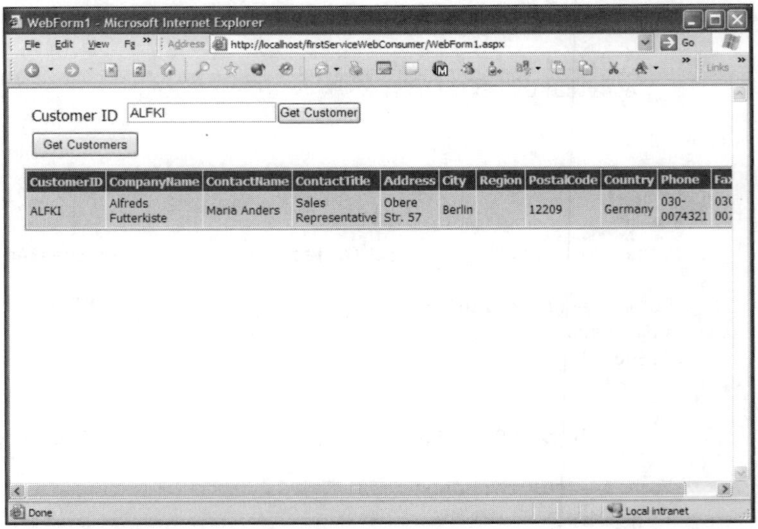

Each time you set the variable `f` to a new instance of a form, you're setting the `MdiParent` property to the current form. This makes it an `MdiChild`. The code for determining the number of `MdiChildren` open is simply the `Length` property of the `MdiChildren` class. Because the form is an object, you can use the `For Each` method to iterate through its collection to retrieve properties, methods, and events. So, by using the `For Each` method and calling the form's `Close` method, you're firing the `Form_Closing` method of each active form.

To exit the application, you called the `Application.Exit()` method. The `Application` object is similar to the `App` object in Visual Basic 6; it contains information about the current running application. It's important to note that the `Closing` event won't fire when you call the `Application.Exit()` method. So, make sure that you gracefully close your windows, and then call `Application.Exit()`. The code in the `closeAllForms` click event demonstrates the correct way to accomplish that.

Table 3.3 has some common properties of the `Application` object, and Table 3.4 has some common methods of the `Application` object that you'll find useful.

TABLE 3.3 Useful Application Object Properties

Property	*Description*
`AllowQuit`	Gets a value indicating whether the caller can quit this application
`CommonAppDataPath`	Gets the path for the application data that's shared among all users
`CommonAppDataRegistry`	Gets the Registry key for the application data that's shared among all users
`CompanyName`	Gets the company name associated with the application
`CurrentCulture`	Gets or sets the culture information for the current thread
`ExecutablePath`	Gets the path for the executable file that started the application
`LocalUserAppDataPath`	Gets the path for the application data of a local, nonroaming user
`ProductName`	Gets the product name associated with this application
`ProductVersion`	Gets the product version associated with this application
`StartupPath`	Gets the path for the executable file that started the application
`UserAppDataPath`	Gets the path for the application data of a roaming user
`UserAppDataRegistry`	Gets the Registry key of the application data specific to the roaming user

TABLE 3.4 Useful Methods of the Application Object

Method	*Description*
`AddMessageFilter`	Adds a message filter to monitor Windows messages as they're routed to their destinations
`DoEvents`	Processes all Windows messages currently in the message queue
`Exit`	Informs all message pumps that they must terminate, and then closes all application windows after the messages have been processed

TABLE 3.4 continued

Method	*Description*
`ExitThread`	Exits the message loop on the current thread and closes all windows on the thread
`OnThreadException`	Raises the `ThreadException` event
`RemoveMessageFilter`	Removes a message filter from the message pump of the application
`Run`	Overloaded; begins running a standard application message loop on the current thread

Using Inheritance in Windows Forms

If you're a Visual Basic 6 programmer, inheritance is a very exciting new feature that can save you many hours of programming. *Inheritance* enables you to define classes that serve as the basis for derived classes.

Derived classes inherit a base class's functionality and can extend the properties, events, and methods of the base class. They can also override inherited methods with new implementations. All classes created with Visual Studio .NET are inheritable by default. Because the forms you design are really classes, you can use inheritance to define new forms based on existing ones.

A few good examples of inheriting forms are

- Data entry pages could be inherited to be used with different data sources, but keeping the same user interface
- Dialog boxes having a common look and feel, with colors and button locations predefined

Learning how inheritance works with Windows Forms is a great way to learn about inheritance for all classes. As you now realize, a form is just a class, and it inherits from a base class called `System.Windows.Forms.Form`. This base class provides the functionality you need to design Windows Forms applications. The same concepts are used in all designable objects in Visual Studio .NET.

Understanding Inheritance

It's important to understand that a derived class can override an inherited property, event, or method of a base class. The keywords used to define a method indicate this behavior. These keywords are listed in Table 3.5.

TABLE 3.5 Properties Used for Inheriting Objects

Property	*Description*
`Overridable`	Can be overridden
`MustOverride`	Must be overridden in derived class
`Overrides`	Replaces method from base (inherited) class
`NotOverridable`	Can't be overridden (Default)

In the following Visual Basic .NET code snippet, there are two classes. `BaseClass` has an overridable method called `OverrideMethod`. The very first line of the derived class indicates that it inherits from the base class, so there's an `OverrideMethod` that overrides the base class's `OverrideMethod`.

VB.NET

```
Public Class BaseClass
    Public Overridable Sub OverrideMethod( )
        MsgBox("Base OverrideMethod")
    End Sub
End Class

Public Class DerivedClass
    Inherits BaseClass
    Public Overrides Sub OverrideMethod( )
        MsgBox("Derived OverrideMethod")
    End Sub
End Class
```

C#

```
  public class BaseClass
  {

    public virtual void OverrideMethod()
    {
      Messagebox.Show("Base OverrideMethod");
    }
  }



 public class DerivedClass : BaseClass
  {

    public override void OverrideMethod()
    {
      Messagebox.Show("Derived OverrideMethod");
    }
  }
```

There might be situations in which you don't want to completely overwrite the base class's method, but simply want to add some functionality to it. To do so, just add `MyBase.`*`MethodName`*, as the following code snippet demonstrates:

VB.NET

```
Public Overrides Sub OverrideMethod( )
      MsgBox("Derived OverrideMethod")
      MyBase.OverrideMethod
End Sub
```

C#

```
    public override void OverrideMethod()
    {
      Messagebox.Show("Derived OverrideMethod");
      base.OverrideMethod();
    }
```

In Visual Basic .NET, the `MyBase` keyword specified the current base class; in C#, the `base` keyword specifies the base class. Inheritance is everywhere in .NET, and by the end of this book, you'll have a good understanding how all the object-oriented techniques are used in .NET.

Implementing Inheritance with Visual Studio .NET

Every control in the Toolbox has a `Modifiers` property. The `Modifier` specifies the accessibility of the control in the derived forms. For example, when you set the modifier to `Public`, you're indicating that properties of this control can be modified in an inherited form. That means you have complete control over each object on a form, and you can specify what inheritance capabilities can be used. The following list defines each `Modifier`:

- Private—The control can be modified only in the base form
- Protected—The control can be modified only by the deriving form
- Public—The control can be modified only by any form or code module
- Friend—The control can be modified only within the base form's project

To see how this works, you're going to add a new form to the HelloNET application, and then inherit that form. To start, right-click the HelloNET project name in the Solution Explorer and select Add, Add Windows Form. Change the `Name` to `BaseForm`, and click the OK button to add it to your solution.

On the BaseForm in the Windows Forms Designer, drag a few `TextBox` controls and `Button` controls from the Toolbox to the form. In the Properties window, change the `Modifier` for one of the controls on your form to `Public`. Leave the remaining controls properties the same.

From the Build Menu, select Build Solution to make sure that the forms are saved and the controls are up to date. Now you need to add a new form to your application. But instead of adding a Windows Form, you're going to right-click the project name in the Solution Explorer, and select Add, Add Inherited Form. This brings up the Add New Item dialog as if you were adding a regular form.

In the Add New Item dialog, change the `Name` to `InheritedForm`, and click the OK button. Now the Inheritance Picker dialog pops up, as shown in Figure 3.15.

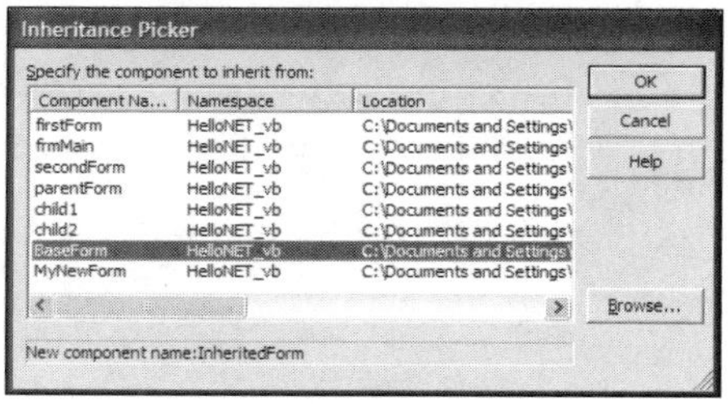

FIGURE 3.15

The Inheritance Picker dialog box.

From the Inheritance Picker, select the `BaseForm` form and click the OK button. You'll notice that every form in your solution is also listed. Because a form is a class, and every class can be inherited, you can inherit any form.

After the `InheritedForm` is added to the solution, notice that you can't double-click the controls that aren't set to `Public`. Notice also that all the properties for the controls are disabled in the Properties window. By setting modifiers on controls, and making their properties overridable, you can implement a very robust inheritance mechanism for your Windows Forms solutions.

Using Common Dialog Controls

The Common Dialog controls in Windows Forms enable you to perform dialog-related tasks. Table 3.6 lists the available Common Dialog controls.

TABLE 3.6 Common Dialog Controls

Control	*Description*
`ColorDialog`	Displays the color picker dialog box that enables users to set the color of an interface element
`FontDialog`	Displays a dialog box that enables users to set a font and its attributes
`OpenFileDialog`	Displays a dialog box that enables users to navigate to and select a file
`PrintDialog`	Displays a dialog box that enables users to select a printer and set its attributes
`PrintPreviewDialog`	Displays a dialog box that shows how a `PrintDocument` object appears when printed
`SaveFileDialog`	Displays a dialog box that allows users to save a file

The Common Dialog controls are nonvisual controls that are added to a form. After you add a control, you can use its properties and methods to display the dialog. Listing 3.6 uses the `Filter` property of `OpenFileDialog` to prompt the user for cursor files.

LISTING 3.6 Using `OpenFileDialog`

VB.NET

```
' Display an OpenFileDialog so the user can select a Cursor.
Dim openFileDialog1 As New OpenFileDialog()
openFileDialog1.Filter = "Cursor Files|*.cur"
openFileDialog1.Title = "Select a Cursor File"
' Show the Dialog.
' If the user clicked OK in the dialog and
' a .CUR file was selected, open it.
If openFileDialog1.ShowDialog() = DialogResult.OK Then
    If openFileDialog1.FileName <> "" Then
        ' Assign the cursor in the Stream to the Form's Cursor property.
        Me.Cursor = New Cursor(openFileDialog1.OpenFile())
    End If
End If
```

C#

```
OpenFileDialog openFileDialog = new OpenFileDialog();
openFileDialog.Filter = "Cursor Files|*.cur";
openFileDialog.Title = "Select a Cursor File";
if (openFileDialog.ShowDialog() == DialogResult.OK &&
    StringType.StrCmp(openFileDialog.FileName, "", false) != 0)
     {
       base.Cursor = new Cursor(openFileDialog.OpenFile());
     }
```

You can also read files using a combination of the `System.IO` classes (you'll learn about them next week) and `OpenFileDialog`, as Listing 3.7 demonstrates.

LISTING 3.7 Opening a File with a `StreamReader` and `OpenFileDialog`

```
' Simple Open
If OpenFileDialog1.ShowDialog() = DialogResult.OK Then
    Dim sr As New System.IO.StreamReader(OpenFileDialog1.FileName)
    MessageBox.Show(sr.ReadToEnd)
    sr.Close()
End If
```

In the Downloads section for the day, I've included a sample application that uses each of the dialogs in different ways.

More About Controls

It's impossible to do a walkthrough of each control, but you now know the basic user interface controls and how to use them. Visual Studio .NET has many amazing new controls that you can use to make your user forms better than ever. Table 3.7 lists the remaining controls in the Toolbox that we didn't touch on today. Most of the controls share common properties with each other, and most are very self-explanatory. If you add a control to a form and aren't sure how to use it, remember to press the Ctrl+F1 key combination to get the dynamic Help for the control.

TABLE 3.7 Controls Available in Windows Forms

Control Name	*Description*
`RichTextBox`	Enables text to be displayed with formatting in plain text or rich text format (RTF).
`LinkLabel`	Displays text as a Web-style link and triggers an event when the user clicks the special text. Usually the text is a link to another window or a Web site.
`StatusBar`	Displays information about the application's current state using a framed window, usually at the bottom of a parent form.
`CheckedListBox`	Displays a scrollable list of items, each accompanied by a check box.
`ComboBox`	Displays a drop-down list of items.
`DomainUpDown`	Displays a list of text items that users can scroll through with up and down buttons.
`ListBox`	Displays a list of text and graphical items (icons).
`ListView`	Displays items in one of four different views. Views include text only, text with small icons, text with large icons, and report view.

TABLE 3.7 continued

Control Name	*Description*
`NumericUpDown`	Displays a list of numerals that users can scroll through with up and down buttons.
`TreeView`	Displays a hierarchical collection of node objects that can consist of text with optional check boxes or icons.
`PictureBox`	Displays graphical files, such as bitmaps and icons, in a frame.
`ImageList`	Serves as a repository for images. `ImageList` controls and the images they contain can be reused from one application to the next.
`CheckBox`	Displays a check box and a label for text. Generally used to set options.
`CheckedListBox`	Displays a scrollable list of items, each accompanied by a check box.
`RadioButton`	Displays a button that can be turned on or off.
`Trackbar`	Allows users to set values on a scale by moving a "thumb" slider along a scale.
`DateTimePicker`	Displays a graphical calendar to enable users to select a date or a time.
`MonthCalendar`	Displays a graphical calendar to enable users to select a range of dates.
`ContextMenu`	Implements a menu that appears when the user right-clicks an object.
`NotifyIcon`	Displays an icon in the status notification area of the taskbar that represents an application running in the background.
`ToolBar`	Contains a collection of button controls.
`Panel`	Groups a set of controls on an unlabeled, scrollable frame.
`GroupBox`	Groups a set of controls (such as radio buttons) on a labeled, nonscrollable frame.
`TabControl`	Provides a tabbed page for organizing and accessing grouped objects efficiently.

Making Your Forms Look Pretty

Making your forms look good is the key to a successful application. There are two useful tools in Visual Studio .NET that will help you put the finishing touches on your forms. They are the Layout toolbar and the Tab Order tool.

The Layout toolbar enables you to align, resize, change spacing, and center controls on the form. Figure 3.16 demonstrates the Layout toolbar after selecting multiple controls on a form.

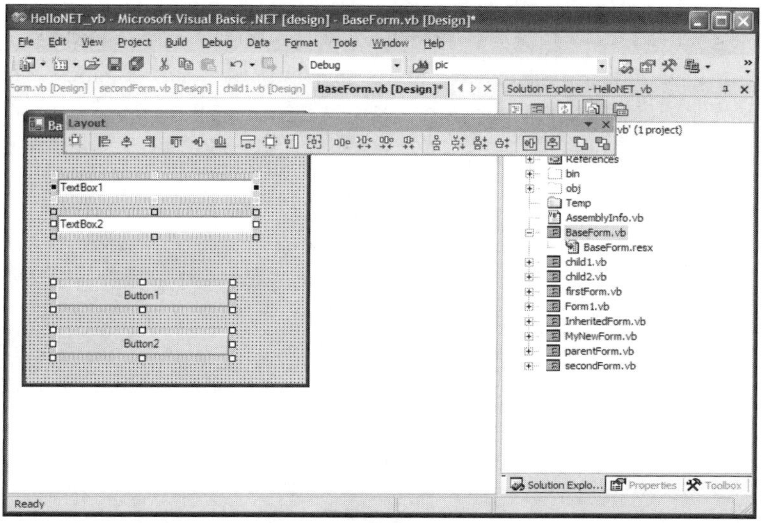

FIGURE 3.16

Using the Layout toolbar to make forms look good.

The Tab Order tool is a massive improvement to setting the order in which controls receive focus on a form. You can still set the `TabOrder` property in the Properties window, but using the Tab Order tool, you can visually set the tab order of controls. To get to the Tab Order tool, you must select a control on the form and then select the Tab Order menu item from the View menu. Figure 3.17 demonstrates the tab order being visually displayed on a form.

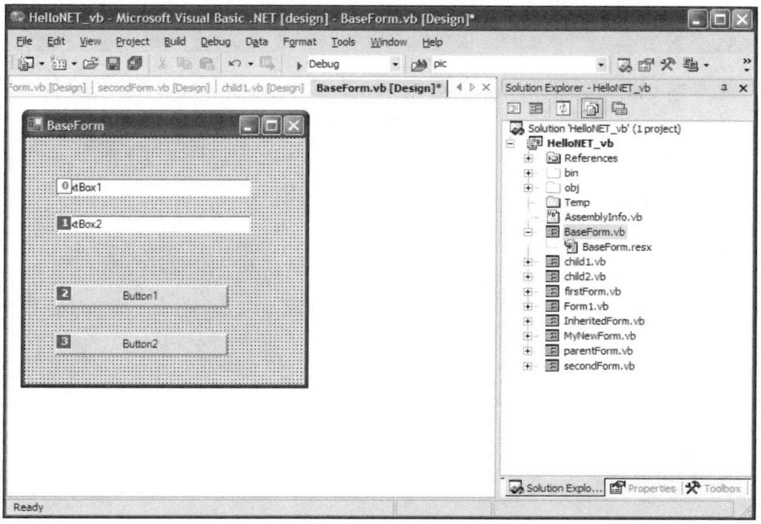

FIGURE 3.17

Setting the tab order visually.

Advanced Windows Forms

There are two advanced features in Windows Forms that are beyond the scope of this book, but are worth noting. The first is shaped forms. In Windows Forms, a form can take on any shape that you specify. Using the power of GDI+, you can specify point structures and clip regions that determine how a form should look. Figure 3.18 demonstrates a shaped form at runtime.

FIGURE 3.18

A shaped Windows Form.

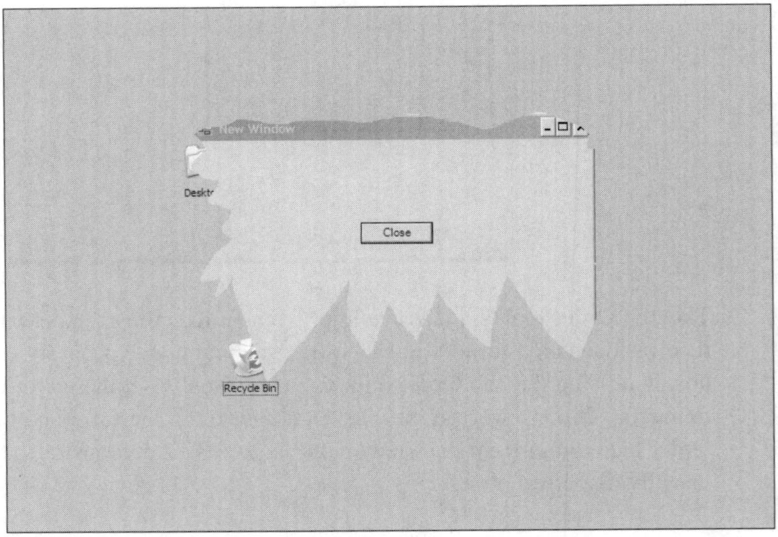

The second and most revolutionary aspect of Windows Forms is the ability to write Windows Forms applications that load dynamically through HTTP. Similar to a Web Form, a properly designed Windows Forms application can trickle down to the client machine. There are a few ways to accomplish this, but the fact that you can write a robust Windows Forms application and have it load over the Internet like an ASP.NET application is outstanding.

In addition to the Downloads section for today, I've included a demo of how this can be achieved. For more information, see the resources in the "Q&A" section at the end of the day.

Summary

Today you learned basic and advanced features of Windows Forms. By using the tools and controls in Visual Studio .NET, you can write user-friendly and intuitive applications faster than ever. Although you didn't learn everything in one day, by end of this week and next week, you'll have written about 20 Windows Forms applications, so your lesson on the power of Windows Forms is just beginning.

Q&A

Q I want to be able to use control arrays to handle multiple events. Where did that functionality go?

A Control arrays do not exist in Visual Basic .NET. Each control you add has its own event that you can write code for. You can, however, handle multiple events with a single method. You did this earlier with the `genericClick` event in the forms exercises. You can also use the `Handles` keyword to indicate what events a method should consume, as the following code demonstrates:

```
Private Sub Button5_Click(ByVal sender As System.Object, _
  ByVal e As System.EventArgs) _
  Handles Button5.Click, Button3.Click, Button4.Click, Button2.Click

End Sub
```

Q Can I use ActiveX controls from Visual Basic 6 in my .NET Windows Forms applications?

A Yes, you can. Although the interop between COM and .NET has some overhead, the functionality is built in. To add an ActiveX control to the Toolbox, you can right-click on the Toolbox and select Customize. From this dialog, you can select the ActiveX controls to add to your application. Most third-party vendors have .NET certified controls. For some of the more popular controls, visit `http://www.infragistics.com` and `http://www.componentone.com`.

Q Windows Forms are awesome. Where can I get more details? The QuickStart tutorials only take me so far.

A Microsoft has a Web site specifically for Windows Forms. Check out `http://www.windowsforms.net` to get tons of great information about developing forms applications.

3

Quiz

1. The Windows Forms classes are located in the ________________ namespace.
2. By setting the ______________ property in a control, I can make sure that my code is not changed if someone inherits my form.
3. The _____________ property returns an array of `MdiChildren` in an MDI application.
4. What are the properties in the Properties window that enable you to specify the location, docking, and resizing capabilities of a control?
5. True or False: I can tell many controls to perform the same method by setting the `SameMethod` property in the Properties window.
6. True or False: The Windows Forms Designer Generated code should not be changed.
7. The ____________ argument and the ____________ argument are always passed as parameters to events for a control.

Quiz Answers

1. `System.Windows.Forms`.
2. You need to change the `Modifiers` property to `Private`.
3. The `MdiChildren` property will allow you to loop through the collection of `MdiChild` forms in your application. You can use the `MdiChildren.Length` property to determine the number of open `MdiChildren` in you application.
4. The `Dock`, `Alignment`, and `Location` properties allow you to control how and where controls are positioned on your forms.
5. False. There is no `SameMethod` property. In order to have your controls perform the same function, use the Handles keyword in VB.NET or simply create a new delegate in C#.
6. True. You can change the Windows Forms Designer Generated code, but you risk the Forms designer changing it once you switch back to Design view.
7. `System.Object and System.EventArgs`.

Exercises

1. To expand on the form events that occur when opening and closing forms, add code to the `child1` and `child2` forms to display a messages in each of the key events that occur when a form is created and when a form is destroyed.
2. Using the `Application` class, create a new form that contains a `ListBox` control and add the following properties to it:
   - `CommonAppDataPath`
   - `CommonAppDataRegistry`
   - `CompanyName`
   - `ExecutablePath`
   - `ProductName`
   - `ProductVersion`
   - `StartupPath`
   - `UserAppDataPath`
   - `UserAppDataRegistry`

   Hint: After you add the `ListBox` control to the form, you need to add code in the `Form_Load` event using the following syntax:

   ```
   ListBox1.Items.Add(Application.CommonAppDataPath)
   ListBox1.Items.Add(Application.StartupPath)
   ```
3. Using the `Splitter` control, the Panel control, and the knowledge you have gained about docking today, create an Explorer-style application.

   Hint: The `Splitter` control has a `Dock` property that dictates whether it should be a horizontal or vertical splitter.
4. Experiment with the `TabControl`, `DateTimePicker`, and `ErrorProvider` controls. Add the controls to a form, and press Ctrl+F1 to view the help files on these controls.

WEEK 1

DAY 4

Deploying Windows Forms Applications

Yesterday you learned how to create Windows Forms applications. Today, you learn how to create a setup project that deploys a Windows Forms application to an end user's machine. If you're familiar with the Setup project type in Visual Basic 6, you'll be shocked and amazed at how easy and reliable it is to create setup projects in .NET. Today, you learn how to

- Create a Windows Installer package using Visual Studio .NET
- Create custom setup actions in installer packages
- Create a license agreement custom dialog
- Deploy the .NET Framework with your application

Introduction to Application Deployment

Deploying an application always seems like it's such a simple process to an end user. All the end user needs to do is double-click `Setup.exe` and the program he's trying to install works like magic and installs the files needed for the application. As a developer, you know that creating deployment projects with the tools provided by Microsoft has been a nightmare.

Using Visual Basic 6 Setup and Deployment Wizard to deploy forms-based applications was a frightening thought. When an installation was complete on a target machine, you had to cross your fingers, and pray that when the machine rebooted there would be no blue screen of death, and that some core operating system file would not be accidentally overwritten by your installation package. This opened up the market for third-party deployment applications, for which most companies simply give in and pay big dollars.

With the advent of Visual Studio .NET, there are no longer issues with deploying applications using the tools provided by Microsoft.

It's easy to understand why deploying applications was so difficult before .NET. All components and applications on a machine needed to be registered in the Windows Registry. Any time the Registry is involved, there are going to be complications. With .NET, the Registry goes away. There's no need to register an application or component to make it work. The .NET Framework provides the runtime that all .NET applications need to run. So, if the .NET Framework is installed on the machine, your application runs without needing any extra handling.

This is a huge feature of .NET. The fact that you can literally copy a folder that contains an application from machine A to machine B, and just be able to run, saves a lot of configuration and deployment headaches.

In addition to the core technology in .NET making the deployment of applications a snap, the actual installation technology has improved as the operating systems have improved. The Windows Installer technology is responsible for handling installation services in Windows.

Note

> Windows Installer files have an `.msi` extension. When I refer to an MSI package, it's the same as a Windows Installer file.

Introduction to the Microsoft Windows Installer Service

The Windows Installer is the technology behind handling all setup and deployment in Windows Me, Windows XP, Windows 2000, and Windows .NET Server. Windows Installer packages can also run on earlier versions of Windows, but the technology is built into the newer Windows version.

Windows Installer packages are predefined databases that contain information about what must be installed on a deployment target. Whereas the Visual Basic 6 Setup and Deployment Wizard used script files to determine the order of each component and files that needed to be installed, a Windows Installer package contains information about *what* must be installed, not *how* it should be installed.

The Installer service keeps track of every application that's installed on a computer, allowing you to uninstall, repair, or reinstall a package based on the state of the machine. This also gives you the ability to roll back installations. For example, if an installation is at 90% and the installation is canceled, all changes made to the computer are rolled back. The installation is not left in a flux state.

4

Using the tools in Visual Studio .NET, you can create Windows Installer packages that set properties and conditions, create custom dialogs, handle user preference input, and even include a product registration with the installation package.

> If your organization uses Windows 2000 Server or Windows .NET Server, a technology called Group Policy is built into Active Directory. Using Group Policy, an administrator can define what Windows Installer packages each client machine should have, and the setup is automatic when a user logs in to her machine.
>
> This is taken to the next level with Active Directory. If you delete a file that was installed, and attempt to launch the application's executable, the Windows Installer service verifies that the file exists on the client machine. If it doesn't, it's retrieved from the server. You can also update version information on assemblies and the Windows Installer server always checks for new versions on the server. Using Microsoft Servers and Windows Installer provides a bulletproof mechanism for keeping applications current and working.

Understanding the Deployment Projects Templates

Visual Studio .NET provides templates for creating deployment projects. In the New Project dialog, there is a Deployment Projects node that contains the available templates for creating deployment projects. Figure 4.1 displays the Deployment Projects node of the New Project dialog.

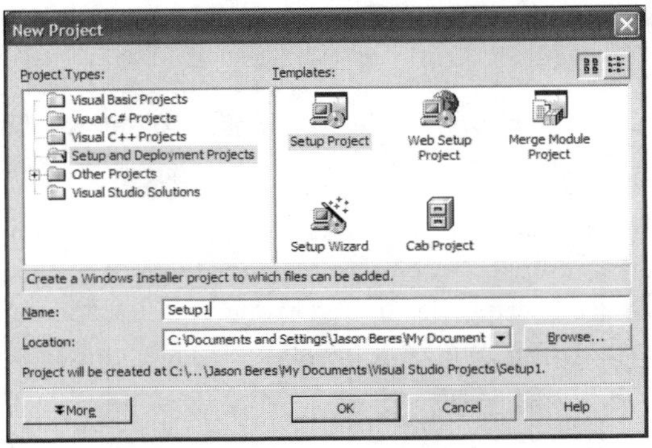

FIGURE 4.1
The Deployment Projects node in Visual Studio .NET.

The following is a list of deployment project types:

- Setup Project—Creates an empty setup project that you can customize.
- Web Setup Project—Creates a setup project with options set for deploying Web applications. You learn about this project type on Day 6, "Deploying ASP.NET Applications."
- Merge Module Project—Creates a merge module, which normally contains applications assemblies. Merge modules are a major feature in Windows Installer, and you'll learn how to implement a merge module later today.
- Setup Wizard—A basic wizard that enables you to choose deployment options for a project.
- Cab Project—Creates Internet-deployable cabinet (CAB) files. You learn how to create and implement CAB files in Day 6.

Creating a Windows Installer Package

The easiest way to create a new MSI package is from an existing application. To see this work, you need to create a new Windows Forms project.

Open Visual Studio .NET, create a new Windows Forms Application project, and name it InstallerTest as shown in Figure 4.2.

After the project is created, you can add a deployment template to your solution. To do so, right-click the InstallerTest solution name in the Solution Explorer, and select Add, Add New Project from the contextual menu. When the New Project dialog pops up, select the Setup and Deployment Projects node, and then Setup Project. Change the name to InstallerTestSetup as shown in Figure 4.3, and click the OK button to add the new project to your solution.

FIGURE 4.2

Creating the InstallerTest application.

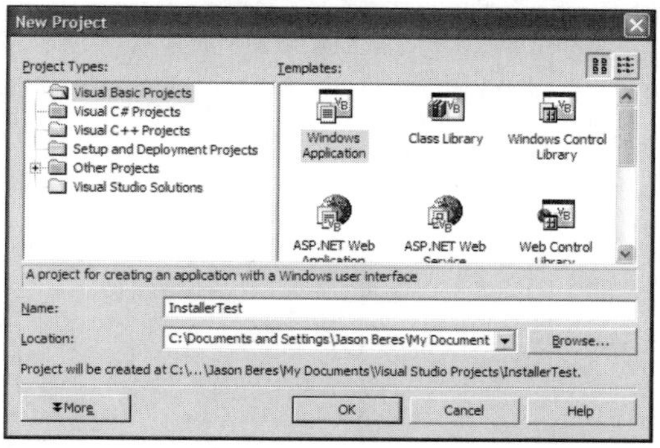

FIGURE 4.3

Adding a new setup project to your solution.

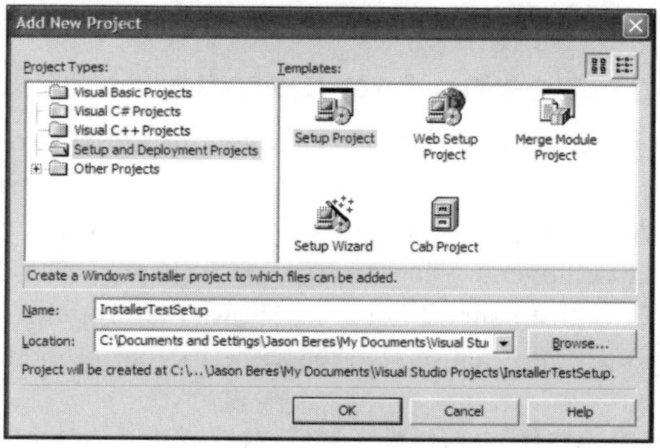

After the new project is created, your Solution Explorer and main window should look like Figure 4.4.

You're now looking at the interface that you'll use to create the MSI package. Everything that you need to create the setup project can be done with this designer, which is known as the File System Editor (FSE).

Using the FSE, you create virtual objects that are stored in the MSI package you create. During the installation of your MSI package, the files and directories created using the FSE are created on the target machine. The navigation of the FSE is the same as using Windows Explorer: The left pane contains the hierarchy of the directory, and the right pane contains the details. Each item in both panes has a contextual menu that pops up with a right-click, giving you action options to perform, such as creating directories, adding files, creating shortcuts, and specifying build options.

FIGURE 4.4
The InstallerTest solution after adding a setup project.

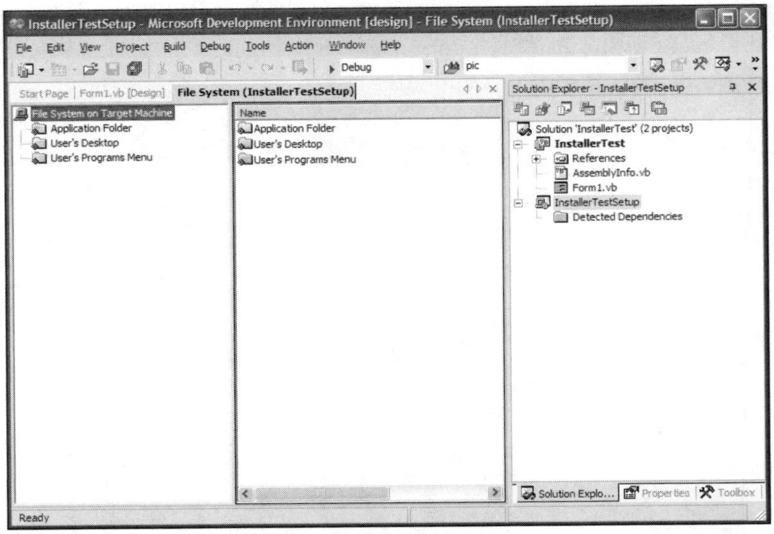

Setting Properties on the Installer Package

The next step is to set properties on the installation project. To do so, select the InstallerTestSetup project name in the Solution Explorer, and press the F4 key to get to the Properties window. The properties you set here define what information is displayed in dialogs during the setup, and what information is displayed in the Add/Remove Programs applet of Control Panel. Figure 4.5 shows the Properties window after I customized it with my own information. Do the same to your properties.

Adding the Application Output to the Installer Package

Now that some properties are set, you must tell the Installer project what the primary output is to install. In this case, it's your InstallerTest Windows Forms project. Note that the project wasn't automatically added when you added the deployment project to your solution. You must always add the files to be installed.

To add the InstallerTest application to this installer package, right-click on Application Folder on the File System Editor. From the contextual menu, select Add, Project Output, as Figure 4.6 demonstrates.

When you select the Add Project Output option, you're prompted with the Add Project Output Group dialog, as Figure 4.7 shows.

FIGURE 4.5

Setting properties in the InstallerTestSetup project.

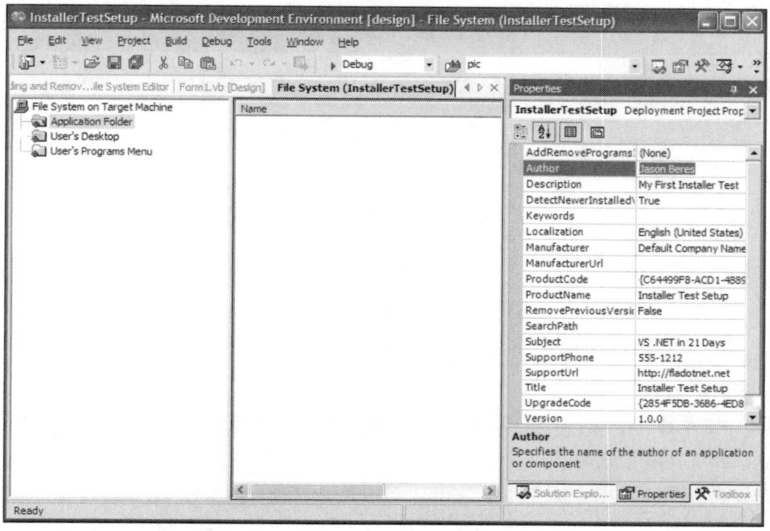

FIGURE 4.6

The Add Project Output menu selection.

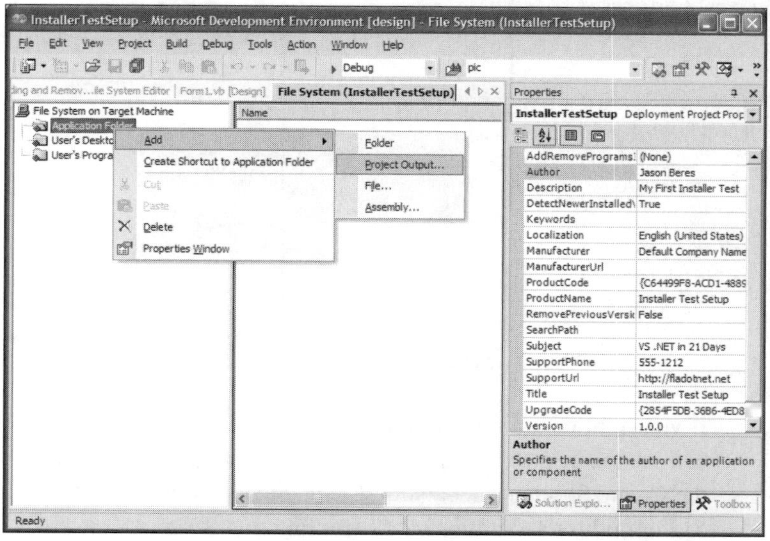

By default, the active project in the solution is in the Project drop-down list. Click the OK button on the Add Project Output Group dialog box to add the InstallerTest application to this setup package.

At this point, the primary output has been added to the InstallerTestSetup project. Your application should look like Figure 4.8.

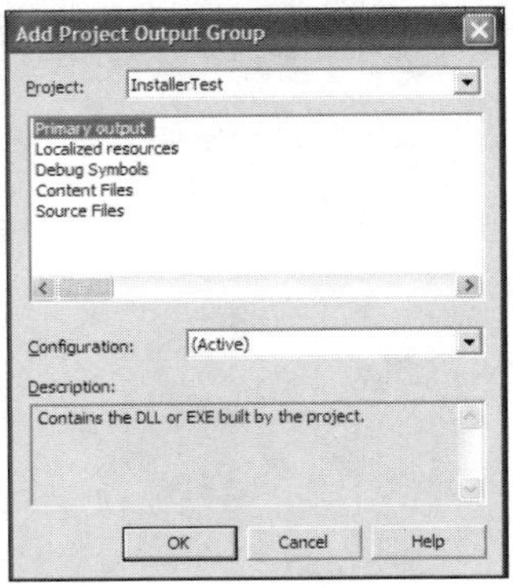

FIGURE 4.7
The Add Project Output Group dialog.

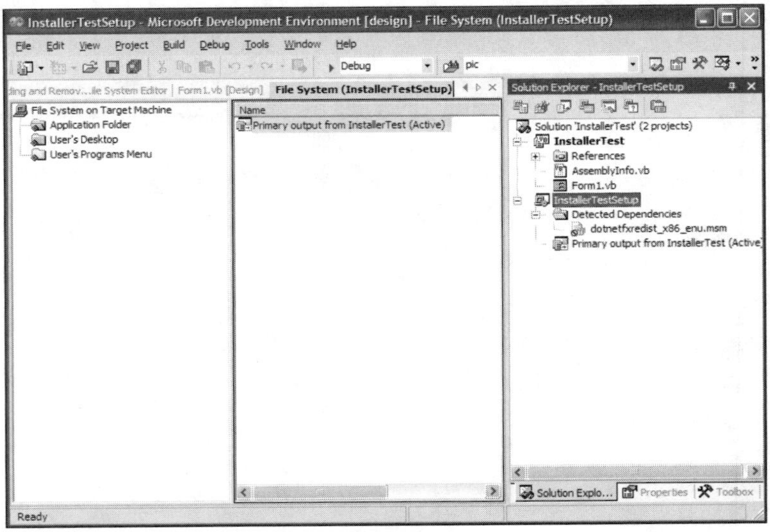

FIGURE 4.8
Solution after adding the primary output.

If you right-click on the primary output in the right pane of the File System Editor, you can see the available options for the output assembly. From the contextual menu, click the Create Shortcut menu item. Change the shortcut name to Installer Test. Your File System Editor should now look like Figure 4.9.

After you create the shortcut, you can drag it to the folders in the left pane of the File System Editor. Anything you add to the folders, be it a file, shortcut, or anything, will be added during the installation. Remember that the File System Editor is a virtual view of the target machine. Drag the shortcut to the User's Desktop node in the left pane.

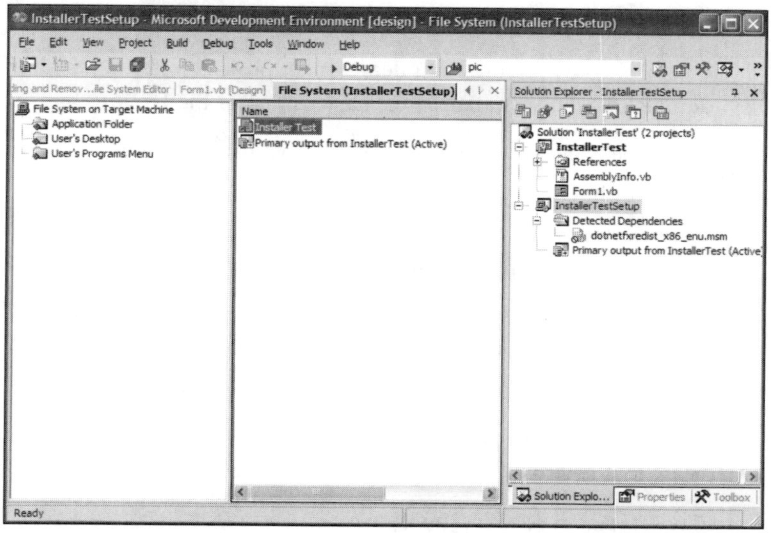

FIGURE 4.9

File System Editor after creating a shortcut for the primary output.

If you right-click the shortcut, and select Properties from the contextual menu, you'll see some of the available properties that you can set. Change the `Description` property to `My First Test Of Installing`, as Figure 4.10 demonstrates.

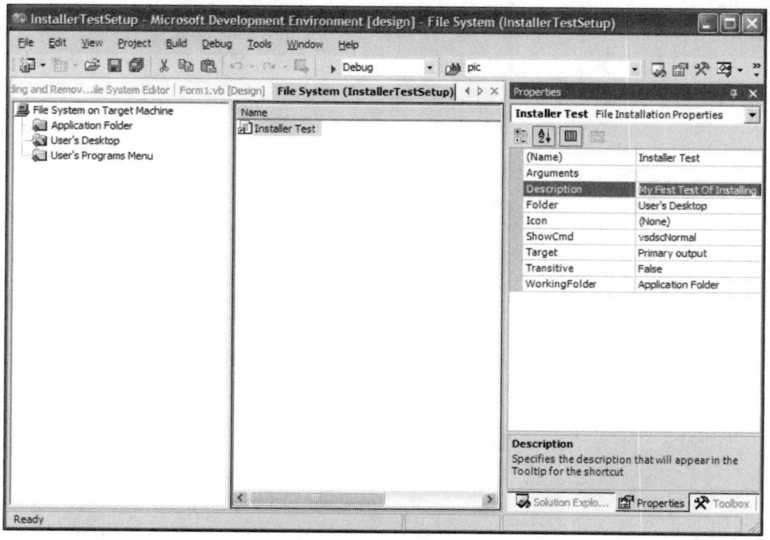

FIGURE 4.10

Setting properties on a shortcut.

Creating Custom Actions

One of the key features that deployment projects offer is the ability to create custom actions for your installation package. Some of the features are

- Associating a file extension with your application
- Adding Registry keys based on user input
- Setting launch conditions, such as file dependencies or version requirements for dependent applications
- Installing custom files based on user selections during setup
- Creating databases or other objects programmatically
- Launching applications when installation is complete

To test this, you're going to create a Registry key and a version launch condition, specifying that Microsoft Word version 9.0 or greater is required by your application.

Creating a Registry Key

To create a Registry key, click the View main menu, and then select Editor, Registry as Figure 4.11 demonstrates.

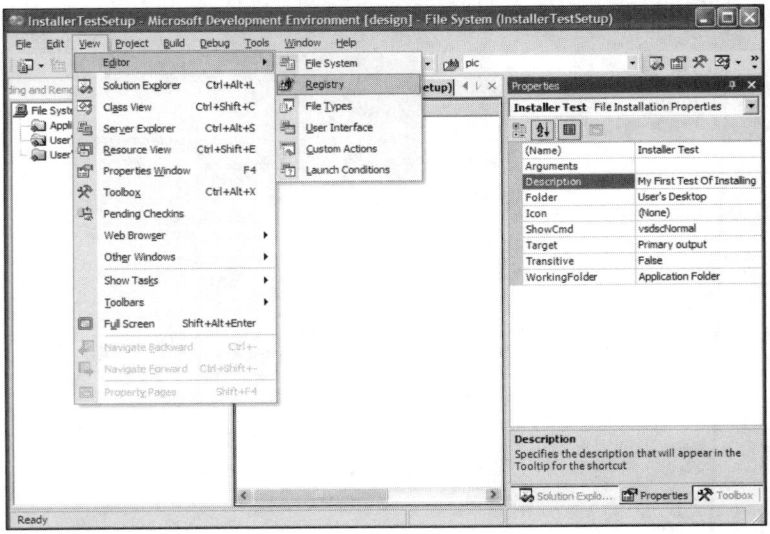

FIGURE 4.11
Getting to the Registry Editor.

You're now in the virtual Registry Editor. From this screen, you have complete control over what Registry keys you add to your application. Figure 4.12 demonstrates the Registry Editor.

FIGURE 4.12

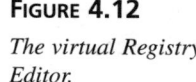

The virtual Registry Editor.

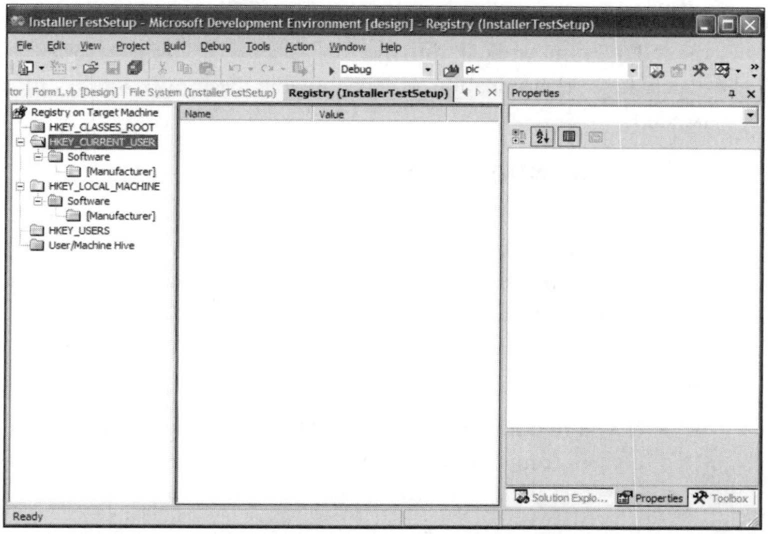

Right-click the HKEY_CURRENT_USER node and select Add Key from the contextual menu. Add a key named `TestKey`.

After the key is added, right-click on `TestKey` and select New, String Value from the contextual menu. Name the new string value ScreenPref. In the Properties window, change the `Value` property to `Maximize`. Your Registry Editor should now look like Figure 4.13.

FIGURE 4.13

Registry Editor after entering ScreenPref key.

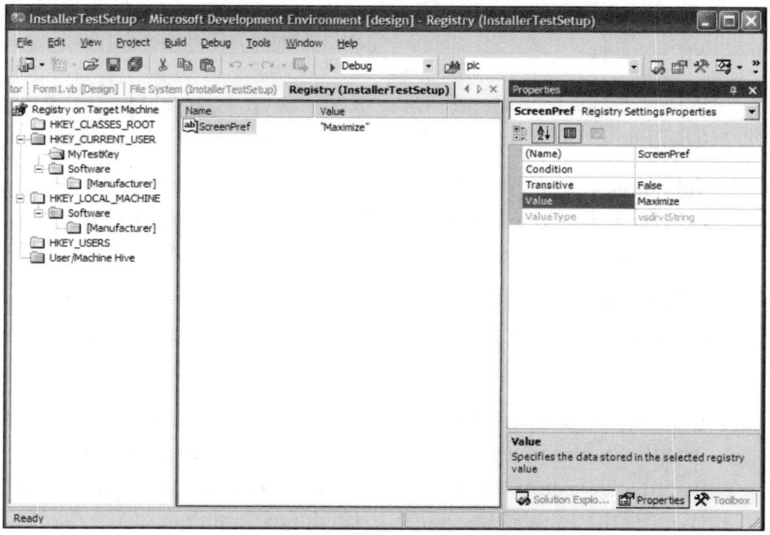

After you add keys and values to the Registry, you can access them using the classes in the .NET Framework. Using the Registry Editor is a great way to set default user preferences. In your application, you can enable the user to modify the user preferences as needed.

Adding a Launch Condition

Adding a launch condition forces the installer to check for the existence of a file, application, or dependency before installation starts. In this step of setting up the test installer, you're going to make sure that Microsoft Word version 9.0 is installed on the deployment target. This is just an example of what you can do with a launch condition, but there are hundreds of reasons why this is a great feature. The following list should give you some ideas:

- If you're doing any Microsoft Office automation, the type libraries for Office aren't always compatible. You might specifically need the Word 9.0 type library to make sure that your Word Merge code doesn't crash.
- If you depend on a specific browser version, such as Internet Explorer 5.0 or higher, you can stop the installation if that version does not exist on the machine.
- If you're using a specific version of Microsoft Data Access Components (MDAC), you can ensure that they're on the machine before installation.
- If the machine doesn't have the .NET Framework installed, your application won't run, so you need a launch condition to check this.
- If your application uses Active Directory, it will work only on Windows XP or greater, so you must check the OS version before installing.

To test this, select Editor, Launch Conditions from the View menu, as demonstrated in Figure 4.14.

When the Launch Condition Editor is open, right-click on the Requirements for Target Machine node and select Add File Launch Condition, as Figure 4.15 demonstrates.

Take note of the other launch conditions. From this menu, you can create conditions for checking the existence of the .NET Framework, specific Registry settings, specific IIS settings, and Windows Installer version launch conditions.

After you add the file launch condition, a new item named Search For File1 is placed under the Search Target Machine node. If you select this item, you'll notice the Properties window appears, and you can set the conditions for the file search.

Figure 4.16 demonstrates how to add version information, filename, and directory information for this search. Notice the `Depth` property is changed to `2`. That means I want the installer to search two levels deep inside the Program Files folder. The more depth you specify, the longer the search will take to complete.

FIGURE 4.14

The Launch Conditions menu selection.

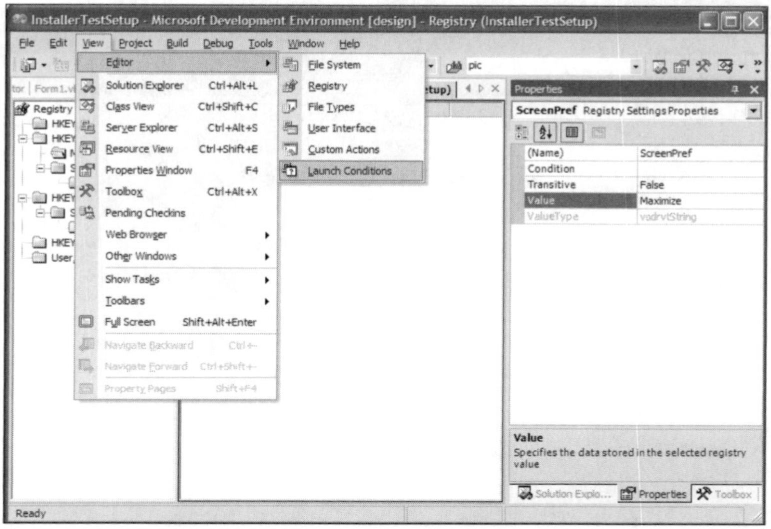

FIGURE 4.15

Adding a file launch condition.

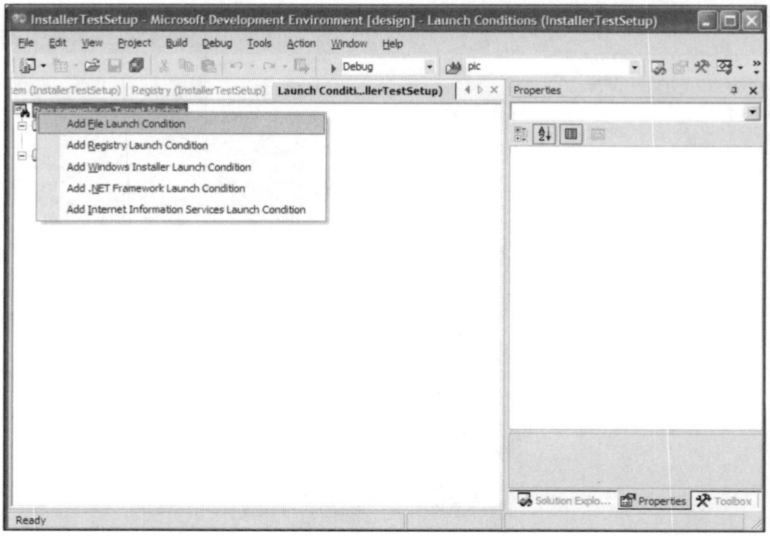

Because I know that Word 9.0 is on my machine, my install will succeed when I test it. You should change the Word 9.0 file search to another file and set the properties accordingly if you want to attempt another search. To verify the `FileName`, `MinVersion`, and `MaxVersion` properties, I used my Windows Explorer to find `WinWord.exe` and viewed its properties, as Figure 4.17 demonstrates.

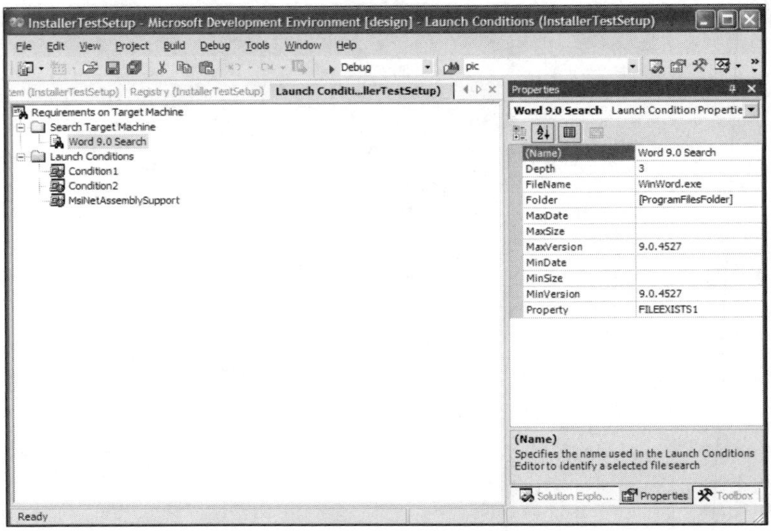

FIGURE 4.16
Setting the Word Search launch conditions.

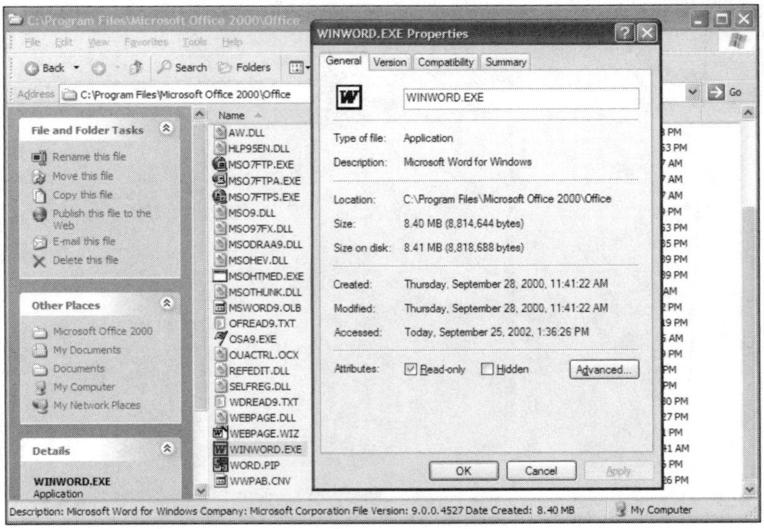

FIGURE 4.17
Filename and version information for MS Word.

To complete the version and file search for Word, you need to change the `Condition1` item that was added under the Launch Conditions node when you added the file search. `Condition1` has an `Error` property that you can set to prompt the user if the installation will fail. You can also set the `Property` property in the Word 9.0 Search node to a friendlier name, and use that `Property` name as the `Condition` property for the launch condition. Change the `Error` property to a useful error message based on the file you're searching for.

Using Custom Dialogs During Installation

The Dialog Editor enables you to add custom dialog options for the installation package. These could range from simple license agreement prompts to complex installation options. To see what options are available, select Editor, User Interface from the View menu to get the Dialog Editor, as shown in Figure 4.18.

FIGURE 4.18

The User Interface menu selection.

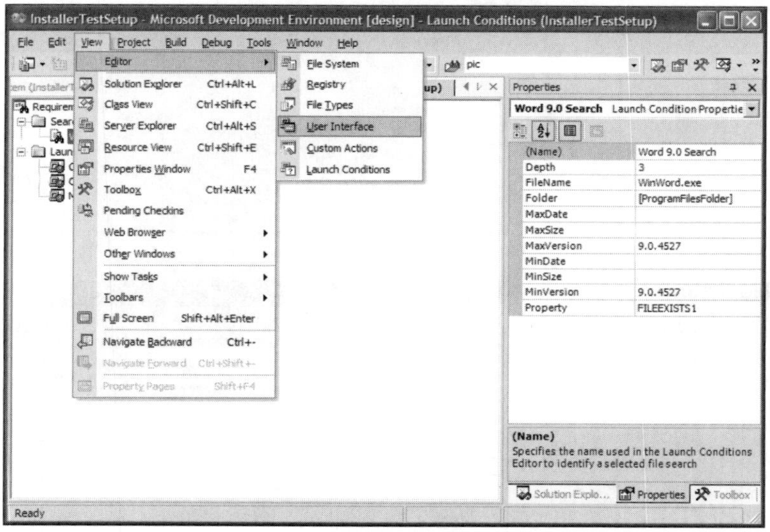

You can see in Figure 4.19 that the standard dialog boxes already exist in the setup package. To add custom dialogs, you can right-click the node that you want the dialog box to appear under and select Add Dialog.

After you select Add Dialog from the contextual menu, you are prompted with the Add Dialog dialog box, as Figure 4.20 demonstrates.

From the Add Dialog dialog box, select the License Agreement dialog box. This adds the default license agreement screen to your installation. The license agreement dialog has a `LicenseFile` property that you can select to indicate what the license file is. This file must be a rich text format (RTF) file, and must be included with the installation. For this example, you don't need to add a license agreement, so you can just leave the `LicenseFile` property blank. My goal is to get you comfortable with the different available options.

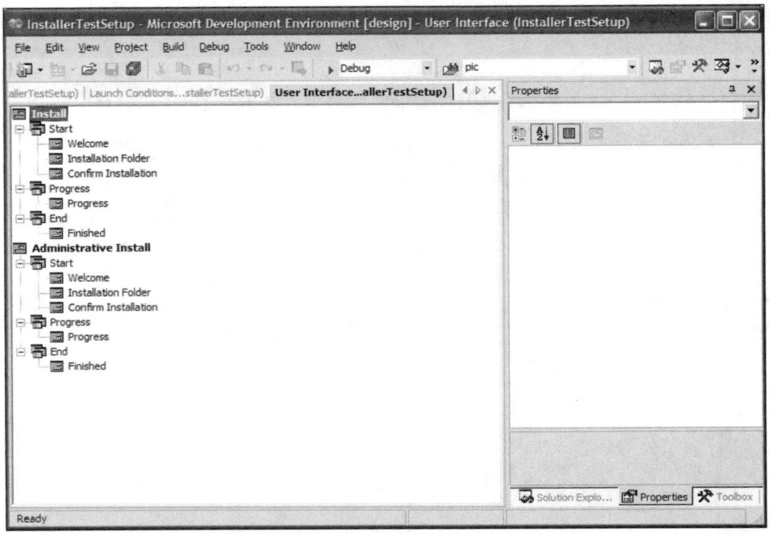

FIGURE 4.19
Standard dialog boxes are already added.

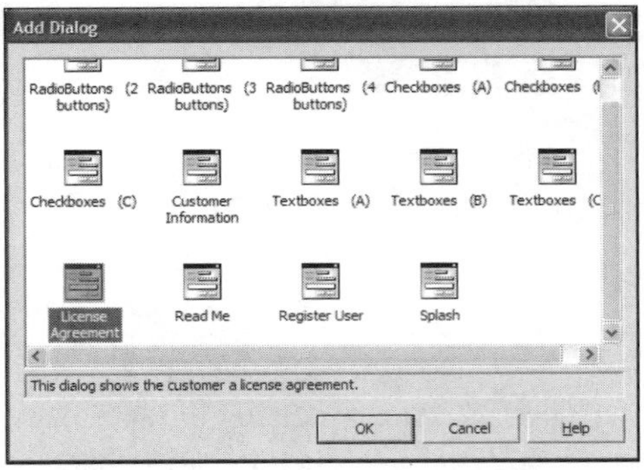

FIGURE 4.20
The Add Dialog dialog box.

When you add the custom dialog, it ends up as the last dialog in the node you added it to. Because a license agreement should logically appear before the installation actually begins, you should right-click the License Agreement node, and select Move Up from the contextual menu. You can manipulate the order in which all screens appear by moving them up or down.

Building the Application

You've now completed the basics in building a solid installation package. The next step is to build the MSI package. Within the Visual Studio .NET integrated development environment (IDE), select the Install menu item from the Project menu. This enables you to test the installation as you're creating it. If you're testing different launch conditions and dialogs, using the Install and Uninstall menu items is a good idea. You're going to be brave and just build the whole solution, and test it from the command line.

Before you select Build Solution from the Build menu, right-click on the TestInstallerSetup project in the Solution Explorer and select Properties from the contextual menu. Figure 4.21 is the properties dialog for the installer solution.

FIGURE 4.21

Build configuration properties.

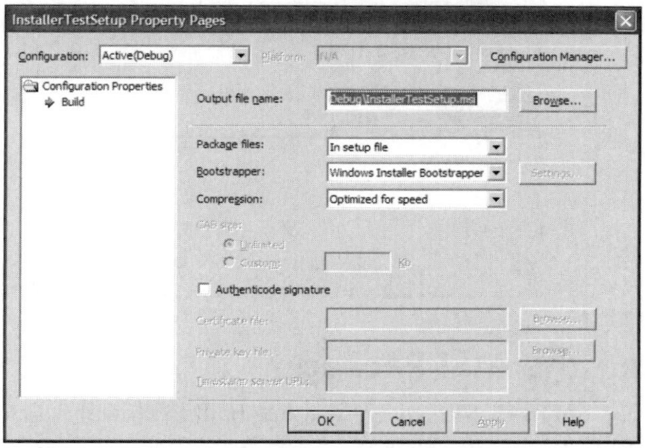

Notice the various configurations you can set. You can also include an Authenticode certificate for your installation. This guarantees the source of your installation if you need it to be trusted by a client machine.

To build the package, select Build Solution from the Build menu. Doing so builds the `TestInstaller.exe` file and it creates `TestInstallerSetup.msi`. If you view the results of the build in the Output window, you'll notice a message that the .NET Framework is required to make this installation work. By default, the 20MB redistribution package for the .NET Framework isn't included in the output. You'll learn how to factor that in during the next section. If any errors are encountered during the build, you're notified of them through the Task Window.

After the project is built, you can navigate to the folder where the MSI package was created to view the output. Figure 4.22 is where the MSI output was put on my machine.

You'll notice that there's an MSI package, a `Setup.exe` file, and two other EXE files. The files named `InstMisA.exe` and `InstMsiW.exe` are version-specific Windows Installer setup packages. When you deploy an application, the launch condition for the Windows Installer makes sure that the target machine has the correct Windows Installer version installed.

FIGURE 4.22

Browsing to the setup files.

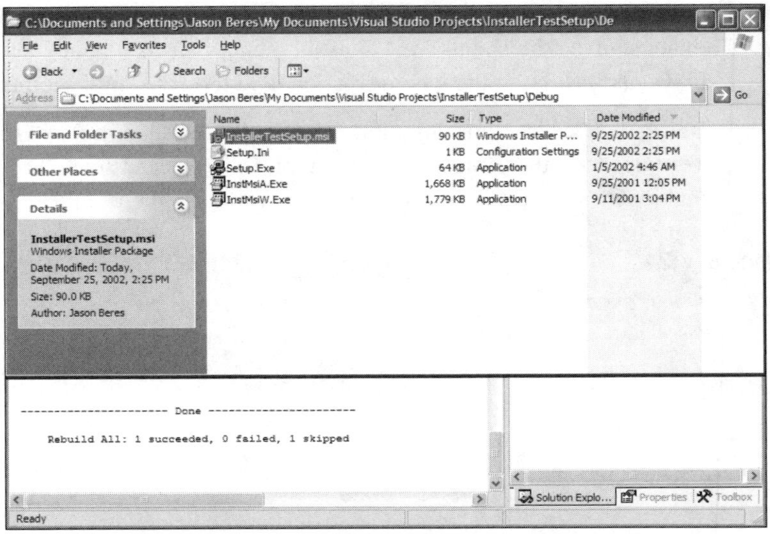

Running the MSI Package

Now you can run the MSI package you just built to view the dialogs and the behavior of the installation. So, double-click the `TestInstallerSetup.msi` file in the file system. The first screen you should see is shown in Figure 4.23, which welcomes you to the setup for your project.

FIGURE 4.23

The Welcome screen for TestInstallerSetup.

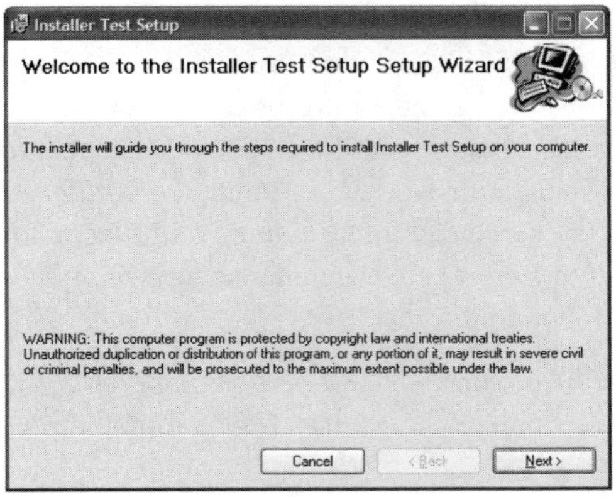

If you click Next, you'll see the custom dialog box you added that makes the user select I Agree in order to continue. Figure 4.24 shows the License Agreement dialog.

FIGURE 4.24

The custom License Agreement dialog box.

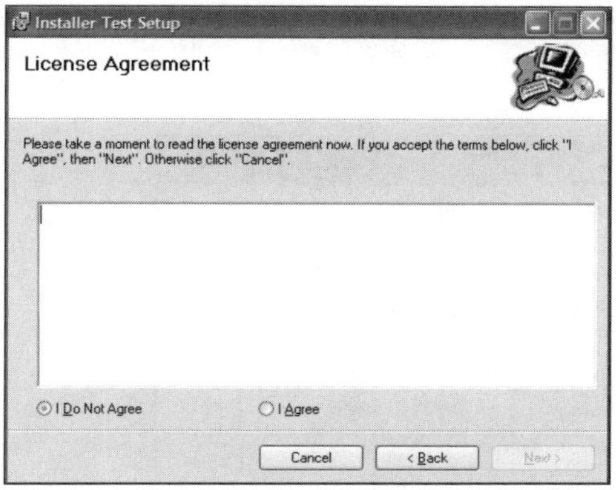

Finish the installation by clicking Next for each screen you're given. These are the default dialogs that always appear unless you explicitly delete them from the Dialogs Editor. If you want an installation to occur with no user interaction, you can delete the dialogs from the Dialog Editor, and the setup will still be functional.

After the setup is complete, you should have a new shortcut on your desktop for the application. If you double-click the shortcut, you should see the single form of your application pop up.

Just like that, you have a complete installation package. Now open up the Control Panel, and select the Add or Remove Programs icon. If you scroll down, you'll see the Test Setup Installer as Figure 4.25 shows.

FIGURE 4.25

Your application in Add or Remove Programs.

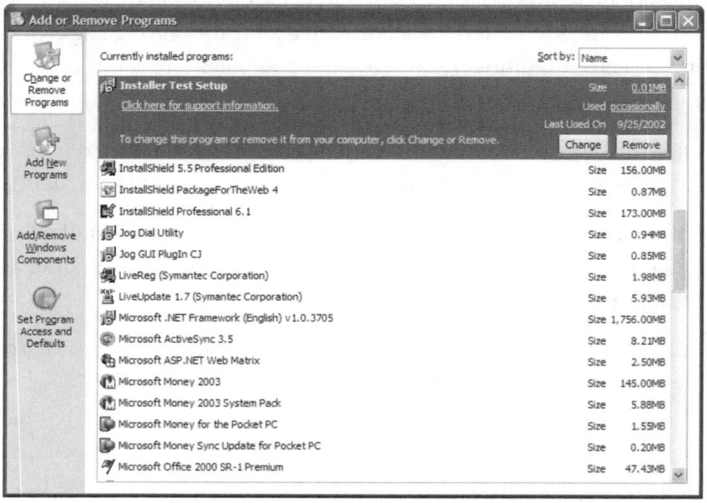

If you click the hyperlink that says Click Here for Support Information, you'll see something like Figure 4.26.

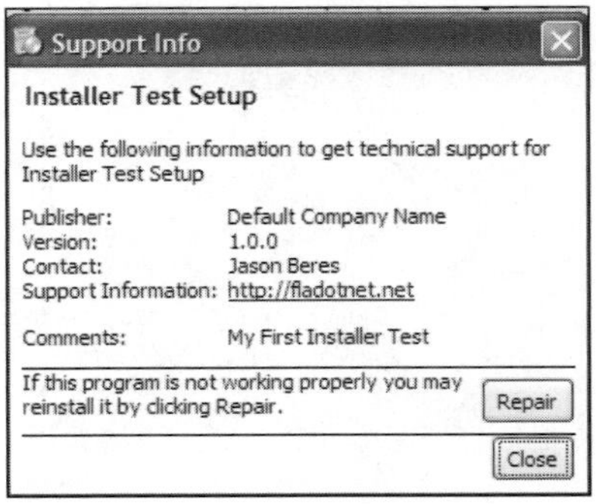

FIGURE 4.26
The Support page for your application.

The properties that you set during the creation of the installation package can be seen. So, it's important that you fill out support information details because they're now part of the Windows Installer package.

Adding Merge Modules to Your Setup

Merge modules are another method of packaging a component for redistribution. The beauty of merge modules is that they're independent installation components that contain all the necessary logic to successfully install, but they can't be installed on their own. They must be part of an MSI package. Like the setup project you created earlier, you can create a merge module project with resources, dependencies, launch conditions, and custom actions. Merge modules are very useful for pre-packaging components that must be shared across multiple resources on a computer, or just as a mechanism of breaking apart a large installation.

There's a Merge Module project template that you can use to create your own merge modules, or you can add a merge module to your setup project if it already exists.

To find out how to add a merge module, return to the InstallerTestSetup project and get to the File System Editor by right-clicking on the project name and selecting View, File System Editor from the contextual menu.

Next, select Add, Merge Module from the Project main menu. You're now prompted with the Add Module dialog that Figure 4.27 displays.

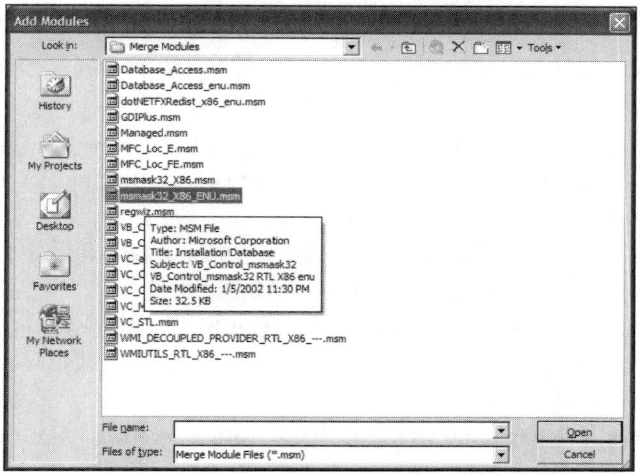

FIGURE 4.27

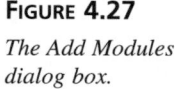

The Add Modules dialog box.

In the `C:\Program Files\Common Files\Merge Modules` folder there are predefined merge modules for several components. Select the `msmask32_X86_ENU.msm` as shown in Figure 4.27. Notice that merge modules have an `.msm` extension. After the file is selected, it can be seen in your Solution Explorer.

4

When you build the application, the MSMakedEdit control's merge module will be included with the MSI package, and it will install as part of your package.

If the installation of the merge module fails, the complete installation fails because the merge module is part of the package. From your point of view, it's just another component to include in your deployment package.

Summary

Today you learned how to use the robust deployment capabilities included in Visual Studio .NET. Creating an application deployment package is no longer a punishment—it's a pleasure. Using the tools in Visual Studio .NET, you can completely customize the look and feel of a deployment package, and include custom actions and conditions that guarantee a successful project rollout.

Q&A

Q You had me add a Registry entry using the Registry Editor, but the setup never used it. Why?

A Although you can customize the setup to use the Registry, the main goal of the Registry Editor is to create entries for your applications at installation, not at the time your application is running.

Q You mentioned that we're going to learn about the .NET Framework redistribution, but you didn't cover it. What gives?

A As part of your exercises at the end of the day, you're going to download a Knowledge Base article that walks you through the deployment of the .NET runtime.

Q What else is there to learn? This stuff is awesome, but the tool looks so cool, there must be more!

A You are correct! When you get to Day 6, you're going to build on what you learned today and take some extra steps to really make your installations great. Remember, the concept for deployment between Windows Forms applications and ASP.NET applications is identical—you use the same tool and have the same features. So, in two days, you just build on what you learned today.

Q My company uses InstallShield to create installation packages. We're moving to .NET, but still have a lot of legacy stuff we need to install. What should we do? Should we use InstallShield or use the Visual Studio .NET installation tools?

A Good question. InstallShield enables you to create merge modules, as does .NET. What you can do is create the merge modules for the legacy applications, and simply add those to a Visual Studio .NET installation project.

Quiz

1. True or False: You can use the Visual Basic 6 Setup and Deployment Wizard to package both .NET and Visual Basic 6 applications.
2. The ________________ template is what I should use to create Windows Forms deployment projects.
3. True or False: You should use a third-party compression utility to makes files smaller before using them in an MSI file.

Quiz Answers

1. False. The Visual Basic 6 Setup and Deployment Wizard only recognizes the .VBP extension as a valid project type.
2. Setup Project Template
3. False. The Windows Installer packages are already compressed.

Exercises

This exercise has to do with deploying the .NET Framework as part of your installation package. Based on your environment, this might or might not be important, but it's a good idea to understand what steps must be taken to ensure the .NET Framework is installed on a client machine to run your applications.

To do this exercise, go to the following link:

`http://msdn.microsoft.com/library/default.asp?url=/library/en-us/dnnetdep/html/dotnetfxref.asp`

This link takes you to a seven-page article that outlines the different methods of getting the runtime installed on client computers. Read this article and follow the steps to understand how to redistribute the .NET Framework.

DAY 5

Writing ASP.NET Applications

Two days ago, you learned about the great innovations of Visual Studio .NET for designing Windows-based applications. Today, you learn how to extend what you discovered about creating Windows applications and by taking it to the Web. ASP.NET is the Web development platform for .NET. Not to be confused with Active Server Pages (ASP), ASP.NET is a major breakthrough in creating robust, scalable, and extensible Web applications. Today, you learn

- What ASP.NET is and how it differs from ASP
- How to use Visual Studio .NET to develop ASP.NET applications
- How to write code-behind for ASP.NET pages
- What server controls are and how they differ from HTML controls
- How to manage session state
- How to use ASP.NET configuration Files

Introduction to ASP.NET

ASP.NET is an object-oriented, event-driven development platform for writing Web-based applications. Before .NET, Active Server Pages was the core Microsoft technology for developing applications that ran through the browser. ASP was a great platform, and it truly revolutionized the way Web applications were written, but it had lots of room for improvement. With ASP.NET, the gap between writing Windows-based applications and Web-based applications has been closed.

Because ASP.NET is based on the .NET Framework, the same classes in the Framework class library (FCL) are available to all .NET-based applications. That means the same coding model that you use to write Windows Forms applications is used to write ASP.NET applications. It also means you can write ASP.NET applications in any .NET language.

One of the drawbacks to writing ASP applications is the scalability issue. Because ASP pages are written in script, the code must be interpreted each time a page is accessed. To improve performance, developers write complex caching schemes, use different session state handling optimizations to improve page throughput, and move code into compiled COM components to increase performance—that all changes with .NET. All ASP.NET applications are compiled. There's no interpreted script of server-side code, and the ASP.NET runtime is a multithreaded asynchronous application, so the core infrastructure is more scalable than ASP. The following bullets highlight some of the major improvements and benefits that ASP.NET gives you, and should also serve as a list of why ASP.NET is so much better than ASP:

- Using the various caching methods in ASP.NET, you can drastically improve application performance with a simple page directive—not any complex code.
- Using the `Web.Config` configuration file, you can implement robust page- and directory-level security without writing code for each page.
- Using Visual Studio .NET, you have the same Code Editor features that Windows Forms applications have, including auto-complete and auto-list members.
- Debugging ASP.NET applications is just like debugging Windows applications. All the great debugging features come from Visual Studio .NET, not the language or type of application you're writing.
- The event-driven model familiar to Visual Basic 6 developers and Windows Forms development is the same in ASP.NET, which makes application development more logical and very rapid.
- Visual Studio .NET provides a vast array of controls, including validation controls, grid controls, and list controls—all of which support data binding.

- ASP.NET provides several ways to implement session state, including page level, session level, and application level. The state data can be stored in memory, in cookies, in a Windows Service process, or in a SQL Server database, giving you great options for designing scalable applications.
- ASP.NET separates the visual pages from the page logic, giving you increased flexibility in how you design and develop applications.
- ASP.NET applications are 100% compiled.

To learn how to use all these great features, let's start writing an ASP.NET application.

Hello ASP.NET!

To create your first ASP.NET application, start Visual Studio .NET. At the Start Page, click the New Project button. In the New Project dialog, select either Visual Basic Project or C# Project, depending on what language you're writing in. From the Template pane, select the ASP.NET Web Application template as shown in Figure 5.1. Change the name of the application to `http://localhost/HelloWeb_vb` or `http://localhost/HelloWeb_cs`, depending on what language you're coding in. Click the OK button to create the application.

FIGURE 5.1

Selecting the ASP.NET Web Application template.

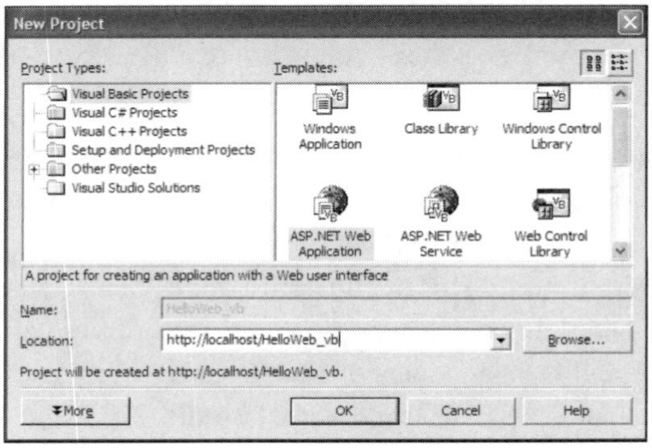

When you create an ASP.NET application, Visual Studio creates the virtual Web directory at the location you specify in the name of the project. In this case, the application was created at `localhost`, which is the default name for the local Web server running on your machine. If you want to create an application on another server, you specify the Web address and project name, and the application is created there. After the application has been created, you should see something like Figure 5.2.

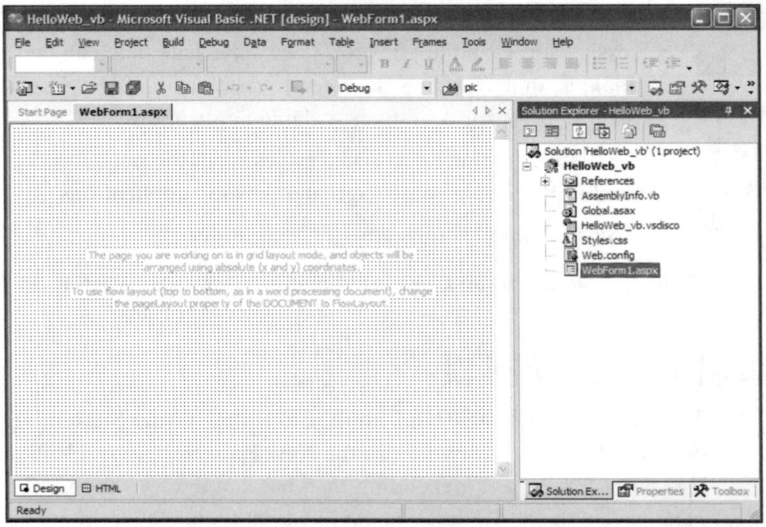

FIGURE 5.2
The HelloWeb application at design time.

You're now in the Visual Studio .NET designer for ASP.NET applications. You'll notice the same look and feel you saw when you were designing Windows Forms applications. The Solution Explorer displays the components of your project, the Properties window, and the Toolbox. All the windows you learned about over the last few days are available. The design environment is the same no matter what type of application you're developing.

To understand where the files are created, navigate to the `\inetpub\wwwroot\helloweb_cs` or `\inetpub\wwwroot\helloweb_vb` directory. When you create new applications in ASP.NET, all the core application files are created directly on the Web server. This is different from writing ASP applications using Visual InterDev, which creates a local copy of files and then creates a copy on the Web server. You use the tools in Visual InterDev to release and refresh copies of files from the Web server. It's extremely important to understand that in ASP.NET and Visual Studio .NET, the files are created directly on the Web server and there's no local copy. Figure 5.3 shows what my directory looks like; yours should look very similar.

If you navigate to the Visual Studio Projects folder under My Documents, you'll see a `HelloWeb_vb` or `HelloWeb_cs` directory, containing only the solution file (with the `.sln` extension). The solution file contains information about where the actual project files are located, so if you're ever having trouble opening a Web project that you didn't create, you can edit the `.sln` file to determine where the project files are located.

FIGURE 5.3

`inetpub` *directory for the HelloWeb application.*

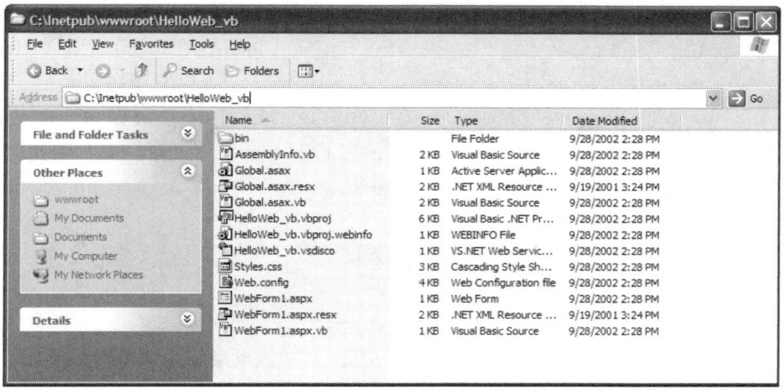

In the Solution Explorer, the files displayed in the hierarchical tree view are only the top-level files in the inheritance hierarchy for each class. That's why more files are listed in the `wwwroot` directory than you see in the Solution Explorer. If you click the Show All Files button on the Solution Explorer toolbar, you can drill into the file hierarchy, as Figure 5.4 demonstrates.

FIGURE 5.4

File hierarchy of a Web application.

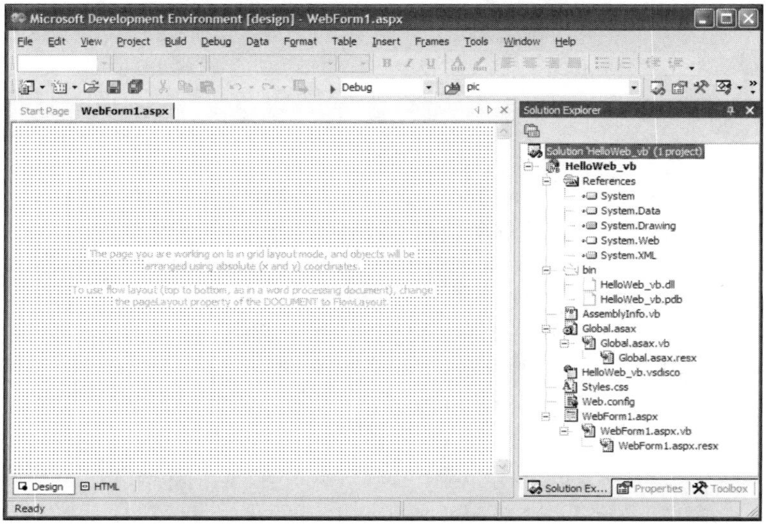

The `Webform1.aspx` file has a `Webform1.aspx.vb` and `Webform1.aspx.resx` underneath it in the tree view. The model for Web Forms is that the ASPX files have a code-behind file, which has the same name of the ASPX file, but with the `.cs` or `.vb` extension based on the language you're coding in. The `.resx` file is the resource file for the ASPX page, which can contain localization information for the Web Form.

All the server events for an ASPX page are handled in the code-behind files, whereas the user interface is contained in the ASPX file itself. Each ASPX page contains page directive attributes that set processing information on the page and indicate the inheritance hierarchy for the page. If you click the HTML button in the lower left of the Web Forms Designer, you're switched to the HTML for the ASPX file. Notice the page directives highlighted across the top of the page, as Figure 5.5 shows.

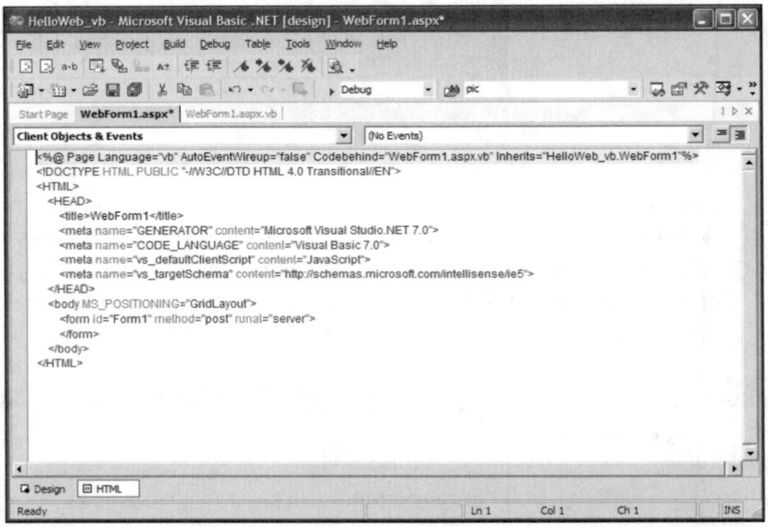

FIGURE 5.5

Page directives for an ASPX page.

The `CodeBehind` attribute contains the `WebForm1.aspx.vb` file, which is the class file under `WebForm1.aspx` in the Solution Explorer. The `Inherits` attribute specifies the `Page` class for `WebForm1` to inherit. This is different from Windows Forms, where a single class file inherits a class that contains the designer information. A `WebForm` has a class file that's physically separated from the designer file, which is actually the ASPX page. The ASPX page has information about what class file it should use to handle its events. The hierarchy of the files in the Solution Explorer is defined by the `Page` directive attributes for each file in the Solution Explorer.

If you click the Design button in the lower-left corner of the HTML designer, you're taken back to the design surface for the ASPX page. To get to the code-behind file, you can double-click the ASPX page (as you do for a Windows Form), you can press the F7 key, or you can double-click the class file in the Solution Explorer. When you get to the code-behind class, you'll see something like Figure 5.6.

FIGURE 5.6

Code-behind for an ASPX page.

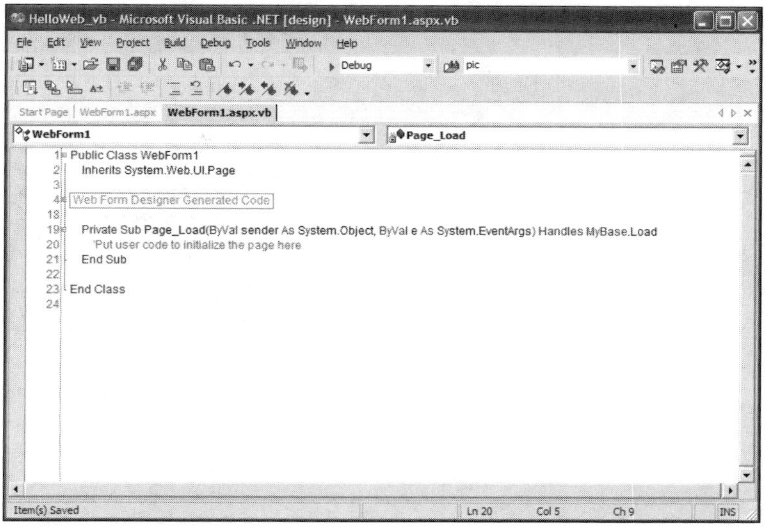

The class file inherits the `System.Web.UI.Page` class. By inheriting this class for the page, all the Web-related methods, properties, and events are available to the code-behind class file.

When an ASP.NET application is compiled, the code-behind files for each ASPX page are compiled into a single assembly with a `DLL` extension and are placed in the `Bin` directory. Each time an ASPX page is called, the ASP.NET runtime on the server creates a class for the ASPX page. The created DLL uses the information in its `Page` directive attributes to determine where to get its events. The combination of the ASPX page's DLL and the solution's DLL make up the HTML that's outputted to the end user's Web browser.

Before we go on to the next section and begin adding controls and code to the `WebForm1.aspx` page, Table 5.1 lists the files that make up a solution and gives a description of what they do for you.

TABLE 5.1 Files That Make Up an ASP.NET Web Application

File Name	*Description*
`Webform1.aspx`	The visual part of the Web Form. You can modify the HTML to pass the user interface of a Web form or drag controls from the Toolbox onto the Web Form.
`WebForm1.aspx.vb` or `WebForm1.aspx.cs`	Code-behind class file that the ASPX file inherits its functionality from.

TABLE 5.1 continued

File Name	*Description*
`Web.Config`	XML-based configuration file for the project. You can set properties on security, caching, state, and tracing information in the `Web.Config` file.
`Global.asax`	Similar to the `Global.asa` file from ASP, the `Global.asax` file contains application-level events for an ASP.NET project.
`Styles.css`	Default style sheet for a project. You can double-click `.css` files to edit them in the Style Sheet Designer.
`AssemblyInfo`	Class file that contains assembly-specific information for the project's assembly output.
`.vdisco`	Discovery file for XML Web services in the application. You learn more about discovery files on Day 13, "XML Web Service in .NET," when you learn about Web services.

Adding Controls to a Web Form

Adding controls to a Web Form is exactly like adding controls to a Windows Form. You visually design a page by dragging predefined controls from the Toolbox onto the Web Form.

Note *Server controls* and *Web controls* are equivalent terms. The term *server controls* is more common in referring to controls that provide server-side event functionality.

When programming in ASP.NET, you have a choice of what types of controls you can use on a Web Form. There are HTML controls and server controls. HTML controls are the same HTML-tag-based controls you use in ASP or a regular HTML page. Server controls offer a richer user interface, and have an object model that you can access in the code-behind class files for an ASPX page.

To get an idea of the controls you can use, click the HTML Controls tab on the Toolbox, and then click the Web Form Controls tab on the Toolbox. Figure 5.7 gives a snapshot that comparing the different types of controls that each Toolbox tab offers.

FIGURE 5.7
HTML controls and Web Forms controls in the Toolbox.

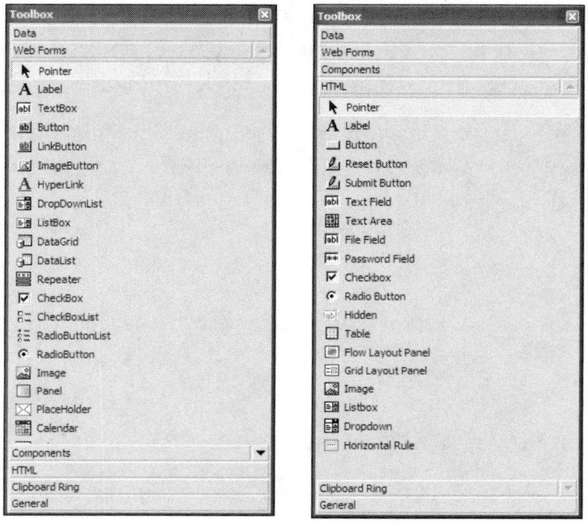

Based on what functionality you're trying to implement, and whether you need to write server events for a control, you can use either HTML controls or server controls. To see the different HTML that's rendered in the designer, drag an HTML text field to the ASPX page and then drag a `TextBox` server control.

If you switch to the HTML view in the designer, you'll see HTML output similar to Listing 5.1.

LISTING 5.1 HTML View Comparing Server Controls and HTML Controls

```
<body>
    <form id="Form1" method="post" runat="server">
        <P>
        <asp:TextBox id="TextBox1" runat="server"></asp:TextBox></P>
        <P> </P>
        <P>  <INPUT type="text"></P>
    </form>
</body>
```

The HTML `<Input>` tag conforms to HTML version 3.2 standards. The server control, however, has an XML-like syntax to define the `TextBox` control and its attributes. All server controls have an `<asp:`*`controltype`* prefix, where *`controltype`* is the class of the control. The `id` attribute is the friendly name for the control, and the `runat` attribute denotes where the control events for the control should occur. By adding the `runat=server` attribute to any control, be it an HTML control or a server control, you

can access the control from the inherited code-behind file. When you add the `runat=server` attribute, the control is declared as an object within the code-behind class file, and you can access the control object model through code within the class file.

If you switch back to the Design view of the page, and then double-click on the ASPX page, you're taken to the code-behind file. At the top of the class file, you'll see the following object declaration:

VB.NET

```
Protected WithEvents TextBox1 As System.Web.UI.WebControls.TextBox
```

C#

```
protected System.Web.UI.WebControls.TextBox TextBox1;
```

Notice that the HTML `Input` control isn't declared in the code-behind file. Because the control does not have a `runat=server` attribute, the declaration isn't created in the code-behind file.

Switch to the HTML view of the `WebForm1.aspx` page and modify the HTML `Input` control to look like this:

```
<INPUT type="text" runat="server" id="HtmlTextBox">
```

Then save the page and switch back to the code-behind class. You'll notice this declaration at the top of the page along with the original `TextBox1`:

VB.NET

```
Protected WithEvents HtmlTextBox As System.Web.UI.HtmlControls.HtmlInputText
```

C#

```
protected System.Web.UI.HtmlControls.HtmlInputText HtmlTextBox;
```

Note

> When you add server controls to an ASPX page, the controls that you add are generated in the code-behind class when you save the ASPX page. If you add new items to the HTML of an ASPX page, or you drag new controls from the Toolbox onto the ASPX page, make sure that you save the page before you go to the code-behind, or you won't see your newly added controls.

When you added the `runat=server` attribute to the HTML tag, you notified the ASPX page that you want to include this item in the class file, and that you want its methods, properties, and events available. Notice that the namespace for the controls is different, however. An HTML control is derived from the `System.Web.UI.HtmlControls` class, whereas a server control is derived from the `System.Web.UI.WebControls` class. Each namespace offers different properties, methods, and events based on the type of control you're using.

Then what's the difference, and why would you use HTML controls instead of server controls? The following bullets highlight the reasons why you would or would not choose one approach or the other:

- Server controls don't expose client events; HTML controls do. In other words, you can't use client-side JavaScript or VBScript with a control that has a `runat=server` attribute.
- Server controls offer a rich object model in the code-behind class that enables you to program Web applications in a way that's similar to writing Windows applications—by responding to events and setting properties.
- If you're migrating an ASP application to an ASP.NET application and aren't familiar with event-driven programming, using HTML controls might seem more familiar to you.
- Both sets of controls offer auto-complete and auto-list members in the HTML view, so that functionality isn't specific to one type of control.
- If you're targeting down-level browsers such as IE 4.0 or Netscape 4.7, IIS automatically renders server controls correctly on such browsers. For example, if you're using a drop-down list control and `AbsolutePositioning` on an ASPX page, the ASP.NET runtime on the server generates HTML 3.2–compliant HTML that positions and HTML `ComboBox` inside a table. It completely changes the code you wrote so it works in the down-level browsers.
- There's overhead associated with using server controls. Because server controls must be part of the compiled assembly and processed by the ASP.NET runtime on the server, it isn't always as efficient as using a straight HTML control.

5

From my experience, you use server controls when you start learning ASP.NET. You have a huge number of capabilities when designing Web-based applications using server controls, and it's the most exciting new feature of ASP.NET. After you get the hang of server controls and HTML controls, you use both to write scalable and robust Web-based applications. Just remember that any HTML tag can have a `runat=server` attribute—a `<TD>` tag, an `<IMG>` tag, any tag. So, if you want to add functionality but need to do it server side, you can simply add the `runat=server` tag and handle events for the object on the server.

Tip

I mentioned that any HTML element can have a `runat=server` attribute. As an example, let's say you have an HTML table, and you need to change the color of a table cell or table row, based on something that occurs in a server event. If you add the `runat=server` attribute to the `TD` HTML element and give it an ID, the code-behind class will have the following declaration:

```
Protected WithEvents TD1 As System.Web.UI.HtmlControls.HtmlTableCell
```

In your code, you can then use a `Select Case` statement or an `If` statement to set `Style` attributes on the `HtmlTableCell` object, as the following code demonstrates:

```
Select Case Request("AlertStatus")
 Case "Red"
   TD1.Attributes.Add("background", "red.jpg")
 Case "Yellow"
   TD1.Attributes.Add("background", "yellow.jpg")
 Case Else
   TD1.Attributes.Add("background", "green.jpg")
End Select
```

Keep in mind that you can do anything with any HTML element in server-side code.

Responding to Server Control Events

The benefit of using server controls is the ease with which you can write server-side code. Using the built-in functionality of the Visual Studio .NET Code Editor with auto-complete and auto-list members is certainly much easier than writing script in a text file. Just as you can handle events in a Windows Form, you can add a control to a Web Form, double-click the control, and then write code for the default event for that control. Because you're dealing with a Web page, there are certain events that can't occur in server-side code. To understand this better, you need to understand how server events are processed.

When a Web page is viewed in a browser, it's just HTML. Because HTML is just a tag-based language that describes how things are supposed to look, it doesn't support any real event processing. This can be extended by certain browsers with Dynamic HTML (or DHTML), which supports JavaScript or VBScript events for HTML elements. That means certain events can occur from a page that's already rendered in the browser. Common events might be `OnMouseOver`, `OnBlur`, and `OnClick`. If a browser supports scripting, you can write script code that responds to events on the client side in the browser.

When using server controls, the event processing takes place on the server. If you write code for the `Click` event of a `Button` server control, the page is posted back to the server and the event is processed. Understanding that the event must occur on the server means that events such as `OnMouseOver` and `OnBlur` can't occur in a server event.

Each time an event is fired for a server control, the whole page is posted back to the server. ASP.NET takes care of remembering the state of the page before and after it's posted back to the server. You learn about how it does that with `ViewState` a little later.

To see how easy it is to write applications using server controls, you'll now write a simple login form. There's no data access yet because you don't get into that until next week, but understanding the page events and how to work with controls are the primary foci of today.

Follow these steps to modify the `WebForm1.aspx` page in your Solution Explorer. Your results should look like Figure 5.9.

1. Make sure that you're in the Web Forms Designer.
2. Delete the HTML text field control and the `TextBox` server control from the form.
3. From the main menu, select Table, Insert, Table. You are prompted with the Insert Table dialog shown in Figure 5.8.

FIGURE 5.8

Insert Table dialog box.

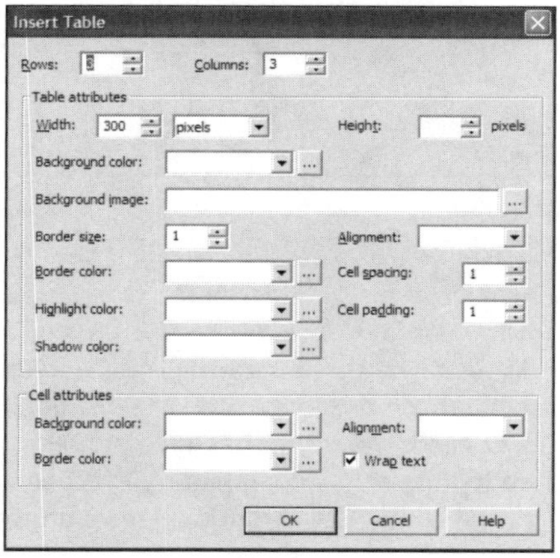

4. Click the OK button to add the default table with three columns and three rows.
5. Drag two `Label` controls from the Web Forms tab of the Toolbox to the first two rows in the first column of the table. Change their `Text` property to `User Name` and `Password`, respectively.

6. Drag two `TextBox` controls from the Web Forms tabs of the Toolbox to the first two rows in the second column of the table. Change their `Name` property to `UserName` and `Password`, respectively.
7. Drag a `Button` control from the Web Forms tab to the third row on the second column in the table, and change its `Text` property to `Log In` and change its `Name` property to `LogIn`.

Your final output will look like Figure 5.9.

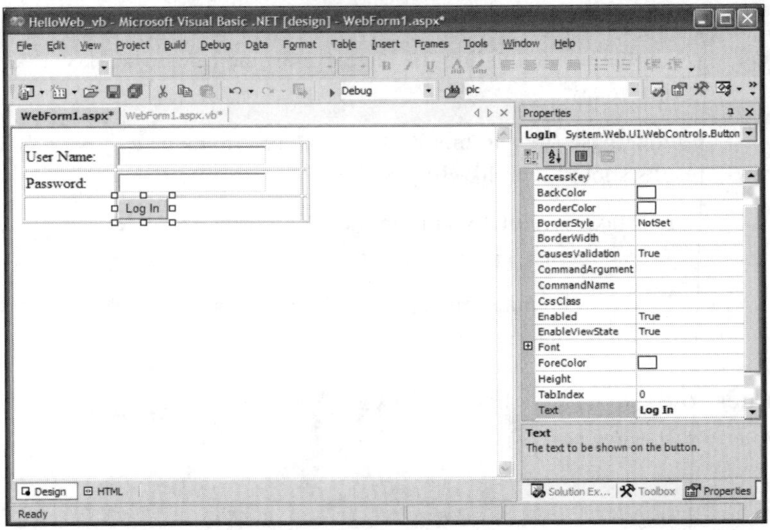

FIGURE 5.9
`WebForm1.aspx` *after adding controls.*

Note

By default, the Web Forms Designer defaults to absolute positioning and grid layout for the designer. That means there's a grid that you can use to line up controls similar to the Window Forms Designer, and that controls are positioned absolutely on the form. Absolute positioning sets the x and y coordinates of each control using the `Style` property. This sort of positioning works great in Internet Explorer, and ASP.NET converts the `Style` properties settings to the correct HTML for down-level browsers such as Netscape Navigator. I'm accustomed to using `Table` to position my HTML elements, so I set my page properties not to use the `FlowLayout` by right-clicking the APX page and setting its Page Layout property to `GridLayout` instead of `FlowLayout`.

Double-click on the Log In button to get to its `Click` event, and add the code in Listing 5.2, which writes out the contents of the `TextBoxes` to the form.

Listing 5.2 `LogIn_Click` Event

VB.NET

```
Private Sub LogIn_Click(ByVal sender As System.Object, _
  ByVal e As System.EventArgs) Handles LogIn.Click

  Response.Write(UserName.Text)
  Response.Write("<br>")
  Response.Write(Password.Text)
  Response.End()

End Sub
```

C#

```
private void LogIn_Click(object sender, System.EventArgs e)
{
  Response.Write(UserName.Text);
  Response.Write("<br>");
  Response.Write(Password.Text);
  Response.End();
}
```

As when you're writing ASP code, you can use the members of the `HttpResponse` class and `HttpRequest` class in the code-behind to read and write HTTP values sent by a browser during a Web request.

If you right-click the `WebForm1.aspx` page in the Solution Explorer and select Build and Browse, the page will be compiled and displayed in the internal browser of Visual Studio .NET. Your IDE should look like Figure 5.10.

Note

> Remember that ASP.NET pages are running from the compiled assembly in the `Bin` directory. So, if you make any changes to your code-behind files, you must rebuild the solution to make sure that you're working with the current version of the files. If you change any of the standard HTML in the ASPX page, it isn't compiled until the page is accessed, so you can select Save All Files from the File menu to make sure that any HTML changes have been saved—you don't need to rebuild the project.

After the page is displayed in the browser, enter values in the `UserName` text box and the Password text box and click the Log In button. The results should look like Figure 5.11.

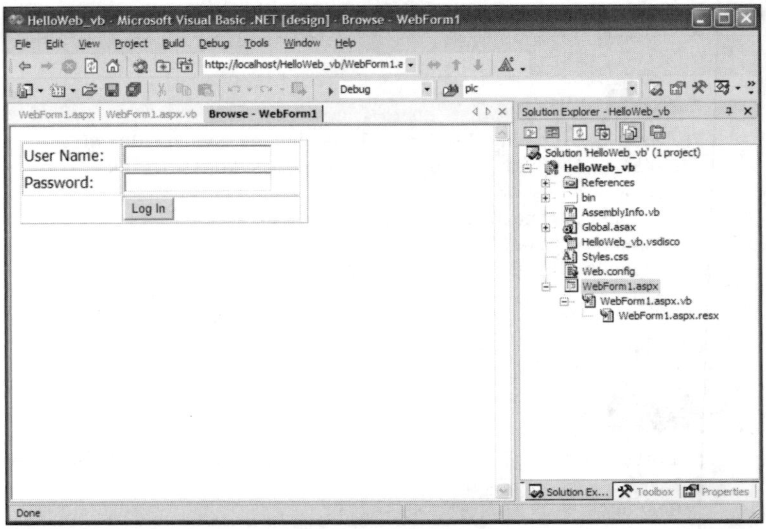

FIGURE 5.10
Browsing to the `WebForm1.aspx` *page.*

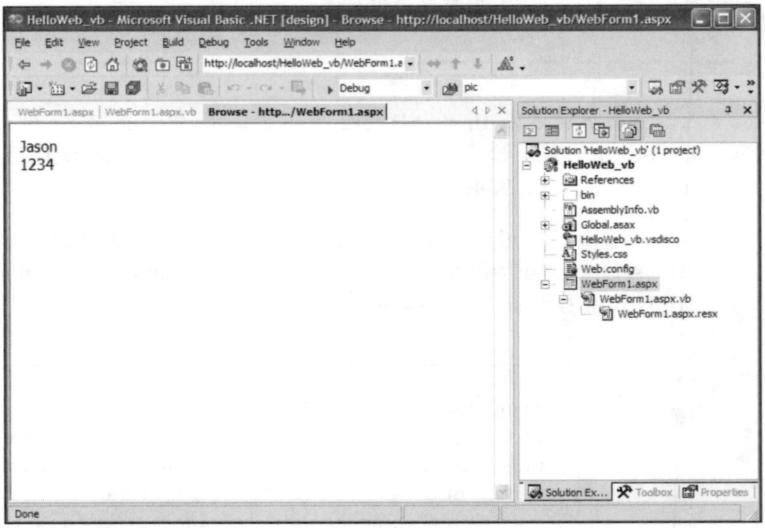

FIGURE 5.11
Results of the `LogIn_Click` *event.*

When you click the Log In button, the page is posted back to the server, and the code for the click event is processed. When you add the server controls to the form, the HTML source looks like Listing 5.3.

Listing 5.3 HTML Code for the `WebForm1.aspx` Page

```
<TABLE id="Table1" cellSpacing="1" cellPadding="1" width="300" border="1">
  <TR>
   <TD>
     <asp:Label id="Label1" runat="server">User Name:</asp:Label></TD>
   <TD>
     <asp:TextBox id="UserName" runat="server"></asp:TextBox></TD>
   <TD></TD>
  </TR>
  <TR>
   <TD>
     <asp:Label id="Label2" runat="server">Password:</asp:Label></TD>
   <TD>
     <asp:TextBox id="Password" runat="server"></asp:TextBox></TD>
   <TD></TD>
  </TR>
  <TR>
   <TD></TD>
   <TD>
     <asp:Button id="LogIn" runat="server" Text="Log In">
     </asp:Button></TD>
   <TD></TD>
  </TR>
</TABLE>
```

As you learned earlier, when you add server controls to a form, they use the `<ASP:>` tag syntax to denote that they're server controls. The `id` attribute is used in the code-behind to respond to events for the control when it's posted back to the server.

When this code is accessed by a browser, the ASP.NET runtime determines how to render the page based on the type of browser that's accessing the page. Because no browsers understand the `<ASP:>` tag syntax, the ASP.NET runtime renders the appropriate HTML to the browser. The HTML in Listing 5.4 shows the HTML rendered to the browser for `WebForm1.aspx`.

5

Listing 5.4 HTML Rendered to the Browser from the `WebForm1.aspx` Page

```
<TABLE id="Table1" cellPadding="1" width="300" border="1">
  <TR>
   <TD>
     <span id="Label1">User Name:</span></TD>
   <TD>
     <input name="UserName" type="text" id="UserName" /></TD>
   <TD></TD>
  </TR>
  <TR>
   <TD>
```

LISTING 5.4 continued

```
    <span id="Label2">Password:</span></TD>
  <TD>
    <input name="Password" type="text" id="Password" /></TD>
  <TD></TD>
 </TR>
 <TR>
  <TD></TD>
  <TD>
    <input type="submit" name="LogIn" value="Log In" id="LogIn" />
  </TD>
  <TD></TD>
 </TR>
</TABLE>
```

Each server control is rendered as an HTML 3.2 standard control. The `Label` control is rendered as a `Span` tag; the `TextBox` control is rendered as an HTML text field element; and the `Button` control is rendered as a Submit button. The Submit button posts the form data back to the server for processing, so when you add a `Button` server control, it's rendered as a Submit button. IIS and the ASP.NET runtime keep track of what events to fire for each control based on the page being browsed and the session ID of the browser session.

Note

> Each ASPX page you add to your solution has a `targetSchema` property. Based on the `targetSchema`, the metadata for the HTML is rendered differently. If you're targeting Internet Explorer 3.02 or Netscape 4.0, you can change the `targetSchema` accordingly.

When you click the Log In button, the event delegate that was wired in the code-behind class is fired, and you retrieve the `Text` property of the `UserName` and `Password` `TextBoxes`. Using the `Write` member of the `Response` class, you write the `Text` values back to the browser. And by calling `Response.End`, you explicitly ended the page processing of this ASP page.

Tip

> By default, the internal browser is used to when you browse ASPX pages from the Solution Explorer. You can change this setting to use whichever browser on your machine you want by select the Browse With option from the right-click contextual menu. I normally change the default browser to my external Internet Explorer browser, and when I'm testing a site that needs to work in Netscape, I browse the pages with Netscape Navigator. IE 6.0, Netscape 4.79, and Netscape 6.2 are all happily installed on my machine.

Now that you understand the basics of writing events for server controls, you're going to use some of the cooler new controls, namely the validation controls that are part of Visual Studio .NET.

Using Validation Controls

Visual Studio .NET comes with built-in validation controls for use in ASPX pages. When you validate a control, you're checking whether a control has data in it and conforms to a specific pattern, (such as an email address), or you're checking the range of data that has been entered.

In ASP, you either had to process the validation on the server and send the page back to the browser if data wasn't correctly entered, or you had to write complex JavaScript to check the validity of control data. ASP.NET has five built-in validation controls in the Toolbox that you can simply drag to a form and associate with a control. Table 5.2 lists the validation controls and gives a description of how you can use each one.

TABLE 5.2 Validation Controls in ASP.NET

Control Name	*Description*
`RequiredFieldValidator`	Forces the user to enter a value into the specified control.
`CompareValidator`	Compares a user's entry against a constant value, or against a property value of another control, using a comparison operator.
`RangeValidator`	Checks that a user's entry is between specified lower and upper boundaries. You can check ranges within pairs of numbers, alphabetic characters, and dates.
`RegularExpressionValidator`	Checks that the entry matches a pattern defined by a regular expression.
`CustomValidator`	Checks the user's entry using validation logic that you write yourself. This type of validation allows you to check for values derived at runtime.

Each validation control has properties specific to the functionality the control provides. For example, the `RequiredFieldValidator` has a `ControlToValidate` property and an `ErrorMessage` property. The `ControlToValidate` property takes the ID of a valid control on the form. The `RegularExpressionValidator` uses the regular expression syntax of .NET to validate the data entered in a control against a regular expression pattern.

Note

> Each validation control has a `Text` property and an `ErrorMessage` property. The `Text` property is like the `Text` property of a `Label` control—it simply displays text. This could be used to display `Required` or an `*` for a `RequiredFieldValidator` control. The `ErrorMessage` property displays if an error occurs in the validation.

To test the validation controls, let's add a new Web Form to your solution. Right-click the project name in the Solution Explorer and select Add, Add Web Form from the contextual menu. When the Add New Item dialog pops up, change the name from `WebForm2.aspx` to `Success.aspx`, as Figure 5.12 demonstrates.

FIGURE 5.12

Add New Item dialog box.

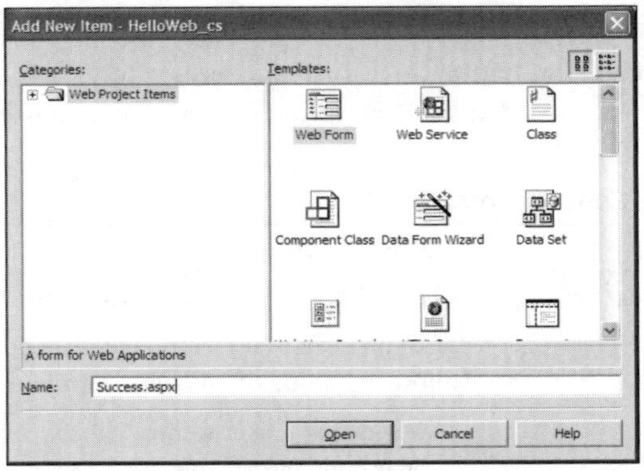

You should now see a new ASPX page called `Success.aspx` is added to your solution, and the `Success.aspx` page should be in the Web Forms Designer. Double-click `Success.aspx` to get to the `Form_Load` event for the page, and add the code in Listing 5.5 to the `Page_Load` event.

LISTING 5.5 Code-Behind for the `Page_Load` Event of the `Success.aspx` Page

VB.NET

```
Private Sub Page_Load(ByVal sender As System.Object, _
 ByVal e As System.EventArgs) Handles MyBase.Load

   Response.Write("<H1>You are now logged in</H1>")

End Sub
```

LISTING 5.5 continued

C#

```
private void Page_Load(object sender, System.EventArgs e)
{
    Response.Write("<H1>You are now logged in</H1>");
}
```

In Listing 5.5, you use the `Response` object's `Write` method to render `You are now logged in`. This page is called from the `WebForm1.aspx page` if the correct username and password are entered.

To modify the `WebForm1.aspx` page, you must do the following:

1. Add a new table row above the Log In button. You can add a new row to the table by clicking inside the cell that contains the Log In button, and then right-clicking and selecting Insert, Row Above from the contextual menu. Most of the options you need for manipulating tables and controls can be accessed by right-clicking on the objects in the designer.
2. In the newly added row, drag a `Label` and `TextBox` from the Web Forms tab of the Toolbox to line up with the other controls in the table. Change the `Text` property of the `Label` control to `Re-Enter Password`, and change the `ID` property of the `TextBox` control to `Password2`.
3. Change the `Text` property of the `Label` control that says `UserName:` to now say `Email Address:`.
4. Drag a `RequiredFieldValidator` control to the form from the Web Form tab of the Toolbox, and place it in the column next to the `Username TextBox`.
5. From the Web Form tab of the Toolbox, drag a `RegularExpressionValidator` control and place it next to the `RequiredFieldValidator` control you just added.
6. From the Web Form tab of the Toolbox, drag a `RequiredFieldValidator` control to the form and place it in the column next to the `Password TextBox`.
7. From the Web Form tab of the Toolbox, drag a `CompareValidator` control to the form and place it in the column next to the `Password2 TextBox`.

Your `WebForm1.aspx` should now look like Figure 5.13.

The next step is to set the properties on the validation controls. Follow these steps to do so:

1. Select the `RequiredFieldValidator1` control, and change the `ControlToValidate` property to `UserName`. Then change the `ErrorMessage` property to `"Email Address Required"`.

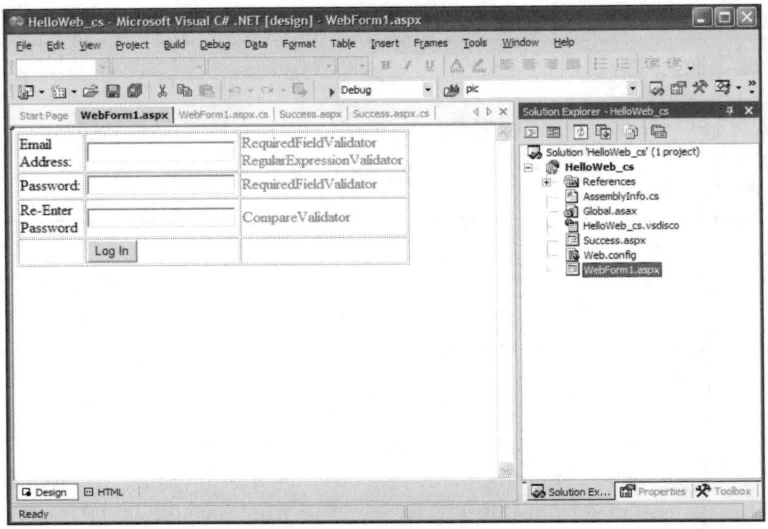

FIGURE 5.13
`WebForm1.aspx` *after adding new controls and validation controls.*

2. Select the `RegularExpressionValidator`. In the `ValidationExpression` property, click the ellipses (...) button to get to the Regular Expression Editor dialog box. Scroll down the list until you see the Internet Email Address regular expression. Select it and click the OK button. Change the `ErrorMessage` property to `"Invalid Email Format"`, and change the `ControlToValidate` property to `Username`.
3. Select the `RequiredFieldValidator2` control, and change the `ControlToValidate` property to `Password`. Then change the `ErrorMessage` property to `"Password Required"`.
4. Select the `CompareValidator1` control, and change the `ControlToCompare` property to `Password`. Change the `ControlToValidate` property to `Password2`, and change the `ErrorMessage` property to `"Passwords do not match"`.

When I mentioned regular expressions earlier, you might've gotten a little scared. But you can see that, once again, the Visual Studio .NET team thought of everything. Using the Regular Expression Editor, you can not only easily select a predefined regular expression for common data formats, but you also get a head start on understanding the regular expression syntax.

The next step is to rename the `WebForm1.aspx` to `Login.aspx`. To do so, right-click `WebForm1.aspx` in the Solution Explorer, and select Rename from the contextual menu. You can now change the name to `Login.aspx`. Make sure that you include the `.aspx` extension, or you'll get an error.

Now that you've set these properties and renamed your form, your `Login.aspx` should look like Figure 5.14.

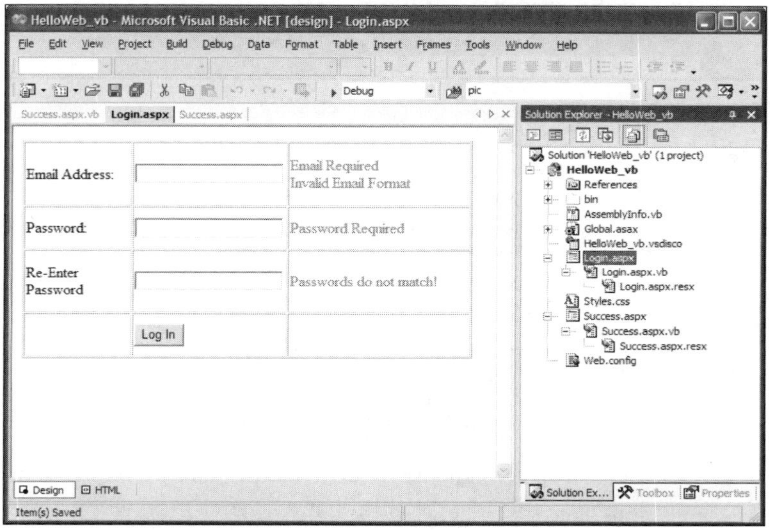

FIGURE 5.14

Notice also that when you renamed your form, the `WebForm1.aspx.vb` *or* `WebForm1.aspx.cs`

Now, double-click the Log In button, and add the code in Listing 5.6.

LISTING 5.6 Code-Behind for the `LogIn_Click` Event in the `Login.aspx` Page

VB.NET

```
Private Sub LogIn_Click(ByVal sender As System.Object, _
 ByVal e As System.EventArgs) Handles LogIn.Click

 If UserName.Text = "jason@fladotnet.net" _
   And Password.Text = "password" Then
   Response.Redirect("Success.aspx")
 Else
  LogIn.Text = "Invalid Data, please retry"
 End If

End Sub
```

C#

```
private void LogIn_Click(object sender, System.EventArgs e)
{
    if (UserName.Text == "jason@fladotnet.net"
```

LISTING 5.6 continued

```
        && Password.Text == "password")
    {
    Response.Redirect(@"Success.aspx");
    }
}
```

> **Tip**
>
> To make your user interface more friendly, you can set the `InitialValue` property of the `RequiredFieldValidator` control to a red asterisk or some other visual clue to the end user that the fields are required. You should also set the `TextMode` property of the `Password` and `Password2` text boxes to `Password` so that the data entered into the field is filled with asterisks, and isn't visible to prying eyes.

Now you can build the solution, right-click the `Login.aspx` page, and select Browse from the contextual menu. After the page is in the browser, test the validation controls. Enter text that isn't an email address, and type different passwords in the `Password` text box and `Password2` text box. When you do so, your form will look something like Figure 5.15.

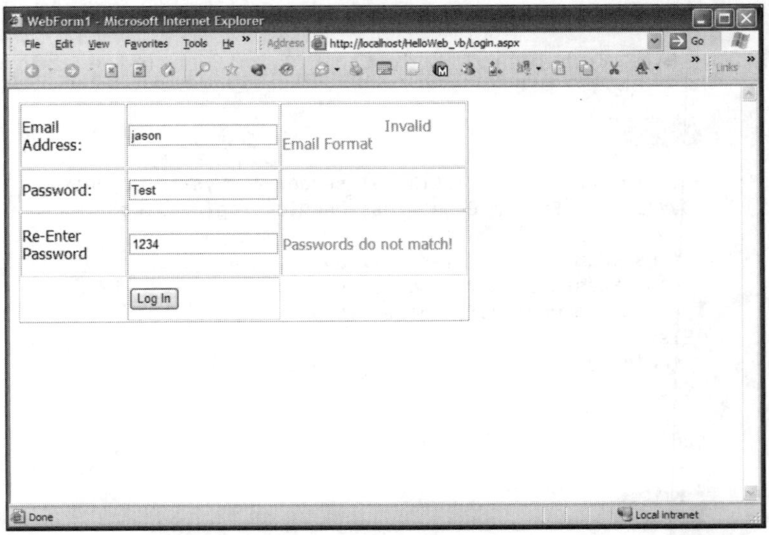

FIGURE 5.15
Testing the `Login.aspx` *validation controls.*

Tip

> You can also press the F5 key to run the application. This starts the application in debug mode. You learn more about debugging on Day 7, "Exceptions, Debugging, and Tracing."

Notice that when you click on the Log In button, the page is never posted to the server. When you place a validation control on a form, ASP.NET automatically adds custom client-side JavaScript when the page is rendered, so the validation occurs on the client and the page isn't posted to the server until the data is correct. Listing 5.7 is the HTML that's rendered to the browser—notice the JavaScript that's been added.

LISTING 5.7 HTML Source with Client-Side JavaScript for Validation Rendered

```
<form name="Form1" method="post" action="Login.aspx"
   language="javascript" onsubmit="ValidatorOnSubmit();" id="Form1">

<script language="javascript"
   src="/aspnet_client/system_web/1_0_3705_288/WebUIValidation.js"></script>

   <P>
    <TABLE id="Table1" width="469" border="1">
     <TR>
      <TD><span id="Label1">Email Address:</span></TD>
      <TD><input name="UserName" type="text" id="UserName" /></TD>
      <TD><span id="RequiredFieldValidator1"
         ➥controltovalidate="UserName"
         errormessage="Email Required"
         evaluationfunction="RequiredFieldValidatorEvaluateIsValid"
         initialvalue=""
         style="color:Red;visibility:hidden;">Email Required</span>
         <span id="RegularExpressionValidator1"
         controltovalidate="UserName"
         errormessage="Invalid Email Format"
      evaluationfunction="RegularExpressionValidatorEvaluateIsValid"
➥validationexpression="\w+([-+.]\w+)*@\w+([-.]\w+)*\.\w+([-.]\w+)*"
      style="color:Red;visibility:hidden;">Invalid Email Format</span>
      </TD>
     </TR>
     <TR>
      <TD><span id="Label2">Password:</span></TD>
      <TD><input name="Password" type="text" id="Password" /></TD>
      <TD><span id="RequiredFieldValidator2"
         controltovalidate="Password"
         errormessage="Password Required"
         evaluationfunction="RequiredFieldValidatorEvaluateIsValid"
         initialvalue=""
```

5

LISTING 5.7 continued

```
            style="color:Red;visibility:hidden;">Password Required</span>
         </TD>
        </TR>
        <TR>
         <TD>Re-Enter Password</TD>
         <TD><input name="Password2" type="text" id="Password2" /></TD>
         <TD><span id="CompareValidator1"
            controltovalidate="Password2"
            errormessage="Passwords do not match!"
            evaluationfunction="CompareValidatorEvaluateIsValid"
            controltocompare="Password"
            controlhookup="Password"
            style="color:Red;visibility:hidden;">
             Passwords do not match!</span>
         </TD>
        </TR>
        <TR>
         <TD></TD>
         <TD><input type="submit" name="LogIn" value="Log In"
            onclick="if (typeof(Page_ClientValidate) == 'function')
            Page_ClientValidate(); "
            language="javascript" id="LogIn" />
         </TD>
         <TD></TD>
        </TR>
       </TABLE>
      </P>
      </P>

<script language="javascript">
<!--
 var Page_Validators =
   new Array(document.all["RequiredFieldValidator1"],
   document.all["RegularExpressionValidator1"],
   document.all["RequiredFieldValidator2"],
   document.all["CompareValidator1"]);
  // -->
</script>


<script language="javascript">
<!--
var Page_ValidationActive = false;
if (typeof(clientInformation) != "undefined" &&
   clientInformation.appName.indexOf("Explorer") != -1) {
  if (typeof(Page_ValidationVer) == "undefined")
    alert("Unable to find script library
      '/aspnet_client/system_web/1_0_3705_288/WebUIValidation.js'.
       Try placing this file manually, or reinstall by running
```

LISTING 5.7 continued

```
        'aspnet_regiis -c'.");
    else if (Page_ValidationVer != "125")
      alert("This page uses an incorrect version of WebUIValidation.js.
        The page expects version 125. The script library is "
        + Page_ValidationVer + ".");
    else
      ValidatorOnLoad();
}

function ValidatorOnSubmit() {
  if (Page_ValidationActive) {
    ValidatorCommonOnSubmit();
  }
}
// -->
</script>

</form>
```

You can see that the HTML output is now vastly different from the output before adding validation controls, and the inserted client-side script was done by ASP.NET.

In the root `wwwroot` directory of your server, there's a folder named `asp_client`, which is used in conjunction with this script to make sure that the validation occurs. If you ever add validation to your pages and you get an error about validation files not being found when the page loads in the browser, make sure that the `asp_client` folder exists in the root of your `wwwroot` directory or in the actual folder of your Web site in the IIS server.

To see what happens with validation controls in Netscape version 4.79, check out Figure 5.16.

When ASP.NET detects that a down-level browser, such as Netscape 4.79, is attempting to access a page that uses validation controls, it simply changes the validation events to occur on the server. You don't need to do anything special to make this happen—it's automatic.

To display a summary of validation errors, you can use the `ValidationSummary` control on a page. This takes all the validation errors on the page, and places them in a nice bulleted list. Figure 5.17 demonstrates the use of a `ValidationSummary` control with the `ShowMessageBox` property set to `True`.

To validate a page in server-side code, you check the `IsValid` property of a page. When you check the `IsValid` property for an entire page, all the validation controls on the page are checked against their respective controls to validate. If they're all okay, processing continues. If there are errors, processing stops and the validation controls or `ValidationSummary` control will be filled.

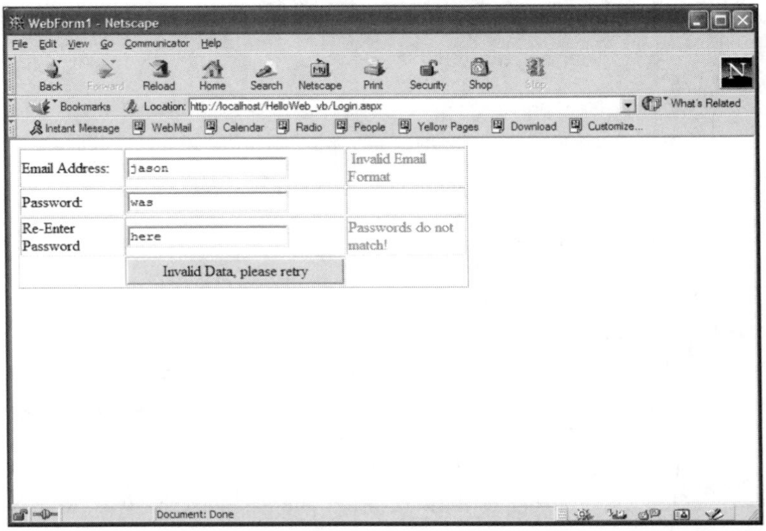

FIGURE 5.16
Running the validation controls in Netscape 4.79.

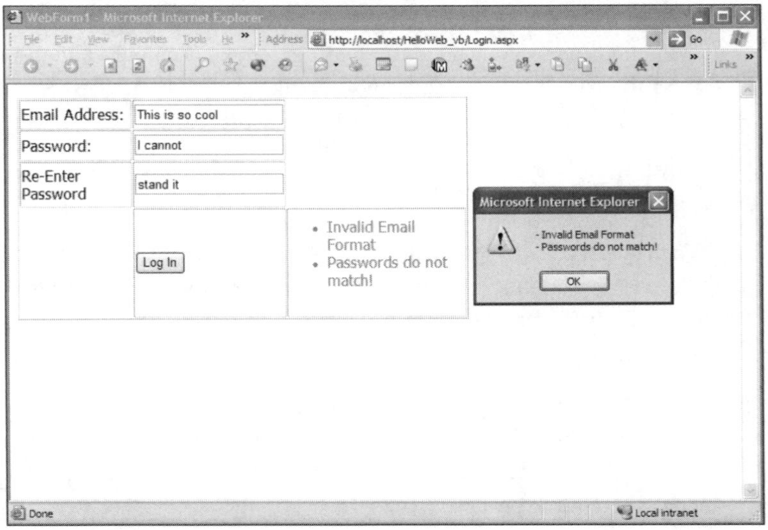

FIGURE 5.17
Using a `ValidationSummary` *control.*

You can use this method of server-side validation checking by setting the `EnableClientScript` property to `False` for each validation control. In Listing 5.8 the

Visual Basic .NET code (used in the `Page_Load` event) checks the `IsValid` property to check controls on the page against their validation controls.

LISTING 5.8 Using the `IsValid` Method of the `Page` Class to Validate a Page

VB.NET

```
If Page.IsValid Then
  If UserName.Text = "jason@fladotnet.net" _
  And Password.Text = "password" Then
   Response.Redirect("Success.aspx")
  Else
   LogIn.Text = "Invalid Data, please retry"
  End If
End If
```

No matter what kind of validation you use, Visual Studio .NET makes it so easy to actually implement validation that you should always include it. Here's a user interface tip: Try to validate controls on the client side. There's nothing worse than going to a Web site, filling out a bunch of fields, clicking a Submit button, and then waiting for someone's slow Internet server to refresh the page just to tell you that you forgot to complete the Zipcode field or State field correctly.

Managing State in ASP.NET Web Applications

The Internet is a stateless application. In a nutshell, that means every call to the server is separate from the next or the previous call. Unlike Windows Forms applications in which you can set global variables and have a bunch of hidden forms open to maintain the state of the data, the Web doesn't afford you that luxury. So, the challenge is to keep track of where the user is in your Web application, and where to take her next. This is done by maintaining state.

State can be maintained in several ways, and some ways are better than others. Where you maintain state can be broken down into two categories: on the client and on the server.

Managing State on the Client

When I say *managing state on the client*, I mean *handling page-level state in the browser*. This can be done in the following ways:

- The `Viewstate` control
- Cookies
- The HTML `Hidden` control
- The browser's query string

Using Cookies

The most familiar way to handle state client-side is by using cookies. Cookies are a key-value paring of collection data that are saved on the client's hard drive. When you need to store information about someone's profile, you normally save a cookie that uniquely identifies him on his machine. If he closes the browser and revisits your site, you check for the cookie in a `Page_Load` event. If it exists, you use it to customize the look and feel of the HTML output. Or, you might simply have a Welcome Back Bob label on your home page, to let the user know he's logged in to your server, or that he's a returning visitor.

Before .NET, cookies were a problem because an end user can decide not to accept cookies on his machine. Because spam emailers and pop-up ads abuse cookies, many people fear them. To get around this, you can modify the `Web.Config` file to use sessionless cookies, meaning the cookie data is encrypted and passed in the query string of the browser, so no data is actually stored on the end user's machine. To change the cookies option in the `Web.Config` file, locate the `sessionState` section of the `Web.Config` file and modify the `cookieless` attribute to `true`, as the following code demonstrates:

```
<sessionState
    mode="InProc"
    stateConnectionString="tcpip=127.0.0.1:42424"
    sqlConnectionString="data source=127.0.0.1;user id=sa;password="
    cookieless="true"
    timeout="20"
/>
```

To access cookies in code, you access the `Cookies` property of the `Request` or `Response` object, depending on whether you're writing a cookie or reading a cookie. The following code snippet checks for a `UserID` cookie. If one doesn't exist, the code writes the cookie out.

VB.NET

```
Dim cookie As HttpCookie = Request.Cookies("UserID")
If cookie Is Nothing Then
  Response.Cookies("UserID").Value = "Jason"
  Response.Cookies("UserID ").Expires = "January 1, 2010"
  Response.Cookies("UserID ").Path = "/"
```

```
Else
  Response.Write(Request.Cookies("UserID")
End If
```

When using the `Cookies` object, you must set the `Expires` property to actually save the cookie. If you don't set the `Expires` property, the cookie is deleted when the user's browser session ends.

> **Note**
>
> In ASP, you could simply check the value of a cookie in server-side VBScript by using this syntax:
>
> ```
> If Request.Cookies("UserID") = "" Then
> ```
>
> This won't work in .NET if the cookie does not exist. You get an error message that says there's no instance of the `Cookie` object. You must explicitly check whether the `HttpCookie` object is Nothing, and then get or set the values of the cookie.

Understanding View State

View state is a new way of storing state data if you're coming from an ASP background. Each control and ASPX page has an `EnableViewState` property, which is set to `True` by default. When a page is processed that has `ViewState` enabled, a hidden field named `Viewstate` is added to the ASPX page and all the page data for the form is preserved in the hidden control. Each time a page is posted back to the server, the contents of the `ViewState` control are updated so that the correct data is in the fields when the same page is rerendered. This makes it so individual controls on a page don't lose their data each time the page is sent to the server.

5

Because `ViewState` is a page-level state management option, the data for each page is simply passed back and forth from the browser to the server inside the page itself. However, this can be problematic for scalability. Because the page data is kept in the hidden control, the page size can grow. For example, if you have a `DataGrid` control that lists all the authors in the Pubs database, all this information is stored in the page's `ViewState` control. Each time the page is rendered to the browser, the amount of data sent down the pipe is literally doubled. To avoid this, you can set the `EnableViewState` property to `False` for the control, thus eliminating the state data from being kept.

If you want to set `ViewState` data in code, you can use a key-value pair similar to a `Cookies` or `Session` object, as the following code demonstrates:

```
Viewstate("UserID") = "Bob"
```

Using the HTML Hidden Control

The HTML `Hidden` control is an HTML element in the Toolbox. Using hidden fields is a common way to store information in ASP. The concept is the same with the HTML `Hidden` control—you can set the `Value` property of the control to store page-specific information.

Using the Query String

Passing data between pages using the query string of the browser is a common way to keep page information safe, while not having to worry about cookies on the client or saving too much data with the `ViewState` control. When you post a page using `HTTP-GET`, which is set using the `Method=Get` attribute on the `Form` tag in the HTML of your page, you automatically send all the data in the fields through the query string of the browser. When you pass values of a form using `HTTP-GET`, the initial control ID is separated from the requested page by an ampersand, and the remaining fields are separated by the question mark character. If you were to pass the data to the `Success.aspx` page using `HTTP-GET` in the code you wrote for the `Login.aspx` page, the query string would look something like this:

```
http://localhost/helloweb_vb?Username=jason@fladotnet&Password=password
```

Of course, it isn't a wise idea to send secret information in plain text through a query string, so using `HTTP-GET` with password information isn't recommended.

Managing State on the Server

To manage state on the server side, you use either session state or application state. When developing in ASP, there are long-winded arguments about how, when, and where to store session-level state. This is because IIS can't scale very well if there are too many session variables in memory. For example, assume that you keep 10 session-level variables for each person who hits your site. On average, you have 1,000 hits an hour. That means IIS has to manage 100,000 unique objects in memory to keep track of each browser's session data. This would kill Web servers. In .NET, this is no longer an issue.

Using Session State

Using session-level state enables you to track variable data for a user throughout his visit to your Web site. Using the `HttpSessionState` class, you can use the same key-value pair syntax for `Session` objects that you use for `ViewState`. Each time a browser hits your site, IIS creates a unique session ID for the browser session if you access the `Session` object in code. If you don't reference the `Session` object in code, IIS doesn't create a unique ID for the end user's session on your site.

Session information is useful to save data between multiple page calls. For example, when I visit my bank's Web site, I must enter my username and password every time I visit, which means the bank isn't storing such high-security data in a cookie. But after I log in to the site, each page I navigate knows who I am, so the data is being passed to all pages for my session through the use of session state. To set or retrieve values for session state, you use this syntax:

```
If Session("UserID") = "Bob" then ...

Reponse.Write(Session("UserID"))
```

After the browser window is closed or the end user navigates to another site, the session data is lost. When the end user returns to the site, you must create new session information based on the user's current session.

In .NET, the `Web.Config` file gives you options as to where session-level state can be stored for a site. By default, session state is stored in the same process as IIS. If you need greater scalability, you can store session state in SQL Server or in an out-of-process state server. To change where the state is stored, you modify the mode attribute in the `sessionState` section of the `Web.Config` file. If you want to store your `Session` data in SQL Server, you modify `Web.Config` to look like this:

```
<sessionState
    mode="SqlServer"
    stateConnectionString="tcpip=127.0.0.1:42424"
    sqlConnectionString="data source=127.0.0.1;user id=sa;password="
    cookieless="false"
    timeout="20"
/>
```

5

You must also supply the correct authentication information, and run a special SQL script that creates database and temporary tables in SQL Server to hold the state data.

In the `Global.asax` file, you can also write code in the `Session_OnStart` and `Session_OnEnd` events. You could use this to ensure that a session-specific event, such as updating a hit counter in a database, is occurring each time a session begins or ends.

Using Application State

Application-level state is the top level in the state management hierarchy. The first time someone accesses your Web site, the `Application` object for the site is created. The `Application` object is alive until the server is rebooted, IIS is restarted, or a new copy of the Web site is deployed. In the `Global.asax` file, there are `Application_OnStart` and `Application_OnEnd` events that you can write code to respond to; they're similar to the `Session_OnStart` and `Session_OnEnd` events. The difference is that application-level variables are global for all sessions for your Web site, not for individual users.

Understanding the Web.Config File

The Web.Config file is an XML-based configuration file that's used by ASP.NET to set options for your application. Each new project you create has its own Web.Config file. Within a project, you can have multiple Web.Config files in different folders, setting up a hierarchy of what settings to use for each folder.

When you're just getting your feet wet with ASP.NET, you'll normally just use the one default Web.Config file on a per-project basis.

As you've seen in the previous section, you can use the Web.Config file to set application-level settings for state management. You can also set security on directories, set up page-and session-level debugging, and store your own custom configuration information.

The biggest benefit to the Web.Config file is that you have a place to store variable data that might have otherwise been kept in application-level or session-level variables in ASP. For example, database connection information, folder locations, and virtual path information can all be stored in the Web.Config file. With an ASPX page, you can retrieve information from the Web.Config file by using the ConfigurationSettings class.

To see how this works, take a look at the custom AppSettings section in the following Web.Config file:

```
<?xml version="1.0" encoding="utf-8"?>
<configuration>
 <appSettings>
   <add key="cn" value="Server=Enterprise;UID=NCC1701D;
     Pwd=CaptJaneway;Database=Ships"/>
   <add key="pics" value="C:\InetPub\storage\"/>
   <add key="picsHTTP" value="http://www.picsserver.com/public/"/>
 </appSettings>
 <system.web>
```

Each of the values stored can be accessed by retrieving the correct key attribute in code. To do this, you would use the following code:

```
sqlCn = ConfigurationSettings.AppSettings("cn")
```

You could also use the GetSettings method to return an array of the items in the AppSettings collection. Storing variable data in the Web.Config file is important for two reasons:

- You don't need to recompile your application if a setting changes; you simply modify the Web.Config file.
- You aren't consuming memory using session- or application-level variables.

Summary

Today you learned the fundamentals of writing ASP.NET applications using Visual Studio .NET. Similar to writing event-driven code in Windows Forms applications, Web Forms offer a major step forward in writing applications that target Web browsers. By having access to the complete FCL in an ASPX page, everything you learned up through today, and everything you learn for the next three weeks, can be applied to Web applications and Windows applications.

Q&A

Q When I look at my Task Manager, there's a process called `ASPNET_WP` that consumes a bunch of memory. What is it?

A The `ASPNET_WP` is the worker process that handles the processing of ASPX files for IIS. This application consumes more and more memory based on the number of users accessing your Web site. It has special permissions to access system files and directories because ASP.NET needs access to system resources on the IIS machine.

Q What's the deal with PostBack events? I see a lot of code in the `Page_Load` events of samples in the SDK that checks to see whether the page is being posted back.

A The `PostBack` event is extremely important to understand. A `Form_Load` event occurs the first time a page is loaded to a client's browser. Most of the time, you're loading fields from a database or setting default values in controls. Because you can write pages that respond to multiple events on the server, the same page may be posted back to the server a number of times. So, by checking the `IsPostBack` property, you can avoid rerunning initialization code in events such as `Form_Load`. The common syntax for checking the `IsPostBack` property is

```
If Not Page.IsPostBack then
   ' Do some page initialization code, this is
   ' the first time the page has been called for this
   ' browser session
Else
   ' The page is being posted back so decide if you want
   ' to do anything there
End if
```

Q I've heard of cool things like caching and user controls. Where can I get more information about those topics?

A In the .NET Framework SDK tutorials that install with Visual Studio .NET, look up the Caching topic under the How do I… section for ASP.NET. There are some great samples of implementing the different caching mechanisms in ASP.NET.

Quiz

1. HTML controls are derived from the ________________ class.
2. True or False: Setting the `Required` field in a `TextBox` control creates client-side JavaScript that forces the end user to enter data into the control.
3. Using the ___________ attribute, server events are automatically wired to my HTML controls.
4. The ____________ object enables me to maintain state for a page.
5. True or False: You can use SQL Server to store page-level state on the client.

Quiz Answers

1. `System.Web.UI.HtmlControls`
2. False: There is no `Required` property for the `TextBox` control. To make a `TextBox` required, you must add a `RequiredFieldValidator` control and associate it with the `TextBox` you wish to make required.
3. `runat=server`
4. `ViewState`
5. False: You would use SQL Server to store server-side session state. On the client, you can use the `HTTPCookies` class to manage session information in the form of browser-based Cookies.

Exercises

1. In the `Login.aspx` page you created earlier, modify the `targetSchema` property of the page and view the source of the output in the browser. What's the difference, if any?
2. ASP.NET has great visual controls, such as the `DataList`, `Repeater`, and `DataGrid`. Using the QuickStart tutorials, look up the samples of those controls, and become familiar with what you can do with them.
3. Using what you learned about session state, add code to the `Login.aspx` page to store username information in a session variable named `UserID`. When you're redirected to the `Success.aspx` page, retrieve the `UserID` session variable and display it on the page.

WEEK 1

DAY 6

Deploying ASP.NET Applications

When you learned how to deploy Windows Forms applications two days ago, I mentioned that the deployment of Windows Forms and Web Forms applications is identical. Using the Windows Installer technology built into Visual Studio .NET, the method of deployment for all applications is the same. However, in ASP.NET applications, there are a couple more options for deployment based on the deployment target you have. Today, you learn

- The ASP.NET-specific deployment options
- How to use the Visual Studio .NET Copy Project dialog box
- How to manually deploy an ASP.NET application using XCopy deployment
- How to extend deployment functionality using Deployment Projects and Windows Installer

Introduction to ASP.NET Deployment

Like Windows Forms applications, the solution for an ASP.NET application contains all the information about the project that the installation package needs. Because of this, you can use simple methods (such as XCopy) or more robust methods (such as Windows Installer) to deploy an application. The decisions you need to make when determining how to deploy your applications to a Web server are

- Does the application already exist on the Web server?
- Do special Registry entries need to be made for COM components when I deploy?
- Do I need to worry about other files that aren't part of my application?

Based on the answers to these questions, your options for deploying an ASP.NET application can vary. The key ingredient to making an ASP.NET application function is Internet Information Server (IIS). IIS is the Web server that serves up Web pages, and it's what the ASP.NET runtime uses to make your ASP.NET applications work.

If you're deploying a Web project for the first time, you can use three methods of deployment:

- Copy Project—This copies the necessary files to a new directory on the Web server. It doesn't configure the Web server.
- XCopy Deployment—This simply uses the DOS XCopy command to copy a file from point A on your development machine to point B on the Web server. You must manually configure the directory and application on IIS to make the Web site accessible.
- Windows Installer—This creates and configures the ASP.NET application on a Web server. Using Windows Installer is the most full-featured and robust way to deploy ASP.NET applications.

You are going to learn how to use each of these methods of deployment.

Note

When you deployed Windows Forms applications two days ago, the last exercise of the day was to go through the installation of the .NET Framework as part of a deployment project. The .NET Framework redistributable is required to run any .NET application, not just Windows Forms. To make your Web project deployments successful, you must install the same .NET Framework redistributable that you used for Windows Forms deployment on the Web server from which you plan to run ASP.NET applications. The 20MB redistribution package has everything that's needed to successfully deploy and run ASP.NET applications on an IIS Web server.

Creating an ASP.NET Application for Deployment

To test the different methods of deploying ASP.NET applications, you must create a new ASP.NET application that you'll use in each of the three methods of deployment today.

Start Visual Studio .NET and click the New Project button on the Start Page. After the New Project dialog pops up, select Visual Basic Projects from the Project Types pane, and then select ASP.NET Web Application from the Templates pane. Change the name of the project to `http://localhost/WebDeploy`.

Figure 6.1 demonstrates what your New Project dialog should look like. Click the OK button to create the application.

FIGURE 6.1

New Project dialog for the WebDeploy project.

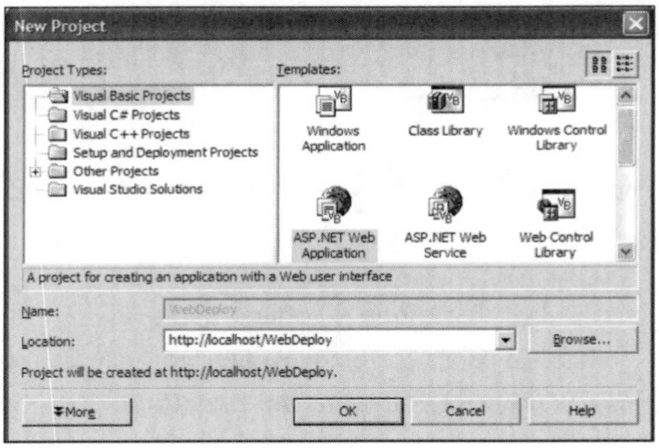

When the application is created, you should see the default `WebForm1.aspx` page in the Web Forms Designer.

Drag a `Label` Web Forms control from the Toolbox to the form, and change its Text property to Project Deployed!.

Your completed `WebForm1.aspx` should look like Figure 6.2.

Now you can save and build the project by selecting Build Solution from the Build menu.

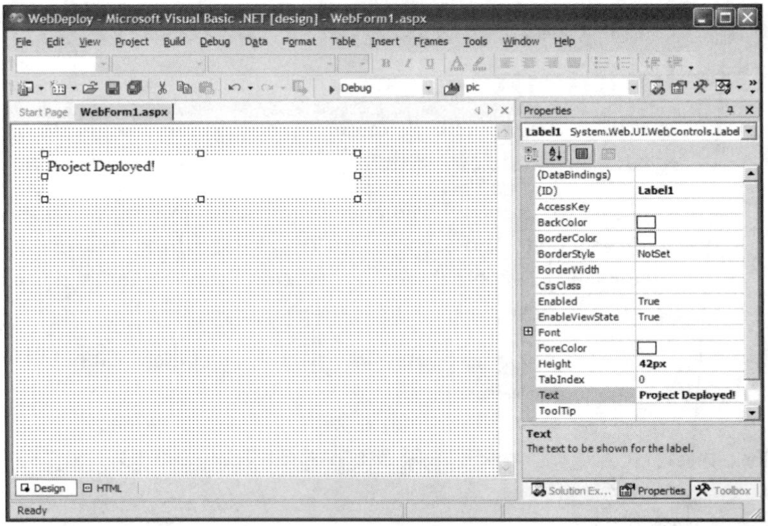

FIGURE 6.2

Completed WebDeploy solution.

Deploying ASP.NET Applications Using Copy Project

The Copy Project method of deploying a project using Visual Studio .NET is a straightforward operation with little room for error. When you use Copy Project, you specify a location to copy files to and how you want the files to be copied.

To use Copy Project, you must have an ASP.NET application open in the Visual Studio .NET IDE. To test out how Copy Project works, from the main menu, select Project, Copy Project. You're prompted with the Copy Project dialog shown in Figure 6.3.

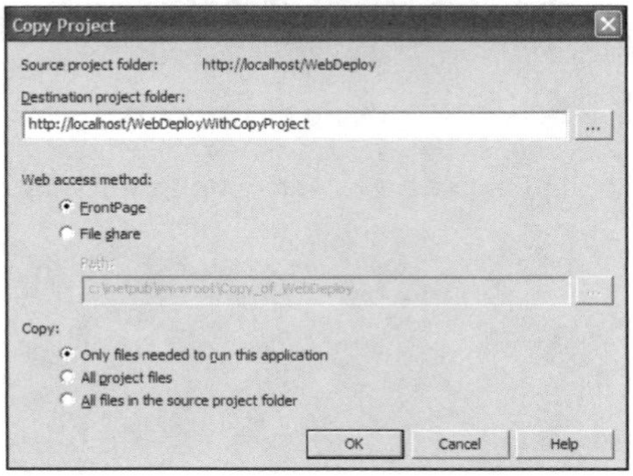

FIGURE 6.3

The Copy Project dialog.

The first thing the Copy Project dialog wants to know is where you want the project deployed. If the directory you plan to deploy to doesn't exist, Copy Project creates it for you. The default settings are also configured in IIS for a new virtual directory. That means as soon as Copy Project is done, you can browse to the URL in the Destination project folder option and your site is active. For this test, change the destination project folder to `http://localhost/WebDeployWithCopyProject`.

After you determine the location of the project, you decide how you want the project files deployed. You set it by selecting either FrontPage or File Share with Web Access Method option button.

If you select FrontPage, you're choosing to deploy your project using HTTP, which is allowed if FrontPage server extensions are installed on the target server. Because they're installed by default on Windows 2000 Servers, Windows 2000 Professional, and Windows XP, this normally isn't an issue. But if the server extensions aren't installed, you get an error and Copy Project fails.

The File Share option is a direct file copy to a shared directory on the Web server. When using this method, Front Page server extensions aren't used and the files are simply copied across the network to the Web server.

Note

> When deploying to your local machine, which you're doing here, all the deployment methods you've learned about always work. When Visual Studio .NET is installed, the IIS on the machine is configured to correctly handle the creation of Web sites, which is what happens every time you create a new ASP.NET Web application. If you have issues using Copy Project when deploying to an external Web server, it's most likely a permission issue. By default, only administrators are allowed write access to the `wwwroot` directory, so you must have your administrator create a special account that allows your login name to physically create directories on the Web server. By default, a VS Developers security group is created when Visual Studio .NET is installed on a computer, and that group has read/write permission on the Web server. The group has no users added by default, so each user who needs access must be added. The problem with this is that you normally won't have Visual Studio .NET installed on the Web server.

The final step to setting your deployment options is what files to copy. You have three choices:

- Only files needed to run this application
- All project files
- All files in the source project folder

The interesting thing about this option is that no matter what option you seem to select, all the files in the source folder are copied. To test this, I added a cursor file, an XML file, and another style sheet, none of which is necessary to run the application. Copy Project decided it would be a good idea to copy them anyway, and it deployed unnecessary files to the Web server.

After you've selected the correct options in the Copy Project dialog, you can click the OK button, and the project is copied to the Web server. If the directory to which you're copying does not exist, it's created.

To check out what just happened, open Control Panel and select the Internet Information Services applet as Figure 6.4 demonstrates.

FIGURE 6.4

Selecting the IIS applet in the Control Panel.

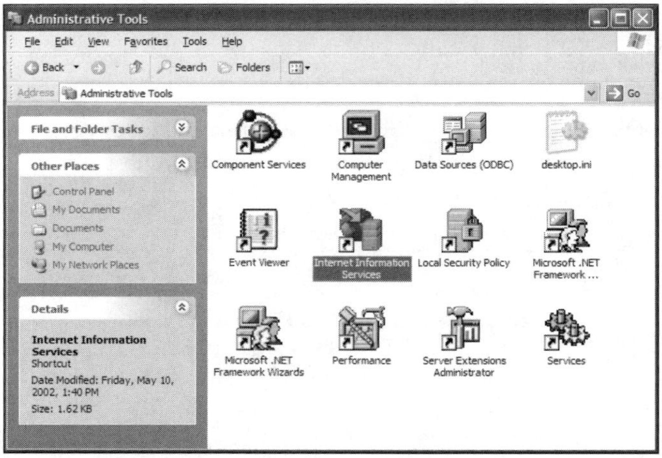

Double-click the IIS applet to open up the IIS Management Console. When IIS is open, drill into the Web Sites node under the name of your local computer in the left pane of the snap-in. Under the Web Sites node is the Default Web Site node. This is the root directory of `\Inetpub\wwwroot` on your machine. If you drill further down, all the Web site folders are listed. Find the `WebDeployWithCopyProject` folder and drill into it, as Figure 6.5 shows.

The folder you're looking at is known as a *virtual directory*. The way the Web server works is that to browse pages, the ASPX, HTML, or any type of document must be running under the isolated memory and protection of the Web server. By creating virtual directories, you're telling IIS that this folder is okay to be browsed from the Web.

FIGURE 6.5

Navigating the IIS snap-in to view virtual directories.

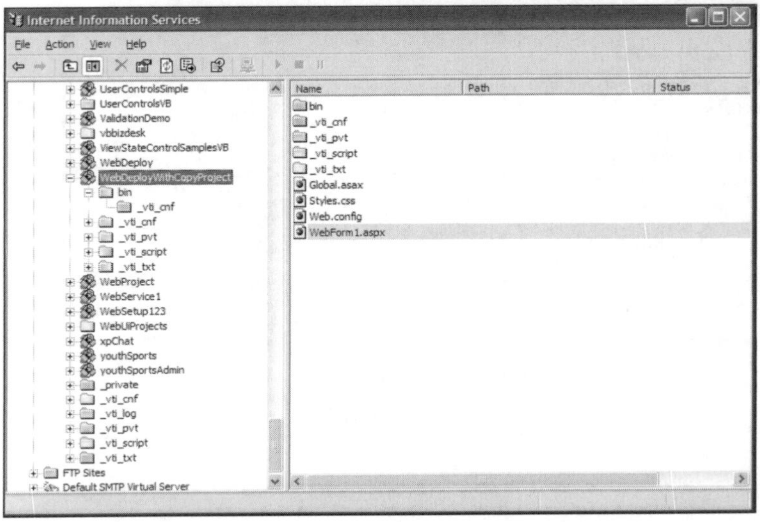

If you right-click the `WebDeployWithCopyProject` node and select Properties from the context menu, you get the project properties dialog for this virtual directory. The default settings of a virtual directory created using Copy Project are the minimal read permissions for a Web site. As you can see in Figure 6.6, the following permissions are given to the site:

- Read Access Only—This means that, from a Web browser, files cannot be uploaded to this site and hackers cannot get in.
- Execute Permissions: Scripts Only—This means only scripted pages can be run from this folder through a browser. Executable files can't be run. This is a high security setting, conforming to the script permissions for the IISUSER account on the local machine.
- Application Protection—Allows this Web application to run in an isolated application process that other applications might or might not be using. This allows good memory protection and consumes minimal server resources.

To test that your application actually runs, close the Properties dialog and right-click `WebForm1.aspx` in the right pane of the snap-in. From the contextual menu, select Browse. Your default page should now be displayed in the browser, as Figure 6.7 demonstrates.

Although Copy Project is a very simple and straightforward mechanism for deploying your site, I see the following drawbacks to using this method of deployment:

FIGURE 6.6

IIS Properties dialog box for the deployment project.

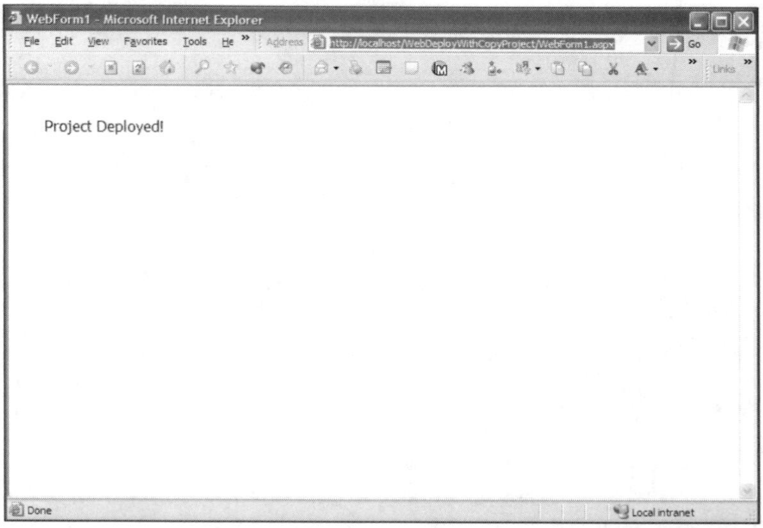

FIGURE 6.7

Viewing your successfully deployed project in the browser.

- It always copies all files, so unless you manually exclude files from a project, they're copied to the server.
- It doesn't register COM components or copy satellite assemblies, such as Crystal Reports, to the target folder.
- There's no differentiation on changed files. In other words, each time you run Copy Project, it attempts to deploy all files, even if they haven't been changed since the last deployment. However, you are prompted with an overwrite warning dialog.

That being said, I think Copy Project is a great way to create and configure a virtual directory. You can always work with your administrator to get other items, such as COM components, deployed to the server.

Note

> Even though it's beyond the scope of this book, the way that COM components can be distributed using .NET is vastly improved. With a new feature called *lazy Registration*, you no longer have to manually create COM component applications in the COM+ snap-in. If you've deployed a COM component to a Web server, the first time you reference it in your code, the component is registered with COM+ and any and all available COM+ attributes can be defined in your code. On Day 14, "Components and .NET," you learn about components in .NET, but we don't get into transactional components and other COM+ features.

Deploying ASP.NET Applications Using Copy

Just when you though DOS was dead, the XCopy utility is back in your vocabulary. The premise of .NET applications is that files used to run an application are never locked in memory. When you start an application, be it an EXE for Windows Forms or an ASP.NET application, a shadow copy of the assemblies is loaded into memory. When methods in assemblies are executed, the shadow copy verifies that it's still the current version of the application and runs as expected.

While an application is running, you can overwrite the files that are being used; they aren't locked in memory. This was a big issue before .NET. If you needed to update a COM DLL that was being used by IIS, you had to stop the IIS server (thus killing all the connections) to install a new DLL version. Not to mention the fact that only one version of a DLL could be used at the same time.

Because .NET doesn't lock assemblies in memory, you can use utilities such as DOS XCopy to simply overwrite what's already in use. At the next request for a page or method in a satellite assembly, the latest version of the assembly is just-in-time compiled (JITted) and the end user sees the most recent updates. This is the biggest reason .NET deployment is such a great move forward in ease of use for developers.

To test this, you're going to manually create a new virtual directory in IIS and deploy the WebDeploy project to it using XCopy.

To start, open Windows Explorer and create a new folder called `XCopyDeploy` on your `C:\` drive, as shown in Figure 6.8.

FIGURE 6.8

Creating an empty directory to prepare for XCopy deployment.

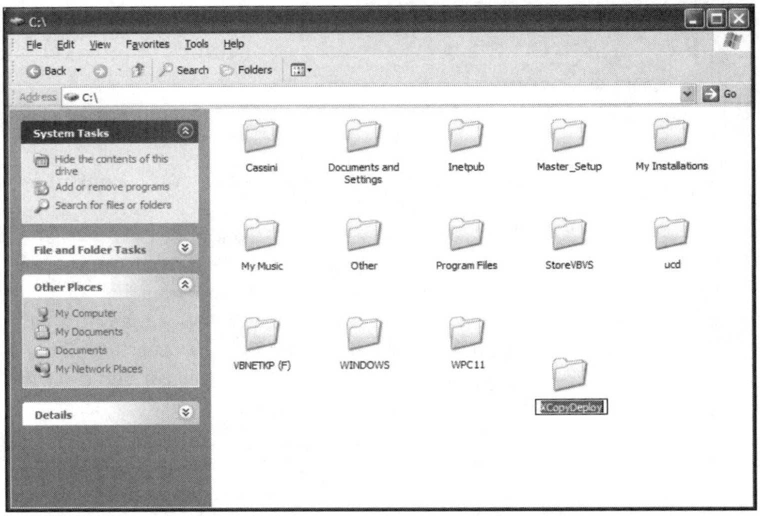

The next step is to configure IIS so it knows this directory can be browsed from the Internet. To do so, open the IIS snap-in that you used earlier. When it's open, right-click on the root node of Default Web Site, and select New, Virtual Directory from the contextual menu. Figure 6.9 shows you where this is in the Tree view.

FIGURE 6.9

Selecting the New Virtual Directory option.

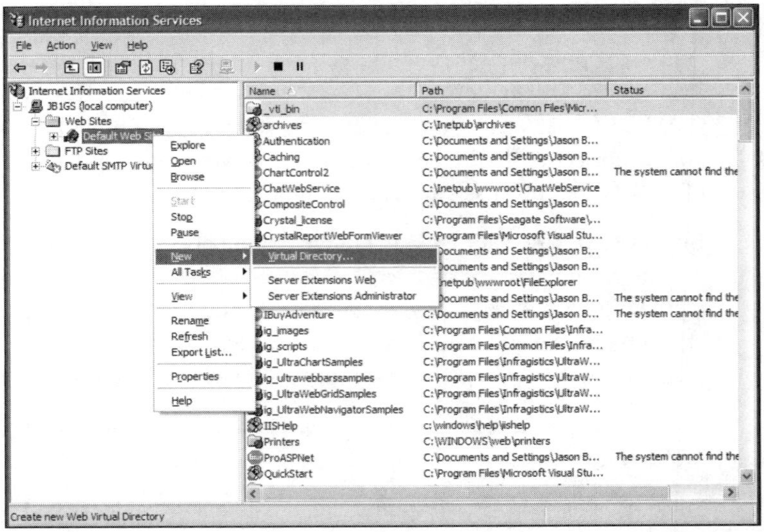

When you create a new virtual directory, you're basically accomplishing what the Copy Project does automatically. You're setting permissions on a directory within IIS that allow it to be accessible from the browser. The New Virtual Directory menu option walks you through a wizard that sets up the directory in IIS.

The first step in the wizard is the Welcome screen shown in Figure 6.10.

FIGURE 6.10

Step 1 in creating the IIS virtual directory.

If you click Next, you're prompted for the alias of the directory. The alias is what's actually typed in the browser address box to gain access to the site. Type in **`XCopyDeploy`** as the alias for this site, as Figure 6.11 demonstrates.

FIGURE 6.11

Setting the alias for the virtual directory.

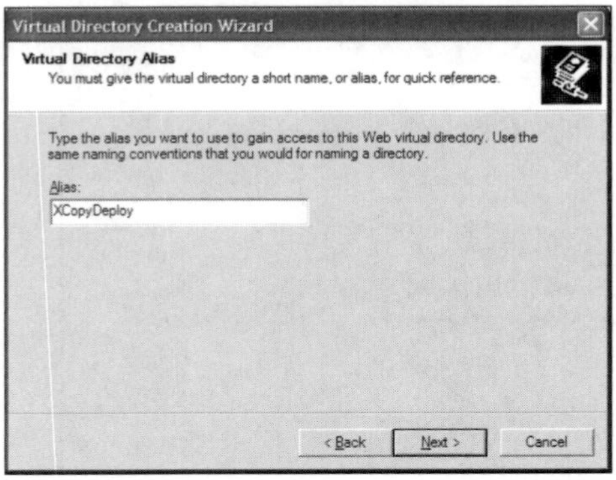

Click the Next button, and you're taken to the next step, which wants to know the physical path of the directory. You created this as `C:\XCopyDeploy`, so enter that into the Directory text box as shown in Figure 6.12. You can also click the Browse button to navigate to the directory on your computer.

FIGURE 6.12

Setting the Web site content directory.

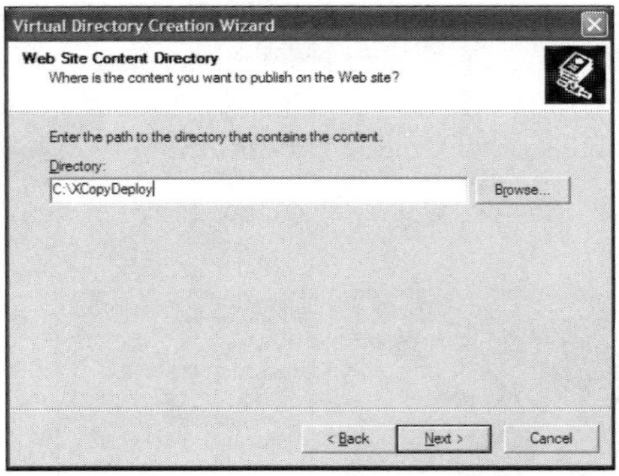

Click Next, and you can set the permissions for the site. By default, the read and script permissions are set. These are what you'll use almost all the time when creating virtual directories. If you set the write permission, hackers can gain access to your computer if they figure out the username and password that has write access. You should use caution when setting write permissions on any folder in IIS. The Browse option allows a directory listing to be automatically created when a user browses to the site. This is common for download sites where a listing of files is all that's needed, and you wouldn't have to do anything special just to list the directory.

For this exercise, leave the defaults that Figure 6.13 displays, and click the Next button.

FIGURE 6.13

Access permissions for the virtual directory.

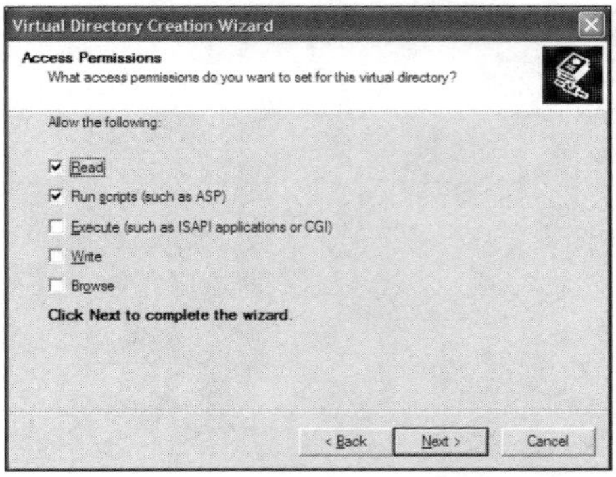

The wizard is now complete, and you should be looking at the Success step that Figure 6.14 presents. Click the Finish button to let IIS create the virtual directory with the settings you've chosen in the wizard.

FIGURE 6.14

Final step in the virtual directory wizard.

The virtual directory has now been created. To check out what was set, drill into the Default Web Site node and find the XCopyDeploy application in the list of available sites.

After you find the `XCopyDeploy` folder, right-click it and select Properties from the contextual menu. You should be looking at something exactly like Figure 6.15.

FIGURE 6.15

Properties dialog for the `XCopyDeploy` *virtual directory.*

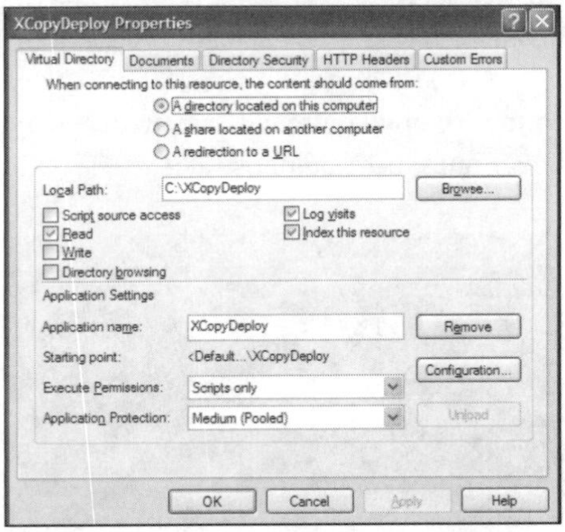

If you compare the settings for this virtual directory and the settings in Figure 6.6, you'll see that they're the same. So, using Copy Project essentially creates a virtual directory in the same manner that the New Virtual Directory Wizard does.

Now you need to use XCopy to copy the files in your solution from the existing `\Inetpub\wwwroot\webDeploy` directory to the `C:\XCopyDeploy` directory.

Of course, XCopy is simply copying files. So, by using Windows Explorer, you can just drag and drop the files from one directory to another. But that isn't very cool: You need to use XCopy.

To do so, open up a command prompt window and navigate to the `WebDeploy` directory. By default, this is at `C:\Inetpub\wwwroot\WebDeploy`. When you're there, type the following `XCopy` command:

```
XCopy *.* C:\XCopyDeploy /s
```

The `/s` is the XCopy switch that copies all files and directories, even empty directories.

Your output in the command window should look like Figure 6.16.

FIGURE 6.16

Results of XCopy deployment in the command window.

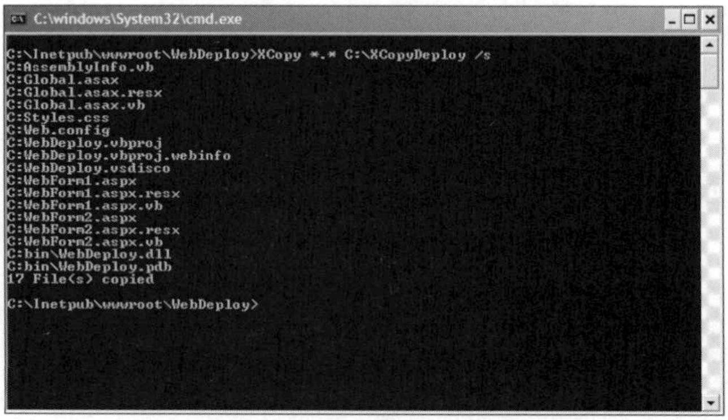

If you need a refresher on the XCopy command-line switches, type in **`/?`** after XCopy, and you'll get a help list, as Figure 6.17 demonstrates.

FIGURE 6.17

Help for XCopy.

Your Web site has now been deployed using XCopy. If you navigate your browser to `http://localhost/XCopyDeploy/WebForm1.aspx`, you'll be looking at your Project Deployed! Message, as Figure 6.18 demonstrates.

FIGURE 6.18

Browsing to the XCopy deployed site.

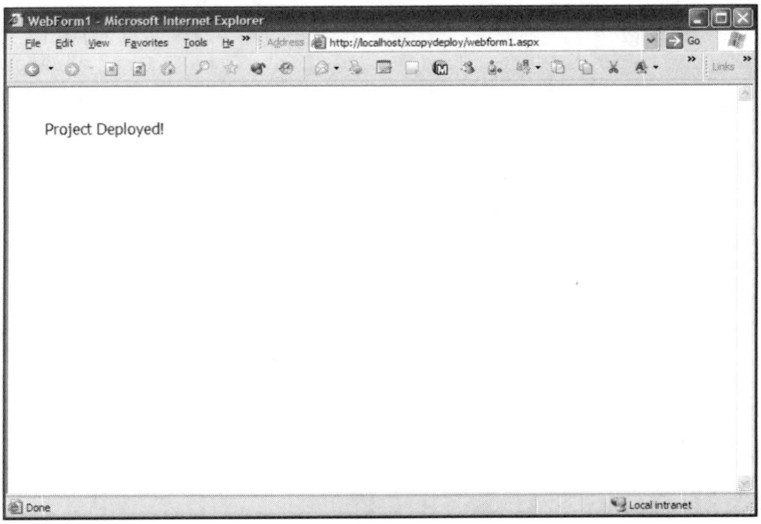

If you open up Windows Explorer and navigate to the `C:\XCopyDeploy` directory, you'll see the files from your solution—all copied and ready to run. Figure 6.19 shows the `XCopyDeploy` directory.

FIGURE 6.19

The `XCopyDeploy` *directory will contain all files copied to run the site.*

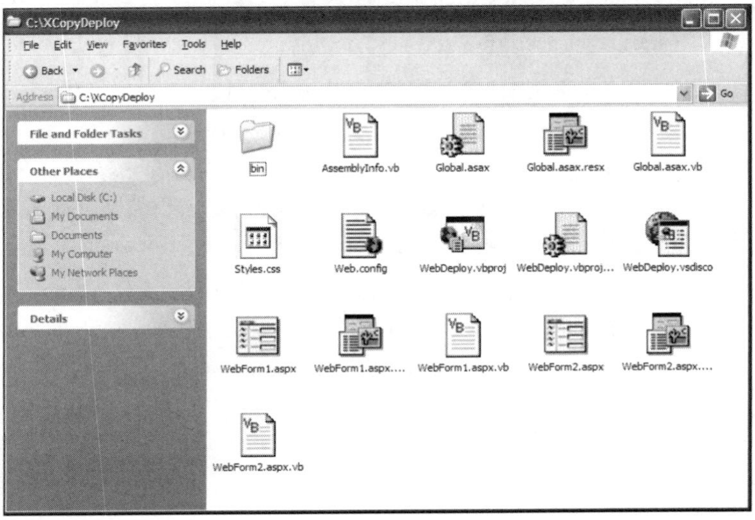

6

As you can see, the XCopy deploy method is the most basic of all deployment options for a .NET application. The main point of this exercise was to give you an understanding on how to create IIS virtual directories and how, by using simple copy methods, you can deploy a complete Web site to a Web server.

To see how .NET really works, go back to the WebDeploy project in Visual Studio .NET and check the `ForeColor` property of `Label1` to `Red`, and change the `FontSize` of `Label1` to `XX-Large`. Then rerun the XCopy command in the command window, and simply click the Refresh button on your browser.

You'll notice the changes are made immediately, and there were no locked files in memory that caused problems when overwriting the assemblies in the `Bin` directory of the `XCopyDeploy` folder.

Using XCopy in a pure .NET solution is great, but if you have components that must be registered on the remote machine, you can't do this from the client that's calling the XCopy command.

Deploying ASP.NET Applications with Windows Installer

The most robust way to deploy any application is to use the Windows Installer technology that's built into Visual Studio .NET. When you learned how to deploy Windows Forms applications, you got a good idea of their power and flexibility when creating MSI packages using Visual Studio .NET. You're now going to extend what you learned two days ago and create an MSI package that can deploy an entire Web site.

To start, you need to add a new deployment project to your WebDeploy solution.

To do so, right-click on the solution name in the Solution Explorer and select Add, New Project as shown in Figure 6.20.

When the New Project dialog pops up, drill into the Setup and Deployment node in the Project Types pane. On the Templates pane, select the Web Setup Project template. Change the name to `MSIWebDeploy` as Figure 6.21 demonstrates.

Exactly like creating a Windows Setup project, the new Web Setup project is added as another project in your Solution Explorer.

The next step is to add the project output to the project. To add the WebDeploy project's output to the MSIWebDeploy project, right-click the MSIWebDeploy project name and select Add, Project Output, as Figure 6.22 shows.

FIGURE 6.20

The New Project contextual menu.

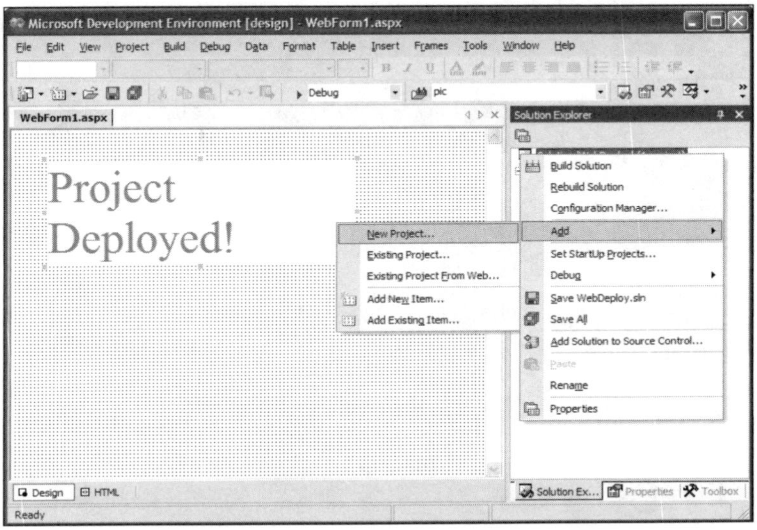

FIGURE 6.21

Creating a new Web Setup project.

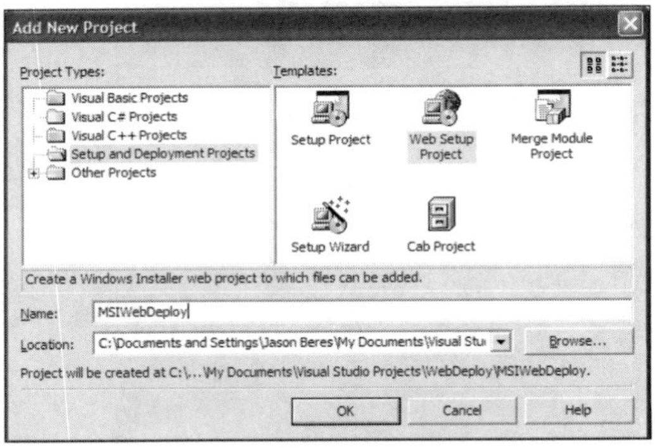

When the Add Project Output dialog pops up, Crtl+click with the mouse and select both Primary Output and Content Files from the list box. This ensures that the assembly in the `Bin` directory is included along with the ASPX files, the `Web.Config` file, and the remaining files that make up the WebDeploy ASP.NET project. From the Configuration dropdown list, change the configuration from Active to Release. You change the configuration of the WebDeploy project in a later step.

Figure 6.23 shows you what the Add Project Output dialog should look like.

After you click the OK button, you're taken back to the File System Editor. If you select the Web Application folder in the left pane of the File System Editor and then press F4 to view its properties, you'll notice the various properties you can modify for the target folder when it's deployed.

FIGURE 6.22

Adding project output to the Web deployment project.

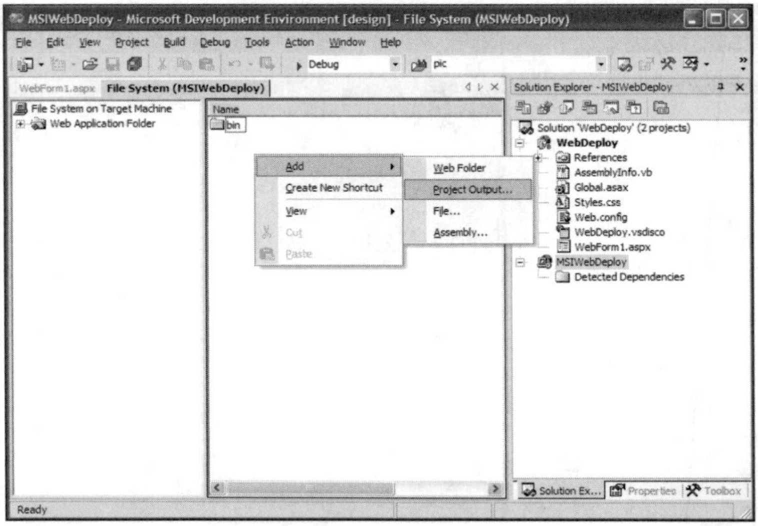

FIGURE 6.23

The Add Project Output dialog box.

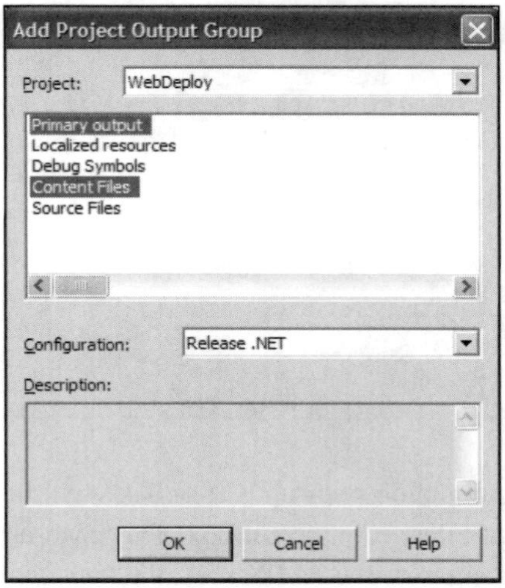

Like the settings of the New Virtual Directory Wizard you used earlier, you can set the different access modes, execute permissions, the port the site works on, and the default document.

Change the `DefaultDocument` property from `default.aspx` to `WebForm1.aspx`, as Figure 6.24 demonstrates.

FIGURE 6.24

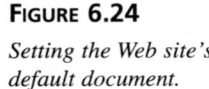

Setting the Web site's default document.

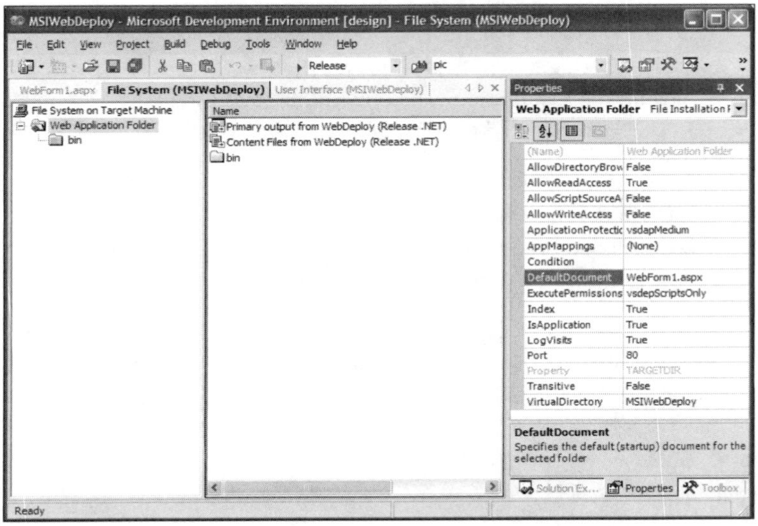

The `DefaultDocument` property updates the settings for the virtual directory as to what page should come up in the browser when a person browses to the site for the first time. Normally, this is `Default.htm`, `Default.aspx`, `Index.htm`, or `Default.asp`, but you can specify other pages that should come up first. When you set the `DefaultDocument` property to `WebForm1.aspx`, the end user can browse to the site and not have to specify the full filename.

Next you want to update the build configuration for this project. To do so, select Configuration Manager from the Build main menu.

When the Configuration Manager dialog pops up, notice that the configuration for the projects are set to Debug. That means when the project is compiled, debug information is created and the output is sent to a Debug folder in the solution. When you're ready to deploy applications, you should change the configuration setting to Release.

In the Configuration Manager dialog, make sure that the MSIWebDeploy and WebDeploy projects are both set to Release. Also make sure that the Build check box is checked for both projects.

At this point, you're ready to build the solution and test the deployment. That's all there is to creating a basic deployment package for an ASP.NET application.

To see how cool this tool is, you're going to extend the functionality of this deployment project and add a custom action that creates a database on the Web server during installation.

Creating a Custom Action

When creating a deployment project, you learned two days ago that you could set conditions on the installation. The conditions might include a file dependency, a specific version of a product, or the existence of the .NET Framework on the deployment target.

You can also extend an installation by adding a custom action. A custom action can be nearly anything you can dream of. Today, you're going to add a console application that creates a database on the target machine. You'll then add the resulting EXE file as a custom action for the deployment project.

To do this, right-click on the solution name in the Solution Explorer and select Add, New Project from the contextual menu. When the Add New Project dialog pops up, select Console Application from the Visual Basic Projects folder (see Figure 6.25).

FIGURE 6.25

Adding a new console application to the solution.

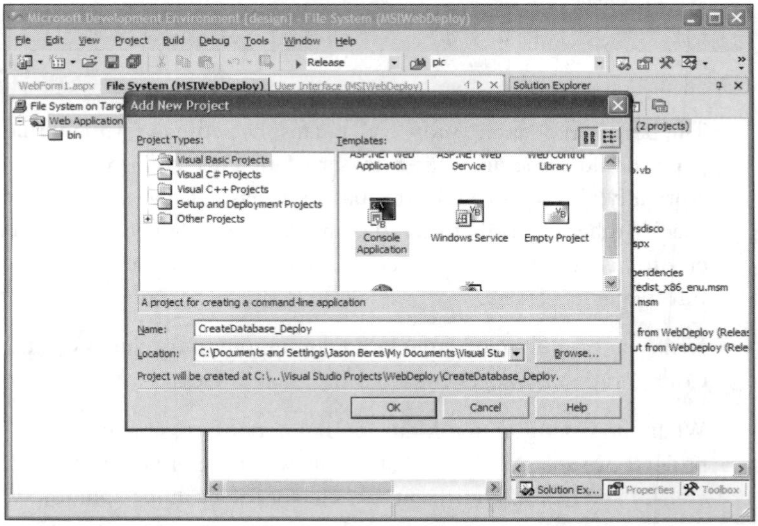

Change the name of the project to CreateDatabase_Deploy, and click the OK button to add the new project to your solution.

After the project is added to your solution, you'll be looking at the `Sub Main` method for the `Module1` module. A console application is a linear, command-window application that has a `Main` method that controls the lifetime of the application. You can accept command-line parameters, add class files, and do pretty much whatever you want with a console application. In this case, you're just going to modify the `Main` method to create a database and a table when it executes.

Add the code in Listing 6.1 to the `Module1` in the console application.

LISTING 6.1 Adding the Create Database Code to `Module1.vb`

VB.NET

```
Imports System.Data.SqlClient

Module Module1

Sub Main()

      Dim cn As New SqlConnection()
      cn.ConnectionString = "uid=sa;pwd=;database=master;server=."
      cn.Open()

      Dim cmd As SqlCommand = New SqlCommand()
      cmd.CommandText = "Create Database Test"
      cmd.Connection = cn

      cmd.ExecuteNonQuery()

      cmd.CommandText = "CREATE TABLE Test.dbo.Table1 " _
         & " ([ID] [int] NOT NULL , [Field1] [varchar] (50)  " _
         & " COLLATE SQL_Latin1_General_CP1_CI_AS NULL) ON [PRIMARY]"

   cmd.ExecuteNonQuery()


End Sub

End Module
```

The code in Listing 6.1 is basic ADO.NET code that you'll learn about next week. The idea is that as this application executes, it creates the database, creates a table in the database, and then ends. A console application is perfect for a custom action because it has a visual screen to which you can write out messages, and it ends all by itself.

If you right-click the CreateDatabase_Deploy project name in the Solution Explorer, the EXE will be built for this Console application.

Next, return to the File System Editor by either selecting the correct tab in the IDE or double-clicking any of the files in the MSIWebDeploy project in the Solution Explorer.

From the File System Editor, select Editor, Custom Actions from the View main menu. This takes you to the Custom Actions Editor.

Right-click on the Install node and select Add Custom Action from the contextual menu. You should now see the Select Item in Project dialog as you see in Figure 6.26.

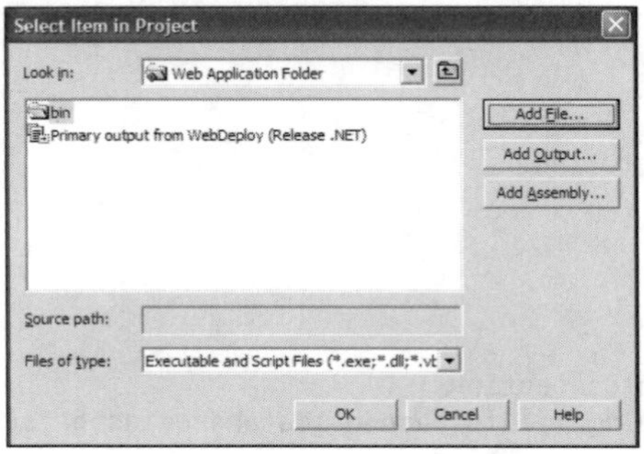

FIGURE 6.26

Select Item in Project to add a custom action.

If you click the Add File button, you can browse to the `CreateDatabase_Deploy` folder to select the `CreateDatabase_Deploy.exe` file from the `Bin` directory. After you've added the file, your dialog box should look like Figure 6.27. The application is now added as a custom action for this project.

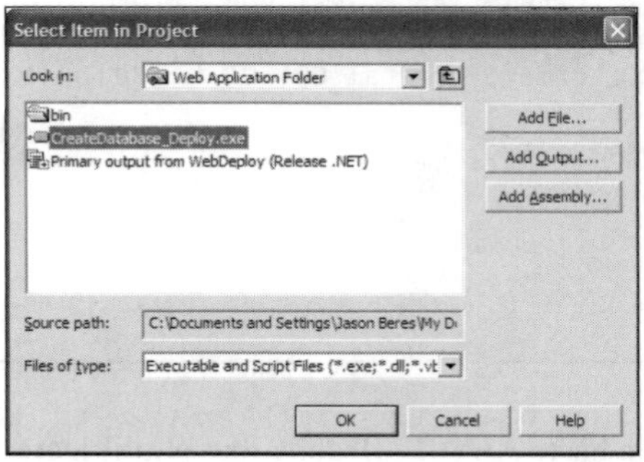

FIGURE 6.27

Adding the `CreateDatabase_Deploy.exe` *file.*

You can now select Build Solution from the Build menu. When you build the solution, the ASP.NET application is built, then the console application is built, and finally the MSI package is built.

If you remember the Project Build Order dialog box from yesterday, you can specify the order in which the projects are built. You can access the build order by right-clicking on the solution name in the Solution Explorer and selecting Project Build Order from the contextual menu.

You've now successfully created the MSI package. To test the installation, you can right-click on the MSIDeploy project name in the Solution Explorer and select Install. This starts the MSI package and guides you through the installation.

Notice that a command window pops up during the installation. This is the console application you wrote; it's creating the database and the table in SQL Server.

By adding custom actions, the sky's the limit in what you can do when creating a custom setup.

Summary

Today you learned about the three methods for deploying ASP.NET applications. Using Copy Project and XCopy deployment have their limits, but they accomplish the task of getting the application files onto a Web server.

Using the deployment projects in Visual Studio .NET is hands-down the best way to deploy any type of application. By extending an installation with custom actions, you can truly create a professional and bulletproof deployment project.

Q&A

Q Is there anything I can't do during a setup using a custom action?

A Not really. Because installation applications take administrative privileges, you have the run of the machine and can do whatever you need to configure the application.

Q Custom actions are going to change my life. Can I have more than one custom action?

A Yes, as a matter of fact, you can have multiple custom actions. You can also have custom actions that occur at different stages of installation or uninstallation. In the Custom Actions Editor, there are four stages of a deployment project's lifetime: install, commit, rollback, and uninstall. Each of these stages can have multiple custom actions. A good example of an uninstall custom action is removing a database that was created during the install. Using the custom dialogs, you can prompt the user for options during install or uninstall, and then base your custom actions on the user's response.

Quiz

1. True or False: After running the XCopy deployment, the only thing you need to change on the newly created virtual directory is the default document that shows up when people browse to the site.

2. True or False: Using Copy Project, the folder on the Web server and the folders in the solution are merged together, creating a new directory with a combination of files.
3. By adding a ______________, I can extend the functionality of my deployment projects using external applications that I write in .NET.

Quiz Answers

1. False. If the virtual directory hasn't been created in IIS, you must do so. If you have any dependent COM components, you must register them on the target machine.
2. False. The folders are overwritten, but you're prompted just in case that isn't your intention.
3. Custom action

Exercises

The method in which the database was created in the custom action is just one way to accomplish the task. My goal was to show you the power of custom actions, not the absolute correct way to create a custom database.

For today's exercise, you're going to view a walkthrough from the software development kit (SDK) that shows you another way to handle database creation during installation using a resource file and custom dialogs.

To get to the walkthrough, search the SDK for Using a Custom Action to Create a Database During Installation.

Follow the project steps, which should take about 30 minutes, to learn about another option when creating custom actions. This exercise is also a good example of passing data from a custom dialog to an external application.

WEEK 1

DAY 7

Exceptions, Debugging, and Tracing

In the previous few days, you've written a lot of code that worked perfectly. I like to think that all my code is perfect, and at the end of these 21 days, the code that you write will be perfect, too. But for those unfortunate times when errors occur in your code, be they from invalid user input, logic errors, or system errors, you must know how to write your applications to handle errors gracefully. Even before errors occur, you need to understand how to use the tools in Visual Studio .NET to debug your applications to avoid errors altogether. Today, you

- Understand why errors occur in applications
- Learn about structured exception handling in .NET and how the common language runtime implements exceptions
- Use `Try`, `Catch`, and `Finally` blocks to avoid runtime errors
- Learn about the differences in features between C# and Visual Basic .NET when handling exceptions
- Learn how to use all the debugging features available in Visual Studio .NET for Windows Forms and ASP.NET applications

Why Errors Happen

In the course of writing any type of computer program, three types of errors can crop up:

- Syntax errors
- Logic errors
- Runtime errors

Let's look at how these errors occur and how you can avoid them.

How to Avoid Syntax Errors

Syntax errors occur when you misspell a variable name, object name, or reference an object incorrectly. Syntax errors are the easiest errors to avoid, because Visual Studio .NET lets you know if a keyword or variable is misspelled. If you're coding in Visual Basic, you can set the `Option Explicit` option on in your Project Properties dialog box, which tells Visual Studio .NET to make sure that all variables you use in your code are declared before they are referenced. This feature isn't available in C#, but you're notified of syntax errors in both C# and Visual Basic .NET by squiggly lines that appear under code that isn't correct after you type a line of code. When a squiggly line appears under your code, you can hover your mouse over the squiggly line and a tooltip lets you know what error is occurring. Figure 7.1 demonstrates this behavior in C# and Figure 7.2 demonstrates this behavior in Visual Basic .NET.

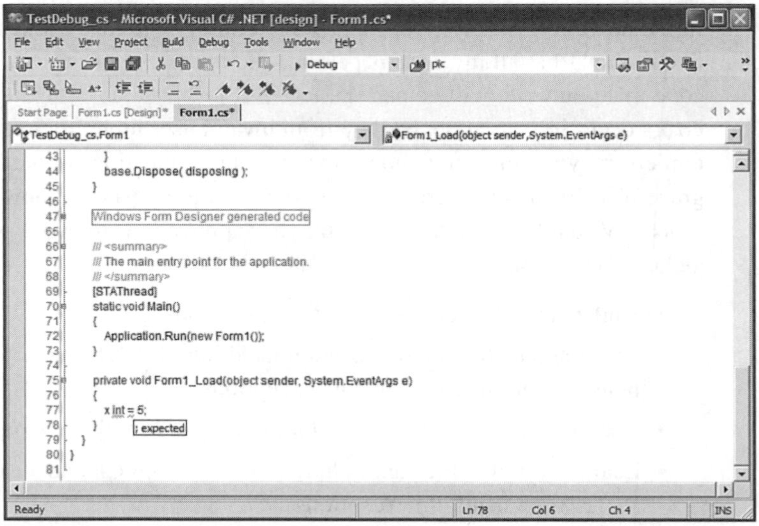

FIGURE 7.1

Visual Studio .NET syntax error notification in C#.

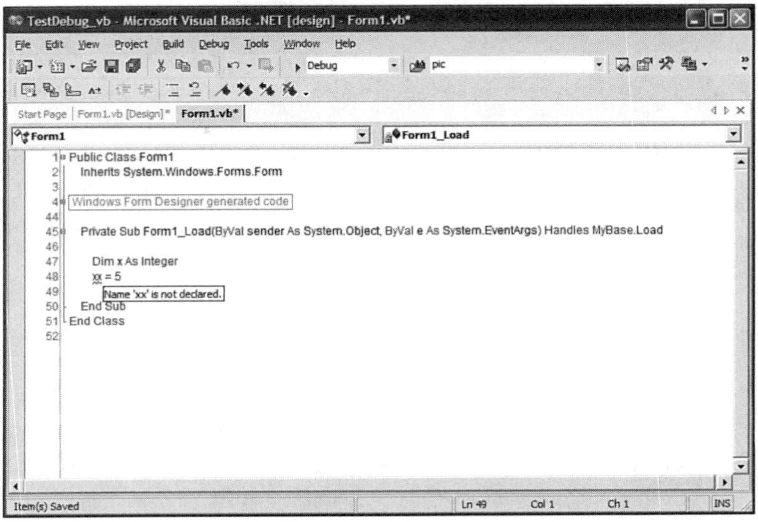

FIGURE 7.2

Visual Studio .NET syntax error notification in Visual Basic .NET.

Note

In Visual Basic .NET, setting `Option Explicit` to `ON` forces you to declare your variables before using them. `Option Explicit` is `ON` by default for new projects. The `Option Strict` setting, which is `OFF` by default, allows narrowing data conversions to take place without a compile error. You should always have `Option Explicit` and `Option Strict ON` to avoid any unexpected errors.

As you can see, it's almost impossible to have syntax errors when using Visual Studio .NET. The IDE always lets you know when something's wrong with the code you just typed. At the other end of the spectrum are logic errors, which can be undetectable.

Tip

To set your project properties for `Option Explicit` and `Option Strict`, right-click your project name in the Solution Explorer and select Properties from the contextual menu. When the property page for your project pops up, select the Build node under the Common Properties node, and you'll see the `Option Explicit` and `Option Strict` options.

How to Avoid Logic Errors

Logic errors are the hardest errors to avoid. Even code written by the most seasoned programmers can contain logic errors. A logic error is a flaw in the way you designed a function, or group of functions, to perform a specific task. Logic errors aren't normally discovered until an application is out in production and being used by end users. This types of error is unavoidable. The only real way to minimize logic errors is to write your applications based on specifications that have been well thought out and clearly defined.

How to Avoid Runtime Errors

Runtime errors are errors that occur at runtime, but aren't handled by an error handler in your code. Runtime errors are the worst type of error that can occur because they directly affect the end user of your application. Runtime errors can also be called laziness errors, because they can be completely avoided simply by implementing some sort of error handling in your code. When an unexpected error occurs and there's no error-handling routine in your application, the application notifies the end user of the error with a very offensive message and crashes immediately. Figure 7.3 shows an example of a runtime error occurring.

FIGURE 7.3

The offensive runtime error notification to the end user.

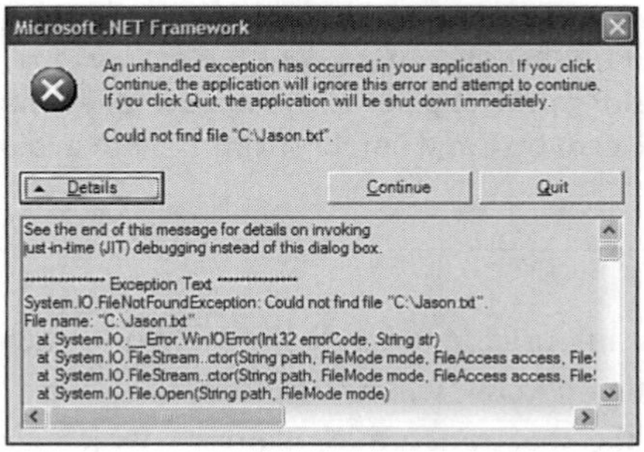

In the code that caused the dialog box shown in Figure 7.3, there was no error handler or any kind of check for the existence of a file when the application attempted to use the `File.Copy` method, so the application aborted. Errors like this are unacceptable, and cause you hours of grief if they aren't avoided, which is why understanding exceptions in .NET and how your application can handle them is so important.

Understanding Exceptions in .NET

When an error occurs in a Visual Basic 6.0 application, the `Err` object fills with information about the last error that occurred. Your application is then thrown that error information, and the error is handled by the `On Error` code you wrote. In Visual Basic .NET, the

Err object still exists, but for backward compatibility only. In C#, the Err object doesn't exist. To make your code compliant with the Common Language Specification (CLS), you must use the exception object from the System.Exception class in the Framework Class Library (FCL).

The Exception object contains the information you need about the last error that occurred in your application. When an error occurs, an Exception object is created. So, when a block of code causes an error, an exception is thrown and the first block of code in the stack that has an exception handler takes care of that exception. If there's no exception-handling code, a runtime error occurs, and your application terminates. Table 7.1 lists the properties of the Exception object.

TABLE 7.1 Properties and Descriptions of the Exception Object

Property Name	*Property Description*
HelpLink	Gets or sets the help file associated with the application
InnerException	Gets a reference to the inner exception
Message	Gets a string representing the error message associated with the exception
Source	Gets or sets the name of the application object that caused the exception
StackTrace	Gets the stack trace identifying the location in the code where the exception occurred
TargetSite	Gets the method name where the exception occurred

Using the properties of the Exception object, you can determine what to do about the exception that occurred. This might be notifying the user with a MessageBox prompt or handling the error and continuing execution in your code.

Note

> Although the information in the Exception object might seem similar to information in the Err object from Visual Basic 6, there are major differences. Exceptions can cross process and machine boundaries. Exceptions are reported the same way in all applications, no matter what language the code is written in or what operating system the code is running on. Finally, exceptions can be traced to the exact line of offending code. Visual Basic 6 offers none of these benefits.

Now that you understand what an exception is, you need to learn how to handle them in code. In .NET, you use structured exception handling (SEH) to help you handle errors in code.

> **Note**
>
> Throughout the day, I refer to *exceptions* and *errors*. These words might seem to equate to the same meaning, but in reality an error causes an exception to be thrown. When an error occurs, the `Exception` object in the common language runtime is filled with information about the error, and your code determines how to handle the exception.

Using Structured Exception Handling

SEH is the control of flow syntax that you use to handle exceptions. SEH isn't a new concept to C++ developers, but it's quite different from the unstructured exception handling mechanism used in previous versions of Visual Basic. The idea behind SEH is that you write code to handle specific or nonspecific errors that could occur as a result of user input, resource availability, or a generic problem that might occur in functions you're writing. With SEH, you can write code to handle errors for specific lines of code; you aren't limited to writing an error-handling routine for a complete subprocedure or function as you were in Visual Basic 6.

> **Note**
>
> Error handling that uses the `On Error Goto` or the `On Error Resume Next` statement is called *unstructured exception handling*.

You write SEH code using `Try/Catch/Finally` blocks in Visual Basic .NET and C#. Using `Try/Catch/Finally` means you're using structured exception handling.

Handling Exceptions with `Try/Catch/Finally`

The syntax for `Try/Catch/Finally` blocks can be explained with the following rules:

- In Visual Basic .NET, each `Try` statement must end with an `End Try` statement and include at least one `Catch` statement or one `Finally` statement.
- In C#, each `try` statement must end with a curly brace, and include at least one `catch` statement or one `finally` statement.

In layman's terms, you're *trying* to execute some code, *catching* an error if one occurs, and *finally* doing something when the code succeeds or fails. The following Visual Basic .NET and C# syntax will give you an idea of what a `Try/Catch/Finally` block might look like:

VB.NET

```
Private Sub Button1_Click(ByVal sender As System.Object, _
    ByVal e As System.EventArgs) Handles Button1.Click

  Try
    ' This is code you are attempting to execute
  Catch
    ' This is code that executes if an exception occurs
  Finally
    ' This is code that runs after the Try or Catch statements
  End Try

End Sub
```

C#

```
private void Form1_Load(object sender, System.EventArgs e)
{
    try
    {
        // This is code you are attempting to execute
    }
    catch
    {
        // This is code that executes if an exception occurs
    }
    finally
    {
        // This is code that runs after the Try or Catch statements
    }
}
```

Understanding the `Catch` Statement

The `Catch` statement filters exceptions based on the code executed in the `Try` statement. There are a few ways to handle `Catch` statements:

- `Catch` a generic error
- `Catch` a specific error, using `Catch As`, based on the type of exception that occurred
- `Catch` a specific error when a criteria is met, using `Catch When` (`Catch When` isn't available in C#)
- In C#, you can specify a specific error in parentheses immediately following the `catch` statement
- `Catch` specific errors using `Catch As` or `Catch When` and then `Catch` a fallback generic error

Note

In C#, you get a compiler error if you attempt to catch a specific exception after having specified a generic `Catch` statement.

To see this in action, create a new Windows Forms project called Exceptions, and add two `TextBox` controls and a two-button control to the default form. Make sure the `Text` property of the `TextBox` controls is blank. Your form should look like Figure 7.4.

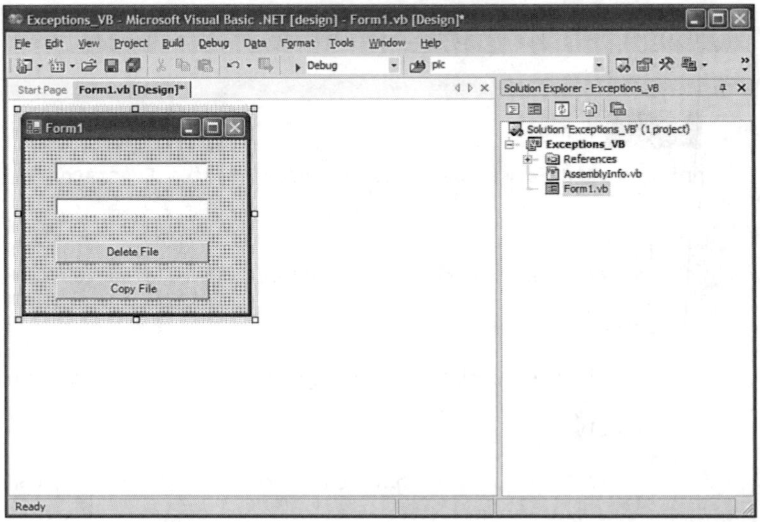

FIGURE 7.4
Default `Form1` for the Exceptions project.

Note

In the following exercise, you use the `System.IO` class, which you learn more about on Day 9, "Using Namespaces in .NET."

Now you're going to add some code that causes exceptions to occur so that you can see the behavior and learn how to handle both a single exception and multiple exception cases. You also learn how the `Finally` statement works.

In the code-behind for the `Button1_Click` event, you write code that attempts to delete the file that's typed into the `textbox1` control. Listing 7.1 shows what the code-behind should look like.

LISTING 7.1 Code-Behind for the `Button1_Click` Event

VB.NET

```
Private Sub Button1_Click(ByVal sender As System.Object, _
    ByVal e As System.EventArgs) Handles Button1.Click

  Try
    System.IO.File.Delete(TextBox1.Text)
  Catch
    MsgBox("An exception occurred!")
  Finally
    MsgBox("Finally we are done!")
  End Try

End Sub
```

C#

```
private void button1_Click(object sender, System.EventArgs e)
{
    try
    {
        System.IO.File.Delete(textBox1.Text);
    }
    catch
    {
        MessageBox.Show("An Exception Occurred");
    }
    finally
    {
        MessageBox.Show("Finally we are done!");
    }
}
```

Tip

In Listing 7.1, you use the fully qualified `System.IO.File` class to execute the `Delete` method. To avoid having to use the fully qualified name each time, use the `Imports` statement to import `System.IO` at the top of the Visual Basic .NET class, and the `using` statement to use the `System.IO` class in your C# class. You can then simply reference the `File.Delete` method without the preceding `System.IO` namespace qualifier.

When you run the code, you get two message box prompts. The first one lets you know that an error occurred, and the second one lets you know that the code is finally done. To break it down, here's exactly what happened:

- The code in the Try statement attempted to delete a file.
- An error occurred, and the exception object filled with the error information and was thrown to the application.
- A MessageBox popped up to say that an error occurred.
- A MessageBox popped up to say that you're finally done.

You can see that the Catch statement executed correctly, but why did the Finally statement execute also? Because in SEH, the Finally statement *always* executes—no matter what. Even if no exception is thrown, the Finally statement code executes. This is useful for cleaning up any resources that you used in the Try statement. For example, if you opened a file stream or database connection, you know that you need to close that resource, so you can always put that type of resource cleanup code in the Finally statement.

How to Filter Specific Exceptions

In the previous example, you used a generic Catch statement to get information about the last error that occurred. But there will be many times when you'll want to react to a specific error that occurred. In such cases, you can use the Catch As statement. When you use Catch As, you're filtering the exception handling based on a specific exception class. Listing 7.2 enhances the code from Listing 7.1 to look for a specific exception object.

LISTING 7.2 Enhanced Code Utilizing the Catch As Statement

VB.NET

```
Try

  System.IO.File.Delete(TextBox1.Text)

Catch ex1 As System.IO.FileNotFoundException

  MessageBox.Show("File is not found")
  MessageBox.Show(ex1.Message)

Catch ex2 As System.IO.PathTooLongException

  MessageBox.Show("Path is too long")
  MessageBox.Show(ex2.Message)

Catch ex3 As System.IO.DirectoryNotFoundException

  MessageBox.Show("Directory Not Found")
  MessageBox.Show(ex3.Message)
```

LISTING 7.2 continued

```
Catch ex As System.Exception

  MessageBox.Show("This is a generic exception handler")

Finally

  MessageBox.Show("Finally we are done!")

End Try
```

C#

```
try
{
    System.IO.File.Delete(textBox1.Text);
}
catch (System.IO.FileNotFoundException ex1)
{
    MessageBox.Show("File is not found");
    MessageBox.Show(ex1.Message);
}
catch (System.IO.PathTooLongException ex2)
{
    MessageBox.Show("Path is too long");
    MessageBox.Show(ex2.Message);
}
catch (System.IO.DirectoryNotFoundException ex3)
{
    MessageBox.Show("Directory not found!");
    MessageBox.Show(ex3.Message);
}
catch (System.Exception e)
{
    MessageBox.Show("This is a generic exception handler");
}
finally
{
    MessageBox.Show("Finally we are done!");
}
```

When you run this code now, type in an invalid filename in `Textbox1`, and then click the Delete File button. The Output window will have the following message:

```
Directory Not Found
Could not find a part of the path "D:\MyText.txt".
```

When the error occurs and the exception is thrown, the first `Catch` statement that has the handler for the particular thrown exception executes. For this reason, you must always attempt to catch in order from the most specific exception to the least specific exception. If the more specific `Catch` statements can't handle the exception, you always have the generic `System.Exception` fallback exception handler.

In the .NET Framework class library (FCL), each class has specific exception classes that define what could possibly go wrong when using that class. Those are the `Exception` classes derived from `System.Exception`. So, how do you know what exceptions can occur when? If you look up the `File.Delete` method in the .NET Framework SDK, you'll see not only how to use the syntax for `File.Delete`, but also the exceptions that can be thrown from using the `File.Delete` method. Figure 7.5 gives you an idea of what to look for when trying to figure what exceptions can occur in a class.

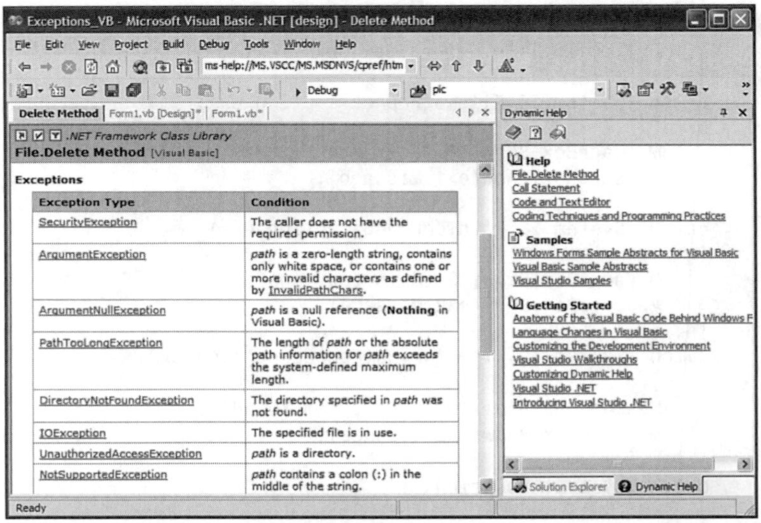

FIGURE 7.5

.NET SDK help file for the `File.Delete` *method showing exceptions.*

Note

If you're using COM components written in unmanaged code, your .NET code maps the `HRESULTS` from the COM component to the correct .NET Framework `Exception` class. You don't have to worry about converting types of exceptions from .NET to non-.NET code; the interoperability classes in .NET handle the conversion of `HRESULTS` to `Exceptions` for you automatically. On Day 14, "Components and .NET," you learn all about interoperating with unmanaged code such as COM components.

Using Visual Basic. NET Exception-Handling Extensions

Visual Basic .NET has two extensions that you can use to handle exceptions: the `Catch When` and `Exit Try` statements.

The `Catch When` statement can be used to look for other criteria besides the exception information—possibly a variable value or a condition of the exception itself. The `Exit Try` statement simply exits the `Try` statement at a certain point. Listing 7.3 shows how to use the `Catch When` and `Exit Try` statements.

LISTING 7.3 Using `Catch When` and `Exit Try`

VB.NET

```
Dim x As Integer = 5

Try

  System.IO.File.Delete(TextBox1.Text)

Catch ex As System.Exception When x = 7

  MessageBox.Show("Please fill in a filename to delete")

Catch ex1 As Exception When x = 5

  If Today.Date = "7/29/2002" Then
    Exit Try
  End If

  MessageBox.Show("You are level 5")

Finally

  MessageBox.Show("Done!")

End Try
```

The first thing Listing 7.3 does is create an integer variable named `x`, and set it to a value of `5`. There are generic exception handlers in the `Try/Catch` block, but the `When` clause tests for the value of `x`. Because `x = 5`, you're prompted with `You are level 5`. If you happen to change your system date to 7/29/2002 and rerun the code, you'll never get the `You are level 5` prompt, because the `Exit Try` statement executes before the next line of code.

Note

> Even though Listing 7.3 uses the Exit Try statement, the `Finally` code still executes. The `Finally` code executes no matter what—all the time.

Up to this point, you've learned everything you need to know about handling exceptions in .NET with structured exception handling. Now you'll see how to use the tools in Visual Studio .NET to effectively debug your code before you deploy it so that you can avoid exceptions.

Raising an Exception

In Visual Basic 6, you could use the `Err.Raise` statement to raise an error to your applications. In .NET, you `Throw` an `Exception` to your application. When you need to cause an error based on the state of your application, you use the `Throw` statement with a new instance of the appropriate exception class. The following code demonstrates how to `Throw` a new `Exception` based on the Boolean return value of the `File.Exists` method:

VB.NET

```
Try
  If Not Directory.Exists("D:\Test") Then
    Throw New DirectoryNotFoundException()
  End If
Catch ex As Exception
  MessageBox.Show(ex.Message)
End Try
```

C#

```
try
{
 if (!Directory.Exists(@"D:\Test"))
  {
   throw new DirectoryNotFoundException();
  }

}
  catch (System.Exception ex)
  {
   MessageBox.Show(ex.Message);
  }

finally
{

}
```

books and unopened music within 30 days from any Barnes & Noble store. For merchandise purchased with a check, a store credit will be issued within the first seven days. Without an original receipt, a store credit will be issued at the lowest selling price. With a receipt, returns of new and unread books and unopened music from bn.com can be made for store credit. Textbooks after 14 days or without a receipt are not returnable. Used books are not returnable.

Valid photo ID required for all returns, (except for credit card purchases) exchanges and to receive and redeem store credit. With a receipt, a full refund in the original form of payment will be issued for new and unread books and unopened music within 30 days from any Barnes & Noble store. For merchandise purchased with a check, a store credit will be issued within the first seven days. Without an original receipt, a store credit will be issued at the lowest selling price. With a receipt, returns of new and unread books and unopened music from bn.com can be made for store credit. Textbooks after 14 days or without a receipt are not returnable. Used books are not returnable.

Valid photo ID required for all returns, (except for credit card purchases) exchanges and to receive and redeem store credit. With a receipt, a full refund in the original form of payment will be issued for new and unread books and unopened music within 30 days from any Barnes & Noble store. For merchandise purchased with a check, a store credit will be issued within the first seven days. Without an original receipt, a store credit will be issued at the lowest selling price. With a receipt, returns of new and unread books and unopened music from bn.com can be made for store credit. Textbooks after 14 days or without a receipt are not returnable. Used books

Barnes & Noble Bookseller
590 East Golf Road
Schaumburg, Il. 60173
(847) 310-0450
12-27-06 S02508 R004

Sams Teach Yourself Visu	39.99
9780672324215	
Christmas Fun: More Than	2.00
9781561569168	
DISCOUNT 4.98 - 2.98	
SUB TOTAL	41.99
SALES TAX	3.67
TOTAL	**45.66**
AMOUNT TENDERED	
CASH	**20.00**
GIFT CARD REDEEM	**27.18**
Card # 504507858536811	
AUTH CODE: #000000	
BALANCE REMAINING	.00
TOTAL PAYMENT	47.18
CHANGE	1.52

Thank you for Shopping at
Barnes & Noble Booksellers
#15234 12-27-06 12:30P BMG

Tip

> In both C# and Visual Basic .NET, you can have multiple `Try/Catch/Finally` blocks in a single function. You can also nest `Try/Catch/Finally` blocks. If you're attempting to handle an exception, you might want to include an exception handler for the exception handler!

Tip

> There's some overhead in the execution cycles for the CPU when using SEH. You should always test for errors, but you can avoid using SEH for every line of code by using some smart programming techniques. For example, if you're writing code that's deleting or copying a file, you should check for the existence of the file outside of an exception handler. If the file doesn't exist, you can simply prompt the user, not raise an exception.

Using Visual Studio .NET to Debug Applications

Visual Studio .NET and the .NET Framework give you all the tools you need to debug your applications while you're designing them. In this section, you learn how to use the `Debug` object on the FCL. You also learn how to use all the output windows in Visual Studio .NET to track exactly what's happening to your application when it's running.

Understanding the `Debug` Class

The `Debug` class is specifically used to aid you in determining the runtime state of your code via user-defined output and alerts. At design time, you use the properties and methods of the `Debug` class to write debug code. The `Debug` class uses one or more listeners to output debug information to a stream. The default output stream in Visual Studio .NET is the Output window. So, for example, any time you use the `Debug.Writeline` method in a Windows Form or ASP.NET application, the data is sent to the Output window by default. If you want the stream to go somewhere other than the Output window, you can add a new listener to the `Listener` collection and direct the output elsewhere, such as an event log or a text file.

Note

> The `Debug` class is found in the `System.Diagnostics` namespace.

Note

> Any code written using the `Debug` class shows up in the build only if the current build configuration is set to Debug. When the build configuration is set to Release, the compiler doesn't include the debug code in the built version.

In Visual Basic 6, you used the `Debug.Print` statement all over your code to output specific information about variable values or message data. The Debug class takes this a step further and gives you a full range of capability for outputting debug information. Before we get into any code, let's examine the properties and methods of the `Debug` class as listed in Tables 7.2 and 7.3, respectively.

TABLE 7.2 Properties of the Debug Class

Property	*Description*
`AutoFlush`	Gets or sets a value indicating whether `Flush` should be called on the listeners after every write
`IndentLevel`	Gets or sets the indent level
`IndentSize`	Gets or sets the number of spaces in an indent
`Listeners`	Gets the collection of listeners that is monitoring the debug output

TABLE 7.3 Methods of the `Debug` Class

Method	*Description*
`Assert`	Checks for a condition and displays a message if the condition is false
`Close`	Flushes the output buffer and then closes the listeners
`Fail`	Emits an error message
`Flush`	Flushes the output buffer and causes buffered data to write to the `Listeners` collection
`Indent`	Increases the current `IndentLevel` by one
`Unindent`	Decreases the current `IndentLevel` by one
`Write`	Writes information about the debug to the trace listeners in the `Listeners` collection
`WriteIf`	Writes information about the debug to the trace listeners in the `Listeners` collection if a condition is true
`WriteLine`	Writes information about the debug to the trace listeners in the `Listeners` collection and adds a linefeed character to the end of the output
`WriteLineIf`	Writes information about the debug to the trace listeners in the `Listeners` collection if a condition is true and adds a linefeed character to the end of the output

As you can see, there are many more options available to you with the Debug class than there were with the Visual Basic 6 `Debug` object.

To see the `Debug` class in action, you're going to modify the default form in the Exceptions project you started earlier in the day. Add a new `Button` to the default `form1` and set the `Text` property to `"Write Debug Information"`. For the code-behind for the new button, enter the code in Listing 7.4, which uses some of the properties and methods of the `Debug` class.

LISTING 7.4 Using the `Debug` Class to Output Debug Information

VB.NET

```
Private Sub Button3_Click(ByVal sender As System.Object, _
      ByVal e As System.EventArgs) Handles Button3.Click

  ' Declare a generic variable for testing
  Dim X As Integer = 5

  ' Create a new file stream
  Dim fOut As Stream = File.Create("C:\ConsoleOutput.txt")

  ' Create a new listener using the file stream as the output
  Dim textListener As New TextWriterTraceListener(fOut)

  ' Add the listener to the Listeners collection
  Debug.Listeners.Add(textListener)

  Debug.WriteLine("This is going to a text file")

  ' Increase the Indent level on the output by 1
  Debug.Indent()

  Debug.WriteLine(Date.Now)
  Debug.WriteLine("The date was just sent to the file")

  ' Use the WriteLineIf to test for a value of False
  Debug.WriteLineIf(X = 7, "X = 7")

  ' Use the WriteLineIf to test for a value of True
  Debug.WriteLineIf(X = 5, "X = 5")

  ' Flush the listener out
  textListener.Flush()

End Sub
```

LISTING 7.4 continued

C#

```
private void button3_Click(object sender, System.EventArgs e)
{
int x = 5;

System.IO.Stream fOut = System.IO.File.Create(@"C:\csConsoleOut.txt");

System.Diagnostics.TextWriterTraceListener textListener = new
        System.Diagnostics.TextWriterTraceListener(fOut);

System.Diagnostics.Debug.Listeners.Add(textListener);

System.Diagnostics.Debug.WriteLine("This is going to a text file");
System.Diagnostics.Debug.Indent();
System.Diagnostics.Debug.WriteLine(System.DateTime.Now);
System.Diagnostics.Debug.WriteLine("The date was sent to the text file");
System.Diagnostics.Debug.WriteLineIf(x == 7, "X = 7");
System.Diagnostics.Debug.WriteLineIf(x == 5, "X = 5");

textListener.Flush();

}
```

Tip

The `System.Diagnostics` class is added to a new Visual Basic .NET project by default. If you create a C# project, you must add the `using System.Diagnostics` statement to avoid typing the fully qualified name as Listing 7.5 does.

When you run the project, the default Output window displays the following:

```
This is going to a text file
  7/21/2002 3:03:30 PM
  The date was just sent to the file
  X = 5
```

If you look at your C drive, you'll find the output text for the custom listener. Figure 7.6 shows what it should look like (other than the date and time being different).

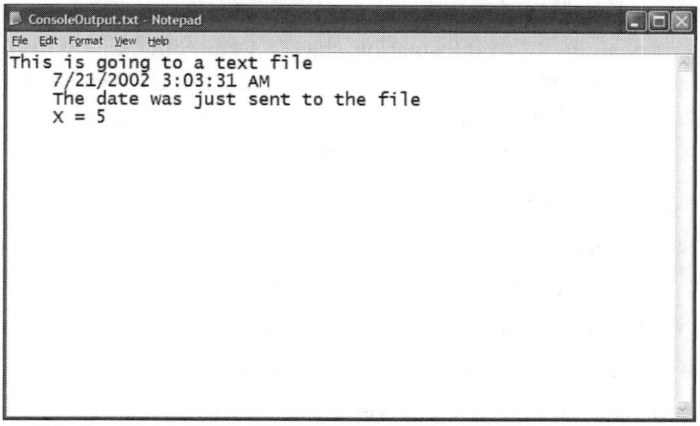

FIGURE 7.6
Text file output of Listing 7.5.

So, to break down what happened in the code:

- Created a new file on the file system called `ConsoleOutput.txt`
- Created a new `TextWriterTraceListener` object, and set its output to the `ConsoleOutput.txt` file you created
- Added the new listener to the `Listeners` collection
- Wrote out some debug information using the `Debug.Writeline`, `Debug.Indent`, and `Debug.WritelineIf` methods
- Called the `Flush` method of your custom listener to flush the buffer of debug data, writing it to the file

There you have it: a new way to keep track of what's happening during the execution of your application without having to use intrusive `MessageBox.Show` prompts or stopping code execution with breakpoints.

Using Breakpoints to Debug Code

Visual Studio .NET enables you to set predetermined points in your code that cause execution to stop so that you can examine the state of the application. Breakpoints stop your code only when you're running it in the Visual Studio .NET IDE; after the code is deployed, breakpoints are ignored.

By default, a breakpoint stops executing code at the exact line at which it's set. The condition that causes the application to break can be set for a number of circumstances, which we look at in a second. Breakpoints can be set only on a line of *executable code*, which doesn't include empty lines or variable declarations that neither instantiate an object nor assign a value to the newly declared variable. You set breakpoints to examine what's going on with any running object in your code. They enable you to see what state variables are in, what information objects are holding, and what threads your application is running on. After you set a breakpoint and your code stops executing, you can modify certain variables to see how your code reacts—thus minimizing that chance that errors will occur after your application is deployed.

Breakpoints can be set in the following five ways:

- Use the mouse to click on the margin to the left of the line where the breakpoint should be set
- Place the cursor on the line where the breakpoint should occur and press F9
- Select New Breakpoint from the Debug menu
- Right-click the line of code where the breakpoint should be set and select New Breakpoint or Insert Breakpoint on the contextual menu
- Place the cursor on the line where the breakpoint should occur and press Ctrl+B to bring up the Breakpoint properties dialog and set the breakpoint

After a breakpoint is set, the line of code on which you set the code to break is easily identified by a burgundy-colored line that spans the line. Figure 7.7 shows this in action.

FIGURE 7.7
Setting a breakpoint.

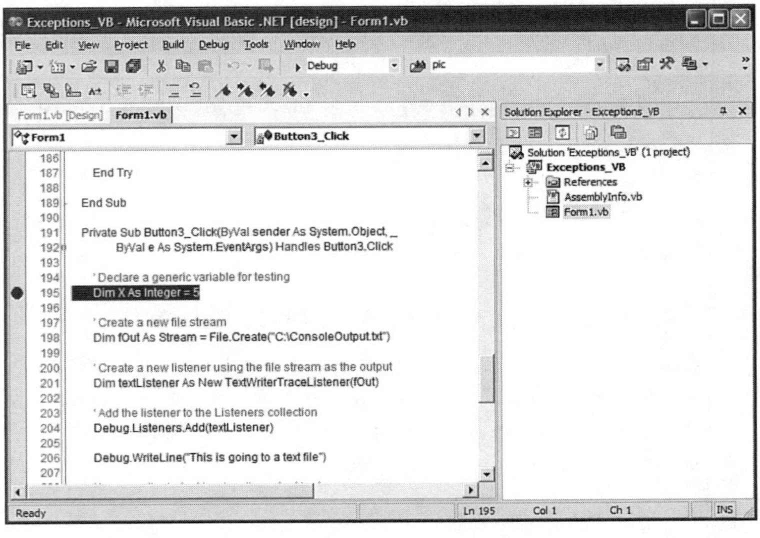

Breakpoints can also be either removed permanently, or disabled so that they don't break the running code but can be easily enabled at any time.

To remove breakpoints, you can

- Use the mouse to click on the margin to the left of the line where the breakpoint is currently set
- Place the cursor on the line where the breakpoint occurs and press F9
- Right-click the line of code where the breakpoint should be removed and click Remove Breakpoint from the context menu
- Select Clear All Breakpoints from the Debug menu

To disable/enable breakpoints, you can

- Right-click the line of code where the breakpoint should be disabled (enabled) and select Disable (Enable) Breakpoint from the contextual menu
- Select Disable (Enable) All Breakpoints from the Debug menu

Tip

If you haven't set a breakpoint, but still want to enter break mode, you can

- Press Ctrl+Break at any time while the application is running
- Select Break All from the Debug menu

After you set a breakpoint, you might or might not want the code to break automatically—you might want to set some sort of condition. You can do so with the Breakpoint Properties dialog box, which you can open by right-clicking the breakpoint that you've set and selecting Properties from the contextual menu. By default, an enabled breakpoint always causes the application to break. Figure 7.8 shows the Breakpoint Properties dialog box.

FIGURE 7.8

The Breakpoint Properties dialog box.

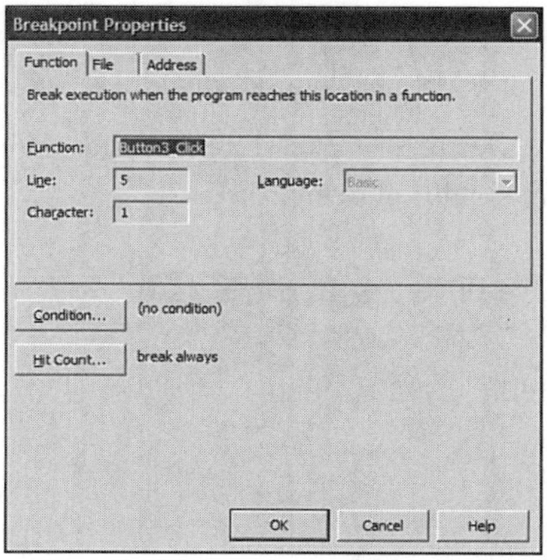

To set a condition for when the Breakpoint will break, use the Condition button or Hit Count button.

The Condition Button Details

Breakpoint conditions cause the execution to break only when the condition has been met. The condition can be any expression that can be evaluated in the current scope of the breakpoint. The condition is further evaluated for either being `True` or having changed since the breakpoint condition was last evaluated. When the expression or state condition is met, the breakpoint causes code execution to break on that line. Figure 7.9 is an example of setting a condition to break the code when the variable `X` is equal to `22`. If the variable `X` never contains the value of 22, the condition is never met and the code execution never breaks.

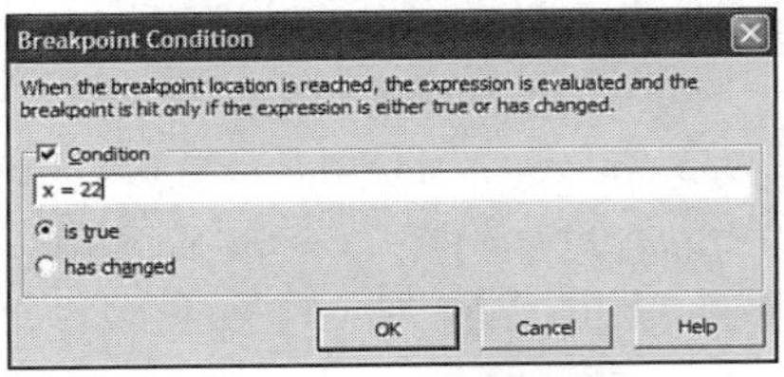

FIGURE 7.9

Setting a condition for a breakpoint.

The Hit Count Button Details

In addition to (or instead of) specifying a condition that breaks execution, a breakpoint can be set to break only when the hit count expression is `True`. The expression must consist of one of the following options:

- `Break Always`
- Break when the hit count is equal to
- Break when the hit count is a multiple of
- Break when the hit count is greater than or equal to

The Breakpoint Hit Count dialog enables you to set the expression and related value. Figure 7.10 shows a hit count condition being set.

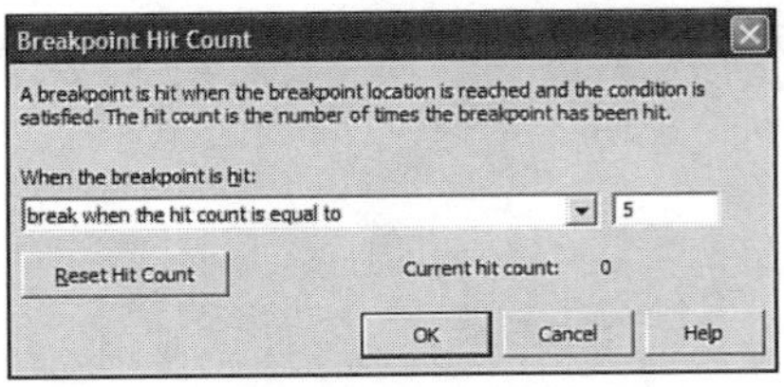

FIGURE 7.10

Setting a hit count expression.

Effective use of breakpoints can accelerate debugging time because it allows your application to run normally and stop at the exact line of code (and with the proper conditions) that you're trying to debug. Therefore, time isn't wasted needlessly stepping through code and reviewing the state of every variable in the application. After you hit a breakpoint, you're in break mode, and you can use the Debug windows to examine the state of your application.

Using the Debug Windows in Break Mode

When your application hits a breakpoint, several very useful debug windows become available that enable you to view and update variables, run local methods, and evaluate expressions. Each of the Debug windows is available only while in break mode, and can be opened by selecting Debug, Windows from the main menu.

Note

When I refer to the current scope of the application in the following sections, it should be noted that, by default, the current scope is the line of executable code where the application entered break mode. Visual Studio .NET enables you to change the current scope at any time while in break mode to review application state at locations other than the scope of current execution.

To change the current scope, simply set the program, thread, and stack frame values in the address toolbar. The Program list box displays all programs that are attached to the current debugger, the Thread list box displays all running threads for the program selected in the program list box (only one item for single-threaded applications). The Stack Frame list box displays the call stack for the thread selected in the Thread list box. When the current scope is changed to a location other than the current execution, the debugger highlights the last line that the application executed for that call stack in green. Otherwise, current execution code is highlighted in yellow by default. You can also change the current scope by using the Call Stack window.

Now let's go through each of the Debug windows and describe how you can use each one to debug your application effectively.

Using the Command Window

The Command window is perhaps the most valuable Debug window that Visual Studio .NET provides. The command window has two modes: command mode and immediate.

When the Command window is in immediate mode, you can evaluate an expression, execute a statement, or print any variable's value in the current scope.

By default, the command window is in command mode. To determine which mode the Command window is currently in, use the following table:

	Caption	*Command Prompt*
Command Mode	Command Window	>
Immediate Mode	Command Window - Immediate	None

To change the command window to immediate mode, simply type **`immed`** at the command prompt and press the Enter key. To change to command mode, type **`>cmd`** at the command prompt and press the Enter key.

The command window is available only while in break mode, and commands are evaluated in the language of the current scope. The Command window allows one command per line and doesn't allow you to modify and run previous commands as was the case with Visual Basic 6.0. It does, however, enable you to quickly recall previous commands by pressing the up and down arrows. Figure 7.11 gives you an idea of what kind of commands you can use in the Command window.

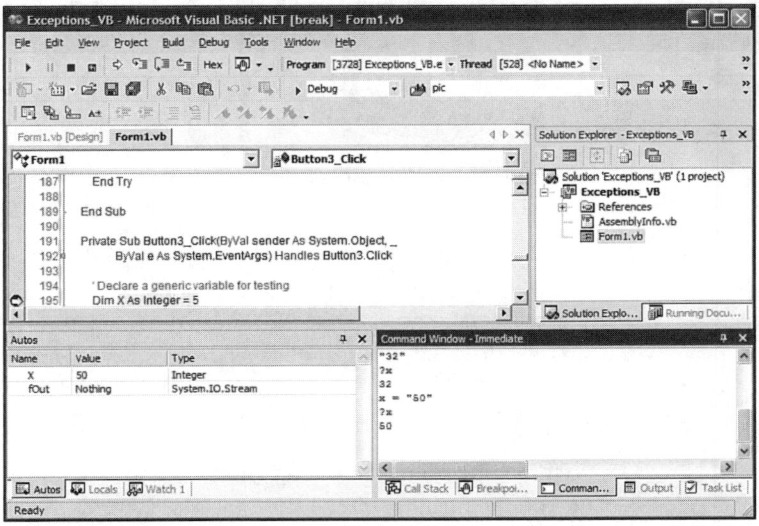

FIGURE 7.11

Using the Command window.

Using the This/Me Window

The This/Me window enables you to view and modify data members of the object that's within the current scope. If code is currently being executed in something other than an object (BAS module in Visual Basic), the This/Me window is empty. The window is named This in C# and Me in Visual Basic.

By double-clicking in the value cell of the data member, you can edit the current value of that member and it's changed for the existing execution scope. Figure 7.12 shows the Me window.

FIGURE 7.12

The Me window in action.

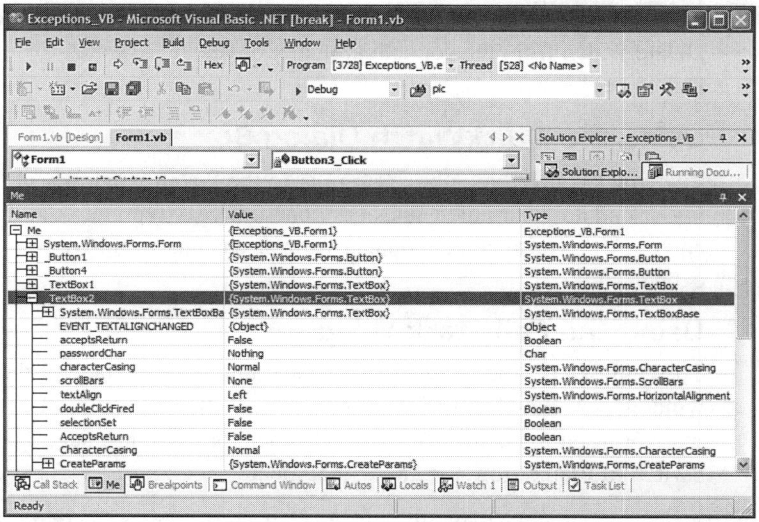

Using the Autos Window

The Autos window is similar to the This/Me window in that you can view and update application variables in the current scope. The difference is that the Autos window displays variables used in the current statement and the previous statement for C++ and C#, or the current statement and the three statements on either side of the current statement for Visual Basic. Only primitive values can be changed in the Autos window. Changing values is done in the same fashion as in the This/Me window: Double-click on the value cell of the variable to change and type the updated value.

Using the Locals Window

The Locals window is similar to the Autos window in every way except the variables that it displays. The Locals window displays all variables that are local to the current scope, whereas the Autos window displays a subset of those variables that appear around the current statement.

Using the Watch Window

The Watch window is similar to the Local and Autos window in its utility. Once again, the difference is in the variables it displays. By default, the Watch window doesn't display any variables. You're actually setting a variable or expression to watch. When a watch condition is met, the execution stops and your application enters break mode. Any variable or expression that you want to continuously review can be added to the Watch window by right-clicking on the item you want to add, and selecting Add Watch from the contextual menu. You may also type in the empty Name column of the Watch window to add your expression. To delete a watch, right-click on the watch to delete and click Delete Watch from the contextual menu, or select the watch to delete and press the Delete key.

Using the QuickWatch Dialog Box

The QuickWatch dialog box is similar to the Watch window, but is most useful in viewing or updating variable values only one time. By typing in the expression to evaluate and clicking Recalculate, you can view or change (primitives only) the value of the expression.

Using the Call Stack Window

The Call Stack window gives you a view into the call stack of the application. From this window, you can change the current scope of the application by double-clicking the item that you want to change to in the call stack, or by right-clicking the item and selecting Switch to Frame from the contextual menu.

Another interesting capability of the Call Stack window is that you can right-click any item in the call stack, and select Run to Cursor from the contextual menu. Doing so runs the application until it gets to the point in the call stack at which you clicked. This capability makes it very easy to maneuver through the application when you're buried in the call stack.

The information displayed in the Call Stack window can be turned on or off by right-clicking in the Call Stack window, and then choosing the appropriate column in the contextual menu to toggle. Your choices for the call stack are

- Module names
- Parameter types
- Parameter names
- Parameter values
- Line numbers
- Byte offsets
- Memory window

Using the Disassembly Window

The Disassembly window displays the native assembler code of the current scope. For you hardcore programmers who like to know everything that's going on under the hood, the Disassembly window enables you to view processor-level commands for your application. Not only can you view your own code, but you can also view the assembly code running in your .NET debugger. The window enables you to show or hide information such as the memory address location relative to the beginning of the function, source code, code bytes (actual byte code used by the processor to execute the instruction), symbol names (associated with the memory address), and line numbers. The Disassembly window gives you the following functionality:

- Jump to the source code associated with the assembly instructions displayed
- Add a quick watch based on an assembly instruction
- Insert a breakpoint
- Jump to the next line of execution (in the event that you've wandered off in the code)
- Run to cursor
- Set next statement

In addition to opening the disassembly window by selecting Window, Disassembly from the Debug menu, you can right-click in the source code window and choose Go to Disassembly from the contextual menu.

Using the Threads Window

The Threads window displays information about all threads running in the debugger. Using this window, you can see which threads are running, their scheduling priority, and current state of the thread. By right-clicking in the Threads window and selecting Freeze, you can suspend activation of a running thread. You can also select Thaw on a suspended thread to resume normal activation. You can view the code associated with a thread by right-clicking on the thread and selecting Switch to Thread from the contextual menu. The Threads window is most useful when you're debugging multithreaded applications.

Using the Modules Window

The Modules window displays information regarding all currently loaded program files. The information displayed is

- Name of the module (that is, `.dll` or `.exe` filename)
- Address in memory where the module is located (starts)
- Path of the module in the file system
- Order in which the modules were loaded
- Version number of the module that's loaded
- The `ProgramID` and name of the PE that owns the module
- Time that the module was created

- Whether or not debug information has been loaded for the module (symbols loaded means you can step through source code to debug; otherwise, you can only step through disassembly)

In addition to the information in the preceding list, the Modules window can be used to tune your application's performance. A module that appears in the Modules window with a red exclamation point and asterisk next to it has been loaded at a relocated base address because another module was already using its base address space. When this occurs, the processor must spend extra clock cycles to point itself to the adjusted address, which causes decreased performance. When this occurs, consider changing the base address of the module that has been relocated.

Now that you understand what the Debug windows can offer you on your road to perfect code, let's take a look at how you can step through code after you're actually in break mode.

Stepping Through Code

While in break mode, the Visual Studio .NET IDE enables you to step through the code to see the actual execution path through the application. This is extremely useful because it gives you a chance to check for logic errors and view variable contents throughout execution. To step though code, you can use the Debugging toolbar shown in Figure 7.13, or you can right-click anywhere in the code window and select any of the options discussed next.

FIGURE 7.13

The Debugging toolbar.

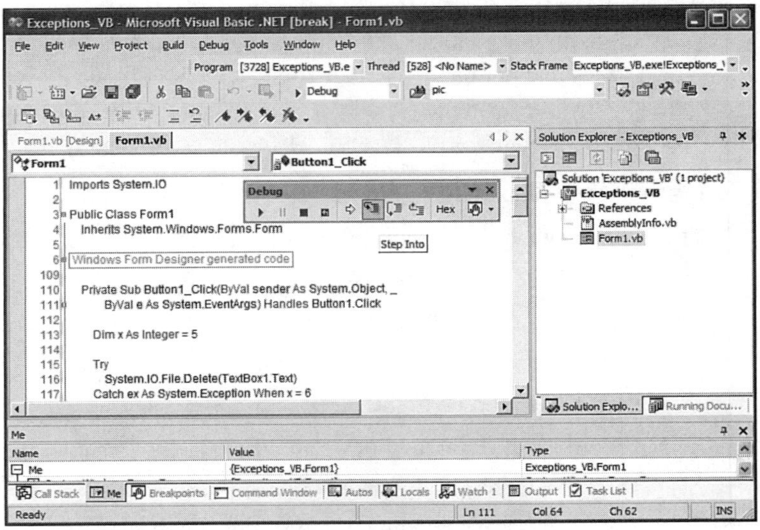

Step Into

While stepping through code, it will eventually happen that the next line of executable code is a property or method call. When you reach this point using the Step Into option, the debugger goes into the property or method call that's called.

Step Over

If you want to ignore what code is running inside a property or method call, it's useful to Step Over the call. In this way, the code that's called is run normally, and you re-enter break mode when execution gets to the next line of code after the call that you stepped over.

Step Out

If you find yourself in a property or method call that you don't care to be in and don't want to step through each line of code to get out, use Step Out. Doing so causes the application to execute normally, and re-enter break mode on the next line of code after the call of the property or method that you were in when you stepped out.

Run to Cursor

Run to Cursor enables you to choose a position at some point ahead of the current line of execution at which the application should re-enter break mode. That is to say, the application executes normally until it reaches the point of execution.

Set Next Statement

Sometimes you might find that you don't want to follow the standard execution path of the application. Perhaps you want to go back in the code execution or skip a line. This can be done by using Set Next Statement.

Continue

Continue enables you to exit break mode and execute the rest of the application as normal (until break mode is re-entered later).

Stop Debugging

Use Stop Debugging to end the debug session as well as close the application. When this occurs, the application stops, and the IDE is now in design time.

Restart

While in break mode, you can stop and restart the application. On restart, the application enters break mode at the first line of executable code in your application.

Detach All

Detach All detaches the debugger from all running threads currently used by the debugger. That means the threads continue to run as normal, without the use of the debugger.

Hovering

The debugger also enables you to view values of expressions and object types by hovering the cursor over the selected code. For example, if you have a local variable, `i`, whose value is `10`, you can hover the cursor over the `i` and view the contents (`i = 10`). You can also highlight a line of code, say `i = 50`, and view the results of the expression (`i = 50 = False`). By hovering over objects, you can view the type name of the object or view the function prototype of procedure calls.

Edit and Continue - Not Supported

For those programmers familiar with Visual Basic 6.0 (and earlier), it will come as sad news to discover that Visual Studio .NET doesn't support the capability to edit and continue. Code can no longer be changed while the debugger is in break mode, and execute as normal using the newly entered code. You can change code while in break mode, but an attempt to run the code any further results in a dialog box that asks whether you want to restart the application.

Keyboard Shortcuts Visual Studio and Visual Basic Versions

Table 7.4 gives you an idea of what shortcuts are available in Visual Basic .NET and C#, and how they compare to Visual Basic 6 debugging shortcuts.

TABLE 7.4 Keyboard Shortcuts in C# and Visual Basic .NET Compared to Visual Basic 6

	Keyboard Shortcut Layouts		*Debug Menu*	*Context Menu*
	Default	**VB6**		
Continue	F5	F5	Continue	
Break All	Ctrl+Alt+Break	Ctrl+Break	Break All	
Stop Debugging	Shift+F5		Stop Debugging	
Restart	Ctrl+Shift+F5	Shift+F5	Restart	
Detach All			Detach All	
Step Into	F11	F8	Step Into	
Step Over	F10	Shift F8	Step Over	
Step Out	Shift+F11	Ctrl+Shift+F8	Step Out	
Run to Cursor				Run to Cursor
Set Next Statement				Set Next Statement

Tip

> You can change all keyboard mappings by going to Tools, Options, Environment, Keyboard, Keyboard Mapping Scheme.

Summary

Today you learned everything you ever wanted to know about exceptions in .NET: how to handle them and how to effectively debug your applications before you deploy them. As you move forward, remember that you can never have enough error handling in your applications. There's nothing more demeaning to your ego than the phone ringing off the hook with complaining users saying such things as, "A box popped up and then my program disappeared." Runtime errors should be a thing of the past with the tools you have available in Visual Studio .NET. Proper use of the debugging tools gives you full access to the execution environment of your application before it's deployed, so you can always test different circumstances under which your applications might run.

Q&A

Q When I upgrade my Visual Basic 6 application to Visual Basic .NET, can I still use my `On Error Goto` error-handling routines?

A Yes, you can. However, they're provided for backward compatibility only, so you should consider rewriting your error-handling routines to the new structured exception handling in .NET.

Q I'm used to Visual Basic 6 debugging, and I like to change my code while I am in debug mode. Why does .NET make me restart every time I do that now?

A Visual Basic .NET is a compiled language, not interpreted. That means in order for your code to run, the intermediate language must be compiled before it runs—even when you're debugging. So, if you make a change to your code, you must restart the application to re-create the intermediate language code.

Q Exceptions are cool. I like the fact that I help out the user by letting him know what happened. Is there a way I can create my own custom exceptions?

A Yes. If you're writing classes and you want to create custom errors that are raised back to the user, you can inherit from the `Exception` class.

Quiz

1. True or False: In C#, the `Exit Try` statement prevents the `Finally` statement from executing, thus enabling me to avoid any of the code execution in the `Finally` statement.
2. True or False: Using the Immediate and Command windows, I can change the values of variables that are in the current scope of execution.

Quiz Answers

1. False: The `Finally` statement will always execute, no matter what.
2. False: Using the Immediate window, you can modify variable values and evaluate statements that apply to the current scope of the executing code. The Command window allows you to execute Visual Studio .NET commands, such as opening files, adding items, and clearing the editors.

Exercises

1. Expanding on the code you wrote in Listing 7.5, look up the `EventLogTraceListener` class in the .NET Framework SDK and add a custom listener to the application that writes the debug information to the event log as well as the text file.
2. Create a new ASP.NET application with a `CommandButton` and a `TextBox`. In the code-behind for the `Button1_Click` event, add a string variable named `strTest` and an integer variable named `intTest`. Set a breakpoint on the `Page_Load` event for `WebForm1` and use the Me debugging window and the Immediate debugging window to evaluate the variable values on the form. Change the breakpoint properties to enter break mode when the value of `strTest` is equal to `"Test Break Mode"`. While in break mode, change the value of `strTest` and see what the results are by doing a `Response.Write` back to the Web form.
3. In each code listing you write for the remainder of the lessons, look up the `Exception` classes that are related to the methods that you're using, and try to incorporate SEH in all the methods that you write.

Week 1

In Review

Now that week 1 is complete, you have a solid foundation to move forward with writing .NET applications using Visual Studio .NET.

On Day 1, you learned about the .NET Framework and how it fits into the whole vision of .NET, including core services like the common language runtime, garbage collection, just-in-time compilation, and the new Microsoft Intermediate Language. Understanding what .NET can do for you is the first step in moving forward with your 21-day adventure of learning how to use Visual Studio .NET to write applications.

On Day 2, you learned about the features in Visual Studio .NET that make your life as a developer better than ever. You learned about the many windows available to you, how to use Dynamic Help in the IDE as you're coding, and how to generate help files for your applications without much effort. You also saw the various project templates that are available to you when developing applications using Visual Studio .NET.

On Day 3, you learned how Windows Forms applications are written, and how to tackle the new event model in .NET. Using the features in Visual Studio .NET, you learned that rapid application development has never been more rapid when writing Visual Studio .NET applications.

Day 4 introduced you to the new built-in Windows Installer features of Visual Studio .NET. By creating deployment applications, you learned how easy it is to distribute professional, robust, and customized deployment solutions using Visual Studio .NET.

On Day 5, you learned how to write ASP.NET applications. Like creating applications for the desktop, Microsoft Visual Studio .NET gives you a simple drag-and-drop design time interface for creating rich interfaces for the browser. You learned that ASP.NET applications share the same event model as controls on Windows Forms, and you learned how to use code behind to respond to user events using Visual Studio .NET.

Day 6 built on the techniques you learned about on Day 4: using the Windows Installer technology on Visual Studio .NET to deploy Web-based applications. You also learned how Web applications could be deployed using XCopy deployment and the Copy Web tools in Visual Studio .NET.

Your week wrapped up with a whole day about exception handling and debugging. Using the extensive debugging tools in Visual Studio .NET, Day 7 taught you how to use debugging to help avoid application errors in the future. In addition, if errors do crop up, you learned how to implement structured exception handling in Visual Basic .NET and C# to gracefully handle any errors that occur in your applications.

WEEK 2

At a Glance

Week 2 teaches you how to write applications in .NET. Starting with an introduction to the Visual Basic .NET and C# languages, you'll be given what you need to understand and use both syntaxes in your applications. You'll learn about the namespaces in the framework class library, and how to use them in your applications to take advantage of the services available to you in the .NET Framework. Most applications you write in today's business world are component driven, access data in a database, and use XML. So, during this week, you'll also learn everything you need to get up to speed on building components, accessing data with ADO.NET, and reading and parsing XML and using the built-in tools in Visual Studio .NET to write robust data-driven applications.

Week 2 covers the following:

- Day 8 teaches you the fundamentals of Visual Basic .NET and C#. You'll learn about the data types allowed in .NET, how to use decision structures in your applications, how to use the various looping techniques in both languages, and how to use operators in Visual Basic .NET and C#.
- Day 9 teaches you about namespaces in the framework class library, and how they are the foundation of the .NET Framework. You'll learn how to locate information in the SDK about namespaces, and how to reference namespaces in your C# and Visual Basic .NET applications. To learn how to implement namespaces, you'll get an intense lesson on using and accessing the environment using the `System.Enviroment` class and how to read and write files and streams using the `System.IO` namespace in the framework class library.

- Day 10 is your first look at accessing data in .NET. You'll learn about ADO.NET and how it differs from traditional ADO. You'll also learn about the new objects in ADO.NET, such as the `DataReader`, the `DataSet`, and the `DataAdapter`. You'll find out how to use these objects to read and write data from SQL Server, Microsoft Access, and other database servers.
- Day 11 builds on what you learned on Day 10, and teaches you how to use all of .NET's visual tools that aid you in designing and writing data-driven applications. Using tools such as the Server Explorer, you can manage your connections to the database, create tables, views, and stored procedures, and write data forms with little or no code.
- Day 12 teaches you about XML in the .NET Framework. XML is the format of choice for interacting with different systems on intranets and over the Web, and understanding how to read, write, and parse XML using the XML namespaces in .NET is essential. Today, you'll learn about all the key options of working with XML using Visual Studio .NET and the `System.XML` namespace.
- Day 13 explains how to create and consume XML Web services in Visual Studio .NET. XML Web services are a cornerstone of the .NET vision, and today you'll see how and why you should be using XML Web services in your applications.
- Day 14 teaches you about components in the .NET Framework. In .NET, there are different categories of components, and understanding when and why to use the various types is important. You will also learn about the different ways that COM components written in non-.NET languages, like Visual Basic 6 and C++, can still be used in .NET.

WEEK 2

DAY 8

Core Language Concepts in Visual Basic .NET and C#

Last week, you learned about the user interface elements in Windows Forms and ASP.NET applications. You wrote a lot of code, and you might or might not have had a full understanding of what it was doing. Today, you're going to learn about the fundamentals of the Visual Basic .NET and C# languages. By the end of the day, you should see that the difference between the two languages is very minor, and you shouldn't be afraid to use one or the other when you start developing .NET applications. Today, you learn

- What the different .NET languages offer
- Different data types in .NET
- How to declare and use variables
- Different scope options for variables
- How to implement operators

- How to implement looping structures
- How to implement decision structures

Languages in the .NET Framework

On Day 1, "Introduction to the Microsoft .NET Framework," the core message was that as a developer, you have access to a unified set of classes. The classes in the framework class library (FCL) are what you access in your applications to provide various functionalities, such as reading and writing of files, accessing a database, or creating a user interface. No matter the language, the classes in the FCL are available to any language that runs inside the .NET Framework runtime.

Before .NET, programming languages lived inside their own box. Visual Basic had the VBRUN DLLs that provided its runtime, and C++ had its own runtime to make C++ programs work. This caused problems when an application written in one language wanted to talk to an application written in a different language. Data types were different, the way objects were handled was different, and there was a lot of overhead for the system to work between applications just to accomplish simple tasks.

With the advent of .NET, these issues are no longer relevant. Because the .NET Framework exposes a unified set of classes, each .NET language has access to the services offered by those classes in a consistent manner. The way you access data in SQL Server in Visual Basic .NET is the same way you would do it C#, COBOL .NET, Perl .NET, and so on. All the class libraries are accessible by any language. Because of this, understanding how the different languages work is merely an issue of syntax, not functionality.

Today you're going to see the differences between Visual Basic .NET syntax and C# syntax. By the end of the day, you'll probably be scratching your head wondering why there are separate Visual Basic .NET and C# languages, and not just one language. To answer that question, you can look at how long it might have taken you to become familiar with the languages you write in now. If you're coming from a C, C++, or Java background, the syntax and the functionality are different from Visual Basic 6. The goal in having multiple languages in .NET is to get all developers up to speed quickly in the language syntax they prefer. The difference with .NET is that all languages share the same functionality. One language doesn't run any faster than another language. It's much easier to move from Visual Basic 6 to Visual Basic .NET than from Visual Basic 6 to C#. That's why so many languages are supported by the .NET Framework.

Note

> The argument of C# running faster then Visual Basic .NET has been raging since the languages were introduced. Remember that all .NET languages must compile to the Microsoft Intermediate Language (MSIL), and the .NET runtime converts the MSIL to the processor-specific code that actually runs your applications. So, although the MSIL code might not be identical among different languages, the speed at which it runs is the same. There's no "better" language to code in—they're all essentially the same. At the other end of that spectrum, if I create my own .NET language, perhaps Jason#, and my compiler doesn't produce very efficient MSIL, my language might perform worse than others. But in general, the MSIL produced by the language-specific compilers is highly efficient.

Understanding CLS Data Types in Visual Basic .NET and C#

When working with data, such as setting or retrieving values from a form, you must normally take that information and either manipulate it or store it temporarily before you persist it to a database or a file.

In C# and Visual Basic .NET, you use variables to store information. Each variable that you declare is of a certain type, which is defined by the rules of the common type system (CTS). The CTS guarantees type safety between different languages, which was unheard of before .NET. That means when you use a String data type in C#, it's the same String data type that you use in Visual Basic .NET and COBOL .NET.

When I talk about different .NET languages, I mean that a language is considered a .NET language because it follows the rules of the Common Language Specification (CLS). The CTS exists in the CLS, which ensures type safety across all languages that have a .NET suffix. The allowable data types, their language-specific syntax, their CLS type, and their value ranges are listed in Table 8.1.

TABLE 8.1 Data Types in .NET

Visual Basic .NET	*C#*	*CLS Type*	*Bytes*	*Value*
Boolean	bool	`System.Boolean`	4	True or False.
Byte	byte	`System.Byte`	1	0 to 255.
Char	char	`System.Char`	2	0 to 65,535.
Date	DateTime	`System.DateTime`	8	January 1, 1 to December 31, 9999.

TABLE 8.1 continued

Visual Basic .NET	*C#*	*CLS Type*	*Bytes*	*Value*
Decimal	decimal	`System.Decimal`	12	+/- 79,228,162,514,264,337,593,950,335 with no decimal point. +/- 7.9228162512264337593543950335 with 28 places to the right of the decimal point. The smallest nonzero number would be a 1 in the 28th position to the right of the decimal point.
Double	double	`System.Double`	8	-1.797693134862231E308 to -4.94065645841247 for negative values to 4.94065645841247 to 1.797693134862231E308 for positive values.
Integer	int	`System.Int32`	4	-2,147,483,648 to 2,147,483,648.
Long	long	`System.Int64`	8	-9,223,372,036,854,775,808 to 9,223,372,036,854,775,807.
Short	short	`System.Int16`	2	-32,768 to 32,767.
Object	object	`System.Object`	4	An object can hold any variable type.
Single	float	`System.Single`	4	-3.402823E38 to -1.401298E-45 for negative values to 1.401298E-45 to 3.402823E38 for positive values.
String	string	`System.String`	10+(2*Length)	0 to 2 billion Unicode characters (approximately).
User-defined type (structure)	struct	`System.ValueType`	Sum of the size of its members	Each member of the structure has a range determined by its data type and independent of the ranges of the other members.

Note

If you're coming from a Visual Basic 6 background, notice the differences in the data type ranges. In Visual Basic .NET, the Short data type replaces the Integer data type, and the Integer data type replaces the Long data type. The Long data type in Visual Basic .NET is a 64-bit number; in Visual Basic 6, a Long data type was a 32-bit number.

Declaring Variables in Visual Basic .NET and C#

Now that you have an understanding of the CLS-compliant data types in .NET, you need to learn how to use these types in your code by declaring variables. You use a declaration statement to define a variable; you also can optionally set a value for the variable when you declare it.

> **Note**
>
> Today, you won't create an application and follow along. You use the code in the listings throughout the day as part of your exercises at the end of the day. If you want to test the code as you're reading, you can create a Windows Forms application and add the various code listings to the code-behind for button click events.

In Visual Basic .NET, using the `Dim` statement is the simplest way to declare a variable. The following code declares a variable named `intX` as the data type Integer:

```
Dim intX as Integer
```

The format for declaring a variable in Visual Basic .NET is

```
Scope variable_name as DataType
```

The *`Scope`* of the variable defines where the variable can be accessed, the *`name`* is the descriptive name that you give the variable, and the *`DataType`* is any of the CLS-compliant types listed earlier in Table 8.1.

In C#, the format is almost identical, just reversed. The following code declares a variable named `intX` as the C# data type int:

```
int intx;
```

Where the format is

```
Scope DataType variable_name;
```

> **Note**
>
> Remember that C# is a case-sensitive language. If you declare variables named `intX`, `INTX`, `IntX`, and `intx`, you'll have four separate variables. In Visual Basic .NET, they would all be considered the same variable because Visual Basic .NET isn't a case-sensitive language.

In C#, all statements are followed by the semicolon. So, a semicolon must follow a variable declaration, and anything after the semicolon is considered another statement to be checked by the compiler.

In both Visual Basic .NET and C#, you can declare multiple variables in a single statement, as the following code demonstrates:

VB.NET

```
Dim intX, intY, intX as Integer
```

C#

```
int intX, intY, intX;
```

In both examples, the data types for each variable are the integer data type. In Visual Basic .NET, you can specify multiple variables on the same line with different data types. The following code shows the declaration of two variables—one integer and one string:

```
Dim intX as Integer, Dim strName as string
```

You can also set the value of a variable when you declare it. The following code sets the value of the `intX` and `intY` variables, but not the `intZ` variable:

VB.NET

```
Dim intX As Integer = 5, intY = 10, intZ
```

C#

```
int intX = 5, intY = 10, intZ;
```

Understanding Variable Scope

When you declare a variable, you can optionally declare it with an access modifier, which specifies where the variable can be accessed by other elements within your application. This is called the *scope* of the variable.

In C#, the access modifiers are

- `public`—Access is available to any other class or class member in the same project, another referenced project, or another referenced assembly.
- `protected`—Access is limited to the containing class or types derived from the containing class.

- `internal`—Access is limited to the current project.
- `private`—Access is limited to the containing type.

In Visual Basic .NET, the access modifiers are

- `Public`—Access is available to any other class or class member in the same project, another referenced project, or another referenced assembly. At the class level, using `Dim` is the same as using `Public`.
- `Protected`—Access is limited to the containing class or types derived from the containing class.
- `Friend`—Access is limited to the current project.
- `Protected Friend`—Access is limited to derived classes or the same project. This can be used only at the class level when declaring variables, not at the procedure level.
- `Private`—Access is limited to the procedure, class, or structure.

In Listing 8.1, you can see the usage of the different access modifiers. Read the comments within the code to see where the variables can be used.

LISTING 8.1 Implementing Different Access Modifiers for Variables and Classes

VB.NET

```
' Public Class variable accessible to
' any object that derives from this class
Public Class Class1

   ' Public to this class and any class that derives from this class
   Public strName As String

   ' Private to this class only
   Private intX As Integer

   ' Accessible from any class in the project
   Friend intZ As Integer

   ' Private Sub Procedure available to Class1, and NOT
   ' any classes that derive from Class1
   Private Sub Test()

      ' Private to the procedure Test()
      Dim intX As Integer

   End Sub

   ' Public Sub Procedure available to Class1, and
```

LISTING 8.1 continued

```
   ' any classes that derive from Class1
   Public Sub TestPublic()

   End Sub

End Class
```

C#

```
// Public Class variable accessible to
// any object that derives from this class
   public class Class1
   {

      // Public to this class and any class that derives from this class
      public string strName;

      // Private to this class only
      private int intX;

      // Accessible from any class in the project
      internal int intZ;

      public Class1()
      {
         // Add constructor code here
      }

      // Private Sub Procedure available to Class1, and NOT
      // any classes that derive from Class1
      private void Test()
      {
         // Private to the procedure Test
         int intX;
      }

      // Public  Procedure available to Class1, and
      // any classes that derive from Class1
      public void TestPublic()
      {

      }

   }
```

Using Constant Variables

A *constant* is an access modifier that enables you to declare a variable whose value doesn't change throughout the lifetime of your application. The best example of a constant is the value of PI, which is a long number that you might not want to type every time you use it in a mathematical application. The following code declares a constant for the value of PI using the `Const` keyword:

VB.NET

```
Const myPI As Decimal = 3.4799897
```

C#

```
const decimal myPI = 3.4799897;
```

After you declare a constant, you cannot modify its value at runtime. That means the constant's value remains the same for the lifetime of your application.

Using Static and Shared Variables

Static and shared variables are special variable types that retain their values. In C#, the keyword `Static` is equivalent in function to the Visual Basic .NET keyword `Shared`. When you declare a variable as `Static` in C# and `Shared` in Visual Basic .NET, the variable's scope is public or private to the class that it's in, but isn't affected by instances of the class.

For example, when you declare a variable as a type of a specific class, you have access to the class's members, such as public, protected, and friend procedures and variables. If a member of the class is defined as `Static` in C# or `Shared` in Visual Basic .NET, the member is specific to the class, not an instance of the class.

The code in Listing 8.2 uses a `globalCounter` variable and an `Increment` method that aren't affected by the creation of any new instances of the `StaticTest` class.

LISTING 8.2 Using Shared/Static Variables in a Class

VB.NET

```
Public Class StaticTest

   Public Shared globalCounter As Integer

   Public Shared Function Increment() As Integer

      globalCounter += 1
      Return globalCounter

   End Function
```

LISTING 8.2 continued

```
End Class

public class StaticTest
{
   public StaticTest ()
   {
   }
```

C#

```
   public static int globalCounter;

   public static int Increment()
   {
      return ++globalCounter;
   }
}
```

Now declare an instance of `StaticTest`, as this Visual Basic .NET code demonstrates:

```
Dim x As New StaticTest()
Dim c As Integer = x.Increment()
MessageBox.Show(c.ToString)

Dim y As New StaticTest()
c = y.Increment()
MessageBox.Show(c.ToString)
```

Each separate instance of the `StaticTest` class retains the value of the `globalCounter` variable. It's shared across all instances of the class.

Using the `New` Keyword

The `New` keyword in Visual Basic .NET and the `new` keyword in C# are used to create new object instances. In some of the code you've seen today, `New` was used to demonstrate the creation of an instance of a class. Each class file in your project contains *members*, which are simply the methods, variables, properties, and structures that make up the class. To use a class's members, you must create a variable of the type of class you're trying to work with.

Note

This book isn't a lesson on object-oriented programming, and you won't get too heavily into creating your own custom classes. But it's important to understand terms such as *type* and *members*. Earlier, you saw the list of CLS-compliant data types. Each of those data types is simply a *type* in the FCL. When you declare a variable as an integer, you can say that you've declared

8

> a variable of type integer. Each time you create a new class file in your projects, you're creating a new type. By adding properties, methods, structures, and variables to the class, you're creating the members of the class. When an instance of the class is created, it's simply another type to be managed by the common language runtime.

When you use the `New` keyword, you're creating a variable of a specified type and setting its members to their default values. In the case of a base type, such as an integer, creating a new instance of a variable of type integer defaults the variable's value to zero. In the case of a class, all nonstatic or nonshared variables are set to their default values. The `New` keyword is used all the time in .NET. Because you're writing code in class files, you must normally create an instance of that class before you attempt to access any of its members. The following code creates a new instance of `Class1` and makes it available to the variable `X`:

VB.NET

```
Dim x as Class1 = new Class1
' Both of these declarations are equivalent in VB.NET
Dim x as new Class1
```

C#

```
Class1 x = new Class1;
```

After you've declared `X` as a new instance of the class `Class1`, you have access to the members of `Class1` using the dot notation. For example, if `Class1` has a public string variable named `firstName`, you can access it as follows:

VB.NET

```
'  Set the variable
x.firstName = "Jason"

' Retrieve the variable
MessageBox.Show(x.firstName)
```

C#

```
//  Set the variable
x.firstName = "Jason";

// Retrieve the variable
MessageBox.Show(x.firstName);
```

Each time you use the `New` keyword, you're creating an instance of a class. The variable holds the instance, which then has access to all the members in the class instance you've declared.

Understanding Operators

Operators assist you in manipulating data by assigning variable values, retrieving variable values, or comparing variable values. An operator falls into one of the following categories: arithmetic, assignment, bitwise, comparison, concatenation, or logical.

Each time you declare a variable, you're assigning the variable to a value, so you're using an *assignment* operator. When you compare the value of one variable to the value of another variable, you're using a *comparison* operator. When you add numbers together, you're using an *arithmetic* operator. You used operators often last week, and most operators are self-explanatory in what purpose they actually have. If you're coming from a Visual Basic 6 background, you'll be pleasantly surprised by some of the new operators available to you in Visual Basic .NET, so make sure that you read through the following section.

Arithmetic Operators

In grade school, we all learned how to add, subtract, multiply, and divide. These are basic life functions, just like watching Star Trek and eating pizza. Visual Basic .NET offers the arithmetic operators listed in Table 8.2 that handle the dirty work of doing math.

TABLE 8.2 Arithmetic/Multiplicative Operators in Visual Basic .NET and C#

Visual Basic .NET	*C#*	*Description*
+	+	Addition
-	-	Subtraction
*	*	Multiplication
/	/	Division
\	N/A	Integer division
Mod	%	Modulo
^	N/A	Exponentiation
N/A	++	Unary addition
N/A	--	Unary subtraction

Each of the operators for performing mathematical functions is straightforward. The one difference between the languages is the way Visual Basic .NET handles division. The \

integer division operator doesn't return a remainder if one exists when dividing two numbers; the regular / division operator does. Listing 8.3 uses each of the arithmetic operators and returns values from the test variables in the procedure.

LISTING 8.3 Using Arithmetic Operators to Test Values

VB.NET

```
Private Sub testOperators()

   Dim X As Integer = 50
   Dim Y As Integer = 10

   ' Addition - returns 60
   MessageBox.Show((X + Y).ToString())

   ' Subtraction - returns 40
   MessageBox.Show((X - Y).ToString())

   ' Multiplication - returns 500
   MessageBox.Show((X * Y).ToString())

   ' Division - returns 5
   MessageBox.Show((X / Y).ToString())

   ' Modulo - returns 0
   MessageBox.Show((X Mod Y).ToString())

   ' Modulo - returns 10
   MessageBox.Show((Y Mod X).ToString())

   ' Exponent - returns 9.76562E+16
   MessageBox.Show((X ^ Y).ToString())

End Sub
```

C#

```
private void testOperators()
{
   int X = 50;
   int Y = 10;

   // Addition - returns 60
   MessageBox.Show((X + Y).ToString());

   // Subtraction - returns 40
   MessageBox.Show((X - Y).ToString());
```

LISTING 8.3 continued

```
        // Multiplication - returns 500
        MessageBox.Show((X * Y).ToString());

        // Division - returns 5
        MessageBox.Show((X / Y).ToString());

        // Modulo - returns 0
        MessageBox.Show((X % Y).ToString());

    }
```

Assignment Operators

Assignment operators take a value from the right side of the operator and assign it to the value on the left side of the operator. In previous Visual Basic versions, the = sign was the assignment operator, but the language has been enhanced to include some pretty cool new assignment operators. Table 8.3 lists the assignment operators in Visual Basic .NET and C# and their descriptions.

TABLE 8.3 Assignment Operators in Visual Basic .NET and C#

Visual Basic .NET	*C#*	*Description*
=	=	Equals assignment
+=	+=	Addition/concatenation assignment
-=	-=	Subtraction assignment
*=	*=	Multiplication assignment
/=	/=	Division assignment
\=	/=	Integer division
^=	N/A	Exponentiation assignment
&=	+=	String concatenation assignment
N/A	%=	Modulus assignment
N/A	<<=	Left shift assignment
N/A	>>=	Right shift assignment
N/A	&=	Bitwise AND assignment
N/A	^=	Bitwise exclusive OR assignment
N/A	|=	Bitwise inclusive OR assignment

To see some of the assignment operators in action, Listing 8.4 demonstrates the more commonly used assignment operators. The usage of the Visual Basic .NET assignment operators should be pretty exciting if you are coming from a Visual Basic 6 background.

LISTING 8.4 Using Assignment Operators to Test Values

VB.NET

```
Private Sub testOperators()

   Dim X As Integer = 50
   Dim Y As Integer = 10

   Dim z As Integer

   ' Addition - returns 60
   X += Y
   MessageBox.Show(X)

   ' Subtraction - returns 50
   X -= Y
   MessageBox.Show(X)

   ' Multiplication - returns 500
   X *= Y
   MessageBox.Show(X)

   ' Division - returns 50
   X /= Y
   MessageBox.Show(X)

   ' Assignment - returns FALSE
   MessageBox.Show((X = Y).ToString())

End Sub
```

C#

```
private void testOperators()
{

   int X = 50;
   int Y = 10;

   // Addition - returns 60
   MessageBox.Show((X += Y).ToString());

   // Subtraction - returns 50
   MessageBox.Show((X -= Y).ToString());
```

LISTING 8.4 continued

```
    // Multiplication - returns 500
    MessageBox.Show((X *= Y).ToString());

    // Division - returns 50
    MessageBox.Show((X /= Y).ToString());

    // Assignment - returns 10
    MessageBox.Show((X = Y).ToString());

}
```

You'll notice that the Visual Basic .NET code is slightly different from the C# code in the way the operator is handled. In Visual Basic .NET, you must explicitly use the right side of the operator in an expression, so placing all the code in the single `MessageBox` statement doesn't work.

Comparison Operators

Comparison operators evaluate the expression on the right side of the equal sign and return a Boolean true or false based on the comparison of the expressions. Comparison operators also can be grouped in the relational and equality operators group. In all cases, a Boolean true or false is returned to the expression you're attempting to evaluate. Table 8.4 lists the comparison operators in Visual Basic .NET and C# and their descriptions.

TABLE 8.4 Comparison Operators in Visual Basic .NET and C#

Visual Basic .NET	*C#*	*Description*
<	<	Less than
<=	<=	Less than or equal to
>	>	Greater than
>=	>=	Greater than or equal to
=	==	Equal to
<>	!=	Not equal to
`Is`	==	Compare two objects
`TypeOf`	`is`	Compare object reference types
=	==	Compare two strings
&	+	Concatenate Strings
`AndAlso`	&&	Short-circuited Boolean AND
`OrElse`	||	Short-circuited Boolean OR

TABLE 8.4 continued

Visual Basic .NET	*C#*	*Description*
`And`	`&&`	Logical AND
`Or`	`||`	Logical OR
`Not`	`!`	Logical NOT

To see a few of the operators in action, read Listing 8.5 and notice the inline comments that explain why the `MessageBox` prompts will or will not display.

LISTING 8.5 Using Comparison Operators to Test Variable Values

VB.NET

```
Private Sub testOperators()

   Dim X As Integer = 50
   Dim Y As Integer = 10

   If X < Y Then
      ' This never shows, X is NOT less then Y
      MessageBox.Show("X greater than Y")
   End If

   Dim s1 As String = "Bob"
   Dim s2 As String = "bob"

   If s1 = s2 Then
      ' This never shows, Bob does not equal bob
      MessageBox.Show("s1 = s2")
   End If

   If s1 = "Bob" OrElse s2 = "Bob" Then
      ' This shows, s1 or s2 = Bob
      MessageBox.Show("s1 or s2 = Bob")
   End If

End Sub
```

C#

```
private void testOperators()
{

   int X = 50;
   int Y = 10;
```

LISTING 8.5 continued

```
        if (X < Y)
        {
           // This never shows, X is NOT less then Y
           MessageBox.Show("X greater than Y");
        }

        string s1 = "Bob";
        string s2 = "bob";

        if (s1 == s2)
        {
           // This never shows, Bob does not equal bob
           MessageBox.Show("s1 = s2");
        }

        if (s1 == "Bob" || s2 == "Bob")
        {
           // This shows, s1 or s2 = Bob
           MessageBox.Show("s1 or s2 = Bob");
        }
    }
```

You can see that when dealing with strings, checking the equality in C# uses the == operator, whereas Visual Basic .NET uses the = operator.

Using Decision Structures

Now that you have an understanding of the common data types and common operators, you can dig into using decision structures. *Decision structures* are program elements that control the flow of your application based on decisions made about the value of variables or events fired by the user.

Table 8.5 lists the decision structures by group in Visual Basic .NET and C# and gives the keywords that you'll use when implementing decision structures in your code.

TABLE 8.5 Summary of Decision Structures in Visual Basic .NET and C#

Type	*Visual Basic .NET*	*C#*
Selection	`Select Case`	`switch`
Decision	`If...Then`	`if...else`
Looping	`While`	`Do`

8

TABLE 8.5 continued

Type	*Visual Basic .NET*	*C#*
	`Do`	`While`
	`Do Until`	
	`Loop While`	
	`Loop Until`	
Looping structure or collections	`For` `For Each`	`for` `foreach`

We'll go through each of these decision structures so that you can see how to implement them and learn the syntactical difference between Visual Basic .NET and C# when using decision structures.

Using `Select Case` and `Switch`

The `Select Case` statement in Visual Basic .NET and the `switch` statement in C# are the most commonly used decision structures when you have to perform a logical test on multiple variables and act on the true or false returned by the test.

The syntax for the `switch` statement is

```
switch (expression)
{
   case constant-expression:
      statement
      jump-statement
   [default:
      statement
      jump-statement]
}
```

In the `switch` statement, the expression being evaluated is compared to the constant expressions in the `case` clauses. Within each `case` clause, if the expression being evaluated matches the constant expression, you can use a jump statement to transfer control outside of the `switch` statement or inside the `switch` statement. Valid jump statements in C# are listed here:

- `break`—Terminates the closest loop or conditional statement in which it appears. When a `break` statement is hit, control passes to the next valid statement in the expression.
- `continue`—Passes control to the next iteration of the enclosing iteration statement. This is used in looping and `for each` statements.

- `default`—If the expression being evaluated in a `switch` statement doesn't match any of the corresponding `case` constant expressions, the `default` label is used. If there's no `default` label, execution continues after the `switch` statement.
- `goto`—Transfers control to a label within the looping or `switch` statement.
- `return`—Terminates execution of the executing method and passes control back to the original caller.

Although every type of jump statement isn't always used in a switch statement, they can be. The commented code in Listing 8.6 uses the `switch` statement to check a value of a variable.

LISTING 8.6 Using the `switch` Statement to Evaluate an Expression

C#

```
string strName = "Gates";
switch(strName)
{
   case "Ballmer":
      // perform an action if the last name is Ballmer
      break;
   case "Jobs":
      // perform an action if the last name is Jobs
      break;
   case "Gates":
      // perform an action if the last name is Gates
      MessageBox.Show("Gates has been entered");
      break;
   default:
      MessageBox.Show("No Valid Names Entered");
      break;
}
```

In Listing 8.6, the `MessageBox` prompt is displayed when the case `"Gates"` is hit because the value of the `strName` variable is set to `"Gates"`.

The `Select Case` statement in Visual Basic .NET works the same way as the `switch` statement in C#. The syntax for `Select Case` is

```
SelectStatement ::=
   Select [ Case ] Expression StatementTerminator
   [ CaseStatement+ ]
   [ CaseElseStatement ]
   End Select StatementTerminator
```

```
CaseStatement ::=
   Case CaseClauses StatementTerminator
   [ Block ]

CaseClauses ::=
   CaseClause |
   CaseClauses , CaseClause

CaseClause ::=
   [ Is ] ComparisonOperator Expression |
   Expression [ To Expression ]

ComparisonOperator ::= = | < > | < | > | = > | = <

CaseElseStatement ::=
   Case Else StatementTerminator
   [ Block ]
```

You can see that `Select Case` has a few more options than `switch`. These options give you additional flexibility when comparing values and ranges of values. In Listing 8.7, the `Select Case` statement is used to compare different numeric values.

LISTING 8.7 Using `Select Case` to Evaluate an Expression

VB.NET

```
Dim intX As Integer = 50

Select Case intX

   Case Is > 51
      ' perform
   Case 43 Or 57 Or 98
      ' perform an action
   Case 59
      MessageBox.Show("You hit 50")

   Case Else
      ' this is the default if no value is hit

End Select
```

In Listing 8.7, you can see the different uses of `Case Is` and `Or` within a `Case` statement. Based on the value of the expression, the corresponding code in the `Case` statement executes. When an expression evaluates to true and the code for the `Case` statement executes, the next line of code that executes is the line immediately following the `End Select` statement. Like `default` in the `switch` statement, `Case Else` is the optional catchall statement if none of the `Case` expressions evaluates to true.

Using If...Then Statements

You can use `If...Then` statements to execute blocks of code based on the Boolean value of a condition. `If...Then` statements are similar to `switch` and `Select Case` statements, but are better used when the available expressions being evaluated is limited. The syntax for `If...Then` statements in Visual Basic .NET is

```
If condition [ Then ]
   [ statements  ]
[ ElseIf elseifcondition [ Then ]
   [ elseifstatements ] ]
[ Else
   [ elsestatements ] ]
End If
```

The corresponding C# syntax is

```
if (expression)
   statement1
[else
   statement2]
```

Notice that the C# code doesn't actually use the `Then` statement. The `Then` statement is unique to Visual Basic .NET. Visual Basic .NET also uses `ElseIf` as one word, whereas C# just evaluates another `if` statement with the `else` keyword.

If the expression in an `If` or `Else` statement evaluates to true, the code block executes and control is passed to the line of code immediately following the end of the `If` block. Listing 8.8 gives an example of equivalent `If...Then` statements in Visual Basic .NET and C#.

LISTING 8.8 Using an `If...Then` Statement to Evaluate an Expression

VB.NET

```
Dim intX As Integer = 10

If intX > 11 Then
   MessageBox.Show("intX > 11")
ElseIf intX < 5 Then
   MessageBox.Show("intX < 5")
Else
   MessageBox.Show("Fallback code block")
End If
```

LISTING 8.8 continued

C#

```
int intX = 10;

if (intX > 11)
   MessageBox.Show("intX > 11");
else if (intX < 5)
   MessageBox.Show("intX < 5");
else
   MessageBox.Show("Fallback code block");
```

In the C# code, notice that the expression being evaluated in the `if` statement must be enclosed in parentheses. Each `else` statement is followed by another `if` statement enclosed in parentheses, and each code block is a statement ending with a semicolon. In Visual Basic .NET, you don't need to use parentheses to evaluate the expression in the `If` statement. `If` statements can also be nested in both Visual Basic .NET and C#, so if an expression evaluates to true, you can have additional nested `If` statements within the code block that executes the statement. There's no limit to nesting `If` statements, but for readability, you don't want to have too many levels of nested `Ifs`. As I mentioned earlier, if you have many expressions to evaluate, you should consider using a `Select Case` or `switch` statement, which is easier to understand and debug.

Using Looping Structures

Looping structures enable you to perform an action any number of times based on a predetermined variable or until a condition is met. The different looping structures and implementation differences can be broken down as follows:

- `While` in Visual Basic .NET and `while` in C# execute a block of statements while a condition is true.
- `Do...Loop` structures in Visual Basic .NET and the `do` structure in C# execute a block of statements until a condition is satisfied.
- `For...Next` structures in Visual Basic .NET and the `for` structure in C# execute a block of statements a specified number of times.
- `For...Each` structures in Visual Basic .NET and the `foreach` structure in C# execute a block of statements for each item in a collection.

Listing 8.9 demonstrates the `While`, `Do`, and `For Next` loops in Visual Basic .NET and C#. Read the commented code to get an idea of what's happening, and why, when the loop structures execute.

LISTING 8.9 Using Looping Structures in Visual Basic .NET and C#

VB.NET

```
' Use a while loop to perform an action while a condition is true

Dim intX As Integer = 1

While intX < 6
   ' Perform this code while the value of intX is < 6
   intX += 1
End While


' Use a do loop until the while condition is met

Dim intX As Integer
Dim intY As Integer

Do
   ' perform this code block while the value of intY < 10
   intX = intY + 1
Loop While intY < 10


' Use a for loop to repeat the same code block
' until a value is hit, in this case 5

Dim intX As Integer

For intX = 1 To 5
   Console.WriteLine(intX)
Next intX
```

C#

```
// Use a while loop to perform an action while a condition is true
int intX = 1;
while (intX < 6)
   {
   // Perform this code while the value of intX is < 6
   intX++;
   }


// Use a do loop until the while condition is met

int intX;
int intY;

do
```

LISTING 8.9 continued

```
        {
        // perform this code block while the value of intY < 10
        intX = intY++;
        }
    while(intY < 10);


    // Use a for loop to repeat the same code block
    // until a value is hit, in this case 5
    for (int intX = 1; intX <= 5; intX++)
        Console.WriteLine(intX);
```

In several lessons this week, you'll use the various looping structures as you learn more about Visual Studio .NET and the language features of Visual Basic .NET and C#.

Summary

Today you learned the basics of the Visual Basic .NET and C# languages. You learned about variables, how to declare them, and what access modifiers you can use to set the scope of a variable in your applications. You also learned about the common operators that you'll use in all your applications. You finished by learning the basics of decision structures, and how each type of decision structure differs based on the task you're trying to accomplish.

Today's lesson is by no means a reference on the Visual Basic .NET or C# language—there's much more to learn. As you work through this week and next, you'll learn more as you go along, so use today as a starting point in becoming familiar with the syntax and slight differences between C# and Visual Basic .NET.

Q&A

Q What are the caveats, if any, when working with C# versus Visual Basic .NET?

A Visual Basic .NET is a very developer-friendly language, and many of the features of the language are what make it the most widely used programming language in the world. If you're going to develop in C# and have never programmed in C or Java, remember that the language is case sensitive, statements must be terminated by a semicolon, and expressions must be enclosed in parentheses when they're being evaluated. Other than those three items, the rest should be pretty straightforward as you learn to use the language.

Q I'm looking at the help file for C#, and I see unsigned numbers, such as Uint16 and Uint32. Why didn't you mention them in your discussion on data types?

A I tried to stick with the CLS-compliant data types today. C# supports unsigned integers, which are part of the C# language, but aren't part of the common language specification. That means you can use unsigned numeric data types in your code, but they won't be CLS compliant.

Q You said there was more to learn. Where should I go to get more details about the language specifics of C# or Visual Basic .NET?

A *Sams Teach Yourself Visual Basic .NET in 21 Days* and *Sams Teach Yourself C# in 21 Days* are good books about the Visual Basic .NET and C# languages. They both cover variables, operators, classes, and objects in most of the first two weeks of lessons. There are many books on the market that have Visual Basic .NET or C# on the cover, but if you decide to buy one, just make sure that it doesn't wrap several major language features into a single lesson. In *Sams Teach Yourself C# in 21 Days*, each day in the first week is broken down into a major language feature, and the second week covers more advanced object-oriented topics, which I think is great. I highly recommend that book.

Quiz

1. By setting the _____________ of a variable, you can dictate where it can be accessible within an application or assembly.
2. True or False: C# can handle loops faster than Visual Basic .NET because less code must be written.
3. I can simplify my addition code by using the new _____________ operators in Visual Basic .NET.
4. A ___________ loop processes a set of statements until a condition is true.

Quiz Answers

1. Scope
2. False. Both C# and Visual Basic .NET compile to the same IL in most cases, making the performance for any function almost identical.
3. Concatenation
4. `While` loop

Exercises

Because there's way too much to cover in one day, these exercises have you do some additional reading in the .NET Framework SDK.

1. Using the Dynamic Help in the Visual Studio .NET IDE, look up the `System.Convert` and the `System.String` namespaces. Study the new conversion and string manipulation features available to you in the FCL. These are very important classes to become familiar with.
2. Look up *arrays* in Dynamic Help and understand the syntax of arrays and how you can use them to store information.
3. Create a new Visual Studio .NET Windows Forms application. Using what you learned today about operators and decision structures, copy some of the code from the listings into the click event of a button control, and step through the code using the debugging techniques you learned about yesterday. This will help you understand what state the variables are in when you're using the different operators and decision structures.

WEEK 2

DAY 9

Using Namespaces in .NET

On Day 1, when you were introduced to the .NET Framework, we talked about the two core components that make it up. The first core component of the .NET Framework is the common language runtime. The common language runtime handles all the internals of running the .NET Framework, such as memory management, security, and type checking. The second core component is the Framework Class Library (FCL). The FCL contains the actual implementation types that you'll use in your applications. Today, you get a better understanding of what the FCL is made up of and how to effectively use namespaces and classes in your applications. You learn

- What a namespace is
- What the common namespaces are in the FCL
- How to find namespaces in the .NET Framework SDK
- Which of the namespaces in the FCL are responsible for what type of functionality
- How to reference namespaces in your Visual Basic .NET and C# classes
- How to program against namespaces; specifically, you learn about the `System.IO` namespace and the `Environment` class of the `System` namespace

What Are Namespaces?

Namespaces are groups of classes, structures, interfaces, enumerations, and delegates, organized in a logical hierarchy by function, that enable you to access the core functionality you need in your applications.

Note

> The `System` namespace contains all the base types you learned about yesterday, such as Int16, Int32, Decimal, and Short.

Each namespace in the FCL can contain multiple namespaces, or they can contain classes that expose properties and methods that you call in your applications. The namespaces within the FCL are grouped by the functionality they provide, which makes it very easy to find what you're looking for. It can be compared to a phone book, in which you look under B for *bugs*, and are led to exterminators, which helps you find all the information you need to squash all the bugs. Similarly, you look for common words in what a namespace offers, and you'll most likely find the information you need to implement the task you're trying to accomplish.

To separate the top-level namespace from the second-level namespace from the class to the actual property or method, the FCL uses the `.` (period) notation to differentiate the hierarchy. For example, if you want to work with data, and you're using SQL Server, you'll find the `System.Data.SqlClient` namespace. In the `System.Data.SqlClient` namespace are the `SqlDataReader` class and the `SqlDataAdapter` class, among many others. When you reference these object in code, you use the following syntax:

VB.NET

```
Dim rdr as System.Data.SqlClient.SqlDataReader
```

C#

```
System.Data.SqlClient.SqlDataReader rdr;
```

Note

> Namespaces are grouped by functionality. Because a namespace may cross over several different physical assemblies, you can't assume that each type within a specific namespace is in the same physical assembly.

All through Week 1, you used the `System.Web` namespace, the `System.Web.UI` namespace, the `System.Windows.Forms` namespace, and the `System.Windows.Forms.Design` namespace. Each namespace gave you all the base functionality you needed to create ASP.NET and Windows Forms applications. Each time you referenced a form object, either on the Windows Form or the Web Form, you were referencing a type in one of the namespaces I just mentioned. So, you're using namespaces and their types to accomplish everything you need to do when developing .NET applications.

There are a couple things to note about cthe naming conventions you use when working with namespaces:

- Namespaces supplied by Microsoft are prefixed with `System` or `Microsoft` (for example, `Microsoft.VisualBasic` and `System.IO`). The `System` prefix means the namespace has come from the .NET team at Microsoft, and the `Microsoft` prefix means the namespace has come from one of the product groups. An example is `Microsoft.Office.Excel`.
- Third-party namespaces are prefixed by the name of the company that distributes the namespace; for example, `Infragistics.UltraWinGrid`.

When you get to Day 14, "Components and .NET," you learn how to create your own namespaces when writing components. You also see how you can use your own naming convention to avoid name collision with other namespaces in the FCL or third parties.

Finding the Information You Need About Namespaces

Knowing that hundreds of namespaces and housands of classes make up the FCL, you need to know what namespaces offer you the functionality you need to complete the job at hand.

You need to know how to navigate the .NET Framework SDK to find the information you need. But first, let's look at the common namespaces in the FCL and the functionality they offer. This will help you know what to look for when we get to the SDK.

- `System.Data`—This namespace contains the core data access functionality for SQL Server and OLE DB data stores. You learn how to use this namespace tomorrow when we get into accessing data with ADO.NET.
- `System.XML`—The class namespace core XML processing functionality. We cover this namespace on Day 12, "Accessing XML in .NET."
- `System.DirectoryServices`—This namespace gives you programmatic access to all Active Directory objects.
- `System.Messaging`—This namespace exposes Microsoft Message Queue functionality to your applications.

- `System.Globalization`—This namespace gives you the ability to write internationally aware applications. We cover this namespace on Day 15, "Writing International Applications."
- `System.Net`—This namespace supports interfaces for sending and receiving data over the network wire.
- `System.Collections`—This namespace includes support for arrays, lists, dictionaries, and hash tables.
- `System.IO`—This namespace supports stream, file, and directory access functionality. You learn how to use this namespace later today.
- `System.Text`—This namespace provides character encoding, character conversion, and string manipulation functionality.
- `System.Text.RegularExpressions`—This namespace contains full regular expression syntax support.
- `System.Threading`—This namespace provides multithreading support. You learn how to use this namespace on Day 13, "XML Web Services in .NET."
- `System.Reflection`—This namespace gives you programmatic access to assembly type information.
- `System.Drawing`—This namespace gives you access to all the GDI+ drawing capabilities, which are wrappers around the GDI COM interface that Windows uses to paint.
- `System.Windows.Forms`—This namespace enables you to write Windows Forms applications.
- `System.Runtime.InteropServices`—This namespace supports access to COM types. You use this namespace on Day 13.
- `System.Runtime.Serialization`—This namespace supports serialization and deserialization of objects. Serialization and Web services are covered on Day 14.
- `System.Security`—This namespace provides access to the underlying security infrastructure that the .NET Framework runs on top of.
- `System.Web`—This namespace supports the core functionality in ASP.NET, Web Forms, Web server management, and HTTP support.
- `System.Web.Services`—This namespace supports the creation of SOAP-based XML Web services on the client and the server. This is covered in detail on Day 14.

As you can see, there are many top-level namespaces, and the list I provided is only a partial one. I also mentioned that these are the common namespaces. Understanding what each namespace can do for you makes them all equally important, so being familiar with the names helps you know where to look in the SDK when you actually need to use something you've never used before.

Searching the .NET Framework SDK

The .NET Framework SDK and the Visual Studio .NET help file are designed to give you quick and easy access to the information you need to use Visual Studio .NET. The help file is broken down by tasks; for example, Working with Data, and Deploying Applications. Each help topic has a hyperlink on the bottom of the help page that leads you to the namespace where the class you are working with exists or to further reading on the topic.

To test this, open the help file for Visual Studio .NET. After it's opened, you should see tabs across the bottom left of the help screen that say Contents, Index, Search, and Favorites. Click the Index tab, and type **`security`** in the Search box. Your results should look something like Figure 9.1.

FIGURE 9.1
Searching the help file for security.

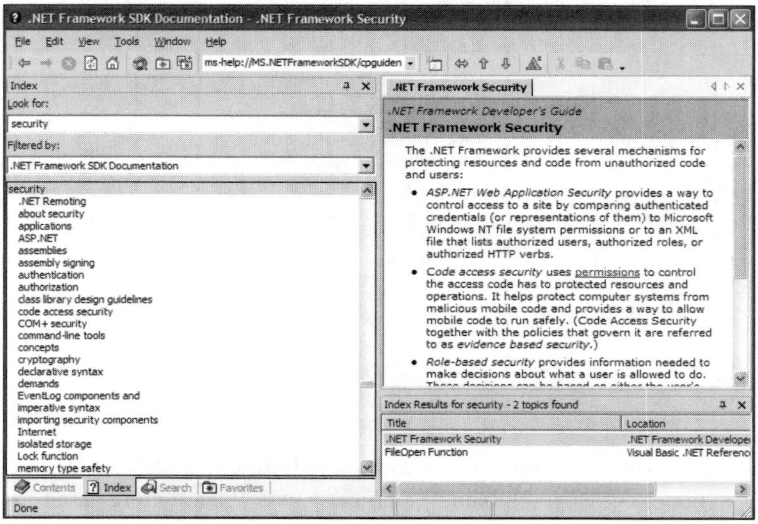

As you can see, a bunch of topics appear for *Security*. If you click the first topic, *.NET Framework namespaces*, you'll see links to all the topics that cover security in the .NET Framework. Doing searches like this helps you understand where things are located in the .NET Framework. Next, do a search for *data* or *collection*, and click around to become familiar with how the help file is cross-referenced with the SDK and samples.

> **Tip**
>
> If you don't see the same tabs in the .NET Framework SDK as Figure 9.1 displays, select View, Navigation from the main menu in the SDK and you can customize what tabs are visible.
>
> If you haven't disabled Dynamic Help in the Visual Studio .NET IDE, you can quickly search for items within the IDE, which you saw in Day 2, "Introduction to Visual Studio .NET."

If you already think you know the namespace you need, you can go directly to the Reference section of the .NET Framework class library in the SDK. Figure 9.2 shows you how to navigate to find the list of every namespace and class in the FCL.

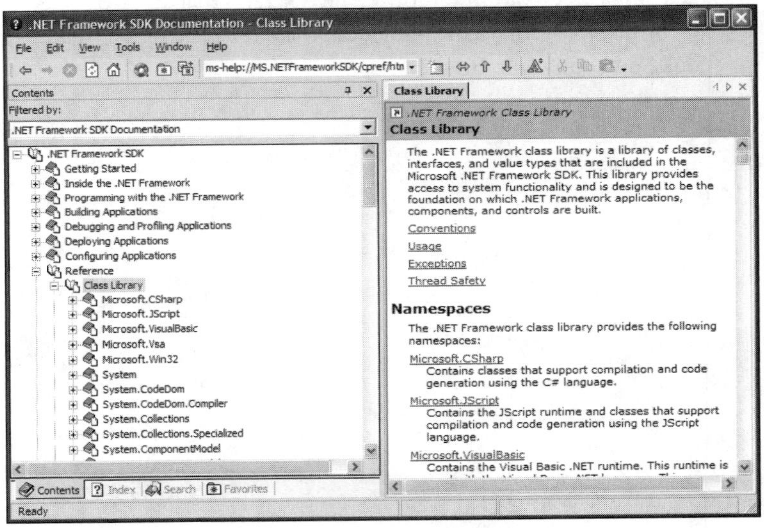

FIGURE 9.2
Navigating to the FCL Reference section in the .NET SDK.

So, now you can see two ways to easily figure out where namespaces and classes are and how to get help on them. Later today, you'll learn more about using the help file. Throughout the rest of this week and next week, you'll reference the SDK help file to do further reading and get a better understanding of where things are in the FCL.

Using Namespaces in Your Applications

Each time you create a new application using Visual Studio .NET, default namespaces are added to the application based on the default functionality of the project type you selected. For example, if you create a Windows Forms application, the `System.Windows.Forms` namespace is automatically added to your project. To see what's added by default to each project you create, you can drill into the References node of the Solution Explorer. An example of the references for a new C# Windows Forms application is shown in Figure 9.3.

FIGURE 9.3

The default references for a C# Windows Forms application.

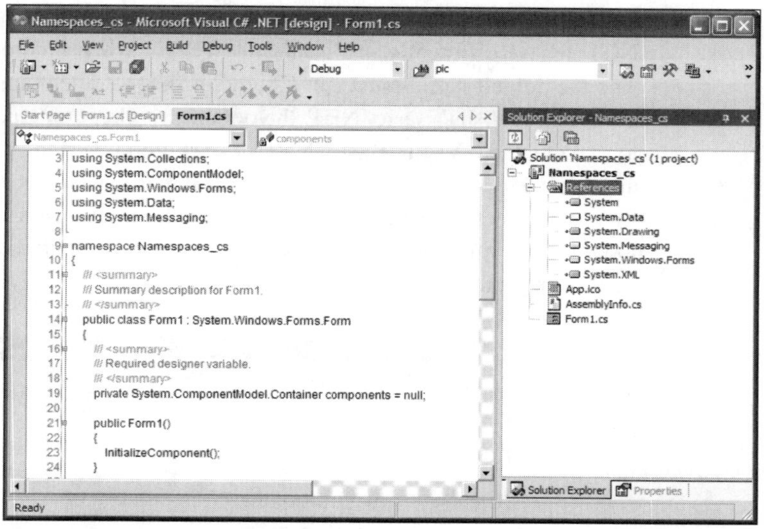

By adding references by default, you can use the `Imports` statement in Visual Basic .NET classes or the `using` statement in C# classes to reference the namespaces that are referenced in your project. That means you can avoid using the fully qualified name every time you're trying to use an object.

However, you can't use the `Imports` or `using` statement on a namespace or class without it first being referenced in the project. So, if you're trying to use a namespace that's not referenced by default, you must add a reference manually. Then you can use the `Imports` or `using` statement to access the object.

To break this down, work through the following steps to see how referencing namespaces matters:

1. Create a new Windows Forms application and call it Namespaces_vb or Namespaces_cs, depending on whether you're using Visual Basic .NET or C#. I refer to this project as the Namespaces project for the rest of this section.
2. On the default `Form1`, double-click the form and scroll to the very top of the class file. If you created a C# application, you'll see the following items:

```
using System;
using System.Drawing;
using System.Collections;
```

```
using System.ComponentModel;
using System.Windows.Forms;
using System.Data;
```

If you created a Visual Basic .NET application, you'll see no `Imports` statements at the top of your class file for the default `Form1`. This is because C# and Visual Basic .NET behave differently in Visual Studio .NET when it comes to how they reference the default namespaces. In C#, the `using` statement appears at the top of each class file. In Visual Basic .NET, the defaults are kept on a per-project basis. If you've created a Visual Basic .NET project, you can right-click the project name and select Properties from the contextual menu. When the Properties page pops up for your project, select the Imports node under the Common Properties tree view node. Figure 9.4 shows the default `Imports` statements that appear on each class for this project.

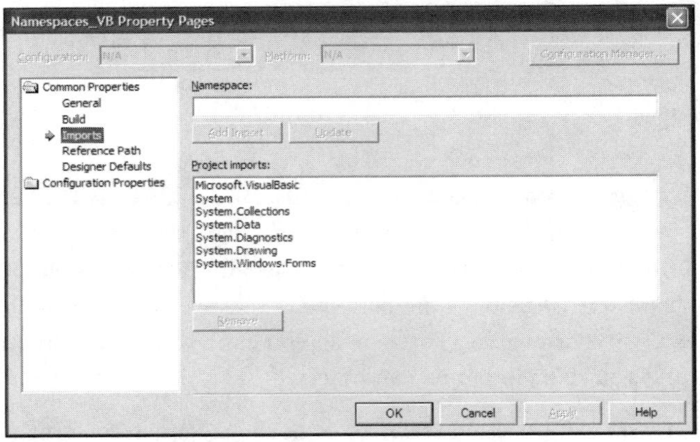

FIGURE 9.4

The default `Imports` *options for a Visual Basic .NET Windows Forms application.*

From this properties page, you can also add additional namespaces that you want to include in your class files for the project you're working on.

When you're writing an application and realize that a namespace you need isn't added, you can add additional namespace references to your application by right-clicking the References node in the Solution Explorer and selecting Add Reference from the pop-up contextual menu. As a test, you need to reference a type from a namespace that isn't added by default to a new project. To demonstrate this, you'll attempt to write some code that references the `System.Messaging` namespace.

In the default form of the Namespaces project you created earlier, double-click the form to get to the code-behind file's `Form1_Load` event. In the `Form1_Load` event, type the following code:

VB.NET

```
Dim m as MessageQueue = New MessageQueue()
```

C#

```
MessageQueue m = new MessageQueue();
```

Notice that the `MessageQueue` object didn't appear in the auto-list members options when you were typing in the `Form1_Load` event. To make this work, you must do two things:

- Add a reference to the `System.Messaging` namespace to your application
- Reference the `System.Messaging` namespace using an `Imports` or `using` statement at the top of your class file

To add a reference to your application, do the following:

1. Right-click the References node of your project in the Solution Explorer.
2. Select Add Reference from the pop-up contextual menu. The Add Reference dialog shown in Figure 9.5 should pop up.

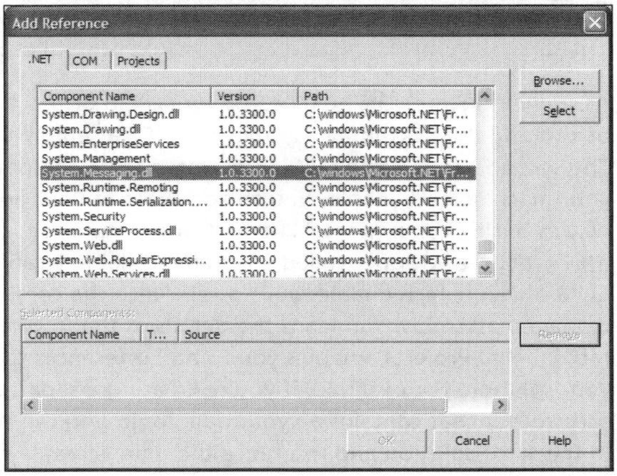

FIGURE 9.5
The Add Reference dialog box.

3. Scroll down on the .NET tab until you see System.Messaging.Dll in the list. Select this assembly and click the Select button. You should now see the `System.Messaging.Dll` in the Selected Components list view.
4. Click the OK button.
5. In your code-behind file for `Form1`, alias the `System.Messaging` namespace with the `Imports` statement in Visual Basic .NET or the `using` statement in C#. Figures 9.6 and 9.7 show you what your C# and Visual Basic .NET solutions should look

like when the `System.Messaging.Dll` is added to your solution and aliased in your class file.

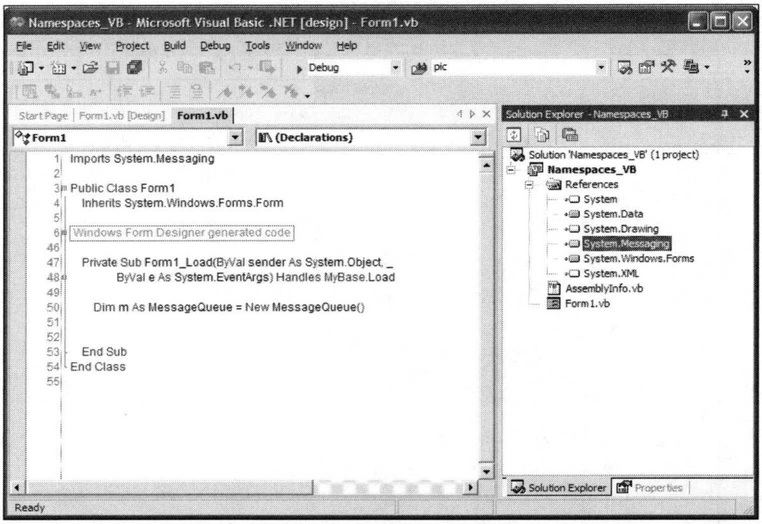

FIGURE 9.6
Visual Basic .NET solution after referencing a new `System.Messaging.dll` *assembly.*

Note

As shown in Figure 9.6, you used the first tab of the Add Reference dialog box to add the `System.Messaging.dll` .NET assembly to your application. The second tab, labeled COM, lists all the COM components registered on your machine and enables you to add them to your application in the same way as a .NET component. When a COM component is added, Visual Studio .NET creates a wrapper called a runtime callable wrapper (RCW) around the COM object, which enables you to reference the component as if it were a managed assembly. You learn the details of the RCW on Day 14. The third tab, labeled Projects, enables you to add references to other applications in your solution. For example, if you're creating a separate assembly for a data access layer that contains all your data logic, you can work on both projects in the same solution and reference the data access layer project in the active project.

Notice that you can now declare new `MessageQueue` objects, and you have the full support of Visual Studio .NET with auto-list members.

Tip

If you're a Visual Basic 6 developer, you can think of the Add Reference dialog in Visual Studio .NET as analogous to the Add Reference dialog in Visual

Basic 6. They accomplish the same thing: They enable you to reference types that aren't part of your application. The underlying difference between them is that when you referenced a new type in Visual Basic 6, the auto list members of the type were the result of the Visual Basic 6 IDE reading information supplied by the COM type library. In .NET, the Visual Studio .NET IDE reads information from the metadata of the assembly by using reflection, which you can learn more about by looking up the `System.Reflection` namespace.

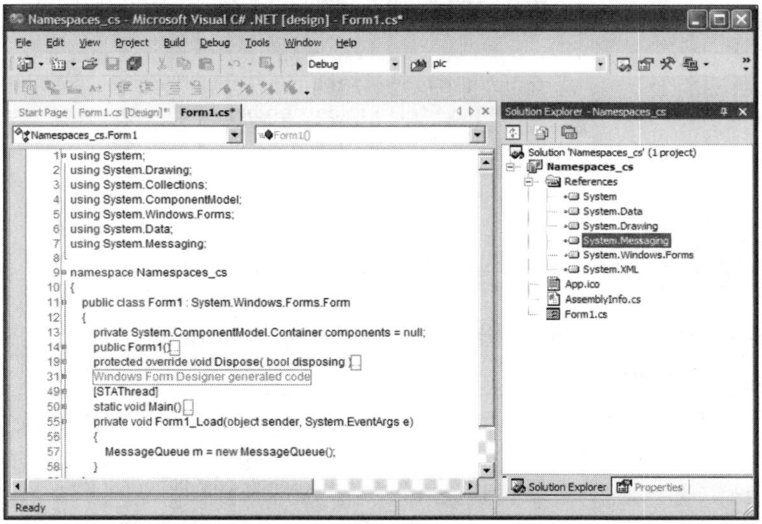

FIGURE 9.7
C# solution after referencing a new `System.Messaging.dll` *assembly.*

You now have an understanding of what namespaces are and how you can use them in your application. You also know how to alias namespaces in your classes and import new namespaces into your solution. Next, you learn about the `Environment` class of the `System` namespace and the `IO` namespace of the `System` namespace.

Working with Your Environment

The `Environment` class of the `System` namespace has properties and methods that enable you to interact with the environment that your application is running in. It also helps you retrieve specific information about the user who is currently logged on to the system that your applications are running on.

If you wrote applications using Visual Basic 6, you know that not many ways were built into the language to get information about the operating system, the version of either the

OS or the version of Visual Basic, or even information about what the current user's name was. In .NET, the `Environment` class gives you more information than you need.

In this section, you learn how to retrieve information about the current state of the operating system and your application. You also learn how to get special operating system and user information, such as where special folders such as My Documents, Application Data, and the Windows directory are located.

Note

> Getting specific information about the logged-in user, such as folder names and locations, is extremely important with Windows 2000 and greater. The idea of a mobile user who has system folders, such as My Documents, located on a server instead of the local machine is common now. The more companies move to thinner clients, the more likely it is that the end user won't have these folders on her local machine, so you need a way to determine where these folders are located. The `Environment` class helps you do just that.

The properties of the `Environment` class are listed in Table 9.1.

TABLE 9.1 The Properties in the `System.Environment` Class

Property	*Description*
`CommandLine`	Gets the command line for this process.
`CurrentDirectory`	Gets and sets the fully qualified path of the current directory; that is, the directory from which this process starts.
`ExitCode`	Gets or sets the exit code of the process.
`HasShutdownStarted`	Indicates whether the common language runtime is shutting down.
`MachineName`	Gets the NetBIOS name of this local computer.
`NewLine`	Gets the newline string defined for this environment.
`OSVersion`	Gets an `OperatingSystem` object that contains the current platform identifier and version number.
`StackTrace`	Gets current stack trace information.
`SystemDirectory`	Gets the fully qualified path of the system directory.
`TickCount`	Gets the number of milliseconds elapsed since the system started.
`UserDomainName`	Gets the network domain name associated with the current user.
`UserInteractive`	Gets a value indicating whether the current process is running in user interactive mode.
`UserName`	Gets the username of the person who started the current thread.

TABLE 9.1 continued

Property	*Description*
`Version`	Gets a `Version` object that describes the major, minor, build, and revision numbers of the common language runtime.
`WorkingSet`	Gets the amount of physical memory mapped to the process context.

Although there are times when you might need to retrieve specific information about environment variables, it might be more common to need to know what logical drives are on a system and the names and locations of the special folders, such as My Documents. You can get this type of information by using the methods of the `Environment` class. Table 9.2 lists the common methods you can use to get specific information about the current environment and the current user.

TABLE 9.2 The Methods in the `System.Environment` Class

Method	*Description*
`Exit`	Terminates this process and gives the underlying operating system the specified exit code.
`ExpandEnvironmentVariables`	Replaces the name of each environment variable embedded in the specified string with the string equivalent of the value of the variable, and then returns the resulting string.
`GetCommandLineArgs`	Returns a string array containing the command-line arguments for the current process.
`GetEnvironmentVariable`	Returns the value of the specified environment variable.
`GetEnvironmentVariables`	Returns all environment variables and their values.
`GetFolderPath`	Gets the path to the system special folder identified by the specified enumeration.
`GetLogicalDrives`	Returns an array of string containing the names of the logical drives on the current computer.

Note

Several methods of the `Environment` class return a string array of information. Whenever a description of a method says something like "Returns a collection" or "Returns an array," you must know the correct way to declare the variable that will hold the returning data, and you must iterate through the data to get each piece of information. The code you write in Listing 9.2 uses the `For Each` method in Visual Basic .NET and the `foreach` method in C# to iterate through the data returned in the string array. The string array was declared by simply adding parentheses after the Visual Basic .NET variable declaration or brackets after the C# variable declaration, like this:

```
Dim myStringArray() as String
```

```
string[] myStringArray;
```

If you forget to add the brackets or parentheses, you'll get an error. Yesterday you learned how to deal with arrays in several different ways. You can refer to that lesson to refresh your memory on all the capabilities of arrays.

Creating the Environment Sample Application

To use the `Environment` class in real life, you're going to write a Windows Forms application that uses most of the properties and methods covered in Tables 9.1 and 9.2. This exercise is very important because you learn how to

- Use the properties and methods of the `Environment` class
- Declare an array and iterate through the items of an array
- Learn the basics of the `ListView` control—a very useful GUI control

Follow these steps to set up the new application. But before you start, look at Figure 9.8 to see what the end result of your form should look like.

1. Create a new Windows Forms application named Environment_Winforms.
2. On the default `form1`, change the following properties using the Properties window:

   `Name` = `mainForm`

   `Text` = `"Environment Settings"`

   `Font` = Tahoma, 10pt

   `StartupPosition` = `CenterScreen`

3. Next, drag a button from the Toolbox onto the form, and change these properties:

   `Name` = `GetEnvironment`

   `Text` = `"Get My Environment"`

4. Drag another button from the Toolbox onto the form, and change these properties:

   `Name` = `GetDrives`

   `Text` = `"Get Logical Drives"`

5. Drag another button from the Toolbox onto the form, and change these properties:

   `Name` = `GetSpecialFolders`

   `Text` = `"Get Special Folders"`

6. Drag a `ListView` object from the Toolbox onto the form, and change these properties:

   `Name` = `EnvironmentListView`

   `Anchor` = `Top, Left, Bottom, Right`

   `Columns` = Click the ellipses button that appears when you click the `Columns` property in the Properties window. The custom designer for adding columns to this list view pops up. Click the Add button on the custom designer twice, and change the `Text` property for the first column to `"Name"` by clicking on the first item on the left list box, which will be called `ColumnHeader1`. After you click the item on the left, you can change the `Text` property on the right side of the designer. Change the `Text` property for the second column to `"Description"`. Click OK to close the custom designer.

   `View` = `Details` (By selecting `Details`, the column headers for the list view are visible. Like using Windows Explorer or My Computer, if you're viewing large icons, small icons, or lists, you won't see the column headers.)

Your newly created `mainForm` should look like Figure 9.8.

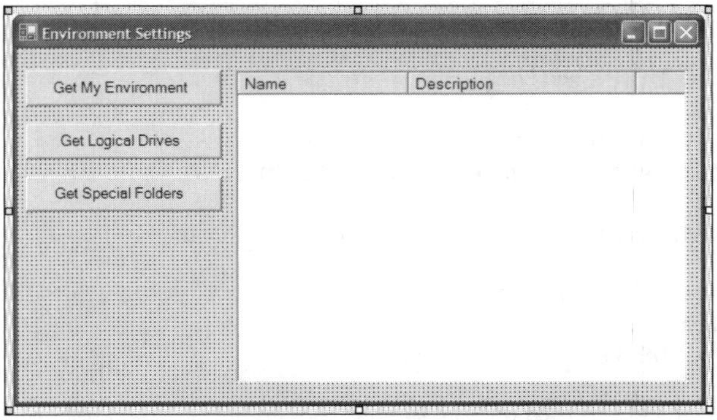

FIGURE 9.8
Environment_WinForms form after adding controls.

Using the Properties of the Environment Class

Now that you've set up the project, you can start writing the code to retrieve environment information. The first thing you'll do is add some code-behind for the Get My Environment button, which gets some of the properties of the `Environment` class listed in

Table 9.1. Double-click the Get My Environment button and add the following code-behind for the GetEnvironment_Click event shown in Listing 9.1.

LISTING 9.1 GetEnvironment_Click Event Code

VB.NET

```
Private Sub GetEnvironment_Click(ByVal sender As System.Object, _
   ByVal e As System.EventArgs) Handles GetEnvironment.Click

 ' Set the cursor to an hourglass
 Me.Cursor = Cursors.WaitCursor

 With EnvironmentListView

  ' Clear the ListView of any existing items
  .Items.Clear()

  ' Create a ListItem variable
  Dim lvi As ListViewItem

  ' Create a new instance of the ListItem variable
  ' and re-use it for each property you add to the ListView
  lvi = New ListViewItem()
  With lvi
   .Text = "Current Directory"
   .SubItems.Add(Environment.CurrentDirectory)
  End With
  .Items.Add(lvi)

  lvi = New ListViewItem()
  With lvi
   .Text = "Machine Name"
   .SubItems.Add(Environment.MachineName)
  End With
  .Items.Add(lvi)

  lvi = New ListViewItem()
  With lvi
   .Text = "OS Version"

   ' NOTE: Call the ToString method to convert the Number
   ' to a string variable for display
   .SubItems.Add(Environment.OSVersion.ToString)
  End With
  .Items.Add(lvi)

  lvi = New ListViewItem()
  With lvi
   .Text = "System Directory"
```

LISTING 9.1 continued

```
            .SubItems.Add(Environment.SystemDirectory)
        End With
        .Items.Add(lvi)

        lvi = New ListViewItem()
        With lvi
            .Text = "Ticks since last shutdown"
            .SubItems.Add(Environment.TickCount)
        End With
        .Items.Add(lvi)

        lvi = New ListViewItem()
        With lvi
            .Text = "User Domain Name"
            .SubItems.Add(Environment.UserDomainName)
        End With
        .Items.Add(lvi)

        lvi = New ListViewItem()
        With lvi
            .Text = "User Name"
            ' NOTE: Call the ToString method to convert the Number
            ' to a string variable for display
            .SubItems.Add(Environment.UserName)
        End With
        .Items.Add(lvi)

        lvi = New ListViewItem()
        With lvi
            .Text = "User Domain Name"
            .SubItems.Add(Environment.Version.ToString)
        End With
        .Items.Add(lvi)
    End With

    ' Set the cursor back to normal
    Me.Cursor = Cursors.Default

End Sub
```

C#

```
private void getEnvironment_Click(object sender, System.EventArgs e)
 {

   // Set the cursor to an hourglass
   this.Cursor = Cursors.WaitCursor;

   // Clear the ListView of any existing items
   EnvironmentListView.Items.Clear();
```

LISTING 9.1 continued

```
        // Create a ListItem variable
        ListViewItem lvi;

        // Create a new instance of the ListItem variable
        // and re-use it for each property you add to the ListView
        lvi = new ListViewItem();

        lvi.Text = "Current Directory";
        lvi.SubItems.Add(Environment.CurrentDirectory);
        EnvironmentListView.Items.Add(lvi);

        lvi = new ListViewItem();
        lvi.Text = "Machine Name";
        lvi.SubItems.Add(Environment.MachineName);
        EnvironmentListView.Items.Add(lvi);

        lvi = new ListViewItem();
        lvi.Text = "OS Version";
        lvi.SubItems.Add(Environment.OSVersion.ToString());
        EnvironmentListView.Items.Add(lvi);

        lvi = new ListViewItem();
        lvi.Text = "System Directory";
        lvi.SubItems.Add(Environment.SystemDirectory);
        EnvironmentListView.Items.Add(lvi);

        lvi = new ListViewItem();
        lvi.Text = "Ticks since last shutdown";
        lvi.SubItems.Add(Environment.TickCount.ToString());
        EnvironmentListView.Items.Add(lvi);

        lvi = new ListViewItem();
        lvi.Text = "User Domain Name";
        lvi.SubItems.Add(Environment.UserDomainName);
        EnvironmentListView.Items.Add(lvi);

        lvi = new ListViewItem();
        lvi.Text = "User Name";
        lvi.SubItems.Add(Environment.UserName);
        EnvironmentListView.Items.Add(lvi);

        // Set the cursor back to normal
        this.Cursor = Cursors.Default;
        }
    }
```

If you press the F5 key to run the application and click the Get My Environment button, you should see something similar to Figure 9.9.

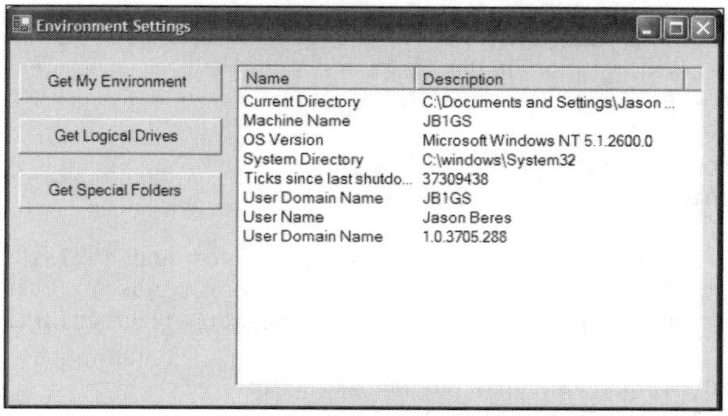

FIGURE 9.9
Output from the `GetEnvironment` *click.*

Here are some key points in the code you just wrote:

- You set the correct mouse cursor to the hourglass by setting the cursor with `Cursor = Cursors.WaitCursor`, and then back to the default cursor by calling `Cursor = Cursor.Default` after the procedure finishes.
- You created a `ListViewItem` variable called `lvi`. For each item you wanted to add to the `ListView` control, you created a new instance of the `ListView` item and set properties on it. The `Text` property is always the first column of the `ListView` control. To add additional columns, you use the `Add` method of the `SubItems` property. After you've added the `Text` and the `SubItems`, you call the `Add` method on the `ListView` to actually display the data. The following snippet does exactly that:

```
lvi.Text = "Current Directory";
lvi.SubItems.Add(Environment.CurrentDirectory);
EnvironmentListView.Items.Add(lvi);
```

- Each `SubItem` you added to the `ListViewItem` retrieved a property of the `Environment` class, such as `CurrentDirectory` or `UserName`.

Using the `GetLogicalDrives` Method

Next, you need to add some code to the click event for the Get Logical Drives button. Double-click the Get Logical Drive button on your form, and add the code shown in Listing 9.2 to the `GetDrives_Click` event that retrieves the drives for the system and displays them in the `ListView` control.

LISTING 9.2 Getting the Logical Drives of Your Environment

VB.NET

```
Private Sub GetDrives_Click(ByVal sender As System.Object, _
  ByVal e As System.EventArgs) Handles GetDrives.Click
```

LISTING 9.2 continued

```
    ' Set the cursor to an hourglass
    Me.Cursor = Cursors.WaitCursor

    ' Clear the ListView
    EnvironmentListView.Items.Clear()

    ' Declare a string array called logicalDrives and call the
    ' GetLogicalDrives method of the Environment class
    Dim logicalDrives As String() = Environment.GetLogicalDrives()

    ' Create a string variable so we can loop
    ' through the array using For Each
    Dim drive As String

    ' Create a ListView Item variable
    Dim lvi As ListViewItem

    ' Look for each drive variable in the logicalDrives string array
    For Each drive In logicalDrives
     With EnvironmentListView
      lvi = New ListViewItem()
      With lvi
       .Text = "Drive Letter"
       .SubItems.Add(drive)
      End With
      .Items.Add(lvi)
     End With
    Next drive

    ' Set the cursor back to normal
    Me.Cursor = Cursors.Default

End Sub
```

C#

```
private void getDrives_Click(object sender, System.EventArgs e)
 {

  // Set the cursor to an hourglass
  this.Cursor = Cursors.WaitCursor;

  // Clear the ListView of any existing items
  EnvironmentListView.Items.Clear();

  // Create a ListItem variable
  ListViewItem lvi;

  // Create a string array variable called logicalDrives
  string[] logicalDrives;
```

Listing 9.2 continued

```
    // Call the GetLogicalDrives method of the Environment class
    logicalDrives = Environment.GetLogicalDrives();

    // Loop thru the collection of drives, and add them to the ListView
    foreach(string drives in logicalDrives)
    {
    // Create a new instance of the ListItem variable
    // and re-use it for each property you add to the ListView
    lvi = new ListViewItem();
    lvi.Text = "Drive Letter";
    lvi.SubItems.Add(drives);
    EnvironmentListView.Items.Add(lvi);
    }

    // Set the cursor back to normal
    this.Cursor = Cursors.Default;

  }
```


If you now run the application by pressing the F5 key, you'll get a list of the logical drives on your system. Building on the previous code you wrote for the `GetEnvironment_Click` event, you're still using the `ListItem` variable to add items to the list view. The differences in what you did are as follows:

- The `GetLogicalDrives` method returns a string array. At this point, you have all the data you need to display in a string array, which makes it easier to write out because you can just write some looping code to do so.
- To loop through the array, you create a drives string variable. With each iteration of the loop (using `For Each` in Visual Basic .NET or `foreach` in C#), you created the new instance of the `ListItem` variable, set the `Text` property to `"Drive Letter"`, and set the `SubItem` to the item in the `logicalDrives` string array you're looping through.
- You call the `EnvironmentListView.Items.Add` method for each item in the array as you looped through, and the item was then displayed in the `ListView`.
- As before, you set the screen cursor to `Wait` at the beginning of the procedure and `Default` at the end to give the user interface some consistency.

Getting Special System Folders with the `SpecialFolder` Enumeration

To finish this `Environment` lesson, you must get the special folders in the system using the `GetFolderPath` method. This method is slightly different from what you used previously because it uses an enumeration called `SpecialFolder` that contains the friendly names of the special folders. As you learned yesterday, enumerations are like arrays, but actually just present information to you in a user-friendly manner, not the underlying numeric value that the information represents. The `SpecialFolder` enumeration contains the path to the following directories on the system:

- `ApplicationData`
- `CommonApplicationData`
- `CommonProgramFile`
- `Cookies`
- `DesktopDirectory`
- `Favorites`
- `History`
- `InternetCache`
- `LocalApplicationData`
- `Personal`
- `ProgramFiles`
- `Programs`
- `Recent`
- `SendTo`
- `StartMenu`
- `Startup`
- `System`
- `Templates`

In Visual Studio .NET, figuring out the enumeration values is very easy, thanks to the auto list members feature. If you don't feel like looking up the enumeration values for the `SpecialFolder` enumeration in the SDK, you can just take a few good guesses, as I did in Figure 9.10.

So, let's now finish the application and get the special folder values. Double-click the Get Special Folders button, and add the code in Listing 9.3 to the `GetSpecialFolders_Click` event in the code-behind.

FIGURE 9.10
Figuring out the `SpecialFolder` *enumeration.*

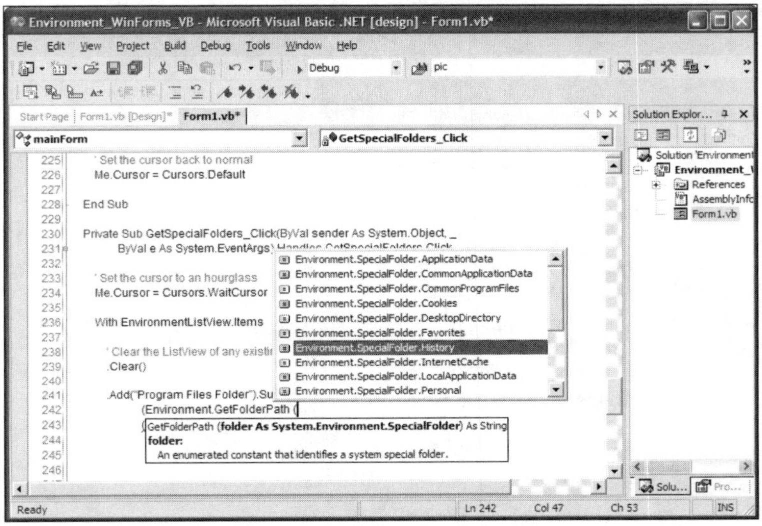

LISTING 9.3 Getting Special Folders from Your Environment

VB.NET

```
Private Sub GetSpecialFolders_Click(ByVal sender As System.Object, _
   ByVal e As System.EventArgs) Handles GetSpecialFolders.Click

 ' Set the cursor to an hourglass
 Me.Cursor = Cursors.WaitCursor

 With EnvironmentListView.Items

  ' Clear the ListView of any existing items
  .Clear()

  .Add("Program Files Folder").SubItems.Add _
    (Environment.GetFolderPath _
    (Environment.SpecialFolder.ProgramFiles))

  .Add("Application Data").SubItems.Add _
   (Environment.GetFolderPath _
   (Environment.SpecialFolder.ApplicationData))

  .Add("Personal Folder").SubItems.Add _
   (Environment.GetFolderPath _
   (Environment.SpecialFolder.Personal))

  .Add("Local Application Data Folder").SubItems.Add _
   (Environment.GetFolderPath _
```

LISTING 9.3 continued

```
    (Environment.SpecialFolder.ApplicationData))

  End With

  Me.Cursor = Cursors.Default

End Sub
```

C#

```
private void getSpecialFolders_Click(object sender, System.EventArgs e)
 {
  // Set the cursor to an hourglass
  this.Cursor = Cursors.WaitCursor;

  // Clear the ListView of any existing items
  EnvironmentListView.Items.Clear();

  // Call the GetFolderPath method, passing the
  // SpecialFolder enumeration variable to get the special Folder
  EnvironmentListView.Items.Add("Program Files").SubItems.Add
   (Environment.GetFolderPath
   (Environment.SpecialFolder.ProgramFiles));

  EnvironmentListView.Items.Add("Application Data").SubItems.Add
   (Environment.GetFolderPath
   (Environment.SpecialFolder.ApplicationData));

  EnvironmentListView.Items.Add("Personal Folder").SubItems.Add
   (Environment.GetFolderPath
   (Environment.SpecialFolder.Personal));

  EnvironmentListView.Items.Add("Local Application Data").SubItems.Add
   (Environment.GetFolderPath
   (Environment.SpecialFolder.LocalApplicationData));

  // Set the cursor back to normal
  this.Cursor = Cursors.Default;

 }
```

Run the application and click the Get Special Folders button. You should see something similar to Figure 9.11.

The code you wrote for the `GetSpecialFolders_Click` event is almost identical to the code you wrote for the `GetEnvironment_Click` click event in Listing 9.1. There are two main differences:

FIGURE 9.11

Output from the `GetFolderPath` *method.*

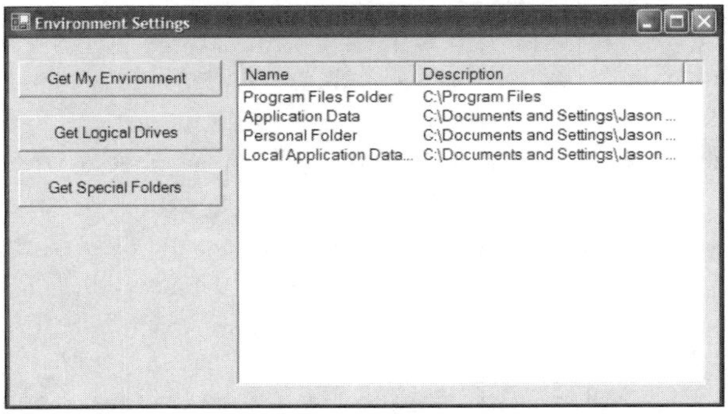

- Instead of creating the `ListItem` variable, you add the `ListItem` and its corresponding `SubItem` in the same line of code. Either method of adding `ListItems` and `SubItems` is acceptable; use the approach that's easiest for you to implement and remember.
- You call the `GetFolderPath` method and use the `SpecialFolder` enumeration to display in the `ListView`, not the properties of the `Environment` class.

You now have a good understanding of how you can use the `Environment` class to retrieve information about the environment that your application is running in. You should also have a good grasp on using the `ListView` control and the `For Each` statement in Visual Basic .NET and the `foreach` statement in C#.

Working with Files and Directories

The `System.IO` namespace contains the basic file I/O functions that enable you to read and write files, list directories, get file information, and manipulate files and directories. Most applications interact with a file in one way or another, and the `System.IO` namespace helps you do so.

In this section, you learn how to

- List directories and files
- Read and write simple text files

Note

In JScript, VBScript, and Visual Basic, you use the `FileSystemObject` to work with files and directories. You can use the `FileSystemObject` in .NET, but because it's a COM object, there's additional resource overhead when calling the `FileSystemObject`'s properties and methods. For this reason, you should always use the managed `System.IO` namespace for all file and directory code.

Inside the `System.IO` Namespace

The `System.IO` namespace contains static (or shared) classes and instance classes that enable you to interact with files, paths, directories, and streams. Streams can be from any type of resource, such as a file on the file system, a network stream, or even a URL from the Internet. You determine which classes in the `System.IO` namespace to use based on the type of stream you're accessing. If you look up the `System.IO` namespace in the SDK help file, you'll see something similar to Figure 9.12, which is a long list of the classes and namespaces that make up the `System.IO` namespace.

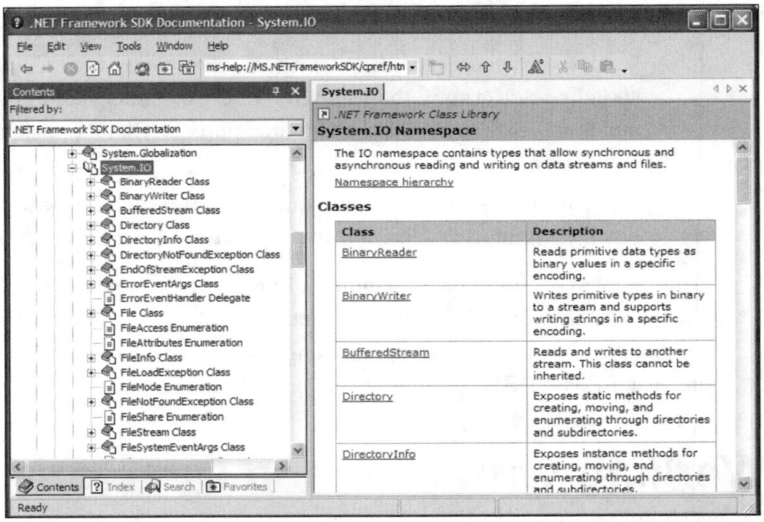

FIGURE 9.12

The `System.IO` *namespace in the .NET Framework SDK.*

Note

Static and *shared* have the same meaning. In Visual Basic .NET, noninstance classes are called *shared*. In C#, noninstance classes are called *static*. All shared or static members are shared across all instances on a class, meaning that you can reference the member without using the `New` constructor for the member you're accessing.

Figure 9.13 is a compact representation of the hierarchy of the `System.IO` namespace. You can see the static (shared) classes and the instance classes in the figure.

As you can see in Figure 9.13, the `System.IO` namespace hierarchy contains many objects that interact with files and the file system. We'll discuss the `File`, `Path`, and `Directory` classes, and the `StreamReader` and `StreamWriter` classes. These are common classes for basic file I/O.

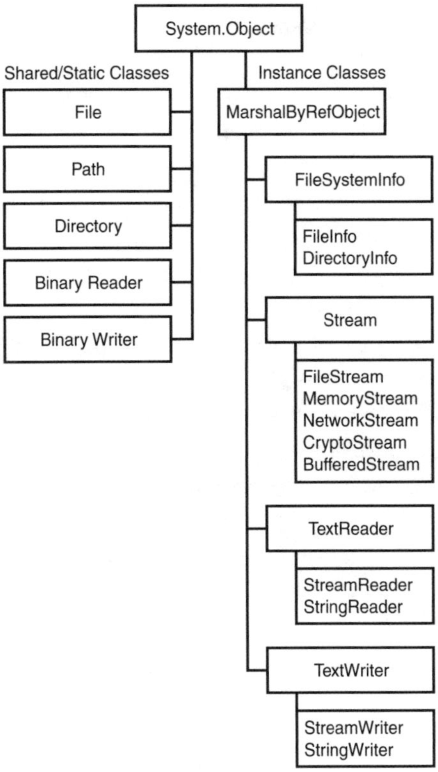

FIGURE 9.13
Compact representation of the `System.IO` *namespace.*

Understanding the `File` Class

The `File` class provides static methods that give you access to files. The instance class `FileInfo` gives you functionality similar to the static `File` class. But because the `File` class is static, it performs security checks each time you access a file object. If you're going to access the same file objects more than once, you should use the `FileInfo` class to avoid the overhead of performing security checks on the same objects each time. Table 9.3 lists the methods of the `File` class and their descriptions.

TABLE 9.3 Methods of the File Class

Method	*Description*
`AppendText`	Creates a `StreamWriter` that appends UTF-8–encoded text to an existing file.
`Copy`	Copies an existing file to a new file.
`Create`	Creates a file in the specified fully qualified path.

TABLE 9.3 continued

Method	*Description*
`CreateText`	Creates or opens a new file for writing UTF-8–encoded text.
`Delete`	Deletes the file specified by the fully qualified path. An exception isn't thrown if the specified file doesn't exist.
`Exists`	Determines whether the specified file exists.
`GetAttributes`	Gets the `FileAttributes` of the file on the fully qualified path.
`GetCreationTime`	Returns the creation date and time of the specified file or directory.
`GetLastAccessTime`	Returns the date and time the specified file or directory was last accessed.
`GetLastWriteTime`	Returns the date and time the specified file or directory was last written to.
`Move`	Moves a specified file to a new location, providing the option to specify a new file name.
`Open`	Overloaded. Opens a `FileStream` on the specified path.
`OpenRead`	Opens an existing file for reading.
`OpenText`	Opens an existing UTF-8–encoded text file for reading.
`OpenWrite`	Opens an existing file for writing.
`SetAttributes`	Sets the specified `FileAttributes` of the file on the specified path.
`SetCreationTime`	Sets the date and time the file was created.
`SetLastAccessTime`	Sets the date and time the specified file was last accessed.
`SetLastWriteTime`	Sets the date and time that the specified file was last written to.

Using the methods of the `File` class is straightforward. The following snippets use some of the methods to get you familiar with the syntax:

VB.NET

```
Imports System.IO

Public Class Class1

 Sub FileClassStuff()

  ' using Exists, Move, SetCreationTime,
  ' SetLastAccessTime, SetLastWriteTime
```

```
  If File.Exists("C:\Junk.txt") Then
   File.Move("C:\Junk.txt", "D:\Junk.txt")
   File.SetCreationTime("D:\Junk.txt", Date.Now)
   File.SetLastAccessTime("D:\Junk.txt", Date.Now)
   File.SetLastWriteTime("D:\Junk.txt", Date.Now)
  End If

  ' using Exists and Delete methods

  If File.Exists("C:\Junk.txt") Then
   File.Delete("C:\Junk.txt")
  End If

 End Sub
End Class
```


C#

```
using System;
using System.IO;

namespace IO_FileClass_CS
{
 public class Class1
 {
  static void Main()
  {

  // using Exists, Move, SetCreationTime,
  // SetLastAccessTime, SetLastWriteTime

  if (File.Exists(@"C:\Junk.txt"))
  {
   File.Move(@"C:\Junk.txt", @"D:\Junk.txt");
   File.SetCreationTime(@"D:\Junk.txt", Date.Now);
   File.SetLastAccessTime(@"D:\Junk.txt", Date.Now);
   File.SetLastWriteTime(@"D:\Junk.txt", Date.Now);
  }

  // using Exists and Delete methods

  if (File.Exists(@"C:\Junk.txt"))
  {
   File.Delete(@"C:\Junk.txt");
  }
  }
 }
}
```

> **Note**
>
> You should always use the `File.Exists` method to check for the existence of files instead of using a `Try/Catch` block to trap the `FileNotFoundException` if the file doesn't exists. This eliminates any of the overhead that might be introduced by using exception handling for actions that could be handled in the language, and not through the use for exceptions.

Understanding the `Path` Class

The `Path` class has methods that enable you to retrieve or modify paths on the operating system. When working with the `Path` class, the methods are smart enough to realize the rules of the operating system that your code is running on. For example, if an OS only allows 256-character pathnames with a 3-character extension, the `Path` class returns `ArgumentException` to let you know that you're doing something wrong. The same code might work perfectly on a system such as Windows XP, which has greater flexibility when working with file paths. Table 9.4 lists the more common available methods to you in the `Path` class.

TABLE 9.4 Methods of the `Path` Class

Method	*Description*
`ChangeExtension`	Changes the extension of a path string.
`Combine`	Combines two path strings.
`GetDirectoryName`	Returns the directory information for the specified path string.
`GetExtension`	Returns the extension of the specified path string.
`GetFileName`	Returns the filename and extension of the specified path string.
`GetFileNameWithoutExtension`	Returns the filename of the specified path string without the extension.
`GetFullPath`	Returns the absolute path for the specified path string.
`GetPathRoot`	Gets the root directory information of the specified path.
`GetTempFileName`	Returns a unique temporary filename and creates a zero-byte file by that name on disk.
`GetTempPath`	Returns the path of the current system's temporary folder.
`HasExtension`	Determines whether a path includes a filename extension.
`IsPathRooted`	Gets a value indicating whether the specified path string contains absolute or relative path information.

As is the `File` class, working with the `Path` class is very straightforward. All methods can be called directly without creating an instance of the `Path` class.

Understanding the `Directory` Class

The `Directory` class exposes methods that enable you to create, delete, move, rename, and enumerate directories and subdirectories. The `Directory` class is also a static class. The `DirectoryInfo` class is the instance class that enables you to create directory instances. Using the `DirectoryInfo` class avoids the overhead of security checks for each directory reference. Table 9.5 lists the common methods of the `Directory` class.

TABLE 9.5 Methods of the `Directory` Class

Method	*Description*
`CreateDirectory`	Creates all directories and subdirectories as specified by path.
`Delete`	Overloaded. Deletes a directory and its contents.
`Exists`	Determines whether the given path refers to an existing directory on disk.
`GetCreationTime`	Gets the creation date and time of a directory.
`GetCurrentDirectory`	Gets the current working directory of the application.
`GetDirectories`	Overloaded. Gets the names of subdirectories in the specified directory.
`GetDirectoryRoot`	Returns the volume information, root information, or both for the specified path.
`GetFiles`	Returns the names of files in the specified directory.
`GetFileSystemEntries`	Overloaded. Returns the names of all files and subdirectories in the specified directory.
`GetLastAccessTime`	Returns the date and time the specified file or directory was last accessed.
`GetLastWriteTime`	Returns the date and time the specified file or directory was last written to.
`GetLogicalDrives`	Retrieves the names of the logical drives on this computer in the form "*<drive letter>*:\".
`GetParent`	Retrieves the parent directory of the specified path, including both absolute and relative paths.
`Move`	Moves a file or a directory and its contents to a new location.
`SetCreationTime`	Sets the creation date and time for the specified file or directory.
`SetCurrentDirectory`	Sets the application's current working directory to the specified directory.
`SetLastAccessTime`	Sets the date and time the specified file or directory was last accessed.
`SetLastWriteTime`	Sets the date and time a directory was last written to.

You'll notice that some of these methods are similar to the methods of the `Environment` class (for example, `GetLogicalDrives`, which returns a string array of drives). Methods such as `SetLastWriteTime` and `GetLastWriteTime` are also similar to the methods of the `File` class. Because files and directories are similar object types, they share methods that perform similar operations.

In the next section, you create a sample application that uses some of the methods of the `Directory` class.

Creating an I/O Sample Application

To use some of the classes in the `System.IO` namespace, you're going to write a Windows Forms application that lists directories and files, writes a list of items from a list box to a text file, and then reads the text file back into a list box. To achieve this, you

- Use the `Directory` class of the `System.IO` namespace
- Use the `StreamWriter` class of the `System.IO` namespace to write to a file
- Use the `StreamReader` class of the `System.IO` namespace to read from a file
- Use arrays
- Use the `ListBox` control

Follow these steps to set up the new application. But before you start, look at Figure 9.14 to see what the end result of your form should look like.

1. Create a new Windows Forms application named IO_VB (if you're using Visual Basic .NET) or IO_CS (if you're using C#).
2. On the default `form1`, change the following properties using the Properties window:

   `Text = "Using the System.IO Namespace"`

   `StartupPosition = CenterScreen`

3. Next, drag a button from the Toolbox onto the form, and change these properties:

   `Name = ListFolders`

   `Text = "List Folders"`

4. Drag another button from the Toolbox onto the form, and change these properties:

   `Name = ListFiles`

   `Text = "List Files"`

5. Drag another button from the Toolbox onto the form, and change these properties:

   `Name = WriteToFile`

   `Text = "Write To ListBox File"`

6. Drag another button from the Toolbox onto the form, and change these properties:

   `Name` = `ReadFromFile`

   `Text` = `"Read ListBox From File"`

7. Drag a `ListBox` from the Toolbox onto the form, and change these properties:

   `Anchor` = `Top, Bottom, Left, Right`

Your completed form should look like Figure 9.14.

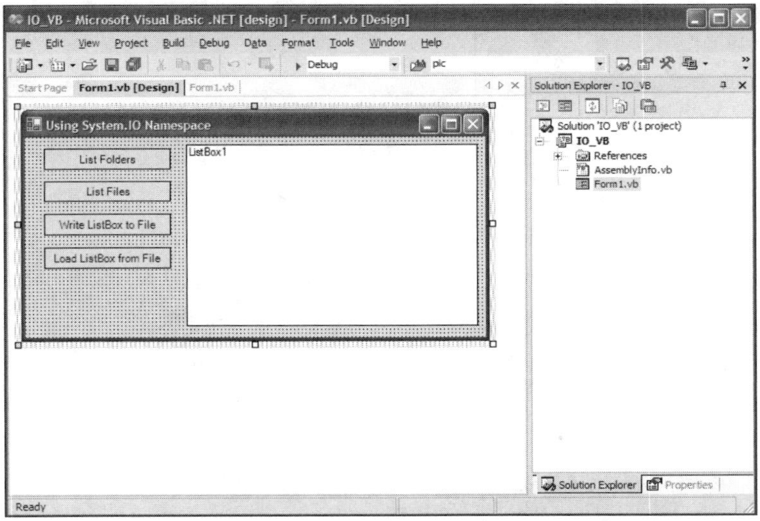

FIGURE 9.14

`Form1.vb` *from the IO application.*

Writing the IO Application Code

Now that you have the project set up, you can start writing the code to retrieve directory information. Double-click the List Folders button and add the code in Listing 9.4 to the code-behind for the `ListFolders_Click` event. This code uses the `Directory.GetDirectories` methods to return an array of directories.

LISTING 9.4 `ListFolders_Click` Event Code

VB.NET

```
Private Sub ListFolders_Click(ByVal sender As System.Object, _
   ByVal e As System.EventArgs) Handles ListFolders.Click

 ' Create a string variable array named
 ' dirs to hold the directory entries for the
```

Listing 9.4 continued

```
        ' special folder Program Files
        Dim dirs As String() = _
          Directory.GetDirectories _
          (Environment.GetFolderPath _
          (Environment.SpecialFolder.ProgramFiles))

        ' Create a string variable for the For Each loop
        Dim dir As String

        ' Loop thru the array of folders and add them to the
        ' ListBox1 using the Items.Add method
        For Each dir In dirs
         With ListBox1.Items
           .Add(dir)
         End With
        Next

       End Sub
```

C#

```
private void listFolders_Click(object sender, System.EventArgs e)
 {

  /* Create a string variable array named
  dirs to hold the directory entries for the
  special folder Program Files */

  string[] dirs =
  Directory.GetDirectories
  (Environment.GetFolderPath
  (Environment.SpecialFolder.ProgramFiles));

  /* Loop thru the array of folders and add them to the
  ListBox1 using the Items.Add method */
  foreach (string dir in dirs)
  {
   listBox1.Items.Add(dir);
  }
 }
```

If you press the F5 key to run the application and click the Get List Folders button, you should see a listing of the subdirectories of your Program Files folder. My output looks like Figure 9.15.

In Listing 9.4, you build on techniques you used in the `Environment` application you created earlier today. You use the `GetFolderpath` method of the `Environment` class to return the location of the Program Files folder. The `Directory.GetDirectories` method returns a string array of folders in the Program Files directory. You then loop through and add them to the list box using the `Items.Add` method. Using the `GetFolderPath` method of the `Environment` class ensures that you won't get an error if the user has a path for Program Files other than `C:\Program Files`.

FIGURE 9.15

Output from the `ListFolders_Click` *event.*

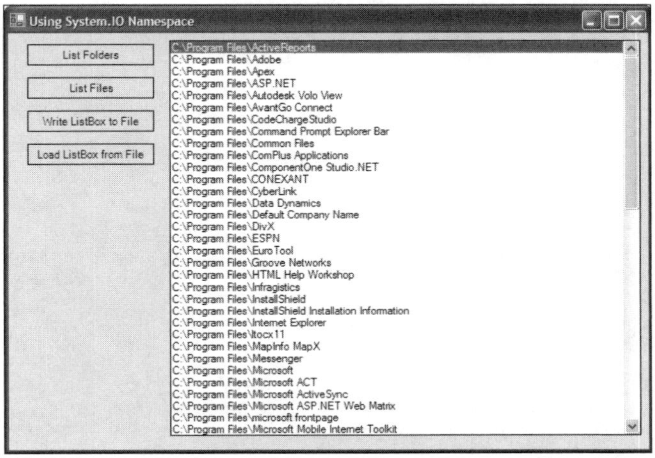

To get folders and files, you use the `GetFileSystemEntries` method of the `Directory` class. Double-click the List Files button and add the code in Listing 9.5 to the `ListFiles_Click` event.

LISTING 9.5 Using the `GetFileSystemEntries` Method

VB.NET

```
Private Sub ListFiles_Click(ByVal sender As System.Object, _
   ByVal e As System.EventArgs) Handles ListFiles.Click

 ' Clear the ListBox
 ListBox1.Items.Clear()

 ' Create a string variable array named
 ' files to hold the directory and file entries for the
 ' special folder My Documents
 Dim files As String() = _
  Directory.GetFileSystemEntries _
  (Environment.GetFolderPath _
  (Environment.SpecialFolder.Personal))

 ' Create a string variable for the For Each loop
```

LISTING 9.5 continued

```
 Dim file As String

 ' Loop thru the array of files and folders and add
 ' them to the ListBox1 using the Items.Add method
 For Each file In files
  With ListBox1.Items
   .Add(file)
  End With
 Next

End Sub
```

C#

```
private void listFiles_Click(object sender, System.EventArgs e)
 {
  // Clear the listBox
  listBox1.Items.Clear();

  /* Create a string variable array named
  files to hold the directory and file entries for the
  special folder My Documents */
  string[] files =
  Directory.GetFileSystemEntries
  (Environment.GetFolderPath
  (Environment.SpecialFolder.Personal));

  /* Loop thru the array of files and folders and add
  them to the ListBox1 using the Items.Add method */
  foreach (string file in files)
  {
   listBox1.Items.Add(file);
  }
 }
```

Now you can run the application by pressing F5 and observe the output. In Listing 9.5, you use the `GetFileSystemEntries` method to return an array of files and directories in the My Documents directory. The `Environment.SpecialFolder.Personal` enumeration returns the correct location of the My Documents folder to list the files and folders. You could also replace the `GetFileSystemEntries` method with the `GetFiles` method to return only the files in the My Documents folder.

Using the `StreamWriter` and `StreamReader` Classes

Up to now, you've used the classes of the `System.IO` namespace to access file system objects. But to read and write data, you must use the methods of the `StreamReader` and `StreamWriter` classes.

In Figure 9.13, you saw a representation of the `System.IO` namespaces and its members. There are classes that handle network streams, crypto streams, binary streams, text streams, and buffered streams. To accomplish basic reading and writing of files, you use the methods of the `StreamReader` and `StreamWriter` classes to complete the I/O project you started earlier. But before we write that code, examine Tables 9.6 and 9.7 to get an idea of what methods are available in the `StreamReader` and `StreamWriter` classes.

TABLE 9.6 Methods of the `StreamReader` Class

Method	*Description*
`Close`	Closes the `StreamReader` and releases any system resources associated with the reader.
`DiscardBufferedData`	Allows a `StreamReader` to discard its current data.
`Peek`	Returns the next available character but doesn't consume it.
`Read`	Reads the next character or next set of characters from the input stream.
`ReadBlock`	Reads a maximum of count characters from the current stream and writes the data to buffer, beginning at *`index`*.
`ReadLine`	Reads a line of characters from the current stream and returns the data as a string.
`ReadToEnd`	Reads the stream from the current position to the end of the stream.

TABLE 9.7 Methods of the `StreamWriter` Class

Method	*Description*
`Close`	Closes the current `StringWriter` and the underlying stream.
`Flush`	Clears all buffers for the current writer and causes any buffered data to be written to the underlying device.
`GetStringBuilder`	Returns the underlying `StringBuilder`.
`ToString`	Returns a string containing the characters written to the current `StringWriter` so far.
`Write`	Writes to this instance of the `StringWriter`.
`WriteLine`	Writes some data as specified by the overloaded parameters, followed by a line terminator.

The `StreamReader` class gives you all the read methods to accomplish reads on a stream after you've opened it. `Read`, `Peek`, `ReadToEnd`, `ReadLine`, and `ReadBlock` all read data from a stream. The `StreamWriter` methods perform the task of writing data to a stream.

`Write` and `WriteLine` are the methods to write data, with the only difference being that the `WriteLine` method adds a line terminator to the end of the line of data you're writing.

To implement the code to loop through the items in the `ListBox` control on your form, double-click the Write To File button, and add the code in Listing 9.6 to the `WriteToFile_Click` event.

LISTING 9.6 Using the `StreamWriter` Class

VB.NET

```
Private Sub WriteToFile_Click(ByVal sender As System.Object, _
   ByVal e As System.EventArgs) Handles WriteToFile.Click

 ' Create a new text file using the StreamWriter class
 Dim sw As New StreamWriter("C:\List.txt")

 ' Create a temp counting variable
 Dim intX As Short

 ' Loop thru the ListBox, grabbing the items and
 ' writing them to the stream using the WriteLine method
 Dim s As String
 For Each s In ListBox1.Items
  sw.WriteLine(s)
 Next

 ' Close the StreamWriter
 sw.Close()

End Sub
```

C#

```
private void WriteToFile_Click(object sender, System.EventArgs e)
 {
  // Create a new text file using the StreamWriter class
  StreamWriter sw = new StreamWriter(@"C:\List.txt");

  /* Loop thru the ListBox, grabbing the items and
  writing them to the stream using the WriteLine method */
  foreach (string s in listBox1.Items)
  {
  sw.WriteLine(s);
  }

  // Close the StreamWriter
  sw.Close();
 }
```

After you run the application, you can check the `List.txt` file in the C drive. It lists the files that are also listed in the `ListBox` in a nice text format. Using the `WriteLine` method of the `StreamWriter` class adds the line terminator after each item it writes out in the `List.txt` file. Figure 9.16 shows the `List.txt` file from my machine.

FIGURE 9.16
The `List.txt` *output from the* `StreamWriter`.

The last step in the code for the I/O application is writing the code-behind for the Read From File button. Listing 9.7 has the code that uses the `StreamReader` class to create a new stream object based on the `List.txt` file you just created in Listing 9.6. Add the code in Listing 9.7 to the code-behind for the `ReadFromFile_Click` event to see this in action.

LISTING 9.7 Using the `StreamReader` Class

VB.NET

```
Private Sub ReadFromFile_Click(ByVal sender As System.Object, _
   ByVal e As System.EventArgs) Handles ReadFromFile.Click

 ' Clear the ListBox
 ListBox1.Items.Clear()

 ' Create a new StreamReader and pass the file
 ' created in the WriteToFile_Click event
 Dim sr As New StreamReader("C:\List.txt")

 ' Use the Peek method to move to the next character
```

LISTING 9.7 continued

```
  ' and the ReadLine method to get the next line
  While sr.Peek <> -1
   With ListBox1.Items
    .Add(sr.ReadLine)
   End With
  End While

  ' Close the StreamReader
  sr.Close()

End Sub
```

C#

```
private void ReadFromFile_Click(object sender, System.EventArgs e)
 {
  // Clear the listBox
  listBox1.Items.Clear();

  /* Create a new StreamReader and pass the file
  created in the WriteToFile_Click event */
  StreamReader sr = new StreamReader(@"C:\List.txt");

  /* Use the Peek method to move to the next character
  and the ReadLine method to get the next line */
  do
  {
   listBox1.Items.Add(sr.ReadLine());
  }
  while (sr.Peek() != -1);

  // Close the StreamReader
  sr.Close();

 }
```

Now run the application to read the data from the file. The first line of code in Listing 9.7 clears the `ListBox`, and then the new `StreamReader` is created based on the file previously created. Using a loop, you're peeking into the file, one line at a time, using the `Peek` method. The `ReadLine` method reads the next line, and adds the string it reads into the `ListBox`. Because `Peek` doesn't consume the bytes of data that it reads, you can keep peeking into a stream while consuming its data with any of the read methods of the stream class. You finally call the `Close` method of the `StreamReader` to release the resource. You should always be diligent about using `Close` on resources that have a `Close` method. Not using `Close` could keep the stream handle open or waste unnecessary resources.

Summary

Today was a long day, but it was filled with valuable information. You learned what namespaces are and how you can use them in your applications. You also saw a breakdown of the key namespaces in the .NET Framework, and you learned how to implement the `System.IO` namespace and the `System.Environment` class. Over the remainder of this week and next week, you'll learn how to implement many more of the core namespaces in .NET, including `System.Data`, `System.XML`, `System.Globalization`, and others.

Some key points to remember from today:

- Be sure to reference assemblies before you use them in your applications.
- Use the `Imports` statement in Visual Basic .NET and `using` statement in C# to avoid using fully qualified names.
- Take time now to familiarize yourself with the .NET Framework SDK and the Visual Studio help files. Doing so will save you hours and hours of time in the future.
- Use the static methods of the `File`, `Directory`, and `Path` classes to do one-off operations. Don't use them for multiple file or directory operations because of the overhead of security checks.
- Use the Toolbox to save cool code snippets! Keep building your personal code library by taking advantage of the drag-and-drop capability of the Toolbox to save snippets for later use.

Q&A

Q I looked in my hard drive, and couldn't find `System.Environment.Dll`. Where is it?

A The classes and namespaces you learn about throughout these 21 days aren't necessarily in a separate DLL or even contained in a single DLL. When you get to Day 14, you'll learn about the global assembly cache and how .NET stores assemblies there.

Q I'm writing in C#. Sometimes, the auto-list members don't show up when I reference a class. Why?

A C# is a case-sensitive language, meaning that you can't use uppercase and lowercase and expect the Visual Studio .NET IDE to figure out what you're trying to type. Visual Basic .NET isn't case sensitive, so it's more friendly in the code window when you're typing along.

Q The I/O application we wrote was cool. But where can I get more information about reading and writing different kinds of files? I know I won't be doing simple text files all the time.

A If you look in the following directory on your machine, you'll find a few more good examples of using I/O:

```
\Program Files\Microsoft Visual Studio .NET\
FrameworkSDK\Samples\QuickStart\howto\samples\io\readwrite
```

You can also find some useful `System.IO` articles at the following links:

`http://msdn.microsoft.com/library/en-us/dnadvnet/html/vbnet07232002.asp`

`http://msdn.microsoft.com/library/en-us/dv_vstechart/html/`
`➥vbtchUseFileStreamObject.asp`

`http://msdn.microsoft.com/library/en-us/dv_vstechart/html/`
`➥vbtchVBAFileIOWhitepaper.asp`

Each of the preceding links offers further information on I/O in .NET. Remember to read all about I/O in the SDK too—there's a ton of good information there.

Quiz

1. The ___________ namespace helps me get information about Active Directory users and computers.
2. To get a list of logical drives on the system, I can use the ____________ method in the `System.Environment` class or the ______________ method in the `System.IO.Directory` class.
3. The only difference between the `Write` and the `WriteLine` methods of the `StreamWriter` class is the __________________ character that the `WriteLine` method uses.
4. True or False: I can use the `Imports` or `using` statement to alias a namespace that isn't imported into my application.
5. How do you add a reference to an assembly that isn't giving you AutoComplete when you're typing in the Code window?

9

Quiz Answers

1. System.DirectoryServices
2. GetLogicalDrives, GetLogicalDrives
3. line terminator
4. True. But, if the assembly is not added to the References node in your Solution Explorer, you will need to make sure to add the assembly as a reference first, then alias it in your class file.
5. Use the Imports statement in VB.NET or the using statement in C# at the top of your class file to reference the namespace you are attempting to use.

Exercises

1. Create a new ASP.NET application using the same code as the I/O application to enable you to select directories and list their contents from the browser. An application like this could be used to list Web site contents and allow users to download files, or as an administration tool for listing files and directories and creating new file and directories.
2. Look up the `FileAttributes` enumeration in the .NET Framework SDK. This enumeration gives the attributes of files on the operating system. Next, write a simple console application that uses the `GetFiles` method of the `Directory` class, and write the code that returns the attributes of the files in the root of your C drive. You can refer to Listing 9.5, where you used the `GetFileSystemEntries` method to retrieve files and folders.
3. Create a new Windows Forms application that enables you to set the `LastAccessTime` and `LastWriteTime` for files on your file system. To accomplish this, add a `TreeView` control, two `DateTimePicker` controls, and a `CommandButton` to the default `Form1` of the new application that you create. The idea is to get and set the values of the `LastAccessTime` and `LastWriteTime` for files in the file system. Here's the code you need to write:
   - Using the methods of the `File` and `Directory` class, fill the `TreeView` with the contents of your C drive.
   - Each time you click a node in the `TreeView`, set the `DateTimePicker` values with the current `LastAccessTime` and `LastWriteTime` values.
   - In the click event for the Set New Times button, add code to reset the `LastAccessTime` and `LastWriteTime` for the selected file.

Your form should look like Figure 9.17.

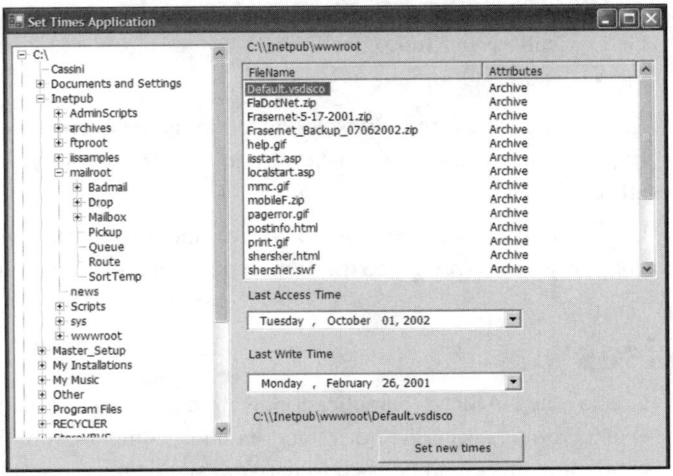

FIGURE 9.17

Sample of the Exercise 3 application.

WEEK 2

DAY 10

Accessing Data with ADO.NET

Most of the applications that you write must access some sort of data store. Today, you learn about data access in .NET. ActiveX Data Objects .NET (ADO.NET) is the technology used in the .NET Framework for all database access. Before .NET, the main technology for data access was ActiveX Data Objects (ADO). ADO was great, but it had its drawbacks. But when there's only one way to do something, as with ADO and accessing data, it's easy to forget about the drawbacks and just work with what you have. Microsoft set out to fix all of these drawbacks in ADO.NET, which was written from the ground up specifically for data access in .NET and the challenges that developers face in the disconnected environment of the Internet. Today, you learn

- The ADO.NET architecture and how it differs from ADO
- How to connect to databases with the `Connection` object
- How to use `DataReaders`
- How to use the `Command` object
- How to use `DataAdapters`
- How to use `DataSets`

- How to filter and sort `DataSets` with `DataViews`
- Databinding fundamentals in Windows Forms

Note

Today, you learn about the ADO.NET classes and how to write data access code. Tomorrow, you'll learn how to use the built in wizards and add-ins in Visual Studio .NET to automate building data access applications. Understanding the ADO.NET classes will help you debug and modify the code written by the wizards that you'll learn about tomorrow. On Day 13, "XML Web Services in .NET," you learn more about databinding controls and Web Forms. Today, we concentrate on understanding ADO.NET and Windows Forms.

Looking Inside ADO.NET

In the .NET Framework class library (FCL), the `System.Data` namespace has all the classes you need to access any type of database or data store. Before .NET, you used ADO to accomplish your data access tasks. ADO was a great technology for data access, but it wasn't designed for disconnected environments such as the Internet. ADO.NET was written from the ground up to include robust support for disconnected applications. The good news for developers is that ADO and ADO.NET have similar syntaxes, so learning how to code ADO.NET will be a snap if you've ever used ADO.

Every data access scenario includes several common operations when accessing databases:

- Connecting to a database
- Selecting one or more records from one or more tables
- Adding, updating, or deleting data in one or more tables

To perform these operations, you use one of the two core ADO.NET namespaces:

- The `System.Data.SqlClient` namespace is optimized for data access with SQL Server 7.0 and SQL Server 2000.
- The `System.Data.OleDb` namespace is optimized for OLE DB data access to databases other than SQL Server, such as Microsoft Access, Excel, dBASE, and so on.
- The System.Data.Odbc namespace is used to connect to ODBC data sources using an ODBC connection string or an ODBC data source name (DSN) that you would set up in the ODBC applet in the Control Panel. For backward compatibility with version 1.0 of the .NET Framework, there is a separate download from Microsoft that will allow version 1.0 clients to use the System.Data.Odbc namespace.
- The System.Data.OracleClient is a managed provider that allows you to access Oracle databases.

Tip

> The `System.Data.SqlClient` namespace speaks the same language that SQL Server speaks, and that's where the performance gains come from when using ADO.NET versus ADO when accessing SQL Server. SQL Server natively uses the tabular data stream (TDS) protocol to read and write data from SQL Server to a stream that's sent over the wire to your applications. In .NET, the `SqlClient` namespace uses the TDS to communicate directly with SQL Server, so there's no overhead in the conversion between the data access code you write and SQL Server consuming those commands. In the past, this created overhead by using unmanaged COM providers. This overhead no longer exists in .NET with the `SqlClient` namespace.

No matter what namespace you use, `SqlClient` or `OleDb`, you must still perform the same tasks to work with any database. You get a connection, execute a command, and either get or set data values. The classes in the `System.Data.SqlClient` namespace are similar in name and functionality to the classes in the `System.Data.OleDb` namespace. For example, to get a `Connection` object, you use the `System.Data.SqlClient.SqlConnection` class if you're accessing SQL Server. For OLE DB, you use the `System.Data.OleDb.OleDbConnection` class. The prefix of `Sql` or `OleDb` is the only difference in the syntax or functionality. For this reason, it's easy to switch between namespaces if the type of database you're using ever changes to or from SQL Server.

Note

> When I refer to SQL Server throughout today's lesson, I'm talking about SQL Server 7.0 and 2000. For SQL Server 6.5 and earlier, you must use the OLE DB namespace to access data.

If you're familiar with the objects in ADO, Figure 10.1 gives you a better understanding of the mapping of ADO to ADO.NET objects.

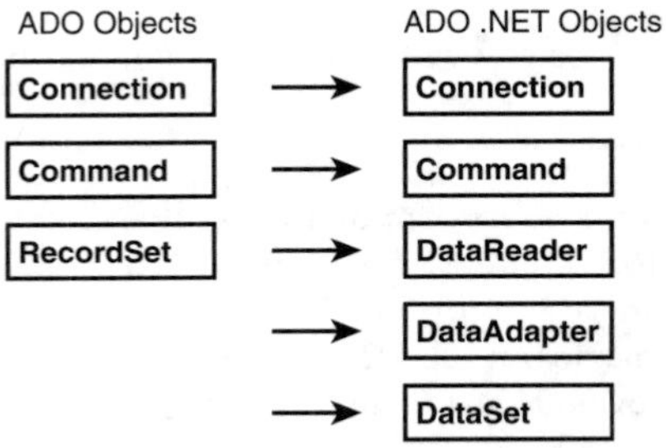

FIGURE 10.1
Mapping ADO objects to ADO.NET objects.

As Figure 10.1 demonstrates, ADO.NET has a few more core objects than ADO. These additional objects give you greater flexibility in designing your applications.

The Connection object is still the same. You set properties on the object and call an Open method to connect to the data source.

The Command object is also practically the same as it was in ADO. You create a Command object to actually hold your SQL statements that select records, insert records, update records, and delete records in the database. The Command object in ADO.NET also supports a Parameters collection that makes it very easy to support parameterized ad hoc queries and stored procedures with input and output parameters.

The DataReader object is for read-only, forward-only data access. This class can be compared to a ForwardOnly cursor in ADO. If you need data as fast as possible with no overhead and that data can be read-only and doesn't need to support paging, a DataReader is the answer.

The DataAdapter is a new ADO.NET object and has no direct correlation to an ADO object. DataAdapters are the Swiss Army Knives of data access objects. The DataAdapter sits between the database and a DataSet object. The DataAdapter's purpose is to be the connected part of a disconnected environment. DataAdapters have InsertCommand, UpdateCommand, SelectCommand, and DeleteCommand properties that enable you to specify how to get or set values in the database. The DataAdapter is responsible for keeping track of the original data that you received from the database and updating any changes that were made since you last connected.

The DataSet is also a brand-new object that doesn't directly map to an ADO object. A DataSet is an in-memory representation of data. The DataSet doesn't directly connect to a database; it's either created dynamically in code or filled with information. DataSets can hold simple, nontyped data from a database or extensible markup language (XML) file, or they can hold complex strongly typed relational data from a database, XML file, or data generated dynamically. DataSets are used in conjunction with DataAdapters. The DataAdapter provides the Connection and Command objects, and the DataSet provides a place for the data to go.

You work with each of these objects in more detail throughout the day.

Note

In ADO.NET, there's no concept of a server-side cursor. A *cursor* is what a database uses to keep track of positioning in a set of records. In ADO, you can specify client-side cursors or server-side cursors. If a cursor is client side, the client side memory is used to keep positional track of records for operations such as moving to the first record, last record, previous record, or next record. If a cursor is server side, the database server keeps track of the positional information for a set of records. Each time a connection is made with the cursor option set to server side, the database server has to consume more resources. If you have many tens or hundreds of users, your database server has to work itself to death just to keep up with the demand of doing all the work server side. In ADO.NET, the server-side cursor doesn't exist, which prevents you from accidentally using cursors on the server.

What Does Disconnected Mean?

I mentioned earlier that ADO.NET is designed for disconnected data access. That doesn't mean you never connect to a database. It means that you have lots of abilities after you disconnect from the data source. Because the database holds all the information about the data, such as field names, data types, and relationships between tables, it's logical to assume that you should be able to access this information after you disconnect from the database. This isn't the case in ADO. However, in ADO.NET, through the use of `DataAdapters` and `DataSets`, you have a complete programming model for maintaining all the schema information that the physical database normally maintains. That means you can get data from the database, disconnect from the database, and are still bound by the rules that are normally enforced when interacting directly with the database. You're physically disconnected from the database, but you still have all the advantages that the database gives you. The `DataSet` object is a true in-memory cache of your database, with a complete hierarchy of objects that enable you to maintain rules, constraints, and relationships between tables that were otherwise impossible using ADO.

Under the hood, XML is used to marshal data to and from ADO.NET objects and the database. Because XML can contain a schema that represents what the data is supposed to look like and what rules it should follow, it's easy to see how ADO.NET can give you this type of flexibility. Understanding how to use the underlying XML isn't important; it's transparent to you when you use ADO.NET. You don't need to know anything about XML to successfully use ADO.NET. In the ADO.NET model, XML is simply considered another source of data. It can be read and written to using ADO.NET without you being aware of what it's actually doing. XML is everywhere in .NET, and the good thing is that you don't have to know how to deal with it because the tools in Visual Studio .NET and the FCL do it for you.

Note

On Day 12, "Accessing XML in .NET," you learn how to access XML using the XML classes on the FCL. On Day 13, you learn how to create and consume XML Web services in .NET. I don't want to minimize the importance and flexibility that XML gives you in the .NET Framework—it's the underlying mechanism through which almost everything communicates. But I want to stress that you don't need to know anything about XML to be productive in .NET.

To give you an idea of how the disconnected model looks, Figure 10.2 shows you how the `DataReader`, `DataAdapter`, and `DataSet` objects fit into data access in ADO.NET.

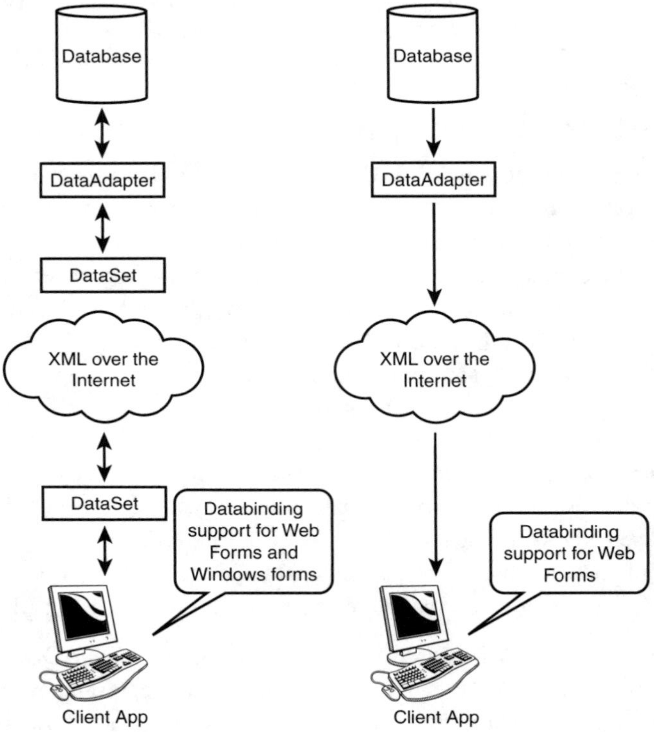

FIGURE 10.2

Data access architecture of ADO.NET.

Databinding is mentioned for the first time in Figure 10.2. In Visual Basic 6 and ASP, databinding was a bad word. There was a lot of overhead and you always needed some sort of data connection to implement databinding. In .NET, databinding is encouraged. The databinding on Windows Forms applications and Web Forms applications is a robust and scalable architecture to use for your presentation tier. You should use databinding wherever possible.

Today, you'll use databinding on Windows Forms first, using `DataAdapters` with `DataSets` and `DataViews`, and then you'll see how to databind controls on Web Forms using `DataReaders`.

Note

> You can't use databinding on Windows Forms using `DataReaders`. If you plan to write an application that uses both Windows Forms and Web Forms, you must implement `DataSets`, not `DataReaders`. With `DataSets`, you can share the code between Windows Forms and Web Forms.

Connecting to a Database

To work with any database, the first thing you must do is connect to it. In ADO.NET, you use the `Connection` object to connect to a database. When accessing SQL Server, the `SqlConnection` class of the `System.Data.SqlClient` namespace contains the connection object that you use to connect to a SQL Server database. The `OleDbConnection` class of the `System.Data.OleDb` namespace contains the connection object for OLE DB data sources.

When connecting to a database, you must specify the server that the database resides on, the database name, and the authentication information for the database. There are several variations of the connection string, so you might see different syntax based on who wrote the connection string code and the type of authentication used if the database is SQL Server.

The following code gives you an example of each of the following types of connection string options:

- Connecting to a Microsoft Access database using the `OleDbConnection` class
- Connecting to a .NET Framework software development kit (SDK) sample Microsoft data engine (MSDE) database with integrated security
- Connecting to a SQL Server database with integrated security
- Connecting to a SQL Server database passing the user ID and password in the connection string

VB.NET

```
' Connect to a Microsoft Access database using the
' System.Data.OleDb.OleDbConnection class
Dim strOleDb As String = _
    "Provider=Microsoft.Jet.OLEDB.4.0;" _
    & "Data Source=..\Northwind.mdb"
Dim cnOleDb As New OleDbConnection()
cnOleDb.ConnectionString = strOleDb
cnOleDb.Open()

' Connect to the MSDE SDK database using  the
' System.Data.SqlClient.SqlConnection class
```

```
' with Integrated Security
Dim strMSDE As String = _
    "Server=(local)\NetSDK;DataBase=Northwind;" _
    & "Integrated Security=SSPI"
Dim cnMSDE As New SqlConnection()
cnMSDE.ConnectionString = strMSDE
cnMSDE.Open()

' Connect to a local SQL Server database using  the
' System.Data.SqlClient.SqlConnection class
' with Integrated Security
Dim strSQL As String = _
    "Server=localhost;DataBase=Northwind;" & _
    "Integrated Security=SSPI"
Dim cnSQL As New SqlConnection()
cnSQL.ConnectionString = strSQL
cnSQL.Open()

' Connect to a local SQL Server database using  the
' System.Data.SqlClient.SqlConnection class
' passing userid and password in the connection string
Dim strSQL1 As String = _
    "Server=localhost;DataBase=Northwind;" & _
    "uid=sa;pwd=password"
Dim cnSQL1 As New SqlConnection()
cnSQL1.ConnectionString = strSQL1
cnSQL1.Open()
```

C#

```
// Connect to a Microsoft Access database using the
// System.Data.OleDb.OleDbConnection class
string strOleDb;
strOleDb =
   @"Provider=Microsoft.Jet.OLEDB.4.0;Data Source=..\Northwind.mdb";
OleDbConnection cnOleDb = new OleDbConnection();
??? Author added parenthesis after OleDbConnection - Jason
cnOleDb.ConnectionString = strOleDb;
cnOleDb.Open();

// Connect to the MSDE SDK database using  the
// System.Data.SqlClient.SqlConnection class
// with Integrated Security
string strMSDE;
strMSDE =
   @"Server=(local)\NetSDK;DataBase=Northwind;Integrated Security=SSPI";
SqlConnection cnMSDE = new SqlConnection;()
??? Author: added parenthesis after SqlConnection
cnMSDE.ConnectionString = strMSDE;
cnMSDE.Open();

// Connect to a local SQL Server database using  the
```

```
// System.Data.SqlClient.SqlConnection class
// with Integrated Security
string strSQL;
strSQL =
   @"Server=localhost;DataBase=Northwind;Integrated Security=SSPI";
sqlConnection cnSQL = new SqlConnection();
??? Author: added parenthesis after SqlConnection
cnSQL.ConnectionString = strSQL;
cnSQL.Open();

// Connect to a local SQL Server database using  the
// System.Data.SqlClient.SqlConnection class
// passing userid and password in the connection string
string strSQL1;
strSQL1 = @"Server=localhost;DataBase=Northwind;uid=sa;pwd=";
SqlConnection cnSQL1 = new SqlConnection();
cnSQL1.ConnectionString = strSQL1;
cnSQL1.Open();
```


The connection string differences are not that noticeable. You can see the difference between `OleDbConnection` and `SqlConnection` is that with SQL Server, you pass the server name (in this case, `localhost`), the database name, and either the integrated security constant or the actual user ID and password. With the `OleDbConnection`, you specify the physical path to the database, and most importantly, the OLE DB provider name. Based on the type of OLE DB provider you're using, the connection string might vary. For example, using Microsoft Access, you must specify the physical path to the database. If you're using Oracle or SQL Server 6.5, you must specify a connection string similar to SQL 7.0 or SQL 2000.

Table 10.1 lists the common properties of a `SqlConnection` object and an `OleDbConnection` object.

TABLE 10.1 Properties of the `Connection` Object

Property	*Description*
`ConnectionTimeout`	Gets the time to wait while trying to establish a connection before terminating the attempt and generating an error
`Database`	Gets the name of the current database or the database to be used after a connection is open
`DataSource`	Gets the name of the instance of SQL Server to which to connect
`PacketSize`	Gets the size (in bytes) of network packets used to communicate with an instance of SQL Server
`ServerVersion`	Gets a string containing the version of the instance of SQL Server to which the client is connected
`State`	Gets the current state of the connection
`WorkstationId`	Gets a string that identifies the database client

Tip

When you open a `Connection` object, you must always explicitly close it. Calling `Close` or `Dispose` on a `Connection` object ensures that the connection is sent back to the connection pool. Connection pooling is automatic in .NET, so you gain performance by closing connections and letting .NET send the connection back to the pool. When you attempt to create a new connection, resources are consumed on the server. To avoid the overhead of creating a new connection for each call on the database server, the .NET managed providers keep a pool of connections available for the next connection attempt to the server, thus avoiding the overhead of connection creation on the server. To keep you honest, the `ExecuteReader` method of the `Command` object actually enables you to close the connection with the `CommandBehavior.CloseConnection` parameter when you execute the command.

The `SqlConnection` and `OleDbConnection` classes are overloaded, so you can also pass the connection string when you create the connection as the following Visual Basic .NET code demonstrates:

VB.NET

```
Dim cn As New SqlConnection( _
    "Server=localhost;DataBase=Northwind;" _
    & "uid=sa;pwd=password")
```

Note

In the remainder of the examples, you use the .NET Framework SDK MSDE database that's installed with the Quick Start tutorials that come with Visual Studio .NET. If you haven't installed the Quick Start tutorials that are part of the .NET Framework SDK, navigate to `\Program Files\Microsoft Visual Studio .NET\FrameworkSDK\StartHere.htm` and follow the instructions on how to install the SDK files.

Now that you can connect to a database, you can start writing some code that retrieves data.

Note

You'll be using the `System.Data.SqlClient` namespace and the `System.Data.OleDb` namespace in the code you write for the rest of the day. Make sure that you remember to alias these namespaces with the `Imports` or `using` statement at the top of your class files as you follow along with the code examples.

Using the Command Object and DataReaders

The Command object is used to execute SQL statements against a database. The SQL statements can be ad hoc text or the name of a stored procedure in SQL Server. The SqlCommand class is responsible for SQL Server access, and the OleDbCommand class is responsible for OLE DB data sources.

You create a Command object in one of two ways:

- By calling the CreateCommand method of a Connection object
- By creating an instance of the SqlCommand or OleDbCommand class, and passing a valid Connection object to the Command instance

After you create a Command object, you set properties that indicate what the SQL statement is, the timeout, the connection information, and parameters if there are any in your SQL statement. Table 10.2 lists the common properties of the SqlCommand class and the OleDbCommand class.

TABLE 10.2 Common SqlCommand and OleDbCommand Properties

Property Name	*Description*
CommandText	Gets or sets the SQL statement or stored procedure to execute at the data source
CommandTimeout	Gets or sets the wait time before terminating an attempt to execute a command and generating an error
CommandType	Gets or sets a value indicating how the CommandText property is interpreted
Connection	Gets or sets the OleDbConnection or SqlConnection used by this instance of the OleDbCommand or SqlCommand
DesignTimeVisible	Gets or sets a value indicating whether the command object should be visible in a customized Windows Forms Designer control.
Parameters	Gets the OleDbParameterCollection or SqlParameterCollection
Transaction	Gets or sets the transaction in which the OleDbCommand or SqlCommand executes
UpdatedRowSource	Gets or sets how command results are applied to the DataRow when used by the Update method of the DataAdapter

After you set up the Command object and specify a SQL statement or stored procedure name in the CommandText property, you call one of the methods listed in Table 10.3 to execute your SQL statement against the database.

TABLE 10.3 Execute Methods of the `SqlCommand` and `OleDbCommand` Classes

Method Name	*Description*
`ExecuteReader`	Executes commands that return rows. For increased performance, `ExecuteReader` invokes commands using the Transact-SQL `sp_executesql` system stored procedure. As a result, `ExecuteReader` might not have the desired effect if used to execute commands such as Transact-SQL `SET` statements.
`ExecuteNonQuery`	Executes commands such as Transact-SQL `INSERT`, `DELETE`, `UPDATE`, and `SET` statements.
`ExecuteScalar`	Retrieves a single value from a database. This does not include aggregate values.
`ExecuteXmlReader` (SQL Server Only)	Sends the `CommandText` to the `Connection` and builds an `XmlReader` object. You can also include `FOR` XML statements when using a Transact-SQL statement with SQL Server.

Each of the methods of the `Command` object gives you a different type of action based on the requirements.

To read the data after you executed a `Command` with `ExecuteReader`, you create a `DataReader` object that holds the data returned from the database. The `DataReader` comes in two flavors, `SqlDataReader` and `OleDbDataReader`, and you choose one or the other depending on the type of database you want to access.

To see how this all works, Listing 10.1 demonstrates how to connect to a database, how to use the `Command` object, and how to read data from a `DataReader` object.

LISTING 10.1 Using `Connection`, `Command`, and `DataReader` Objects to Retrieve Data

VB.NET

```
Dim cn As New SqlConnection( _
   "Server=(local)\NetSDK;DataBase=pubs;" _
   & "Integrated Security=SSPI")

         ' Create a SqlDataReader object
         Dim dr As SqlDataReader

         ' Create a new SqlCommand object
         Dim cmd As New SqlCommand()

         ' Set the Select statement in the CommandText property and
```

LISTING 10.1 continued

```
        ' set the Connection property to the "cn" SqlConnection object
        ' you just created
        With cmd
            .CommandText = "Select au_lname, au_fname from Authors"
            .Connection = cn
        End With

        ' Open the Connection
        cn.Open()

        ' Call the ExecuteReader method of the Command object
        dr = cmd.ExecuteReader(CommandBehavior.CloseConnection)

        ' Use this for concatenating the data from the database
        Dim strName As String

        ' Call the Read method of the DataReader to loop thru the records
        While dr.Read
            ' Add the items to the ListBox1 control
            strName = dr("au_lname") & ", " & dr("au_fname")
            MessageBox.Show(strName)
        End While

        ' Close the connection
        cn.Close()
```

C#

```
SqlConnection cn = new SqlConnection
  (@"Server=(local)\NetSDK;DataBase=pubs;Integrated Security=SSPI");

// Create a SqlDataReader object
SqlDataReader dr;

// Create a new SqlCommand object
SqlCommand cmd = new SqlCommand();

// Set the Select statement in the CommandText property and
// set the Connection property to the "cn" SqlConnection object
// you just created

cmd.CommandText = "Select au_lname, au_fname from Authors";
cmd.Connection = cn;

// Open the Connection
cn.Open();

// Call the ExecuteReader method of the Command object
dr = cmd.ExecuteReader(CommandBehavior.CloseConnection);
```

LISTING 10.1 continued

```
// Use this for concatenating the data from the database
string strName;

// Call the Read method of the DataReader to loop thru the records
while (dr.Read())
   {
     // Add the items to the ListBox1 control
     strName = dr.GetString(0) + ", " + dr.GetString(1);
     MessageBox.Show(strName);
     listBox1.Items.Add(strName);
    }

// Close the Connection object
cn.Close();
```

After you have called the `ExecuteReader` method, you use the `Read` method of the `DataReader` class to loop through the records. Each time a record is read, the position in the `Reader` is advanced to the next record. This makes it easy to use the `While` statement to read each row. The `Read` method returns a `False` value when there are no more records to read, and your code execution continues after the `While` loop. Remember, a `DataReader` is a forward-only set of records, so you can't move backward in the `DataReader`.

You can also implement other looping techniques for reading data from a `DataReader`, as the following Visual Basic .NET code demonstrates:

VB.NET

```
Do Until dr.Read = False
        ' do something with the data
Loop
```

If you compare the Visual Basic .NET and C# code for Listing 10.1, you'll notice a difference in the way the actual data is retrieved from the current record on the `Read` method of the `DataReader`. The Visual Basic .NET code uses the actual field name, and the C# code uses the `GetString` method with the ordinal position of the field you're attempting to access. When reading data with a `SQLDataReader`, you have different methods of accessing the specific data type in the field of the current row. Table 10.4 is a very compact list of some of the methods in the `SqlDataReader` class that get values based on data type.

TABLE 10.4 Methods of the `SqlDataReader` Class

Method Name	*Description*
`GetSqlBinary`	Gets the value of the specified column as a `SqlBinary`
`GetSqlBoolean`	Gets the value of the specified column as a `SqlBoolean`
`GetSqlByte`	Gets the value of the specified column as a `SqlByte`
`GetSqlDateTime`	Gets the value of the specified column as a `SqlDateTime`
`GetSqlDecimal`	Gets the value of the specified column as a `SqlDecimal`
`GetSqlDouble`	Gets the value of the specified column as a `SqlDouble`
`GetSqlGuid`	Gets the value of the specified column as a `SqlGuid`
`GetSqlInt16`	Gets the value of the specified column as a `SqlInt16`
`GetSqlInt32`	Gets the value of the specified column as a `SqlInt32`
`GetSqlInt64`	Gets the value of the specified column as a `SqlInt64`
`GetSqlMoney`	Gets the value of the specified column as a `SqlMoney`
`GetSqlSingle`	Gets the value of the specified column as a `SqlSingle`
`GetSqlString`	Gets the value of the specified column as a `SqlString`

There are many other methods to retrieve all the data types for SQL Server and OLE DB data sources. It isn't important to list them all here. When you're writing the code in the Visual Studio .NET integrated development environment (IDE), you get the list of possible members for the `DataReader` class. You'll know if you're using the wrong method when an exception occurs. A safe bet is to use either the numeric ordinal position of the data in the row with the `GetString` method, or the field name and put the field data into a string. You can then use the `System.Convert` class to manipulate the data. There's some overhead in doing that, but if you aren't sure of the data type or how to handle it, you can still get the data you need.

Using `ExecuteNonQuery` with a `Command` Object

The `ExecuteNonQuery` method is used when you aren't returning any data, as in the case of an `Insert`, `Update`, or `Delete`. Listing 10.2 demonstrates the use of `ExecuteNonQuery` using a `Command` object and a `DataReader`.

LISTING 10.2 Using `ExecuteNonQuery` with a `Command` Object

VB.NET

```
Sub DoNonQuery()

    Dim cn As New SqlConnection( _
```

LISTING 10.2 continued

```
            "Server=(local)\NetSDK;DataBase=pubs;" _
            & "Integrated Security=SSPI")


        Dim cmd As New SqlCommand()

        With cmd
            .CommandText = "Delete from Authors where au_lname = 'Smith'"
            .Connection = cn
            .CommandType = CommandType.Text
        End With

        Try
            cn.Open()
            cmd.ExecuteNonQuery()

        Catch ex As Exception

            MessageBox.Show(ex.Message)

        Finally

            If cn.State = ConnectionState.Open Then
                cn.Close()
            End If

        End Try

    End Sub
```

C#

```
private void DoNonQuery()
   {
      SqlConnection cn = new SqlConnection
       (@"Server=(local)\NetSDK;DataBase=pubs;Integrated Security=SSPI");
      SqlCommand cmd = new SqlCommand();

      cmd.CommandText = "Delete from Authors where au_lname = 'Smith'";
      cmd.Connection = cn;
      cmd.CommandType = CommandType.Text ;

      try
         {
            cn.Open();
            cmd.ExecuteNonQuery();
         }
         catch (Exception ex)
         {
            MessageBox.Show(ex.Message);
```

LISTING 10.2 continued

```
            }
            finally
            {
               if (cn.State == ConnectionState.Open)
               {
                  cn.Close();
               }
            }
        }
```

The code in Listing 10.2 is almost identical to the code in Listing 10.1. You created a `Connection` object, a `Command` object, and then executed the `Command`. The difference is in the type of SQL statement. When you perform an `Insert`, `Update`, or `Delete` on a database, you don't expect a result set back. By calling the `ExecuteNonQuery` method, you're saving resources on the server. Because no data is coming back, there's no need to call the `ExecuteReader` method to hold the returning data stream.

You also check the `State` property of the `Connection` object. This is a safe way to close the `Connection` if it's open. By wrapping this code in a `try/catch` block, you catch any error that might occur when you open the connection and execute the command. The `finally` block makes sure that the connection is closed when you're done with it.

Using Windows Controls with `DataReaders` and `Command` Objects

Now that you have a handle on the basics of the `Connection`, `Command`, and `DataReader` objects, you can start the Windows Forms project that you'll build for the rest of the day.

To begin, create a new C# or Visual Basic .NET Windows Forms application and call it DataAcess_vb or DataAccess_cs, depending on the language you want to use. I refer to the project as DataAccess.

Follow these steps to create the controls for the default `Form1`. Figure 10.3 gives you an example of where we're going with this form.

Follow these steps to create the GUI:

1. Drag a `TabControl` from the Toolbox to the form and set the following properties:

   `Dock: Fill`

   `TabPages`—Click the ellipses to bring up the TabPage Collection Editor. Click the Add button three times to add three pages. For the pages, set the `Text` property to the following:

`Readers and Adapters`

`DataGrid Binding`

`Simple Data Entry`

Click OK to close the TabPage Collection Editor.

2. Drag four `CommandButtons` to `TabPage1` and set these properties:

   Button1:

   Text: `Using a DataReader`

   Name: `UseDataReader`

   Button2:

   Text: `Using a DataSet`

   Name: `UseDataSet`

   Button3:

   Text: `Show Checked Items`

   Name: `ShowCheckedItems`

   Button4:

   Text: `DataBind with DataSet`

   Name: `DataBindWithDataSet`

3. Drag a `ListBox` control from the Toolbox to `TabPage1`.
4. Drag a `CheckedListBox` control to `TabPage1`.
5. Drag a `ComboBox` control from the Toolbox to `TabPage1`.
6. Drag three `Label` controls from the Toolbox to `TabPage1`.

Refer to Figure 10.3 to see how to arrange everything. You add controls to the second and third tabs later today.

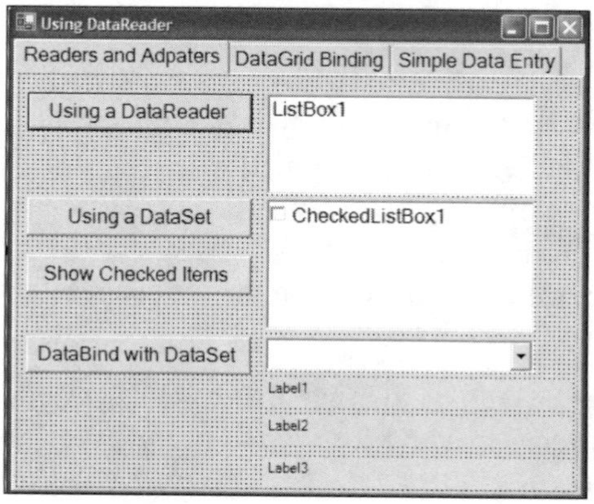

FIGURE 10.3

Form1 of the DataAccess project.

The goal of this project is to give you an understanding of how to get data from a database and, after you have the data, what you can do with it. To start, let's use what you learned earlier about `DataReaders` and write the code for the `UsingDataReader` click event. Listing 10.3 is similar to Listing 10.1; the only difference is that you're adding the data to the `ListBox1` control as you call the `Read` method of the `SqlDataReader` class. Double-click on the Using a DataReader button and add the code from Listing 10.3.

LISTING 10.3 Populating a `ListBox` from a `DataReader`

VB.NET

```
Private Sub UseDataReader_Click(ByVal sender As System.Object, _
                ByVal e As System.EventArgs) Handles UseDataReader.Click

        ListBox1.Items.Clear()

        Dim cn As New SqlConnection( _
                        "Server=(local)\NetSDK;DataBase=pubs;" _
                        & "Integrated Security=SSPI")

        ' Create a SqlDataReader object
        Dim dr As SqlDataReader

        ' Create a new SqlCommand object
        Dim cmd As New SqlCommand()

        ' Set the Select statement in the CommandText property and
        ' set the Connection property to the "cn" SqlConnection object
        ' you just created
        With cmd
            .CommandText = "Select au_lname, au_fname from Authors"
            .Connection = cn
        End With

        ' Open the Connection
        cn.Open()

        ' Call the ExecuteReader method of the Command object
        dr = cmd.ExecuteReader(CommandBehavior.CloseConnection)

        ' Use this for concatenating the data from the database
        Dim strName As String

        ' Call the Read method of the DataReader to loop thru the records
        While dr.Read
            ' Add the items to the ListBox1 control
            strName = dr("au_lname") & ", " & dr("au_fname")
            ListBox1.Items.Add(strName)
```

LISTING 10.3 continued

```
        End While

    End Sub

    Private Sub UseDataSet_Click(ByVal sender As System.Object, _
            ByVal e As System.EventArgs) Handles UseDataSet.Click

        ' Create a connection
        Dim cn As New SqlConnection( _
                   "Server=(local)\NetSDK;DataBase=pubs;" _
                   & "Integrated Security=SSPI")

        ' Create a new SqlDataAdapter object.
        ' The overloaded constructor allows you to set the SQL Statement
        ' and the connection object or connection string at the time
        ' you create the SqlDataAdapter object
        Dim da As SqlDataAdapter = New SqlDataAdapter _
            ("SELECT au_id, au_lname + ', ' + au_fname As
           FullName FROM Authors", cn)

        ' Create a new DataSet to hold the data from the SqlDataAdapter
        Dim ds As DataSet = New DataSet("Authors")
        da.Fill(ds, "Authors")

        ' Create a DataRow object
        Dim dr As DataRow

        ' Loop thru the table rows and add the items
        ' in each dataset table row to the CheckedListBox
        For Each dr In ds.Tables("Authors").Rows
            CheckedListBox1.Items.Add(dr("FullName"))
        Next

    End Sub
```

C#

```
private UseDataReader_Click(object sender,
        System.EventArgs e)
   {

      listBox1.Items.Clear();

      SqlConnection cn = new SqlConnection
       (@"Server=(local)\NetSDK;DataBase=pubs;Integrated Security=SSPI");

      // Create a SqlDataReader object
      SqlDataReader dr;
```

LISTING 10.3 continued

```
        // Create a new SqlCommand object
        SqlCommand cmd = new SqlCommand();

        // Set the Select statement in the CommandText property and
        // set the Connection property to the "cn" SqlConnection object
        // you just created

        cmd.CommandText = "Select au_lname, au_fname from Authors";
        cmd.Connection = cn;

        // Open the Connection
        cn.Open();

        // Call the ExecuteReader method of the Command object
        dr = cmd.ExecuteReader(CommandBehavior.CloseConnection);

        // Use this for concatenating the data from the database
        string strName;

        // Call the Read method of the DataReader to loop thru the records
        while (dr.Read())
                {
        // Add the items to the ListBox1 control
        strName = dr.GetString(0) + ", " + dr.GetString(1);
        listBox1.Items.Add(strName);
    }
```


Next, you write code for the `SelectedIndexChanged` event of the `ListBox1` control. Because this is the default event for that type of control, you can double-click the control on the form and the code window takes you to the event. The code in Listing 10.4 is what must be added to the `SelectedIndexChanged` event for the `ListBox1` control.

LISTING 10.4 `SelectedIndexChanged` Code for the `ListBox1` Control

VB.NET

```
Private Sub ListBox1_SelectedIndexChanged _
            (ByVal sender As System.Object, _
            ByVal e As System.EventArgs) _
            Handles ListBox1.SelectedIndexChanged

        ' Display where the event came from
        Label1.Text = "ListBox1_SelectedIndexChanged"

        ' Display the selected item
        Label2.Text = ListBox1.Items(ListBox1.SelectedIndex)
```

LISTING 10.4 continued

```
        ' Display the index
        Label3.Text = ListBox1.SelectedIndex
    End Sub
```

C#

```
private void listBox1_SelectedIndexChanged(object sender,
        System.EventArgs e)
   {
      // Display where the event came from
      label1.Text = "ListBox1_SelectedIndexChanged";

      // Display the selected item
      label2.Text = listBox1.Text;

      // Display the index
      label3.Text =listBox1.SelectedIndex.ToString();
   }
```

Listing 10.4 retrieves the data from the `ListBox`. The `Index` changes each time the position changes in a `ListBox`, so you often need to know what the data actually represents. Listing 10.4 has nothing to do with data access; rather, it's an example of what you can do with data after you retrieve it.

To see what happens, press the F5 key to run the application. When Form1 pops up, click the Using a DataReader button. You'll see that the `ListBox` loads with the records from the database. As you click different items in the `ListBox`, the labels display the selected items in the `ListBox` control.

Your results should look like Figure 10.4.

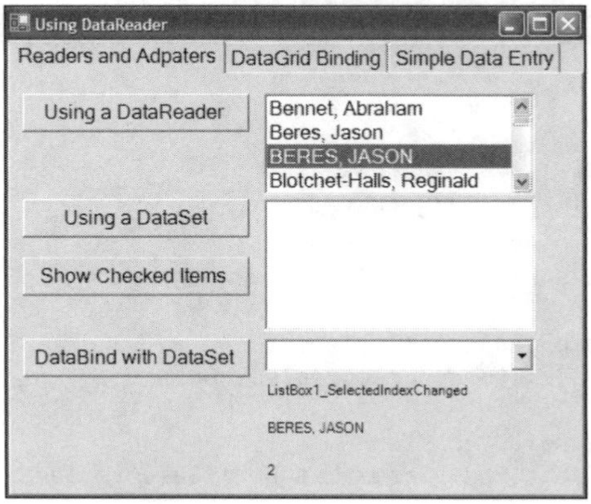

FIGURE 10.4

Results from running the `UsingDataReader` *code.*

Using DataReaders is a common task that will make up most of your data access code. DataReaders offer an extremely fast and low-overhead method of getting data to and from a database, thereby increasing scalability and reducing server resources.

Using DataAdapters and DataSets

If you need more flexibility than a DataReader offers, you can use a DataSet object as a container for records from the database. In Figure 10.2, you saw where the DataSet fits in a disconnected data access scenario. The DataSet itself doesn't connect to a database; it simply holds data and table information in its DataTables collection. To get data into a DataSet, you use a DataAdapter. The DataAdapter supplies the methods and properties to connect to a database, retrieve data, and populate the DataSet with that data. There are two key methods of the DataAdapter object: Fill and Update. The Fill method takes a DataSet and DataTable parameter to fill the records from a Command object's SQL statement. You still use a Command object when dealing with DataAdapters—that remains constant when doing any type of data access. The Command object always contains the SQL statements that interact with the data source.

When accessing SQL Server, you should use the SqlDataAdapter class, and when accessing other data sources, use the OleDbDataAdapter class.

To see how this works, the following code snippet uses DataAdapter, Command, and DataSet objects to retrieve data from the Authors table. This code assumes the existence of a valid connection named cn.

VB.NET

```
' Create a new SqlDataAdapter object.
Dim da As SqlDataAdapter = New SqlDataAdapter()

' Create a Command Object and pass a valid Connection object
Dim cmd As New SqlCommand("Select * from Authors", cn)

' Set the SelectCommand property to the Command object
da.SelectCommand = cmd

' Create a new DataSet to hold the data from the SqlDataAdapter
Dim ds As DataSet = New DataSet()

' Call the Fill method to execute the Command
' and load the data into the DataSet.
da.Fill(ds, "Authors")
```

C#

```
// Create a new SqlDataAdapter object.
```

```
SqlDataAdapter da = new SqlDataAdapter();

// Create a Command Object and pass a valid Connection object
SqlCommand cmd = new SqlCommand("Select * from Authors", cn);

// Set the SelectCommand property to the Command object
da.SelectCommand = cmd;

// Create a new DataSet to hold the data from the SqlDataAdapter
DataSet ds = new DataSet();

// Call the Fill method to execute the Command
// and load the data into the DataSet.
da.Fill(ds, "Authors");
```

The `Fill` method of the `DataAdapter` class actually does all the work. When the method is called, it refreshes the data in the `DataSet` based on the `Command` object's SQL statement. Although the code assumes there's a valid `Connection` object named `cn`, there's no code to call the `Open` method on the `Connection` object. A nice feature of the `DataAdapter` class is it checks to see whether a connection is open and, if it isn't, it opens one for you implicitly. After the `Fill` method is completed, the connection is closed automatically for you.

The `Update` method of the `DataAdapter` object, which you learn about tomorrow, compares original values in the `DataSet` against what the user modified and sends those records back to the database. The `UpdateCommand` and `DeleteCommand` properties on the `DataAdapter` handle this work. Through `UpdateCommand` and `DeleteCommand`, the `DataAdapter` supports batch updates. *Batch updating* means you can be disconnected for a long period of time and successfully update multiple rows and tables with a single `Update` call.

Note

> When you learn about the visual database tools in Visual Studio .NET tomorrow, you'll learn more about the various methods for updating data using a `DataSet` and `DataAdapter`. Today, we're just going to cover how to retrieve data from a `DataSet`, how to loop through the collection or rows that are returned, and how to bind data to Windows Forms.

The constructor for the `DataAdapter` is overloaded, so you can pass the SQL statement directly when creating the new `DataAdapter` instance. The following Visual Basic .NET code creates a `SqlDataAdapter` and passes a query and `Connection` object all at once.

VB.NET

```
Dim da As SqlDataAdapter = New SqlDataAdapter("SELECT * from Customers", cn)
```

Now that you have a basic understanding of what a `DataSet` and `DataAdapter` can do, you can continue working on the DataAccess application you started earlier.

Writing Data Access Code with a `DataAdapter`

You're now going to write the code for the Using a DataSet button. What you write here is very similar to the code snippet you saw earlier that demonstrated the general syntax of using a `DataAdapter`, but now you're going to iterate through the data you retrieve from SQL Server and load it into the `CheckedListBox1` control. Double-click the Using a DataSet button on the default Form1 to get to the code window, and add the code in Listing 10.5 to the `UseDataSet_Click` event of the form.

LISTING 10.5 `UseDataSet_Click` Event Code

VB.NET

```
Private Sub UseDataSet_Click(ByVal sender As System.Object, _
        ByVal e As System.EventArgs) Handles UseDataSet.Click

    ' Create a connection
    Dim cn As New SqlConnection( _
            "Server=(local)\NetSDK;DataBase=pubs;" _
            & "Integrated Security=SSPI")

    ' Create a new SqlDataAdapter object.
    ' The overloaded constructor allows you to set the SQL Statement
    ' and the connection object or connection string at the time
    ' you create the SqlDataAdapter object
    Dim da As SqlDataAdapter = New SqlDataAdapter _
        ("SELECT au_id, au_lname + ', ' + au_fname As FullName FROM Authors", cn)

    ' Create a new DataSet to hold the data from the SqlDataAdapter
    Dim ds As DataSet = New DataSet("Authors")
    da.Fill(ds, "Authors")

    ' Create a DataRow object
    Dim dr As DataRow

    ' Loop thru the table rows and add the items
    ' in each dataset table row to the CheckedListBox
    For Each dr In ds.Tables("Authors").Rows
        CheckedListBox1.Items.Add(dr("FullName"))
    Next

End Sub
```

LISTING 10.5 continued

C#

```
private void UseDataSet_Click(object sender, System.EventArgs e)
  {
     // Clear the items
     checkedListBox1.Items.Clear();

     // Get the connection
     SqlConnection cn = new SqlConnection
      (@"Server=(local)\NetSDK;DataBase=pubs;Integrated Security=SSPI");

     /* Create a new SqlDataAdapter object.
     The overloaded constructor allows you to set the SQL Statement
     and the connection object or connection string at the time
     you create the SqlDataAdapter object */
     SqlDataAdapter da = new SqlDataAdapter
       ("SELECT au_id, au_lname + ', ' + au_fname As
          FullName FROM Authors", cn);

     // Create a new DataSet to hold the data from the SqlDataAdapter
     DataSet ds = new DataSet("Authors");
     da.Fill(ds, "Authors");

     // Loop thru the table rows and add the items
     // in each dataset table row to the CheckedListBox
     foreach (DataRow dr in ds.Tables["Authors"].Rows)
     {
      checkedListBox1.Items.Add(dr["FullName"]);
     }
  }
```

Next, you need to write the code for the `CheckedListBox_SelectedIndexChanged` event. This code is similar to the code you wrote for the `ListBox1_SelectedIndexChanged` event with the exception of using the `GetItemChecked` method of the `CheckListBox` control to determine whether an item is checked. Double-click the `CheckListBox` control and add the code in Listing 10.6 for the control's `SelectedIndexChanged` event.

LISTING 10.6 `SelectedIndexChanged` Code for the `CheckedListBox` Control

VB.NET

```
Private Sub CheckedListBox1_SelectedIndexChanged _
               (ByVal sender As System.Object, _
               ByVal e As System.EventArgs) _
               Handles CheckedListBox1.SelectedIndexChanged
```

LISTING 10.6 continued

```
        ' Display where the event came from
        Label1.Text = "CheckedListBox1_SelectedIndexChanged"

        ' Display the selected item
        Label2.Text = CheckedListBox1.Items(CheckedListBox1.SelectedIndex)

        ' Display if the item is checked or not
        Label3.Text = "Checked = " & CheckedListBox1.GetItemChecked _
                    (CheckedListBox1.SelectedIndex)

    End Sub
```

C#

```
    private void checkedListBox1_SelectedIndexChanged(object sender,
          System.EventArgs e)
       {
          // Display where the event came from
          label1.Text = "CheckedListBox1_SelectedIndexChanged";

          // Display the selected item
          label2.Text = checkedListBox1.Text;

          // Display if the item is checked or not
          label3.Text = "Checked = " +
              checkedListBox1.GetItemChecked(checkedListBox1.SelectedIndex);
       }
```

If you press F5 to run the project and click the Using a DataSet button, you should see something similar to Figure 10.5.

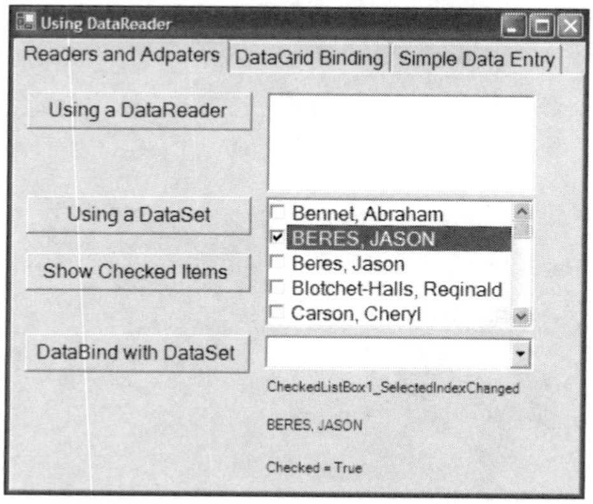

FIGURE 10.5
Running the Using a DataSet command.

In the UseDataSet_Click event, you created a SqlDataAdapter and passed the ad hoc select statement and Connection object to its overloaded constructor. You then created a new DataSet object, and called the Fill method of the SqlDataAdapter to hold the data from the database. The DataTable in this case is called Authors, and the second parameter of the Fill method is the name of the DataTable. This can be any friendly name that you choose. The idea behind the DataTable is that a DataSet can hold multiple sets of records from multiple data sources, and you need a way to reference the DataTables in the DataSet container in your code. The For Each loop uses a DataRow variable to loop through the collection of DataRows in the DataTable and adds the row item FullName to the CheckedListBox control.

It sounds like a lot to remember, but remember these bullets and you'll always know what to do with a DataSet:

- DataSets contain DataTable objects from one or more data sources.
- The DataTables collection in the DataSet has a DataRows collection.
- You can use any number of looping techniques to iterate through the collection of DataRows in a DataTable that are in a DataSet.

You can see by my description that a hierarchy exists in the DataSet. There are more than tables and rows; there are also columns, constraints, and relationships. Figure 10.6 gives you an idea of the hierarchy of objects in a DataSet.

FIGURE 10.6
DataSet *object hierarchy.*

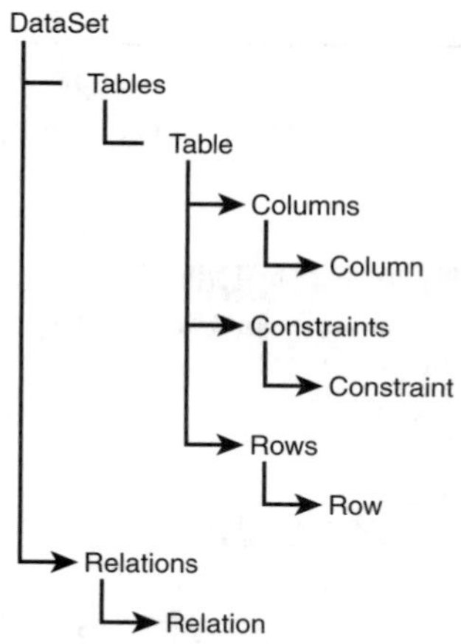

> **Note**
>
> You can dynamically create `DataSets` in memory and with `DataRows` that contain any type of information. On Day 13, you learn how to create `DataSets` that aren't getting information directly from a database, and why this is an extremely powerful feature of the `DataSet` class.

Next, you need to see how you can use databinding with a `DataSet` to make your life even easier.

Using Databinding with `DataSets`

In Visual Basic 6, *databinding* means that you can get data from a database and bind that data to various controls. This is still true in Visual Studio .NET, except that binding data to controls has been taken to new heights.

Most controls that exists in the Toolbox can be bound to a data source, and the data source doesn't have to be a database. It can be an array, a Web service, an XML file, a resource file—almost anything. The nice thing is that the model for databinding is consistent no matter what the source of data is. You tell a control what property you want to bind, you pass the control a data source and, like magic, the information appears. This type of flexible binding makes it very easy to write 100% data-driven applications.

There are two ways to bind a control to a data source:

- From the `DataBinding` property in the Properties window of the control
- Writing code to implement databinding

Tomorrow, when you learn about the data wizards in Visual Studio .NET, you'll use the Properties window in Visual Studio .NET to specify databinding properties. Today, you learn how to databind a `DataSet` to a `ComboBox` control and a `DataGrid` control by using ADO.NET code.

Understanding Simple and Complex Binding

There are two types of binding scenarios: simple binding and complex binding. *Simple binding* is when you set the `DataSource` property of a single control to a single field in a `DataSet`. *Complex binding* means you bind multiple rows and fields to a single control. Complex binding is most common in list controls and grid controls.

The following code snippet demonstrates how to implement simple databinding on a `TextBox` control. The `DataBindings` collection has methods such as `Add` that enable you to set what field you want to bind from a `DataSet`. After the databindings on a control are set, you don't have to worry about setting the `Text` property of the control—it is automatically filled by whatever the data happens to be in the `DataSet`.

VB.NET

```
' Create a connection
Dim cn As New SqlConnection( _
    "Server=(local)\NetSDK;DataBase=northwind;" _
    & "Integrated Security=SSPI")

' Create a new SqlDataAdapter and pass the SQL Statement
' that gets the ID and Name from the Authors table and connection object
Dim da As SqlDataAdapter = New SqlDataAdapter _
    ("SELECT * from Customers", cn)

' Create a new DataSet
Dim ds As DataSet = New DataSet("Customers")

' Call the Fill method to load the DataSet
da.Fill(ds, "Customers")

' Add DataBinding to the TextBoxes
TextBox2.DataBindings.Add("Text", ds.Tables("Customers"), "CompanyName")
TextBox3.DataBindings.Add("Text", ds.Tables("Customers"), "Address")
TextBox4.DataBindings.Add("Text", ds.Tables("Customers"), "City")
```

C#

```
// Get the connection
SqlConnection cn = new SqlConnection
  (@"Server=(local)\NetSDK;DataBase=northwind;Integrated Security=SSPI");

// Create a new SqlDataAdapter and pass the SQL Statement
// that gets the ID and Name from the Authors table and connection object
SqlDataAdapter adp = new SqlDataAdapter("SELECT * from Customers", cn);

// Create a new DataSet
DataSet ds = new DataSet("Customers");

// Call the Fill method to load the DataSet
adp.Fill(ds, "Customers");

// Add DataBinding to the TextBoxes
textBox2.DataBindings.Add("Text", ds.Tables["Customers"], "CompanyName");
textBox3.DataBindings.Add("Text", ds.Tables["Customers"], "Address");
textBox4.DataBindings.Add("Text", ds.Tables["Customers"], "City");
```

Because most controls have a `Text` property, including a `Form` and `Label`, you can quickly set up simple binding to display data from a database or other source.

To finish up the DataAccess project, you're going to implement complex binding on a ComboBox control and a DataGrid control.

When binding to a ComboBox, you set two properties: the DisplayMember and ValueMember. The DisplayMember is what actually displays in the ComboBox, whereas the ValueMember is an underlying unique value for the row being displayed. This is normally the primary key from the database.

For the Authors table, the primary key that uniquely differentiates each row is the au_id field. au_id would be the ValueMember field. To write the binding code for the DataAccess application, double-click the DataBind with DataSet button to get to the BindWithDataSet event in the code window. Listing 10.7 is the code that handles the click event for this button.

LISTING 10.7 BindWithDataSet Click Event Code

VB.NET

```
Private Sub BindWithDataSet_Click(ByVal sender As System.Object, _
            ByVal e As System.EventArgs) Handles BindWithDataSet.Click

  ' Create a connection
    Dim cn As New SqlConnection( _
             "Server=(local)\NetSDK;DataBase=pubs;" _
             & "Integrated Security=SSPI")

  ' Create a new SqlDataAdapter and pass the SQL Statement
  ' that gets the ID and Name from the Authors table and connection object
    Dim da As SqlDataAdapter = New SqlDataAdapter _
 ("SELECT au_id, au_lname + ', ' + au_fname As FullName FROM Authors", cn)

  ' Create a new DataSet
  Dim ds As DataSet = New DataSet("Authors")

  ' Call the Fill method to load the DataSet
  da.Fill(ds, "Authors")

  With ComboBox1
      ' Set the DataSource property of the ComboBox
      ' to the DataSet
      .DataSource = ds.Tables("Authors")

      ' Set the DisplayMember, this will be what is loaded
      ' into the ComboBox and is visible to the user
      .DisplayMember = "FullName"

      ' Set the ValueMember, this is to associate the
```

LISTING 10.7 continued

```
        ' display data with a unique ID that represents this row in the
        ' the DataSet
        .ValueMember = "au_id"

    End With

End Sub
```

C#

```
private void BindWithDataSet_Click(object sender, System.EventArgs e)
   {
      // Clear the items
      comboBox1.Items.Clear();

      // Get the connection
      SqlConnection cn = new SqlConnection
       (@"Server=(local)\NetSDK;DataBase=pubs;Integrated Security=SSPI");

      /* Create a new SqlDataAdapter object.
      The overloaded constructor allows you to set the SQL Statement
      and the connection object or connection string at the time
      you create the SqlDataAdapter object */
      SqlDataAdapter da = new SqlDataAdapter
        ("SELECT au_id, au_lname + ', ' + au_fname As
          FullName FROM Authors", cn);

      // Create a new DataSet to hold the data from the SqlDataAdapter
      DataSet ds = new DataSet("Authors");
      da.Fill(ds, "Authors");

      // Set the DataSource property of the ComboBox
      // to the DataSet
            comboBox1.DataSource = ds.Tables["Authors"];

      // Set the DisplayMember, this will be what is loaded
      // into the ComboBox and is visible to the user
      comboBox1.DisplayMember = "FullName";

      // Set the ValueMember, this is to associate the
      // display data with a unique ID that represents this row in the
      // the DataSet
      comboBox1.ValueMember = "au_id";
   }
```

In each of the previous exercises, you wrote code to retrieve the information from the `ListBox` control and you displayed that in the `Label` controls. When you bind data to a control, the way you retrieve values from the bound list controls is slightly different from a nonbound list control. This is because the control can contain information for many fields, not just what's displayed. The following `ComboBox1_SelectedIndexChanged` code fills the labels with the `DisplayMember` and `ValueMember` of the currently selected item in the `ComboBox`.

To add the code in Listing 10.8, double-click the `ComboBox1` control to get the `ComboBox1_SelectedIndexChanged` event.

LISTING 10.8 Retrieving Values from a Bound `ComboBox` Control

VB.NET

```
Private Sub ComboBox1_SelectedIndexChanged( _
        ByVal sender As Object, _
        ByVal e As System.EventArgs) _
        Handles ComboBox1.SelectedIndexChanged

    ' Display where the event came from
    Label1.Text = "ComboBox1_SelectedIndexChanged DataBound"

    ' Display the selected item
    Label2.Text = ComboBox1.Text

    ' Display the Value member
    Dim itm As DataRowView
    itm = ComboBox1.SelectedItem
    Label3.Text = CType(itm("au_id"), String)

End Sub
```

If you run the application by pressing F5 and you click on the DataBind with DataSet button, you should see something similar to Figure 10.7.

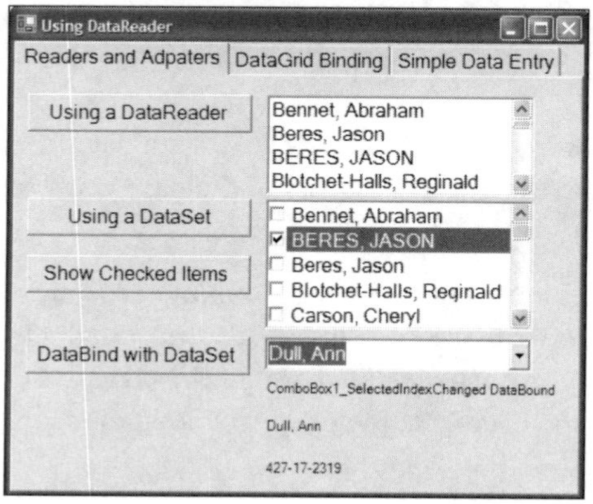

FIGURE 10.7
Running the `BindingToDataSet` *code.*

When you click the DataBind with DataSet button, the `ComboBox1` control is filled with the authors' names, which is the `DisplayMember` property, and the `SelectedIndexChanged` event of the control retrieves the `au_id` field stored in the `ValueMember` property. With only a few lines of code, you simplified your development by binding data directly from the `DataSet` object.

Binding to a `DataGrid` Control

To finish off the DataAccess application, you're going to bind a `DataSet` to a `DataGrid` control. To set this up, you need to add a `DataGrid` and `ComboBox` control to the `TabControl1` control.

Follow these steps to set up the rest of the project:

1. In design mode, click the second tab on the `TabControl1` control.
2. Drag a `ComboBox` control from the Toolbox to the `TabPage2` control.
3. Drag a `DataGrid` control from the Toolbox to the `TabPage2` control.

Your form should resemble Figure 10.8.

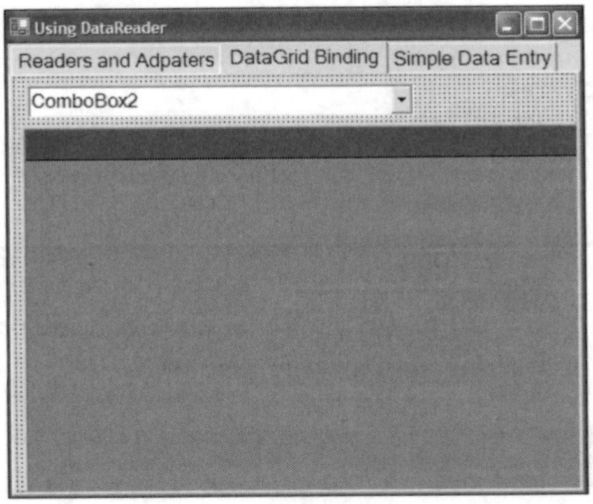

FIGURE 10.8
Form after adding `DataGrid` *and* `ComboBox` *controls to* `TabPage2`.

Next, you must write the code to fill the `DataGrid` with data from a `DataSet`. The `ComboBox` is there for the exercises at the end of the day; you won't do anything with it now.

To fill the `DataGrid`, you're going to write code in the `TabIndexChanged` event of the `TabControl1` control. To write the code that loads the grid, double-click `TabControl1` to get to the `TabControl1_TabIndexChanged` event. The code in Listing 10.9 binds the `DataGrid` control with the data from the Orders table in the Northwind database.

LISTING 10.9 `TabControl1_SelectedIndexChanged` Event Code

VB.NET

```
Private Sub TabControl1_TabIndexChanged _
        (ByVal sender As Object, _
        ByVal e As System.EventArgs) _
        Handles TabControl1.SelectedIndexChanged

    ' Check to see what tab we are on,
    ' if it is the 2nd tab, then do the databinding for the grid
    If TabControl1.SelectedTab.TabIndex = 1 Then

        ' Create a new connection object
        Dim cn As New SqlConnection( _
              "Server=(local)\NetSDK;DataBase=northwind;" _
              & "Integrated Security=SSPI")

        ' Create a new SqlDataAdapter and pass the SQL Statement
        ' and connection object
        Dim da As SqlDataAdapter = New SqlDataAdapter _
            ("SELECT * from Orders", cn)

        ' Create a DataSet to hold the SqlDataAdapter data
        Dim ds As DataSet = New DataSet("Orders")

        ' Call the Fill method to load the DataSet
        da.Fill(ds)

        ' Set the DataSource property of the grid
        ' to bind the data from the DataSet
        DataGrid1.DataSource = ds

    End If

End Sub
```

C#

```
private void tabControl1_TabIndexChanged(object sendert,
      System.EventArgs e)
  {
      // Check to see what tab we are on,
      // if it is the 2nd tab, then do the databinding for the grid
      if (tabControl1.SelectedTab.Text  == "DataGrid Binding");
      {
         // Get the connection
         SqlConnection cn = new SqlConnection
          (@"Server=(local)\NetSDK;DataBase=northwind;
              Integrated Security=SSPI");
```

LISTING 10.9 continued

```
            // Create a new SqlDataAdapter and pass the SQL Statement
            // and connection object
            SqlDataAdapter da = new SqlDataAdapter
                 ("SELECT * from Orders", cn);

            // Create a DataSet to hold the SqlDataAdapter data
            DataSet ds = new DataSet("Orders");

            // Call the Fill method to load the DataSet
            da.Fill(ds);

            // Set the DataSource property of the grid
            // to bind the data from the DataSet
            dataGrid1.DataSource = ds;

        }
    }
```

The code is identical to all the `SqlDataAdapter` code you've written today. You create a `Connection` and a `Command`, and call `Fill` on the `DataAdapter`. The only difference is that you set the `DataSource` property of the `DataGrid` to the `DataSet` object.

If you run the code by pressing F5 and click the second tab, you should see results like Figure 10.9.

FIGURE 10.9
Complex binding to a `DataGrid` *control.*

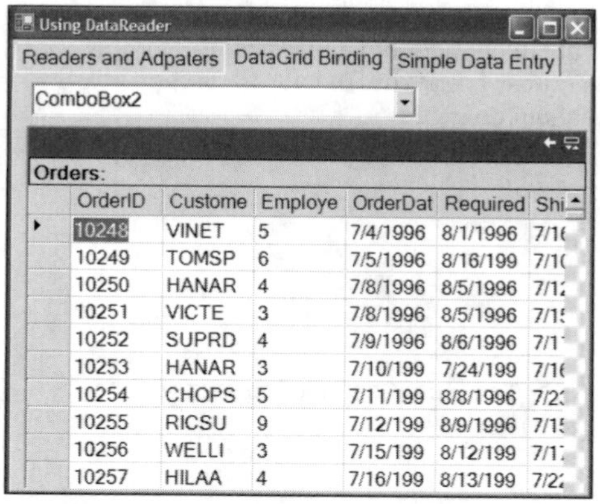

Like magic, you have a `DataGrid` filled with data from a SQL Server database.

As you can see, implementing simple and complex databinding is very simple. By setting a few properties in any control in the Toolbox, you can quickly create a data-driven user interface.

Summary

Today you learned all the basics of accessing data with ADO.NET. Like most of the object models in the FCL, Microsoft seems to have thought of everything, and ADO.NET is no different. Choosing the wrong data access strategy when developing applications can spell disaster for scalability and functionality. With ADO.NET, you have many options to choose from when deciding how to get data to and from any type of data store.

If you need fast, read-only access, use a `DataReader`.

If you need complex relational data that must be disconnected from a data source, use `DataSets` and `DataAdapters`.

Tomorrow you continue learning about using ADO.NET through the Visual tools in Visual Studio .NET. Everything you learned today serves as a foundation for your work tomorrow and the rest of the week.

Q&A

Q I don't get it. Why doesn't a `DataReader` support databinding on Windows Forms? It seems like so much less code to write!

A It's true that using `DataReaders` amounts to writing less code. To bind to a control in Windows Forms, the class must expose the `IList` or `IListSource` interface of the `System.ComponentModel` namespace. A `DataReader` is an unbuffered stream of data that does not support these interfaces.

Q You kept mentioning scalability. How can I achieve maximum performance and scalability in my data access applications?

A Even though applications might be hindered by the hardware they're running on, writing efficient code also makes a big difference. Follow these tips to maximize your code performance:

- Always open database connections as late as possible and close them as early as possible.
- Use `DataReaders` for read-only forward-only data access as much as possible. `DataReaders` are the most efficient way to access data from a database in .NET.
- Don't pass large `DataSet` objects over the network. Doing so affects the network performance, which in turn affects your application performance.

- Use stored procedures for all `Selects`, `Inserts`, `Updates`, and `Deletes`. Stored procedures are compiled in SQL Server, whereas ad hoc queries aren't. Using stored procedures improves data access performance.

Q I keep getting errors when I attempt to reuse a connection object after I implement a `DataReader`. Why?

A Each time a `DataReader` is associated with a `Connection` object, the relationship is exclusive until you explicitly close the `DataReader` object using the `Close` method of the `DataReader`. Doing so releases the `Connection` object for reuse with another `Command` object.

To get more information online, open the following link. It takes you to the Diving Into Data Access column of the Microsoft Developers Network (MSDN).

`http://www.msdn.microsoft.com/library/en-us/dndive/html/data06132002.asp`

This series of articles gives you tons of great examples on different data access techniques, and discusses more advanced topics such as handling multiple tables in a `DataSet` and how to manage relationships in a `DataSet`.

Quiz

1. The ______________ object in ADO.NET handles the execution of SQL statements for the `DataReader` and `DataAdapter` classes.
2. The `DataReader` is used for forward-only reading of data. To be able to reuse data from a database, manipulate the __________ class.
3. True or False: The `SqlDataAdapter` and `OleDataAdapter` share the same functionality.
4. True or False: You don't need to use a `Connection` object with the `DataAdapter` class because it handles all connection information for you.
5. True or False: The `DataBindings` collection in .NET only supports `DataSets` and XML files for simple and complex binding to the `Label` control, the `DataGrid` control, and the `TextBox` control.
6. In Web Forms, I can use the _____________ object and the ___________ object to bind controls to a data source.

Quiz Answers

1. `Command`
2. `DataSet`
3. False. The answer is misleading, though. The two classes share about 98% of the same functionality, with `DataType` classes being the main difference.

4. False. You still must set connection parameters. The DataAdapter explicitly opens a connection for you. You don't have to use connection.open.
5. False. You can use the DataBindings collection with many controls, and the only complex binding mentioned in the question would be the DataGrid control.
6. DataSet, DataReader

Exercises

1. In the DataAccess application you wrote today, you added a button named ShowCheckedItems to TabPage1. Write the code that iterates through the CheckedListBox and return the items that are checked. To get started, look up the GetItemChecked method in the SDK. This should give you a hint about how to proceed with the code.
2. We didn't delve too much into the Command.Parameters collection today. Being able to send parameters to a stored procedure is extremely important. To get familiar with the syntax, examine the following Visual Basic .NET code:

```
With cmd.Parameters
    .Add("@au_id", SqlDbType.VarChar, 11).Value = TextBox1.Text
    .Add("@au_fname", SqlDbType.VarChar, 20).Value = TextBox2.Text
    .Add("@au_lname", SqlDbType.VarChar, 20).Value = TextBox3.Text
    .Add("@phone", SqlDbType.Char, 12).Value = TextBox4.Text
    .Add("@address", SqlDbType.VarChar, 40).Value = TextBox5.Text
    .Add("@city", SqlDbType.VarChar, 20).Value = TextBox6.Text
    .Add("@state", SqlDbType.Char, 2).Value = TextBox7.Text
    .Add("@zip", SqlDbType.Char, 5).Value = TextBox8.Text
    .Add("@contract", SqlDbType.Int).Value = "1"
End With
```

   Now, open up the completed DataAccess solution and study the code in the AddAuthor_Click event. This is the model for adding parameters to the Command object and passing them to a stored procedure. In the SDK file, look up the SqlDbType enumeration, and learn why it's important when dealing with creating parameters and how the data types in .NET map to the data types in SQL Server. After tomorrow's exercises, you'll have a better understanding of parameters, and you'll be using them more throughout the week.

3. When you added the ComboBox to TabPage2, you didn't write any code for it. You're now going to write code that
   - Binds the Customers table from the Northwind database to the ComboBox2 on TabPage2
   - Filters the DataGrid based on the CustomerID that's selected from ComboBox2

To get started, add a `DataView` variable named `dv` directly under the `Public Class Form1` declaration. Your code should look like this:

```
public class Form1 : System.Windows.Forms.Form
{
    private DataView dv;
```

Or, if you're using Visual Basic .NET, your code should look like this:

```
Public Class Form1
    Inherits System.Windows.Forms.Form
    Private dv As DataView
```

The `DataView` object is reused in several `Form1` methods, so making it globally available to the class is important.

Next, create a method in your code called `Load_Customers`. The `Load_Customers` method mimics the code you wrote for the `BindWithDataSet_Click` event except it works with the Northwind database and the Customers table, not the Authors table in the Pubs database.

In the `Load_Customers` method, do the following:

- Create a connection to the Northwind database.
- Create a `SqlDataAdapter` that selects all `Customers` from the Customers table.
- Call the `Fill` method of the `SqlDataAdapter` using the name Customers as the `DataTable` for the `DataSet`.
- Set the `ComboBox2 DataSource` to the `DataSet` you just created.
- Set the `ValueMember` of the `ComboBox` to the `CustomerID` field.
- Set the `DisplayMember` to the `ComboBox` to the `CustomerID` field.

Next you must write code in the `SelectedIndexChanged` event of `ComboBox2` that uses the `RowFilter` event of the `DataView` object to filter the `DataView` and rebinds the `DataView` to the `DataGrid`.

The following code accomplishes that task:

VB.NET

```
Private Sub ComboBox2_SelectedIndexChanged(ByVal sender As System.Object, _
        ByVal e As System.EventArgs) Handles ComboBox2.SelectedIndexChanged

    ' Set the RowFilter property on the DataView
    dv.RowFilter = "CustomerID Like '" & ComboBox2.Text & "%'"

    ' Re-set the datasource to the filtered data
    DataGrid1.DataSource = dv

End Sub
```

C#

```
private void comboBox2_SelectedIndexChanged(object sender, System.EventArgs e)
   {
      // Set the RowFilter property on the DataView
      dv.RowFilter = "CustomerID Like '" + comboBox2.Text + "%'";

      // Re-set the datasource to the filtered data
      dataGrid1.DataSource = dv;
   }
```

To finish up, modify the code you wrote earlier in the `TabControl1_TabIndexChanged` event to bind the `DataGrid` to the `DataView` instead of the `DataSet`.

The following code hint will help you do this:

```
dv = New DataView(ds.Tables(0), "", "", DataViewRowState.OriginalRows)
```

To get a better understanding of the `DataView` object, look up `DataView` in the SDK and explore its capabilities.

When you're done, you have a complete mechanism for filtering records in a `DataSet` using the `DataView` object.

Your application should look something like Figure 10.10 when you are finished.

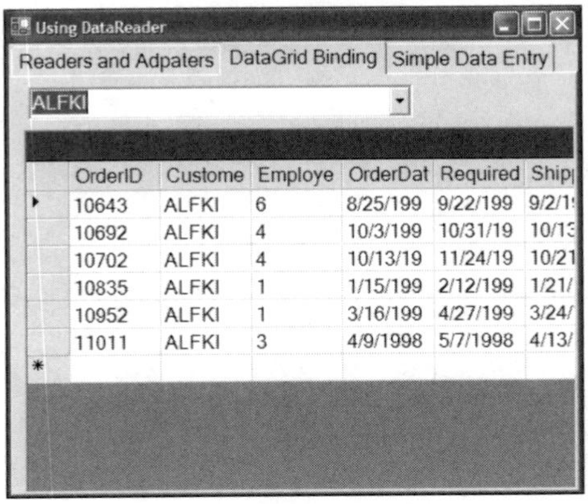

FIGURE 10.10
The results from exercise 3.

WEEK 2

DAY 11

Understanding Visual Database Tools

Yesterday you learned the ins and outs of ADO.NET. Although you had to write some code to work with data, you saw how easy it is to write data access applications using ADO.NET. Today, you learn that you can write complete data-driven applications without writing any code. Using the visual tools in Visual Studio .NET, including the Server Explorer, you can create database connections, manage databases, create tables, views, and stored procedures, and use wizards to generate forms automatically. Today is broken down into three main sections. You learn how to

- Use the Server Explorer to manage databases and `Connection` objects, including creating views, stored procedures, and debugging stored procedures
- Create a data-driven form using the Server Explorer
- Use the DataForm Wizard to create a data-driven data entry form

Managing Databases with the Server Explorer

The Server Explorer in Visual Studio .NET is your door to server resources on your local machine or other network computers that you have the authority to connect to. In Day 2, "Introduction to Visual Studio .NET," you got a rundown on the different parts of the Server Explorer, but we held off on anything that has to do with databases until today.

To start working with the Server Explorer, create a new Visual Basic .NET or C# Windows Forms application called DataTools_vb or Datatools_cs, depending on what language you're using. I refer to the application as simply DataTools throughout the rest of the day. After your project is open, you should see the Server Explorer on the left side of your screen. If you don't, select Server Explorer from the View pull-down menu or use the Ctrl+Alt+S keyboard shortcut.

> **Note**
>
> The Server Explorer isn't included in the Standard Edition of Visual Studio .NET.

As you learned earlier in Week 1, the Server Explorer contains nodes that enable you to drill into the enterprise features of your machine. The design goal of the Server Explorer is to make your life easy—to give you access to all the servers and services you need when writing enterprise applications. If the Server Explorer didn't exist, you'd need to have several Microsoft Management Console sessions open to view SQL Server databases, message queues, event logs, performance counters, and services. You might not use those features in every application, but having them handy is an extremely nice feature.

The top-level node of the Server Explorer is Data Connections. The Data Connections node is responsible for handling the `OleDbConnection` and `SqlConnection` controls on the Data tab in the toolbox. You learn more about managing items in the node later today.

If you drill into the Servers node, you'll see the SQL Servers node for the SQL Servers on your machine. Figure 11.1 shows what the SQL Server nodes looks like on my computer.

FIGURE 11.1
The SQL Servers node of the Server Explorer.

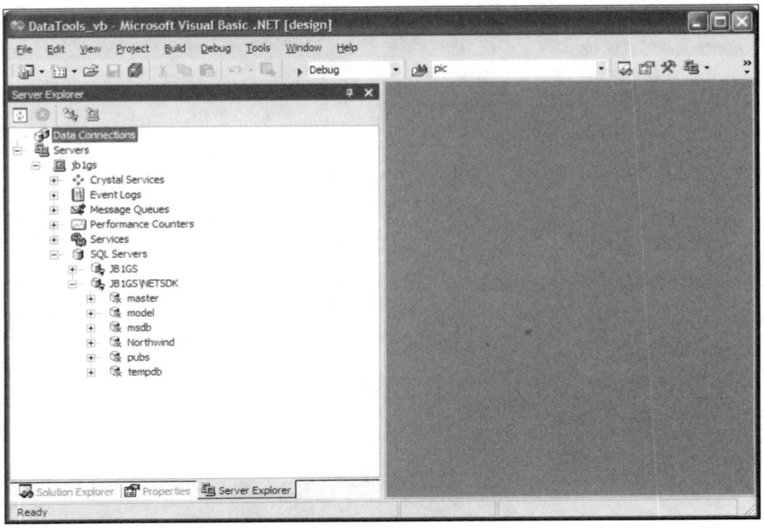

On my computer, I've installed SQL Server 2000 Developer Edition as well as the .NET SDK MSDE database. The nice thing about the Server Explorer is that if you don't have SQL Server installed, you still have a great management tool for MSDE databases because MSDE doesn't come with the Enterprise Manager tool that SQL Server has. You can see in Figure 11.1 that each node under the server instance name contains the names of all the databases in this instance of SQL Server. If you're attempting to connect to another server, you must right-click the top-level Servers node. This prompts you for the server name to connect to. If you're attempting to connect to other servers, you must be on the same domain, but you can change the security context with which to log in to the server. This maintains security across network resources.

If you have multiple instances of SQL Server installed on your machine, you can right-click the SQL Servers node and connect to as many instances of SQL Server as you want. More nodes are added for each server instance, as shown in Figure 11.1.

When you click any of the nodes under the Server Explorer, you can right-click any of the objects to get the available options for working with the selected item. You also have a new menu item on the main menu—Database—which gives you the same options as right-clicking on the nodes for the individual databases. To see this in action, drill into the Northwind database, and then drill into tables and right-click on the Categories table, as Figure 11.2 demonstrates.

FIGURE 11.2

Context menu for database options.

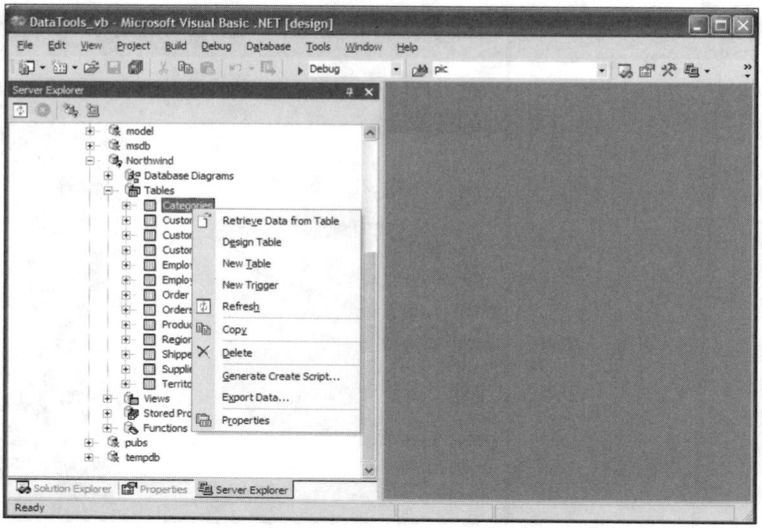

If you select the Retrieve Data from Table item from the contextual menu, you'll see something like Figure 11.3.

FIGURE 11.3

Opening a table from the Server Explorer.

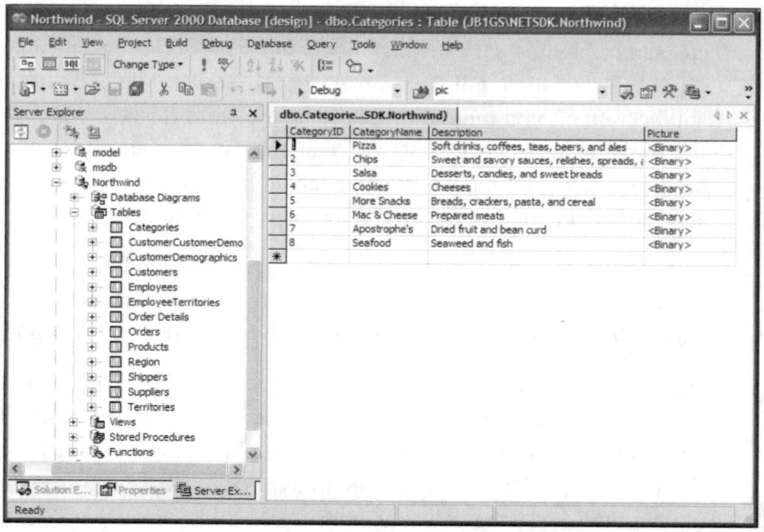

From here, you can add, edit, and delete records from the Categories table. Table 11.1 describes what you can do from the Server Explorer for each type of object in SQL Server.

TABLE 11.1 Options for Manipulating SQL Server Objects from the Server Explorer

Object	*Description of Available Options*
Database	Close the existing connection for the selected database.
	Change the login context for the selected database.
	Create a new database in the selected SQL Server or MSDE instance.
	Generate SQL scripts for the selected database or other SQL Server objects.
Tables	Create a new table in the selected database.
	Retrieve data from the selected table.
	Design the selected table using the Table Designer.
	Create a new trigger on the selected table.
	Delete the selected table.
	Copy the selected table. You can then paste the object onto a form, which creates `SqlConnection` and `SqlDataAdapter` objects on the form for the selected table.
	Generate SQL scripts for the selected table or other SQL Server objects.
	Export to table data into the SQL Server Bulk Copy format.
Views	Retrieve data from the selected view.
	Design the selected view. This brings up the Query Designer window for the selected view, enabling you to visually design the view.
	Create a new view. This brings up the Query Designer window so that you can visually create the new view.
	Create a new trigger for the selected view.
	Copy the selected view. You can then paste the object onto a form, which creates `SqlConnection` object and `SqlDataAdapter` objects on the form.
	Delete the selected view.
	Generate SQL scripts for the selected view or other SQL Server objects.
Stored Procedures	Create a new stored procedure.
	Alter the selected stored procedure.
	Run the selected stored procedure.
	Step into the selected stored procedure with the debugger.
	Copy the selected stored procedure. You can then paste the object onto a form, which creates `SqlConnection` objects and `SqlDataAdapter` objects on the form for the selected stored procedure.
	Delete the selected stored procedure.
	Generate SQL scripts for the selected table or other SQL Server objects.
Functions	Create a new inline function.
	Create a new scalar-valued function.
	Create a new table-valued function.

If you've ever used the SQL Server Enterprise Manager, you'll notice that the functionality and designers are almost identical in Visual Studio .NET. With the exception of defining users and roles, you can do almost the same things with Visual Studio .NET that you can with Enterprise Manager.

Using the Table Designer

To see how the Table Designer works, right-click on the Categories table and select Design Table from the contextual menu. The Table Designer should appear as shown in Figure 11.4.

FIGURE 11.4

Table Designer in Server Explorer.

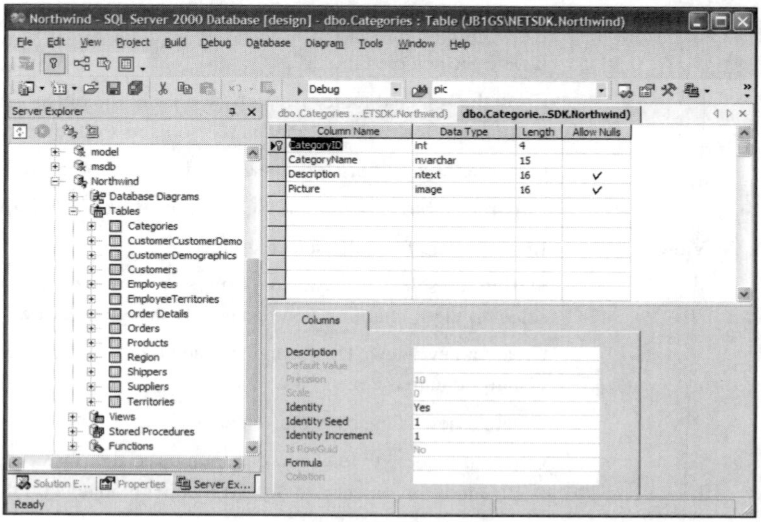

The Table Designer for altering tables and adding new tables is identical. Some of the key capabilities you have are

- Add and modify column names
- Modify data types for columns
- Modify the precision and scale for numeric types
- Set identity fields and the identity increment and identity seed
- Set the `IsRowGuid` property to define the row's data type as GUID
- Set the default collation for the table
- Set the primary key, foreign keys, and clustered and nonclustered indexes for the table

- Set relationship properties between the selected table and other tables
- Define check constraints for the columns in the table

When using the Table Designer, changes you make aren't applied unless you save the table. If this is the first time you've seen the Table Designer, you can play around with the different available options without affecting anything.

Tip

> When using the Table Designer, you can either right-click when you're inside the designer to get the contextual menu with available options, or you can use the Table toolbar that opens when you're in Table Design mode.

Using the View and Query Designer

The View and Query Designer enables you to easily create queries and views visually. Views are useful objects in SQL Server that enable you to create complex queries with multiple tables and joins. After the view is saved, you reference it as if it were a single table. For example, consider the following complex `Select` query:

```
SELECT dbo.[Order Details].OrderID, dbo.[Order Details].ProductID,
dbo.Products.ProductName, dbo.[Order Details].UnitPrice,
dbo.[Order Details].Quantity, dbo.[Order Details].Discount,
CONVERT(money, (dbo.[Order Details].UnitPrice *
dbo.[Order Details].Quantity) *
(1 - dbo.[Order Details].Discount) / 100) * 100 AS ExtendedPrice
FROM
dbo.Products INNER JOIN dbo.[Order Details] ON
dbo.Products.ProductID = dbo.[Order Details].ProductID
```

If you had to use it over and over in your application, it could become difficult to remember the exact syntax. If you save this query as a view named `vw_GetOrderDetailsExtended`, you can simply use this in your code:

```
Select * from vw_ GetOrderDetailsExtended
```

Using views can separate your data access functionality from your data access code. To test the creation of a new view, right-click the Views node and select New View. The Add Table dialog shown in Figure 11.5 is the first thing to pop up.

From the Add Table dialog, select the Customers table and click Add, and then select the Orders table and click Add. Now that both tables are added, click the Close button to close the Add Table dialog.

Now the Query Designer appears with the Customers and Orders table added. To select the columns that will be in your query output, simply choose them by checking the box to the left of the column name. The Query Designer is broken up into the four panes described in Table 11.2.

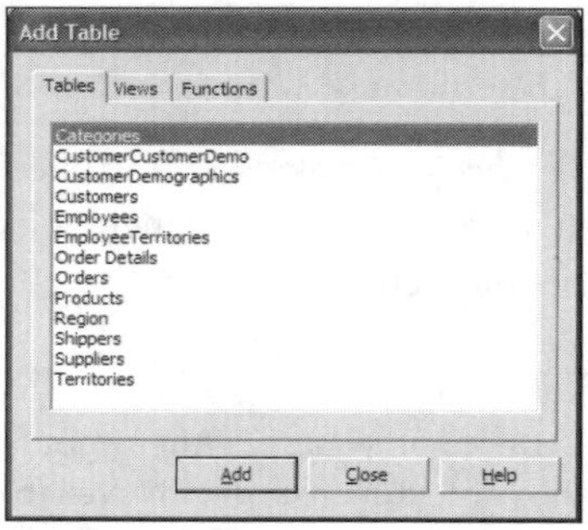

FIGURE 11.5
Add Table dialog for the Query Designer.

TABLE 11.2 The Query and View Designer Panes

Pane Name	*Description*
Diagram pane	Displays the tables and joins between tables that are added to the query.
Grid pane	Creates a data grid that displays selected columns, sorts, and filters for the query.
SQL pane	Displays the auto-generated SQL statement as you select and deselect column names from the Diagram pane. You can also type SQL statements that otherwise would not be able to be created visually, such as union joins.
Results pane	Shows the output of the query in a data grid.

Tip

You can add additional tables, views, and functions to the query you're designing by dragging and dropping from the Server Explorer onto the Diagram pane.

By either right-clicking anywhere in the designer or using the Query drop-down menu from the main menu, you can

- Execute the query by selecting Run
- Verify the SQL syntax of the query
- Add additional tables to the query
- Get the Properties page for the query to define `Group By` clauses, `Distinct` clauses, encrypt the view, bind the view to a table schema, or modify the view's indexes

Figure 11.6 shows the Query and View Designer in action after adding the Customers and Orders table, selecting some fields, and selecting Run from the Query drop-down menu.

FIGURE 11.6

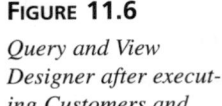

Query and View Designer after executing Customers and Orders query.

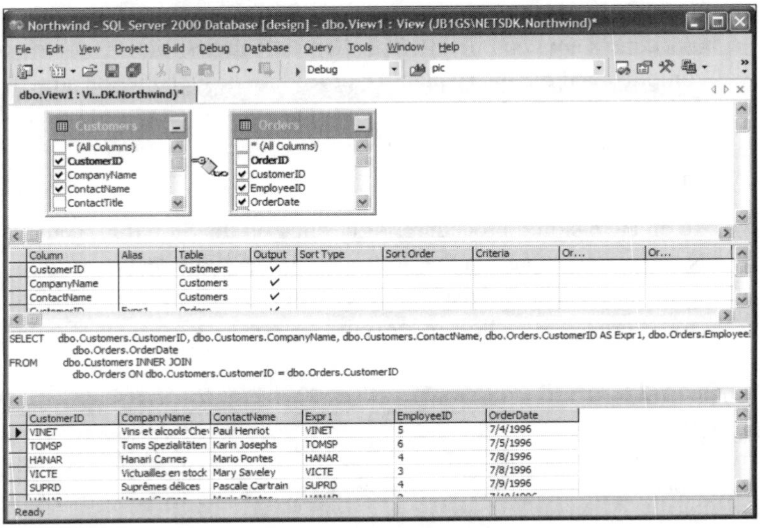

After running the View and making sure it's okay, you can close the designer window. As the designer window closes, it prompts you to save the view as View*X*, where *X* is a number. If you click Yes, you're prompted for a more friendly name. Give the view you just created the name `vw_CustomerOrders` when prompted. After the view is saved, it appears under the Views node of your Northwind database.

Caution

> If you aren't familiar with the encryption options in views and stored procedures in SQL Server, don't mess with them. When you encrypt a view or stored procedure, you can't decrypt it. There's no such thing as decrypting an object in SQL. You would have to use the `Alter` statement with the original SQL statement with the `With Encryption` option commented-out of the SQL statement. So, unless you remember the exact syntax of your SQL statements, it's best not to encrypt your views or stored procedures.

Using the Stored Procedure Designer and Debugger

Stored procedures are the best way to access your data to improve performance and scalability. Every time you run a query against SQL Server, it goes through several steps to parse and analyze the query. The internal SQL Server Query Analyzer determines the best options based on the tables in your query on getting the data back to you. This consumes resources on the database server.

By saving your queries as stored procedures, you can avoid this overhead because stored procedures are compiled in SQL Server. The first time a stored procedure executes, it's compiled and the query plan for procedure is added to the stored procedure cache in SQL Server. When subsequent calls are made to the stored procedure, it can grab the optimized and compiled query plan from the cache, giving you massive performance gains.

To create a stored procedure, right-click on the Stored Procedures node for the Northwind database in the Server Explorer, and select New Stored Procedure. The designer for creating the stored procedure appears. Figure 11.7 shows a newly created stored procedure called `sp_GetCustomerOrders`.

FIGURE 11.7

Using the Stored Procedure Designer to create a new stored procedure.

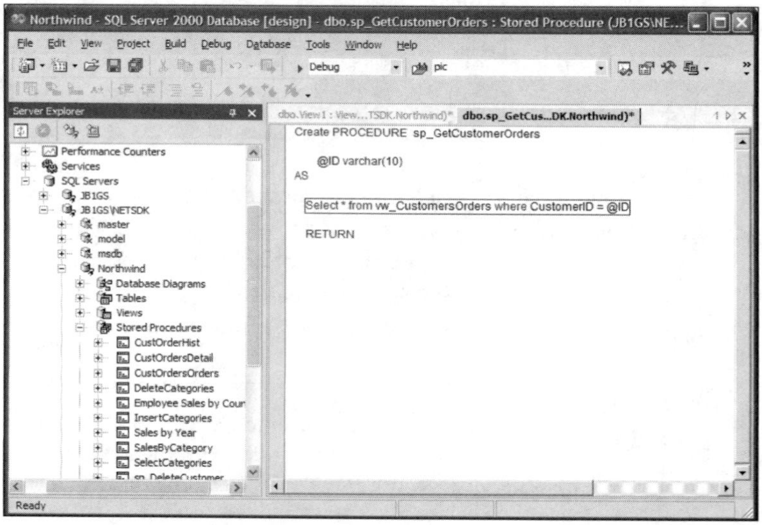

The SQL statement in Figure 11.7 is as follows:

```
Create Procedure sp_GetCustomerOrders
  @ID varchar(10)
AS
  Select * from vw_CustomerOrders where CustomerID = @ID
Return
```

This procedure gets all the records from the view you created earlier whose `CustomerID` matches the `@ID` parameter being passed to the stored procedure.

Before you run the stored procedure, you must save it. You can either click the Save button on the main toolbar, or select Save sp_GetCustomerOrders from the File menu.

Now you can right-click in the designer window and select Run Stored Procedure, as Figure 11.8 demonstrates.

FIGURE 11.8

Running the stored procedure from the Stored Procedure Designer.

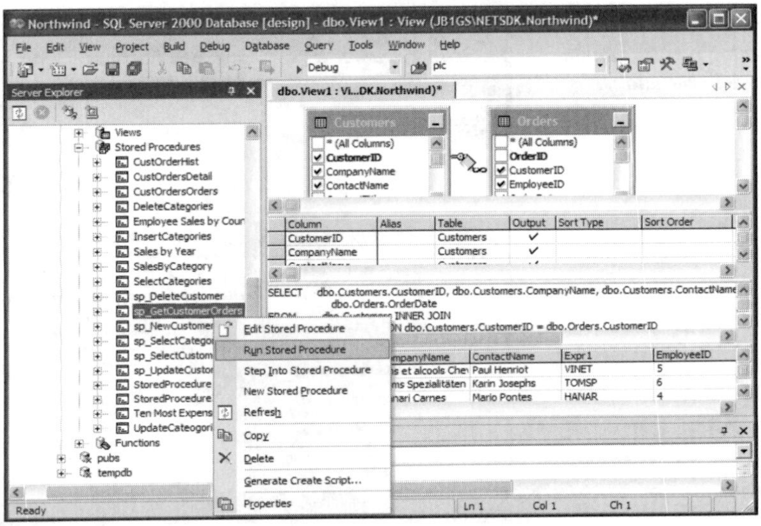

Notice the other options available in the context menu. You have the ability to use all the robust debugging tools in Visual Studio .NET to set breakpoints and step through your stored procedures. This is an extremely powerful feature that can save you hours of time when working with stored procedures.

11

There's also an Insert SQL option on the contextual menu. If you click it, the View and Query designer pops up so that you can visually create stored procedures just as you can views.

When you run this stored procedure, the Run Stored Procedure dialog pops up and asks you for the `@ID` parameter. Type in **`ALFKI`** for the `@ID` parameter as shown in Figure 11.9.

After you click the OK button, the stored procedure executes, and the results are displayed in the Database Output window as Figure 11.10 shows.

Like magic, your stored procedure executes and you see the results. Visual Studio .NET could not have made creating views and stored procedures any easier.

Tip

> When creating views and stored procedures, you should prefix them with `vw` for a view or `sp` for a stored procedure. This enables you and others to know they're not actually accessing a table, which is useful because there are rules for running updates, inserts, and deletes against views.

FIGURE 11.9

Dialog box for running stored procedures.

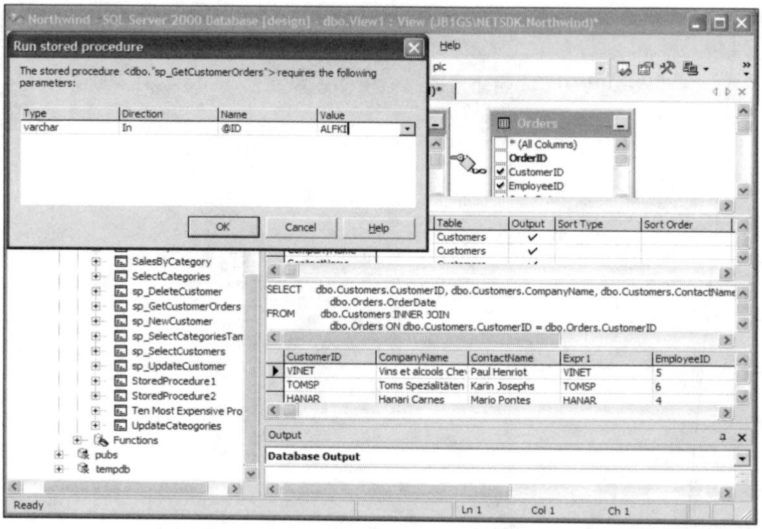

FIGURE 11.10

Stored procedure results in the Database Output window.

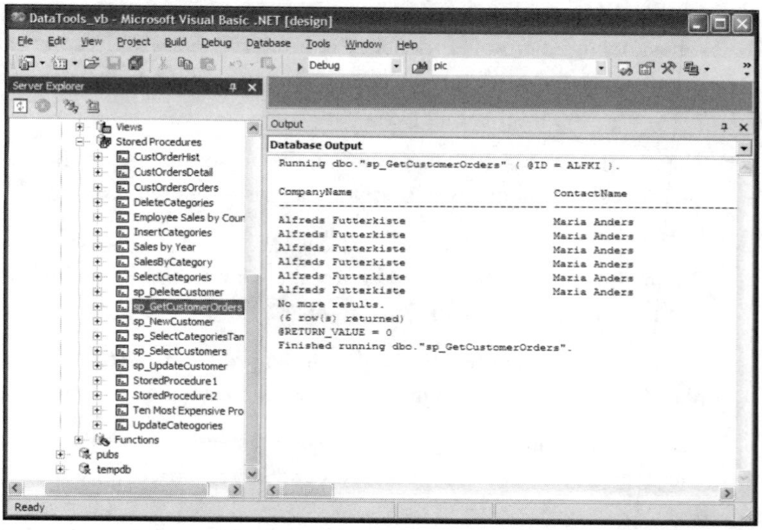

Note

By default, `MSSDI98.DLL` (which is needed to attach to the SQL Debugger) isn't installed in the correct path when MSDE is installed. This means stored procedure debugging doesn't work until you copy `MSSDI98.DLL` to the `\BINN` directory of the SQL Server Desktop Engine directory. This is normally under `Program Files\Microsoft SQL Server`. If you can't find it, perform a search for `BINN`—it's the only directory named `BINN` on your computer.

> Also, if SQL Server 2000 is already installed and you're using the MSDE database, as I am, debugging won't work. The DLL versions installed with SQL Server and MSDE are different, so you must make sure that the latest version of `MSSDI98.DLL` is in your `BINN` directory.

Now that you have a handle on how to use the database tools in the Server Explorer, you can create data-driven forms that take advantage of the features in the Server Explorer.

Building Data-Driven Forms with the Server Explorer

As you learned yesterday, databinding is everywhere in .NET. You can literally bind any type of data source to any type of object. Using the Server Explorer in .NET, you can set up quick-and-dirty data entry forms with just a few lines of code.

To see how to use the Server Explorer to create a data entry form, double-click the default `Form1` in the DataTools project that you've been working with.

After the form is in the Forms Designer, drag the Categories table from the Northwind database in the Server Explorer onto the form. A `SqlConnection` object and a `SqlDataAdapter` object are added automatically to your form. Figure 11.11 is what your project should look like at this point.

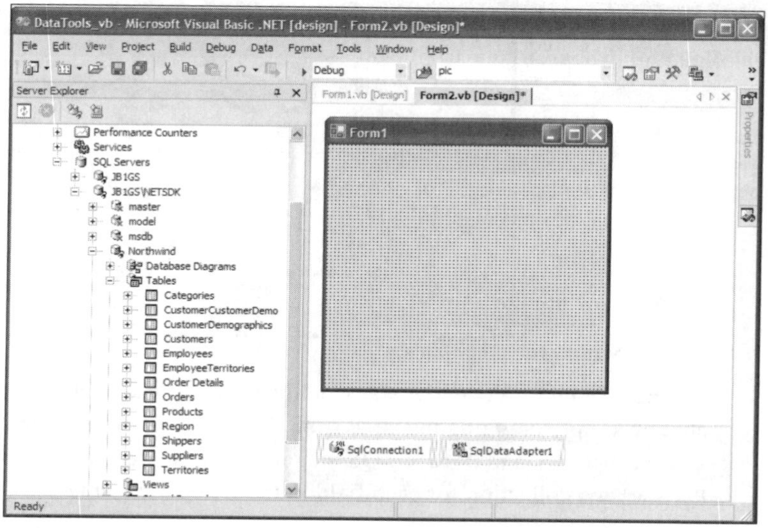

FIGURE 11.11
Project after Categories is added from the Server Explorer.

Note

The `SqlConnection` and `SqlDataAdapter` objects that were added to your form are the same objects you learned about yesterday. Yesterday, you created these objects in code; today, you're using them as design-time components. On the Data tab of the Toolbox, you'll notice there are design-time components for each of the SQL and OLE DB objects you created programmatically yesterday. There's no difference between creating ADO.NET objects through code and using them as components from the Toolbox. If you use the components from the Toolbox, you have more design-time visual tools to work with the ADO.NET objects and data sources.

Now that the `Connection` object and `DataAdapter` object have been added automatically, you have the connection to the database and the object that you can use in conjunction with a `DataSet` to move data back and forth between SQL Server.

To see what actually happened, double-click on the form, and drill into the Windows Forms Designer region in the Code window. You'll see lines and lines of code that you didn't write. A snapshot of what was generated is shown in Figure 11.12.

FIGURE 11.12

ADO.NET code generated by Server Explorer objects.

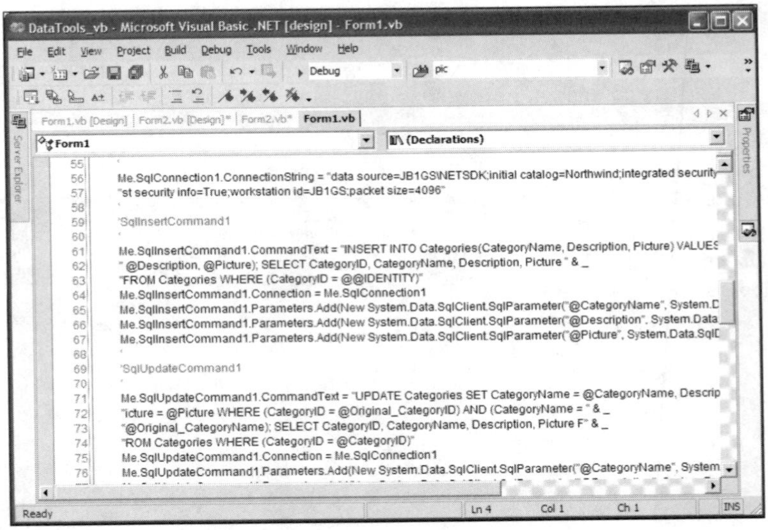

All the ADO.NET code that you would have otherwise had to write yourself was generated by simply dragging the table from the Server Explorer onto the form. The `Select`, `Insert`, `Update`, and `Delete` SQL statements were created along with the `SqlCommand` `Parameters` collection for each field in the Categories table.

Next, you must create a DataSet to hold the data that the DataAdapter is going to retrieve for you. In ADO.NET, there are two types of DataSets: typed and nontyped. A typed DataSet contains strong type information about the fields and the allowable data types. When you create a typed DataSet, you can reference the field names in the DataSet as you would any other property—by using the dot syntax.

A nontyped DataSet does not contain strong type information about the fields in the DataSet. The main difference to you is how the field names are referenced when working with the DataSet. When using the SqlDataAdapter component from the Toolbox or when it's automatically generated for you by the Server Explorer, you can easily generate a typed DataSet for the DataAdapter.

To generate a typed DataSet for the SqlDataAdapter1 that was added to Form1, right-click SqlDataAdapter1 and select Generate DataSet from the contextual menu. The Generate Dataset dialog box now pops up. You should see something like Figure 11.13.

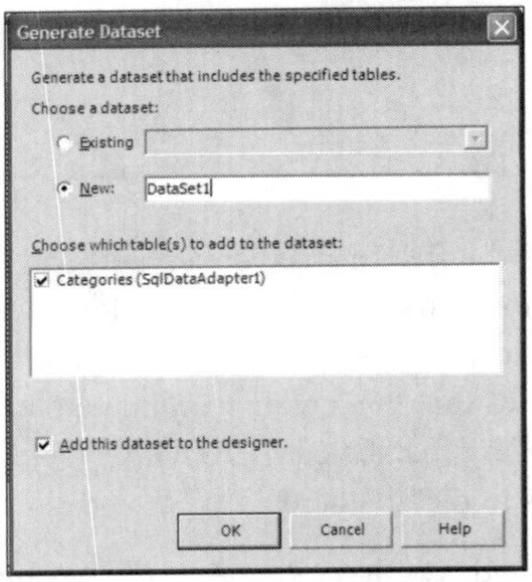

FIGURE 11.13
The Generate Dataset Dialog box.

Because DataSets can contain data from multiple sources, you're given the option either to use an existing DataSet in your project or to create a new DataSet. For this exercise, select the New option and type **DataSet1** in the Name box. Leave the Categories (SqlDataAdapter1) option checked, and leave Add This Dataset to the Designer checked. After you click the OK button, you'll notice a new Dataset11 object is added to your form.

If you look in your Solution Explorer, you'll see the DataSet1.xsd file has been added to your solution. This is the XML schema that represents the typed dataset for the DataSet component that the Generate DataSet tool just created. If you double-click the DataSet1.xsd file, you'll see the XML schema that represents your data. If you see the Dataset schema, but not as an XML schema, click the XML button at the bottom of the Schema Designer to view the actual XML representation of the schema for the typed `DataSet` component. Figure 11.14 shows the auto-generated schema.

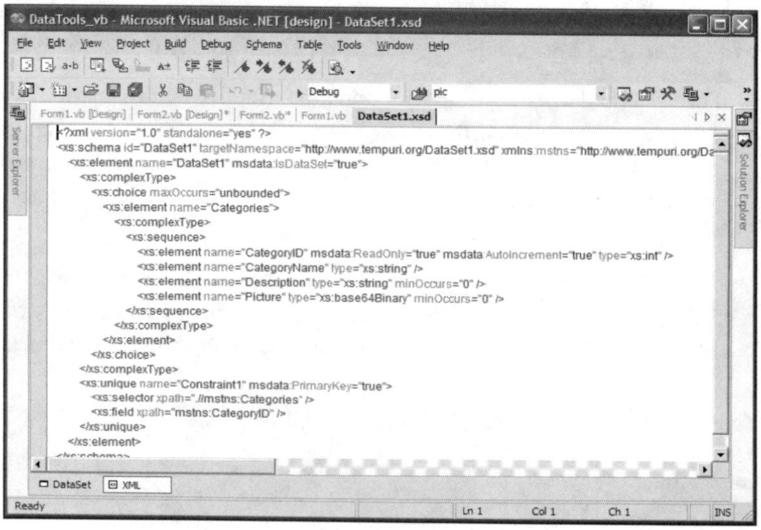

FIGURE 11.14

XSD schema generated from the `SqlDataAdapter` *for the* `DataSet`.

Notice that the XSD file defines the field names, data types, and primary key constraints. The `DataSet` uses this file to know what kind of data is allowed and how it should store that data. Tomorrow, when you learn about XML in .NET, you'll create your own XSD files and use them with XML files that you create to validate data types against XML data. Because the data format being marshaled by ADO.NET is XML, it's only natural that it would use XML schemas to dictate the data types and rules for the data.

Now that the XSD file is generated, you have `Connection`, `DataAdapter`, and `DataSet` components ready to go for this form, but you haven't done any coding.

Before you write the four lines of code to actually use the data you have just created, right-click on `SqlDataAdapter` and select Preview Data from the contextual menu. The Data Adapter Preview window pops up. This window enables you to view the actual data before using it. Figure 11.15 shows the output after clicking the Fill Dataset button on the Preview form.

If you have multiple `DataSets` on the form, they show up in the Target dataset drop-down list. This form is useful for simply viewing the data that's available from the `DataAdapter` object. Click the Close button to close the Preview dialog.

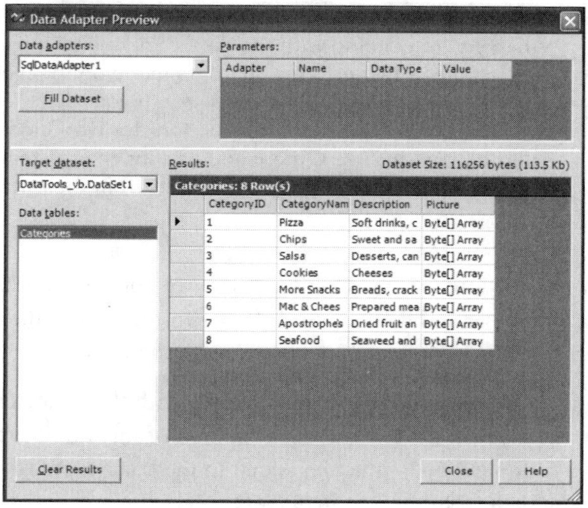

FIGURE 11.15

Previewing data from the `DataAdapter`.

Next, right-click the `DataSet11` component on your form and select Dataset Properties from the context menu. The Dataset Properties dialog pops up. This dialog, shown in Figure 11.16, contains the field details that the `DataSet` uses, based on the strongly typed dataset you created from the `SqlDataAdapter`. You can drill into the table and select the fields to view the properties. If you modify the XSD file, the Dataset Properties dialog box reflects those changes.

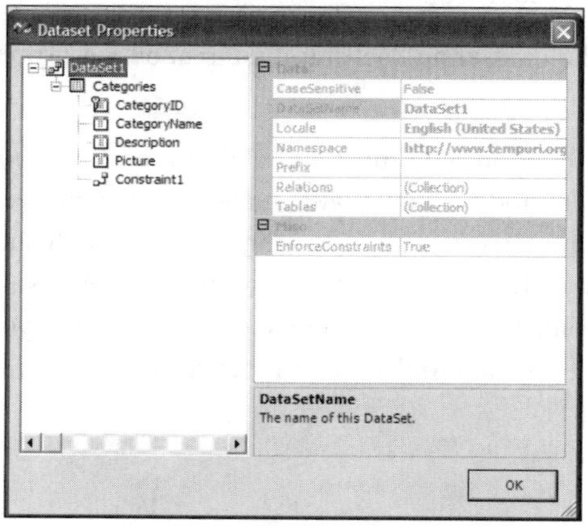

FIGURE 11.16

The Dataset Properties dialog box.

Tip

> When you're working with the data components shown in the nonvisible controls area of your forms, the Data menu on the main menu changes its options based on the object you select. If you click the `DataSet11` component, the Data menu has all the options for working with `DataSets`. If you select `SqlDataAdapter1`, the menu options change to those for `DataAdapters`. The same is true for all the components from the Data tab in the Toolbox.

To finish up this section, you must add a `DataGrid` control from the Toolbox to your Form1. After you've added the `DataGrid` to the form, modify the `Anchor` properties of the `DataGrid` so that it automatically resizes with the form.

Now you must write the code that loads the grid with the data from the dataset. As you learned yesterday, you must call the `Fill` method of the `DataAdapter` to load data into a `DataSet`. The following code must be added to the `Load` event of your form to fill the dataset with the data from the `DataAdapter`:

VB.NET

```
SqlDataAdapter1.Fill(DataSet11, "Categories")
DataGrid1.DataSource = DataSet11
```

C#

```
sqlDataAdapter1.Fill(DataSet11, "Categories");
dataGrid1.DataSource = DdataSset11;
```

You're simply filling the dataset and setting the `DataSource` property of the grid to the dataset.

Before you run the application, you must add code to the `Closing` event to the form. This code calls the `Update` method of the `DataGrid` and the `Update` method of the `DataAdapter`. By calling `Update` in the `Closing` event of the form, you're telling the `DataAdapter` to use the auto-generated `Update` command that was created to send the changed data to the database, thus persisting your changes that you make in the grid. The following code should be added to the `Closing` event of the form:

VB.NET

```
DataGrid1.Update()
SqlDataAdapter1.Update(DataSet11)
```

C#

```
dataGrid1.Update();
sqlDataAdapter1.Update(DataSet11);
```

Now, run the application by pressing the F5 key. You should see something like Figure 11.17.

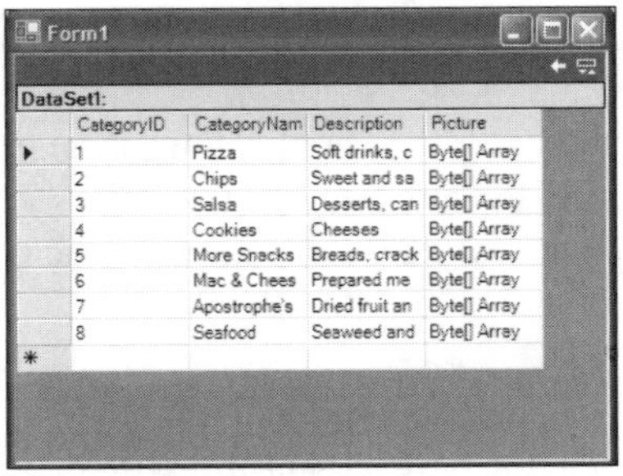

FIGURE 11.17
The Categories form generated by the Server Explorer.

If you modify some of the data, close the form, and rerun the application, you'll see that your changes are saved to the database. If you compare the data in Figure 11.15 to the data in Figure 11.17, you'll notice that I've changed some of the data, and it has successfully persisted to the database.

To recap what just happened:

- You dragged the Categories table from the Server Explorer on to your form.
- Visual Studio .NET auto-generated a `SqlConnection` component, a `SqlDataAdapter` component, and all the ADO.NET code that's necessary to select, insert, update, and delete data from the Categories table.
- You used the built-in Generate DataSet tool in Visual Studio .NET to create a strongly typed dataset based on the information in the `DataAdapter`.
- You added a `DataGrid` to your form to display the Categories table data.
- You added two lines of code to fill the dataset from the `DataAdapter` and bind the dataset to the `DataGrid` control.
- You added two lines of code to call the `Update` method on the `DataAdapter`, which in turn executed the auto-generated `Update` command for the fields that you modified in the `DataGrid`.

Creating quick-and-dirty forms from the Server Explorer is extremely simple, but the results are extremely useful. Next, you're going to learn how to create slightly more functional forms without writing any code at all—not even four lines.

Note

> In the next section, you learn about the DataForm Wizard. The code generated by the DataForm Wizard can be used to extend the exercise you just completed by implementing `Insert` and `Delete` functionality.

Using the DataForm Wizard to Create Data Entry Forms

The Data Form template for Windows Forms applications is an extremely powerful tool for creating full-featured data access forms. This section walks you through the wizard and available options for creating a new data entry form for the Customers table in the Northwind database.

Note

> ASP.NET applications also have a DataForm Wizard, but it isn't as robust as the Windows Forms wizard. In the exercises at the end of the day, you create an ASP.NET application that uses the DataForm Wizard to create a Web page, but the databinding technology between the Internet and Windows is different. Because the Web is stateless, it's more efficient to use `DataReaders` to bind data. ASPX pages are read-only in essence, so binding data to a Web form is a one-way street—you're outputting data for display. There's no efficient way to keep track of the contents of a dataset over HTTP calls. You would need to store the dataset in a viewstate for each Web form, which could become very inefficient for large datasets. For this reason, the DataForm Wizard for Windows Forms is much more robust than the Web Forms DataForm Wizard.

Using the DataForm Wizard

In your DataTools application, right-click the project name in the Solution Explorer and select Add New Item from the contextual menu. Select Data Form Wizard from the Add New Item dialog, and name it `CustomersDataEntry`, as shown in Figure 11.18.

After you click the OK button, the Welcome to the DataForm Wizard dialog appears. You should see something like Figure 11.19.

Click the Next button to begin the wizard.

The first step in the wizard is to choose the dataset that will hold the databinding. You have two options on this screen: Either create a new dataset or use an existing dataset. As you saw earlier in the day, you're offered the datasets that exist in your project.

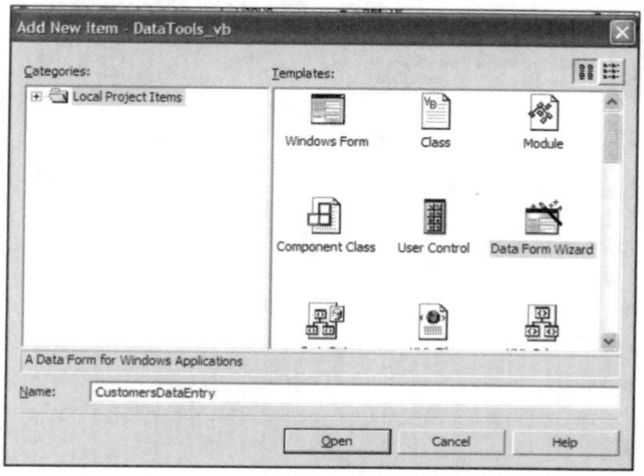

FIGURE 11.18

Adding the Data Form Wizard to your application.

FIGURE 11.19

The DataForm Wizard Welcome Screen.

11

As a rule of thumb, you should use separate `DataAdapters` and `DataSets` for each table that you work with. Because a `DataAdapter` generates SQL commands for `Insert`, `Update`, and `Delete`, it can do so for single tables. In the past, you created joins to work with multiple tables. Now, you create multiple datasets that are linked together by a `DataRelation` object. The `DataRelation` object links multiple tables in multiple `DataSets` and enforces constraints as if you were working directly with the database server. Because the `DataSet` object can be strongly typed and it's essentially an in-memory cache of the database, the `DataRelation` can enforce rules set up by the schemas or you can programmatically define constraints that the `DataRelation` must enforce. For the purpose of our data entry form, you're going to create a new `DataSet` named `dsCustomers`, as Figure 11.20 demonstrates.

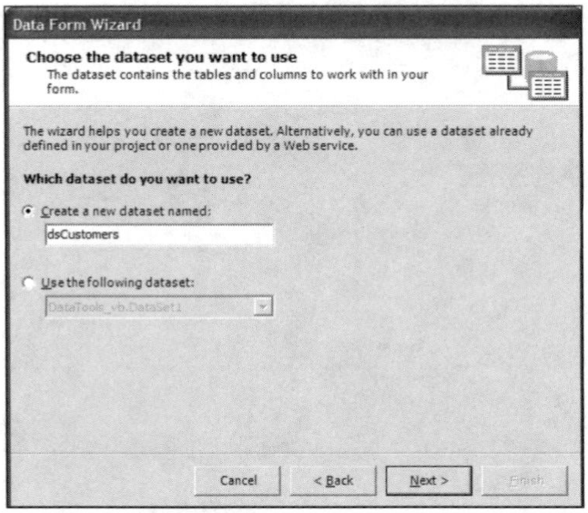

FIGURE 11.20

Choosing the dataset from the Data Form Wizard.

Now that you've named the `DataSet`, click the Next button to select a `Connection` object. At this point, you might or might not have connections available. At the very beginning of today's lesson, I mentioned the top-level node in the Server Explorer, named Data Connections. The Data Connections node keeps track of `Connection` objects that have been added through using the data components in the Toolbox. After you create a connection, you can reuse it for other forms and it is available in other projects. Because this is just a reference to a connection, you aren't actually using it unless you reference it. If you've used the Data Form Wizard before or have dragged a `Connection` object onto a form, you'll most likely see a connection in the Available Connections drop-down list. If there are no connections to choose, you must click the New Connection button, which brings up the Data Link Properties dialog shown in Figure 11.21.

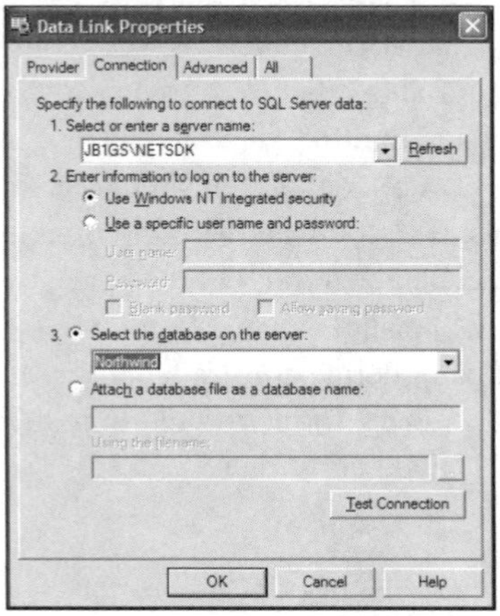

FIGURE 11.21

Adding a new connection with the Data Form Wizard.

This is the same connection properties dialog used for all data and ODBC connections in Windows. Select the name of your server from the Server Name drop-down. Click the Use Windows NT Integrated Security option button, and then select the Northwind database from the Select the Database on the Server drop-down.

Click the Test Connection button just to make sure that it works, and then click the OK button to close the dialog. Next, you must choose the tables or views that this form will use. Because we're creating a data entry form for customers, select the Customers table from the left-side tree view and move it to the Selected Items node, as Figure 11.22 shows.

FIGURE 11.22

Selecting the table or view in the Data Form Wizard.

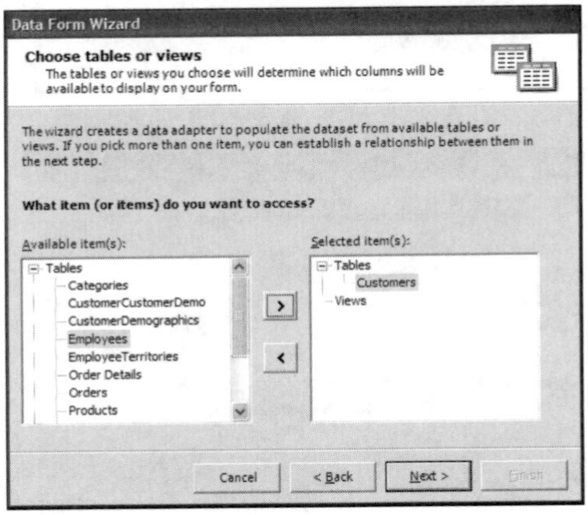

After you click the Next button, you'll notice a slight delay, and you'll see a new XSD file named `dsCustomers.xsd` in your solution. Because you have the main ingredients that Visual Studio .NET needed to create the typed dataset, it went ahead and created the XSD file and added it to your solution.

Figure 11.23 is the next step in the wizard, which enables you to choose which fields you want displayed on the form.

Notice that you have the option for master and detail tables. If you created a `DataSet` that had more than one table, the `TableRelation` would be set up at this point. Because you're using only one table, the detail table option is disabled.

Click the Next button to get to the final step of the wizard. At this point, you decide what type of form you want to create. Figure 11.24 shows the available options.

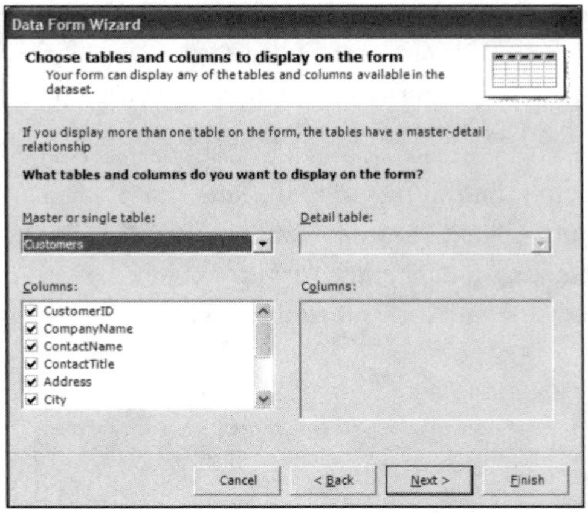

FIGURE 11.23
Choosing the fields to display on the form.

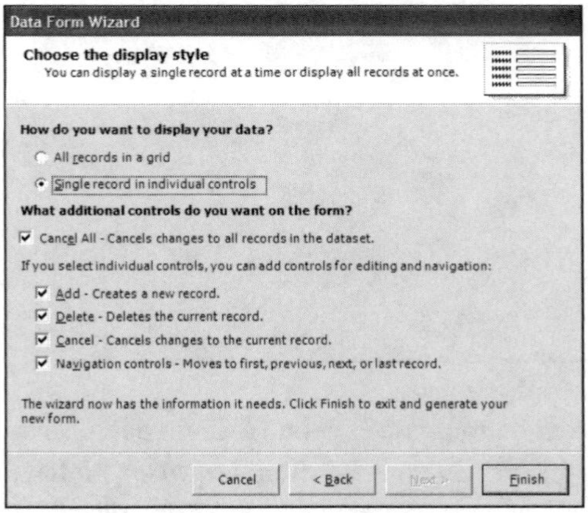

FIGURE 11.24
Choosing the display style of the Data Form Wizard–generated form.

At this point, you have several options based on what functionality you want to give to the end user. Select the Single Record in Individual Controls option for this form. After you click the Finish button, the form is created and you should have something that looks very close to Figure 11.25.

You can see that the `Connection`, `DataAdapter`, and `DataSet` objects were added to the form, and that all of the correct controls needed to make the form functional have been added.

If you click on the `TextBox` associated with the `CustomerID` field and view the `DataBindings` property in the Properties window, you'll see that the fields available in `objdsCustomers` are listed as available bindable fields. Figure 11.26 shows the `DataBindings` property in the Properties window.

FIGURE 11.25

The results of running the Data Form Wizard.

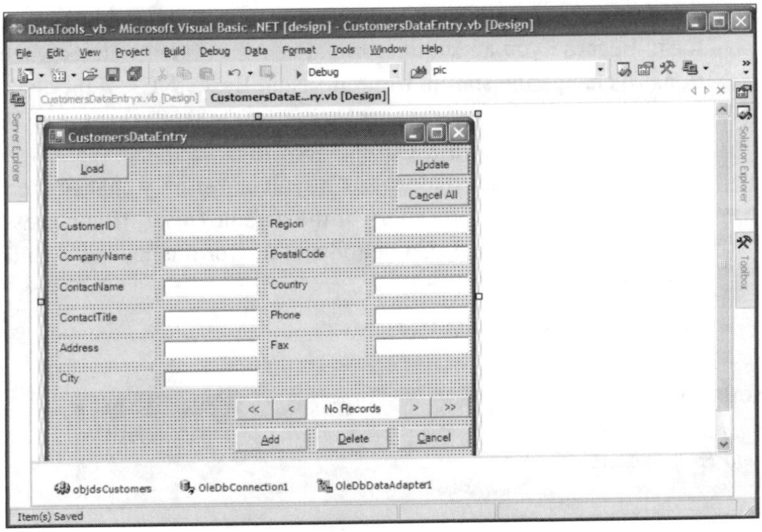

FIGURE 11.26

Viewing the `DataBindings` *properties.*

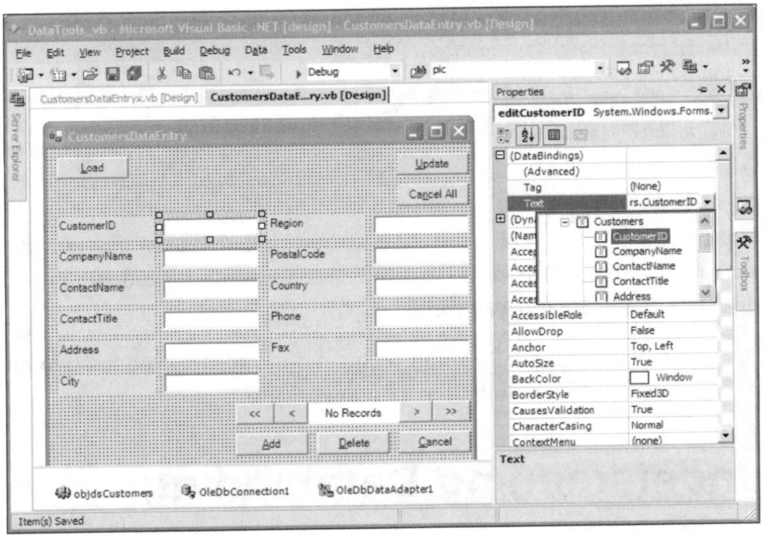

When you add `DataSets` to a form, the fields from the strongly typed dataset are automatically available as bindable objects for all controls on the form. Because each control has a `DataBindings` property, you can bind the fields from the `DataSet` to any control on the form.

To run the application, you must change the `StartUp` object to the `CustomersDataEntry` form. Because you added the form after `Form1`, `Form1` starts when you run the application. To change the startup form in Visual Basic .NET, right-click on the project name in the Solution Explorer and select Properties. In the Properties dialog, change the `Startup` object in the drop-down list from `Form1` to `CustomersDataEntry` and click the OK button to close the Properties dialog. In C#, you can simply change the code that loads the correct form in the `Main` procedure of the default `Form1`. If you press F5 to run the application, you can click the Load button and the form is loaded with the data from the Customers table.

Your final output should look like Figure 11.27.

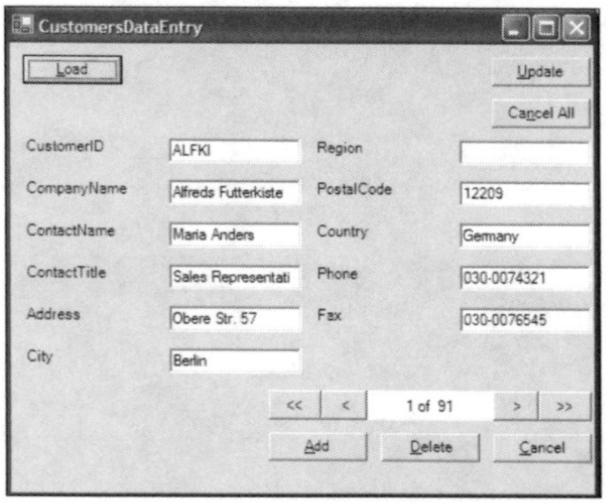

FIGURE 11.27
Final output from the Data Form Wizard.

If you change some data and click the Update button, the new data is persisted back to the database. The Data Form Wizard writes all the code that you need to create a fully functional data-driven form.

To understand what's going on behind the scenes, you need to understand what is happening with databinding in Windows Forms.

Understanding Databinding

In Visual Basic 6, the `RecordSet` object gives you the ability to bind data from a database to text boxes, data grids, and labels. The `RecordSet` keeps track of the positioning through its event model. You simply call methods such as `MoveFirst`, `MoveNext`, `MovePrevious`, and `MoveLast` to navigate records in the `RecordSet`, and the `RecordSet` magically handles it for you.

In .NET, the `DataSet` binds its data to controls. Because the DataSet is simply a container of data, it has no knowledge of positioning. To implement code like `MoveFirst` and

MoveNext, you must set up a BindingContext for the controls that are being databound. .NET uses the inherited CurrencyManager class to internally handle the navigation within the BindingContext of the DataSet and the controls that it's binding to.

To understand this better, consider the following Visual Basic .NET code for the btnNavNext that the Data Form Wizard created:

```
Private Sub btnNavNext_Click(ByVal sender As System.Object, _
      ByVal e As System.EventArgs) Handles btnNavNext.Click

  Me.BindingContext(objdsCustomers, "Customers").Position = _
      (Me.BindingContext(objdsCustomers, "Customers").Position + 1)
  Me.objdsCustomers_PositionChanged()

End Sub
```

To navigate, the current position must be maintained within the DataSet. You can keep track of this yourself, but it's easier to let the Position property of the BindingContext class handle the positioning for you. When controls are databound on a Windows Form, they're part of the BindingContext of the form, so using the Position property is an easy way to handle navigation.

Summary

Today you gained a lot of practical knowledge about the tools available in Visual Studio .NET to work with databases, and how to use those tools to create data-driven applications with Windows Forms.

Using the Server Explorer to work with databases can save you lots of time; everything you need is right in front of you in an easy-to-use interface. The Query and View Designers, used in conjunction with the Stored Procedure Designer and Debugger can help you create efficient and scalable data access applications.

When you need to create fully functional, robust data-driven forms, use the Data Form Wizard in .NET. Even if you aren't writing Windows Forms applications, you can run the wizard and examine the auto-generated code to learn more about the DataAdapter and how it uses Select, Insert, Update, and Delete commands.

Q&A

Q You had me write all this code yesterday. What should I do: write the code or use the wizards?

A When designing Windows Forms applications, using the wizards is a highly effective and efficient way to write all your data access code. Most developers like to separate their data logic into components, but the Data Form Wizard isn't an effective way to do that. Either way, if you're new to ADO.NET, using the tools in Visual Studio .NET to learn the syntax for data access is a good idea.

Q You said `DataReaders` are lightweight and incur less overhead cost. But everything I learned today used `DataSets`, not `DataReaders`. Why?

A Because `DataReaders` don't support databinding, they're not very useful in Windows Forms, where you can use databinding for all your data presentations.

Q What happens if my data requirements change and I need to change the code that the wizard created for the `InsertCommand`, `SelectCommand`, `DeleteCommand`, and `UpdateCommand` properties on the `DataAdapter`?

A Your best bet is to run the Configure Adapter Wizard from the Data menu. This enables you to easily change the queries or stored procedures for the `DataAdapter`, and let the Configuration Wizard rewrite the data access code.

Quiz

1. Using the _____________, you can manage SQL Server databases, OLEDB connections, Windows event logs, and Microsoft message queues.
2. True or False: Using the Server Explorer to manage my SQL Servers is a good idea, but there are security risks because everyone with Visual Studio .NET can see my SQL Servers.
3. To create a data-driven form with Visual Studio .NET, I should add a ________ first, and then a ____________, and finally I can add controls to my forms and set the data bindings on the controls.

Quiz Answers

1. Server Explorer
2. False. The Server Explorer in Visual Studio .NET does *not* enable you to bypass any permissions that you would otherwise not be granted using SQL Server security or Windows 2000 Authentication. In fact, using Server Explorer is more secure because there's no access to the Security node that SQL Server Enterprise Manager has.
3. `SqlDataAdapter`, `DataSet`

Exercises

1. Run the Data Form Wizard for the Customers table again. This time, select the All Records in a Grid option instead of the individual controls. Observe the differences in functionality, if any exist.
2. Run the Data Form Wizard again. This time, add the Customers and the Orders table to the `DataSet`. You'll be offered a new step in the wizard because more than one table is selected. You have to define the relationship between the two tables based on the `CustomerID` primary key. When the wizard finishes, you should have a master-detail data entry form.

WEEK 2

DAY 12

Accessing XML in .NET

For the last two days, you've learned about data access in .NET. The theme throughout has been how extensible markup language (XML) is everywhere in .NET, but you can write great applications without knowing too much about it. That all changes today. There are times when you need to deal with XML files, and you need to know what to do when that happens. The .NET Framework has broad support for all XML data access scenarios, so if you need to access and manipulate XML, the tools are there to do so. Today you get a crash course on

- What XML is and how it fits into .NET
- Using the Schema Designer in Visual Studio .NET to create XML schemas
- Using the XML Editor in .NET to edit XML files
- Binding schemas to XML files using XML Editor in Visual Studio .NET
- Validating XML data against an XML schema
- Using the `DataSet` to read and write element-based XML data from SQL Server
- Using the `DataReader` and the FOR XML AUTO clause in SQL Server to create attribute-based XML files

- How to read and manipulate XML files using `XmlReaders`
- How to read and manipulate XML files using the XML document object model (DOM) classes in .NET
- Using XPath queries to query nodes in XML files

What Is XML?

XML is a text-based way to describe structured data. Unlike HTML, which uses various markup tags to describe how data should be displayed or rendered in a Web browser, XML is simply data. With the need to move data between systems in a flexible and platform-neutral way, XML has become the standard way to pass data around the Internet. Some of the reasons for this are

- XML is plain text; any computer can understand plain text
- Data in an XML file is self-describing
- Parsing XML documents has become fairly simple
- XML can be transmitted over HTTP
- XML can work across firewalls over HTTP

The data in an XML document is described through the use of elements. Elements create the structure for the document, similar to column names in a database. Within the element tags of an XML document lies the actual data. The element name describes the data in the element. An XML document can also contain attributes, which further describe the data contained in an element. Listing 12.1 is an example of a simple XML document.

LISTING 12.1 Simple XML Document

```
<?xml version="1.0"?>
<!-- This simple data represents food items in a grocery store -->
<GroceryStore>
        <StoreName>Brian's Groceries</StoreName>
        <Departments>
                <Department Name="Breads">
                        <Item ID="B1">
                                <Name>Wonder Bread</Name>
                                <Price>1.29</Price>
                                <New />
                        </Item>
                        <Item ID="B2" Type="Muffin">
                                <Name>Blueberry Muffin</Name>
                                <Price>3.99</Price>
                                <New />
                        </Item>
                </Department>
```

Listing 12.1 continued

```
                <Department Name="Fruits">
                        <Item ID="F1">
                                <Name>Apple</Name>
                                <Price>0.99</Price>
                        </Item>
                </Department>
        </Departments>
</GroceryStore>
```

The XML document can be broken down into several key parts.

The *prolog* of an XML document defines the XML version number and encoding information. This is required for an XML document to be well formed. In Listing 12.1, the prolog is

```
<?xml version="1.0"?>
<!-- This simple data represents food items in a grocery store -->
```

The prolog can contain

- XML comments—XML comments are defined by the `<!--` and `-->` start and end tags. XML comments can be in the prolog or anywhere else within the XML document.
- Namespace declaration—The XML namespace for the current document in the prolog. Like namespaces in .NET, an XML namespace can be used to uniquely identify the contents of the document. In .NET, you can create XML software definition (XSD) files that contain schema information for an XML file.
- XML stylesheet declaration—An XML stylesheet contains information about how the data in the document should be displayed. A stylesheet can contain HTML tags or application logic used to transform the XML document structure to another XML document structure.

The *root element* of the XML document is required. It's the main parent in the XML tree for the document. The `<GroceryStore>` beginning element and `</GroceryStore>` end element define the root element for Listing 12.1.

Tags define the boundary of the data content within an XML document. In an XML document, there are start tags, end tags, and empty tags. The start tag defines the element name, and everything between the start tag and end tag can be considered the data for the element. An empty tag contains no data, but it can contain attributes. *Attributes* are name-value pairs that can be used to further describe the data within an element.

In Listing 12.1, the `Department` element (with start tag `<Department>` and end tag `</Department>`) contains `Item` child elements, which also contain `Name` and `Price` child elements. The `Department` element has a `Name` attribute, and the `Item` element has an `ID` attribute and a `Type` attribute. The first two Items for the `Department Bread` have empty elements named `New`.

As Listing 12.1 demonstrates, XML documents use a tree-like hierarchy to describe the data they contain. Using the tools and namespaces in .NET, you can quickly and easily parse XML documents such as Listing 12.1.

XML in .NET

Visual Studio and the .NET Framework have built-in support for designing schemas, editing and creating XML files, and a complete set of class libraries for writing applications that need to read and write XML.

The core XML classes in .NET are compliant with the W3C standards for XML, XSLT 1.0, XPath 1.0, DOM Level 1 and DOM Level 2, namespaces, XSD 1.0, and XSD schema. That compliance means interoperability between different systems isn't an issue.

In .NET, all XML-specific classes are in the `System.Xml` namespace. The `System.XML` namespace is a complete XML parser with extensible classes that enable you to work with XML in any number of ways. The abstract `XmlReader`, `XmlWriter`, and `XmlDocument` classes provide parsing, reading, writing, and validation for XML documents, respectively. The `XslTransform` and `XPathDocument` classes provide XSLT stylesheet transformation capabilities. Using the `DataSet` class in ADO .NET, you can create `Dataset` containers that can read and write XML documents and XML schemas by using the `XmlReader`, `XmlWriter`, or `XmlDocument` classes. Using the `DataSet` class to work with XML documents is extremely simple and efficient.

Figure 12.1 puts the different classes in the `System.XML` namespace in perspective.

FIGURE 12.1

XML objects in the `System.XML` *namespace.*

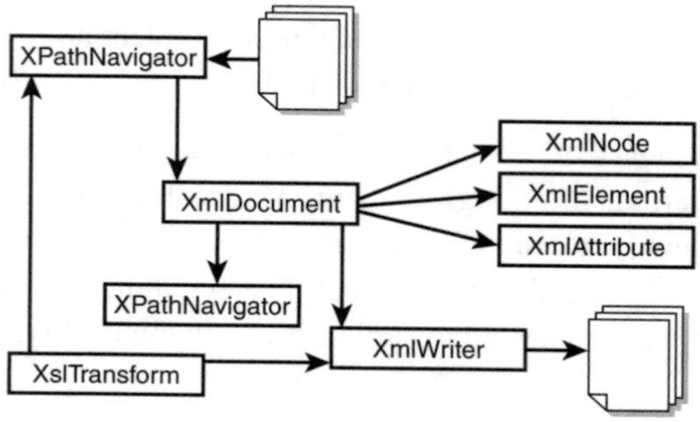

Before getting into the specific classes you can use to manipulate XML documents, you learn how to use the tools in Visual Studio .NET to create and edit XML schemas and XML documents.

Using the XML and Schema Designers

Visual Studio .NET gives you everything you need to effectively work with XML documents and XSD schemas. Using the Schema Designer, you can create XML schemas and link them to XML documents. Normally, a schema can be created directly from a database, but if you're not using a database and you need a relational way to represent data, you can build schemas directly in Visual Studio .NET. A schema contains all the information needed to describe any type of relational data that you're working with.

To test this, create a new project named XML_vb or XML_cs, depending on the language you're using. After the project is open, right-click the project name in the Solution Explorer and select Add New Item from the contextual menu. Select XML Schema and change the name to `EmployeesSchema` as shown in Figure 12.2.

FIGURE 12.2
Adding the `EmployeesSchema` *to your project.*

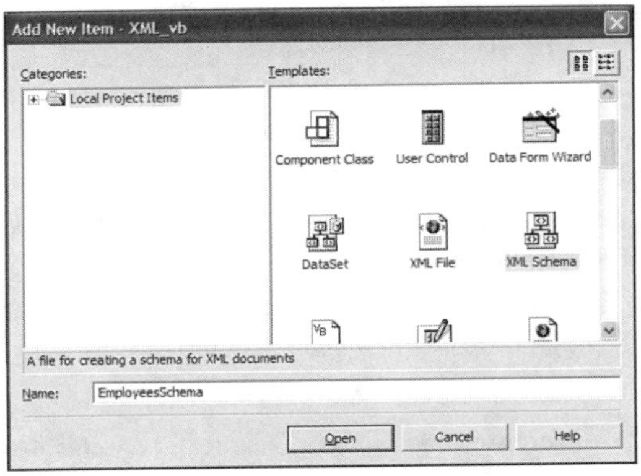

After you click Open, the schema is added to your project and the Schema Designer is brought up. If you look at the Toolbox, you'll see that the controls in the Toolbox are now specifically related to designing XML schemas. Figure 12.3 is what you should see at this point.

Each item in the toolbox is a schema-specific object that you can drag onto the design surface in the designer to create the structure of your data. Table 12.1 gives you a breakdown of the items in the Toolbox and what each one can do.

12

FIGURE 12.3
The Schema Designer and XML Schema Toolbox tab.

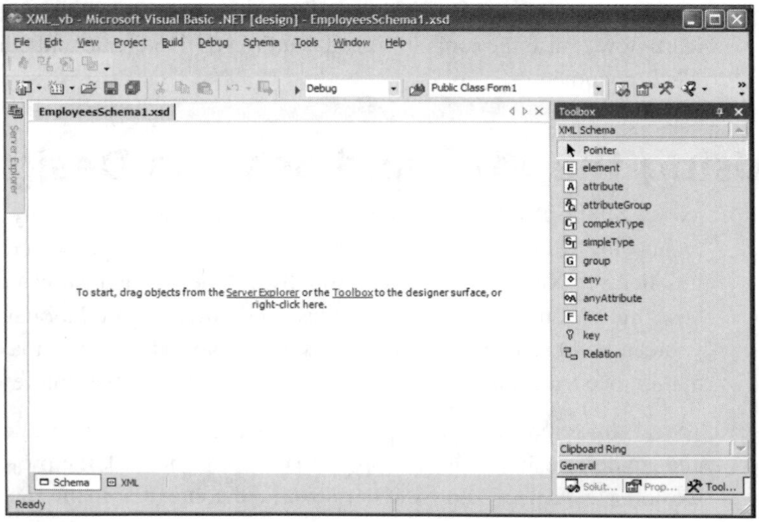

TABLE 12.1 XML Schema Toolbox Items

Toolbox Item	*Description*
`Element`	Creates an `Element` that can be global, added to other `Elements`, added to `Groups`, or used to construct `complexTypes`.
`Attribute`	Creates an attribute that can be global, added to `Elements`, or added to `Groups`.
`attributeGroup`	Creates an `attributeGroup` that can be global, added to `Elements`, or used in the construct of `complexTypes`.
`complexType`	Creates a `complexType` that you can add `Elements`, `Attributes`, `attributeGroups`, `Anys`, and `anyAttributes` to.
`simpleType`	Creates a `simpleType` that you can add `Facets` to.
`Group`	Creates groups that can be global, added to other `Groups`, `Elements`, or `complexTypes`.
`Any`	Creates an `Any` element that can be added to `Elements`, `complexTypes`, or `Groups`.
`anyAttribute`	Creates an `anyAttribute` element that can be added to `Elements`, `attributeGroups`, or `complexTypes`.
`Facet`	Creates a `Facet` that can be added to a `simpleType`. A facet is used to further restrict the definition of a simple type.
`Key`	Launches the Edit Key dialog box that's used to create keys when added to an element.
`Relation`	Launches the Edit Relation dialog box that's used to define relationships between elements. You can use this to create one-to-many relationships in XML schemas and datasets.

Now that you have an idea of the types of objects that can be added to the schema, you can start designing the Employees schema.

Creating the Employees Schema

The goal of this section is to guide you through the creation of a schema using the designer, to link the schema to an XML document, and use the XML document and schema in an application.

You've already added an XSD file to your application and named it EmployeesSchema. Now, you need to use the items in the XML Schema toolbox to create the types that make up the XML document.

Using Simple Types to Create the ZipCode Field

The first step is to create a simpleType named ZipCode. The ZipCode type uses a regular expression syntax to create a constraint for the field. To do this:

- Drag a simpleType from the Toolbox onto the designer.
- Change the simpleType name to ZipCode.
- Click to the next column and select positiveInteger from the data type drop-down list.
- Click to the second row, and select facet from the drop-down list in the first column.
- Click to the next column and select pattern from the drop-down list.
- Click to the third column and type **"\d{5}"**.

You've now created a simple type named ZipCode that uses a regular expression pattern to enforce a rule that says that anything entered into this field should be five numeric positive numbers. If you switch to the XML view by clicking the XML button on the lower left of the screen, you'll see that the definition of the ZipCode type looks something like this:

```
<xs:simpleType name="ZipCode">
        <xs:restriction base="xs:positiveInteger">
                <xs:pattern value="\d{5}" />
        </xs:restriction>
</xs:simpleType>
```

You learned about validation controls in ASP.NET on Day 5, "Writing ASP.NET Applications." RegularExpressionValidator controls use regular expression syntax to generate the client-side JavaScript that enforces the validation rules for the server controls associated with the validation control. In schemas, you create a Facet type with a pattern to implement any type of pattern for a data type. This is almost identical to using a constraint in a SQL Server table.

Tip

> To learn more regular expressions, create a new ASP.NET application and add a `RegularExpressionValidator` control to the Web Form. In the Properties dialog box for the control, select the `ValidationExpression` property to view the syntax for the various options. For example, to validate an Internet email address, the regular expression syntax is `"\w+([-+.]\w+)*@\w+([-.]\w+)*\.\w+([-.]\w+)*"`.

Creating the Address Complex Type

Now you create the `Address complexType` to hold address information for the `Employees`. This is a `complexType` because in the schema, it can contain any of the types listed in Table 12.1. If you're in XML view, click the Schema button to return to the Schema Designer. To create the `Address` type, follow these steps:

1. Drag a `complexType` from the Toolbox onto the designer.
2. Change the name from `complexType1` to `Address`. Don't select a data type from the second column.
3. Click to the next row, and select `element` from the drop-down list in the first column. In the second column, type **`Name`** for the `Element` name, and select `String` as the data type from the drop-down list in the third column.
4. Click to the next row, and select `element` from the drop-down list in the first column. In the second column, type **`Street`** for the `Element` name, and select `String` as the data type from the drop-down list in the third column.
5. Click to the next row, and select `element` from the drop-down list in the first column. In the second column, type **`State`** for the `Element` name, and select string as the data type from the drop-down list in the third column.
6. Click to the next row, and select `element` from the drop-down list in the first column. In the second column, type **`Zip`** for the `element` name, and select `ZipCode` as the data type from the drop-down list in the third column. The `Zip` element now follows the rules you've defined for the `ZipCode` simple type.

Next you must create the main elements that make up the data for each customer. The `ZipCode` and `Address` are basically data types that are used for each `Employee`. If you compare this to tables in a database, the `Address` type would be a child table to an `Employee` parent table.

Creating the Main `Employee` Elements

To create the main elements for the `Employee` schema, follow these steps:

1. Drag an `element` type from the Toolbox onto the design surface.

2. Change the name from `element1` to `Employee`. Leave the Data Type column blank. This will be the main `Employee` element for each record in the XML document.
3. Click to the next row, and select `Element` from the drop-down list in the first column. In the second column, type **`Email`** for the `element` name, and select `String` as the data type from the drop-down list in the third column.
4. Click to the next row, and select `element` from the drop-down list in the first column. In the second column, type **`Password`** for the element name, and select `String` as the data type from the drop-down list in the third column.
5. Click to the next row, and select `element` from the drop-down list in the first column. In the second column, type **`HomeAddress`** for the element name, and select `Address` as the data type from the drop-down list in the third column. At this point, notice that the `Address` complex type you created earlier is connected to the `HomeAddress` element you just added. You can see that the hierarchy of the XML document is starting to take shape.
6. Click to the next row, and select `element` from the drop-down list in the first column. In the second column, type **`OtherAddress`** for the `element` name, and select `Address` as the data type from the drop-down list in the third column. Again, an `Address` type is connected to the `OtherAddress` element just added.

You've now defined the elements to hold the employee data and employee address information. If you switch to the XML view of the designer, you'll see something like this:

```
<xs:simpleType name="ZipCode">
        <xs:restriction base="xs:positiveInteger">
                <xs:pattern value="\d{5}" />
        </xs:restriction>
</xs:simpleType>
<xs:complexType name="Address">
        <xs:sequence>
                <xs:element name="Name" type="xs:string" />
                <xs:element name="Street" type="xs:string" />
                <xs:element name="State" type="xs:string" />
                <xs:element name="Zip" type="xs:string" />
        </xs:sequence>
</xs:complexType>
<xs:element name="Employee">
        <xs:complexType>
                <xs:sequence>
                        <xs:element name="Email" type="xs:string" />
                        <xs:element name="Password" type="xs:string" />
                        <xs:element name="HomeAddress" type="Address" />
                        <xs:element name="OtherAddress" type="Address" />
                </xs:sequence>
        </xs:complexType>
</xs:element>
```

The last step in creating the schema is to add the root element. To be well-formed XML, all XML documents must have a root element.

Adding the Root Element to the `EmployeeSchema`

There is no root element type in the toolbox. The root element of any XML document is just another element, so to add the root element to the schema:

- Drag an `elementType` onto the designer and change the default `elementType1` name to `EmployeeList`.
- Select the `Employee` type you created in the previous section and drag it onto the second row of the `EmployeeList` element.

You've now defined `EmployeeList` as the root element for the `Employee` type.

The schema you have just created should look like Figure 12.4.

FIGURE 12.4

The `EmployeesSchema` *XML schema.*

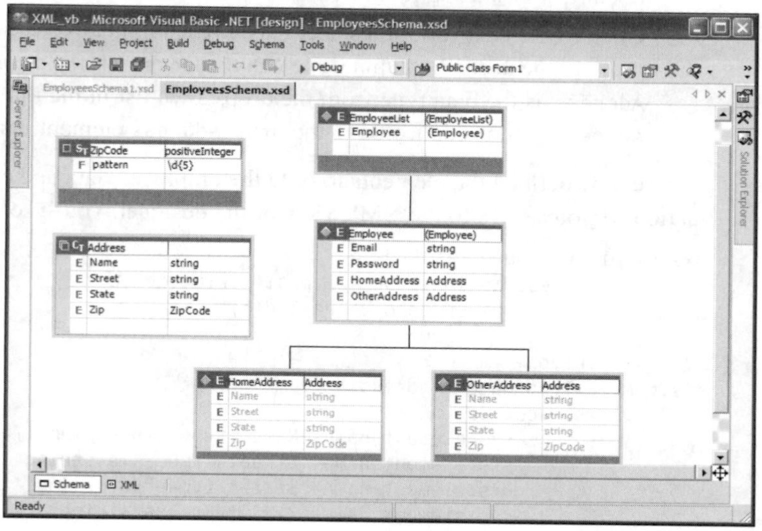

If you switch to the XML view of the designer, you'll see the XML schema definition for the `EmployeesSchema` that Figure 12.5 depicts. Using the designer to create XML schemas is obviously much easier than hand-coding the complete schema shown in Figure 12.5.

Next, you need to associate the schema with an XML document.

FIGURE 12.5

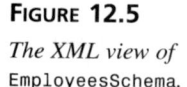

The XML view of `EmployeesSchema`.

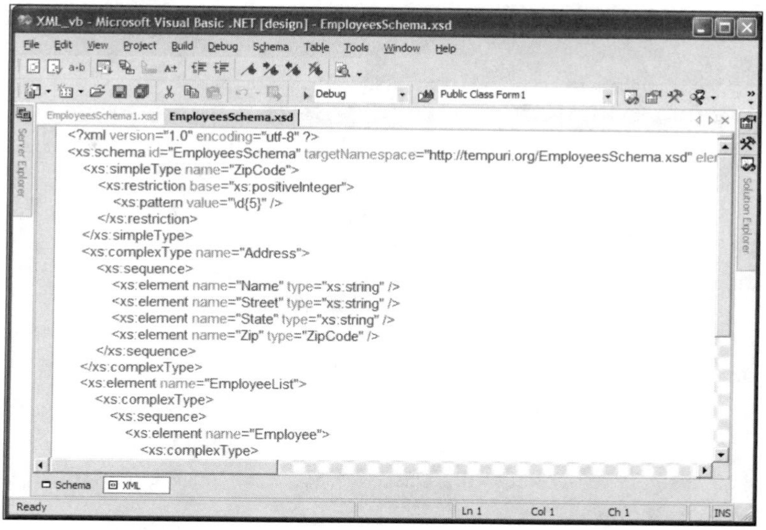

Adding the `Employees` XML Document

To add the XML document that uses the `EmployeesSchema`, right-click on your project name in the Solution Explorer and select Add New Item from the contextual menu. Select XML File from the Add Item dialog, and name it `Employees` as Figure 12.6 demonstrates.

FIGURE 12.6

Adding the `Employees` *XML file.*

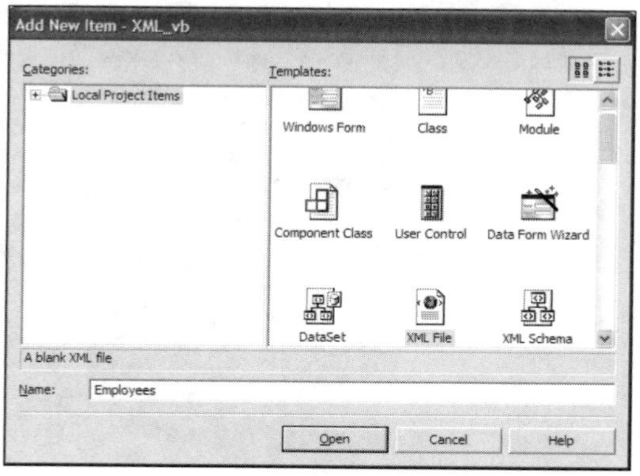

After the `Employees.xml` file is added, you must associate it with the `EmployeesSchema`. To do so, right-click the XML file in the XML Designer and select Properties from the contextual menu. When the Properties dialog pops up, you can select the schema from Target Schemas drop-down list, as Figure 12.7 demonstrates. After you select `EmployeesSchema`, click the OK button to close the Properties dialog box.

FIGURE 12.7

Associating `EmployeesSchema` *with the* `Employees` *XML document.*

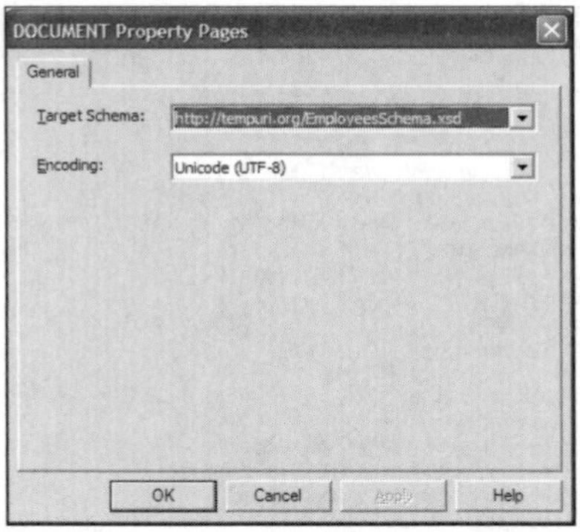

Now that the `Employees` XML file has a schema, the XML Designer in Visual Studio .NET shows its true power. If you click the Data button in the lower-left corner of the designer to switch to the Data view, you can see the hierarchy of data that the schema has set up.

From this point, you can add, edit, and delete records just as if this were a regular database table. Figure 12.8 is the Data view after adding an `Employee` record. Notice that `HomeAddress` and `OtherAddress` are children to the `Employee` main element.

FIGURE 12.8

Adding data to the XML file using the Data view.

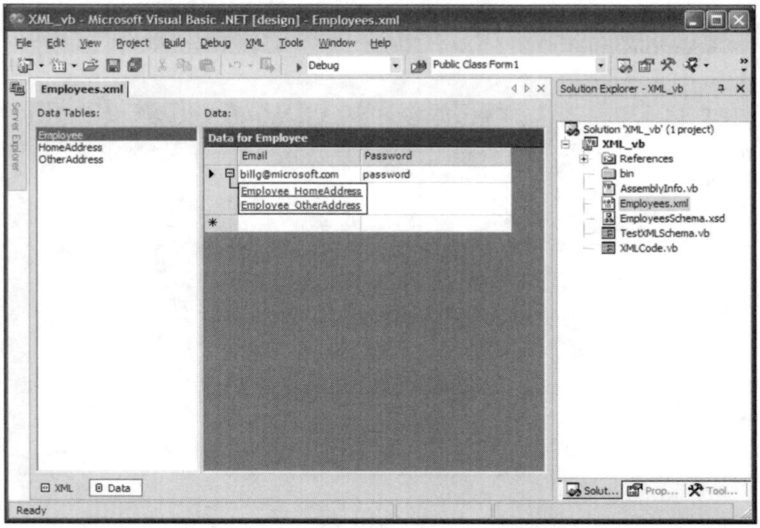

Next, you can write an application that actually reads and writes data from this XML file.

Using the Employees XML File in an Application

Earlier you learned that the `DataSet` class can natively read and write XML files using `XmlReaders` and `XmlWriters`. Table 12.2 lists the XML-specific methods that you can use when working with XML files and schemas with the `DataSet` class.

TABLE 12.2 XML Methods in the `DataSet` Class

Method Name	*Description*
`GetXml`	Returns the XML representation of the data stored in the `DataSet`.
`GetXmlSchema`	Returns the XSD schema for the XML representation of the data stored in the `DataSet`.
`InferXmlSchema`	Infers the XML schema from the specified `TextReader` or file into the `DataSet`.
`ReadXml`	Reads an XML schema and data into the `DataSet`.
`ReadXmlSchema`	Reads an XML schema into the `DataSet`.
`WriteXml`	Writes XML data and, optionally, the schema, from the `DataSet`.
`WriteXmlSchema`	Writes the `DataSet` structure as an XML schema.

I mentioned earlier that you could create an XML schema from database tables that already exist. Using the `WriteXmlSchema` method, you could have created the `EmployeesSchema` from SQL Server tables, if the tables existed, and then set up a relationship between the tables using the Schema Designer. Most of the time you deal with database, not schemas and XML files, so using methods of the `DataSet` class can expedite your schema creation time.

To use the `Employees` schema in an application, you're going to write some code that reads the XML schema and XML file into a `DataSet`, and then you're going to bind the `DataSet` to a `DataGrid`. Because the `DataGrid` enables you to add, edit, and delete records, you'll modify the data in the `DataGrid` and write it back to an XML file.

To do so, add a new form to your solution named `TestXmlSchema` and add three `CommandButtons` and a `DataGrid` control from the Toolbox. Arrange the controls on the form so that they look like Figure 12.9, and name the `CommandButtons` `LoadXML`, `DisplaySchema`, and `SaveXML`, respectively.

Double-click the Load XML File button to get to the click event for the control. Add the code in Listing 12.2 to handle the click events for the three buttons.

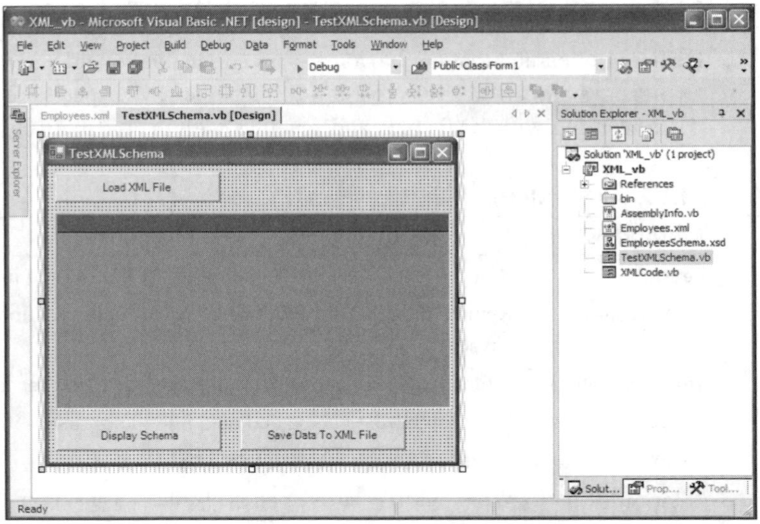

FIGURE 12.9
The `TestXmlSchema` *form after arranging controls.*

LISTING 12.2 Code for the `TestXmlSchema` Form

VB.NET

```
Dim ds As New DataSet("MyFile")

Private Sub LoadXMLFile_Click(ByVal sender As System.Object, _
        ByVal e As System.EventArgs) Handles LoadXMLFile.Click

    ' Read the XML Schema into the DataSet
    ds.ReadXmlSchema("../EmployeesSchema.xsd")

    ' Read the XML file into the DataSet
    ds.ReadXml("../Employees.xml")

    ' Bind the grid to the DataSet
    DataGrid1.DataSource = ds

End Sub

Private Sub DisplaySchema_Click(ByVal sender As System.Object, _
            ByVal e As System.EventArgs) Handles DisplaySchema.Click

    ' Call the GetXmlSchema method to display the loaded schema
    MessageBox.Show(ds.GetXmlSchema)

End Sub
```

LISTING 12.2 Continued

```
    Private Sub SaveXML_Click(ByVal sender As System.Object, _
            ByVal e As System.EventArgs) Handles SaveXML.Click

        ' Write out the data in the grid to a new XML file
        ds.WriteXml("NewXmlFile.xml")

    End Sub
```

C#

```
private DataSet ds = new DataSet();

private void LoadXML_Click(object sender, System.EventArgs e)
   {
      // Read the XML Schema into the DataSet
      ds.ReadXmlSchema(@"../EmployeesSchema.xsd");

      // Read the XML file into the DataSet
      ds.ReadXml(@"../Employees.xml");

      // Bind the grid to the DataSet
      dataGrid1.DataSource = ds;
   }

private void DisplaySchema_Click(object sender, System.EventArgs e)
   {
      // Call the GetXmlSchema method to display the loaded schema
      MessageBox.Show(ds.GetXmlSchema());
   }

private void SaveXML_Click(object sender, System.EventArgs e)
   {
      // Write out the data in the grid to a new XML file
       ds.WriteXml(@"NewXmlFile.xml");
   }
```

12

The code is straightforward based on what you already know about `DataSets` and XML files. You simply write code to load the XML file and schema, and then write the data in the grid to a new file after you've changed information in the grid. The click event that calls the `GetXmlSchema` method displays the schema for the `DataSet`. If you click this before loading the XML and schema into the grid, you'll see that a default schema is still available when there's nothing in the `DataSet`.

Run the application by pressing the F5 key. After the application starts, add some data to the rows in the grid. You'll notice the hierarchy of the XML schema is completely maintained; the `DataGrid` looks exactly as it did in the XML Designer. Figure 12.10 is what the `TextXmlSchema` form should look like at runtime.

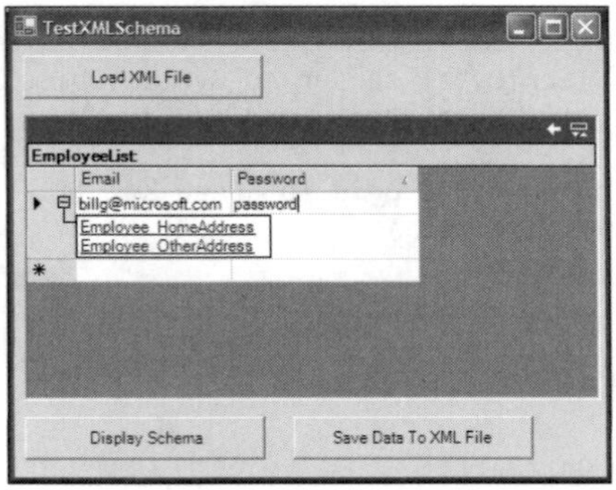

FIGURE 12.10

Running the `TextXmlSchema` *application.*

If you add a new row to the grid, add an `OtherAddress` but not a `HomeAddress`. You'll test XML validation in the Visual Studio .NET XML designer. Also, when you enter data into the grid, attempt to add an invalid `ZipCode`, such as alphanumeric characters. You'll notice that the `DataGrid` enforces the rules of the schema, and reverts to the previous value in the grid if you try to enter data that disagrees with the schema definition.

After adding some data, click the Save Data To XML File button. In the `Bin` directory of your project, you should see the `NewXmlFile.Xml` file that you just saved.

Note

If the `Bin` directory isn't visible, click the Show All Files button on the Solution Explorer toolbar. You might also have to click the Refresh button on the Solution Explorer toolbar to see the `NewXmlFile.xml` file.

Double-click the `NewXmlFile.Xml` to open it in the designer. You should see the new records that you added to the `DataGrid`. To validate the XML file against the `EmployeesSchema` XSD file, select the Validate XML Data option from the XML menu. The XML file is validated against the schema. If there are any errors, which there should be, they appear in the Task List window just as any other build error would. Figure 12.11 shows you what the errors should look like if you didn't enter a `HomeAddress` for an employee.

Note

When validating XML files, the Validate XML Data menu option appears only if you're in the XML view of the XML Designer.

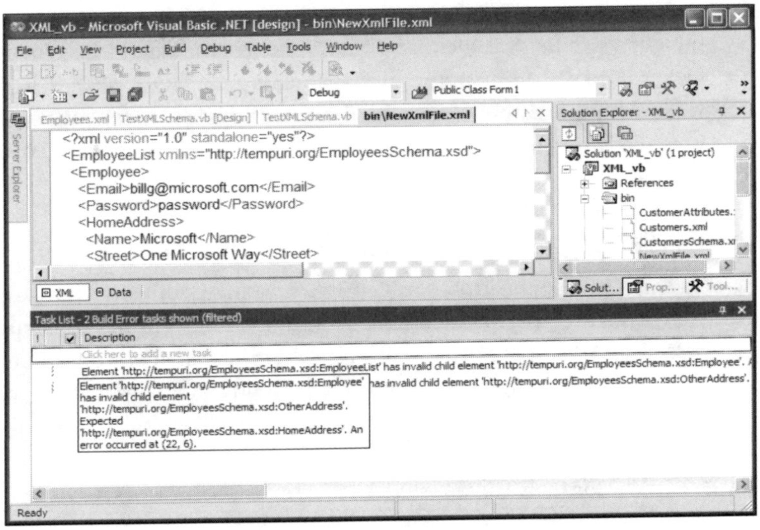

FIGURE 12.11
Results of validating the XML file against the schema.

You just finished a complete application that can add, edit, and delete records based on an XML schema and XML file created using Visual Studio .NET. Next, you're going to learn to how to use the `System.XML` classes to work with XML data in code.

Reading and Writing XML Files

12

The abstract `XmlReader` and `XmlWriter` classes of the `System.XML` namespace provide reading and writing functionality for XML files. `XmlReaders` are implemented in three main classes that provide forward-only processing of XML files. Table 12.3 lists the implementations of the `XmlReader` class.

TABLE 12.3 `XmlReader` Classes in the `System.XML` Namespace

Class	*Description*
`XmlTextReader`	Fastest implementation of `XmlReader`. It checks for well-formed XML, but doesn't support data validation. This reader cannot expand general entities and doesn't support default attributes.
`XmlValidatingReader`	Implementation of `XmlReader` that can validate data using DTDs or schemas. This reader can also expand general entities and supports default attributes.
`XmlNodeReader`	Implementation of `XmlReader` that reads XML data from an `XmlNode`.

The `XmlReader` classes are noncached forward-only readers. If you need to parse XML in memory, use the `XmlDocument` class. The `XmlDocument` class loads an XML file in memory as a tree-like hierarchy, similar to using the DOM objects in the MSXML parser. To work with the different variations of parsing XML files, you're going to write code that uses the different navigation techniques of the `XmlWriter`, `XmlReader`, and `XmlDocument` classes.

Creating the `XMLCode` Test Form

To the XML application you've been working with, add a new form named `XMLCode` by right-clicking your project name, selecting Add from the contextual menu, and then selecting Add New Form. Table 12.4 describes the controls and the `Text` and `Name` properties you must add to the form. When you're done, your form should look like Figure 12.12.

TABLE 12.4 Controls for the `XMLCode` Form

Control	*Name*	*Text*
`CommandButton`	`GetXmlFromDataSet`	Get XML From DataSet
`CommandButton`	`GetXmlDataReader`	Get XML DataReader
`CommandButton`	`LoadXmlFromFile`	Load XML From File
`CommandButton`	`SimpleXmlTextReader`	Simple XmlTextReader
`CommandButton`	`XmlTextReaderByNode`	XmlTextReader By Node
`CommandButton`	`XmlTextReaderAttributes`	XmlTextReader Attributes
`CommandButton`	`UsingXmlDocument`	Using XmlDocument
`CommandButton`	`XPathSelectNodes`	XPath SelectNodes
`CommandButton`	`DOMXmlAttributes`	DOM XmlAttributes
`RichTextBox`	`XmlOut`	Leave Blank

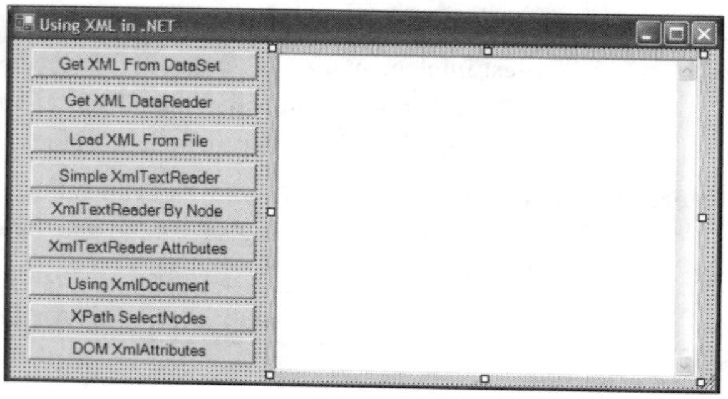

FIGURE 12.12
`XMLCode` *form after adding controls.*

You must also alias the following namespaces in this form:

- `System.Data.SqlClient`
- `System.IO`
- `System.Text`
- `System.Xml`

Now that the form is created, you'll write code to create the XML files you'll be working with.

Using a `DataSet` to Create XML Files and Schemas

Earlier today you created an XML file based on rules you defined in an XML schema file. I mentioned that this could have been done just as easily using methods of the `DataSet` class. To create an XML file and schema based on the Customers table in the Northwind database, double-click the Get XML from DataSet button and add the code in Listing 12.3.

LISTING 12.3 Using the `WriteXml` and `WriteXmlSchema` Methods of the `DataSet` Class

VB.NET

```
Private Sub GetXmlFromDataSet_Click(ByVal sender As System.Object, _
            ByVal e As System.EventArgs) Handles GetXmlFromDataSet.Click

    ' Check to see if the files exist, is they do, Delete them
    If File.Exists("Customers.xml") Then
        File.Delete("Customers.xml")
    End If

    If File.Exists("CustomersSchema.xml") Then
        File.Delete("CustomersSchema.xml")
    End If

    ' Create a DataSet to hold the XML
    Dim ds As DataSet = New DataSet("NorthwindCustomers")

    ' Connect to the database
    Dim cn As SqlConnection = New SqlConnection( _
            "database=northwind;server=.\NetSDK;Integrated Security=SSPI")

    ' Set the DataAdapter to get the data
    Dim adp As New SqlDataAdapter("Select * from Customers", cn)

    ' Fill the DataSet with the DataAdapter command
    adp.Fill(ds, "Customer")
```

LISTING 12.3 continued

```
        ' call the WriteXml and WriteXmlSchema methods
        ds.WriteXml("Customers.xml")
        ds.WriteXmlSchema("CustomersSchema.xml")

    End Sub
```

C#

```
private void GetXmlFromDataSet_Click(object sender, System.EventArgs e)
   {
      // Check to see if the files exist, is they do, Delete them
      if (File.Exists(@"Customers.xml"))
      {
              File.Delete(@"Customers.xml");
      }

      if (File.Exists(@"CustomersSchema.xml"))
      {
              File.Delete(@"CustomersSchema.xml");
      }

      // Create a DataSet to hold the XML
      DataSet ds = new DataSet("NorthwindCustomers");

      // Connect to the database
      SqlConnection cn = new SqlConnection
        (@"database=northwind;server=.\NetSDK;Integrated Security=SSPI");

      // Set the DataAdapter to get the data
      SqlDataAdapter adp = new SqlDataAdapter("Select * from Customers", cn);

      // Fill the DataSet with the DataAdapter command
      adp.Fill(ds, "Customer");

      // call the WriteXml and WriteXmlSchema methods
      ds.WriteXml(@"Customers.xml");
      ds.WriteXmlSchema(@"CustomersSchema.xml");
   }
```

Run the application and execute the code you just wrote. If you drill into the `Bin` directory of the solution, you'll see the two new XML files that your code created. Using the `WriteXml` and `WriteXmlSchema` methods of the `DataSet` class, you created the XML file and XML schema for the Customers table in the Northwind database. If you double-click the XML files in the Solution Explorer, you'll see the XML that was created in the XML designer. You'll notice that using the `WriteXml` and `WriteXmlSchema` methods creates XML files using `Elements`—there are no attributes in the created files.

To create attribute-based XML files, you can use a `DataReader` with the `For XML Auto` clause in T-SQL and a `FileStream` to generate the XML file.

Using `For XML Auto` to Create Attribute-Based XML Files

To create an attribute-based XML file, you can use many techniques. The `XmlTextWriter` class could be used, but there's an easier way. Listing 12.4 demonstrates how to use the `For XML Auto` Transact-SQL clause to return XML from SQL Server. After the data is returned in a `SqlDataReader`, you can loop through the data and write it out to a stream. To ensure that the resulting XML is well formed, you add the prolog information and the root element's start and end tags. Double-click on the Get XML DataReader button and add the code in Listing 12.4.

LISTING 12.4 Creating an Attribute-Based XML File

VB.NET

```
Private Sub GetXmlDataReader_Click(ByVal sender As System.Object, _
     ByVal e As System.EventArgs) Handles GetXmlDataReader.Click

     ' Create a stream to write to
     Dim sr As New StreamWriter("CustomerAttributes.xml")

     ' Add the XML prolog and Root element
     sr.WriteLine("<?xml version='1.0' standalone='yes' ?>")
     sr.WriteLine("<TransformedCustomers>")

     ' Connect to the database
     Dim cn As SqlConnection = New SqlConnection( _
             "database=northwind;server=.\NetSDK;Integrated Security=SSPI")
     cn.Open()

     ' Use the For XML Auto clause
     Dim cmd As New SqlCommand("Select * from customers for XML Auto", cn)

     ' Declare the DataReader to read the data
     Dim dr As SqlDataReader = cmd.ExecuteReader

     ' Loop thru the DataReader, writing out the file
     While dr.Read
         ' Get each chunk of XML as the reader reads it
         sr.Write(dr(0))
     End While

     ' Write the End Element
```

12

LISTING 12.4 continued

```
        sr.WriteLine("</TransformedCustomers>")

        ' Flush and Close the Stream
        sr.Flush()
        sr.Close()
    End Sub
```

C#

```
    private void GetXmlDataReader_Click(object sender, System.EventArgs e)
       {
            // Create a stream to write to
            StreamWriter sr = new StreamWriter(@"CustomerAttributes.xml");

           //  Add the XML prolog and Root element
            sr.WriteLine("<?xml version='1.0' standalone='yes' ?>");
            sr.WriteLine("<TransformedCustomers>");

            //  Connect to the database
            SqlConnection cn = new SqlConnection
             (@"database=northwind;server=.\NetSDK;Integrated Security=SSPI");
            cn.Open();

            //  Use the For XML Auto clause
            SqlCommand cmd = new SqlCommand(@"Select * from customers for XML Auto",
➥cn);

            //  Declare the DataReader to read the data
            SqlDataReader dr = cmd.ExecuteReader();

            //  Loop thru the DataReader, writing out the file
             while (dr.Read())
             {
                // Get each chunk of XML as the reader reads it
                sr.Write(dr.GetString (0));
             }

            //  Write the End Element
            sr.WriteLine("</TransformedCustomers>");

            //  Flush and Close the Stream
            sr.Flush();
            sr.Close();
       }
```

If you run the application now and run the `GetXMLDataReader` code, you'll have a new XML file in your Bin directory named `CustomerAttributes.xml`. If you compare this file to the `Customers.xml` file you created in Listing 12.3, you'll see the XML format looks quite different, but the way they are handled in the Data view of the XML Designer is exactly the same. They're both examples of well-formed XML documents.

The amount of actual text, or size in bytes, of an XML file that's purely using elements is much larger than an XML file created using attributes. If the amount of data being passed over the wire is critical, you should consider using attributes for flat XML files instead of elements.

The `ReadXml` method of the `DataSet` you used earlier to load the `Employees.xml` file behaves the same for XML documents based on elements or attributes.

To read the complete XML file as a stream, you can use the `GetXml` method of the `DataSet` class. Listing 12.5 loads the `Customers.xml` file into a `DataSet`, and then uses the `GetXml` method of the `DataSet` class to display the data in the textbox. Add the code in Listing 12.5 to the `LoadXml` click event.

LISTING 12.5 Loading XML to a String Using the `ReadXml` and `GetXml` Methods of the `DataSet` Class

VB.NET

```
Private Sub LoadXMLFile_Click(ByVal sender As System.Object, _
            ByVal e As System.EventArgs) Handles LoadXMLFile.Click

    ' Create a new DataSet
    Dim ds As New DataSet()

    ' Load the XML file into the DataSet with the ReadXml method
    ds.ReadXml("Customers.xml")

    ' Send the XML to the textbox
    XmlOut.Text = ds.GetXml()

End Sub
```

C#

```
private void LoadXMLFile_Click(object sender, System.EventArgs e)
   {
      // Create a new DataSet
      DataSet ds = new DataSet();

      // Load the XML file into the DataSet with the ReadXml method
      ds.ReadXml(@"Customers.xml");

      // Send the XML to the textbox
      XmlOut.Text = ds.GetXml();
   }
```

In Listing 12.5, the `ReadXml` method is used to fill the `DataSet` with the data from the XML file. After the `DataSet` is loaded, the `GetXml` method is called to output the XML data to the text box. When you run the application and execute the code, the data from the XML file is simply displayed in the text box, and you should see something similar to Figure 12.13.

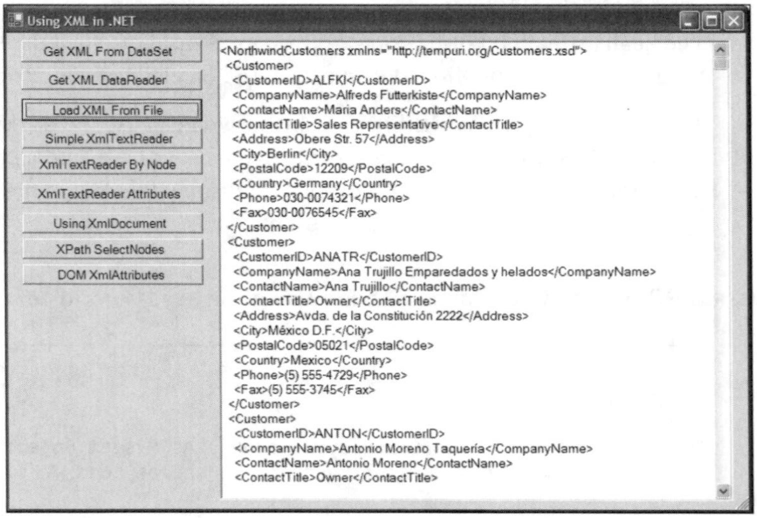

FIGURE 12.13

Output from the `GetXml` *method of the* `DataSet` *class.*

After an XML file is loaded into the `DataSet`, you can treat it like any other `DataTable` in the `DataSet`. You can loop through tables, rows, and columns just as you did over the last two days when you learned how to work with `DataSets` in ADO.NET. Remember that XML is data. After data is in a `DataSet`, the methods to interact with it are the same no matter what the datasource is.

Using the `XmlTextReader` Class

The `XmlTextReader` class can be compared to the `DataReader` class of the `System.Data` namespace. `DataReaders` are read-only, forward-only unbuffered streams of data from a database. `XmlReaders` are read-only, forward-only unbuffered streams of data from XML files. The `XmlTextReader` class provides robust functionality for reading XML files that are element based or attribute based.

The `Read` method of the `XmlTextReader` class reads the XML stream until a `False` value is returned to indicate the end of the file has been reached. While reading the file, you can check the `NodeType` property to determine what node you're reading and what kind of node it is. Table 12.5 lists the `NodeType` enumeration and descriptions of the different types of nodes.

TABLE 12.5 The `NodeType` Enumeration

Node Name	*Description*
`Attribute`	An `Attribute` node can have the following child node types: `Text` and `EntityReference`. The `Attribute` node doesn't appear as the child node of any other node type. It isn't considered a child node of an `Element`.
`CDATA`	`CDATA` sections are used to escape blocks of text that would otherwise be recognized as markup. A `CDATA` node cannot have any child nodes. It can appear as the child of the `DocumentFragment`, `EntityReference`, and `Element` nodes.
`Comment`	A `Comment` node can't have any child nodes. It can appear as the child of the `Document`, `DocumentFragment`, `Element`, and `EntityReference` nodes.
`Document`	A document object that, as the root of the document tree, provides access to the entire XML document. A `Document` node can have the following child node types: `XmlDeclaration`, `Element` (maximum of one), `ProcessingInstruction`, `Comment`, and `DocumentType`. It can't appear as the child of any node types.
`DocumentFragment`	A document fragment. The `DocumentFragment` node associates a node or subtree with a document without actually being contained within the document. A `DocumentFragment` node can have the following child node types: `Element`, `ProcessingInstruction`, `Comment`, `Text`, `CDATA`, and `EntityReference`. It can't appear as the child of any node types.
`DocumentType`	A `DocumentType` node can have the following child node types: `Notation` and `Entity`. It can appear as the child of the `Document` node.
`Element`	An `Element` node can have the following child node types: `Element`, `Text`, `Comment`, `ProcessingInstruction`, `CDATA`, and `EntityReference`. It can be the child of the `Document`, `DocumentFragment`, `EntityReference`, and `Element` nodes.
`EndElement`	Returned when `XmlReader` gets to the end of an element.
`EndEntity`	Returned when `XmlReader` gets to the end of the entity replacement as a result of a call to `ResolveEntity`.
`Entity`	An `Entity` node can have child nodes that represent the expanded entity (for example, `Text` and `EntityReference` nodes). It can appear as the child of the `DocumentType` node.
`EntityReference`	An `EntityReference` node can have the following child node types: `Element`, `ProcessingInstruction`, `Comment`, `Text`, `CDATA`, and `EntityReference`. It can appear as the child of the `Attribute`, `DocumentFragment`, `Element`, and `EntityReference` nodes.
`None`	This is returned by the `XmlReader` if a `Read` method hasn't been called.

TABLE 12.5 continued

Node Name	*Description*
`Notation`	A `Notation` node can't have any child nodes. It can appear as the child of the `DocumentType` node.
`ProcessingInstruction`	A `ProcessingInstruction` node cannot have any child nodes. It can appear as the child of the `Document`, `DocumentFragment`, `Element`, and `EntityReference` nodes.
`SignificantWhitespace`	White space between markup in a mixed content model or white space within the `xml:space="preserve"` scope.
`Text`	The text content of a node. A `Text` node can't have any child nodes. It can appear as the child node of the `Attribute`, `DocumentFragment`, `Element`, and `EntityReference` nodes.
`Whitespace`	White space between markup.
`XmlDeclaration`	The `XmlDeclaration` node must be the first node in the document. It can't have child nodes. It is a child of the `Document` node. It can have attributes that provide version and encoding information.

To implement a simple `XmlTextReader` that outputs only the text or data value for a node, you can use the `NodeType` as the `XmlReader` reads the XML stream. The code in Listing 12.6 uses an `XmlTextReader` to read the `Customers.xml` file to output only `Text` node types. Add the code in Listing 12.6 to the Simple `XmlTextReader` click event.

LISTING 12.6 Implementing a Simple `XmlTextReader` and Checking the `NodeType` Property

VB.NET

```
Private Sub SimpleXmlTextReader_Click(ByVal sender As System.Object, _
            ByVal e As System.EventArgs) Handles SimpleXmlTextReader.Click

    ' Load the XML file into a new XmlTextReader
    Dim xr As New XmlTextReader("Customers.xml")
    Dim sb As New StringBuilder()

    ' Read the file, getting the Text nodes, which is the actual data
    While xr.Read
        ' Check the XmlNodeType enumeration for Text
        If xr.NodeType = XmlNodeType.Text Then
            ' Get the Value of the Text nodetype
            sb.Append(xr.Value)
            ' Append the carriage return
            sb.Append(ControlChars.CrLf)
```

LISTING 12.6 continued

```
        End If
    End While

    ' Output to the textbox
    XmlOut.Text = sb.ToString

    ' Close the XmlTextReader
    xr.Close()

End Sub
```

C#

```
private void SimpleXmlTextReader_Click(object sender, System.EventArgs e)
   {
      // Load the XML file into a new XmlTextReader
      XmlTextReader xr = new XmlTextReader(@"Customers.xml");
      StringBuilder sb = new StringBuilder();

      // Read the file, getting the Text nodes, which is the actual data
      while (xr.Read())
      {
         // Check the XmlNodeType enumeration for Text
         if (xr.NodeType == XmlNodeType.Text)
         {
            // Get the Value of the Text nodetype
            sb.Append(xr.Value + "\n");
         }
      }

      // Output to the textbox
      XmlOut.Text = sb.ToString();

      // Close the XmlTextReader
      xr.Close();
   }
```

After you call the `Read` method in Listing 12.6, you check the `NodeType` property. If `NodeType` is equal to `NodeType.Text`, the value is appended to the string builder. If you run the application and execute the code, you'll see something similar to Figure 12.14.

By outputting only the `Text` node type, you're getting rid of the XML tags that describe the data.

If you need to output specific data, such as the `CompanyName`, you can check the `Name` property of the current element. The code in Listing 12.7 reads each element, and adds only the `CompanyName` values to the string builder for output to the text box. Add the code in Listing 12.7 to the `XmlTextReaderByNode` click event.

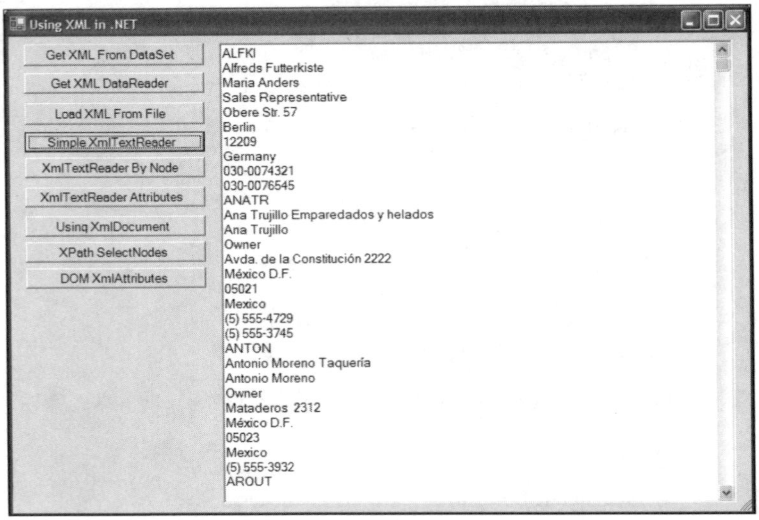

FIGURE 12.14

The `XmlReader` *outputting only* `Text` `NodeType`*s.*

LISTING 12.7 Reading XML Elements by Name

VB.NET

```
Private Sub XmlTextReaderByNode_Click(ByVal sender As System.Object, _
                ByVal e As System.EventArgs) Handles XmlTextReaderByNode.Click

    ' Load the XML File
    Dim xr As New XmlTextReader("Customers.xml")
    Dim sb As New StringBuilder()

    ' Retrieve data based on a specific Node Name
    While xr.Read
        ' Ignore any non-character data
        If xr.ReadString.Length > 0 Then
            ' Check the name of the Element
            If xr.Name = "CompanyName" Then
                ' Read the String with the ReadString() method
                sb.Append(xr.ReadString())
                ' Append the carriage return
                sb.Append(ControlChars.CrLf)
            End If
        End If
    End While

    ' Display in the textbox
    XmlOut.Text = sb.ToString

End Sub
```

LISTING 12.7 continued

C#

```
private void XmlTextReaderByNode_Click(object sender, System.EventArgs e)
{
        // Load the XML file into a new XmlTextReader
        XmlTextReader xr = new XmlTextReader(@"Customers.xml");
        StringBuilder sb = new StringBuilder();

        // Read the file, getting the Text nodes, which is the actual data
        while (xr.Read())
        {
                // Ignore any non-character data
                if (xr.ReadString().Length > 0)
                {
                // Check the name of the Element
                        if (xr.Name == "CompanyName")
                        {
                          // Read the String with the ReadString() method
                          sb.Append(xr.ReadString() + "\n");
                        }
                }
        }

        // Output to the textbox
        XmlOut.Text = sb.ToString();

        // Close the XmlTextReader
        xr.Close();
}
```

12

When you run this code, you get only the `CompanyName` values from the XML file, as Figure 12.15 demonstrates.

Using the Name property along the with NodeType is extremely useful for getting data values for specific elements.

Working with Attributes and the `XmlTextReader`

Until now, you've used only the element-based `Customers.xml` file. But you'll often need to deal with attributes in an XML file. Using the `GetAttribute` method of the `XmlTextReader` class returns a specific attribute in a node.

When the reader reads a node using the `Read` method, it reads all the information in the node. So, if there are attributes in the node, it looks at them as a collection. By checking the `HasAttributes` and `AttributesCount` properties, you can determine whether a node has attributes, and use the `GetAttributes` method to grab the data values for the attributes you're looking for.

FIGURE 12.15

Retrieving elements by name using the `XmlTextReader` *class.*

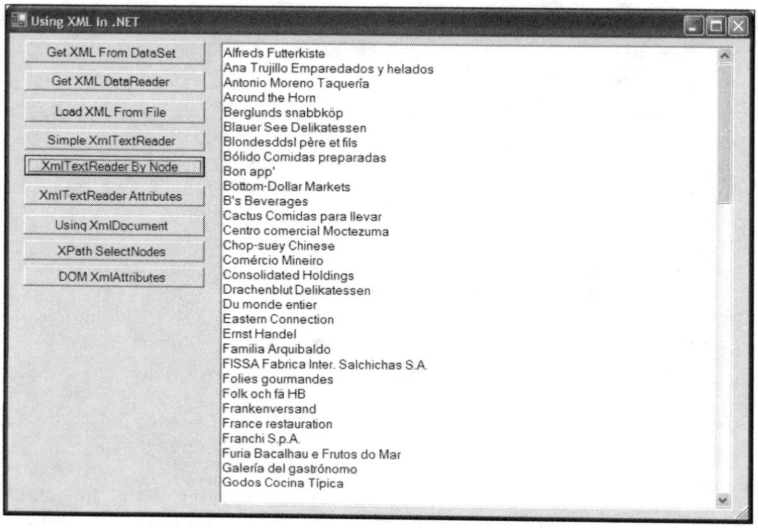

Listing 12.8 uses the `GetAttributes` method to accomplish the same thing that Listing 12.7 did: retrieve `CompanyName`. The difference is that the XML file you're reading is the attribute-based file, not the element-based file. The code iterates through all the attributes for each node and outputs them to the text box. Add the code in Listing 12.8 to the `XmlTextReaderAttributes` click event.

LISTING 12.8 Using the `GetAttributes` Method

VB.NET

```
Private Sub XmlTextReaderAttributes_Click(ByVal sender As System.Object, _
          ByVal e As System.EventArgs) Handles XmlTextReaderAttributes.Click

    ' Load the XML file into a new XmlTextReader
    Dim xr As New XmlTextReader("CustomerAttributes.xml")
    Dim sb As New StringBuilder()

    ' Read the file
    While xr.Read
        ' Only look at Elements
        If xr.NodeType = XmlNodeType.Element Then
            ' That have attributes
            If xr.HasAttributes Then
                ' With an AttributeCount > 0
                If xr.AttributeCount > 0 Then
                    sb.Append(ControlChars.CrLf)
```

LISTING 12.8 continued

```
                        ' Write out the CompanyName
                        sb.Append(xr.GetAttribute("CompanyName"))
                        sb.Append(ControlChars.CrLf)
                        ' Loop thru the Attributes and write them out
                        Dim intX As Integer
                        For intX = 0 To xr.AttributeCount - 1
                            sb.Append("***")
                            ' Get the Attribute
                            sb.Append(xr.GetAttribute(intX))
                            sb.Append(ControlChars.CrLf)
                        Next
                    End If
                End If
            End If
        End While

        ' Output to the textbox
        XmlOut.Text = sb.ToString
        'Console.WriteLine(sb.ToString)

        ' Close the XmlTextReader
        xr.Close()
    End Sub
```

C#

```
private void XmlTextReaderAttributes_Click
        (object sender, System.EventArgs e)
   {
        // Load the XML file into a new XmlTextReader
        XmlTextReader xr = new XmlTextReader(@"CustomerAttributes.xml");
        StringBuilder sb = new StringBuilder();

        // Read the file, getting the Text nodes, which is the actual data
        while (xr.Read())
          {
            // Only look at Elements
            if (xr.NodeType == XmlNodeType.Element)
               {
               // That have attributes
               if (xr.HasAttributes)
               {
               // With an AttributeCount > 0
               if (xr.AttributeCount > 0)
                  {
                  // Write out the CompanyName
                  sb.Append(xr.GetAttribute("CompanyName"));
                  for (int i = 0; i < xr.AttributeCount; i++)
                     {
```

12

LISTING 12.8 continued

```
                sb.Append("***");
                sb.Append(xr.GetAttribute(i) + "\n");
              }
            }
          }
      }
    }
  // Output to the textbox
  XmlOut.Text = sb.ToString();
  // Close the XmlTextReader
  xr.Close();
  }
```

The code in Listing 12.8 first checks to see whether the current node has attributes. If it does, the code makes sure that the count is greater then zero, and then loops through the attributes using the index of the attribute within the node. If you run this now and execute the code, you'll see something like Figure 12.16.

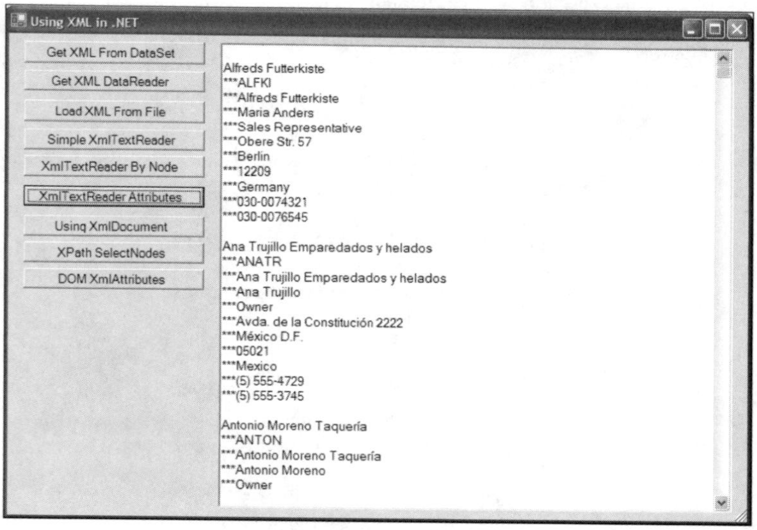

FIGURE 12.16
Using attributes with the `XmlTextReader` *class.*

Reading attributes is just as easy as reading elements in an XML file. More complex XML files use a combination of elements and attributes to describe the data, so understanding how to work with each type of node is important.

Summary

Today you learned about XML in the .NET Framework. Using the tools available in Visual Studio .NET, you can create XML schemas and use those schemas with XML files quickly and easily. If you need to process XML files, you can use the classes in the `XmlTextReader` to process large XML files with very little overhead. No matter what type of XML document you have to work with, the classes in the `System.XML` namespace have all the functionality you need.

Q&A

Q You showed me a couple ways to load XML documents. Which is the best way to load an XML document?

A The best way might not be the easiest way. Using the `XmlDocument` class with DOM gives you great flexibility, but at the cost of resources. Using the `XmlTextReader` is super fast and efficient, but it's a forward-only stream, so you might find it limited. Loading an XML document into a `DataSet` is easy too, but you must be familiar with navigating tables and rows in a `DataSet` to work effectively with the XML document. So, the short answer is that there's no *single* best way; there's only a best way based on what you need to do with the data and what syntax you are familiar with.

Q Why go through all the trouble of creating schemas in the designer when I can just use the `WriteXmlSchema` method of the `DataSet` class?

A Using the `WriteXmlSchema` method is an easy way to get a schema from tables in a database, but it might not build the schema correctly based on the hierarchy you're looking for. If you build a few more schemas with the Schema Designer, you'll realize it's as easy as creating a table in SQL Server and calling `WriteXmlSchema`.

12

Q You aren't showing me how to do any of this in ASP.NET. Why?

A All the code you wrote today can be cut and pasted directly into an ASP.NET application and run without modification. The `DataGrid` in Windows Forms correctly displays the hierarchy of the data, but the Web Forms `DataGrid` doesn't, so I wanted you to get an idea of what the data looks like in real life, not in the flat grid on a Web page. It's very easy to see how to write data back to an XML file using the DataGrid. This is still possible in ASP.NET, but not with the grid control.

Q I'm hungry for more XML. Where do I go next?

A If you're a hardcore XML developer, a must-have book on the shelf is *XML for ASP.NET*, by Dan Wahlin. That book covers pretty much everything you'd ever need to know about XML and .NET. I highly recommend it.

Online, the MSDN XML Developer Center is jam-packed with XML programming information. You can find it at the following URL:

`http://www.msdn.microsoft.com/library/default.asp?url=/nhp/default.asp?contentid=28000438`

Also on Microsoft.com is the XML series of online seminars. I recommend viewing the seminar about transforming XML with XSLT in .NET, which is important but beyond the scope of this book:

`http://support.microsoft.com/default.aspx?scid=kb;en-us;q326069`

If you need some other great examples of using XSLT to transform XML, check out the XSLT Stylesheet Library at `http://www.xmlpitstop.com`. There are tons of great examples of transforming XML with XSLT in .NET.

Quiz

1. True or False: XML files are better than flat text files because they can be transmitted easily over the Internet.
2. All XML-specific classes are found in the __________ namespace.
3. Name the three main classes for reading forward-only XML data.
4. Using the __________ Transact SQL clause, you can easily create attribute-based XML files from SQL Server.
5. Using the __________ method of the `XmlTextReader` class, you can get the attribute data value of a node.

Quiz Answers

1. False. XML files are better at defining hierarchical data, and they are self-describing with XML schemas. Both text files and XML files can be transmitted over the Internet.
2. `System.Xml`
3. `XmlTextReader`, `XmlValidatingReader`, `XmlNodeReader`
4. `FOR XML AUTO`
5. `GetAttribute`

Exercises

1. Open the solution file for the XML app that you just completed and do the following:
   - Go to the code for the Using XML Document button. If you do not have Dynamic Help on, click Help from the main menu and select Dynamic Help. Read the SDK file on the `XmlDocument` class to familiarize yourself with its capabilities.
   - Set a breakpoint on the `Load` method of the `xDoc` variable in the `XPathSelectNodes` click event. Step through the code and examine how the `SelectNodes` and `SelectSingleNode` methods behave compared to the `XmlTextReader` methods when retrieving node values.
   - Run the code for the `DOMXmlAttribute` click event. Using the Dynamic Help, familiarize yourself with the `XmlAttribute`, `XmlNode`, and `XmlNodeList` objects in the SDK.
   - Read about the differences of using the `XmlReader` classes versus the `XmlDocument` classes when working with XML files.
2. Create a new ASP.NET Web Application. Using the databinding techniques you learned about over the last few days, do the following:
   - Add a `ComboBox` and `DataGrid` to the default WebForm1.aspx page.
   - Load the `Customers.xml` file into a `DataSet`, and then bind the `DataSet` to a `DataGrid`.
   - Load the `ComboBox` with the `CustomerID` field using an `XmlReader`, and add the `CustomerID` to the `Items` collection of the `ComboBox`.

   This will help you become familiar with using ASP.NET and loading XML files on Web pages.

WEEK 2

DAY 13

XML Web Services in .NET

Yesterday you learned about XML and how it's a flexible and extensible mechanism for working with data. Today you learn how extensible markup language (XML) can be used in a distributed architecture. By using XML Web services as your means of distributing application functionality, you can take what used to be available only on your computer and make it available to the whole world. Best of all, you don't have to write any extra code to make it happen. Today, you learn

- What XML Web services are
- How to create Web services using Visual Studio .NET
- How to pass data from SQL Server via Web services
- How to consume an XML Web service from a Windows Forms application
- How to consume an XML Web service from an ASP.NET application
- How to consume an XML Web service from VBScript in DHTML

What Are XML Web Services?

XML Web services are application components that can expose functionality over hypertext transfer protocol (HTTP) using the simple object access protocol (SOAP). Using Web services, you have the ability to expose methods in your applications to anyone on the Internet.

Before .NET, one of the biggest challenges developers had to work around was getting data from their servers to another server without compromising security. If you had a component that returned customer information, and you wanted to let someone outside your network access that component, your task wasn't easy. You had to configure the distributed component object model (DCOM) and somehow manage to let the caller of the component authenticate on your server, create an instance of the component, and then call methods on the component. This wasn't easy to implement, so there was a lot of code written to work around the limitation of exposing application functionality in a safe way.

With XML Web services, these limitations are no longer an issue. By wrapping application logic into a Web service, anyone can access the methods in your components over port 80 using HTTP. No special configuration needs to be in place. When a call is made to a Web service, the information is passed back to the caller using XML. Yesterday, you learned how XML is the best way to pass data around the Internet because it's just plain text. Web services take advantage of this by using XML as the backbone of the core Web service infrastructure.

Besides the technical aspects of not having to open any special ports, risk security holes, or configure DCOM to allow others access to application functionality, Web services give you the ability to write cross-platform applications immediately. Any application running written in any language running on any operating system can make a Web service request. It's just like calling any URL on the Internet. How it's implemented is irrelevant; the fact that you can send and receive information in a simple and secure manner is what matters.

Understanding How Web Services Work

Web services are built on open Internet standards and protocols. The common protocols that make Web services work are HTTP and SOAP. Understanding the internals of these protocols isn't important. Like TCP/IP (transmission control protocol/Internet protocol) and IPX (internetwork packet exchange) define how data is transferred over a network, HTTP defines how data is passed over the Internet and SOAP defines how XML must look when being consumed as a Web service being transmitted over HTTP.

- Web services description language (WSDL) is an XML-based contract that defines what methods are contained in a Web service. WSDL can be compared to a type library for a COM component; it lets you know methods are available in the Web service to consume. Because WSDL files are XML based, any client can read them to find out what the Web service offers.
- DISCO, or discovery, files provide a mechanism to discover what Web services are available at a particular site. If you have a Web site and you want to expose a number of Web services, you can create a DISCO file that can be queried by others to find out what your site offers. Discovery files aren't required to make a Web service work; they just provide a mechanism to find out what's available on a specific Web site.
- Universal description, discovery, and integration (UDDI) is a distributed repository application programming interface (API) for Web services. The global community of the Internet needed a mechanism for people to find what Web services are available, so the UDDI repository was created. UDDI is the Yellow Pages for Web services. You can go to `http://www.uddi.org` and search for Web services by type, functionality, industry, or company. If your large corporation needs its own Web services Yellow Pages, you can write your own UDDI directory using the UDDI software development kits (SDKs) available from Microsoft.

To summarize, Web services are application components that can be consumed over the Internet using open standards. You can use tools of the UDDI repository to search for Web services, or you can discover what Web services are available at specific sites if the sites provide a DISCO file. When you find a Web service, you can inspect its functionality through its WSDL file. Every aspect of creating and consuming Web services uses XML, so they're both cross-platform and cross-language.

Creating Your First Web Service

Creating a Web service is as easy as creating any other type of application using Visual Studio .NET. To create your first Web service project, start Visual Studio .NET and select New Project from the Start Page. Select the Visual Basic Projects or C# Projects folder from the New Project dialog, depending on what language you're writing in, and then scroll down and select ASP.NET Web Service. Change the project name from `http://localhost/WebService1` to `http://localhost/firstService_vb` or `http://localhost/firstService_cs`, depending on what language you're using. Figure 13.1 demonstrates what you should be looking at right now.

FIGURE 13.1

New Project dialog box.

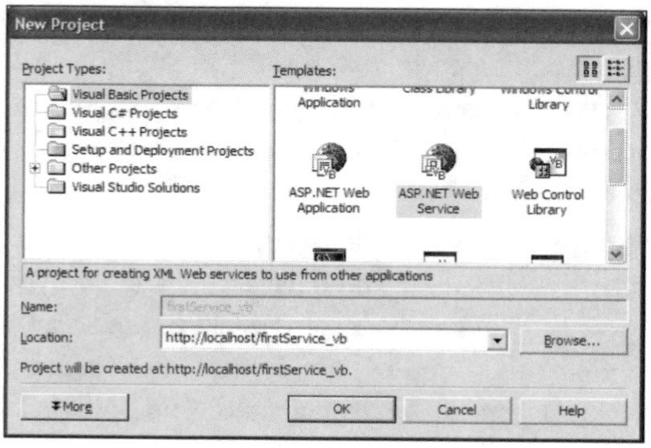

If you click OK, the new project is created and you're presented with the Web services component designer as Figure 13.2 shows.

FIGURE 13.2

Web services designer surface.

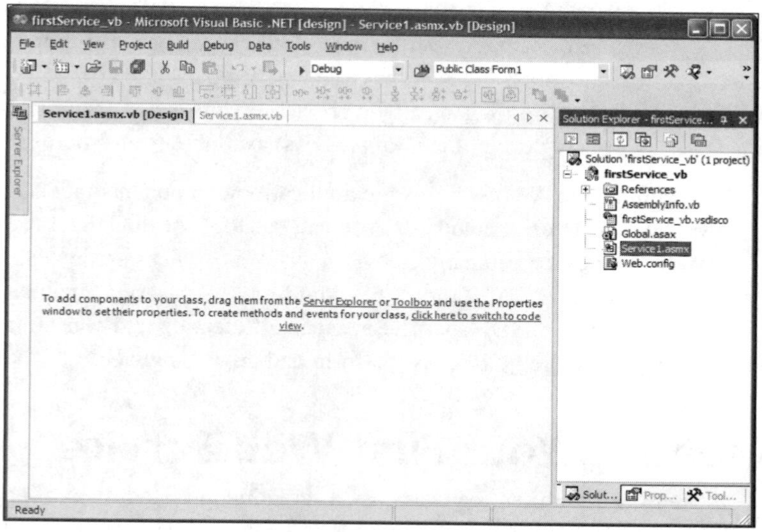

From this point, you can modify properties, add items from the toolbox, or switch to the Code view. If you look at the Properties window for this new Web service, you'll notice the name isn't firstService, it's Service1. Service1 is the default name for all new Web services added to a project. When you created the project firstService, you created the Internet Information Server (IIS) virtual directory named firstService to contain the Web service named Service1. For now, you can leave the name Service1 as it is.

On the designer, click the link that switches you to Code view. You should see something similar to Figure 13.3 if you created a Visual Basic .NET project.

FIGURE 13.3

The Code view of an XML Web service.

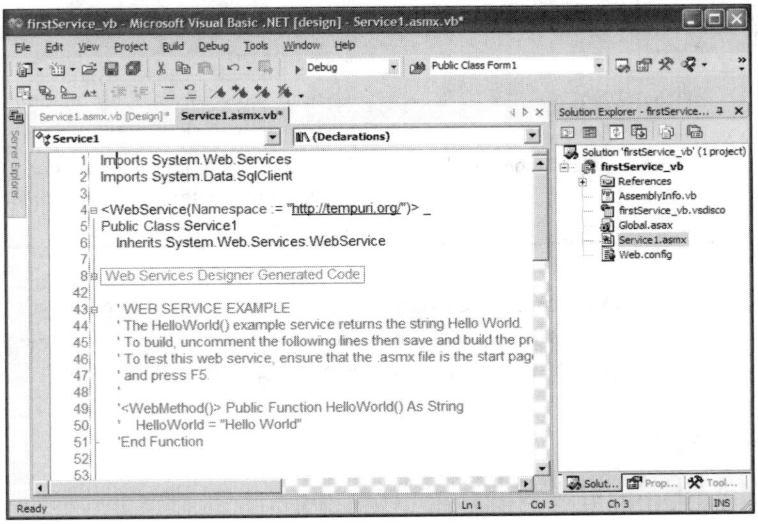

You're now in the code-behind file for the Web service named Service1. Web services in Visual Studio .NET have a .ASMX extension, so naturally the code-behind would be either ASMX.VB (for Visual Basic .NET) or ASMX.CS (for C#). It follows the same pattern as ASPX pages in Web applications. The code-behind file simply tacks on the language extension to the designer file.

If you look at the code in the class file, you'll notice that the `System.Web.Services` namespace is imported into this class.

The `System.Web.Services` namespace contains classes that enable you to create Web services using Visual Studio .NET that work with the ASP.NET engine and allow ASP.NET and Windows Forms applications to consume Web services. The four main classes in the `System.Web.Services` namespace are listed in Table 13.1.

TABLE 13.1 Classes of the `System.Web.Services` Namespace

Class	*Description*
`WebMethodAttribute`	Adding this attribute to a method within an XML Web service created using ASP.NET makes the method callable from remote Web clients
`WebService`	Defines the optional base class for XML Web services, which provides direct access to common ASP.NET objects, such as application and session state

TABLE 13.1 continued

Class	*Description*
`WebServiceAttribute`	Used to add additional information to an XML Web service, such as a string describing its functionality
`WebServiceBindingAttribute`	Declares the binding one or more XML Web service methods implemented within the class implementing the XML Web service

Simply importing the `System.Web.Services` namespace doesn't make this a Web service. The class file must inherit the `WebService` class. So, in the `Service1.asmx` file, the following code makes this class a Web service:

VB.NET

```
Imports System.Web.Services

<WebService(Namespace := "http://tempuri.org/")> _
Public Class Service1
    Inherits System.Web.Services.WebService
```

C#

```
using System.Web.Services;

namespace firstService_cs
{
   public class Service1 : System.Web.Services.WebService
```

All this is done automatically by Visual Studio .NET when you create a new Web service project or you add an ASMX file to your application.

The `Namespace` attribute points to `http://www.tempuri.org/`. This is the default namespace for all new Web services created with Visual Studio .NET. You should change it before you deploy your Web service application. The namespace defines what data is in the Web service and what rules the data should follow. It's the same concept that you learned about yesterday when you created XML schema definition (XSD) files for the XML files in your project. In that case, the namespace defined what the XML should look like; the namespace for a Web service defines what the Web service should look like.

Notice the commented-out `HelloWorld` method in the `Service1` class. This sample method is in every new ASMX file in Visual Studio .NET. The `HelloWorld` method looks like any other method in the class files you worked with until today, with the exception of the `WebMethod` attribute. By prefixing a method name with the `WebMethod` attribute, it becomes available to the outside world.

> **Note**
>
> Attributes are tags that enable you to further define objects in an application. The attribute information is then examined at runtime through reflection, letting the language-specific compiler determine what to do with the attribute information. In the case of the `WebMethod` attribute, the ASP.NET engine knows to make the method available to remote callers. In C#, attributes are enclosed in brackets, *`[attributename]`*, and in Visual Basic .NET, they're enclosed by less-than/greater-than signs, *`<attributename>`*.

To make the `HelloWorld` method available to the outside world, uncomment the method. Make sure that you also uncomment the `WebMethod` attribute. Before you run the application, you must add two more methods that you'll consume later—it'll also give you an idea of how to use Web services in a real-world scenario.

Listing 13.1 has two methods: `GetCustomers` and `GetCustomerByID`. Both use ADO.NET that you learned about over the past few days. Add these methods to the class file for `Service1.asmx`.

LISTING 13.1 Code to Get SQL Data from the `Service1.asmx` File

VB.NET

```
<WebMethod()> Public Function GetCustomers() As DataSet

    Dim cn As New SqlConnection( _
               "Server=jb1gs\NetSDK;Database=pubs;" _
               & "Integrated Security=SSPI")

    Dim da As SqlDataAdapter = New SqlDataAdapter _
        ("SELECT * from Authors", cn)

    Dim ds As DataSet = New DataSet()
    da.Fill(ds, "Customers")

    Return ds

End Function

<WebMethod()> Public Function GetCustomerByID _
                (ByVal ID As String) As DataSet

    Dim cn As New SqlConnection( _
               "Server=jb1gs\NetSDK;Database=pubs;" _
               & "Integrated Security=SSPI")

    Dim da As SqlDataAdapter = New SqlDataAdapter _
        ("SELECT * from Authors where au_id = ?", cn)

    da.SelectCommand.Parameters.Add("au_id", ID)

    Dim ds As DataSet = New DataSet()
    da.Fill(ds, "Customers")
```

LISTING 13.1 continued

```
    Return ds

End Function
```

C#

```
[WebMethod]
public DataSet GetCustomers()
{
        SqlConnection cn = new SqlConnection
           (@"Server=jb1gs\NetSDK;Database=Northwind;Integrated Security=SSPI");
        SqlDataAdapter da  = new SqlDataAdapter("SELECT * from Customers", cn);
        DataSet ds = new DataSet();
        da.Fill(ds, "Customers");
        return ds;
}

[WebMethod]
public DataSet GetCustomerByID(string ID)
{
        SqlConnection cn = new SqlConnection();
           (@"Server=jb1gs\NetSDK;Database=Northwind;Integrated Security=SSPI");

        SqlDataAdapter da  = new SqlDataAdapter();
           (@"SELECT * from Customers where CustomerID = @CustomerID", cn);

        da.SelectCommand.Parameters.Add("@CustomerID",
        SqlDbType.VarChar, 15).Value = ID;

        DataSet ds = new DataSet();
        da.Fill(ds, "Customers");
        return ds;
}
```

Note

In version 1.0 of the .NET Framework, the HTTP-GET, HTTP-POST and SOAP protocols were enabled by default for accessing Web Services when Visual Studio .NET was installed. In version 1.1 of the .NET Framework, the HTTP-POST and SOAP protocols are enabled by default, but not the HTTP-GET protocol. This was done for security reasons. To enable HTTP-GET for your Web Services, and to successfully do the exercises today, you need to modify the Web.Config file to allow the HTTP-GET protocol to be used. To do this, open the Web.Config file, and add the following section to after the <globalization> tag at the end of the Web.Config file:

```
<webServices>
    <protocols>
        <add name="HttpGet"/>
    </protocols>
</webServices>
```

You can also enable and disable specific protocols in the machine.config file, which will affect all projects for an entire machine. To learn more about the configuration files, and how they can affect your applications, look up Configuration Options under XML Web Services in the Dynamic Help file.

Press F5 to run the application. The browser now opens with the auto-generated Service Help Page, as shown in Figure 13.4.

FIGURE 13.4

Service Help page for a Web service.

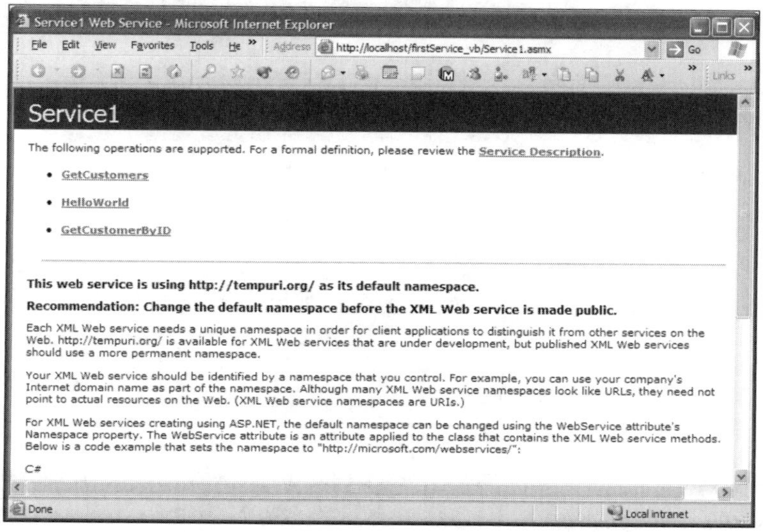

The Service Help Page provides you with a list of all the methods that are available in the Web service and some sample code that shows the implementation of the Web service in C# and Visual Basic .NET. Any time you reference an ASMX file without any parameters, you get the Service Help Page. Notice that the three methods you added to the class file are listed. If you didn't include the `WebMethod` attribute in one of the method declarations, you won't see it in the list.

The URL that the browser is pointing to is simply the name of the server, the project name, and then the ASMX filename.

If you click the `GetCustomerByID` link, you're taken to the Service Description page. The Service Description page gives you the WSDL grammar of how to access this method via SOAP, HTTP-GET, or HTTP-POST. That's a nice feature, but you really don't need to know any of that if you're using Visual Studio .NET to consume the Web service. Figure 13.5 is what the Service Help page looks like for the `GetCustomerByID` method.

Notice that because the method accepts a parameter, you're given a text box to fill in the `CustomerID` parameter. If your Web service methods accept parameters, there will be a text box for each parameter. This is a great feature that makes it very easy to test your methods before you deploy your Web services.

For the `CustomerID` method, type in **`ALFKI`**. Now, you can click the Invoke button to actually run the `GetCustomerID` method.

FIGURE 13.5

The Service Help page.

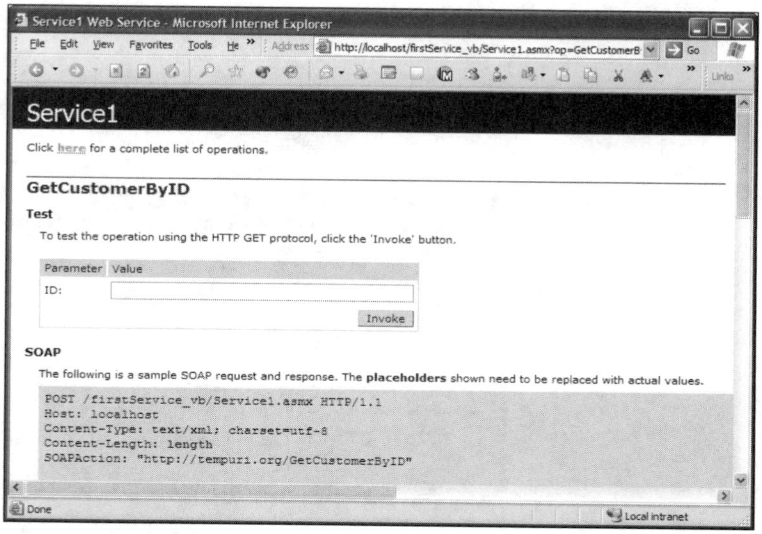

FIGURE 13.6

XML returned from the HelloWorld Web service.

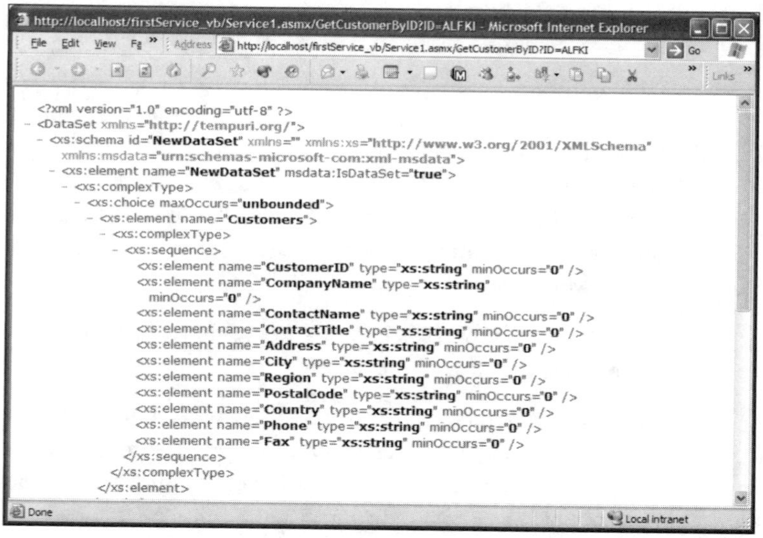

The results are an XML file that's returned through the browser, as Figure 13.6 demonstrates.

Notice that the URL has the name of the ASMX file and then the method name you're trying to call:

```
http://localhost/firstService_vb/Service1.asmx/HelloWorld
```

This is the standard syntax to reference a method in a Web service. If the method expects parameters, you use the same query string syntax that you use for any URL that expects parameters. As an example, the following code assumes that a parameter named `ID` and a parameter named `ZipCode` are being passed to the `HelloWorld` method:

```
http://localhost/firstService_vb/Service1.asmx/HelloWorld?ID=1&ZipCode=33486
```

The next step is to consume the Web service from a client application and do something useful with the XML that's returned.

Consuming XML Web Services

Every time we come upon XML in this book, I mention that you don't have to know about XML to get anything done with XML. That still holds true. Although an XML Web service returns XML, the controls, classes, and tools in Visual Studio .NET natively read and write XML, so you don't need to understand the XML part—you only need to understand how to get the data from the XML part.

There are probably 50 ways to consume a Web service from any number of client applications. You can use Visual Basic 3, Visual Basic 4, Visual Basic 5, Visual Basic 6, Delphi, FLASH, C++, PowerBuilder—you name it. Because the implementation simply returns text in XML format, anything that can read text can consume a Web service. That's the whole point of a Web service: It can be created and consumed by anything.

The rest of the day focuses on four ways to consume a Web service, which I think are 99.9% of what you'll ever run into. You learn how to consume a Web service from

- An ASP.NET application
- A Windows Forms application
- A console application
- An HTML page from client-side VBScript/JavaScript

Consuming a Web Service from an ASP.NET Application

The idea behind a Web service is to be able to access application components from any type of application anywhere. To see how this works, you're going to create a new ASP.NET Web application and call the three methods of the firstService application you just finished creating.

To start, open a new instance of Visual Studio .NET and create a new ASP.NET Web application named firstServiceWebConsumer in either Visual Basic .NET or C#, whichever language you prefer (see Figure 13.7). Click the OK button to create your new project.

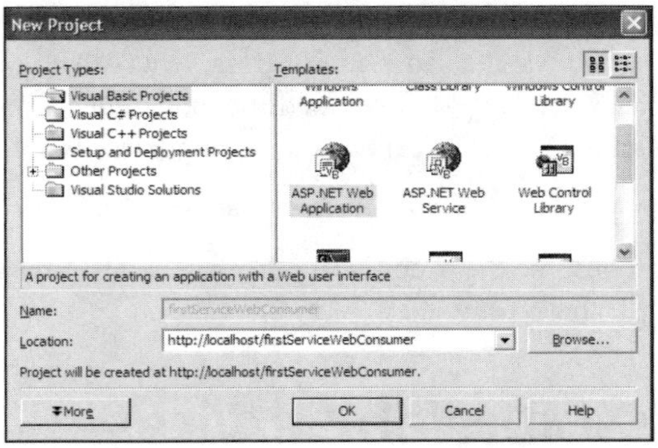

FIGURE 13.7
Creating the Web service Web consumer.

After the project is created, you must reference the Web service you created earlier. This is accomplished in a similar manner to adding a reference to an assembly.

If you right-click the References node on the Solution Explorer, you have two options: Add Reference and Add Web Reference, as Figure 13.8 demonstrates. Select Add Web Reference from the contextual menu.

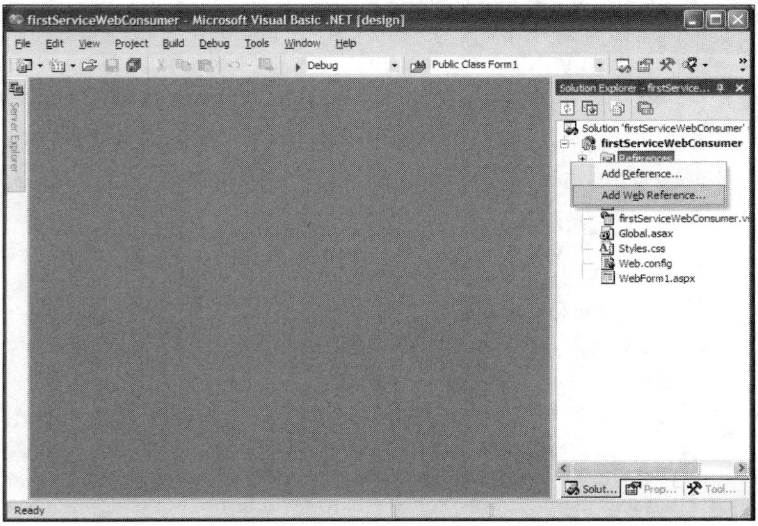

FIGURE 13.8
The Add Reference option in the Solution Explorer.

The Add Web Reference dialog pops up as shown in Figure 13.9.

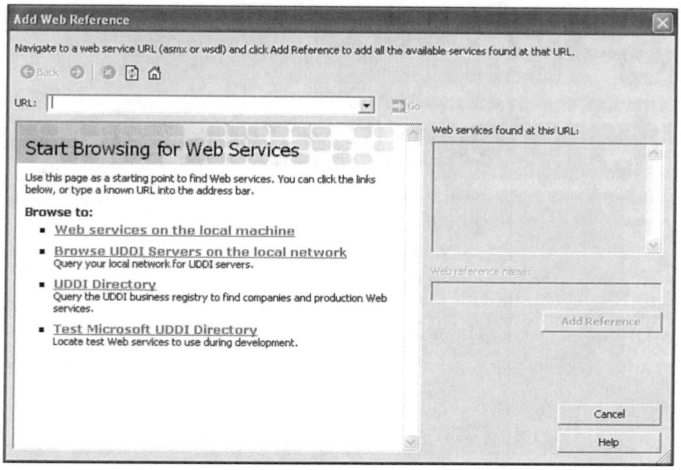

FIGURE 13.9

The Add Web Reference dialog box.

The Add Web Reference dialog has several features. You can search the UDDI directory that was discussed earlier today. You can also search the Test Microsoft UDDI Directory. Microsoft has several Web services, such as the Knowledge Base search service, that you can test and implement in your own applications.

Because you don't want to do either of the available options, you must type the URL of the Web service you want to consume. In the Address box, type

`http://localhost/fistService_vb/Service1.asmx`

or

`http://localhost/fistService_cs/Service1.asmx`

depending on what you named your project earlier.

After you type in the address and press Enter, you should see something similar to Figure 13.10, which is the Service Help Page for the Web service named `Service1.asmx`.

From here, you have the same capabilities that you did when you ran the Web service from the project earlier. You can view the service descriptions, invoke the Web services, and inspect additional information that you might need about implementing the Web service. To add this reference to your project, click the Add Reference button. Your Solution Explorer should now look like Figure 13.11.

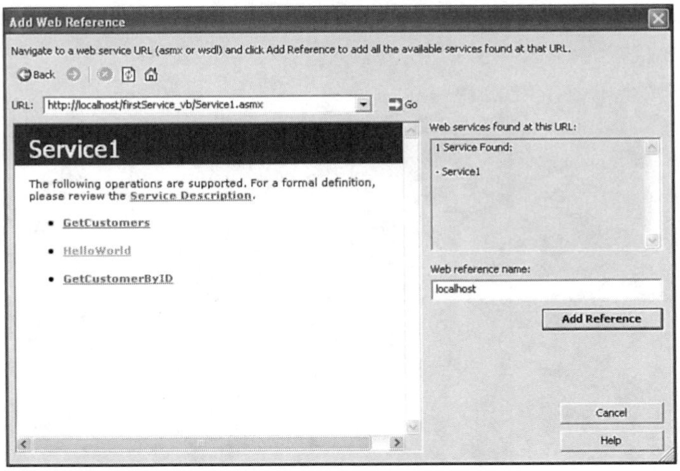

FIGURE 13.10
Service Help page for `Service1.asmx`.

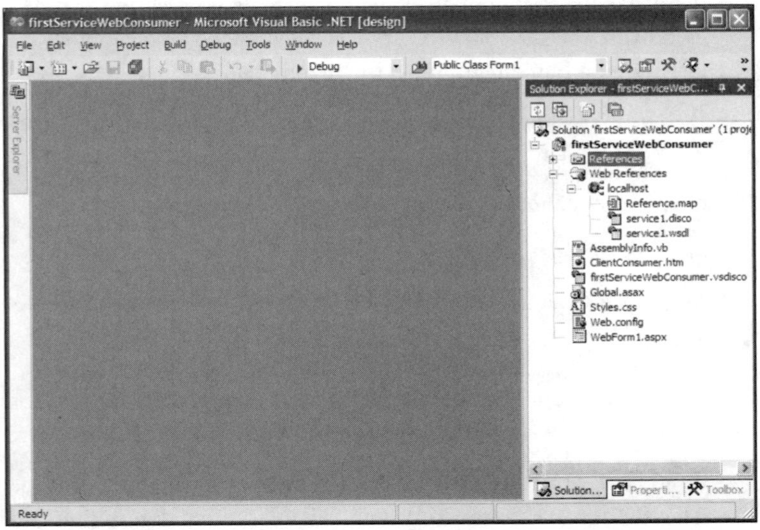

FIGURE 13.11
Solution after adding a Web reference for `Service1.asmx`.

Tip

When you add the Web reference, the Web server name where the Web service is located shows up in the Solution Explorer under Web References. You can right-click on the name of the Web server (in this case, `localhost`) and change it to something more familiar or recognizable.

Now that you've added the Web reference, you can reference the methods in the Web service as you would any other method in a class. Remember that the WSDL file can be considered a type library for a Web service. In .NET, the term *proxy* is to refer to the metadata of an object, but not necessarily the object itself. When you add a reference to a Web service created in .NET, a WSDL proxy is added to your solution. The WSDL file contains all the type information that your application needs to invoke the Web service.

For this exercise, the Web service and consumer are on the same machine. This might or might not be true in real life. Either way, you should always use the actual DNS name or IP address of the Web service when you add it through the Add Web Reference dialog. That way, if you move the consumer to another machine, the Web Reference is still valid.

To access the methods in the newly added Web reference, follow these steps to prepare the default `WebForm1.aspx` page. The outcome should look something like Figure 13.12.

1. Drag a `Label` control onto the form and set the `Text` property to `Customer ID`.
2. Drag a `TextBox` control to the right of the `Label` control and change its `Name` property to `CustomerID`.
3. Drag a `CommandButton` control to the form, change its `Name` property to `GetCustomer` and change the `Text` property to `Get Customer`.

FIGURE 13.12

Webform1 after adding new controls.

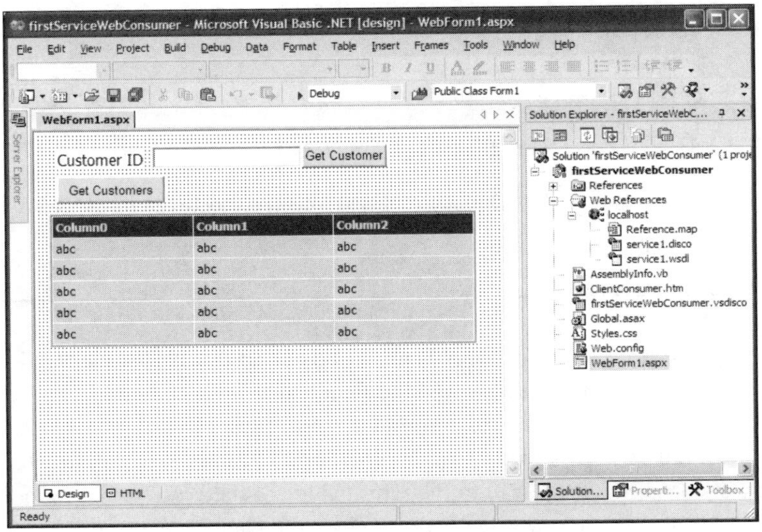

4. Drag a `CommandButton` control to the form, change its `Name` property to `GetCustomers`, and change the `Text` property to `Get Customers`.

5. Drag a `DataGrid` control to the form. You can right-click the `DataGrid` and select AutoFormat from the contextual menu to select a nice color scheme.

Now that you've added the controls and the form is all set, double-click the Get Customer button to get to the code-behind for the `GetCustomer` click event.

In Listing 13.2, you take the `CustomerID` information from the `CustomerID TextBox` and pass it to the `GetCustomer` method of the Web service.

LISTING 13.2 Code-Behind for the `GetCustomer` Click Event

VB.NET

```
Private Sub GetCustomer_Click(ByVal sender As System.Object, _
        ByVal e As System.EventArgs) Handles GetCustomer.Click

    Dim ws As New localhost.Service1()

    DataGrid1.DataSource = ws.GetCustomerByID(CustomerID.Text.Trim)

    DataGrid1.DataBind()

End Sub
```

C#

```
private void GetCustomer_Click(object sender, System.EventArgs e)
{
   localhost.Service1 ws = new localhost.Service1();

   DataGrid1.DataSource = ws.GetCustomerByID(CustomerID.Text.Trim().ToString());

   DataGrid1.DataBind();
}
```

The code in Listing 13.2 is amazingly simple. All you need to do is create an instance of the Web service reference, and then call the method on the reference like any other class. Because the `DataGrid` control natively reads a `DataSet` and data returned from an XML Web service is read as either XML or a `DataSet`, you can just set the DataSource property of the `DataGrid` to the return value of the Web service, and the `DataGrid` understands the return value. After you set the DataSource of the `DataGrid`, you can call the `DataBind` method of the `DataGrid` and the data appears in the grid.

Listing 13.3 has the code you should add to the `GetCustomers` click event, which returns all the customers in the Customers table.

LISTING 13.3 Code-Behind for the `GetCustomers` Click Event

VB.NET

```
Private Sub GetCustomers_Click(ByVal sender As System.Object, _
        ByVal e As System.EventArgs) Handles GetCustomers.Click

    Dim ws As New localhost.Service1()

    DataGrid1.DataSource = ws.GetCustomers()

    DataGrid1.DataBind()

End Sub
```

C#

```
private void GetCustomers_Click(object sender, System.EventArgs e)
{
   localhost.Service1 ws = new localhost.Service1();

   DataGrid1.DataSource = ws.GetCustomers();

   DataGrid1.DataBind();

}
```

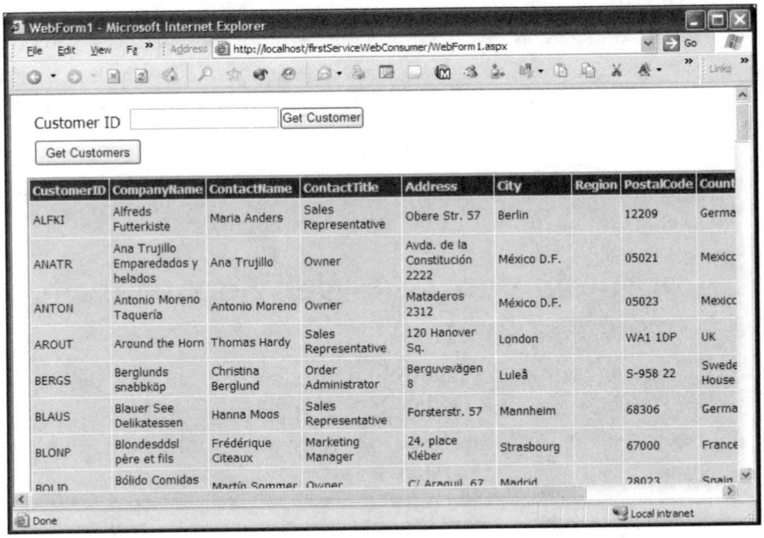

FIGURE 13.13
Results of the `GetCustomers` *method.*

Now that you've written the code for both `Click` events, you can press F5 to run the application.

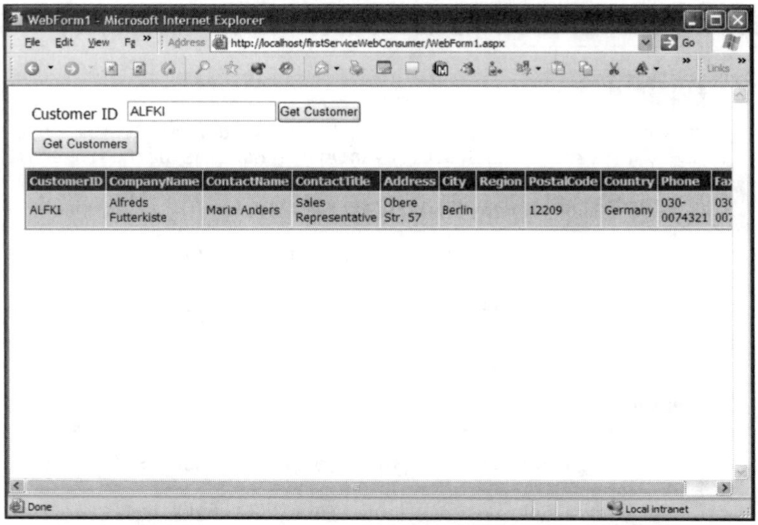

FIGURE 13.14

Results of the `GetCustomer` *method.*

When `WebForm1` is in the browser, click the Get Customers button. Your results should look like Figure 13.13.

Next, enter the `CustomerID` **`ALFKI`** into the `TextBox` control and click Get Customer. You should see something similar to Figure 13.14.

Just like that, you've consumed data from a Web service. You've also seen how to pass a variable to a method in a Web service. It's no different than working with any other object, except that methods can be called on a remote server and data is retrieved with no special settings on your part. It's truly a powerful tool.

If you don't want to simply bind the data to a `DataGrid`, you can save the data to a file, load it into a stream, or bind it to other controls.

Consuming an XML Web Service from a Windows Forms Application

Consuming a Web service from a Windows Forms application is identical to consuming a Web service from an ASP.NET Web application. You need to add a Web reference to the project, create an instance of the proxy class, and call the methods that you need to consume.

To test this, create a new Windows Forms application and name it firstServiceFormsConsumer_vb or firstServiceFormsConsumer_cs, depending on the language you're coding in.

When the project is loaded, add a ComboBox and a RichTextBox to the default form1. Change the Name property of the ComboBox to cbo, and change the Name property of the RichTextBox to rtb.

Next, add the Web reference to the project exactly as you did for the ASP.NET Web application. Right-click the References node in the Solution Explorer, select Add Web Reference from the contextual menu, and enter the URL to the ASMX file.

When that's done, you can write some code to consume the Web service. You're going to load the return data from the Web service into a DataSet, and then bind the DataSet to the ComboBox. On the SelectedIndexChanged event of the ComboBox, you'll call the GetCustomerByID Web service, and pass the Text property of the ComboBox to the method.

Listing 13.4 shows the code you should add to both the Form_Load event and the SelectedIndexChanged event of the ComboBox.

LISTING 13.4 Code for Windows Forms Events to Consume Service1.asmx

```
Private Sub Form1_Load(ByVal sender As System.Object, _
            ByVal e As System.EventArgs) Handles MyBase.Load

    Dim ws As New localhost.Service1()

    Dim ds As DataSet

    ds = ws.GetCustomers

    cbo.DisplayMember = "CustomerID"

    cbo.DataSource = ds.Tables(0)

End Sub

Private Sub cbo_SelectedIndexChanged(ByVal sender As System.Object, _
            ByVal e As System.EventArgs) Handles cbo.SelectedIndexChanged

    Dim ws As New localhost.Service1()

    Dim ds As DataSet

    ds = ws.GetCustomerByID(cbo.Text)

    rtb.Text = ds.GetXml
```

LISTING 13.4 continued

```
End Sub
```

C#

```
private void Form1_Load(object sender, System.EventArgs e)
   {
      localhost.Service1  ws =  new localhost.Service1();

      DataSet ds;

      ds = ws.GetCustomers();

      cbo.DisplayMember = "CustomerID";

      cbo.DataSource = ds.Tables[0];
   }

private void comboBox1_SelectedIndexChanged
      (object sender, System.EventArgs e)
   {
      localhost.Service1  ws =  new localhost.Service1();

      DataSet ds;

      ds = ws.GetCustomerByID(cbo.Text);

      rtb.Text = ds.GetXml();
   }
```

If you run the application by pressing the F5 key, the `Form_Load` event calls the Web service and grabs all the customers. The databinding used in the form load is the same code you used two days ago when you wrote the DataAccess application. Because the return type from the Web service is a `DataSet`, you can just set the `DataSet` equal to the data

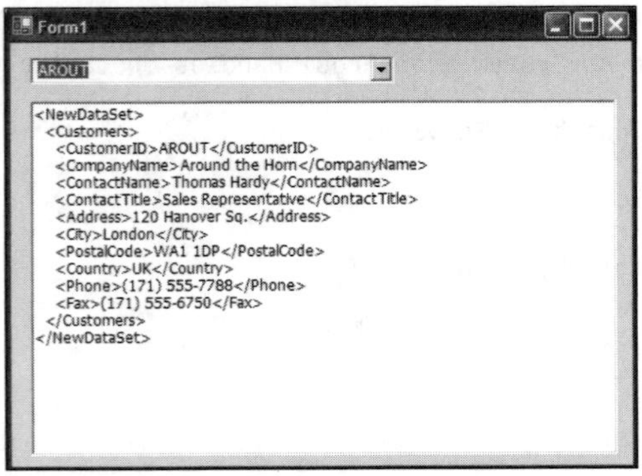

FIGURE 13.15
Consuming the Web service from Windows Forms.

coming back from the Web service. After the `ComboBox` is bound, the `SelectedIndexChanged` event fires and the `GetCustomerID` method of the Web service proxy is invoked each time you select another item. The `GetXml` method that you learned about yesterday loads the XML string into the `RichTextBox` control.

Your output should look something like Figure 13.15.

Each time you select another `CustomerID` from the `ComboBox`, the XML changes.

Because both methods from the Web service are returning a `DataSet`, you have the full power of the `DataSet` class at your fingertips. You can save the XML to a file, load the XML into an `XMLDocument` object, or use an `XMLTextReader` to read through the nodes. Everything you learned yesterday about working with XML can be applied to the results from an XML Web service.

If the return type is a string, integer, or even a serialized class, you can handle it accordingly. If a client is non-.NET, the data is just XML, so it can be treated like an XML file.

Consuming a Web Service from VBScript

There are a few ways to invoke a Web service from VBScript or JavaScript. A DHTML behavior is available for download from the Web Workshop on MSDN, or you can simply use XMLHTTP to call the Web service asynchronously.

To test it, add a new HTML form to the ASP.NET Application you were working with earlier.

On the HTML form, add an HTML `TextBox`, an HTML `Button`, and two HTML `Labels`.

FIGURE 13.16

Creating the HTML form to consume a Web service.

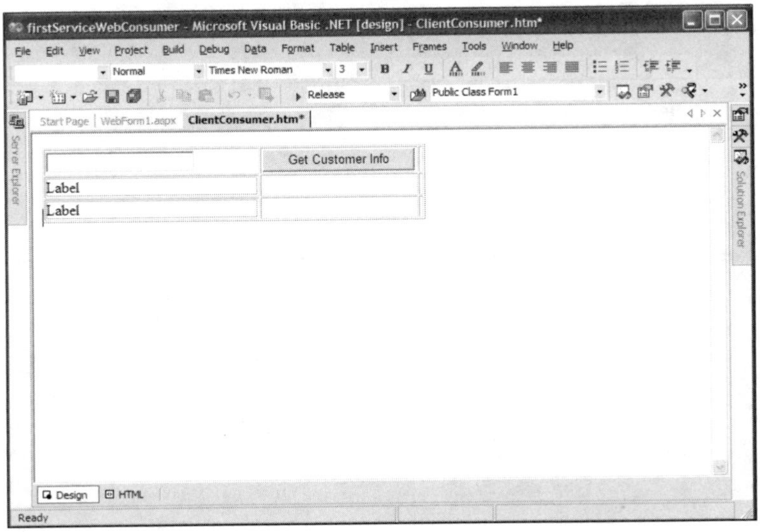

13

The HTML Labels are actually HTML DIV elements, so you can interact with them from the client.

Set the ID and NAME property of one of the Labels to customerID and set the other to companyName.

Your HTML form should look something like Figure 13.16.

Next, double-click on the Button1 that was added, and you're taken to the client-side HTML Button1_OnClick subprocedure. Add the code in Listing 13.5 to the onclick event for Button1.

LISTING 13.5 Client VBScript Code for Calling a Web Service

```
Sub Button1_onclick

  Dim strResults, objXML, strURL, objNodes

  set objXML = CreateObject("Microsoft.XMLDOM")

  objXML.async = false

  strSQL = "http://localhost/firstService_vb/Service1.asmx/
            GetCustomerByID?ID=" & Text1.value

  objXML.load(strSQL)

  objNodes =  objXML.xml

  set objNodes = objXML.selectNodes("//NewDataSet")

  For Each objNode In objNodes
    customerID.innerText  = objNode.selectSingleNode("CustomerID").text
    companyName.innerText  = objNode.selectSingleNode("CompanyName").text
  Next

  set objNodes = Nothing
  set objXML = Nothing

End Sub
```

In the VBScript, you create an XMLDOM object and call its Load method. The Load method takes the URL of the Service1.asmx file, and uses HTTP-GET to pass the ID parameter in the query string to the Web service. Because the caller isn't a .NET client, it's script, the DOM (document object model) can simply consume the XML data as an XML document and use SelectNodes to get the Nodes collection it's looking for. In the

GetCustomerByID method, you didn't specify a name for the DataSet, so the parent node is named the default: NewDataSet.

The XML being parsed is

```
<?xml version="1.0" encoding="utf-8" ?>
<DataSet xmlns="http://tempuri.org/">
<xs:schema id="NewDataSet" xmlns=""
     xmlns:xs="http://www.w3.org/2001/XMLSchema"
     xmlns:msdata="urn:schemas-microsoft-com:xml-msdata">
<xs:element name="NewDataSet" msdata:IsDataSet="true">
<xs:complexType>
<xs:choice maxOccurs="unbounded">
<xs:element name="Customers">
<xs:complexType>
<xs:sequence>
  <xs:element name="CustomerID" type="xs:string" minOccurs="0" />
  <xs:element name="CompanyName" type="xs:string" minOccurs="0" />
  <xs:element name="ContactName" type="xs:string" minOccurs="0" />
  <xs:element name="ContactTitle" type="xs:string" minOccurs="0" />
  <xs:element name="Address" type="xs:string" minOccurs="0" />
  <xs:element name="City" type="xs:string" minOccurs="0" />
  <xs:element name="Region" type="xs:string" minOccurs="0" />
  <xs:element name="PostalCode" type="xs:string" minOccurs="0" />
  <xs:element name="Country" type="xs:string" minOccurs="0" />
  <xs:element name="Phone" type="xs:string" minOccurs="0" />
  <xs:element name="Fax" type="xs:string" minOccurs="0" />
  </xs:sequence>
  </xs:complexType>
  </xs:element>
  </xs:choice>
  </xs:complexType>
  </xs:element>
  </xs:schema>
<diffgr:diffgram xmlns:msdata="urn:schemas-microsoft-com:xml-msdata"
          xmlns:diffgr="urn:schemas-microsoft-com:xml-diffgram-v1">
<NewDataSet xmlns="">
<Customers diffgr:id="Customers1" msdata:rowOrder="0">
  <CustomerID>ALFKI</CustomerID>
  <CompanyName>Alfreds Futterkiste</CompanyName>
  <ContactName>Maria Anders</ContactName>
  <ContactTitle>Sales Representative</ContactTitle>
  <Address>Obere Str. 57</Address>
  <City>Berlin</City>
  <PostalCode>12209</PostalCode>
  <Country>Germany</Country>
  <Phone>030-0074321</Phone>
  <Fax>030-0076545</Fax>
</Customers>
</NewDataSet>
```

13

```
</diffgr:diffgram>
</DataSet>
```

After the XML is in the DOM, you can specify what nodes you want to display. Using `SelectSingleNode` retrieves the correct node, and enables the data to be displayed in the `DIV`, as the following code demonstrates:

```
customerID.innerText  = objNode.selectSingleNode("CustomerID").text
```

If you enter different `CustomerIDs` from the Northwind database and click the button, the data shows up. Also, notice that the browser doesn't refresh. This processing is being done asynchronously, so the client side never needs to refresh the browser.

This capability using Web services and client-side script opens up a ton of possibilities for writing great browser-based applications.

Summary

Today you learned about the premiere technology of the .NET Framework. XML Web services are the foundation of what .NET's all about. The ability to develop scalable, loosely coupled, cross-platform and cross-language applications is now a reality when developing XML Web services with Visual Studio .NET. Even though the infrastructure of building and consuming Web services is complex, Visual Studio .NET hides all the complexity and makes it very easy to develop robust Web service–based applications.

Q&A

Q Web services are cool. Are they efficient? It seems like a lot of XML coming down the pipe.

A Web services are a little chunky in file size. The main benefit of Web services is they are cross-platform and cross-language. If saving every bit of network bandwidth is an issue and you're running a complete Microsoft server and client solution, you should look at .NET remoting using binary TCP formatters. .NET remoting is highly efficient.

Q How does early binding occur? How does .NET know all the methods in the Web service?

A When you reference the ASMX file and add the WSDL to your solution, Visual Studio .NET creates a proxy class that's built in the language of your project and contains all the properties and methods that are read from the WSDL file. If you click the Show All Files button on the Solution Explorer toolbar, you'll see a `Reference.Map` file with the attached `Reference.vb` or `Reference.cs` file that contains the information that Visual Studio .NET needs to accomplish early binding.

Q I'm hungry for more! Where can I get hard-core Web services information?

A There are tons of great resources on the Web. Check the following links for examples and Web service information:

`http://www.msdn.microsoft.com/webservices/`

The At Your Service column on MSDN is also great:

`http://www.msdn.microsoft.com/library/default.asp?url=/library/en-us/dnservice/html/service09032002.asp`

Dan Wahlin also has great resources, including information about using the Google Search Web service and the Amazon.com Web services, at

`http://www.xmlforasp.net/content.aspx?content=codebank&codeType=webservices`

Quiz

1. What must a class inherit for it to be considered a Web service?
2. To make a method available to the outside world, I must add the ______________ attribute to my methods.
3. An XML Web service can be consumed as a __________ or an ______ file natively by a .NET application.

Quiz Answers

1. The class must inherit `System.Web.Services.WebService`.
2. `Webmethod`
3. `DataSet`, XML

13

Exercises

1. Create a new ASP.NET Web application and duplicate the functionality of the Windows Forms application you created earlier today.
2. Create a new Web service named MathService. Add a function that accepts two numeric values and returns a numeric value that's the result of multiplying the two input values.
3. Create a new Web service that has all the data from the Customers table and the Orders table in the Northwind database. The `DataSet` that's returned should have

WEEK 2

DAY 14

Components and .NET

Reusability is what makes writing applications in .NET better than other development environments. This week you've written a lot of code that could be modified slightly and be reused in all of your applications. All the extensible markup language (XML) and ADO.NET code that you wrote has standard functionality that you could share among multiple applications. By writing components, you can write code that can be shared among multiple forms or classes in your applications or across multiple applications. Today, you learn

- What a component is in .NET
- How to determine what types of components to write and when
- How to write reusable code in .NET assemblies
- How to write and implement your own namespaces
- How to use unmanaged COM DLLs in .NET

Introduction to Components

Components mean different things to different people. To me, a component is code that's compiled into a dynamic link library (DLL) that can be shared across applications. Even if the DLL isn't shared across applications, it provides me with the ability to encapsulate my application logic into specific parts. I might have a data access component, a utility component, and a security component. By splitting apart the core functionality of my applications in separate DLLs, I can modify the behavior of the application without modifying the code in the user interface.

This type of development is especially effective in traditional Active Server Pages (ASP) applications. Because ASP is script, and not compiled, you could achieve performance gains by putting code in DLLs and having the ASP application call methods in the DLLs. Doing so avoids the overhead of Internet Information Server (IIS) having to process the thousands of lines of script code that would have existed inside the ASP page itself.

Writing components is done using the ActiveX DLL template in Visual Basic 6. By implementing methods, properties, and events in class modules, you can compile your code into a component object model (COM) DLL and use it anywhere you need it. You create reusable objects, as long as the DLL is registered correctly on that machine that's attempting to consume it.

In .NET, the concept of writing components is the same, but it's taken to the next level. Because the core of .NET is based on inheritance, you can inherit from specific classes to give your component the functionality you want. Depending on what type of component you need to write, you can inherit from different base classes to expose functionality to your component that you would have had to write if you were using Visual Basic 6.

> Being new to .NET, you'll hear a lot about the performance gains in code execution for ASP.NET Web applications because the code is compiled. You learned in Day 1, "Introduction to the Microsoft .NET Framework," that after code has been just-in-time (JIT) compiled, it's in the machine language for the specific processor it's running on. That begs the question, "Why write components separate from my ASP.NET code if it's all compiled anyway?" The short answer is you don't have to. After code is compiled, it can run no faster, so your code being compiled in a component or a code-behind makes no performance difference. The biggest reason to write components is to separate the business logic and the data logic from the user interface logic. This makes maintaining applications easier and provides a clear division of labor for team development. Plus, by separating the code from the content, you can reuse your components in other applications. So, in my opinion, you should separate your implementation code from user interface code as much as possible.

Understanding the Component Types

As you've seen this week, Visual Studio .NET provides designers that make working with objects easier. When you added an XML schema to your project two days ago, you were given the Schema Designer. When you need to create a Web service, there was a designer that enabled you to drag objects from the Toolbox onto the Web service. The same holds true for building components with Visual Studio .NET. Depending on that type of project you create or what type of items you add to your projects, Visual Studio .NET provides a Component Designer that enables you to drag and drop items from the Toolbox onto the design surface and expose objects to your component.

This makes it simple to create complex components without having to implement all the code. You can create several types of applications that are considered to be components, based on the interfaces they expose and how they're compiled.

Class Library applications are a template in the New Project dialog. When you create a Class Library application, it's almost the same as adding a class library to your application. The only difference is that you can add classes to any type of application, whereas a Class Library project template is used to specifically compile to a managed DLL (an *assembly* in .NET terms) that can be consumed by other applications. With Class Library applications, you can implement the functionality of any other type of component that we discuss today. By inheriting from different base classes, you're exposing specific functionality to the application.

For example, when you learned how to create Web services yesterday, your class file inherited the `System.Web.Services.WebService` class. This made specific ASP.NET functionality available to the class to implement the class as a Web service. The class also implemented the `System.ComponentModel.IContainer` interface. By exposing this interface to the class, you were given the designer surface to add nonvisual controls or components to the Web service. Even though a Class Library application is a blank slate, you can literally create any type of object with it.

If you create a Class Library application and you want to use the Component Designer to add components from the Toolbox to your class, you can add a component class to your project or you can inherit the correct class that gives you the designer that you need.

The component classes inherit from the `System.ComponentModel.Component` class. When you add a component class to your solution, the class automatically exposes specific methods that assist in the creation of a component; namely, a designer, the `New` method, the `Dispose` method, and initialization code for the class itself.

To give you an idea of what the difference is between a Class Library project template and adding a new component class to an existing class library application, look at the difference between the generated code for a Class Library application and the code generated for the component class item in Listings 14.1 and 14.2.

LISTING 14.1 Default Code for a Class in a Class Library Application

VB.NET

```
Public Class Class1

End Class
```

C#

```
using System;

namespace ClassLibrary4
{
        /// <summary>
        /// Summary description for Class1.
        /// </summary>
        public class Class1
        {
                public Class1()
                {
                        //
                        // TODO: Add constructor logic here
                        //
                }
        }
}
```

LISTING 14.2 Default Code for a Component Class Template

VB.NET

```
Public Class Component1
    Inherits System.ComponentModel.Component

#Region " Component Designer generated code "

    Public Sub New(Container As System.ComponentModel.IContainer)
        MyClass.New()

        'Required for Windows.Forms Class Composition Designer support
        Container.Add(me)
    End Sub

    Public Sub New()
```

LISTING 14.2 continued

```
        MyBase.New()

        'This call is required by the Component Designer.
        InitializeComponent()

        'Add any initialization after the InitializeComponent() call

    End Sub

    'Component overrides dispose to clean up the component list.
    Protected Overloads Overrides Sub Dispose(ByVal disposing As Boolean)
        If disposing Then
            If Not (components Is Nothing) Then
                components.Dispose()
            End If
        End If
        MyBase.Dispose(disposing)
    End Sub

    'Required by the Component Designer
    Private components As System.ComponentModel.IContainer

    'NOTE: The following procedure is required by the Component Designer
    'It can be modified using the Component Designer.
    'Do not modify it using the code editor.
    <System.Diagnostics.DebuggerStepThrough()> Private Sub InitializeComponent()
        components = New System.ComponentModel.Container()
    End Sub

#End Region

End Class
```

C#

```
using System;
using System.ComponentModel;
using System.Collections;
using System.Diagnostics;

namespace ClassLibrary4
{
   /// <summary>
   /// Summary description for Component1.
   /// </summary>
   public class Component1 : System.ComponentModel.Component
   {
      /// <summary>
      /// Required designer variable.
      /// </summary>
```

LISTING 14.2 continued

```
        private System.ComponentModel.Container components = null;

        public Component1(System.ComponentModel.IContainer container)
        {
            /// <summary>
            /// Required for Windows.Forms Class Composition Designer support
            /// </summary>
            container.Add(this);
            InitializeComponent();

            //
            // TODO: Add any constructor code after InitializeComponent call
            //
        }

        public Component1()
        {
            /// <summary>
            /// Required for Windows.Forms Class Composition Designer support
            /// </summary>
            InitializeComponent();

            //
            // TODO: Add any constructor code after InitializeComponent call
            //
        }

        #region Component Designer generated code
        /// <summary>
        /// Required method for Designer support - do not modify
        /// the contents of this method with the code editor.
        /// </summary>
        private void InitializeComponent()
        {
            components = new System.ComponentModel.Container();
        }
        #endregion
    }
}
```

As you can see, much more code is added based on the type of template you're adding to your application. There are slight differences between the Visual Basic .NET and C# code, but that's purely in the implementation, not the functionality.

Visual Studio .NET incorporates the plumbing code that helps you write the application faster. Because you don't have to remember what you should inherit from, or what syntax is used for each type of component, or what interfaces to implement, you can concentrate on writing the implementation code, not the plumbing code.

The following component project templates have design time–generated code that's specific to the implementation of the class:

- Windows Control Library—Used to create Windows Controls. This class inherits from the `System.Windows.Forms.UserControl` class and exposes the `System.ComponentModel.IContainer` class that gives you a design surface to drag Toolbox items onto and exposes base class events for all controls in Windows Forms. This template is for designing new Windows Controls and extending existing Windows Controls.
- Web Control Library—Used to create Web Controls. This class inherits the `System.Web.UI.WebControls.WebControl` class. This template doesn't give you a design surface to work with, so you must implement the control extensibility without the help of a designer.
- ASP.NET Web Service—Used to create Web service applications. This class inherits the `System.Web.Services.WebService` class and exposes the `System.ComponentModel.IContainer` interface to give you a design surface and make available ASP.NET-specific functionality to your application.
- Windows Service—Used to create applications that run as Windows services. This class inherits the `System.ServiceProcess.ServiceBase` class, and exposes the `System.ComponentModel.IContainer` interface to give you a design surface and specific functionality to work with Windows services.

The following project template is considered a component but doesn't give you a design surface as part of the project template:

- Class Library

The following project item is considered a component, but doesn't have a project template but does provide implementation code:

- Transactional Component—Used to create serviced components designed for COM+. These classes inherit the `ServicedComponent` class and the default implementation gives you commented code on using `SetComplete`, `SetAbort`, and `AutoComplete` to write components that are transactional.

Each of the project templates I just described is also implemented as items that you can add to your existing applications. To see what types of items you can add to a project, you can right-click on any project name in the Solution Explorer and select Add, New Item. You're prompted to select from the list of available items to add, as Figure 14.1 demonstrates.

The bottom line is that no matter what type of component you're creating, it's still a class file. The specific implementation of the class is what differentiates each type of component in .NET. To understand how a component can be consumed by other applications, you're now going to create a Class Library component, which will make up most of the component development you'll do in real life.

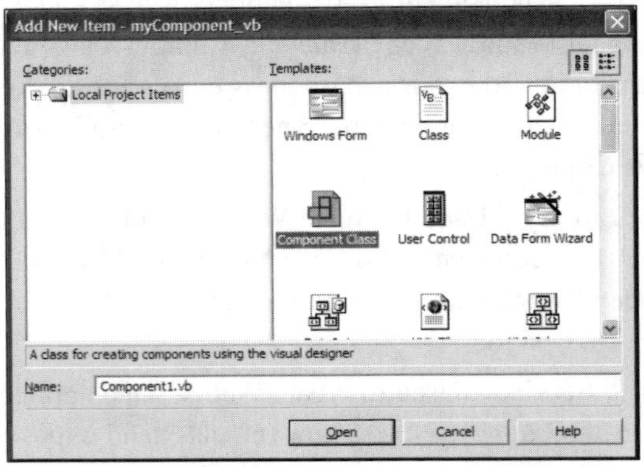

FIGURE 14.1
The Add New Item dialog box.

Creating a Class Library Application

To create your new component, start Visual Studio .NET and create a new Class Library application called myComponent_vb or myComponent_cs, depending on what language you're writing in.

In the myComponent application, you're going to write simple methods and properties that are exposed to consumers of the component. You are also going to create a namespace for your component. By default, the namespace name is normally the name of the application. You're going to change this to implement your own namespace.

To implement the functionality of your component, type the code in Listing 14.3 in the default `Class1` class that's added to the Class Library application.

As you're entering the code, read the comments for each item to understand how it's being used. You're going to add methods that return a dataset; two methods that have the same name, but have different in and out parameters, and you're going to implement read/write and read-only properties. The functionality you implement here is common to what you would need to do in real-world scenarios.

LISTING 14.3 Code for the `myComponent` Class

VB.NET

```
' You are using SQL Server, so you must import the
' SqlClient namespace
Imports System.Data.SqlClient
```

LISTING 14.3 continued

```
' This is your top-level namespace
Namespace Sams

    ' This is the child namespace for the Sams namespace
    Namespace Day14

        ' The name of the class, NewClass
        Public Class NewClass

            ' These are private variables to be used when
            ' setting and retrieving the Properties
            Private m_Fname As String
            Private m_LName As String

            ' A function that returns a DataSet to the caller
            Function GetAuthors(ByVal ConnectionString As String) _
                    As DataSet
                Dim cn As SqlConnection =
                    New SqlConnection(ConnectionString)
                Dim cmd As New SqlCommand("Select * from Authors", cn)
                Dim adp As New SqlDataAdapter()
                adp.SelectCommand = cmd
                Dim ds As DataSet
                adp.Fill(ds, "Authors")
                Return ds
            End Function

            ' Generic Math Function with Integer as return value
            Function DoMath(ByVal num1 As Integer, _
                ByVal num2 As Integer) As Integer

                Return num1 * num2

            End Function

            ' Generic Math Function with Integer as return value
            Function DoMath(ByVal num1 As Integer, _
                 ByVal num2 As Integer, ByVal num3 as Integer) As Integer

                Return num1 * num2

            End Function

            ' Read/Write property for FirstName
            Property FirstName()
                Get
                    Return m_Fname
                End Get

                Set(ByVal Value)
                    m_LName = Value
```

LISTING 14.3 continued

```
                End Set
            End Property

            'Read/Write property for LastName
            Property LastName()
                Get
                    Return m_Fname
                End Get

                Set(ByVal Value)
                    m_Fname = Value
                End Set
            End Property

            ' Read-only property to return the full name
            ReadOnly Property FullName()
                Get
                    Return m_Fname & " " & m_LName
                End Get
            End Property

        End Class

    End Namespace

End Namespace
```

C#

```
using System;
using System.Data;
using System.Data.SqlClient;

namespace Sams
{
   namespace Day14
   {
      public class NewClass
      {
         public NewClass()
         {
         }
         // These are private variables to be used when
         // setting and retrieving the Properties
         string m_Fname;
         string m_Lname;

         // A function that returns a DataSet to the caller
         public System.Data.DataSet getCustomers(string ConnectionString)
         {
```

LISTING 14.3 continued

```
        SqlConnection cn = new SqlConnection
           (ConnectionString);
        SqlDataAdapter da  = new SqlDataAdapter
            ("SELECT * from Authors", cn);
        DataSet ds = new DataSet();
        da.Fill(ds, "Authors");
        return ds;
    }

    // Generic Math Function with Integer as return value
    public int doMath(int num1, int num2)
    {
        return num1 * num2;
    }

    // Generic Math Function with Decimal as return value
    public int doMath(int num1, int num2, int num3)
    {
        return num1 * num2 * num3;
    }

    // Read/Write property for FirstName
    public string firstName
    {
        get
        {
            return m_Fname;
        }
        set
        {
            m_Fname =value;
        }
    }

    // Read/Write property for LastName
    public string lastName
    {
        get
        {
            return m_Lname;
        }
        set
        {
            m_Lname = value;
        }
    }

    // Return the Fullname value
    public string FullName
    {
        get
```

LISTING 14.3 continued

```
                {
                    return m_Fname + " " + m_Lname;
                }
            }
        }
    }
}
```

As you're writing components, remember that the Class view gives you a bird's-eye view of what your classes contain. If you're coding in C#, you can use the Class view to add types to your class very easily. Figure 14.2 shows the right-click power of the Class view to add a new property to a C# class file.

FIGURE 14.2

Using the Class view to add types to your class file.

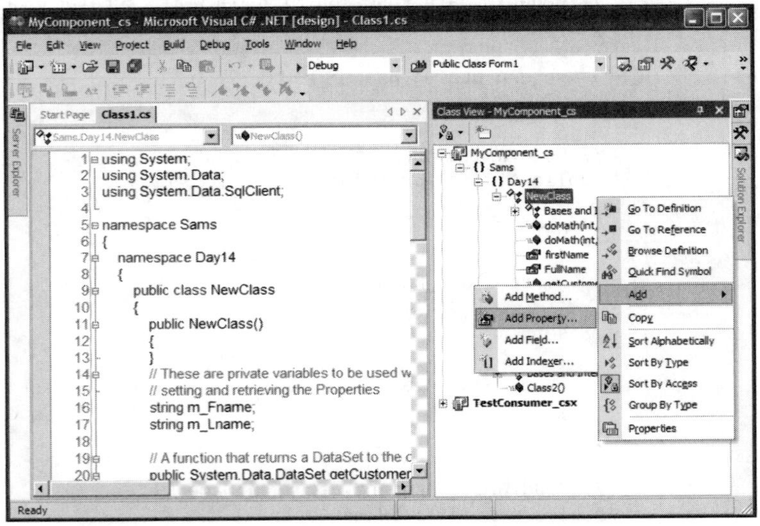

After you select New Property from the contextual menu, the Add Property Wizard screen enables you to easily add a type name, data type, return value, and any comments that you would like to with the type, as Figure 14.3 demonstrates. Using the Class view in C# to add types to your classes makes doing so fast and simple.

Now that you've written the code for the class, you need to compile the application into an assembly. But before you do that, you might want to update the `AssemblyInfo` file in your solution. The `AssemblyInfo` file contains attributes that describe your component. By specifying the correct data in the attribute, those properties are compiled into the assembly, and they can be viewed by consumers of the assembly.

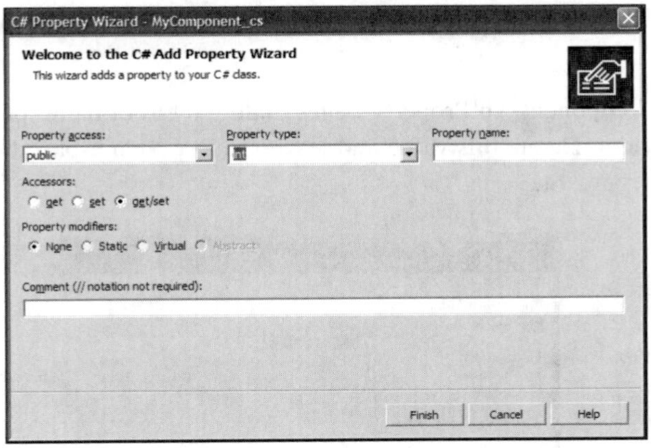

FIGURE 14.3
The C# Add Property Wizard.

If you double-click the `AssemblyInfo.vb` or `AssemblyInfo.cs` file in your solution, you should see something like Figure 14.4. Figure 14.4 is the `AssemblyInfo.vb` for a Visual Basic .NET project.

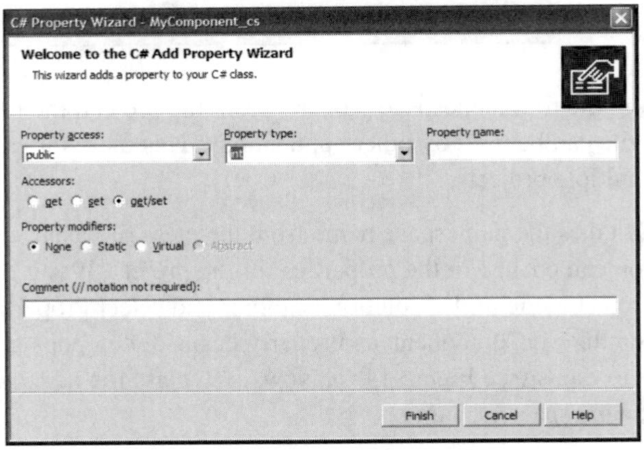

FIGURE 14.4
Modifying the `AssemblyInfo` *attributes.*

Change the following assembly attributes to the listed values:

- `AssemblyTitle`—myComponent
- `AssemblyDescription`—My first .NET component
- `AssemblyProduct`—Made with Visual Studio .NET

14

Next, you need to modify the root namespace of the component. If you're coding in C#, you don't have to worry about it: C# takes the namespace information from the class file itself. In Visual Basic .NET, you must right-click on the project name in the Solution

Explorer, and select Properties from the contextual menu to get to the Project Properties dialog.

In the myComponent_vb Property Pages dialog, the root namespace is set to myComponent. Delete this value and leave the Root namespace box blank, as demonstrated in Figure 14.5.

FIGURE 14.5

Removing the root namespace in the Property Pages dialog.

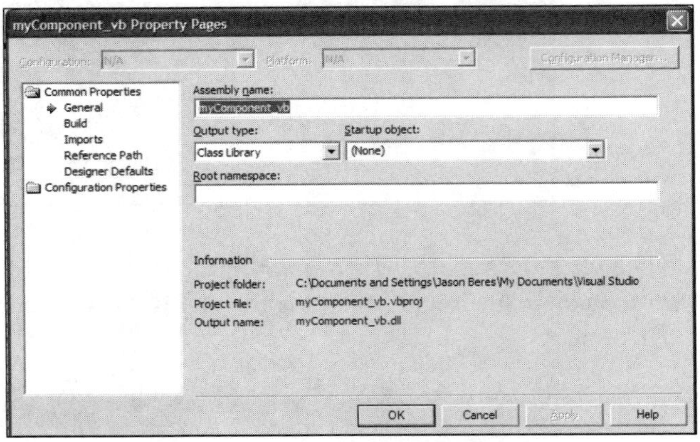

By removing the root namespace property from the project, the namespace defined in your class file can be used by other applications. This makes it easy to create namespaces that span multiple projects.

Because C# takes the namespace name from the class file itself, there's still a useful property you can change in the properties for the project. If you're coding in C#, right-click the project name in the Solution Explorer and select Properties from the contextual menu. When the MyComponent_cs Property Pages dialog pops up, change the default namespace to Sams (see Figure 14.6). Now, each class file added to your application has the default namespace of Sams.

Now you're ready to build the component. If you right-click the project name in the Solution Explorer and select Build from the contextual menu, your component will be compiled into a managed DLL.

The next step is to consume the DLL from a client application.

Consuming the Class Library Application

To consume the DLL you just created from another application, you can simply add another project to your solution. Adding multiple projects to a single solution makes it very easy to debug. You can set breakpoints in any of the projects, and as they're hit, the code execution stops. This even works if the components are written in a different language from the consumer of the component.

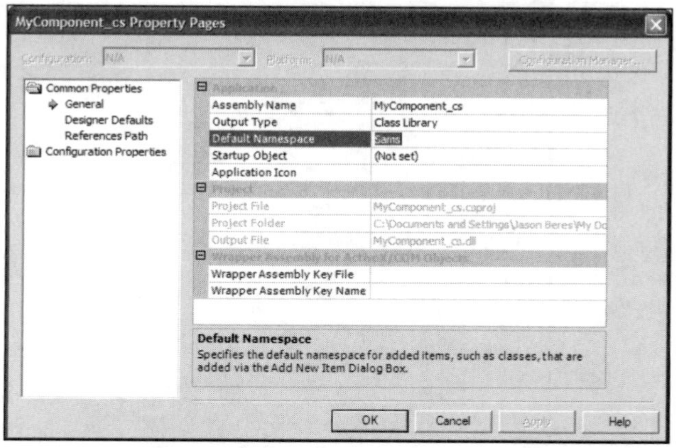

FIGURE 14.6
Setting the default namespace in a C# project.

To test this, right-click the myComponent solution in the Solution Explorer, and select Add, New Project from the contextual menu. When the Add New Project dialog pops up, select a new Windows Forms application, and name it TestConsumer_vb or TestConsumer_cs, depending on the language you're writing in. Figure 14.7 demonstrates this. You now have two projects in your solution.

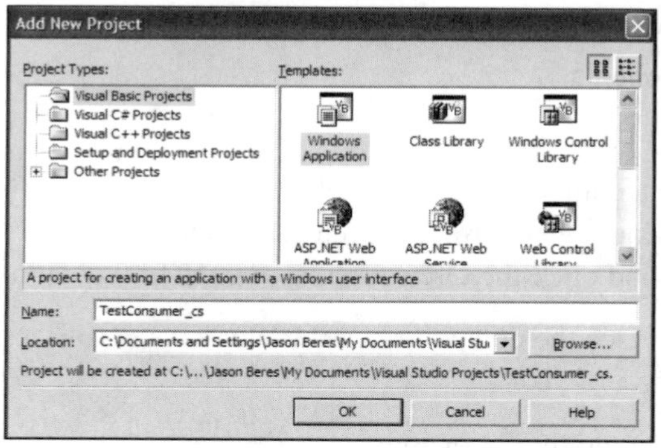

FIGURE 14.7
Adding a new project to the myComponent solution.

Next, you need to tell the solution that the TestConsumer project is the startup project. That means when you press the F5 key to run the application, the Windows Forms application starts, not the Class Library application.

To do this, you can right-click the TestConsumer project name in either the Solution Explorer or the Class view, and select Set As StartUp Project from the contextual menu, as Figure 14.8 shows.

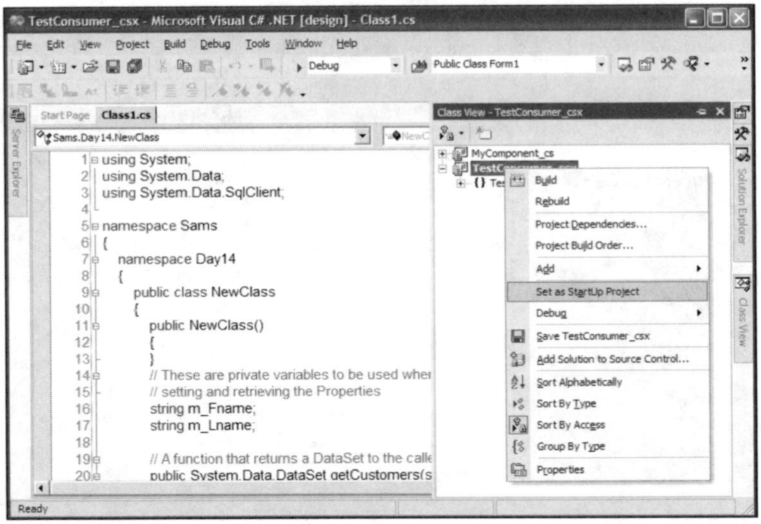

FIGURE 14.8

Setting a startup project.

After you set the startup project, it appears in bold in the Solution Explorer.

To consume the component, you must add a reference to it in the TestConsumer project. To do so, right-click the References node in the Solution Explorer and select Add Reference from the contextual menu. As you learned a few days ago when we discussed namespaces, you can add three types of references to an application:

- .NET component
- COM component
- Project

Because you have a component in your solution, you can click the Projects tab, and you'll see the myComponent project in the list. Select the myComponent project, click the Select button, and click the OK button, as Figure 14.9 demonstrates.

Now you can reference the component in the Windows Forms application as you would any other assembly.

To set up your form, do the following:

1. Drag a `TextBox` from the Toolbox to the form.
2. Drag another `TextBox` control from the Toolbox to the form.
3. Drag a `CommandButton` control from the Toolbox to the form, and set its Text property to DoMath and set its Name property to DoMath.
4. Drag another `CommandButton` control from the Toolbox to the form, and set its Text property to DoName and set its Name property to DoName.

5. Drag a `DataGrid` control from the Toolbox to the form.

Arrange the controls so that they look something like Figure 14.10.

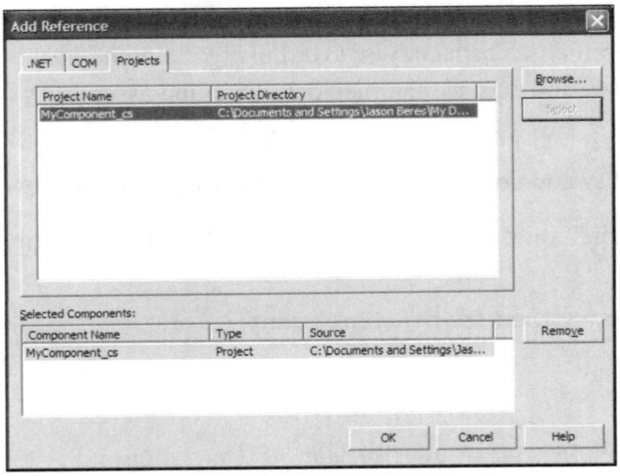

FIGURE 14.9
Adding your component to the TestConsumer application.

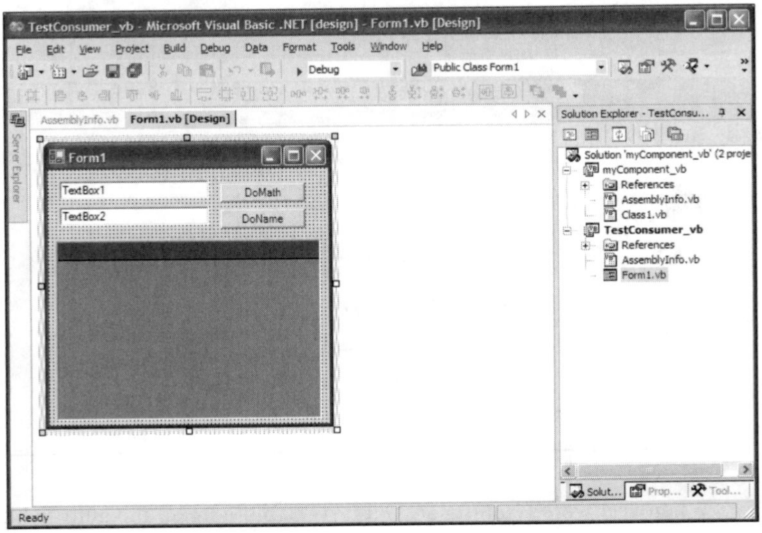

FIGURE 14.10
Form1 of the TestConsumer application after adding controls.

Next, double-click the form to get to the code-behind for Form1.

At the top of the class file, alias your component with the `Imports` statement in Visual Basic .NET or the `using` statement in C#. Your code should look like the following:

14

VB.NET

```
Imports Sams.Day14
```

C#

```
using Sams.Day14;
```

By adding the component as a reference, it's available to your application. And by correctly setting up the namespace, you avoid using the name of the physical file as you did in Visual Basic 6, and can use the metadata from the assembly to determine the correct namespace.

Now, you need to add code to the DoMath and DoName click events.

If you double-click on the DoMath button, add the code in Listing 14.4.

LISTING 14.4 Code for the `DoMath_Click` Event

VB.NET

```
Private Sub DoMath_Click(ByVal sender As System.Object, _
        ByVal e As System.EventArgs) Handles DoMath.Click

    Dim x As New NewClass()

    MessageBox.Show(x.DoMath(TextBox1.Text, TextBox2.Text))

End Sub
```

C#

```
private void DoMath_Click(object sender, System.EventArgs e)
{
   NewClass x = new NewClass();
   int retVal;
   retVal = (x.doMath(Convert.ToInt32(textBox1.Text),
               Convert.ToInt32(textBox2.Text)));
   MessageBox.Show(retVal.ToString());
}
```

When you were typing along, you probably noticed the auto-list members and auto-complete available to you. After you create a new instance of the component class, all the properties, methods, and events are available to the application consuming the component.

You were also introduced to a very cool object-oriented feature in .NET called *overloading*. When a method is overloaded, it means there are multiple methods with the same name, but they have different data types for the input parameters or return values. They also can have a different number of input parameters. In the `DoMath` method you created in your component, there were two `DoMath` methods: one had two input parameters and the other had three. Depending on the data you pass to the method, .NET correctly figures out the correct method to use with the least amount of overhead.

> **Note**
>
> The input parameters and return values of a method are known as the method's *signature*.

Figure 14.11 shows the power of the Visual Studio .NET integrated development environment (IDE) when using components. Notice that the methods and properties for your component are listed, as well as a tooltip indicating that the method is overloaded and how many overloaded methods it has.

FIGURE 14.11

Using auto-complete with your component in .NET.

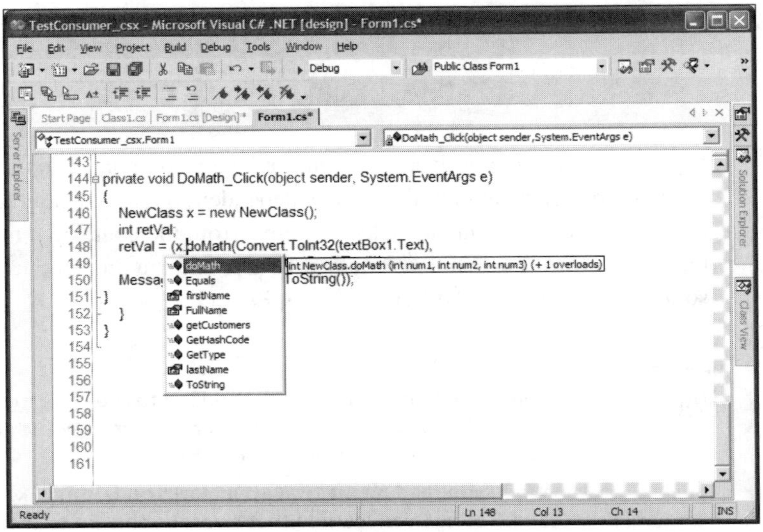

Now if you press F5 to run your application and click the DoMath button, you get a `MessageBox` back with the value.

Another extremely powerful tool is the Project Build Order property. Let's say that you have more than one component, and certain components depend on other components being successfully built before they can be built. If you have a bunch of projects in your Solution Explorer, you can set the order in which they're built by right-clicking on the solution name and selecting Project Build Order from the contextual menu. You get a dialog like the one in Figure 14.12 that enables you to specify the order in which the components should be built.

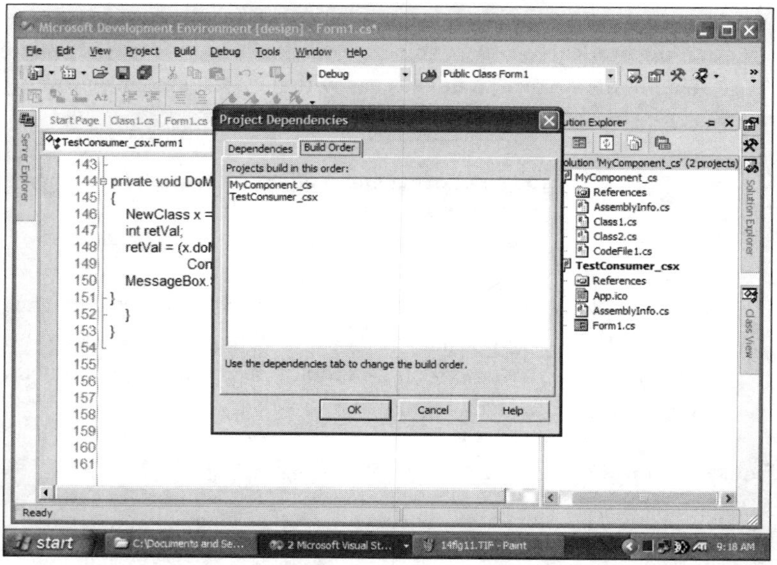

FIGURE 14.12
Specifying the build order for a solution.

If you have multiple projects in a solution and a component in one of the projects is giving you problems, and nothing else is dependent on it, you can right-click on the project name of the component and select Remove from the contextual menu. Doing so removes the project form the solution. You can always add the project back by right-clicking the solution and selecting Add, Add Exiting Project.

Note

You might want to add error handling to the code to make sure that the data being passed to the component is correct. Which brings up a good point: What about errors in the component?

When you read about `Try/Catch` blocks on Day 7, "Exceptions, Debugging, and Tracing" you learned that errors bubble up to the first method in the calling chain that has an error handler. If you're writing the components and consuming them in your own applications, you can implement error handling wherever you want because you're the only one using the component. If you plan to distribute the component for others to use, you can't assume that they'll implement error handling. That means you should handle errors in the component itself by using the `Throw` statement if an error occurs. The following snippet should refresh your memory regarding what you learned about handling errors on Day 7:

```
Try
Catch e as Exception
    Throw e
Finally
```

By throwing the exception to the caller, you're passing the correct error information and you're making sure that your code isn't causing the system to crash.

Note

You write code to consume the rest of the methods and properties in your component in the exercises at the end of the day.

Now you know how to create a component in .NET using the Class Library template and consume that component from a client application. You can see that creating and debugging components in the .NET IDE is very simple by adding another project to your solution. The Class Library template makes up most of the component development that you'll do. Creating components using the design surfaces is a great Visual Studio .NET feature, but you're normally encapsulating specific application functionality into separate pieces, so you don't necessarily need a designer to do that.

In the future of the mobile world, you might implement most of your components as Web services, so the functionality can be exposed outside of your organization.

Interoperating with Unmanaged Code

Chances are fairly high that you have lots of code that isn't written in .NET. If this code is compiled to a DLL, it can be consumed by a .NET application almost transparently.

Note

Remember that .NET code is considered managed code, running in the managed environment of the .NET Framework. Any code that isn't written in a .NET language and doesn't natively run in the .NET Framework is considered unmanaged code.

The .NET Framework can access unmanaged code through a proxy called the runtime callable wrapper (RCW). The RCW is a proxy class that defines how the types should be marshaled from the unmanaged component to the managed application. The process of creating the RCW can be automatic, done via Visual Studio .NET, or manual, using a command-line tool named `tlbimp.exe`. `tlbimp` of the tool's name is short for type library importer.

After the RCW has been created, the .NET application that's accessing the COM component has no idea that it isn't interacting with a managed assembly. Because the RCW handles all the plumbing with the common language runtime and your application, all you must do is reference the component as you would any other assembly. The .NET Framework handles the hard part of marshaling types and objects between two different infrastructures. This includes COM errors, which are thrown in COM as `HRESULT`, and translated to managed exceptions in .NET.

Another term for the RCW is *interop assembly*. When you create the RCW via the `tlbimp.exe` utility, you're creating a managed assembly, known as the interop assembly, which is built using metadata from the COM components type library. Because most COM objects expose their functionality through type libraries, the type information that .NET needs to interact with the component can be retrieved without much difficulty.

Creating an Interop Assembly with `tlbimp.exe`

The `tlbimp.exe` utility is a console application that creates an interop assembly based on the type library of a COM DLL. The `tlbimp.exe` utility is located in the Framework SDK directory in Program Files. Or you can access it by opening the Visual Studio .NET command prompt from the Start menu.

The following code demonstrates the usage of `tlbimp`:

```
tlbimp [COM-Dll-Filename] /[options]
```

Based on what you're trying to accomplish with the interop assembly, you can pass different switches to the command line for `tlbimp.exe`. Table 14.1 lists the options for `tlbimp.exe`.

TABLE 14.1 Command-Line Switches for `tlbimp.exe`

Option	*Description*
`/asmversion:`*`versionnumber`*	Specifies the version of the assembly to create.
`/delaysign`	Tells `tlbimp` to sign the assembly using delayed signing.
`/help`	Displays help options for `tlbimp.exe`.
`/keycontainer:`*`containername`*	Signs the assembly with a strong name using the public/private key pair found in the key container specified in the *`containername`* parameter.
`/nologo`	Suppresses the Microsoft startup banner display.
`/out:`*`filename`*	Specifies the name of the output file to be created. By default, the output file has the same name as the COM DLL, but you're warned if you attempt to overwrite the file if it exists in the same path.
`/primary`	Produces a primary interop assembly for the type library.

TABLE 14.1 continued

Option	*Description*
`/publickey:`*`filename`*	Specifies the file containing the public key to use to sign the resulting assembly.
`/reference:`*`filename`*	Specifies the assembly file to use to resolve references to types defined outside of the current type library.
`/silent`	Suppresses the display of success messages.
`/strictref`	Doesn't import a type library if the tool cannot resolve all references defined within the current assembly or assemblies specified with the `/reference` option.
`/sysarray`	Imports any COM-style `SafeArrays` as a managed `System.Array` class type.
`/unsafe`	Produces interfaces without .NET Framework security checks. You shouldn't use this option unless you're aware of the risks of exposing code as unsafe.
`/verbose`	Displays additional information about the imported type library when `tlbimp.exe` is run.
`/?`	Displays help on the syntax for `tlbimp.exe`.

After you run `tlbimp.exe` and pass it the COM component and the desired interop assembly output filename, you have a .NET assembly, as the following snippet demonstrates:

```
tlbimp ComComponent.dll /out:dotNetInteropAsembly.dll
```

After the interop assembly is created, it can be referenced in a .NET application like any other assembly. But for it to work, the COM component still needs to be registered on the client machine that's accessing the interop assembly. The `tlbimp.exe` utility does not convert the DLL to a managed assembly; it simply reads the type library of the COM component and creates an assembly with enough metadata for the common language runtime to use the COM component. Calls made to the interop assembly from a .NET application are actually passed from the interop assembly to the COM component, and the common language runtime marshals the correct data types to your managed code.

When you create an interop assembly using `tlbimp.exe`, you're most likely going to install the interop assembly to the global application cache (GAC) so that it can be used across multiple applications.

If you want to use the COM component in only a single application, you can directly reference the COM component in your Visual Studio .NET solution.

Referencing a COM Component Directly with Visual Studio .NET

To see how to use a COM component in .NET by using the power of Visual Studio .NET, you'll create and directly reference a COM component using the Visual Studio .NET IDE. This process is different from using `tlbimp.exe` because it creates a managed assembly for you. So, you reference the managed assembly as a .NET component, not as a COM component.

To make this work, follow these steps:

1. Create a Visual Basic 6 ActiveX DLL project named MyComComponent.
2. Rename the default `Class1` file to `MyComClassFile`.
3. Add the following method to the `MyComClassFile`:

```
Public Function DoMath(num1 As Integer, _
                 num2 As Integer) As Integer

    DoMath = num1 * num2

End Function
```

4. Compile the DLL to your `C:\` drive.

Note

> If you don't have Visual Basic 6 on your machine, I've included the DLL in the `Day14` folder of the downloadable code.

Your Visual Basic 6 application should look like Figure 14.13.

Next, open Visual Studio .NET and create a new Windows Forms application and call it COMConsumer_vb or COMConsumer_cs, depending on the language you're writing in.

When the application is open, right-click the References node in the Solution Explorer and select Add Reference.

When the Add Reference dialog pops up, click the COM tab. Scroll down until you find MyComComponent. Highlight it and click Select as Figure 14.14 demonstrates.

After you click the OK button to close the Add Reference dialog, the component is visible in the References node of your solution.

The process you have just gone through created the RCW and exposed this component to the managed application. To verify this, right-click on the MyComComponent in the References node and select Properties from the contextual menu. The Properties window displays a few key items that differentiate this from managed .NET assemblies: The `Type` is `ActiveX`, there's a GUID associated with the component, and the `Name` property is prefixed with `Interop`. Figure 14.15 shows you what the properties look like on my machine.

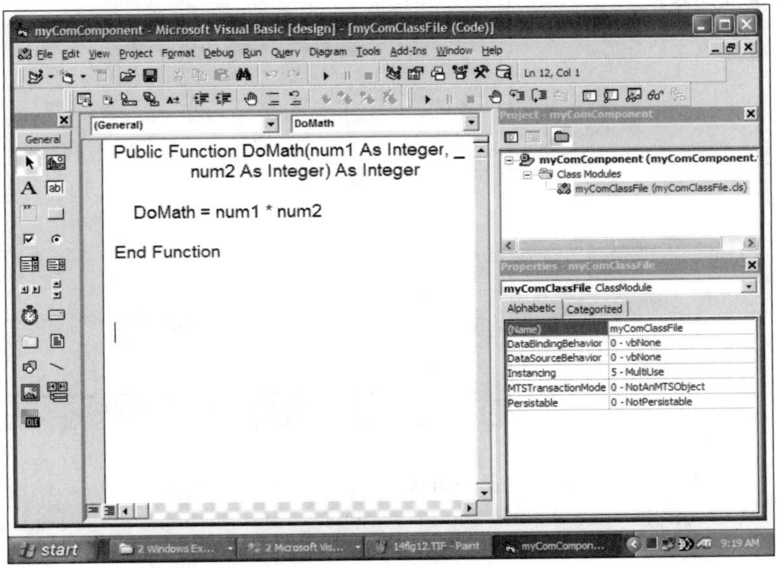

FIGURE 14.13

Creating an ActiveX DLL in Visual Basic 6.

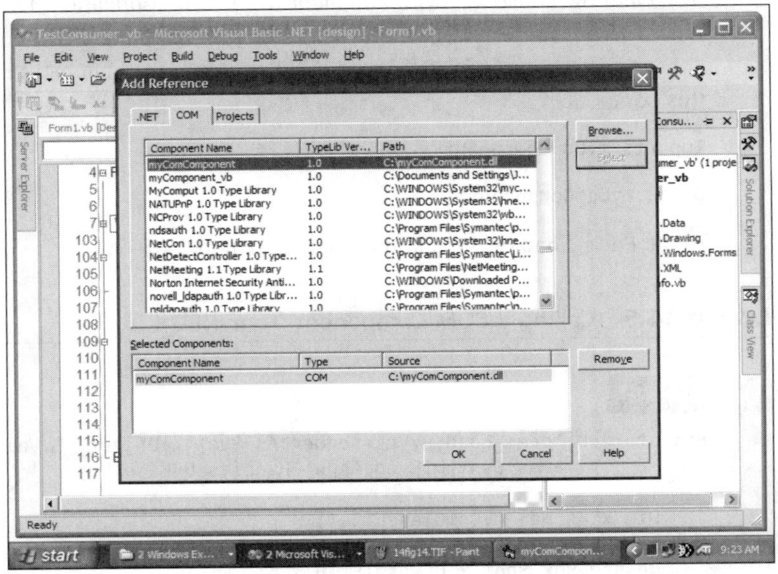

FIGURE 14.14

Adding a COM component to a Visual Studio .NET solution.

14

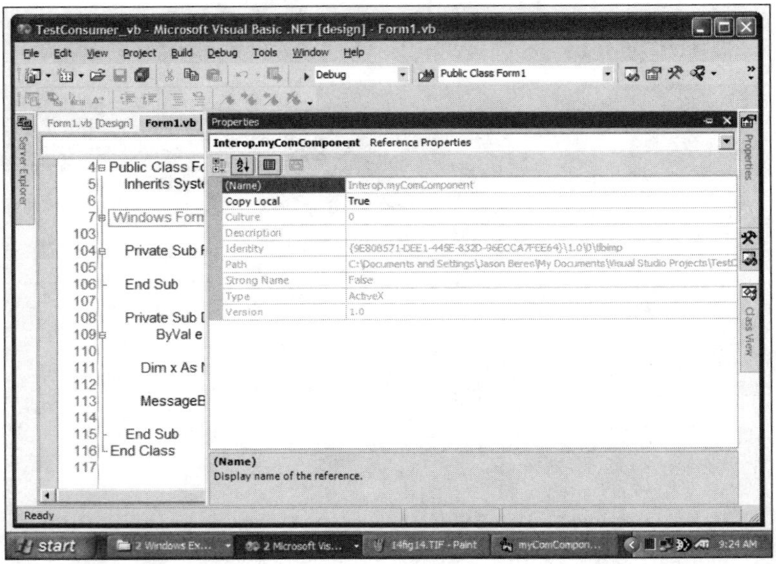

FIGURE 14.15
Properties of a COM component referenced through Visual Studio .NET.

If you look at the properties for any of the other assemblies in the References node, you'll notice that the type is Assembly, and the name is the namespace that the assembly represents.

You can now consume this component from your application. Double-click the default Form1 to get to the code window and add an alias to the COM component using the `Imports` statement in Visual Basic .NET or the `using` statement in C#. The syntax for this component is

```
Imports myComComponent
```

```
using myComComponent;
```

In the `Form_Load` event, add the code in Listing 14.5.

LISTING 14.5 Calling a COM Component from .NET

VB.NET

```
Private Sub Form1_Load(ByVal sender As System.Object, ByVal _
            e As System.EventArgs) Handles MyBase.Load

    Dim x As New myComClassFile()

    MessageBox.Show(x.DoMath(5, 6))

End Sub
```

LISTING 14.5 continued

C#

```
private void Form1_Load(object sender, System.EventArgs e)
   {

         myComClassFileClass x = new myComClassFileClass();
         short val1;
         short val2;
         val1 = 5;
         val2 = 6;
         short retVal;
         retVal = x.DoMath(ref val1, ref val2);
         MessageBox.Show(retVal.ToString());

   }
```

If you run the application by pressing the F5 key, you get a `MessageBox` that returns the value `30`, which is what the COM component was supposed to do: multiply two numbers.

As you can see, exposing a COM component to a .NET application is very simple. You can either create an interop assembly using the `tlbimp.exe` utility, or you can directly reference a COM DLL through the Add References dialog in Visual Studio .NET.

Summary

Today you learned how to implement components in .NET. By going through the example of creating the Class Library application, you saw that creating a reusable piece of code is not a difficult task. You also gained a basic understanding of how to use your existing COM components in a .NET application. You now know that the code you wrote before you started using .NET can still be accessed in a number of ways by using the tools provided by Visual Studio .NET.

Q&A

Q I think I understand all the different types of component templates in .NET, but when do I actually need the ones that have a designer and when should I just use a Class Library application?

A It all depends on what you need. Most of my development involves breaking apart functionality into Class Library applications and then using the Class Libraries in different applications. The functionality exposed by the designers enables you to create visual components for Windows Forms and Web Forms. You can create nonvisual components by creating component classes and using items in the Components tab of the Toolbox. You create a component class in the exercises later today.

Q The C# code for the COM interoperability seemed different than the Visual Basic .NET code. Why is that?

A The answer isn't simple. C# handles interop slightly different from Visual Basic .NET, so if you're seriously considering hard-code COM interop, you need to get a good book on the subject. We barely scratched the surface today. The best book that I know of is

.NET and COM: The Complete Interoperability Guide, written by Adam Nathan and published by Sams Publishing.

There are other books out there about COM interop, but this one is by far the best. It's 1,608 pages of COM interop fun.

Q I have a lot of Visual Basic 6 code that returns ADO recordsets to ASP pages. I want to use these DLLs in my ASP.NET applications. Can I pass an ADO recordset to a .NET application?

A Yes, you can. The `DataSet` class can decipher ADO recordsets. Do a search in the software development kit (SDK) for ADO, and you'll find an example. There's also a good example of this in the Quick Start tutorials that come with the .NET SDK and are available online at `http://www.gotdotnet.com`.

Q I need more details about creating components and controls. What can I do next?

A When you get to exercise 3 later today, you'll find the walkthroughs for creating all types of .NET components. The SDK has tons of information about where to go next.

If you want to get another great book by Sams Publishing, I suggest *Creating Custom Controls for ASP .NET*, by Doug Seven and Donnie Mack.

Quiz

1. The ____________________________ interface gives me a design-time surface when I create components.
2. The _____________ utility will create an interop assembly that I can use as a managed assembly in .NET.
3. True or False: Using `tlbimp.exe` creates a managed assembly based on the type library of a COM component that I can reference in a .NET application. If I just

directly reference a COM component in Visual Studio .NET, the code is just converted to .NET code and I don't need an interop assembly.

Quiz Answers

1. `System.ComponentModel`
2. `Tlbimp.exe`
3. False. If you simply reference the COM component from VS.NET, the RCW is created behind the scenes for you. You must still make sure that the COM component is correctly registered on the target machine. No code conversion is happening; the wrapper is simply created.

Exercises

1. In the TestConsumer project you created earlier today, you didn't implement code for all the methods and properties you wrote in the myComponent Class Library application. Do the following to finish off the application:
   - In the `Form_Load` event, write code that calls the `GetAuthors` method and fill the `DataGrid` on the form with the results. This demonstrates how to pass ADO.NET data from a component to a client application.
   - In the `DoName_Click` event, add code that sets the `FirstName` and `LastName` properties and then display the `FullName` property in a `MessageBox`. This demonstrates how to set and retrieve properties in a component.
2. Create a new ASP.NET application with a `DataGrid`, a `TextBox`, and a `CommandButton`.

   Add a Class Library project to the solution. In the class library, create two methods with the following characteristics:
   - A `GetAuthors` method that retrieves all authors from the Pubs database. This method should return a `SqlDataReader`.
   - A `GetAuthorByID` method that takes the `Au_ID` field as a parameter to retrieve a specific author from the database. This method should return a `SqlDataReader`.

   In the code-behind for the ASPX page that has the `CommandButton` and the `TextBox`, write code that fills the `DataGrid` with the results from the component based on the `SqlDataReader` that's returned.

The goal of this exercise is to get you familiar with passing ADO.NET data to an ASP.NET application and using databinding with a data from a component. You might recall doing something almost exactly like this over the last few days, so reuse as much code that you've already written as you can.

3. Open the Visual Studio .NET SDK and do a search for walkthroughs. You should get to a screen that looks something like Figure 14.16.

FIGURE 14.16

Searching the SDK for walkthroughs.

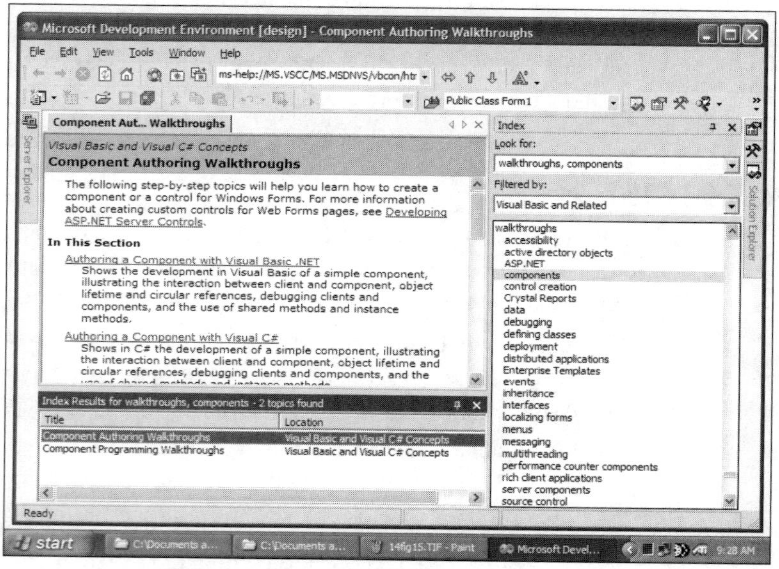

To better understand the concept of creating instances of a component with the `New` keyword, do the "Authoring a Component with Visual Basic .NET" or the "Authoring a Component with Visual C#" walkthrough.

If you're interested in creating controls for Web Forms or Windows Forms applications, the component authoring walkthroughs contain many great examples and information about taking the next step in component development.

WEEK 2

In Review

Week 2 covered many very cool topics. You learned about data access, I/O, and XML. You also learned how to write your first component in .NET, and how technologies such as ADO.NET and XML Web services can dramatically improve the way you write your applications.

On Day 8, you learned about the fundamentals of the Visual Basic .NET and C# languages. You learned about variables, data types, decision structures, and looping techniques. After going through the code on Day 8, you probably realized that Visual Basic .NET and C# aren't so different after all.

Day 9 introduced you to namespaces in .NET, and how they make up the framework class library. You learned that each namespace can have child namespaces, and that the classes in each namespace are the objects that you interact with in your code. You also learned how to use the SDK help files to get information about namespaces.

Day 10 was your first look at data access in .NET using ADO.NET. ADO.NET is the next-generation data access technology to access any type of data store using .NET. You learned that `DataReaders` provide a highly efficient mechanism for getting forward-only, read-only data, and `DataAdapters` and `DataSets` allow a robust disconnected environment for literally any type of application.

Day 11 built on Day 10 with an introduction to the visual database tools in Visual Studio .NET that aid you in developing data-driven applications. Using tools such as the Server Explorer, you learned how to manage your SQL Server databases and write data-driven applications with almost no code.

On Day 12, you learned how to work with XML in .NET. Using the `System.XML` namespace, you learned that reading, writing, and parsing XML is a trivial task when working with Visual Studio .NET.

On Day 13, you learned about XML Web services, a cornerstone of the .NET vision. You learned that using XML Web services to build an application enables you to expose your application's methods to any other type of application running on any other type of operating system. You also learned how to return datasets with SQL Server data from a Web service, and how to call Web services from the client script in an HTML page.

Day 14 wrapped up the week with a lesson on components in .NET. You learned how designers work in Visual Studio .NET, and about the options you have when building components using the different project templates in Visual Studio .NET. You also learned how to create your own namespaces, and how to use legacy COM components in managed code using Visual Studio .NET.

WEEK 3

At a Glance

Week 3 teaches you about the more interesting and exciting features of Visual Studio .NET. You'll start the week by learning how to write internationally aware applications, and how to write macros and add-ins to customize and extend the Visual Studio .NET environment using the automations features of the IDE. You'll also learn about the new reporting capabilities using the built-in Crystal Reports for .NET. In addition, you'll learn how to use Microsoft Application Test Center to stress test your applications. You'll finish the week with a lesson on using Visual SourceSafe from Visual Studio .NET and how to use object role modeling and Visio to create conceptual data models.

Week 3 covers the following:

- Day 15 teaches you how to use the `System.Globalization` namespace in the framework class library to write applications that are culturally sensitive. You'll learn how to modify the culture settings of a computer based on user preference, and how to alter the running threads' culture information to write language-specific applications.
- Day 16 teaches you how to write macros for Visual Studio .NET. Like macros in Microsoft Word or Microsoft Excel, the macros in Visual Studio .NET simplify your life by making repetitive tasks automatic inside the IDE.
- Day 17 builds on your macro knowledge and teaches you how to write separate add-in applications. Add-ins are separate COM-based applications written in .NET that give you full reign over the functionality of the

Visual Studio .NET IDE. You'll learn how to create interactive forms that can access the Toolbox and Code Editor in Visual Studio .NET.

- Day 18 introduces you to Crystal Reports for Visual Studio .NET. You'll learn how to write data-driven reports for both Windows Forms and ASP.NET applications, and how to use the special Report Viewer component to view reports in both types of applications.
- Day 19 teaches you how to use Microsoft Application Test Center. Using the specific testing techniques that you learn today, you'll be able to effectively determine how your ASP.NET applications will perform when they're used outside the development environment. Understanding benchmarks such as how long a page takes to load when one user hits it versus one thousand users hit it will help you fine-tune your code to work for the optimal target environment.
- Day 20 covers the code management features supplied by Microsoft Visual SourceSafe. Keeping your code versioned and safe from destruction will help you sleep better at night. Learning how to use Visual Studio .NET's built-in tools to manage your code will make your development cycle worry-free and flexible.
- Day 21 introduces you to conceptual data design with Visio. Using a technology called *object role modeling*, you'll learn how to break down application processes into regular sentences. Then you'll find out how to take those sentences and plug them into Visio to create a data model that can be used to automatically create any ODBC database, including SQL Server and Oracle.

WEEK 3

DAY 15

Writing International Applications

With the world coming closer together with the Internet, it's logical that software should recognize different localized cultural information, such as correct date, time, and currency formatting. Visual Studio .NET has built in-tools and classes that enable you to write applications that are truly international, and allow you to handle multiple localizations in a single application. Doing so makes your apps truly global in nature. Today, you learn

- What makes an application global
- How to retrieve culture-specific information
- How to write applications that handle multiple cultures
- How to use resource files in your application

Introduction to Globalization

A globalized application is one that works in any locale it's installed in. That means if you develop an application on a computer with English - United States as the regional settings in the Control Panel, your application also functions correctly on a computer where the regional settings are Spanish - Mexico. This isn't a trivial issue, but understanding how to localize your applications using .NET will make your life easier.

When you write code, you're concentrating on the user interface and the application logic. Most of the time, you don't expect that anyone outside of your company or your country will use your application. However, if the possibility exists, you must take specific steps to make sure that when the application runs in another locale, it makes sense to the end user.

When writing applications for different locales, you must make sure that you're writing in a culture- and language-neutral manner. That means you aren't hard-coding number and string formatting for dates, times, and currencies. It also means that user interface elements, such as the `Text` properties on labels, make sense. In other words, saying "Hello" in English takes less space on a label than saying "Bonjour" in French. Making your code and interface culture- and language-neutral is the first step in ensuring that your application works in other locales.

The next things you need to worry about are the resources that the application needs when it runs in another locale. A *resource* is anything that might display on a form, be it a text string or a bitmap. When you write culture-neutral code, you're setting user interface text through resources, not through hard-coded properties.

After you build the application, the final step is to test the various locales that you've prepared for and make sure that they work correctly.

Using .NET, there are several different ways to create global applications with relative ease. The first thing you need to understand is the `CultureInfo` class.

Using the `CultureInfo` Class

The `CultureInfo` class provides culture-specific information about the locale of the operating system running your application. To give you an idea of what the `CultureInfo` class does, you can look at your own computer's regional settings.

In the Control Panel, the Regional and Language Settings applet is the place to view and change how regional information should be displayed on your computer. This includes date, time, currency, currency symbol information, as well as your keyboard layout.

Figure 15.1 demonstrates the Regional and Language Settings dialog box for my computer.

FIGURE 15.1

Regional settings for English (United States).

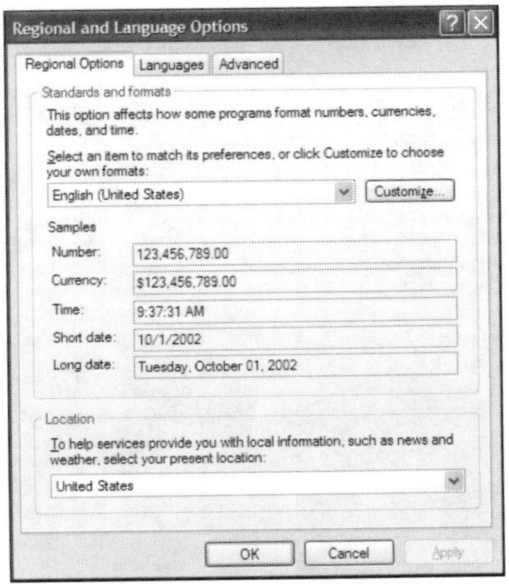

Because I installed Windows XP and I live in Florida, the locale for my computer is English (United States). I could have changed this to whatever I wanted during installation of Windows XP, or I could go to the Control Panel and modify it. Because the locale is en-US, the standard date, time, and currency formats are used throughout Windows.

If I want to see what the regional information would look like in another locale, I can change the settings to another locale in the Control Panel. Figure 15.2 shows I'm changing the locale to Tatar.

FIGURE 15.2

Modifying my locale to Tatar.

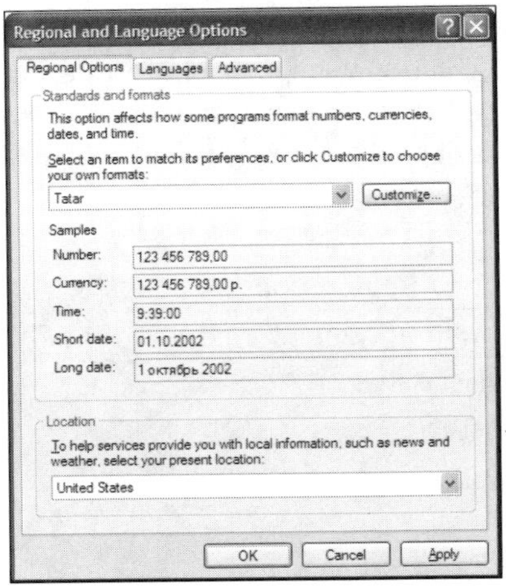

After the locale is changed, Windows takes on a new look for the regional settings of Tatar. If I look at my Outlook Calendar, it doesn't display the months and times as it would in the United States—it displays them as it would for Tatar. Figure 15.3 shows Outlook after changing my locale to Tatar.

FIGURE 15.3

Outlook Calendar after changing the locale to Tatar.

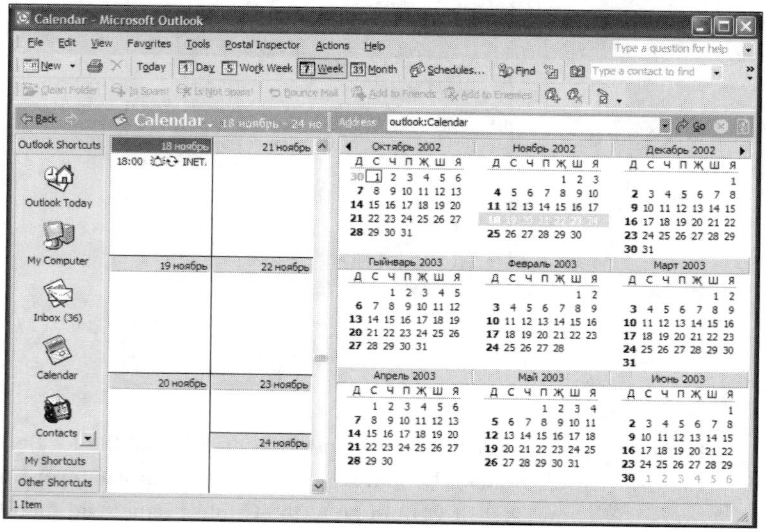

As you can see, Outlook is written with globalization in mind. The dates and months aren't specific to any region; they're determined by the locale settings in the Control Panel. This is how you should write applications that can span the globe. The `CultureInfo` class gives you the flexibility to do this.

In Windows and the .NET Framework's `System.Globalization` namespace, there are predefined culture names that comply with the RFC 1766 standard *languagecode-Country/regioncode* format for determining the culture you're working in. To make sense of this, look at the compact version of `CultureInfo` names and language-country/region combinations listed in Table 15.1.

TABLE 15.1 `CultureInfo` Names and Region Codes

Culture Name	*Language-Country/Region*
"" (empty string)	Invariant culture
`af`	Afrikaans
`af-ZA`	Afrikaans - South Africa

TABLE 15.1 continued

Culture Name	*Language-Country/Region*
sq	Albanian
sq-AL	Albanian - Albania
ar	Arabic
ar-DZ	Arabic - Algeria
ar-BH	Arabic - Bahrain
ar-EG	Arabic - Egypt
ar-QA	Arabic - Qatar
ar-SA	Arabic - Saudi Arabia
ar-SY	Arabic - Syria
ar-TN	Arabic - Tunisia
ar-AE	Arabic - United Arab Emirates
ar-YE	Arabic - Yemen
hy	Armenian
hy-AM	Armenian - Armenia
az	Azeri
Cy-az-AZ	Azeri (Cyrillic) - Azerbaijan
Lt-az-AZ	Azeri (Latin) - Azerbaijan
eu	Basque
eu-ES	Basque - Basque
be	Belarusian
be-BY	Belarusian - Belarus
bg	Bulgarian
bg-BG	Bulgarian - Bulgaria
ca	Catalan
ta	Tamil
ta-IN	Tamil - India
tt	Tatar
tt-RU	Tatar - Russia
te	Telugu
te-IN	Telugu - India
th	Thai
th-TH	Thai - Thailand

TABLE 15.1 continued

Culture Name	*Language-Country/Region*
`tr`	Turkish
`tr-TR`	Turkish - Turkey
`uk`	Ukrainian
`uk-UA`	Ukrainian - Ukraine
`ur`	Urdu
`ur-PK`	Urdu - Pakistan
`uz`	Uzbek
`Cy-uz-UZ`	Uzbek (Cyrillic) - Uzbekistan
`Lt-uz-UZ`	Uzbek (Latin) - Uzbekistan
`vi`	Vietnamese
`vi-VN`	Vietnamese - Vietnam

Table 15.1 should give you a good idea of where this is going. Every possible culture code is available for you to use. Later, you're going to write code to actually list them all.

Understanding that you have access to specific cultures isn't enough to write global code. You must use the methods and properties of the `CultureInfo` class to make sure that you're displaying the correct information on your forms. Table 15.2 lists the common properties available to you in the `CultureInfo` class, and Table 15.3 lists the common methods that you can take advantage of when using the `CultureInfo` class.

TABLE 15.2 Common Properties of the `CultureInfo` Class

Property	*Description*
`Calendar`	Gets the default calendar used by the culture
`CompareInfo`	Gets the `CompareInfo` that defines how to compare strings for the culture
`CurrentCulture`	Gets the `CultureInfo` that represents the culture used by the current thread
`CurrentUICulture`	Gets the `CultureInfo` that represents the current culture used by the `ResourceManager` to look up culture-specific resources at runtime
`DateTimeFormat`	Gets or sets a `DateTimeFormatInfo` that defines the culturally appropriate format of displaying dates and times

15

TABLE 15.2 continued

Property	*Description*
`DisplayName`	Gets the culture name in the format `"<languagefull> (<country/regionfull>)"` in the language of the localized version of .NET Framework
`EnglishName`	Gets the culture name in the format `"<languagefull> (<country/regionfull>)"` in English
`InstalledUICulture`	Gets the `CultureInfo` that represents the culture installed with the operating system
`InvariantCulture`	Gets the `CultureInfo` that's culture-independent (invariant)
`IsNeutralCulture`	Gets a value indicating whether the current CultureInfo represents a neutral culture
`IsReadOnly`	Gets a value indicating whether the current `CultureInfo` is read-only
`LCID`	Gets the culture identifier for the current `CultureInfo`
`Name`	Gets the culture name in the format `"<languagecode2>-<country/regioncode2>"`
`NativeName`	Gets the culture name in the format `"<languagefull> (<country/regionfull>)"` in the language that the culture is set to display
`NumberFormat`	Gets or sets a `NumberFormatInfo` that defines the culturally appropriate format of displaying numbers, currency, and percentages
`OptionalCalendars`	Gets the list of optional calendars that can be used by the culture
`Parent`	Gets the `CultureInfo` that represents the parent culture of the current `CultureInfo`
`TextInfo`	Gets the `TextInfo` that defines the writing system associated with the culture
`ThreeLetterISOLanguageName`	Gets the ISO 639-2 three-letter code for the language of the current `CultureInfo`
`ThreeLetterWindowsLanguageName`	Gets the three-letter code for the language as defined in the Windows API
`TwoLetterISOLanguageName`	Gets the ISO 639-1 two-letter code for the language of the current `CultureInfo`
`UseUserOverride`	Gets a value indicating whether the current `CultureInfo` uses the user-selected culture settings

TABLE 15.3 Common Methods of the `CultureInfo` Class

Method	*Description*
`ClearCachedData`	Refreshes cached culture-related information
`Clone`	Creates a copy of the current `CultureInfo`
`CreateSpecificCulture`	Creates a `CultureInfo` that represents the specific culture that's associated with the specified name
`GetCultures`	Gets the list of supported cultures filtered by the specified `CultureTypes`
`GetFormat`	Gets an object that defines how to format the specified type
`ReadOnly`	Returns a read-only wrapper around the specified `CultureInfo`
`ToString`	Overridden; returns a string containing the name of the current `CultureInfo` in the format `"<languagecode2>-<country/regioncode2>"`

As you can see, the whole idea of the `CultureInfo` class is to give you the ability write global applications. To see how you can use this in code, you're going to write a Culture Info Browser application that uses the methods and properties of the `CultureInfo` class.

Writing the Culture Info Browser Application

The Culture Info Browser application uses the methods and properties in the `CultureInfo` class to give you specific information about the formatting of numbers, dates, and strings for each culture on your computer.

To get started, create a new Windows Forms application named Globalization_vb or Globalization_cs, depending on the language you're using.

When the default `form1` comes up in the designer, follow these steps to complete the user interface:

1. Change the `Text` property of the form to `Culture Info Browser`.
2. Change the `Font` property of the form to `12pt Tahoma`.
3. Drag a `ListBox` control to the form. Change the `Name` property to `lb`, and set the `Dock` property to `Left`.
4. Drag a `Splitter` control to the form. It should automatically dock against the `ListBox`.
5. Drag a `ListView` control to the form. Change the `Name` property to `lv`, and set the `Dock` property to `Fill`.

The user interface is now complete. You have a form that resizes its child controls correctly, and uses a splitter bar to enable resizing between the controls on the form. Your completed form should look like Figure 15.4.

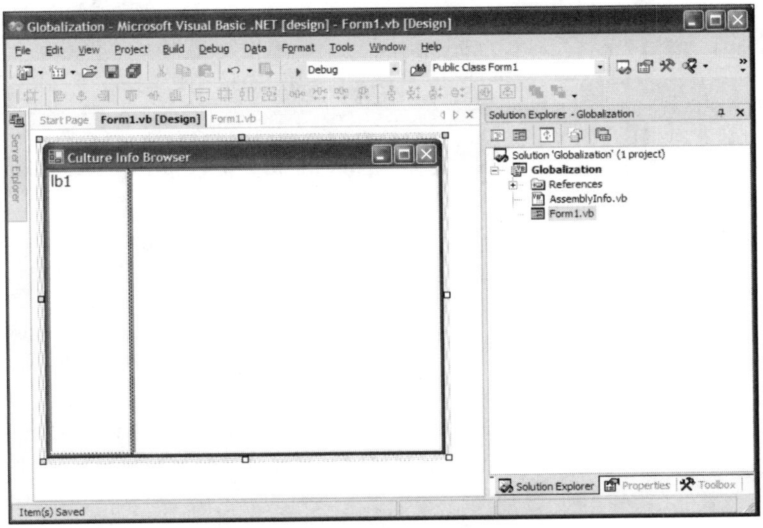

FIGURE 15.4

The Culture Info Browser application at design time.

The next step is to add some code. Double-click the form to get the `Form_Load` event. Before you add any code, you must add the `System.Globalization` namespace to this class. So, scroll to the top of the `form1` class file, and add the `Imports` or `using` statement for the `System.Globalization` namespace. Listing 15.1 is what the top of your class file should look like.

LISTING 15.1 Aliasing the `System.Globalization` Namespace

VB.NET

```
Imports System.Globalization

Public Class Form1
   Inherits System.Windows.Forms.Form
```

C#

```
using System.Globalization;

namespace Globalization_cs
{
```

Next, you fill the ListBox with all the available cultures on your machine. The `CultureInfo` class has a `CultureType` enumeration, which returns an array to the `CultureInfo` type that contains information about each culture you specify in the filter. The filter can be any `CultureType` listed in Table 15.4.

TABLE 15.4 `CultureType` Members

Member Name	*Description*
`AllCultures`	Refers to all cultures.
`InstalledWin32Cultures`	Refers to all cultures that are installed in the system.
`NeutralCultures`	Refers to cultures that are associated with a language but aren't specific to a country/region. The names of these cultures consist of the lowercase two-letter code derived from ISO 639-1. For example: `"en"` (English) is a neutral culture. The invariant culture is included in the array of cultures returned by `CultureInfo.GetCultures` with this value.
`SpecificCultures`	Refers to cultures that are specific to a country/region. The names of these cultures follow the RFC 1766 standard in the format `"<languagecode2>-<country/regioncode2>"`, where `<languagecode2>` is a lowercase two-letter code derived from ISO 639-1 and `<country/regioncode2>` is an uppercase two-letter code derived from ISO 3166. For example, `"en-US"` (English - United States) is a specific culture.

To test this, add the code in Listing 15.2 to the `Form_Load` event of your form.

LISTING 15.2 Getting the `CultureInfo` in the `Form_Load` Event

VB.NET

```
Private Sub Form1_Load(ByVal sender As System.Object, _
   ByVal e As System.EventArgs) Handles MyBase.Load

   ' Create a CultureInfo Variable
   Dim cu As CultureInfo

   ' Loop through the CultureTypes Enumeration
   ' and list the Culture Name in the Listbox
   For Each cu In CultureInfo.GetCultures _
     (CultureTypes.InstalledWin32Cultures)
      lb1.Items.Add(cu.Name)
   Next
End Sub
```

Listing 15.2 continued

C#

```
private void Form1_Load(object sender, System.EventArgs e)
{
   //   Create a CultureInfo Variable
   //   Loop through the CultureTypes Enumeration
   //   and list the Culture Name in the Listbox
   foreach (CultureInfo cu in
      CultureInfo.GetCultures
      (CultureTypes.InstalledWin32Cultures))
   {
      lb.Items.Add(cu.Name);
   }
}
```

The code in Listing 15.2 loops though the enumeration to retrieve the names in the `InstalledWin32Cultures` enumeration, and adds them to the list box.

To view the properties of the culture that you click on in the list box, add the code in Listing 15.3, which uses the properties of the `CultureInfo` class to retrieve the values for the selected region code.

Listing 15.3 Retrieving the `CultureInfo` Properties for the Selected Culture

VB.NET

```
Private Sub lb1_SelectedIndexChanged(ByVal sender As System.Object, _
  ByVal e As System.EventArgs) Handles lb1.SelectedIndexChanged

   ' Get the Culture listed in the Listbox control
   Dim cu As String = CType(lb1.SelectedItem, String)

   ' Declare an instance of the CurrentCulture class,
   ' passing the selected listbox item
   Dim ci As New CultureInfo(cu)

   ' Set the cursor to an hourglass
   Me.Cursor = Cursors.WaitCursor

   ' Set the View property, and add 2 columns
   lv.View = View.Details
   lv.Columns.Add("Property", 300, HorizontalAlignment.Left)
   lv.Columns.Add("Value", 300, HorizontalAlignment.Left)

   ' Create a string array to hold the DayNames
   Dim Days() As String
   Days = ci.DateTimeFormat.DayNames
```

LISTING 15.3 continued

```
        ' Create a string array to hold the MonthNames
        Dim Months() As String
        Months = ci.DateTimeFormat.MonthNames

        ' Looping variable
         Dim intX As Integer

        With lv.Items
            ' Clear the ListView of any existing items
            .Clear()

            ' Add items to the list base on the
            ' ci CultureInfo class variable
            .Add("Name").SubItems.Add(ci.Name)
            .Add("Display Name").SubItems.Add(ci.DisplayName)
            .Add("English Name").SubItems.Add(ci.EnglishName)
            .Add("LCID").SubItems.Add(ci.LCID)
            .Add("Long Date Format").SubItems.Add _
                (ci.DateTimeFormat.LongDatePattern.ToString)
            .Add("Native Name").SubItems.Add(ci.NativeName)
            .Add("Text Info").SubItems.Add(ci.TextInfo.ToString)
            .Add("3 Letter ISO Lang Name").SubItems.Add _
                (ci.ThreeLetterISOLanguageName)
            .Add("3 Letter Windows Name").SubItems.Add _
                (ci.ThreeLetterWindowsLanguageName)
            .Add("2 Letter ISO Name").SubItems.Add(ci.TwoLetterISOLanguageName)

            ' Add the Days of the week
            For intX = 0 To Days.Length - 1
                .Add("Day " & intX + 1).SubItems.Add(Days(intX))
            Next

            ' Add the Months of the year
            For intX = 0 To Months.Length - 1
                .Add("Month " & intX + 1).SubItems.Add(Months(intX))
            Next
        End With

        ' Set the mouse cursor back to normal
        Me.Cursor = Cursors.Default

    End Sub
```

C#

```
private void lb_SelectedIndexChanged(object sender, System.EventArgs e)
{
    // Get the Culture listed in the Listbox control

    string cu = lb.Text;
```

LISTING 15.3 continued

```
// Declare an instance of the CurrentCulture class,
// passing the selected listbox item
CultureInfo ci = new CultureInfo(cu);

// Set the cursor to an hourglass
this.Cursor = Cursors.WaitCursor;

// Set the View property, and add 2 columns
lv.View = View.Details;
lv.Columns.Add("Property", 300, HorizontalAlignment.Left);
lv.Columns.Add("Value", 300, HorizontalAlignment.Left);

// Create a string array to hold the DayNames
string[] days;
days = ci.DateTimeFormat.DayNames;

// Create a string array to hold the MonthNames
string[] months;
months = ci.DateTimeFormat.MonthNames;

// Clear the ListView of any existing items
lv.Items.Clear();

// Add items to the list base on the
// ci CultureInfo class variable
lv.Items.Add("Name").SubItems.Add(ci.Name);
lv.Items.Add("Display Name").SubItems.Add(ci.DisplayName);
lv.Items.Add("English Name").SubItems.Add(ci.EnglishName);
lv.Items.Add("LCID").SubItems.Add(ci.LCID.ToString());
lv.Items.Add("Long Date Format").SubItems.Add
     (ci.DateTimeFormat.LongDatePattern.ToString());
lv.Items.Add("Native Name").SubItems.Add(ci.NativeName);
lv.Items.Add("Text Info").SubItems.Add(ci.TextInfo.ToString());
lv.Items.Add("3 Letter ISO Lang Name").SubItems.Add
     (ci.ThreeLetterISOLanguageName);
lv.Items.Add("3 Letter Windows Name").SubItems.Add
     (ci.ThreeLetterWindowsLanguageName);
lv.Items.Add("2 Letter ISO Name").SubItems.Add
     (ci.TwoLetterISOLanguageName);

// Add the Days of the week
for(int x = 0; x < days.Length -1; x++)
{
   lv.Items.Add("Day " + Convert.ToString(x+1)).SubItems.Add(days[x]);
}

// Add the Months of the year
for(int x = 0; x < months.Length -1; x++)
{
   lv.Items.Add("Month " +
       Convert.ToString(x+1)).SubItems.Add(months[x]);
```

LISTING 15.3 continued

```
        }

        // Set the mouse cursor back to normal
        this.Cursor = Cursors.Default;
    }
```

Press the F5 key to run the application. Click around the list box in the left pane of the form, and you'll notice the different culture-specific formatting available.

Figure 15.5 demonstrates the `CultureInfo` properties for the Malay region.

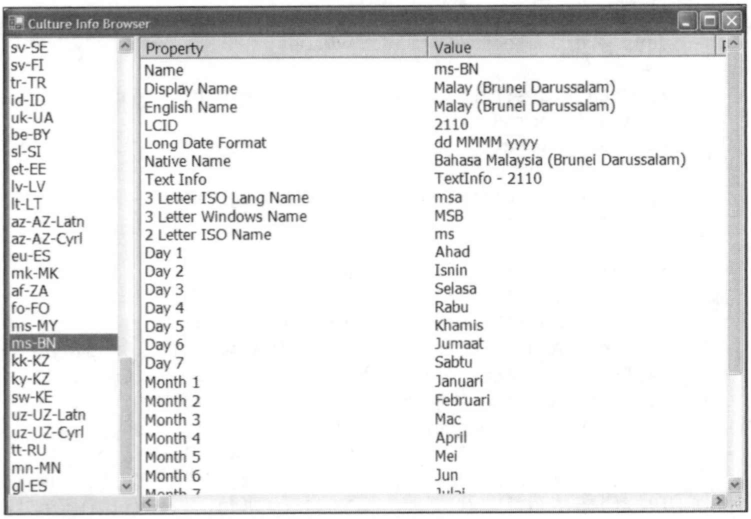

FIGURE 15.5
Running the Culture Info Browser application.

After you create the instance of the `CultureInfo` class, the `ci` variable has full access to the properties and methods of the `CultureInfo` class. Notice the arrays you returned: a `days` array and a `months` array, which contain the correct day and month spelling for the selected culture, respectively. You saw earlier how Outlook handles a different locale setting, so now you understand how it knows where to get the information.

There are many more properties that you didn't display. As you saw when you were typing the code, the auto-complete feature in Visual Studio .NET comes in very handy again when learning about a new class. Figure 15.6 shows the auto-list members in action for the `ci` variable, which is an instance of the `CultureInfo` class.

I joke about guessing when you aren't sure about what properties and methods to use, but guessing is a sure way to learn what a class offers. Go ahead and try some of the other properties that you didn't list in the `ListView` control. It's an excellent way to learn.

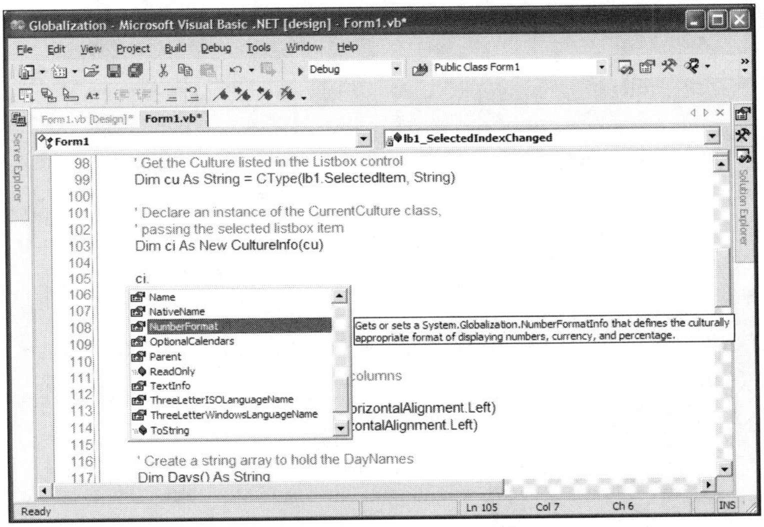

FIGURE 15.6
Visual Studio .NET auto-list members in action with the `CultureInfo` *class.*

I mentioned the Outlook Calendar again, and it seems to make sense that when you change a locale in the Control Panel, the entire operating system should reflect those changes. When you write code in .NET, the .NET Framework looks at the `CurrentCulture` of the current thread that's running your application to determine what locale information to use.

So, by changing the `CurrentCulture` of the `CurrentThread`, you can actually see the differences in what your code would look like running in a different locale. This is why writing language- and locale-neutral code is so important. Consider the following Visual Basic .NET code:

```
Dim i As Integer = 100

Console.WriteLine(i.ToString("c", _
 System.Threading.Thread.CurrentThread.CurrentUICulture.NumberFormat))

Console.WriteLine(i.ToString(Date.Now, _
 System.Threading.Thread.CurrentThread.CurrentUICulture.DateTimeFormat))

Console.WriteLine(FormatCurrency(i))
```

When I run this on my normal English (United States) locale, the numbers are displayed as I expect. When I run it after changing the locale to Tatar (Russia), the numbers also look as I'd expect. There are different formats for the numbers and dates, as the following output shows:

```
100,00 ?.
10011,02002 13:14:18
100,00 ?.
```

When dealing with applications that use the `CultureInfo` class, the data is based on the `CurrentCulture` of the running thread. So, you can modify the running thread's current culture to actually see how your data would look running on another locale.

To make this work, you must modify the `CurrentUICulture` property of the `CurrentThread`. On a Windows Form, this can be done before the `InitializeComponent` method call by using the code listed in Listing 15.4.

LISTING 15.4 Changing the `CurrentUICulture` in the Class Constructor

VB.NET

```
System.Threading.Thread.CurrentThread.CurrentUICulture = _
  New System.Globalization.CultureInfo("tt-RU")
```

C#

```
System.Threading.Thread.CurrentThread.CurrentUICulture =
 new System.Globalization.CultureInfo("tt-RU");
```

By modifying the running thread's `CurrentUICulture` to `ìtt-RUî`, the form correctly formats the data based on the `ìtt-RUî` localization properties.

That's why the Culture Info Browser is so important. It's one thing to see how things look in a nice demo, but you can actually implement the correct culture formatting by altering the `CurrentUICulture` on any running thread in any .NET application.

Note

Because the `System.ReadMyMind` namespace isn't in the .NET FCL yet, you're normally going to write applications that enable the end user to set a preference on what locale she wants to use. One of my customers has offices in Monaco, Greece, Australia, and the United States, so there are four different locales I need to worry about. But even though a person using my application might be in Monaco, it doesn't mean he necessarily wants the European date and currency formats. So, I need to let the users choose what they want. By letting them do so, I can guarantee that each screen they look at is user-friendly to their preference because I can modify the culture information for all the formatting in the application.

The next step in understanding globalization is the use of Visual Studio .NET's built-in tools that handle localization resources.

Managing Resource Files with Visual Studio .NET

Built into the Visual Studio .NET IDE is the ability to write completely global applications through the use of resource files.

Resource files are XML-based files that describe a form. Each time you add a new form to an application, a `.resx` file accompanies the form in the Solution Explorer. Normally, this file contains only basic information about the form, and doesn't do a whole lot. Figure 15.7 is the `form1.resx` file for the Culture Info Browser form you wrote earlier.

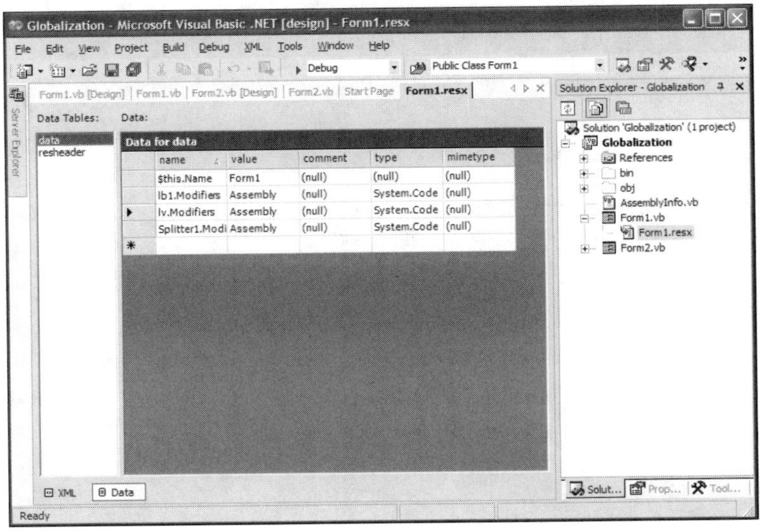

FIGURE 15.7

The `form1.resx` file in the XML Designer.

When you add controls to a form, the Windows Forms Designer adds code to the class file to set the various properties that you set in the Properties window. For the `form1.vb` file in the Culture Info Browser, the Windows Forms Designer–generated code looks like Listing 15.5.

Listing 15.5 Windows Forms Designer–Generated Code for the `form1.vb` Class File

VB.NET

```
Friend WithEvents lb1 As System.Windows.Forms.ListBox
Friend WithEvents Splitter1 As System.Windows.Forms.Splitter
Friend WithEvents lv As System.Windows.Forms.ListView

<System.Diagnostics.DebuggerStepThrough()> _
Private Sub InitializeComponent()
   Me.lb1 = New System.Windows.Forms.ListBox()
   Me.Splitter1 = New System.Windows.Forms.Splitter()
   Me.lv = New System.Windows.Forms.ListView()
   Me.SuspendLayout()
   '
   'lb1
   '
   Me.lb1.Dock = System.Windows.Forms.DockStyle.Left
   Me.lb1.ItemHeight = 19
   Me.lb1.Name = "lb1"
   Me.lb1.Size = New System.Drawing.Size(84, 308)
   Me.lb1.TabIndex = 3
   '
   'Splitter1
   '
   Me.Splitter1.Location = New System.Drawing.Point(84, 0)
   Me.Splitter1.Name = "Splitter1"
   Me.Splitter1.Size = New System.Drawing.Size(3, 310)
   Me.Splitter1.TabIndex = 4
   Me.Splitter1.TabStop = False
   '
   'lv
   '
   Me.lv.Dock = System.Windows.Forms.DockStyle.Fill
   Me.lv.Location = New System.Drawing.Point(87, 0)
   Me.lv.Name = "lv"
   Me.lv.Size = New System.Drawing.Size(321, 310)
   Me.lv.TabIndex = 5
   '
   'Form1
   '
   Me.AutoScaleBaseSize = New System.Drawing.Size(8, 20)
   Me.ClientSize = New System.Drawing.Size(408, 310)
   Me.Controls.AddRange(New System.Windows.Forms.Control() _
           {Me.lv, Me.Splitter1, Me.lb1})
   Me.Font = New System.Drawing.Font("Tahoma", 12.0!, _
            System.Drawing.FontStyle.Regular, _
            System.Drawing.GraphicsUnit.Point, CType(0, Byte))
   Me.Name = "Form1"
```

LISTING 15.5 continued

```
        Me.Text = "Culture Info Browser"
        Me.ResumeLayout(False)

    End Sub
```

Each time a control is added or a property is set, the designer updates the code in the class file automatically. That works very well when you're writing applications that will be used in one language and one locale. However, it doesn't work well when you consider that your application might be running all around the world.

To solve this problem, each form you add to a project has a `Localizable` property. When set to True, `Localizable` alters the way the designer keeps track of the objects on your forms.

Creating the Resources Project

To test this out, create a new project named Resources_vb or Resources_cs, depending on your language. Drag two `Label` controls, two `Button` controls, and two `TextBox` controls to the form and arrange them as they're shown in Figure 15.8.

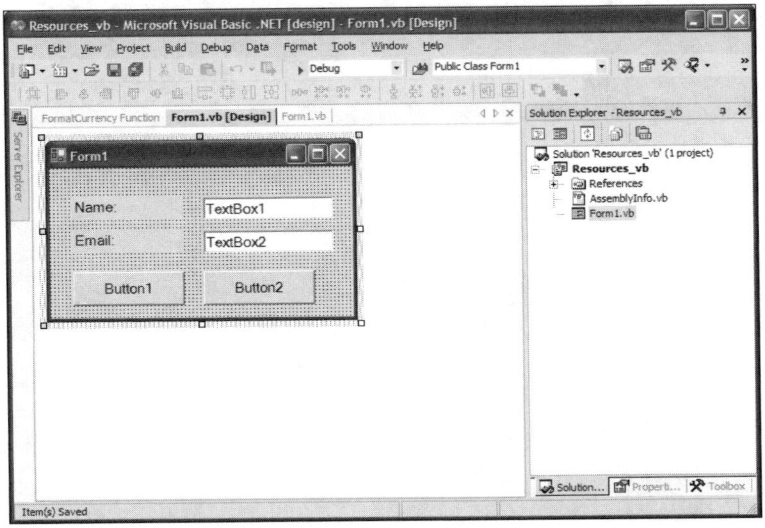

FIGURE 15.8
`Form1` *of the Resources application.*

If you examine the code in the `form1` class file that was generated by the Windows Forms Designer, you'll notice nothing unusual. The controls are added, and the names and locations of the controls on the form are coded into the class file.

Your goal is to make this form work for the default locale of your operating system and the `fr-FR` locale. That means when an end user in France sees your form, the controls must display different information based on the language and formatting of the French end user's locale. The layout of the controls must also change for the French locale because the words are comprised of more characters in French than they are in English.

To make this work, change the following properties in the default `form1`:

- `Localizable: True`
- `Language: French`

You've now told the IDE that this form uses resource files to manage the objects on the form. If you drill open the `form1.resx` file in the XML Designer, you'll notice that instead of just keeping track of the basic form information, it now keeps track of all properties of all the objects on the form. Your `form1.resx` should resemble Figure 15.9.

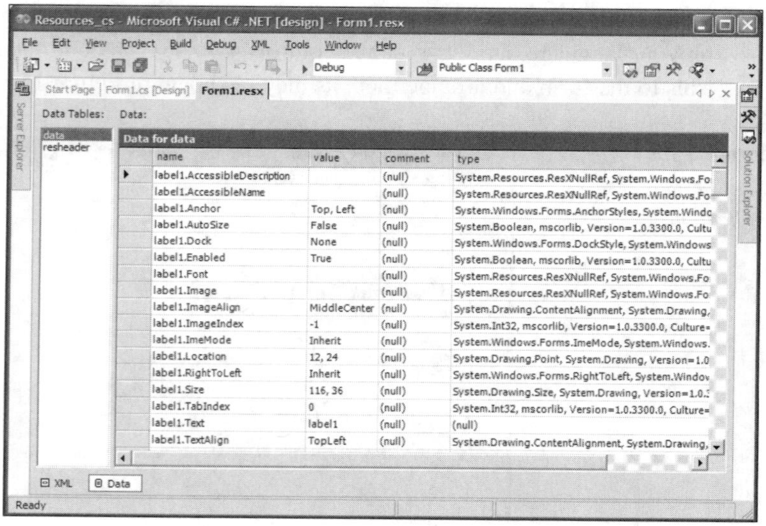

FIGURE 15.9
`form1.resx` *after setting* `Localizable` *to* `True`.

If you drill into the Windows Forms Designer–generated code in the `form1` class file now, you'll see something much different from normal. Listing 15.6 is a portion of the designer-generated code for the C# version of the project.

LISTING 15.6 C# Windows Forms Designer–Generated Code for the `Form1.cs` Class

C#

```
private void InitializeComponent()
{
```

15

LISTING 15.6 continued

```
System.Resources.ResourceManager resources =
      new System.Resources.ResourceManager(typeof(Form1));

this.label1 = new System.Windows.Forms.Label();
this.label2 = new System.Windows.Forms.Label();
this.textBox1 = new System.Windows.Forms.TextBox();
this.textBox2 = new System.Windows.Forms.TextBox();
this.button1 = new System.Windows.Forms.Button();
this.button2 = new System.Windows.Forms.Button();
this.SuspendLayout();
//
// label1
//
this.label1.AccessibleDescription =
  ((string)(resources.GetObject("label1.AccessibleDescription")));
this.label1.AccessibleName =
  ((string)(resources.GetObject("label1.AccessibleName")));
this.label1.Anchor =
  ((System.Windows.Forms.AnchorStyles)
  (resources.GetObject("label1.Anchor")));
this.label1.AutoSize =
  ((bool)(resources.GetObject("label1.AutoSize")));
this.label1.Dock = ((System.Windows.Forms.DockStyle)
   (resources.GetObject("label1.Dock")));
this.label1.Enabled = ((bool)(resources.GetObject("label1.Enabled")));
this.label1.Font = ((System.Drawing.Font)
    (resources.GetObject("label1.Font")));
this.label1.Image = ((System.Drawing.Image)
    (resources.GetObject("label1.Image")));
this.label1.ImageAlign = ((System.Drawing.ContentAlignment)
    (resources.GetObject("label1.ImageAlign")));
this.label1.ImageIndex = ((int)
    (resources.GetObject("label1.ImageIndex")));
this.label1.ImeMode = ((System.Windows.Forms.ImeMode)
    (resources.GetObject("label1.ImeMode")));
this.label1.Location = ((System.Drawing.Point)
    (resources.GetObject("label1.Location")));
this.label1.Name = "label1";
this.label1.RightToLeft = ((System.Windows.Forms.RightToLeft)
    (resources.GetObject("label1.RightToLeft")));
this.label1.Size = ((System.Drawing.Size)
    (resources.GetObject("label1.Size")));
this.label1.TabIndex = ((int)(resources.GetObject("label1.TabIndex")));
this.label1.Text = resources.GetString("label1.Text");
this.label1.TextAlign = ((System.Drawing.ContentAlignment)
    (resources.GetObject("label1.TextAlign")));
this.label1.Visible = ((bool)(resources.GetObject("label1.Visible")));
```

Because the form is localizable, the objects' properties are being tracked in the `.resx` file. The class knows where to get the information it needs at runtime by creating an instance of the `ResourceManager` class, as this code demonstrates:

```
System.Resources.ResourceManager resources =
   new System.Resources.ResourceManager(typeof(Form1));
```

After the `ResourceManager` is created, the `GetString` or `GetObject` method is called to retrieve the correct property settings at runtime.

To see how this works, change the controls of the default `form1` to look like Figure 15.10. The idea here is that you're creating an English version of your application, and then creating a French version.

FIGURE 15.10
`form1` *after changing controls to the French version.*

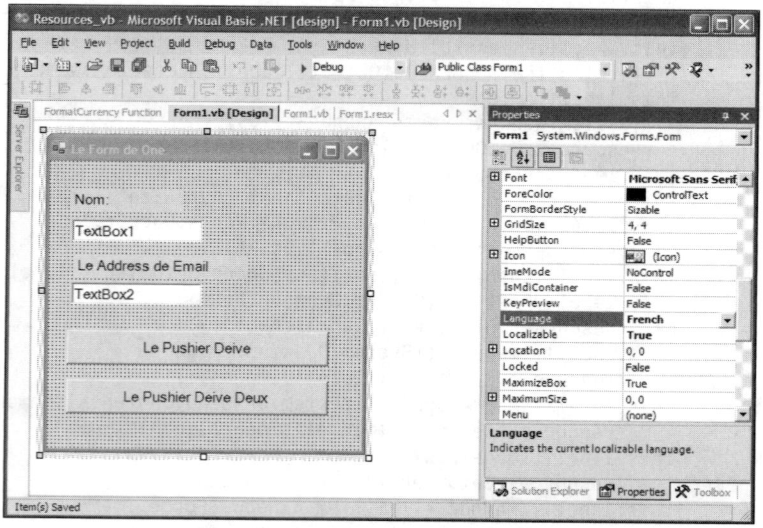

Notice that you've moved the controls on the form and modified the text. The key is in the Properties window. `Localizable` is set to `True`, and `Language` is set to French.

If you change the `Language` property back to `(default)`, the form defaults back to its original layout, as Figure 15.11 demonstrates.

In the Solution Explorer, expand all the nodes as I did in Figure 15.11. You'll see an additional `.resx` file under `form1`. You'll also see an additional folder created with the locale name in the `Bin` directory and a `Resources.dll` for the folder.

Visual Studio .NET tracks each locale that you add to the form, and creates satellite assemblies that are deployed to the end user's machine based on the locale she's using.

FIGURE 15.11

Default `form1` *after switching back to the default locale.*

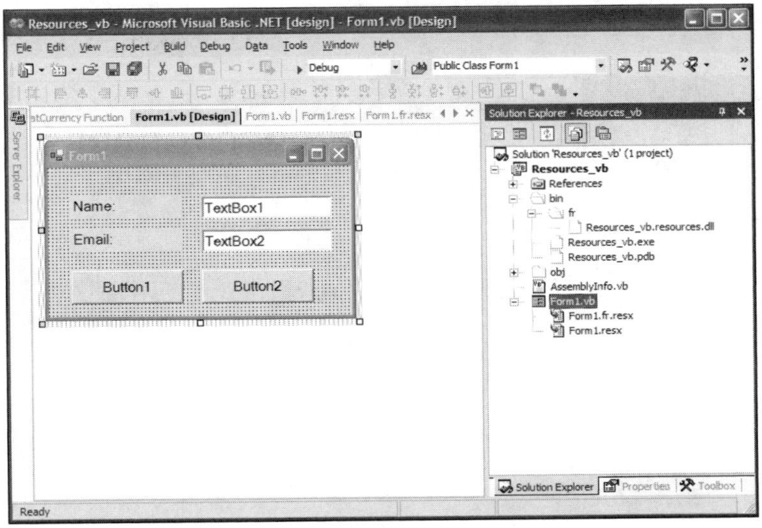

When you modify the culture for the current thread of the application, the correct form is displayed, and you don't have to worry about how culture-specific information will look on the forms you're creating.

In Visual Studio .NET, the default locale is the locale set in the Control Panel for the operating system that your application is running on. This is important to understand. I'm in the English (United States) locale, which is *not* the default locale for someone running my application in Spain. The default locale is known as the *fallback locale*, meaning that if the .NET runtime can't determine the locale of the system running your application, the defaults that you set at design time will be used.

If you really want your application to work on `en-US` and `fr-FR`, you must explicitly select the English (United States) locale from the list, and then select the French (France) locale.

You now need to add some code to the form so that you can test the different locales. Add the code in Listing 15.6 to the `Form_Load` event of the default `form1`. This code simply displays the date and a number in the currency of the current thread's locale. Make sure that you add the `System.Threading` and `System.Globalization` namespaces to the top of your class file before you add the code in Listing 15.7.

LISTING 15.7 Displaying the Correct Date and Time Format for the Current Locale

VB.NET

```
Private Sub Form1_Load(ByVal sender As System.Object, _
  ByVal e As System.EventArgs) Handles MyBase.Load

   Dim i As Integer = 100

   TextBox1.Text = i.ToString("c", _
    Thread.CurrentThread.CurrentUICulture.NumberFormat)

   TextBox2.Text = i.ToString(Date.Now, _
    Thread.CurrentThread.CurrentUICulture.DateTimeFormat)

End Sub
```

C#

```
private void Form1_Load(object sender, System.EventArgs e)
{

int i = 100;

textBox1.Text = i.ToString("c",
 Thread.CurrentThread.CurrentUICulture.NumberFormat);

textBox2.Text = i.ToString(DateTime.Now.ToString(),
 Thread.CurrentThread.CurrentUICulture.DateTimeFormat);

}
```

By getting the `CurrentUICultureNumberFormat` and `CurrentUICultureDateTimeFormat`, you're globalizing the application. You aren't dependent on anything, except what you dictate should be the current culture. That means your application is 100% portable to any locale setting in the world. If you press F5 to run the application, you should see something similar to Figure 15.12.

What you actually did was format the date and time using the fallback locale, which would be whatever the Control Panel happens to be set to.

To force the French locale, modify the `Sub New` in the default `form1` to look like Listing 15.8. This code modifies the current thread's locale setting.

FIGURE 15.12

Running the Resources application with the fallback locale.

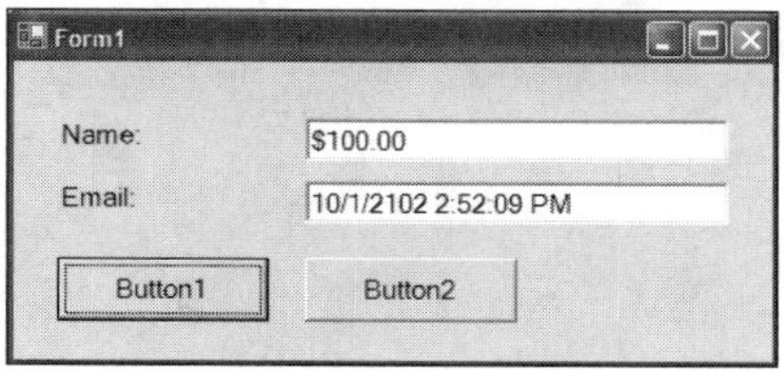

LISTING 15.8 Modifying the `CurrentUICulture` in the `Form1` Class Constructor

VB.NET

```
Public Sub New()
   MyBase.New()

   Thread.CurrentThread.CurrentUICulture = _
    New CultureInfo("fr-FR")

   'This call is required by the Windows Form Designer.
   InitializeComponent()
   'Add any initialization after the InitializeComponent() call
End Sub
```

C#

```
public Form1()
{
   //
   // Required for Windows Form Designer support
   //

Thread.CurrentThread.CurrentUICulture =
 new CultureInfo("fr-FR");

   InitializeComponent();

   //
   // TODO: Add any constructor code after InitializeComponent call
   //
}
```

If you press F5 to run the application now, you'll see something like Figure 15.13.

By forcing the locale to French (French), the correct form is displayed. You did nothing special to completely change the look and feel of the application except modify the `Language` property at design time.

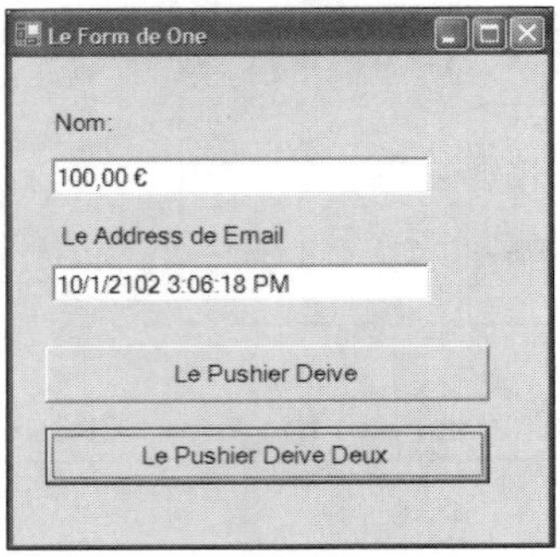

FIGURE 15.13

Running the Resources application after modifying the locale.

Using Other Resource Managers

There are two other ways to implement the resource files for creating global applications. The first method is the use of the WinRes Resource File Editor. This is a Windows Forms tool that enables you to open the `.resx` file of a form, modify the properties of the form, and save the `.resx` file as a different locale. This is an immensely powerful tool when multiple developers are working on different locales for different forms. WinRes can be accessed by typing **`WinRes.exe`** at the Visual Studio command prompt, or by navigating to the `Bin` directory of the Visual Studio .NET SDK on your hard drive. Figure 15.14 shows the default `form1.resx` file opened in the WinRes tool, and the Save As dialog prompting for the correct locale to which to save the `.resx` file.

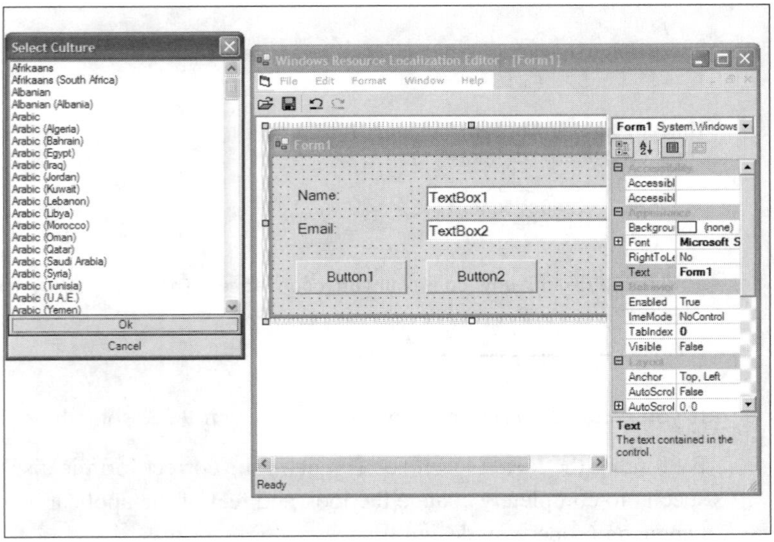

FIGURE 15.14

The WinRes tool in action.

The second method for separating out the locale-specific data from the user interface is to add an assembly resource file to your project. You can do this through the standard Add New Item dialog, as Figure 15.15 demonstrates.

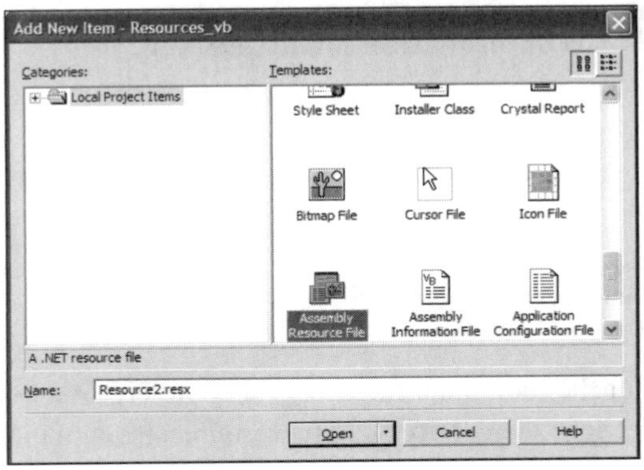

FIGURE 15.15
Adding a resource assembly file to your application.

A resource assembly file is an-XML based file that contains the same information that's tracked automatically by the Windows Forms Designer when `Localizable` is set to `True`. The only drawback is that you're entering the data into the XML file manually, and then writing all the code using the `ResourceManager` class's `GetString` and `GetObject` methods to display the correct data based on the locale. This is a flexible alternative, but of the three approaches to globalizing an application, it's by far the most tedious.

Summary

Today you learned how to make your applications global. By using a combination of the `CultureInfo` class of the `System.Globalization` namespace and the Visual Studio .NET IDE, you can very easily create world-class globalized applications.

If you need to work in teams, using only the Visual Studio .NET IDE might not be the best alternative. Using a tool such as WinRes enables you to spread the creation of locale-specific resource files to other developers.

The goal is to write language- and culture-neutral applications, and using the tools provided by Visual Studio .NET makes this possible.

Q&A

Q Is it possible to have multiple forms with multiple locales running in the same Windows Forms application?

A Yes, that's 100% possible. Because the running thread defines the `CurrentUICulture`, you can create a new thread in your application to display another locale. The following pseudo-code does just that:

```
Sub Main()
   Dim t1 as new Thread(AddressOf DoLocale1)
   Dim t2 as new Thread(AddressOf DoLocale2)
End Sub

Sub DoLocale1()
   t1.CurrentUICulture = New CultureInfo(ìes-ESî)
End Sub

Sub DoLocale2()
   t2.CurrentUICulture = New CultureInfo(ìtt-RUî)
End Sub
```

In the code for the individual threads, you could create a new `ResourceManager` instance to retrieve the culture specific resources from the XML-based resource assembly file.

Q This stuff seems easy enough. Is there anything you aren't telling me?

A Not really. The only thing left to study is how to write language-neutral code for things such as sorting and string comparisons. Each language is very different in those respects. If you need to do only a basic display of data, and make sure that the formatting is correct, you can use today's lesson chapter as your tutor. If your needs are greater than that, the Framework SDK has a huge amount of information about globalization.

If you do a search for globalization or `CultureInfo` or `System.Globalization`, you'll find everything that you'll ever need to know about globalization in .NET.

Quiz

1. The ____________________ enumeration contains the information I need to get the culture information installed on my computer.
2. The _____________ locale is always a fallback resource if I can't get the correct locale on a machine.
3. What are the properties that will get me the correct month and day names for a specific locale?

Quiz Answers

1. `CultureType`
2. Default. This is the locale set in the Control Panel's Regional and Language options applet.
3. The `DateTimeFormat.MonthNames` and the `DateTimeFormat.DayNames` methods of the `CultureInfo` class returns arrays of the correct days and months for a specific culture.

Exercises

1. Expanding on the Resources application you created earlier, add two more languages to the form by selecting different culture names from the `Language` property drop-down list.

   Notice the `.resx` files added to your solution, and the additional directories and assemblies added to your `Bin` directory.
2. Look up WinRes in the .NET Framework SDK help file.

   Attempt to open the `form1.resx` file from the Resources application in the WinRes tool. After modifying the form in the designer, save the `.resx` file to a locale that you haven't used yet. Then modify the code in the form to use the culture you just saved in the WinRes tool.

WEEK 3

DAY 16

Using Macros in Visual Studio .NET

As you have learned in the previous two weeks, Visual Studio .NET offers you a huge leap forward in productivity gains compared to other development environments. Today we focus on automating common tasks that you do every day. If you're a power user, you might have experience in creating macros using Microsoft Office. The same power and flexibility that Office gives you to create macros is available in Visual Studio .NET to help get your work done quicker. Today, you learn

- The different models Visual Studio .NET gives you to increase productivity
- How to use the Macro Explorer
- How to use the Macros IDE
- How to record macros
- How to write your own macros

Introducing Extensibility

Extensibility is the concept of extending your existing environment to do things that are otherwise not there. For example, the Tools menu in Visual Studio .NET has a list of external applications that can be accessed from the integrated development environment (IDE). You can also add your own external tools to the Tools menu. This gives you greater flexibility in getting your hands on what you need faster. Using the automation model built into Visual Studio .NET, you can extend the IDE with internal tools and windows without ever leaving the environment you're working in.

Visual Studio .NET has a complete automation object model that makes all of this possible. Depending on the task, you might want to create a macro, create an add-in, or utilize the Visual Studio Integrator Program (VSIP).

Today we focus on macros, and tomorrow you learn about add-ins. But before we get into the world of macros, it's important to understand the three different automation options, and why you would or would not use them for your automation needs.

Macros

Macros are the least flexible of the extensibility objects that you can use in Visual Studio .NET. That isn't a bad thing at all; in fact, I think it's great. Because macros offer the most basic capability to repeat common tasks, they're super easy to start using without a learning curve. When I say *least flexible*, I mean that you can't do certain things with macros—that's why add-ins exist. When you create a macro, you record your keystrokes and mouse clicks for a common task that you want to automate. After the recording is completed, you save the macro, and either add it to a toolbar or create a shortcut key for it, and you simply run the macro to complete the same task that you recorded. I can think of about 1,000 great candidates for macros, and you'll learn about some of them throughout the day.

Add-ins and Wizards

Add-ins are applications that are compiled and become part of the IDE. You can create an add-in with any component object model (COM) compatible language, such as Visual Basic .NET or C#. Because add-ins are COM objects, they must be registered in Windows before you can access them through Visual Studio .NET.

Add-ins are used to extend the functionality of the IDE itself. An add-in might or might not have an interface or a menu location. You can access add-ins in Visual Studio .NET by selecting the Add-in Manager from the Tools menu. After an add-in is registered on the local machine, it shows up in the Add-in Manager dialog box. One add-in, the Web hosting provider upload utility, is included in Visual Studio .NET. As you might be able to ascertain from its name, this add-in automates the process of uploading your Web project to your Web host of choice. You should consider using add-ins when you need to create advanced functionality within the IDE. You can also use add-ins to create custom property pages for Visual Studio .NET Tools, Options dialog box, to create tool windows like the toolbox, and to dynamically enable and disable menu commands in the IDE.

Wizards are similar to add-ins. Because wizards have been available in every Microsoft product since Office 2.0, you're most likely familiar with what they can do. A wizard provides a set of steps, some of which might be optional, to lead a user through a complicated task. Tomorrow, you learn about add-ins and their project template in Visual Studio .NET, which is actually called the Add-In Wizard!

The Visual Studio Integrator Program

The Visual Studio Integrator Program goes beyond macros and add-ins. VSIP enables third parties to integrate special features directly into Visual Studio .NET. When independent software vendors (ISVs) and corporate developers want to participate, they fill out a form on Microsoft's Web site, which is submitted to Summit Software. Microsoft then grants a license to the approved vendor. When approved, you receive the necessary tools to participate in the VSIP. Using this software development kit (SDK), you can develop your own custom code editors, design surfaces, new project types, and advanced debuggers. A good example of a VSIP is Great Plains Software, the accounting software arm of Microsoft. Great Plains has a custom IDE that enables you to extend its software using Visual Studio.

Now that we've taken a brief look at the various automation offerings in Visual Studio .NET, you can learn how to extend the IDE using macros.

Introducing Macros in Visual Studio .NET

Macros are typically made up of multiple simple tasks that you need to do repetitively. Macros are written in Visual Basic .NET and have their own development environment, called the Macros IDE. In Visual Studio .NET, macros are referred to as *VSMacros*.

Developing macros also provides an excellent way to learn the Visual Studio .NET automation model, which you can then use to develop more complex automation tasks such as add-ins. Macros can be as simple or complex as you want them to be. As you learn more about macros, you'll see that some things aren't possible—which is when you must convert your macro to an add-in.

To create macros, the Visual Studio .NET IDE provides you with a macro recorder and the Macros IDE. You use the macro recorder to record the task that you're doing, and you can edit or debug the code generated from the macro in the Macros IDE. For most macros, you won't need to use the Macros IDE at all, but it's there to give you the ability to extend what the recorder has done using the extensibility model in Visual Studio .NET. You can also create macros from scratch using the Macros IDE. After today, you'll realize how simple it is to write macros, and you might split your time between recording a basic macro with the recorder and sprucing it up in the Macros IDE.

When you record a macro, the recorder watches which windows you work in and what tasks you're doing in those windows, and makes a "tape" of your actions. When you finish recording, you can give the macro a friendly name and it's forever added to the Macro Explorer, which provides the same functionality for macros that the Solution Explorer provides for Visual Studio .NET solutions.

Using the Macro Explorer

To become familiar with the Macros environment, create a new Windows Forms application and name it LearnMacros_vb or LearnMacros_cs, depending on your language. Macros in Visual Studio .NET only understand Visual Basic .NET, so the actual macro code that you create and examine today is in Visual Basic .NET. You can still use macros with any project template and any language in Visual Studio .NET.

The Macro Explorer is your window for managing macros in Visual Studio .NET. To open the Macros Explorer, you can press the Alt+F8 key combination, or select Other Windows, Macro Explorer from the View menu. From the Macro Explorer, you can

- View, edit, and run your macros
- View, edit, and run the macro samples that come with Visual Studio .NET
- Create new macro projects
- Load or unload macro projects

Figure 16.1 shows the Macro Explorer with the MyMacros default project and the Samples project that comes with Visual Studio .NET expanded.

To record macros and perform other macro management, you can access the Macro options by selecting the Tools, Macros menu as shown in Figure 16.2.

To get an idea of what the Macro Explorer can do and how to work with macros, you need to record your first macro.

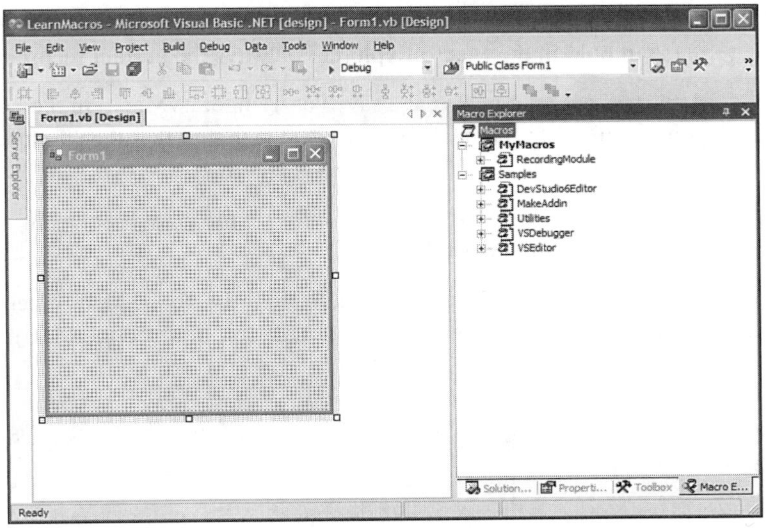

FIGURE 16.1
The Macro Explorer.

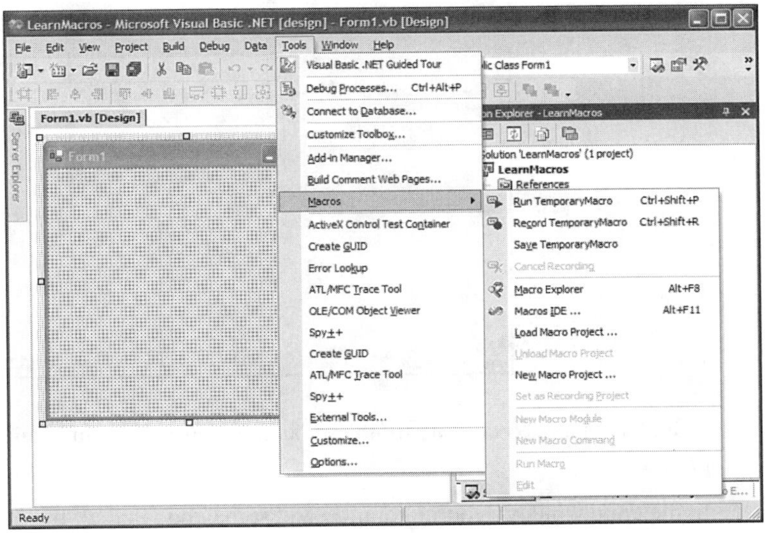

FIGURE 16.2
Use the Tools menu to get to macros options.

Recording a Macro

Each macro is contained within a macro project. You can have one macro or multiple macros in a macro project. When you record a macro, you must set Recording Project in the Macro Explorer. This is done by right-clicking on a macro project name in the Macro

Explorer and selecting Set As Recording Project from the contextual menu. The project name in bold in the Macro Explorer is always the current recording project.

After you record a macro, it's saved as TemporaryMacro in the Macro Explorer. At this point, you must rename the macro to something other then TemporaryMacro or it will be recorded over the next time a macro is recorded.

To record your first macro, double-click on the default `form1` in the Windows Forms Designer to get the Code Editor.

Next, select Record TemporaryMacro from the Tools, Macro menu. At this point, the recording of your new macro has started. You'll notice the Macro Recording toolbar pops up in the IDE, as Figure 16.3 shows.

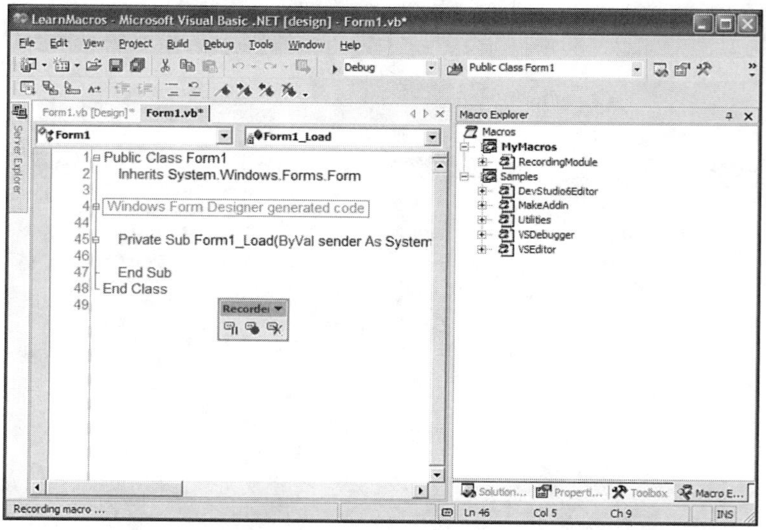

FIGURE 16.3
The Macro Recording toolbar.

From the Macro Recording toolbar, you can pause, stop, and cancel the recording process.

In the code window, you're going to add some code that all methods should have: a `Try/Catch` block for correct error handling. Add the code in Listing 16.1 to the `Form_Load` event of the default `form1`.

LISTING 16.1 Adding the `Try/Catch` Block to the `Form_Load` Event

VB.NET

```
Try
```

LISTING 16.1 continued

```
        Catch ex as Exception

            MessageBox.Show(ex.Message)

        Finally

    End Try
```

C#

```
try
{

}
catch(Exception ex)
{
    MessageBox.Show(ex.Message);
}
```


After you've typed in the code, click the Stop button on the Macro Recording toolbar. The macro has now been recorded and stored as TemporaryMacro in the Current Recording module within the Macro Explorer as shown in Figure 16.4.

FIGURE 16.4

The TemporaryMacro after recording.

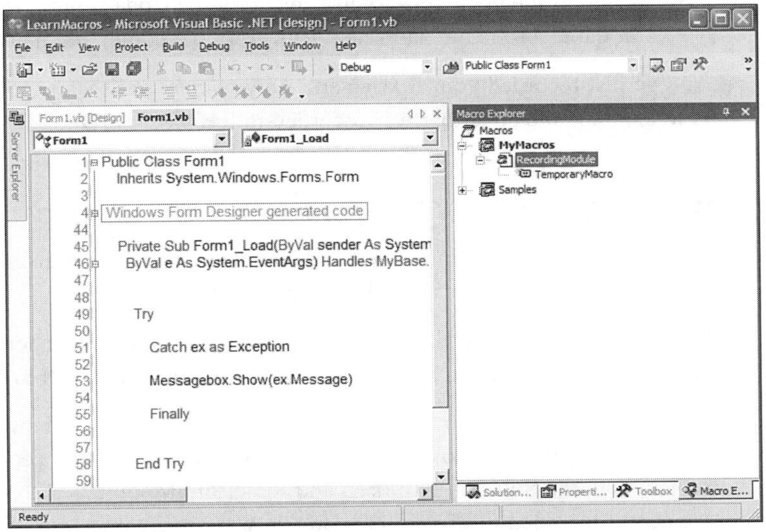

Now that the macro is recorded, you must rename the TemporaryMacro to something meaningful. In the Macro Explorer, right-click on TemporaryMacro and select Rename from the contextual menu. Rename the macro to TryCatchBlock, as Figure 16.5 shows.

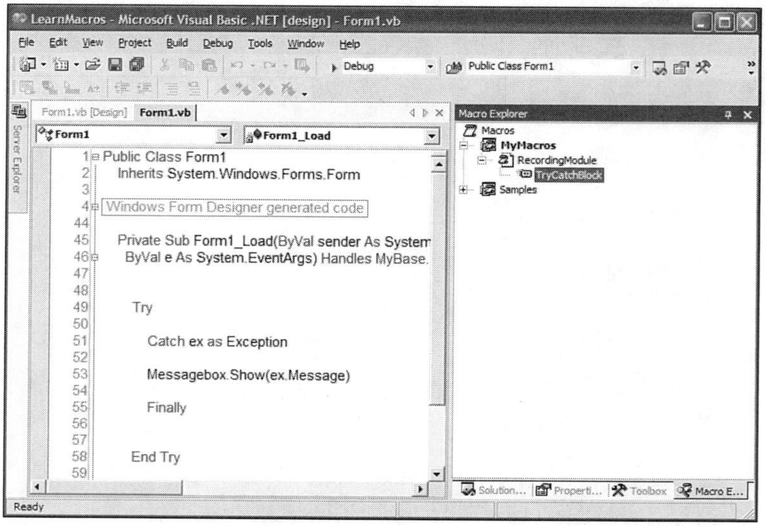

FIGURE 16.5
Renaming TemporaryMacro to TryCatchBlock.

Now you can test your macro.

1. First, delete the `Try/Catch` block code that you just added in the code window.
2. Next, from the Macro Explorer, double-click the TryCatchBlock macro. Now watch as the code appears like magic in the Code Editor. You can also right-click on the macro name and select Run from the contextual menu to run the macro.

You've just recorded your first macro. As you can see, it isn't too difficult. The next step is to examine the code that was recorded in the Macros IDE.

Using the Macros IDE

The Macros IDE is the integrated development environment that Visual Studio .NET uses to manage macro projects and write macro code.

To get to the Macros IDE, right-click on the TryCatchBlock macro in the Macro Explorer and select Edit. You should now be looking at something similar to Figure 16.6.

The Macros IDE is a separate IDE from Visual Studio .NET. However, it shares the same look and feel and has most of the same functionality. You can see that the MyMacros project is in the Solution Explorer, and RecordingModule is the default module name for the newly recorded macros. The code that was generated automatically is shown in Listing 16.2.

.NET IDE. Using the properties, methods, and events of the EnvDTE object, you can create your own macro code or modify the code generated by the macro recorder.

If you look at the References node of a project in the Macros IDE, you'll notice that the following objects are referenced:

- `EnvDTE`
- `Microsoft.Vsa`
- `Office`
- `System`
- `System.Windows.Forms`
- `VSLangProj`
- `VsMacroHierarchyLib`

Most of those objects are COM objects that are also used in other Microsoft applications. You can see that the macro and extensibility that is being used in Visual Studio .NET is giving you some of the same functionality that you have in Office.

When you looked at the code generated for the TryCatchBlock macro, the first item in the module was the `Imports` statement that imported the `EnvDTE` namespace. The `EnvDTE` namespace has the properties, methods, and events that you use to manipulate the Visual Studio .NET IDE. The code that did the actual typing of the `Try/Catch` block was using the `ActiveDocument` property of the `DTE` object. The `DTE` object is the design time environment object of the current Visual Studio .NET IDE. All the objects you work with are under `DTE` in the object hierarchy.

The remaining code in the macro you recorded uses the `DTE.ActiveDocument.Selection` property to retrieve the selected area of the topmost window in the IDE. Using methods such as `LineUp`, `LineDown`, and `Text`, the text that you typed can be repeated by this macro.

You use two classes in the `DTE` object to accomplish most of your macro work: the `Document` object and the `TextSelection` object. Before you get into the objects of the `EnvDTE` object, you must create a new macro project to which you can add the code you write for the rest of today.

Creating a New Macro Project

To create a new macro project, close the Macros IDE and return to the LearnMacro Visual Studio .NET project.

From the Macro Explorer, right-click the topmost node and select New Macro Project, as Figure 16.7 demonstrates.

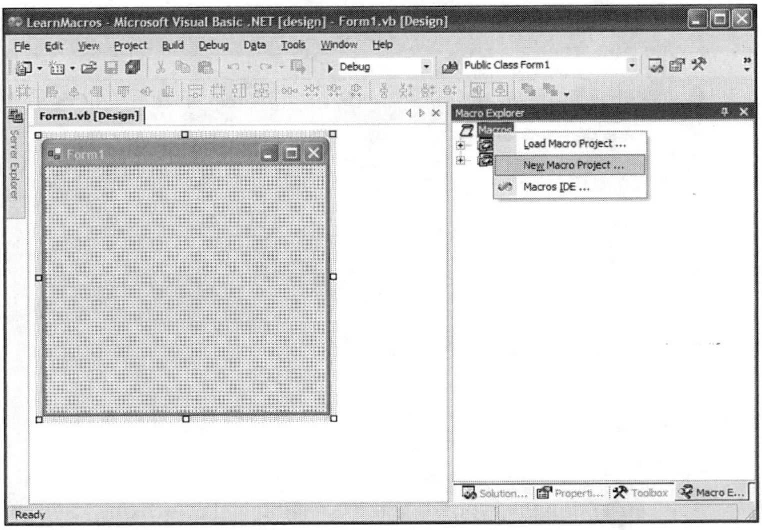

FIGURE 16.7
The New Macro Project menu.

When the New Macro Project pops up, name the new project Utilities as Figure 16.8 shows.

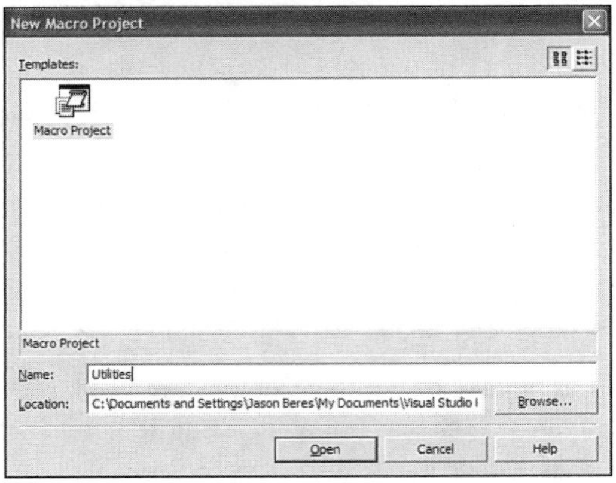

FIGURE 16.8
The Add New Macro Project dialog box.

After the new macro project is added to the Macro Explorer, right-click on the default Module1 in the Utilities project. Select Rename from the contextual menu and rename the module to VSMacros, as shown in Figure 16.9.

Next, right-click the VSMacros module and select Edit. You're now in the Macros IDE, as Figure 16.10 demonstrates.

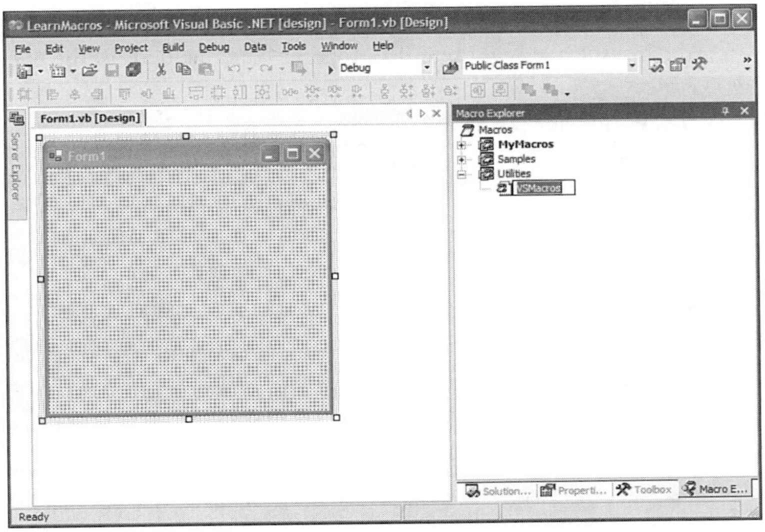

FIGURE 16.9

Renaming the Module1 module to VSMacros.

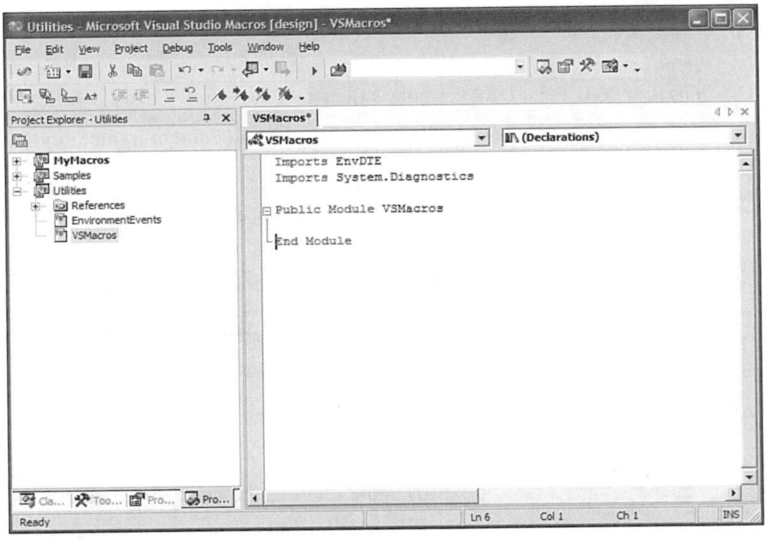

FIGURE 16.10

The Utilities project in the Macros IDE.

In the next section, you're going to learn about the `Document` and `TextSelection` objects and add code to the VSMacros module.

Working with the `Document` Object

When you refer to the `ActiveDocument` in a macro, the `EnvDTE` returns a `Document` object for the `ActiveDocument`. Using the properties, methods, and events of the returned `Document` object enables you to manipulate the IDE.

To get an idea of what the `Document` object gives you, examine Tables 16.1 and 16.2, which respectively present the properties and methods of the `Document` object.

TABLE 16.1 Properties of the `Document` Object

Property	*Description*
`ActiveWindow`	Returns the current active window, or the topmost window if no others are active; returns `Nothing` if no windows are open
`Collection`	Returns the `Documents` collection
`DTE`	Returns the top-level extensibility object
`Extender`	Returns the requested extender object if it's available for this object
`ExtenderCATID`	Returns the extension category ID (CATID) for the object
`ExtenderNames`	Returns a list of available extenders for the object
`FullName`	Returns the full path and filename of a document
`Kind`	Returns a GUID string indicating the kind or type of the object
`Name`	Returns the filename of the object without the path
`Path`	Returns the path, without the filename, for the directory containing the document
`ProjectItem`	Returns the `ProjectItem` object associated with the given object
`ReadOnly`	Returns whether the document in memory can be edited
`Saved`	Returns `True` if the object has been saved since last being changed
`Selection`	Returns the current selection in the active window associated with this document (or the topmost window of the document if none is active)
`Windows`	Returns a `Windows` collection containing the windows that display in the object

TABLE 16.2 Methods of the `Document` Object

Method	*Description*
`Activate`	Moves the focus to the current item and makes it active
`Close`	Closes the open document and optionally saves it
`NewWindow`	Creates a new window in which to view the document
`Object`	Returns an interface or object that can be accessed by name at runtime
`Redo`	Re-executes the last action that was undone by the `Undo` method or the user
`Save`	Saves the document
`SaveAll`	Saves all documents currently open in the environment
`Undo`	Reverses the action last performed by the user in the document

An example of using the `Document` object properties to retrieve information about the document in the active code window is presented in Listing 16.3. Add this code to the VSMacros module as the `GetDocumentInfo` subprocedure.

LISTING 16.3 Using the `ActiveDocument` Property to Retrieve Document Properties

VB.NET

```
Sub GetDocumentInfo()
    If (DTE.ActiveDocument.ReadOnly) Then
        MsgBox("This document is Read Only")
    Else
        MsgBox("This document is Writable")
    End If

    MsgBox("Document name = " & DTE.ActiveDocument.Name)
    MsgBox("Document full name = " & DTE.ActiveDocument.FullName)
    MsgBox("Document path = " & DTE.ActiveDocument.Path)
End Sub
```

Remember that the `ActiveDocument` property actually returns a `Document` object. To modify this to make your coding less wordy, you can create a variable of type `Document` and reference the object using a variable. Listing 16.4 shows the altered code to use the `Document` object. Add the code in Listing 16.4 to your VSMacros module as the `GetDocumentInfo2` subprocedure.

LISTING 16.4 Using the `Document` Object to Retrieve Document Properties

VB.NET

```
Sub GetDocumentInfo2()

    ' Create a Document variable
    Dim doc As Document

    If (doc.ReadOnly) Then
        MsgBox("This document is Read Only")
    Else
        MsgBox("This document is Writable")
    End If

    MsgBox("Document name = " & doc.Name)
    MsgBox("Document full name = " & doc.FullName)
    MsgBox("Document path = " & doc.Path)
End Sub
```

By creating the `Document` variable, you still have the nice features of auto-complete and auto-list members; you just don't have to type in `DTE.ActiveDocument` each time you want to reference the document in the active window.

The `Document` object also is a member of the `Documents` collection. Because Visual Studio .NET enables you to have many windows open, you can write macros that use the `Save` and `Close` methods of the `Document` object while iterating through the `Documents` collection of the `Windows` property of the `Document` object. The code in Listing 16.5 is a useful snippet that saves and closes all the open windows in the IDE. Add the code in Listing 16.5 to your VSMacros module.

LISTING 16.5 Saving and Closing a Document Using the Methods of the `Document` Object

VB.NET

```
Sub CloseAllWindows()

    Dim doc As Document

    For Each doc In DTE.Windows.DTE.Documents
        doc.Save()
        doc.Close()
    Next

End Sub
```

By iterating through the `Documents` collection, you can use the `Save` and `Close` methods to take care of your open windows. This is cool because as your projects become larger, you have a bunch of tabs across the top of your designer. When you close a project, the state of the open windows is remembered for the next time you open the project. By closing all the windows, the project will have no windows open the next time you start it, which makes the startup time shorter.

The `Documents` collection also has a few methods that alleviate having to use the `Save` and `Close` methods on each open document. Table 16.3 lists the methods of the `Documents` collection.

TABLE 16.3 Methods of the `Documents` Collection

Method	*Description*
`CloseAll`	Closes all open documents in the environment and optionally saves them
`Item`	Returns an indexed member of a collection
`SaveAll`	Saves all documents currently open in the environment

Working with the `TextSelection` Object

The `TextSelection` object is the second most useful object when working with macros and the IDE. The `TextSelection` object directly reflects editor commands in the Visual Studio .NET IDE.

Table 16.4 lists the properties of the `TextSelection` object and Table 16.5 lists its methods.

TABLE 16.4 Properties of the `TextSelection` Object

Property	*Description*
`ActivePoint`	Returns the current endpoint of the selection
`AnchorPoint`	Returns the origin point of the selection
`BottomPoint`	Returns the point at the end of the selection
`DTE`	Returns the top-level extensibility object
`IsActiveEndGreater`	Indicates whether the active point is equal to the bottom point
`IsEmpty`	Indicates whether the anchor point is equal to the active point
`Mode`	Sets or returns a value determining whether dragging the mouse selects in stream mode or block mode
`Parent`	Returns the parent object; in this case, the `TextDocument` object
`Text`	Returns the selected text
`TextPane`	Returns the text pane that contains the selection
`TextRanges`	Returns a `TextRanges` collection with one `TextRange` object for each line or partial line in the selection
`TopPoint`	Returns the top end of the selection

TABLE 16.5 Methods of the `TextSelection` Object

Method	*Description*
`ChangeCase`	Changes the case of the selected text.
`CharLeft`	Moves the object the specified number of characters to the left.
`CharRight`	Moves the object the specified number of characters to the right. The default is one character.
`ClearBookmark`	Clears any unnamed bookmarks on the current line.
`Collapse`	Collapses the selection to the active point.
`Copy`	Copies the selection to the clipboard.
`Cut`	Copies the selected text to the clipboard and deletes it from its original location.

TABLE 16.5 continued

Method	*Description*
`Delete`	Deletes the selected text.
`DeleteLeft`	Deletes a specified number of characters to the left of the active point.
`DeleteWhitespace`	Deletes white space horizontally or vertically around the current location.
`DestructiveInsert`	Inserts text that overwrites the existing text.
`EndOfDocument`	Moves the object to the end of the document.
`EndOfLine`	Moves the object to the end of the current line.
`FindPattern`	Searches for the given pattern from the active point to the end of the document.
`FindText`	Searches for the given text from the active point to the end of the document.
`GoToLine`	Moves to the beginning of the indicated line and selects the line if requested.
`Indent`	Indents the selected lines by the given number of indentation levels.
`Insert`	Inserts the given string at the specified location.
`InsertFromFile`	Inserts the contents of the specified file at the current location.
`LineDown`	Moves the selected line down a specified number of lines.
`LineUp`	Moves the selected line up a specified number of lines.
`MoveToAbsoluteOffset`	Moves the active point to the given 1-based absolute character offset.
`MoveToDisplayColumn`	Moves the active point to the indicated display column.
`MoveToLineAndOffset`	Moves the active point to the given position.
`MoveToPoint`	Moves the active point to the given position.
`NewLine`	Inserts a line break at the active point.
`NextBookmark`	Moves to the location of the next bookmark in the document.
`OutlineSection`	Creates an outlining section based on the current selection.
`PadToColumn`	Fills the current line with white space to the given column.
`PageDown`	Moves the active point a specified number of pages down in the document, scrolling the view.
`PageUp`	Moves the active point a specified number of pages up in the document, scrolling the view.
`Paste`	Inserts the clipboard contents at the current location.
`PreviousBookmark`	Moves to the location of the previous bookmark in the document.
`ReplacePattern`	Searches for the given pattern in the selection and replaces it with new text.

TABLE 16.5 continued

Method	*Description*
`ReplaceText`	Searches for the given pattern in the selection and replaces it with new text.
`SelectAll`	Selects the document.
`SelectLine`	Selects the line containing the active point.
`SetBookmark`	Sets an unnamed bookmark on the current line.
`SmartFormat`	Formats the indicated line of text based on the current language.
`StartOfDocument`	Moves the object to the beginning of the document.
`StartOfLine`	Moves the object to the beginning of the current line.
`SwapAnchor`	Exchanges the positions of the active point and the anchor point.
`Tabify`	Converts spaces to tabs in the selection according to your tab settings.
`UnIndent`	Removes indents from the selected text by the number of indentation levels given.
`Untabify`	Converts tabs to spaces in the selection according to the user's tab settings.
`WordLeft`	Moves the object the specified number of words to the left.
`WordRight`	Moves the object the specified number of words to the right. The default is one word.

Using the `TextSelection` object, you can modify the TryCatchBlock macro you created earlier. Listing 16.6 shows how to use the `TextSelection` object to create a better `Try/Catch` macro. Add the code in Listing 16.6 to your VSMacros module.

LISTING 16.6 Adding the `Try/Catch` Block with Streamlined Code to the VSMacros Module

VB.NET

```
Sub TryCatchBlock_vb()

    Dim txt As TextSelection = _
        DTE.ActiveDocument.Selection
    With txt
        .Text = "Try"
        .NewLine(3)
        .Text = "Catch ex as Exception"
        .NewLine(2)
        .Text = "Finally"
        .NewLine(2)
```

LISTING 16.6 continued

```
        .LineUp(False, 7)
    End With

End Sub
```

C#

```
Sub TryCatchBlock_cs()

    Dim txt As TextSelection = _
        DTE.ActiveDocument.Selection

    With txt
        txt.Text = "try"
        .NewLine()
        .Text = "{"
        .NewLine(2)
        .Text = "}"
        .NewLine()
        .Text = "catch (System.Exception ex)"
        .NewLine()
        .Text = "{"
        .NewLine(2)
        .Text = "}"
        .LineUp(False, 5)
    End With

End Sub
```

In Listing 16.6, you're creating a `TextSelection` variable based on the `ActiveDocument.Selection` property. Then, using straightforward Visual Basic .NET code, you're doing exactly what the Macro Recorder did earlier. You can see that the code you write is much cleaner than what the Macro Recorder generates. They both accomplish the same thing though: They add a `Try/Catch` block to your code window without you having to do it manually!

To test the code, select Close and Return from the File menu. You're now back at the Visual Studio .NET IDE, and you can double-click on your macros to test them. Your Macro Explorer should look like Figure 16.11 at this point.

The next step is to make your macros more accessible by creating a toolbar for them.

FIGURE 16.11

The Macro Explorer with the Utilities project.

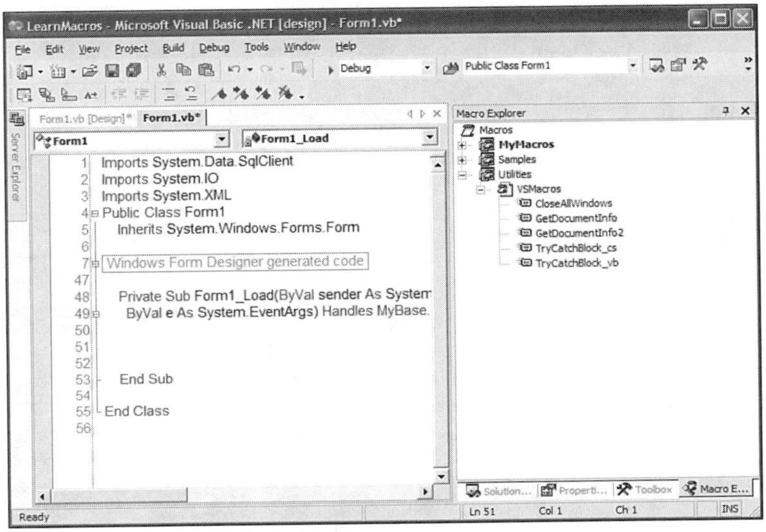

Creating a Macros Toolbar

Creating a toolbar for macros in Visual Studio .NET is exactly like creating a macros toolbar in an Office application.

The first step is to right-click on the Visual Studio .NET toolbar area to get the list of available toolbars. Then select Customize, as Figure 16.12 demonstrates.

FIGURE 16.12

The Toolbars menu.

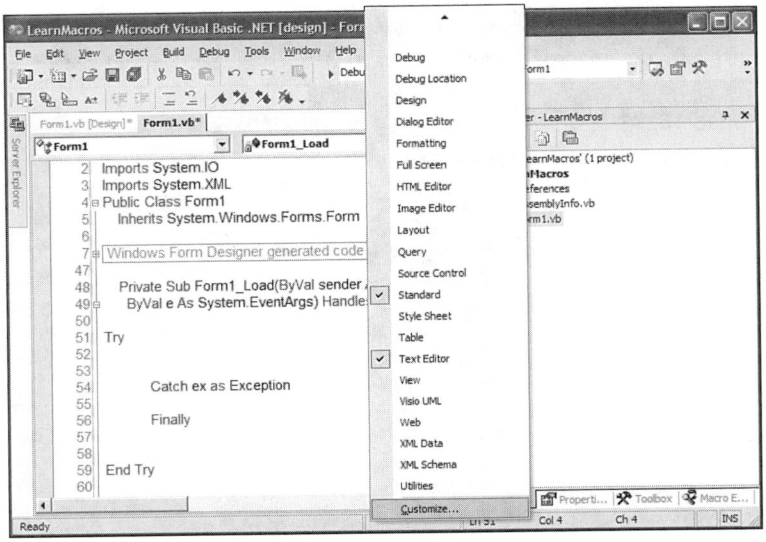

After you click Customize, the Customize dialog pops up. Click the New button, and type **`Utilities`** in the input box, as Figure 16.13 shows.

FIGURE 16.13

Adding the Utilities toolbar.

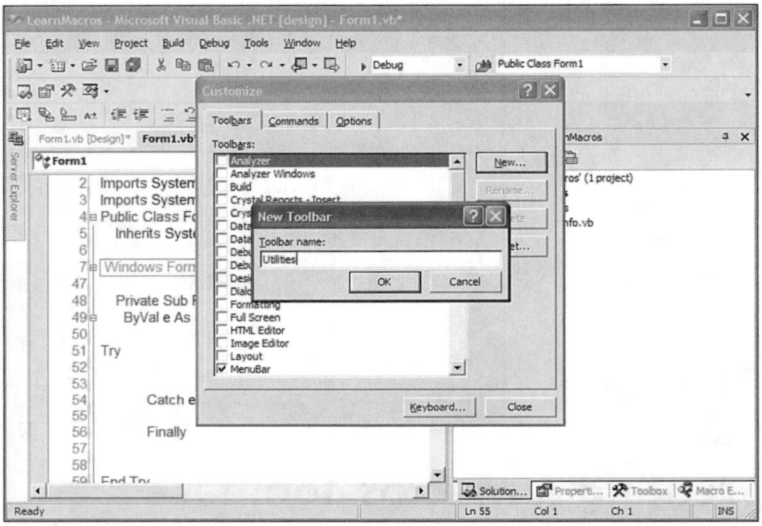

After you add the new toolbar, you'll see an empty toolbar next to the dialog box. Click the Commands tab on the Customize dialog. On the left Categories pane, scroll down until you see Macros. Select Macros, and you'll see the Macro projects listed in the Commands list box.

Scroll down in the Commands list box until you see the Utilities.VSMacros project that all your macros are in. Figure 16.14 is what you should see on your screen.

FIGURE 16.14

Finding the Utilities.VSMacros commands.

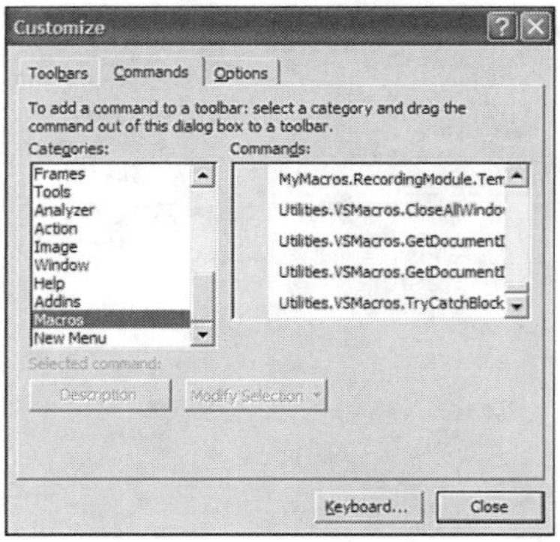

When you see the commands, drag the items to the new toolbar as shown in Figure 16.15.

FIGURE 16.15

Adding commands to the new Utilities toolbar.

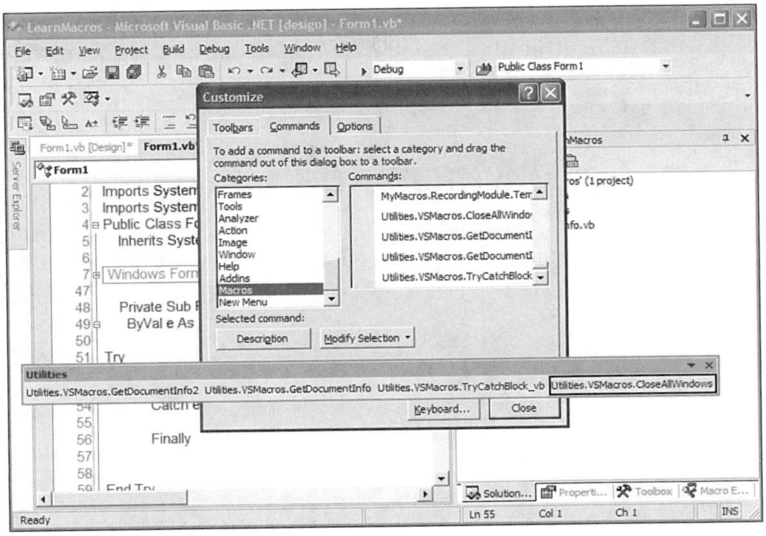

Because the descriptions are too long to be logical, you can right-click each item in the toolbar, and change its name to something less wordy. Notice that you can also add an icon to your toolbar item using the contextual menu.

Figure 16.16 shows my completed toolbar with an icon on the GetDocumentInfo2 macro, as well as the automatic tooltip that's provided by the IDE.

FIGURE 16.16

The completed Macro toolbar in action.

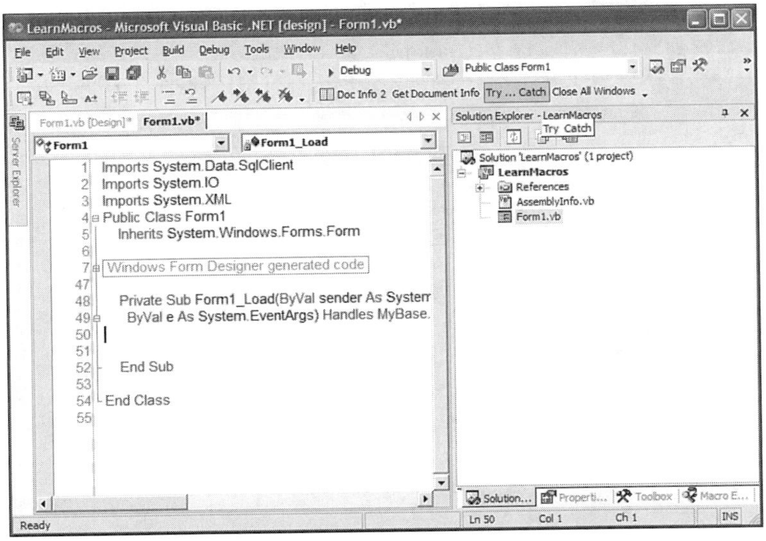

So, your work has come full circle: You created a macro using the recorder, rewrote it using the objects in the DTE class, and finally you created a toolbar to access your macros faster than going to the Macro Explorer.

More Cool Macro Ideas

To keep your excitement about macros going, I want to give you some ideas for moving forward with them, and show you a few more code snippets to test in your VSMacros module. Because you created a `Try...Catch` block, you could create macros for

- `If...Then...Else` blocks
- `For...Next` loops
- Variable declarations
- `While` Loops

Adding an `Imports` or `Using` Statement

Almost all classes I write use the `System.Data.SqlClient` namespace, and maybe the `System.IO` namespace or `System.XML` namespace. To add text to the top of your file, you can use the `StartOfDocument` method, as in Listing 16.7.

LISTING 16.7 Adding `Imports/Using` Statements to Class Files

VB.NET

```
Sub StartOfDocumentExample()
    Dim txt As TextSelection = DTE.ActiveDocument.Selection

    With txt
        .StartOfDocument()
        .Text = "Imports System.Data.SqlClient" & vbCrLf
        .Text = "Imports System.IO" & vbCrLf
        .Text = "Imports System.XML" & vbCrLf
    End With
End Sub
```

C#

```
Sub StartOfDocumentExample()
    Dim txt As TextSelection = DTE.ActiveDocument.Selection
    With txt
        .StartOfDocument()
        .Text = "using System.Data.SqlClient;" & vbCrLf
```

LISTING 16.7 continued

```
        .Text = "using System.IO;" & vbCrLf
        .Text = "using System.XML;" & vbCrLf
    End With
End Sub
```

When you run this macro, the correct code is added to the top of your class file.

Working with the Task List

You can add new task items to the Task List in Visual Studio .NET using the `TaskItems` object. The code in Listing 16.8 will prompt you for a task, and then add it to the Task List. This is a very cool macro, and it might give you more ideas about how to use the Task List.

LISTING 16.8 Automating the Addition of Task Window Items

VB.NET

```
Sub AddNewTask()
    Dim win As Window = DTE.Windows.Item _
            (Constants.vsWindowKindTaskList)
    Dim TL As TaskList = win.Object
    Dim TLItem As TaskItem


    Dim strTask As String
    strTask = InputBox("Please enter the Task")

    If strTask.Trim.Length > 0 Then
        ' Add a task to the Task List.
        TLItem = TL.TaskItems.Add(" ", " ", strTask, _
            vsTaskPriority.vsTaskPriorityHigh, _
            vsTaskIcon.vsTaskIconUser, True, , 10, , )
    End If
End Sub
```

Notice that the code in Listing 16.8 also uses the `InputBox` function to prompt you for the description of the task. Using the `InputBox` function enables you to retrieve information from the user to use in your code.

This is also useful for prompting the user for iterations, variable scope, or other items that you might want to write macros for.

Creating a Code Library

Creating a code library is a great idea to preserve all the great work you do everyday. Using macros, you can save the code you write to a SQL Server table.

The macro in Listing 16.9 copies the selected text in the Code Editor, prompts you for a description, and then inserts the text into a database. You must add a reference to the `System.Data` assembly in the References node of the Macros project for this to work. Then add the `Imports System.Data` and `System.Data.SqlClient` at the top of the VSMacros module.

LISTING 16.9 Writing Code Snippets to SQL Server

VB.NET

```
Sub AddToCodeLibrary()

    Dim code As String
    Dim txt As TextSelection = DTE.ActiveDocument.Selection

    code = txt.Text
    Dim cn As SqlConnection = _
     New SqlConnection _

     ("Integrated Security=SSPI;database=Utilities;server=jb1gs\netsdk")


    cn.Open()

    Dim cmd As New SqlCommand()
    cmd.CommandType = CommandType.StoredProcedure

    Dim desc As String
    desc = InputBox("Enter a description for this code snippet")

    With cmd
        .Connection = cn
        .CommandText = "insert_CodeSnippets"
        .Parameters.Add("@code_1", _
           SqlDbType.VarChar, 5000).Value = code
        .Parameters.Add("@description_2", _
           SqlDbType.VarChar, 100).Value = desc
        .ExecuteNonQuery()
    End With

    MsgBox("Code added to the database")
```

LISTING 16.9 continued

```
        cn.Close()
        cn = Nothing

    End Sub
```

I created a database named Utilities and a table named Code to hold all of my data. The SQL script for the table and stored procedure are given in Listing 16.10.

LISTING 16.10 SQL Script for Adding a Utilities Table to SQL Server

```
CREATE TABLE [dbo].[CodeSnippets] (
        [ID] [int] IDENTITY (1, 1) NOT NULL ,
        [Code] [varchar] (5000) COLLATE SQL_Latin1_General_CP1_CI_AS
                                ➥NOT NULL ,
        [Description] [varchar] (100) COLLATE SQL_Latin1_General_CP1_CI_AS
                                      ➥NOT NULL ,
        [DateAdded] [datetime] NOT NULL
) ON [PRIMARY]
GO


CREATE PROCEDURE [insert_CodeSnippets]
        (@Code_1          [varchar](5000),
         @Description_2          [varchar](100))

AS INSERT INTO [Utilities].[dbo].[CodeSnippets]
         ( [Code],
           [Description])

VALUES
        ( @Code_1,
          @Description_2)
GO
```

Now you can start saving your code to a SQL Server database and keep it forever. Tomorrow, you're going to learn how to grab the code you saved to the database and create a tab for it in the Toolbox—then the code will be there for you to drag into the code window when you need it.

Summary

Today you learned how macros can automate repetitive tasks and extend the built-in functionality of the IDE. Using the macro recorder, you can get a good idea of how the extensibility objects work. After you're familiar with the syntax of the different objects, you can use the Macros IDE to further customize the macros that you write.

Q&A

Q I tried to record a macro that added a task item, but nothing was recorded. Why?

A The macro recorder can record only certain events in the IDE. Some items, such as the Task List, are not available.

Q Where can I get more information about macros?

A The Visual Studio .NET SDK has a section on macros, but it's very brief. Do a search in the SDK for DTE, and you'll find all the goodies that pertain to the extensibility objects and macros.

Quiz

1. The _________ namespace gives you access to the properties, methods, and events of the Visual Studio .NET IDE.
2. The ______________ is the central repository for all macro projects.
3. True or False: C# can be used to write macros, but Visual Basic .NET just works better in the Macros IDE.

Quiz Answers

1. `EnvDTE`
2. Macro Explorer
3. False. You can't use C# in the Macros IDE.

Exercise

To learn more about macros, test all the macros that are included in the Samples node of the Macro Explorer. Microsoft has supplied about 50 sample macros that an excellent learning tools (and they also do some pretty cool things).

WEEK 3

DAY 17

Automating Visual Studio .NET

Yesterday you learned about the extensibility options in Visual Studio .NET. By creating macros, you interacted with the integrated development environment (IDE) and you learned how to manipulate the text editor. Today, you take the next step in Visual Studio .NET automation and learn how to create add-ins. Add-ins are like macros in that they extend what you can do with the IDE. But when you use add-ins, you have access to more objects that you can use to control the environment. Today, you learn

- What add-ins are
- How to use the Add-Ins Project Wizard
- How to use forms in add-ins
- How to interact with the Toolbox through automation

Introducing Add-ins

Yesterday, when you created your first macro, you learned how to interact with the IDE using the objects in the `EnvDTE` namespace. All the code you wrote was in Visual Basic .NET, and the overall access you had to objects in the Visual Studio .NET IDE through the automation objects was limited. For example, using the macro recorder, you couldn't automate adding a task to the Task List. You could, however, add a task directory by accessing the `TaskItems` object. Using add-ins, you can write code in C# or Visual Basic .NET, and you have complete control over all objects in the Visual Studio .NET automation namespaces.

Add-ins are applications in their own right. The only difference between an add-in and a standalone application is that an add-in is hooked into the Visual Studio .NET IDE. By creating an add-in, you literally have complete programmatic control over whatever you want to do inside the Visual Studio .NET IDE. Compiled as COM applications, add-ins use the `IDTExtensibilty2` interface, which is part of the `EnvDTE` namespace. The automation model gives you programmatic access to the following groups of items:

- Project solution wizards
- All items available in the Add New Item dialog in Visual Studio .NET
- All Code Editor objects and designer objects
- The Toolbox, its tabs, and the items in Toolbox tabs
- All windows in Visual Studio .NET that are accessible from the View, Other Windows menu items, including the Output window, all debugging windows, and all Find and Search windows
- All debugging objects
- All events that take place in Visual Studio .NET, such as closing and opening of forms, classes, and designers

That means the sky's the limit when creating an add-in. As with macros, the idea is to use add-ins to extend the IDE in ways that help you become more productive.

To use an add-in, it must be registered with the component object model (COM). That means an add-in must be installed on the computers that are to use it. You can't XCopy deploy an add-in. If you did, you'd have to manually register the add-in with the Windows Registry. A cool feature in Visual Studio .NET is that the Add-ins Project Wizard creates a Windows Installer file for you when you create an add-in project, so you can create your installation package simply by building the add-in.

When an add-in is installed, it can be accessed from the Tools, Add-in Manager menu item. When you select the Add-in Manager menu item, the Add-in Manager dialog pops up, as Figure 17.1 demonstrates.

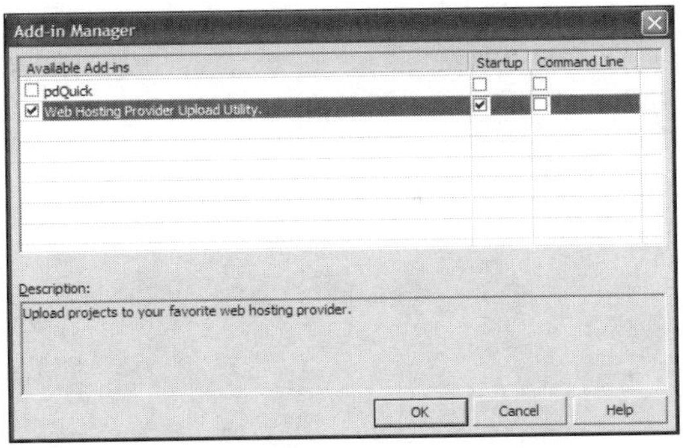

FIGURE 17.1
The Add-In Manager in Visual Studio .NET.

You can see in Figure 17.1, the Web Hosting Provider Upload Utility is selected and is set to load when Visual Studio .NET starts. The Web Hosting Provider Upload Utility is an add-in that's installed with Visual Studio .NET and extends the IDE by helping you upload ASP.NET applications to your Web hosting service. The other add-in in the list is called pdQuick—I downloaded it from the Web. I thought it was really cool because it added a `Try/Catch` block to my code. After I realized how easy it is to do that with a macro, I decided to write my own. Based on what you learned yesterday, you can do the same thing on your own, too! After an add-in is installed, you can uninstall it through Add/Remove Programs in the Control Panel.

To get an understanding of what you can do with add-ins, you're going to create a simple add-in that interacts with the IDE. When that's done, you'll create an add-in that expands on the code snippet macro that you wrote yesterday.

Creating Your First Add-in

To create your first add-in, open Visual Studio .NET and click the New Project button on the Start Page. In the Project Types dialog, expand the Other Projects node and then select the Extensibility Projects node. In the Templates pane, you'll see the Visual Studio .NET Add-in and the Shared Add-in templates. Select the Visual Studio .NET Add-in template and change its name to FirstAddin_vb or FirstAddin_cs, depending on the language you're writing in, as shown in Figure 17.2.

After you click the OK button, the Add-in Project Wizard dialog pops up. This wizard guides you through setting the default properties for your new add-in. Figure 17.3 shows the Welcome screen for the Add-in Project Wizard.

Click Next to get to step 1 of 6 in the wizard. In this step, you decide on the language in which you want to write the add-in. You can choose Visual Basic .NET, C#, or C++, as Figure 17.4 demonstrates. Select the language you're most comfortable with and click Next.

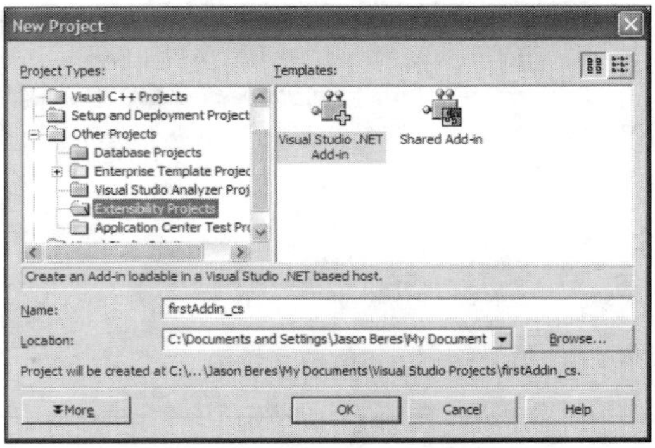

FIGURE 17.2

The Extensibility Projects node in the New Project dialog.

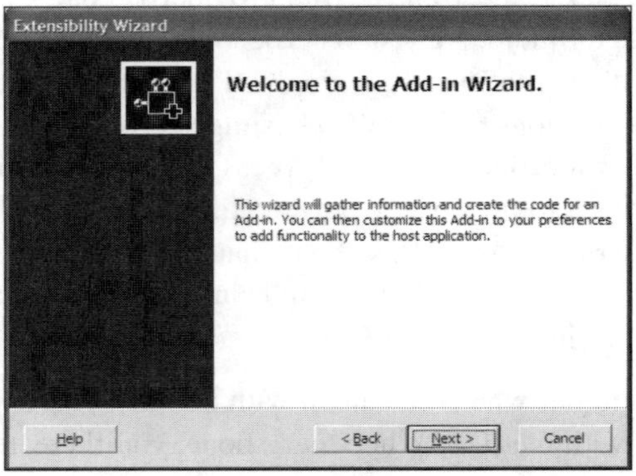

FIGURE 17.3

The Add-in Project Wizard welcome screen.

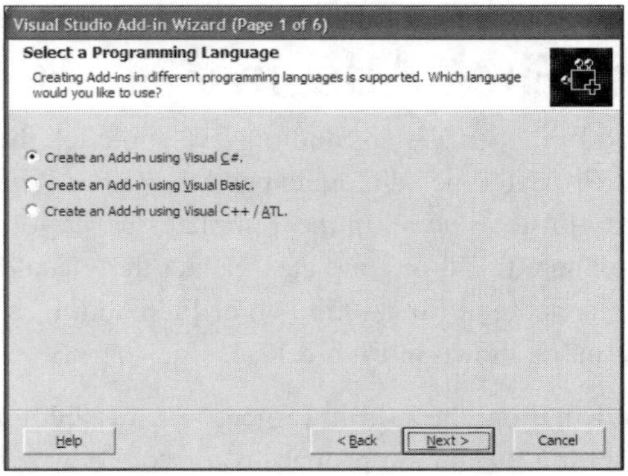

FIGURE 17.4

Choosing the language the add-in will be written in.

In step 2, shown in Figure 17.5, you select the host environment for the add-in: You can choose either the Macros IDE or Visual Studio .NET. Because this add-in won't be needed in the Macros IDE, make sure that Visual Studio .NET is the only option selected.

FIGURE 17.5

Selecting the add-in's host application.

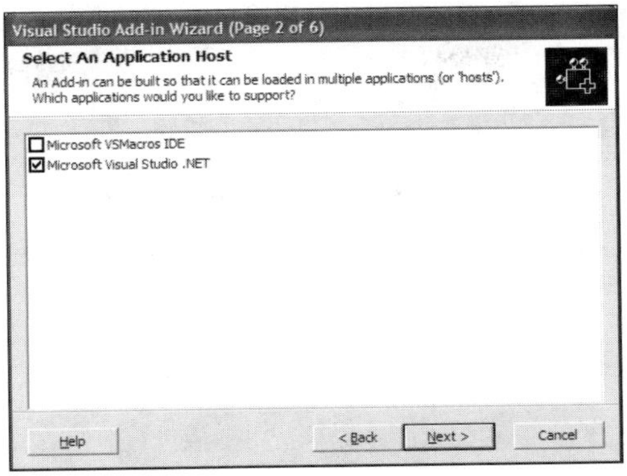

After you click Next to get to step 3 of 6 in the wizard, you're prompted for the name and description of your add-in. Figure 17.6 shows the information I added for my first add-in.

FIGURE 17.6

Entering a name and description for the add-in.

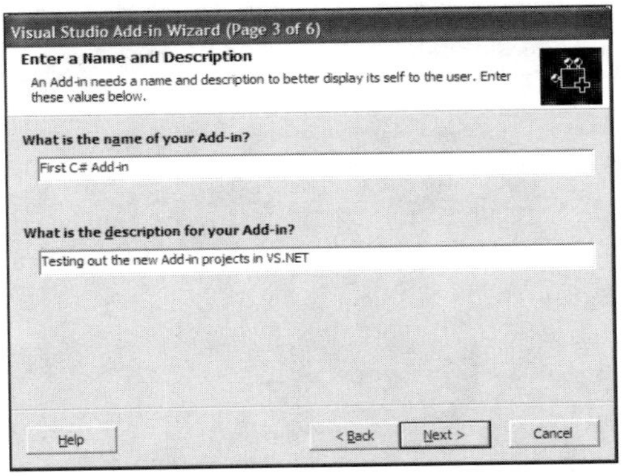

Click Next to get to step 4 of 6 in the wizard. This step has several options that determine how your add-in will be used. If you check the first option, a Tools menu item is automatically created for you when the add-in is installed and running. Make sure that this option is checked. The second group of options dictates how the add-in is used. If the add-in pops up a modal window during a build process, you must uncheck the My Add-in Will Never Put up a Modal IU option. To make your add-in start automatically when Visual Studio .NET starts, you can check the second option. For the purpose of the add-in you're writing here, check this box.

The final option sets the Windows Installer options regarding how the add-in is to be installed. If the add-in is meant for all users of a computer, check this box. For the add-in you're writing today, you can leave this option checked. This option doesn't impact the code you're writing for the add-in. Your add-in options should look like Figure 17.7.

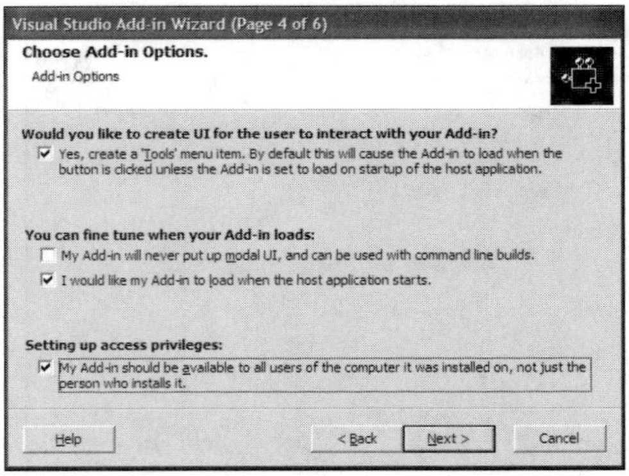

FIGURE 17.7

Setting the add-in options.

After you click Next, you're taken to the Help About information page for the add-in. Check the Yes box, and modify the template information for the Help About dialog that will be generated for your add-in. I changed my information to look like Figure 17.8.

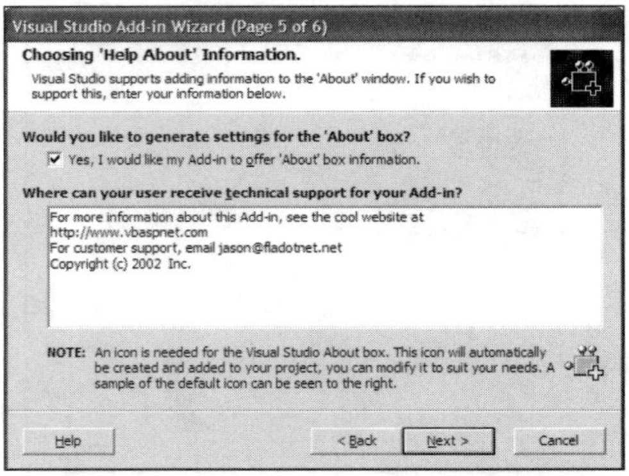

FIGURE 17.8

Adding Help About dialog box information.

Click Next to get to the Summary page of the wizard. This screen, shown in Figure 17.9, gives you a summary of the options you selected while creating the add-in. If there's something you want to change, you can click Back at this point and modify your settings.

When you click the Finish button, the FirstAddin solution is created. Figure 17.10 shows the FirstAddin solution after the Add-in and Windows Installer Deployment projects have been created.

The wizard process creates the plumbing code that's needed to make your add-in function. This includes hooking into the IDE and creating dummy entries for the different events that can occur in the lifetime of the add-in. Let's go through the code that was generated to better understand the capabilities of the add-in.

FIGURE 17.9

Summary page for the Add-in Project Wizard.

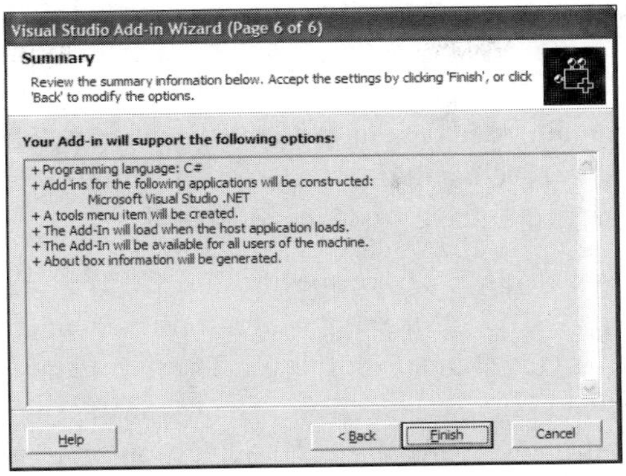

FIGURE 17.10

The FirstAddin solution after running the Add-in Project Wizard.

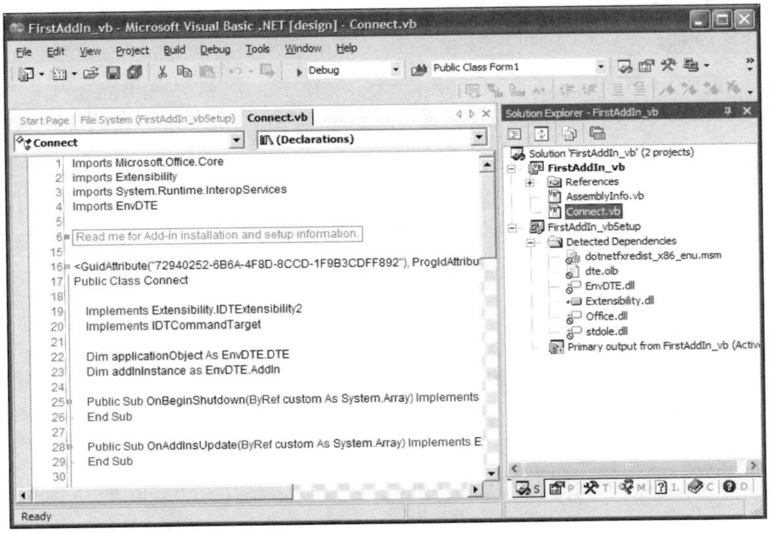

Understanding the Life Cycle of an Add-in

When you create a new add-in, the wizard takes care of writing all the code that connects the add-in to the IDE. If you drill into your Solution Explorer, you'll see the `Connect.vb` or `Connect.cs` class file. This class is responsible for handling the interaction between your code and the instance of the IDE that the add-in is connecting to. Notice the namespaces referenced at the top of the class file:

- `Microsoft.Office.Core`
- `Extensibility`

- `System.Runtime.InteropServices`
- `EnvDTE`

These namespaces are unique to dealing with the extensibility objects in the IDE, and the `InteropServices` namespace handles the interaction with COM at runtime. All the IDE-specific objects are located in the `EnvDTE` namespace.

In the class declaration, `GuidAttribute` specifies the COM globally unique identifier (GUID) for this add-in. Each COM component must have a unique ID in the Registry; that unique ID lives with the component forever. The wizard automatically creates a unique GUID for each add-in that you create. The following snippet shows the GUID and the program ID attribute for the Visual Basic version of my add-in:

```
<GuidAttribute("72940252-6B6A-4F8D-8CCD-1F9B3CDFF892"),
      ProgIdAttribute("FirstAddIn_vb.Connect")> _
Public Class Connect
```

If no GUID exists, the add-in can't be installed into the Registry. When you use the Windows Installer deployment project that the Add-in Project Wizard created as part of this solution, it uses the GUID to register the add-in component with COM.

The `Connect` class itself implements two interfaces: `IDTExtensibility2` and `IDTCommandTarget`. In COM, an interface represents the methods, properties, and events that are exposed to a caller of a COM component. The reason a GUID must exist for a COM component is to maintain the validity of the exposed interfaces. If the interface to a component changes, the GUID must change. An interface might change as the result of a method parameter value or a return value changing. This is one of the reasons COM was such a pain in the neck: It was too difficult to maintain a consistent interface without breaking the functionality of existing components.

By exposing the two aforementioned interfaces, the `Connect` class can directly interact with the events that occur within the IDE. Those events are what make up the life cycle of the add-in. The events that occur are

- `OnConnection`
- `OnStartupComplete`
- `OnAddInsUpdate`
- `QueryStatus`
- `Exec`
- `OnBeginShutdown`
- `OnDisconnection`

Each event has a predefined method that you can write code for in the `Connect` class.

Note

> Each of the methods for the life cycle of an add-in handles its corresponding event that fires in the `Connect` class. When I refer to the `OnConnection` method, I mean that the host application is firing that event and the method in the `Connect` class file is consuming that event.

Understanding the `OnConnection` Method

The `OnConnection` event is fired when the add-in is first loaded. When you used the wizard to create the add-in, you had the option of having the add-in load at the time Visual Studio .NET starts. Enabling that selection fires the `OnConnection` event. The `OnConnection` event also fires when the add-in is loaded through the Add-in Manager dialog and when the `Connect` property of the `Connect` class is set to true. This event sets the object instances that you use in either the `Connect` class itself or that you pass as a parameter to other classes that must use this instance hook. The key object being created in the `OnConnection` event is the `applicationObject` and the `addInInstance` object that you use to work with the IDE. This Visual Basic .NET code snippet is when the objects are actually created:

```
applicationObject = CType(application, EnvDTE.DTE)
addInInstance = CType(addInInst, EnvDTE.AddIn)
```

At this point, the IDE environment is set to an object and you can work with it.

The code in Listing 17.1 is the C# and Visual Basic .NET code that the wizard generates to make the connection into the IDE possible. The comments in the code will give you help on how to make sure that the `OnConnection` event fires.

LISTING 17.1 Wizard-Generated Code for the `OnConnection` Event That Connects Your Add-in to the IDE

VB.NET

```
Public Sub OnConnection(ByVal application As Object, _
        ByVal connectMode As Extensibility.ext_ConnectMode, _
        ByVal addInInst As Object, ByRef custom As System.Array) _
        Implements Extensibility.IDTExtensibility2.OnConnection

   applicationObject = CType(application, EnvDTE.DTE)
   addInInstance = CType(addInInst, EnvDTE.AddIn)

   If connectMode = Extensibility.ext_ConnectMode.ext_cm_UISetup Then
      Dim objAddIn As AddIn = CType(addInInst, AddIn)
      Dim CommandObj As Command

      ' When run, the Add-in wizard prepared the registry for the Add-in.
```

LISTING 17.1 continued

```
        ' At a later time, the Add-in or its commands may become
        ' unavailable for reasons such as:
        '   1) You moved this project to a computer other than the one
        ' it was originally created on.
        '   2) You chose 'Yes' when presented with a message
        ' asking if you wish to remove the Add-in.
        '   3) You add new commands or modify commands already defined.
        ' You will need to re-register the Add-in by building
        ' the FirstAddIn_vbSetup project,
        ' right-clicking the project in the Solution Explorer,
        ' and then choosing install.
        ' Alternatively, you could execute the ReCreateCommands.reg
        ' file the Add-in Wizard generated in
        ' the project directory, or run 'devenv /setup' from a command prompt.
        Try
         CommandObj = applicationObject.Commands.AddNamedCommand(objAddIn, _
             "FirstAddIn_vb", "FirstAddIn_vb", _
             "Executes the command for FirstAddIn_vb", _
             True, 59, Nothing, 1 + 2)

          CommandObj.AddControl(applicationObject.CommandBars.Item("Tools"))
        Catch e as System.Exception
        End Try
     End If
  End Sub
```

C#

```
public void OnConnection(object application,
    Extensibility.ext_ConnectMode connectMode,
          object addInInst, ref System.Array custom)
      {
         applicationObject = (_DTE)application;
         addInInstance = (AddIn)addInInst;
         if(connectMode ==
             Extensibility.ext_ConnectMode.ext_cm_UISetup)
         {
            object []contextGUIDS = new object[] { };
            Commands commands =
                   applicationObject.Commands;
            _CommandBars commandBars =
                   applicationObject.CommandBars;

            // When run, the Add-in wizard prepared the registry
            // At a later time, the Add-in or its commands may
            //    become unavailable for reasons such as:
            //   1) You moved this project to a computer other
            //        than which it was originally created on.
            //   2) You chose 'Yes' when presented with a
            //       message asking if you wish to remove the Add-in.
```

LISTING 17.1 continued

```
            //   3) You add new commands or modify
            //       commands already defined.
            // You will need to re-register the Add-in by
            // building the firstAddin_csSetup project,
            // right-clicking the project in the Solution Explorer,
            // and then choosing install.
            // Alternatively, you could execute the
            // ReCreateCommands.reg file the Add-in Wizard generated in
            // the project directory, or run 'devenv /setup'
            // from a command prompt.
            try
            {
               Command command =
                   commands.AddNamedCommand(addInInstance,
                         "firstAddin_cs", "firstAddin_cs",
                         "Executes the command for firstAddin_cs", true,
                   59, ref contextGUIDS,
                   (int)vsCommandStatus.vsCommandStatusSupported+
                   (int)vsCommandStatus.vsCommandStatusEnabled);
               CommandBar commandBar =
                   (CommandBar)commandBars["Tools"];
               CommandBarControl commandBarControl =
                  command.AddControl(commandBar, 1);
            }
            catch(System.Exception /*e*/)
            {
            }
        }
    }
```

After the `OnConnection` method fires, any menu items and Toolbox items that your add-in creates are added to the IDE. The next stage in processing for the add-in is the `OnStartupComplete` event.

Understanding the `OnStartupComplete` Method

The `OnStartupComplete` event fires when the host IDE is initialized. In Visual Studio .NET, this is when the Start Page can be seen. Any application initialization that must occur for your add-in can happen in the `OnStartupComplete` event. An example of this might be a custom project template. After the Visual Studio .NET IDE starts, you might display a custom project template options dialog, which in turn creates an application. A scenario like this essentially bypasses the normal flow that a developer would go through when creating a new project in Visual Studio .NET. Recall that you can write shared add-ins that interact with other IDEs, not just Visual Studio .NET. So, this event could serve as a general dialog that fires when any Office application starts.

Understanding the `OnAddInsUpdate` Method

The `OnAddInsUpdate` event doesn't exactly correspond to the life cycle of the add-in, but it's important to the events that occur within the `Connect` class file. When an end user modifies the loaded add-ins through the Add-in Manager, the `OnAddInsUpdate` method fires in all *other* add-ins, not the add-in that's being loaded or unloaded. This means if your add-in is dependent on another add-in, you can trap the unloading or loading of a specific add-in.

For example, assume that you have two add-ins: a `FileTransfer` add-in and a `FileMonitor` add-in. The `FileMonitor` add-in might monitor the bytes being sent during a `FileTransfer` method. If the `FileTransfer` add-in is unloaded, there's no reason to continue to watch bytes with the `FileMonitor` add-in. In that case, the `FileMonitor` add-in would trap the `OnAddInsUpdate` event for the unloading of the `FileTransfer` add-in and either stop watching for bytes or unload itself. Conversely, you could automatically load the `FileTransfer` add-in whenever the `FileMonitor` add-in is loaded.

Understanding the `OnBeginShutdown` Method

When the host application that your add-in is running in begins to close, the `OnBeginShutdown` event occurs. This would occur if the user selects the File, Exit menu item or ends the process of the IDE. When this event fires, your add-in is still loaded, but the host is closing. This occurs all the time with add-ins. Because they're loaded most of the time, an end user never goes through the process of closing all the add-ins and then closing the application. The `OnBeginShutdown` event can occur more than once. For example, if the host (the IDE instance running the add-in) has a cancel event for a shut down, such as a prompt of "Are you sure you want to close?", the event fires each time the host attempts to shut down.

Understanding the `OnDisconnection` Method

The `OnDisconnection` method handles the unloading of the add-in. This is the final event to occur in the lifetime of the add-in. It can occur via the Add-in Manager dialog when a user unchecks the Loaded option, when the IDE host is shutting down, or when the `Connect` property of the add-in is set to false. You can trap how the add-in is being disconnected from the host via the `ext_dm` constant. This constant is a parameter passed to the method from the IDE when disconnection occurs. Table 17.1 lists the values that you can trap when this event fires.

TABLE 17.1 Values of the ext_dm Constant

Constant	*Value*	*Description*
`ext_dm_HostShutdown`	0	The add-in was unloaded when the application was closed.
`ext_dm_UserClosed`	1	The add-in was unloaded when the user cleared its check box in the Add-In Manager dialog box, or when the `Connect` property of the corresponding `AddIn` object was set to false.
`ext_dm_UISetupComplete`	2	The add-in was unloaded after the environment setup completed and after the `OnConnection` method returned.
`ext_dm_SolutionClosed`	3	The add-in was unloaded when the solution was closed; received by solution add-ins.

In Listing 17.2, you can see the usage of the `OnDisconnection` event fired from the `Extensibility.IDTExtensibility2.OnDisconnection` event. The code listing demonstrates the VB.NET code; if you're writing in C#, the enumeration for the `DisconnectMode` is identical.

LISTING 17.2 Using the `DisconnectMode` Enumeration to Determine How the Add-in Is Being Closed

VB.NET

```
Public Sub OnDisconnection(ByVal RemoveMode As _
      Extensibility.ext_DisconnectMode, _
      ByRef custom As System.Array) _
      Implements Extensibility.IDTExtensibility2.OnDisconnection

      Select Case RemoveMode
         Case ext_DisconnectMode.ext_dm_HostShutdown

         Case ext_DisconnectMode.ext_dm_SolutionClosed

         Case ext_DisconnectMode.ext_dm_UISetupComplete

         Case ext_DisconnectMode.ext_dm_UserClosed

         Case Else

      End Select
   End Sub
```

In this method, you can perform add-in–specific cleanup code, if necessary.

Understanding the Exec and QueryStatus Methods

The final two events that occur in the Connect class of your add-in don't have to do with the connection, startup, or shutdown of the add-in. They deal with events that fire while the add-in is running. The Exec method is the actual code you write to make up your add-in. In Listing 17.3, the commented code tells where your implementation would go.

LISTING 17.3 The Exec Method in the Connect Class Where You Implement the Core Add-in Functionality

VB.NET

```
Public Sub Exec(ByVal cmdName As String, _
  ByVal executeOption As vsCommandExecOption, _
  ByRef varIn As Object, ByRef varOut As Object, _
  ByRef handled As Boolean) _
  Implements IDTCommandTarget.Exec

   handled = False
   If (executeOption = _
    vsCommandExecOption.vsCommandExecOptionDoDefault) Then
      If cmdName = "FirstAddIn_vb.Connect.FirstAddIn_vb" Then

         ' *******
         ' This is where your code goes that makes up your Add-in
         ' *******

         handled = True
         Exit Sub
      End If
   End If
End Sub
```

C#

```
public void Exec(string commandName,
   EnvDTE.vsCommandExecOption executeOption,
   ref object varIn, ref object varOut, ref bool handled)
{
   handled = false;
   if(executeOption ==
        EnvDTE.vsCommandExecOption.vsCommandExecOptionDoDefault)
   {
      if(commandName == "firstAddin_cs.Connect.firstAddin_cs")
      {
         /*
          *  Your Code Goes Here!
          */
         handled = true;
```

LISTING 17.3 continued

```
            return;
        }
    }
```

The parameters that are passed to the `Exec` method determine how your code can react to the request to execute your Add-in code.

Based on the `vsCommandExecuteOption` parameter passed to the `Exec` method, your code can react to the `Exec` method in a number of ways. Table 17.2 lists the Constants and their descriptions of how the command should execute and how you would respond.

TABLE 17.2 `VsCommandExecuteOption` Constant Values

Constant	*Value*	*Description*
`vsCommandExecOptionDoDefault`	`0`	Performs the default behavior, whether prompting the user for input or not.
`vsCommandExecOptionPromptUser`	`1`	Executes the command after obtaining user input.
`vsCommandExecOptionDoPromptUser`	`2`	Executes the command without prompting the user. For example, choosing the Print button on the toolbar causes a document to print immediately, without user input.
`vsCommandExecOptionShowHelp`	`3`	Shows help for the corresponding command, if it exists, but doesn't execute the command.

Because your add-in can have a number of menu items or toolbar items, each command may be handled in any number of ways. Listing 17.4 demonstrates how you might handle different parameters being passed to the `Exec` method. As before, if you're writing in C#, the constants are the same.

LISTING 17.4 Using the `VSCommandExecOption` Constants in the `Exec` Method

VB.NET

```
Public Sub Exec(ByVal cmdName As String, _
     ByVal executeOption As vsCommandExecOption, _
     ByRef varIn As Object, ByRef varOut As Object, _
     ByRef handled As Boolean) _
     Implements IDTCommandTarget.Exec

      handled = False
      If (executeOption = _
       vsCommandExecOption.vsCommandExecOptionDoDefault) Then
```

LISTING 17.4 continued

```
            If cmdName = "FirstAddIn_vb.Connect.FirstAddIn_vb" Then

               Select Case executeOption
                  Case vsCommandExecOption.vsCommandExecOptionDoDefault

                  Case vsCommandExecOption.vsCommandExecOptionDoPromptUser

                  Case vsCommandExecOption.vsCommandExecOptionPromptUser

                  Case vsCommandExecOption.vsCommandExecOptionShowHelp

               End Select

               ' *******
               ' This is where your code goes that makes up your Add-in
               ' *******

               handled = True
               Exit Sub
            End If
         End If
      End Sub
```

The Boolean value `Handled` indicates whether the code in your `Exec` method was successfully handled. The `QueryStatus` method can check the status of your add-in. In this method, you can see whether the various command items of your add-in are available, visible, enabled or disabled, or hidden.

Now that you have an idea of the different methods and events that can occur in an add-in, you must write some code that takes advantage of the extensibility features in Visual Studio .NET.

Writing Your First Add-in

Now that you have a good understanding of what steps make up the code generated by the Add-in Project Wizard, you're going to write some code that interacts with the Toolbox. To get started, follow these steps:

1. Add a new Windows Form to your FirstAddin project and name it `ToolboxTester`. Change the `Text` property of the form to `Toolbox Tester`, and change the `FormBorderStyle` property to `FixedToolWindow`.
2. Add a `Button` to the form. Change the `Name` property to `ShowToolBoxTabs` and change the `Text` property to `"Show Toolbox Tabs"`.
3. Add a `ListBox` control to the form and change its `Name` property to `lb`.

4. Add a `Button` to the form and change its `Name` property to `AddToolboxItems`. Change its `Text` property to `"Add Toolbox Items"`.

Your completed form should look like Figure 17.11.

FIGURE 17.11
The ToolboxTester form after adding new controls.

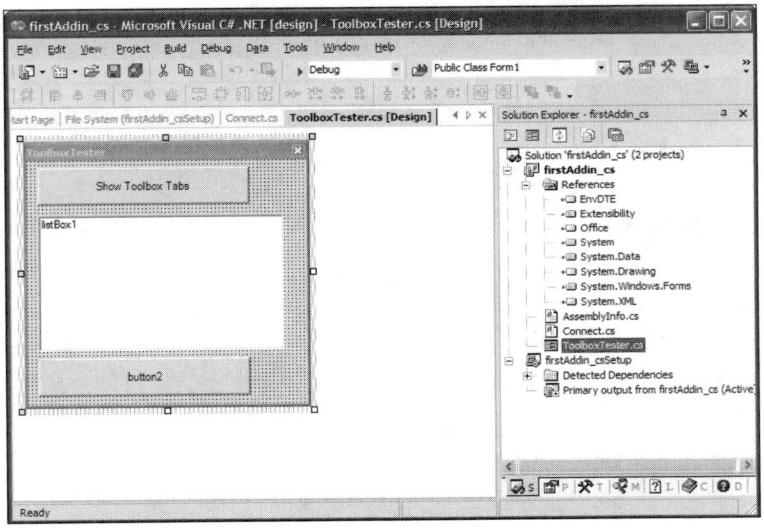

The goal of this add-in is to work with the Toolbox via a custom form that your FirstAddin project loads when Visual Studio .NET starts.

The first step is to notify the `Exec` method in the `Connect.vb` or `Connect.cs` class file that you want to load the new form when the add-in executes. To do so, your `Exec` method should look like Listing 17.5.

LISTING 17.5 The `Exec` Method Code in the `Connect` Class File

VB.NET

```
Public Sub Exec(ByVal cmdName As String, _
 ByVal executeOption As vsCommandExecOption, _
 ByRef varIn As Object, ByRef varOut As Object, _
 ByRef handled As Boolean) _
 Implements IDTCommandTarget.Exec

   handled = False

   If (executeOption = vsCommandExecOption. _
     vsCommandExecOptionDoDefault) Then
```

LISTING 17.5 continued

```
        If cmdName = "firstAddin_vb.Connect.firstAddin_vb" Then

            handled = True

            Dim f As New ToolboxTester(applicationObject)
            f.Show()

            Exit Sub
        End If
    End If
End Sub
```

C#

```
public void Exec(string commandName,
    EnvDTE.vsCommandExecOption executeOption,
    ref object varIn, ref object varOut, ref bool handled)
{
    handled = false;
    if(executeOption ==
        EnvDTE.vsCommandExecOption
        .vsCommandExecOptionDoDefault)
    {
        if(commandName ==
            "firstAddin_cs.Connect.firstAddin_cs")
        {
            handled = true;

            ToolboxTester f = new ToolboxTester(applicationObject);
            f.Show();

            return;
        }
    }
}
```

The code in Listing 17.5 is straightforward. You're simply showing a form. The difference is in the `applicationObject` that you're passing to the `ToolboxTester` form. Because you must tell the form that it's dealing with a specific instance of the IDE, you must pass the `applicationObject` variable to the form that represents this instance of the development tools extensibility (DTE) object. Right now, the project won't build because the `New` constructor in the form isn't expecting a variable to be passed to it.

The next step is to modify the `ToolboxTester` class file to implement the add-in code. Double-click the `ToolboxTester` form to get to the code-behind and add the `using` or `Imports` statement from Listing 17.6 to the top of your class file.

LISTING 17.6 Adding the Correct Namespace Aliases to the `ToolboxTester` Class File

VB.NET

```
Imports System.Text
Imports EnvDTE
Imports System.Runtime.InteropServices
```

C#

```
using System.Text;
using EnvDTE;
using System.Runtime.InteropServices;
```


Adding these namespaces to the class gives you access to the namespaces you need in the code. The most important namespace is the `EnvDTE` namespace, which gives you access to all the automation objects, such as the Toolbox.

Next you must add a class-level variable to hold the `applicationObject`'s `DTE` from the `Connect` class file. Listing 17.7 shows you the `DTE` variable declaration and where you should put it in the class file.

LISTING 17.7 Creating a Class-Level `applicationObject` Variable to Hold This Instance of the IDE Handle

VB.NET

```
Public Class ToolboxTester
   Inherits System.Windows.Forms.Form

   Private applicationObject As EnvDTE.DTE
```

C#

```
public class ToolboxTester : System.Windows.Forms.Form
{
   private _DTE applicationObject;
```

Next you must modify the constructor of the form that will accept the `applicationObject` passed from the `Connect` class file, and then set the local `applicationObject` variable. Listing 17.8 is a modified constructor for the `ToolboxTester` class file.

LISTING 17.8 Modifying the Constructor for the `ToolboxTester` Class to Accept the IDE Instance

VB.NET

```
Public Sub New(ByVal thisDTE As EnvDTE.DTE)

   MyBase.New()

   InitializeComponent()

   applicationObject = thisDTE

End Sub
```

C#

```
public ToolboxTester(_DTE thisDTE)
{

   InitializeComponent();

   applicationObject = thisDTE;
}
```

Now that the `DTE` extensibility object is correctly passed from the `Connect` class file to the `ToolboxTester`, the application builds with no errors. But no code actually does anything yet, so you must add code to the click events for the two buttons you added to the form.

But before doing this, you must look at the Toolbox object that you're using. In the hierarchy of the `DTE` object, the second level is the `Windows` collection. Within the `Windows` collection are the individual collections that make up the objects in the IDE, including the Toolbox. Table 17.3 lists the Toolbox objects that you have access to.

TABLE 17.3 Toolbox Objects and Their Descriptions

Object	*Description*
`Toolbox`	Represents the Toolbox
`ToolboxTabs`	Represents all the tabs in the Toolbox
`ToolboxTab`	Represents a tab in the Toolbox
`ToolboxItems`	Returns a collections of all the items in a tab in the Toolbox
`ToolboxItem`	Represents a single item in a `ToolboxItems` collection

To see how this works, the following code snippet creates a `win` variable that is the current Toolbox in the `DTE.Windows` collection. After the object variable is created, you can create `Toolbox` and `ToolboxTabs` variables, which give you access to the properties, methods, and events of the `Toolbox` objects.

```
' Create an object reference to the IDE's
' ToolBox object.

Dim win As Window = DTE.Windows.Item _
(Constants.vsWindowKindToolbox)

Dim tb As ToolBox = win.Object
Dim tbTabs As ToolBoxTabs

' Create an object reference to the ToolBoxTabs object.
tbTabs = tb.ToolBoxTabs

' List the total number of tabs in the ToolBox.

 MessageBox.Show("Number of ToolBox tabs: " & tbTabs.Count)
```


To display the `ToolboxTabs` in the list box and then add a new `ToolboxTab` to the Toolbox, add the code in Listing 17.9 to the `ShowToolboxTabs_click` event and the `AddToolboxTab_click` event.

LISTING 17.9 Adding the Toolbox Manipulation Code in the `ShowToolboxTabs_click` Event

VB.NET

```
Private Sub showToolboxTabs_Click(ByVal sender As System.Object, _
ByVal e As System.EventArgs) Handles showToolboxTabs.Click

      Dim tb As ToolBox
      tb = applicationObject.Windows.Item _
       (EnvDTE.Constants.vsWindowKindToolbox).Object

      Dim tbi As ToolBoxTab

      For Each tbi In tb.ToolBoxTabs
            lb.Items.Add(tbi.Name)
      Next

End Sub

Private Sub addToolboxTab_Click(ByVal sender As System.Object, _
  ByVal e As System.EventArgs) Handles addToolboxTab.Click

      Dim tb As ToolBox
```

Listing 17.9 continued

```
        Dim tbTab As ToolBoxTab

        tb = applicationObject.Windows.Item _
         (Constants.vsWindowKindToolbox).Object

        tbTab = tb.ToolBoxTabs.Add("New Toolbox Tab")

        tbTab.ToolBoxItems.Add("Code Snippet", "Dim x as integer", _
         vsToolBoxItemFormat.vsToolBoxItemFormatText)

        tbTab.ToolBoxItems.Add("HTML Snippet", "<h1>Hello World</h1>", _
        vsToolBoxItemFormat.vsToolBoxItemFormatHTML)

End Sub
```

C#

```
private void showToolboxTabs_Click(object sender,
   System.EventArgs e)
   {

      ToolBox tb;
      tb = (ToolBox)applicationObject.Windows.Item
        (EnvDTE.Constants.vsWindowKindToolbox).Object;

      foreach (ToolBoxTab tbi in tb.ToolBoxTabs)
      {
        lb.Items.Add(tbi.Name.ToString());
      }
         }

private void AddToolboxItems_Click(object sender,
   System.EventArgs e)
    {

      ToolBox tb;
      tb = (ToolBox)applicationObject.Windows.Item
      (EnvDTE.Constants.vsWindowKindToolbox).Object;

         ToolBoxTab tbTab;
         tbTab = tb.ToolBoxTabs.Add("New Toolbox Tab");

         tbTab.ToolBoxItems.Add("Code Snippet", "Dim x as integer",
         vsToolBoxItemFormat.vsToolBoxItemFormatText);

         tbTab.ToolBoxItems.Add("HTML Snippet", "<h1>Hello World</h1>",
         vsToolBoxItemFormat.vsToolBoxItemFormatHTML);
     }
```

Now that you've written the necessary code for the Toolbox to interact with in your add-in, you need to build the project. The best way to make sure that your add-in works is to install it from the Windows Installer project. In real life, you can just press the F5 key to run the application and a new instance of the Visual Studio .NET IDE starts. After the new IDE instance is open, you can test your add-in. When you close the IDE instance, the add-in project goes out of Debug mode and you can modify your code. This is very handy when it comes to debugging: You can simply step into the add-in code from the other IDE instance.

You're going to install the add-in from the Windows Installer project just to see how the whole process works:

1. Right-click on the FirstAddin project and select Build. Make sure that there are no errors in the Output window.
2. Next, right-click on the FirstAddin_Setup project and select Build from the contextual menu. This creates the Windows Installer MSI package for you.
3. When the build completes, right-click on the installer project and select Install from the contextual menu. This starts the Windows Installer Wizard that an end user would normally see. Go through the steps of installing the add-in on your computer. When the add-in is installed, all the necessary Registry entries are made for the COM interop, and the application directory where your add-in will exist is created.

Now you can test your add-in. Open a new instance of Visual Studio .NET and create a Windows Forms application. You can leave the default name. After the application is created and Visual Studio .NET is open, select the Tools menu. Your add-in should load, as Figure 17.12 demonstrates.

Next, click the menu item. You should see your `ToolboxTest` form pop up. Click the Show Toolbox Items buttons and you'll get a listing of your Toolbox tabs, as shown in Figure 17.13.

If you click the Add Toolbox Item button, a new tab is added and the code snippets you added are added as tab items. Notice that the item you added as HTML isn't available. That's because you aren't viewing an HTML file in the Code Editor. Figure 17.14 is what you see after dragging the Code Snippet item into the Code Editor.

You've now successfully created your first add-in, attached to the IDE, and worked with the Toolbox.

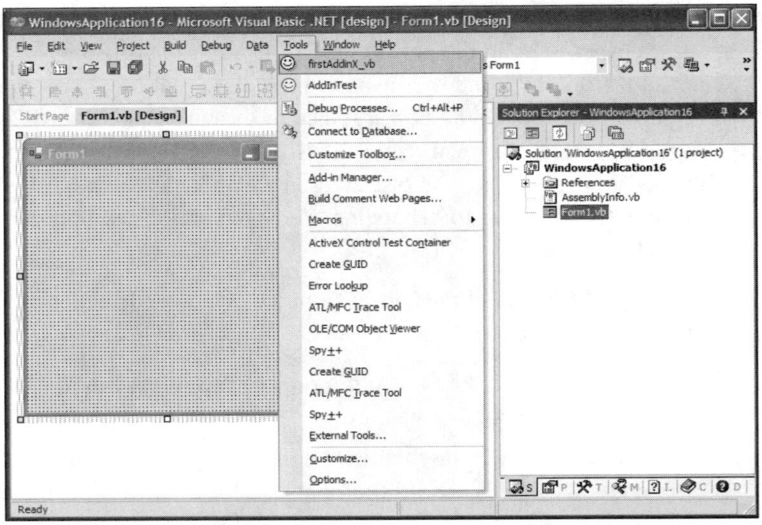

FIGURE 17.12

Your first add-in loaded in the Tools menu.

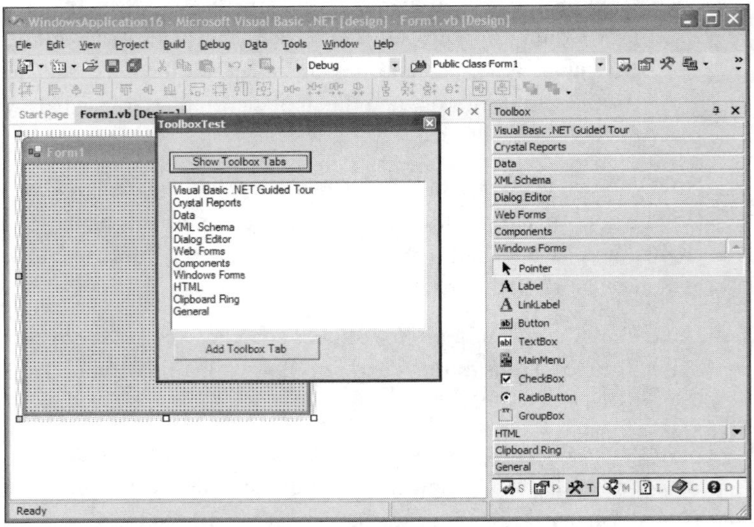

FIGURE 17.13

Getting a list of Toolbox tabs.

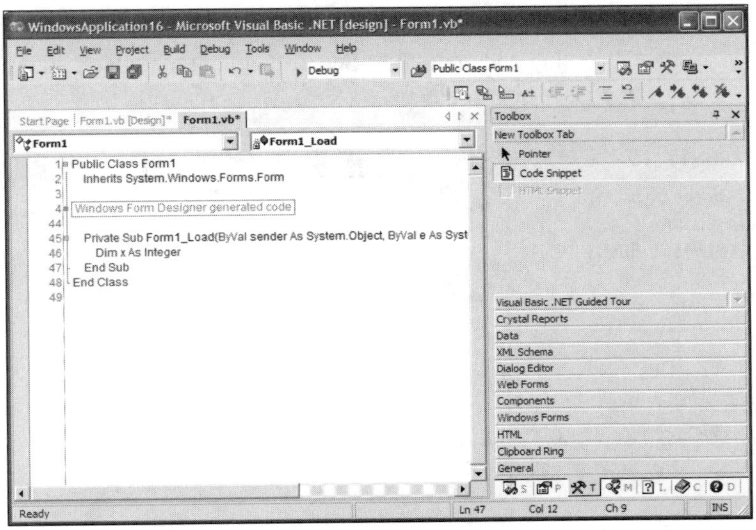

FIGURE 17.14

The new Toolbox tab added with code snippets.

Taking the Next Step with Add-ins

As you can see by the simple add-in that you wrote today, there's a lot you can do with add-ins. The next step in add-in development is to study the other objects that you can work with in add-in projects and the `EnvDTE` namespace.

To start becoming familiar with those objects, search Dynamic Help for the various objects that you can interact with. They might include

- `CommandBars` object
- `OutputWindow` object
- `TextWindow` object
- `TaskList` object
- `CodeDom` namespace

Each of these objects gives you access to the IDE. `CodeDom` is a super-powerful namespace that helps you create methods to add language-specific code to the Code Editor. To see how you would look up the `TextWindow` object in Dynamic Help, Figure 17.15 is an example of searching for the `TextWindow` object.

Some useful add-ins that I can think of are

- Backing up your project to another location on the network
- Zipping and emailing a project or a project file to another developer

- Analyzing the code in your project to create custom help files
- Accessing code in a SQL Server code library, which you're going to build in the exercises later today

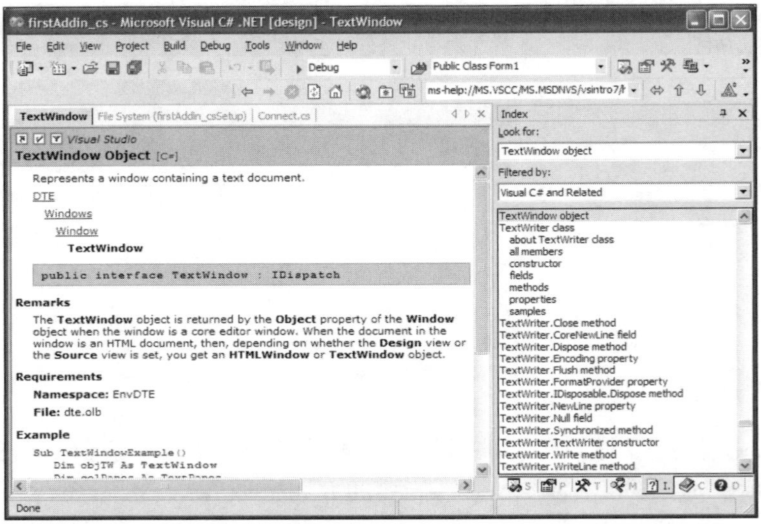

FIGURE 17.15

Searching Dynamic Help for the `TextWindow` *object.*

Summary

Today you learned how to create add-ins in Visual Studio .NET. By creating add-ins, you can programmatically control any aspect of the Visual Studio .NET IDE. You learned how to use the `Toolbox` object today, but some other cool ideas include working with the Task List window, adding custom output to an Output window, or even creating your own toolbars that can have multiple commands in a single add-in.

Q&A

Q Why does the add-in sometimes not show up in the Tools menu when I run the add-in application?

A Make sure that you select Uninstall from the deployment project after you've installed the add-in to test it. Because the Registry is involved, you must make sure that it's cleared out before you attempt to run the new add-in.

Q The Help File for add-ins is sort of confusing. Is my help messed up?

A No, your Help isn't messed up. Someone seems to have forgotten a few things when adding the help for automation. The hierarchy isn't like it is for the other namespaces in the framework class library (FCL), so you have to figure it out on your own. I suggest printing out the object model hierarchy bitmap that you can find in the SDK under Automation. It's a visual representation of the `EnvDTE` objects, and it'll assist you in getting the right information.

Q Add-ins are exciting. Are there any books or good articles about add-ins?

A Information about add-ins is scarce. A-Press publishes a book by Les Smith called *Writing Add-ins for Visual Studio .NET*. It's all Visual Basic .NET code and it walks you through a lot of neat Add-in ideas. You can find some good articles about add-ins at

`http://msdn.microsoft.com/msdnmag/issues/02/02/VSIDE/VSIDE.asp`

Quiz

1. The ____________ namespace contains the automation objects for Visual Studio .NET.
2. The ___________ object can be passed to other classes to encapsulate the current IDE instance.
3. True or False: Because an add-in is all .NET, it's okay to simply delete the directory where it's installed to remove the add-in from another computer.

Quiz Answers

1. `EnvDTE`
2. The `EnvDTE.DTE` object from the `Connect` class is the current IDE instance that you can pass around to other forms or classes in your add-in project.
3. False. All add-ins are implemented as COM components, so they're registered in the Registry. You should use the Add/Remove Programs applet in the Control Panel to remove an add-in.

Exercise

Building on what you started yesterday with the code snippet macro, you're going to create an add-in that retrieves the data from SQL Server where the code snippets exist.

To do this, work through the following steps:

1. Create a new add-in project.
2. Add a new form to the add-in.
3. Add a `ListView` control to the form.

4. Add a `Button` control to the form.
5. On the `Form_Load` event, fill the `ListView` control with the data from the Utilities database in SQL Server where you're saving the code snippets from the macro you created yesterday.
6. When a user selects a code snippet from the `ListView`, add code to the `Button` that asks if the user wants to add the code to a tab in the Toolbox or a directory into the Code Editor.
7. Write code that inserts the code into either the Toolbox or into the Code Editor.

This form actually has only two methods with code: the `Form_Load` event and the `Button_Click` event that handle the interaction. You can get help while you're doing this by using what you learned today about the `Toolbox` object and by looking up the `TextWindow` object in Dynamic Help.

WEEK 3

DAY 18

Using Crystal Reports

Writing professional reports is always a nice touch for a completed application. With Visual Studio .NET, you have the ability to write very professional-looking reports with little or no code using the built-in Crystal Reports designer. Today you learn

- What Crystal Reports is
- The difference between the push model and the pull model for generating reports
- How to use the `CrystalReportViewer` control
- How to print reports
- How to export reports

Why Use Crystal Reports?

Crystal Reports is the integrated reporting tool in Visual Studio .NET. Based on the type of application you're developing—desktop or Web-based—Crystal provides report viewers that integrate into forms to display reports built with the Crystal Reports designer.

For simple reporting, you can bind a report to a viewer and just display it or you can use the rich object model that Crystal exposes to completely control the customization of your reports. Using the Crystal Reports designer is by far the easiest way to create reports out of the box with Visual Studio .NET. In addition to great support for Web Form viewers and Windows Forms viewers, you can also expose Crystal reports as XML Web services. When a report is exposed as a Web service, the caller of the Web service gets the XML representation of the report. This is immensely useful for complex data where it might be easier to use a wizard in Crystal to create a report than it would be to write the database code to generate the correct XML schema information.

When creating reports, you have the option of pulling data from a data source to the report or pushing data from a data source to the report. In the pull model, the database drivers connect to the data source and pull data dynamically. In the pull model, you can design a report and bind it to a viewer at design time. When the report is viewed at runtime, the data is pulled from the data source. The Crystal engine handles the connection details and the actual pulling of the data; no additional code is needed from you. An example of a good pull-model scenario is monthly or quarterly sales data: After the aggregate formulas have been created, the report definition never changes and Crystal can handle getting the data on demand when needed.

In the push model, you write the database connection code; that is, the code that fills the data source with data, and then passes the data to the report. The push model is more flexible than the pull model because you normally design reports on a development machine, and the connection details might change at runtime. In that case, you can specify connection information in the `Web.Config` file or any application configuration file, and dynamically create the data source at runtime. An example of a push model report is Customer Orders By ID, where the ID of the customer can be different each time the report is called. You just pass parameters to the report, and dynamically build the data source at runtime.

When designing reports, you have the option of using the following data sources:

- ADO.NET dataset
- OLEDB data source
- Microsoft Access database

- Microsoft Excel spreadsheet
- Crystal Data Objects

If you're using MSDE or SQL Server databases, the logical choice is to use ADO.NET datasets to push data to a report.

After you've determined the data source of the report, you add different fields to the report to represent your data. As with the full version of Crystal Reports, the Visual Studio .NET version supports bound database fields, formula fields, parameter fields, custom groups, summary fields, running totals, subreports, and custom charts. Based on the type of report you're using, you add various fields to different areas of the report in the report designer to customize your data output.

Now that you understand the basics on what Crystal is, you can start writing your first Crystal Report in Visual Studio .NET.

Creating a Windows Forms Report

The first report you're going to write is a simple bound report using the Windows Forms viewer. To begin, start Visual Studio .NET and create a new Windows Forms application. Change the name of the application to Reports, as Figure 18.1 demonstrates.

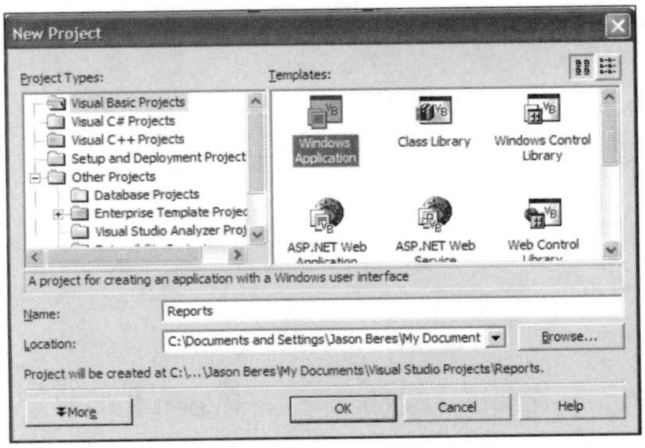

FIGURE 18.1
Creating the Reports Windows Forms application.

After the application is loaded, right-click on the Reports project name in the Solution Explorer and select Add, New Item from the contextual menu. When the New Item dialog box pops up, scroll down until you see the Crystal Report item. Select the Crystal Report item and change its name to `Report1`, as shown in Figure 18.2.

At this point, the Crystal Report Gallery dialog box pops up. Each time you add a new report to your solution, you're prompted with the Report Gallery dialog box from which you can select the type of report you want to create. Most of the time, you'll use the Report Export. The Blank Report option gives you a blank designer with which you can add fields manually. If you choose Existing Report, you can add a report created by someone else in Visual Studio .NET or you can import an existing report that was created with the full version of Crystal Reports.

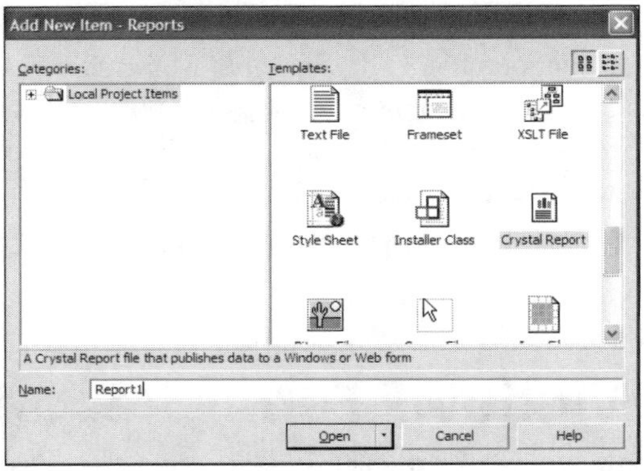

FIGURE 18.2

Adding a new Crystal Report to your application.

By choosing either Report Expert or Blank Report, you can select from the list of templates that give you the basic look and feel of the report. These include

- Standard
- Form Letter
- Form
- Cross-Tab
- Subreport
- Mail Label
- Drill Down

For the purpose of your first report, choose the Report Expert option and then select the Standard expert, as Figure 18.3 demonstrates.

After you choose the Standard Report type, you're taken to the Standard Report Expert. The Expert is a tabbed dialog wizard that guides you through the definition of your report. The Report Experts are what make using Crystal so easy: You answer some questions and, like magic, you have a report that's ready to go.

The first step of the wizard is to set the data source information. Based on the type of report you're creating, the data source can be any type of ODBC connection, OLE DB connections, RDO connection, XML files, an ADO.NET dataset, and so on. For this report, no datasets are defined in the application, so you're going to drill into the OLE DB connections node. When you drill into the node, the OLE DB provider dialog pops up. If you had existing reports with OLE DB connections, they would be listed there. Because this is the first time you're running the Expert, you must fill out the information to get a database connection. Figure 18.4 shows the initial selection screen for the OLE DB provider. Select the SQL Server OLE DB provider as shown.

FIGURE 18.3

Choosing the Report Type from the Report Gallery.

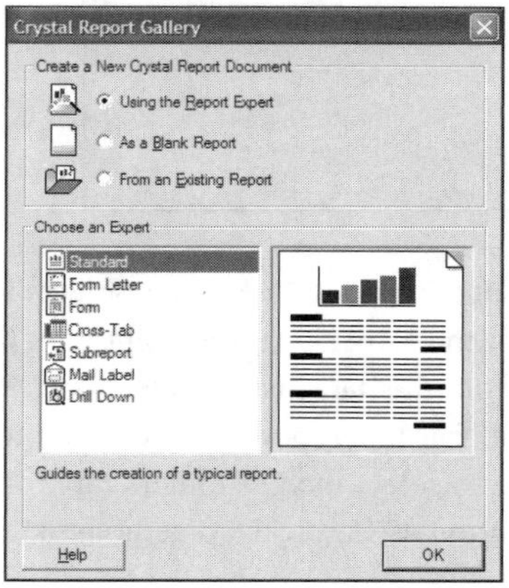

FIGURE 18.4

Selecting the OLE DB provider for your report.

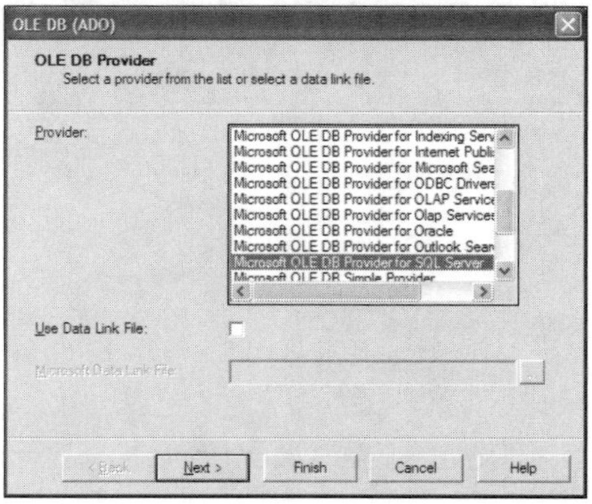

When you click Next after selecting the SQL Server OLE DB provider, you're prompted for the connection information to the SQL Server or MSDE database. For this report, you're going to use the Northwind database in MSDE, so enter the correct `machine name\NETSDK` database, select the Integrated Security check box, and then select Northwind from the Database drop-down list as shown in Figure 18.5.

After you've set the correct login information and selected the Northwind database, click the Finish button on the OLE DB provider dialog.

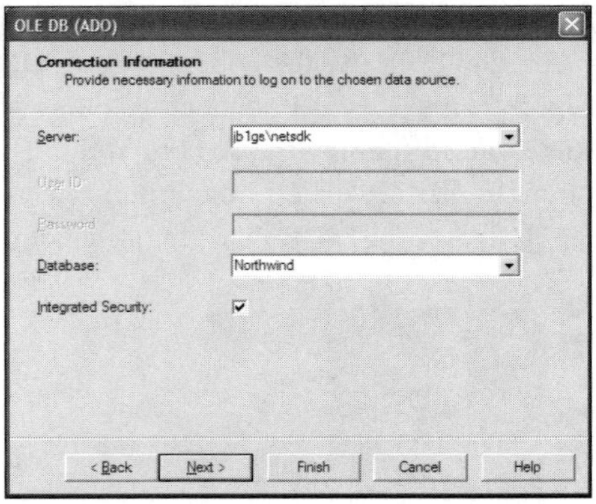

FIGURE 18.5

Setting the connection parameters for the OLE DB connection.

Now that you've defined the connection parameters, the objects from the connection are displayed in the OLE DB node of the Expert. At this point, you have the option to create a command to retrieve the data from the database or select one or more tables from the Tables under the Northwind node. For this report, you're going to create a simple list of names from the Customers table, so select the Customers table from the Northwind database and click the Insert Table button as Figure 18.6 demonstrates.

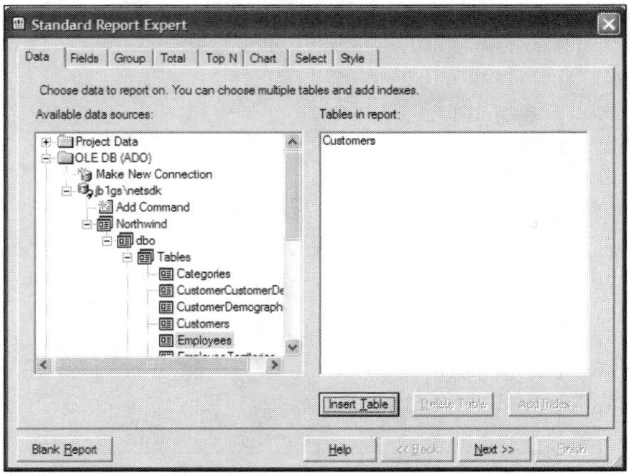

FIGURE 18.6

Selecting the Customers table for the report.

After you click the Next button, you're taken to the Fields tab. Now you can select the fields that you want to bind to your report. From this tab, you can also view the data from SQL Server by clicking the Browse Data button or you can create a formula field by clicking the Formula button. A *formula* is composed of simple or complex selection criteria that you can set for any field in a report. Using either the Crystal Syntax or Basic Syntax, you can create formulas to select data, format data, or create custom summary or aggregate fields. In this report, you won't be using any formulas. Select the following fields and click the Add button:

- `CustomerID`
- `CompanyName`
- `ContactName`
- `ContactTitle`
- `Phone`

The Fields tab should now resemble Figure 18.7.

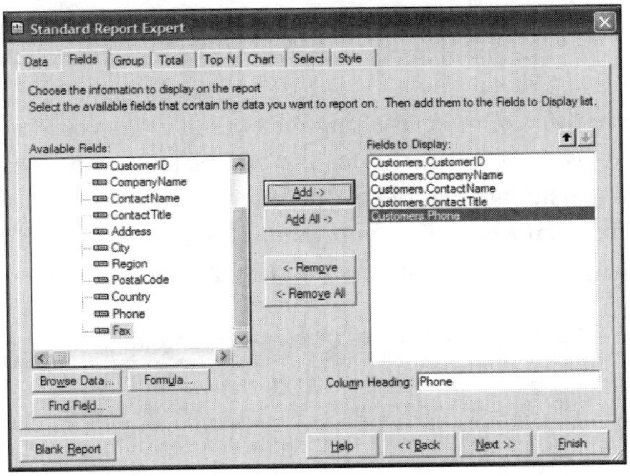

FIGURE 18.7
Selecting the bound fields for your report.

As you select the fields on the Fields tab, you can also modify the Column Heading text box for each corresponding field that you select. This is an easy way to make the column names more user friendly.

After you click the Next button, you're on the Group tab. Grouping is normally a pain in the neck when writing code, but with Crystal it's a simple field selection. Because there's only one table in this report, there's no need to do any grouping. But if you had added the Customers and Orders tables, you could select the `CustomerID` field to group by. This would automatically create a group hierarchy in your report. Your Group tab should look like Figure 18.8.

The next tab is the Total tab. In this report, the data is all alphanumeric customer information, so no automatic summary or total fields are needed. If you click Next again, you're at the Top N tab. From here, you can select the Top N values for any of the calculated fields you selected in the Total tab. These include the Top N, Bottom N, Top Percentage, and Bottom Percentage of the selected fields based on the selected total fields. Because you didn't select any Total fields, the Top N tab won't be available.

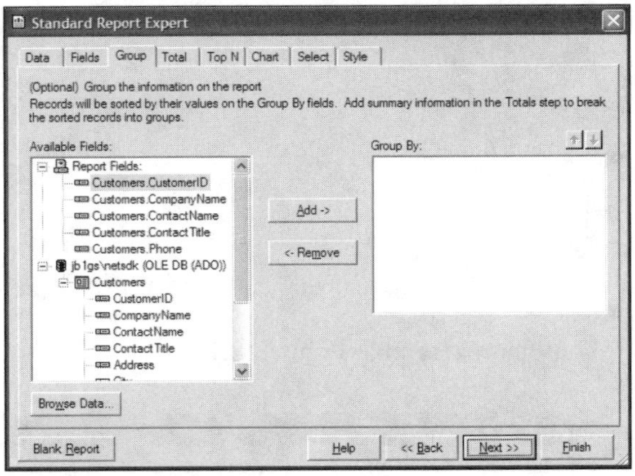

FIGURE 18.8

Selecting the Group By field.

The next step in the wizard is selecting the type of chart you want to display on your report. Charting is a very powerful feature of Crystal that enables you to select a wide variety of chart, including bar, pie, stock, and 3D. Based on the fields selected in a report, you can specify what data you want to display in the chart. Figure 18.9 gives you an idea of what you can do with charting. For this report, you won't need a chart.

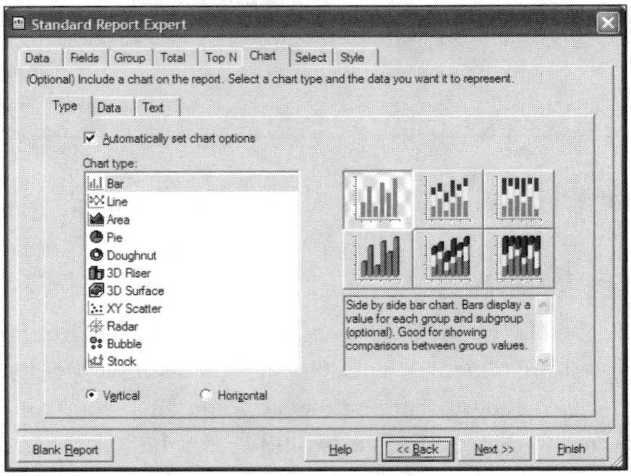

FIGURE 18.9

Selecting the charting option in the Report Expert.

The next tab, Select, enables you to filter data for the report. By choosing fields to select or filter, you can improve the speed of a report or limit the data the end user is expecting. After you've selected a field, either from the Report Fields node or the Connection node, you can specify a number of filtering statements. For example, you can select the `CompanyName` field, and then set the criteria to "greater than or equal to C," which returns all records in the report with a `CompanyName` that start with the letter C or any letter after

C. You can also have multiple criteria, and include filters that are fields not selected for the report itself. For this report, you aren't filtering any data, but Figure 18.10 gives you an idea of the power and flexibility of using the Select tab to define report requirements.

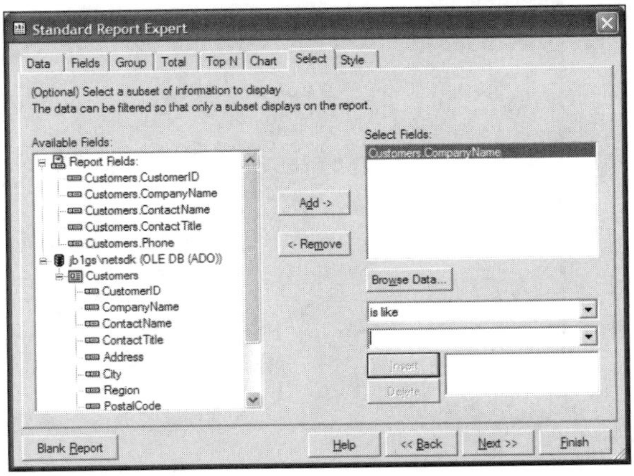

FIGURE 18.10

Using the Select tab to filter records for the report.

If you click Next, you're at the last step of the Expert. On this tab, you can define the title of your report and select the formatting of the report. The options specified here are most useful in a group report, where there are a number of levels of data to display. You can decide whether you want the report data displayed in a table, a drop table, or in different colors and shading. For this report, enter `First Report` as the title and select the Standard report option, as Figure 18.11 demonstrates.

18

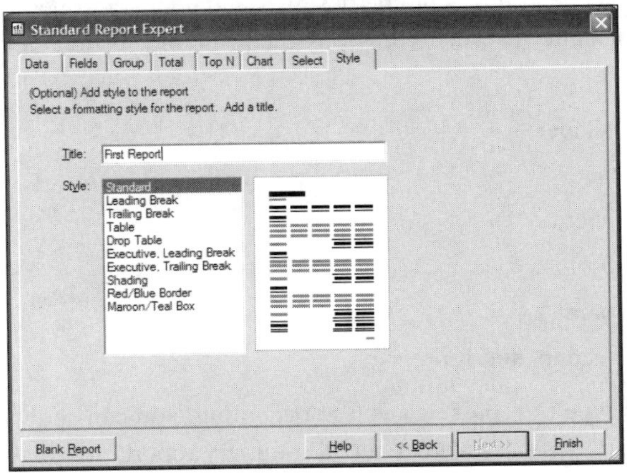

FIGURE 18.11

Selecting the report format and setting the title.

After you click finish, the Expert takes the information you entered and creates your report. Figure 18.12 is what you should see.

FIGURE 18.12

The completed Report1 in the Crystal Designer.

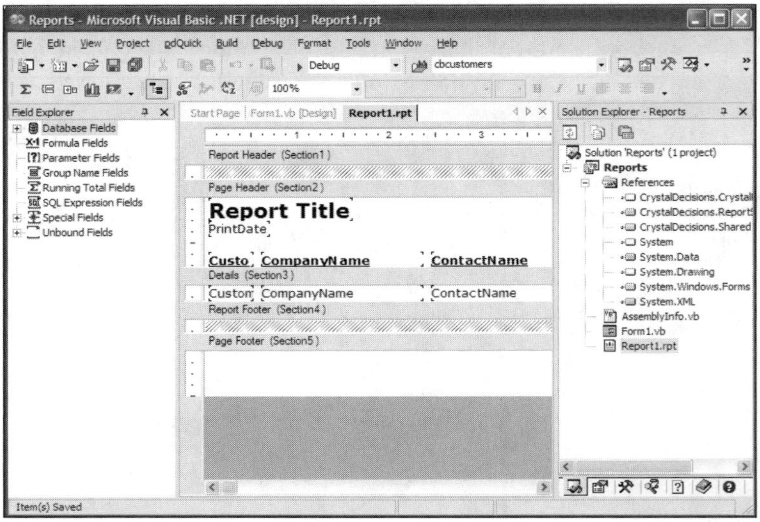

Look in the Solution Explorer, and you'll see that you have a Report1.rpt file. This is the Crystal Report that's in the designer. Each `.rpt` file works like a Web Form; there's a code-behind class file that the `.rpt` file uses to create the report. This class file is automatically generated by the wizard and shouldn't be messed with. This file is altered each time you modify something on the report, so you'd most likely lose any changes that you make to this file.

The Crystal Designer is laid out similarly to any other designer in .NET, and you have the ability to move controls on the designer and change properties. When working with reports, the designer is broken down by the printable sections for a report. Each report contains a

- Report header
- Page header
- Details section
- Report footer
- Page footer
- Group headers and footers

Based on the type of report that you're designing, you can show or hide any of the sections. For example, when you create a Summary report, you may have a group on a month field from the database. To just display the group summary calculations, you can suppress or hide the Details section of the report. Each different report has a Format

Section option that you can access by right-clicking the gray bar that represents the section in the designer. From the Section Expert, you can set different print, page break, and section suppression settings.

The true data manipulation power of Crystal is in the File Explorer, which is docked on the left of the Visual Studio .NET IDE. The File Explorer has the features of the Toolbox, Properties window, and more—all in the window—giving you complete customization of the report you're designing. Let's take a look at each section of the File Explorer to get an idea of what you can do.

Using the Database Fields Node

If you drill into the Database Fields node, you have access to all the fields from the tables you selected in the Expert. The fields that are actually used in the report have a red check mark to the left of each field name. For the report you're creating now, you'll see the Customers table. If there were multiple tables in the report, each table would be listed in the Database Fields node.

From this node, you can drag fields to the designer to include in the report, just as you would drag a control from the Toolbox onto a form. If you right-click any of the fields in the table, you can browse the field data from the data source, or rerun the Select Expert to filter or select specific records. If you decide that you want to add another table to your report, you can select the Add/Remove Database menu item from the right-click contextual menu to modify the database tables. If you remove an existing database that has fields on the report, you must manually remove the fields from the report designer.

Using the Formula Fields Node

By right-clicking the Formula Fields node and selecting New from the context menu, you bring up a prompt for a formula name. After you enter a name and click OK, the Formula Editor dialog pops up. Using the editor, you can define special formula fields to use in your reports. For example, in Figure 18.13, I used the Formula Editor to create a formula that creates a field named `@@formula`, which makes the `CompanyName` field all uppercase if it starts with the letter C.

I mentioned earlier that the syntax can be Basic or Crystal, so depending on your preference, you can use either one. The great thing about the editor is that you can simply double-click any of the hundreds of predefined functions or operators and then just place the database fields that you want to manipulate.

After you've verified the syntax of the formula by using the Verify Syntax button, clicking the Save button adds the formula under the Formula Fields node. From here, you can drag the formula field onto your report as you would any other database field.

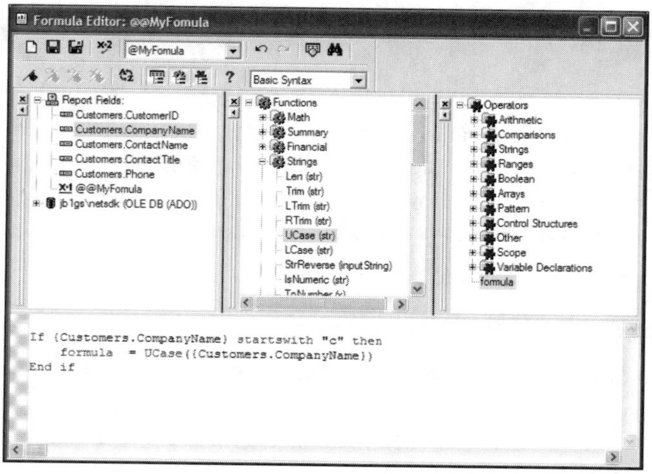

FIGURE 18.13

Adding a custom formula using the Formula Editor.

Using the Parameter Fields Node

Parameter fields enable you to specify parameters that can be passed to a report. For example, you can create a parameter named `@CustomerID`. Then from your C# or Visual Basic .NET code, you could use the Crystal classes to pass the correct values to the report, and the report would filter data based on your parameter. This makes a filtered or multiselect report very easy to implement. If you don't want to write the code to do the filtering, you can use the tools in the Parameter Fields dialog to specify filtering options.

When you right-click on the Parameter Fields node and select New, you're prompted with the Create Parameter Field dialog box shown in Figure 18.14.

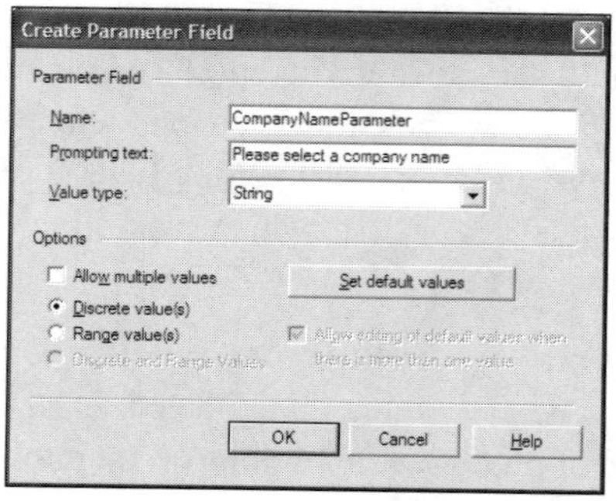

FIGURE 18.14

The Create Parameter Field dialog box.

From this dialog, you specify a name, data type, and type of parameter selection that will occur. If you're passing parameter values in code, you can simply click the OK button and the parameter field will be added to the Parameter Fields node. If you want Crystal to handle the dialog for filtering, you can click the Set Default Values button, which brings up the Set Default Values dialog. From this screen, you can define the filters that you want to occur. In Figure 18.15, I created a filter that will prompt the user with a sorted list of the `CompanyName` fields to choose from. After the user selects a value, Crystal filters the report accordingly. This is a very powerful tool for doing all kinds of filtering for a report.

FIGURE 18.15

Setting the default values for a parameter field.

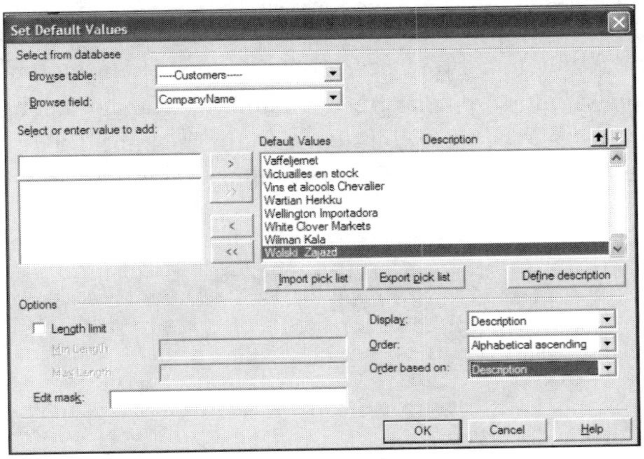

Using the Group Name Fields Node

When you run the Expert for each report, you're given the option of setting groupings on a report. At the initial stage of creation, you might not know exactly how the report will look or what other groupings you might need. By adding a new group from the Group Name Fields dialog, you can further group the data in your report and specify how it should look when grouped. By right-clicking the node and selecting Insert Group, you bring up the Insert Group dialog in Figure 18.16.

FIGURE 18.16

Inserting a new group into a report.

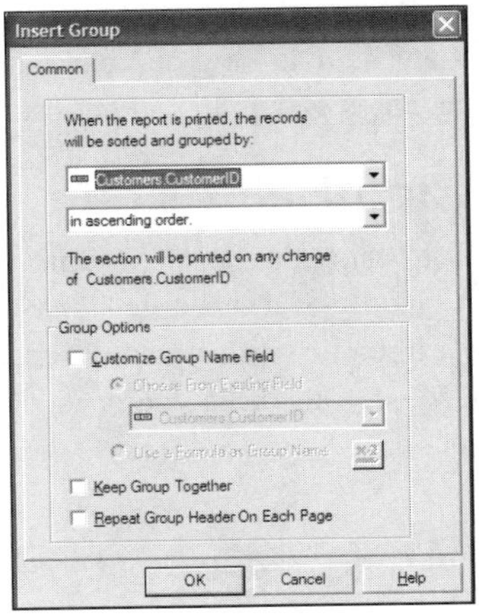

18

The nice thing about this dialog is that you can customize the group by using a formula. For example, if you want to create a new group if the `OrderPrice` of a record is greater than $100.00, you can specify that in a formula, and that group will be created in the report only if the data matches that criteria.

Using the Running Total Fields Node

When dealing with numeric values, a running total is always a nice feature. Using the Running Totals dialog, you can create a number of fancy running total fields that you can add to your report. When you right-click on the Running Total Fields node and select New, you're prompted with the Create Running Total Field dialog shown in Figure 18.17.

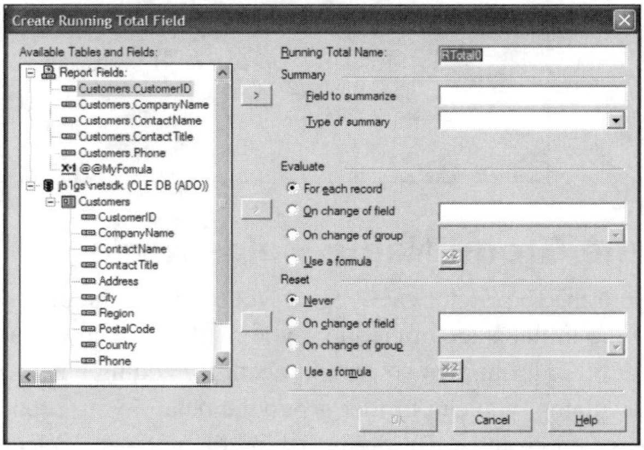

FIGURE 18.17
Creating a running totals field.

Depending on your requirements, you can specify running totals based on each record, a specific value of a record, or when a group changes. You can also reset the running total. Using a combination of a running total field and a group name field, you could drill very deep into data for a report, giving as much grouping and total information as is required.

Using the SQL Expression Fields Node

Adding a SQL expression is similar to using the Formula Editor, but with fewer options. The SQL Expression Editor gives you only SQL-specific syntax options for manipulating data for a field. You can do simple arithmetic or string concatenation of field data, or you can cast and format data in a field. Most of the time you're much better off adding a formula field instead of a SQL expression.

Using the Special Fields Node

The Special Fields node gives you fields that make the report seem like you went the extra mile to make it look good. From this node, you can drag any of the fields in the following list to your report to enhance the output:

Print Date	Page Number	Group Selection Formula
Print Time	Group Number	File Path and Name
Modification Date	Total Page Count	File Author
Modification Time	Report Title	File Creation Date
Data Date	Report Comments	Page N of M
Data Time	Report Selection Formula	Record Number

Using the Unbound Fields Node

Adding an unbound field to your report enables you to programmatically pass fields from your application to the report. When you drag an unbound field to a report, you can specify the data type of the unbound field. You also can use any of the formatting options that you normally have for any other field you add to a report.

18

Using the Windows Forms Report Viewer

Now that you have a report ready to run and you're familiar with the reports designer, you can create a form to actually view your report.

The first step is to add a new form to your solution by right-clicking the project name in the Solution Explorer and selecting Add, Add Windows Form from the contextual menu. You can leave the default Form1.vb or Form1.cs name.

Next, in the Toolbox, scroll down in the Windows Forms tab until you see the `CrystalReportViewer` control. Drag it onto your form, and set the `Dock` property to `Fill` so that it resizes with the form. Your form should look something like Figure 18.18.

The viewer on its own does nothing. You can either set a binding property to specify the report to load or you can programmatically load a report into the viewer. To view the `Report1.rpt` you created, press the F4 key to view the properties for the viewer control and select the `ReportSource` property. If you click the Browse option in the `ReportSource` property, the Open An Existing Crystal Report dialog pops up. Navigate to the correct directory of this solution and select `Report1.rpt`, as Figure 18.19 demonstrates.

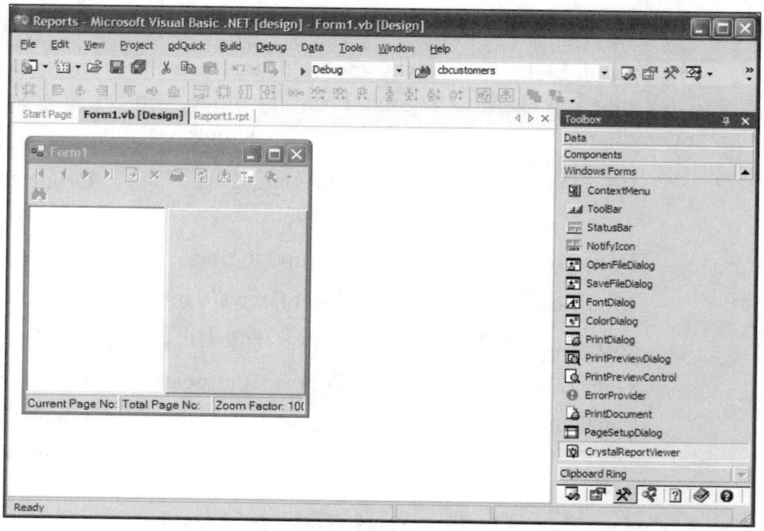

FIGURE 18.18

`Form1` *after adding the* `CrystalReportViewer` *control.*

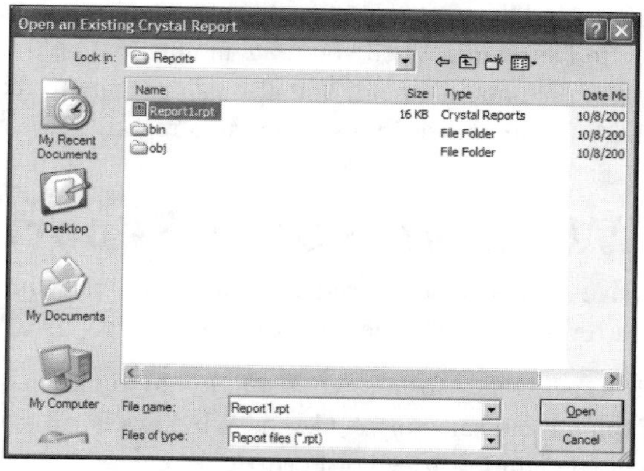

FIGURE 18.19

Selecting the `ReportSource` *for the* `CrystalReportViewer` *control.*

After that property is set, you can press the F5 key to run the application. Like magic, the report that you created is displayed in a nice full-featured report viewer. Figure 18.20 is what you should see now.

The toolbar on the viewer enables you to page through, drill into (if it's a group report), print, and export a report. The exporting features of Crystal are especially useful. You have the option of exporting any report to an Excel spreadsheet, Word document, rich text document, or Adobe PDF document.

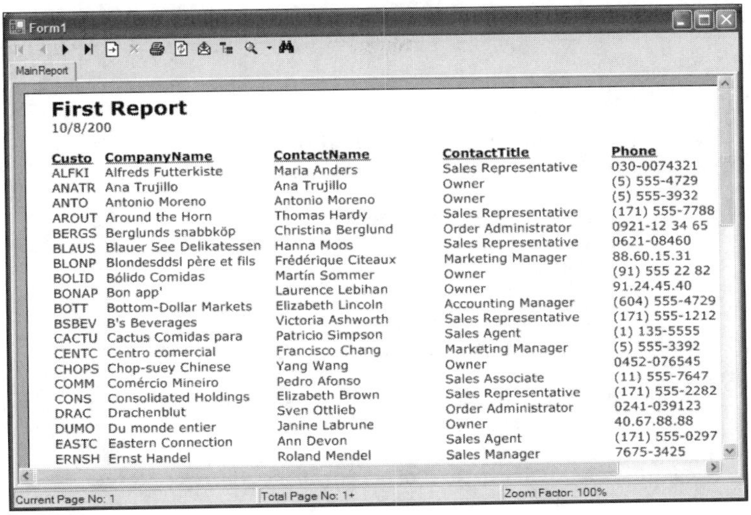

FIGURE 18.20
Viewing the `Report1.rpt` *in the report viewer.*

How to Programmatically Load a Report

You won't normally load reports from the My Documents\ Visual Studio Projects folder on an end user's computer, and the login information and database location are normally different when you deploy a report. For this reason, you must be able to load a report dynamically and set login information at runtime.

Using the `TableLogOnInfo` class of the `CrystalDecisions.Shared` namespace, you have programmatic access to the login information for the database tables in a report. Using the `ReportDocument` class, you can specify a report to load at runtime.

In your applications, you should have a single form named `rptViewer` that has the report viewer control. The report name that the user is requesting is passed in the constructor for the `frmViewer`. It's a good idea to have a folder named Reports in your solution where all the reports are located, so you can use the relative path of the report to load at runtime.

The code in Listing 18.1 can be added to either the `Load` event of the `frmViewer` or after the `InitializeComponent` call in the form's constructor. After calling the `Load` method on the `ReportDocument` object, you set the `ConnectionInfo` properties by looping through the `Tables` collection that exists in the report. To tell the viewer what to load, you simply set the `ReportSource` property just as you did in the properties window for the viewer.

LISTING 18.1 Loading a Crystal Report in Code

VB.NET

```
Private Sub rptViewer_Load(ByVal sender As System.Object, _
   ByVal e As System.EventArgs) Handles MyBase.Load

  Me.Cursor = Cursors.WaitCursor

  Try

  Dim oRpt As New ReportDocument()
  oRpt.Load("..\Reports\" & strReportName)

  Dim tbCurrent As CrystalDecisions.CrystalReports.Engine.Table
  Dim tliCurrent As CrystalDecisions.Shared.TableLogOnInfo

  For Each tbCurrent In oRpt.Database.Tables
    tliCurrent = tbCurrent.LogOnInfo
    With tliCurrent.ConnectionInfo
      .ServerName = "jb1gs"
      .UserID = "sa"
      .Password = ""
      .DatabaseName = "Northwind"
    End With

    tbCurrent.ApplyLogOnInfo(tliCurrent)

  Next tbCurrent

  viewer.ReportSource = oRpt

  Catch ex As Exception
    MsgBox(ex.Message)
  Finally
    Me.Cursor = Cursors.Default
  End Try

End Sub
```

C#

```
private void frmViewer_Load(object sender, System.EventArgs e)
{

CrystalReport1 oRpt = new CrystalReport1 ();
Database oDb;
Tables oTables;
Table oTable;
TableLogOnInfo tliCurrent;
ConnectionInfo oCnInfo = new ConnectionInfo ();
```

LISTING 18.1 continued

```
// Setup the connection information structure to be used
// to log onto the datasource for the report.
oCnInfo.ServerName = "jb1gs";
oCnInfo.DatabaseName = "Northwind";
oCnInfo.UserID = "sa";
oCnInfo.Password = "admin";

//Get the table information from the report
oDb = oRpt.Database;
oTables = oDb.Tables;

//Loop through all tables in the report and
// apply the connection
//information for each table.
for (int i = 0; i < oTables.Count; i++)
{
   oTable = oTables [i];
   tliCurrent = oTable.LogOnInfo;
   tliCurrent.ConnectionInfo = oCnInfo;
   oTable.ApplyLogOnInfo(tliCurrent);
}

crystalReportViewer1.ReportSource = oRpt;
}
```


After the `ConnectionInfo` properties and the `ReportSource` are set, the report will display in the viewer.

Printing a Report Without the Viewer Control

You can bypass the viewer control and print a report directly from a menu item or the click event of a button. Using the `PrintToPrinter` method of the `ReportDocument` class, you can print a loaded report directly to a printer. Listing 18.2 demonstrates how you could accomplish this in the click event of a button. Notice the code comments for the parameters for the `PrintToPrinter` method that sets the properties on the printed document.

LISTING 18.2 Printing a Report with the `PrintToPrinter` Method

VB.NET

```
Private Sub button1_Click(sender As Object, e As System.EventArgs)
   oRpt = New ReportDocument()
```

Listing 18.2 continued

```
      oRpt.Load("C:\Report1.rpt")
      Try
         oRpt.PrintOptions.PrinterName = "\jbnet\hp-color"

         ' The PrintToPrinter method parameters are:
         ' # of copies
         ' Collated
         ' Start Page
         ' End Page
         oRpt.PrintToPrinter(1, True, 1, 1)

      Catch err As Exception
         MessageBox.Show(err.ToString())
      End Try
   End Sub
```

C#

```
   private void button1_Click(object sender, System.EventArgs e)
   {
   oRpt = new ReportDocument();

      oRpt = new ReportDocument();
      oRpt.Load(@"C:\Report1.rpt");

      try
      {
         oRpt.PrintOptions.PrinterName =
             "@\\jbnet\\hp-color";

         // The PrintToPrinter method parameters are:
         // # of copies
         // Collated
         // Start Page
         // End Page
         oRpt.PrintToPrinter(1, true, 1, 1);

      }
      catch(Exception err)
      {
         MessageBox.Show(err.ToString());
      }
   }
```

After you add this code to the click event of a button and modify the location of the printer and the report name, the file prints directly without a viewer control.

Exporting a Report Programmatically

Another useful feature is the ability to export a report document without the end user viewing it first and then clicking the Export button on the toolbar. To do this, you use the `ExportOptions` collection of the `ReportDocument` class to set properties on what you want to export and how it should be exported. The code in Listing 18.3 exports a report file to a PDF file and saves it to disk.

LISTING 18.3 Exporting a Report with Code Using the `Export` Method

VB.NET

```
Private Sub button1_Click(sender As Object, e As System.EventArgs)

   ' The path/location where the exported file will be saved
   Dim exportFilePath As String = "c:\Report1.pdf"

   ' Create an instance of the untyped report object
   oRpt = New ReportDocument()

   ' Load the report from disk
   oRpt.Load(reportFile)

   ' Set the options for saving the exported file to disk
   oDest = New DiskFileDestinationOptions()
   oDest.DiskFileName = exportFilePath

   ' Set the exporting information
   oExport = oRpt.ExportOptions

   ' Set the destination options
   oExport.DestinationOptions = oDest

   ' Set the location, this can be:
   ' DiskFile, ExchangeFolder, MicrosoftMail or NoDestination
   oExport.ExportDestinationType = ExportDestinationType.DiskFile

   ' Set the Export type, this can be:
   ' PDF, Excel, Word Doc, RTF Doc,
   ' HTML 3.2, HTML 4.0 or CrystalReport
   oExport.ExportFormatType = ExportFormatType.PortableDocFormat

   ' Call the Export method to export the report
   oRpt.Export()
   MessageBox.Show("Report Exported!")
End Sub
```

18

LISTING 18.3 continued

C#

```
    private void button1_Click(object sender, System.EventArgs e)
    {

        // The path/location where the exported file will be saved
        string exportFilePath = "c:\\Report1.pdf";

        // Create an instance of the untyped report object
        oRpt = new ReportDocument();

        // Load the report from disk
        oRpt.Load(reportFile);

        // Set the options for saving the exported file to disk
        oDest = new DiskFileDestinationOptions();
        oDest.DiskFileName = exportFilePath;

        // Set the exporting information
        oExport = oRpt.ExportOptions;

        // Set the destination options
        oExport.DestinationOptions = oDest;

        // Set the location, this can be:
        // DiskFile, ExchangeFolder, MicrosoftMail or NoDestination
        oExport.ExportDestinationType = ExportDestinationType.DiskFile;

        // Set the Export type, this can be:
        // PDF, Excel, Word Doc, RTF Doc,
        // HTML 3.2, HTML 4.0 or CrystalReport
        oExport.ExportFormatType = ExportFormatType.PortableDocFormat;

        // Call the Export method to export the report
        oRpt.Export();
        MessageBox.Show("Report Exported!");

    }
}
```

In the commented code in Listing 18.3, you can see the various options for the `ExportFormatType` and the `ExportDestinationType` for the report. These are the same properties that you can set in the viewer control.

Viewing Reports in Web Forms

To view a report in a Web Form, you go through the same process of adding a new report to your ASP.NET applications and designing the report using the Report Expert. After you've designed the report, you must add the `CrystalReportViewer` control from the Web Forms Toolbox tab. At this point, things change slightly.

Earlier, you saw how to programmatically load a report at runtime. The method of loading a report into the Web Form viewer control is the same. If you want to set the `ReportSource` property at design time, you must select the `DataBindings` property from the Properties window of the report viewer. Figure 18.21 demonstrates the DataBindings dialog box for a report viewer. Notice the `ReportSource` property—I've entered the path to a valid report file that I created.

FIGURE 18.21

Setting the `DataBindings` *of a Web report at design time.*

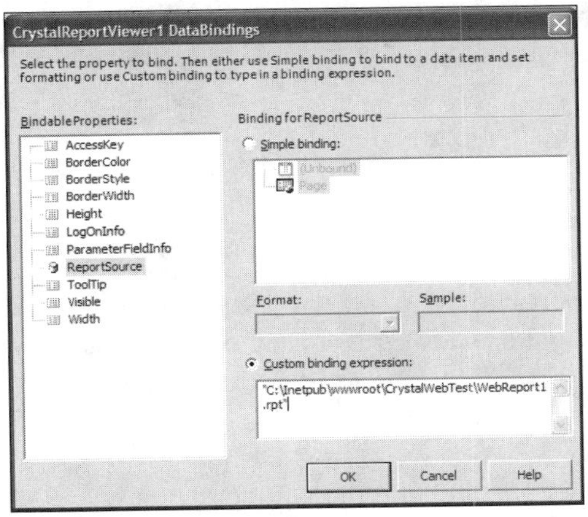

When the `ReportSource` property is set, a report appears in the Web Form with phony data, as Figure 18.22 demonstrates.

At this point, the viewer is aware of the report that it must display. To actually bind that data from the data source to the report, you must call the `DataBind` method of the `Page` class to make the report viewable at runtime. The following C# snippet calls the `DataBind` method:

```
Page.DataBind();
```

This code must go in the `Page_Load` event in the code-behind of the page with the viewer. After the `DataBind` method executes, the report binds to the data source, and loads in the browser viewer. You'll notice in the following code that the `ReportSource` property is set in the viewer object in the HTML of the Web Form:

```
<CR:CrystalReportViewer id=CrystalReportViewer1 "
ReportSource='<%# "C:\Inetpub\wwwroot\CrystalWebTest\WebReport1.rpt" %>'>
</CR:CrystalReportViewer>
```

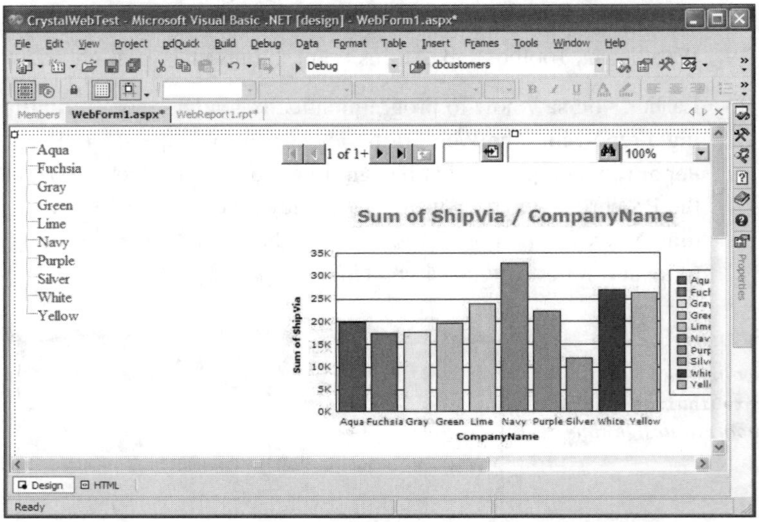

FIGURE 18.22
A report loaded into the Web Form viewer.

When you load a report into the Web Form viewer control, there's no printing capability. That means no Print button shows up on the toolbar for the viewer. You must use the regular File, Print menu to print the reports displayed in the browser.

Summary

Today you learned about the robust reporting capabilities in Visual Studio .NET using Crystal Reports. By adding reports to your ASP.NET and Windows Forms applications, the Report Expert from Crystal guides you through all the steps necessary to create high-quality reports. Using the `CrystalReportViewer` control for the desktop and the Web, you have an easy way to present reports to the end user. You also learned how to export reports to various formats and how to print without using the report viewer controls.

Q&A

Q There are a lot of cool features in Crystal, but no time seems to have been spent on the help file. Where do I find out more information on creating reports?

A The help file that comes with .NET isn't great, but it's pretty good. To get a ton of great help on using Crystal with .NET, go to this link:

`http://support.crystaldecisions.com/updates/default.asp`

Search for samples in the .NET version of Crystal Reports. There are 75 to 100 different samples in Visual Basic .NET, C#, and C++ .NET on all aspects of using Crystal in Visual Studio .NET. It's a very helpful Web site.

Q Crystal is cool, but are there any other reporting tools that integrate with .NET?

A Yes, as a matter of fact, I use ActiveReports from Data Dynamics. It has lots of great features; most notably, the fact that the report object itself has a code-behind class in which you can write code to manipulate report data. In my opinion, ActiveReports gives you more granular control over what the data looks like in a programmatic way, not a wizard-driven way.

Quiz

1. The ________________ determines the default report properties when I add new reports to a solution.
2. Using report ______________, I can customize the presentation of individual fields when they print in a report.
3. Setting the ____________ property in the Windows Forms viewer control, I can set the path of the report to display at runtime or design time.
4. The _______________ node of the File Explorer lets me add items such as page number and report path to my reports.

Quiz Answers

1. Report Expert
2. Formulas
3. `ReportSource`
4. Special Fields

Exercises

1. Using what you learned today about reports in Windows Forms, take the code in Listing 18.1 and create a Web-based reporting application. You should add an ASPX page that enables the user to select a report. Then, using `Reponse.Redirect`, pass the report name to another ASPX page that loads the report dynamically at runtime.

If your preference is to write reports using Windows Forms, you can take the code in Listing 18.1 and add the correct constructor to a form that accepts a report file name to bind to a generic viewer application.

2. Search the Dynamic Help for Crystal Reports. Find the Reporting Off ADO .NET Datasets section. This section walks you through the steps to create a report off a `DataSet` object. Read this walkthrough and try to work it out. If you need more help, you can go to the link in the Q&A and download the samples at the Crystal site for working with `DataSets`.

WEEK 3

DAY 19

Understanding Microsoft Application Center Test

Some of the biggest questions when you develop new applications for the Internet are "How will it perform?" and "Will I need more hardware to support this application?" There have always been stress-testing tools available for Web-based applications, but they're expensive and difficult to implement. With Visual Studio .NET, there is a built-in tool, Application Center Test, that stress-tests your Web applications and gives you the information you need to make sure that the hardware and software you're using are appropriate for the job. Today you learn

- What Application Center Test is
- How to add Application Center Test projects to your Visual Studio .NET solutions
- How to understand Application Center Test results

Introduction to Application Center Test

Application Center Test (ACT) is an enterprise tool integrated into the Visual Studio .NET development environment that allows stress and regression testing of Web projects.

Note Application Center Test is available only in the Enterprise Developer and Enterprise Architect versions of Visual Studio .NET.

ACT enables you to create VBScript or JScript routines to drive testing. Using ACT, you can create complex tests that can run repeatedly to provide baselines for performance and to ensure that software issues haven't crept into the project.

The ACT product distributed with .NET is a subset of the functionality found in Application Center, which is a Microsoft enterprise tool allowing creation and management of clustered Web servers. The Application Center Test in the Application Center suite also allows tests to be run from multiple client computers because the load generated from a single computer is limited by processor, memory, disk, or network connection at some point.

Some features of the main ACT included in Visual Studio .NET are

- Integrates with the Visual Studio .NET integrated development environment (IDE)
- Creates and manages cookies
- Records a test script while browsing with Microsoft Internet Explorer
- Supports testing of secure sockets layer (SSL) Web pages
- Allows several authentication schemes
- Accumulates test data for later analysis
- Allows configurable simultaneous connections to drive the testing from a single computer
- Does *not* allow multiple client computers to be coordinated
- Is *not* appropriate for heavy load testing of scaleable sites

The last two items are part of the full Application Center product.

Strategy for Using ACT

The easiest way to use ACT is from the Visual Studio .NET IDE. You can add an ACT project to your solution and run it directly from Visual Studio .NET. This allows testing and editing of the script, but you don't have the same robust functionality of using ACT outside the Visual Studio .NET environment.

A second way to use ACT is in standalone mode. From the Visual Studio .NET menu, ACT is available under Visual Studio Enterprise Features. Using the standalone program enables you to set many more parameters than using the IDE integrated ACT, such as connections and iterations from the user interface. Using the standalone version also enables you to create specific users that are used to run the test, in addition to the ability to add performance counters.

For creating the test script, a recording tool is included that works like a macro recorder you learned about this week when creating macros in Visual Studio .NET. When you start recording, the recording tool opens a Microsoft Internet Explorer (IE) session, enabling you to manually browse through the target Web site, clicking on the features or links you want to test. As you're clicking around in IE, each click is recorded and the data being downloaded to the browser is recorded. This is the basis for the test.

Tip

> For basic testing, use the integrated version; for more complicated test setup, use the standalone version to help you with settings. The version of ACT that comes with Visual Studio .NET isn't adequate for high-end load testing of Web projects because it doesn't allow multiple client computers to be controlled. You need the full version of Application Center to do that.

If you use the standalone ACT or the integrated ACT, a script file is created that you'll probably want to modify and tune. When you take a careful look at the script, you'll see that it's pretty simple. All features of ACT and the interaction with the browser can be scripted.

As you'll see later, all the ACT settings except the scripts are stored in XML files. If you're motivated enough and can remember last week when you learned how to work with XML, you can modify the XML files to adjust to interfaces in any way you choose.

Understanding ACT Projects, Users, Tests, and Connections

Much of today focuses on using projects, users, tests, and connections in ACT.

A *project* may contain one or more tests. A project may be opened or created with the standalone tool or from the Visual Studio .NET IDE. They share a common file format and both have the file extension `.act`.

Note

> Note that you can't have the same ACT project file open simultaneously with both the standalone tool and the Visual Studio .NET IDE.

Users are agents that are started and run tests. They generate the load and simulated Web site access. Normally (and always if you run only from the Visual Studio .NET IDE), users are generated as needed automatically by the program. If you use the standalone program, you can define your own users. This enables you to create accounts, assign names, passwords, and user rights, and also to manipulate and reuse cookies.

Connections are used to send requests and receive responses from the target Web server.

Tests are what you run. A test is a VBScript or JScript file that executes. `Test` is the main ACT object and is used to modify, control, and monitor a test.

If you start the ACT standalone tool, you'll see a number of sample projects, ranging from simple to complex, with some of them targeted at the Visual Studio .NET Web samples.

Creating a New ACT Project

To see the overall use of ACT within the framework of Visual Studio .NET, you'll create a new ASP .NET Web application, add an ACT project to the solution, and then add and run a test. Later today, you'll learn about the additional control you have in the standalone version of Application Center Test.

To start, create a new ASP.NET Web application and name it ActWebTest. On the default `Webform1`, add a `Label` server control. Set the `Text` property of the `Label` control to ACT Web Test. Figure 19.1 shows what your project should look like at this point.

So far, you've just added a single control to the default `Webform`. Keep in mind that as you add more controls and objects to a Web Form, you'll see different results in the tests.

The next step is to add an ACT project to your existing solution. To do this, right-click on the ActTestWeb project name in the Solution Explorer, and then select Add, New Project. The Add New Project dialog pops up. From the Project Types pane on the left side of the dialog, drill into the Other Projects node, and select Application Center Test Projects. As Figure 19.2 demonstrates, only one template is shown: ACT Project.

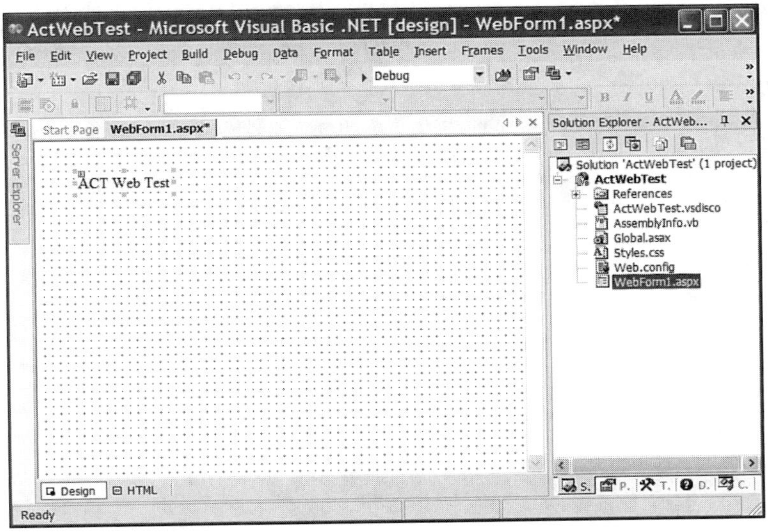

FIGURE 19.1

The ActWebTest project with the `Label` *control on the default form.*

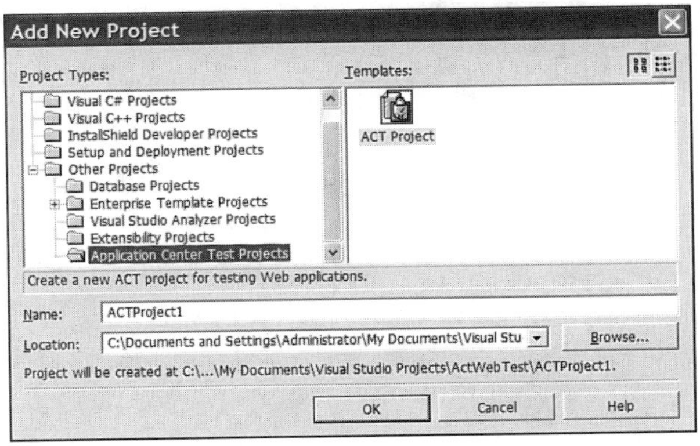

FIGURE 19.2

ACT project templates in the Add Project dialog.

If you select the Act Project template and click the OK button, the new ACT Project will be added to your solution. Accept the defaults, but note where it's being saved so you can open it later outside the Visual Studio .NET environment. Now that you've added the ACT project to the solution, your Solution Explorer should resemble Figure 19.3.

The next step is to add a test to ACTProject1. To do this, right-click on the ActProject1 in the Solution Explorer and select Add, New Item. The Add New Item dialog now pops up, as Figure 19.4 demonstrates.

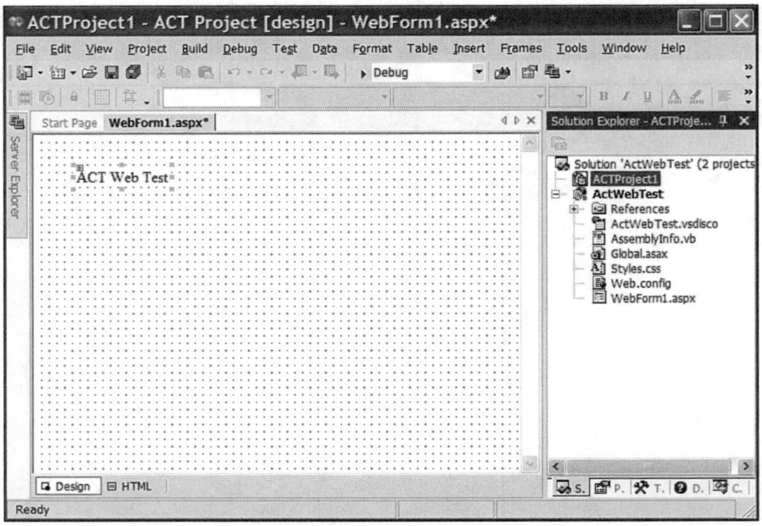

FIGURE 19.3

Solution after adding the ACT project.

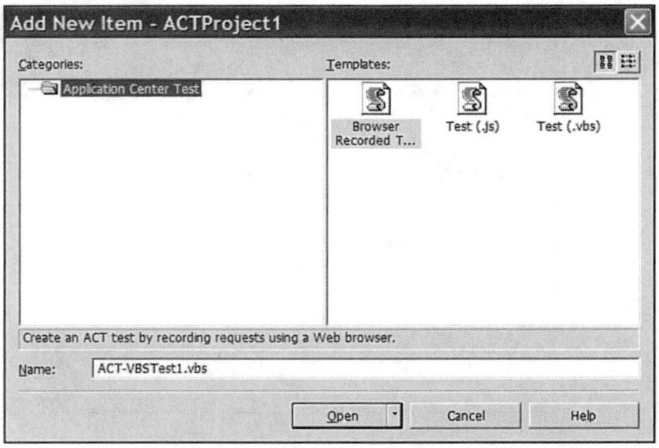

FIGURE 19.4

The Add New Item dialog for an ACT test.

Three test templates are displayed: Browser Recorded Test (.vbs), Test (.js), and Test (.vbs). The last two create blank test script files that you can fill in using either JScript or VBScript.

From the Add New Item dialog box, choose Browser Recorded Test. The recording dialog box pops up as shown in Figure 19.5.

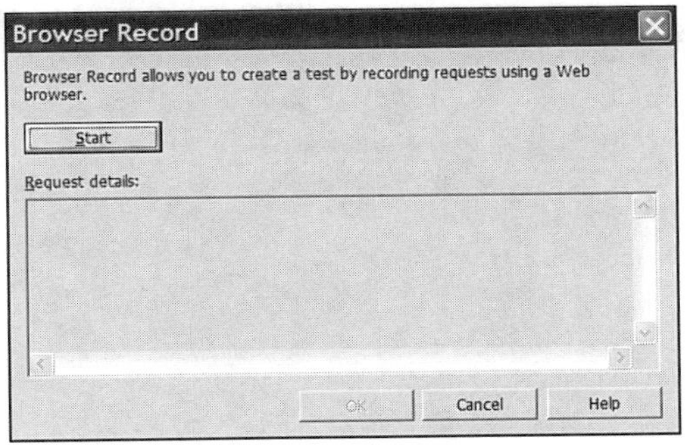

FIGURE 19.5
The Browser Record dialog.

Press the Start button to begin recording. After pressing the Start button, a new Web browser session is opened to the address `About:Blank`, as Figure 19.6 shows.

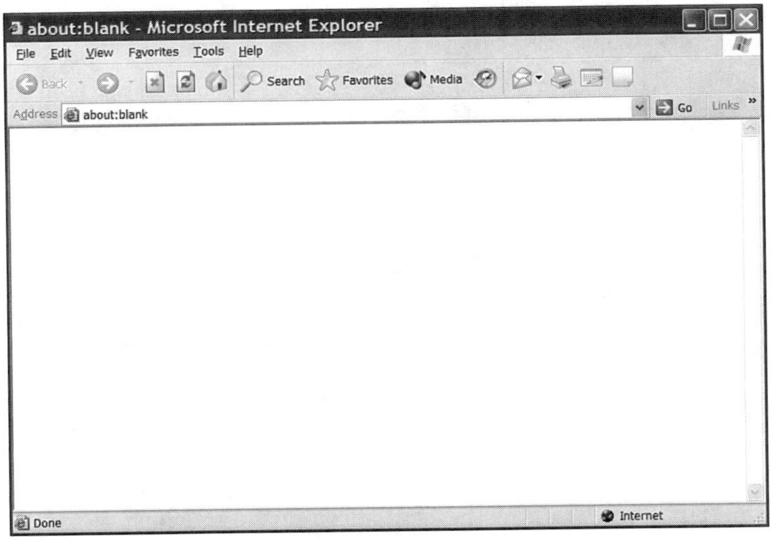

FIGURE 19.6
`About:Blank` *starts the new test session.*

Because the browser opens up to the `About:Blank` page, you must navigate to the URL of the test site. Type **`http://localhost/ActWebTest/WebForm1.aspx`** in the Address box. Figure 19.7 is the page you created earlier.

Now that you've browsed to the page, you can stop the recording process. To stop the recording, go back to the Visual Studio .NET IDE and click the Stop button. Then click the OK button as Figure 19.8 demonstrates.

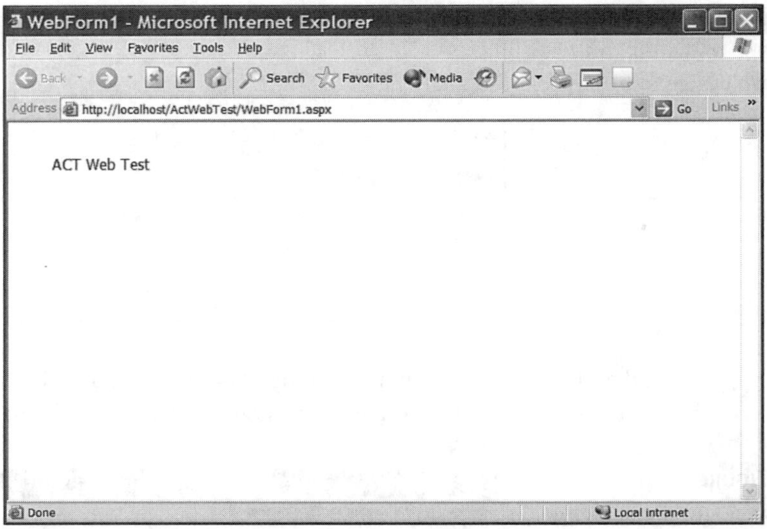

FIGURE 19.7
Browsing to the test page.

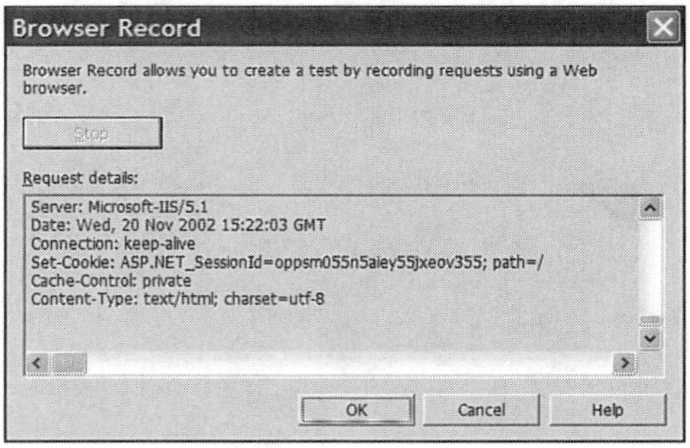

FIGURE 19.8
Stopping the test recording.

Visual Studio .NET now displays the VBScript that was generated from the recording process. Figure 19.9 shows what you should be looking at now. You go through the script code in detail later today, but for a single browse to a page, it consists of a `Main sub` routine that calls the `SendRequest1` subroutine. If you browse to multiple pages, click a submit button or other controls, or if the pages contain images and other objects that must be downloaded from the Web site, more subroutines are generated. When I first tested this, I was also downloading email from my MSN email account, and all the activity for that was recorded also. So, the actual script that's generated gives you all the activity on the machine when the test is run, not just the information about browsing to the test application you created.

FIGURE 19.9

VBScript generated from the test recording.

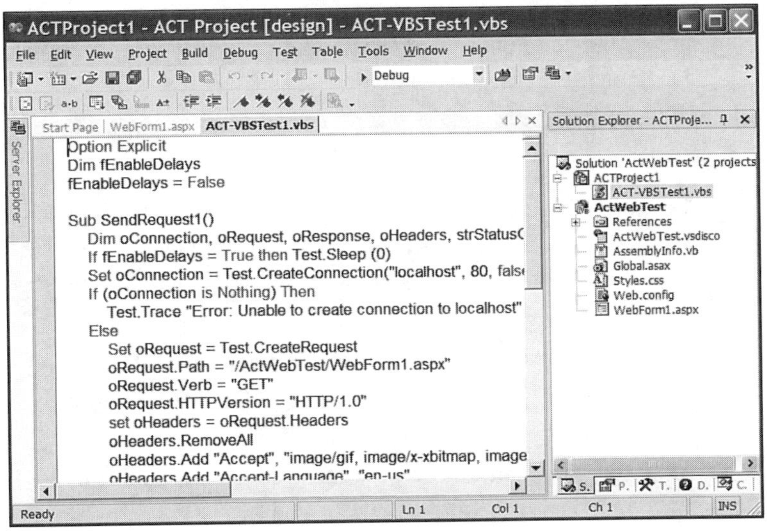

Now that the test has been generated, you need to actually run it. First, you must set some of the properties for the test. Right-click on the test (the default name in this case is ACT-VBSTest1.vbs) and display the properties as in Figure 19.10.

FIGURE 19.10

Properties of the VBS script file.

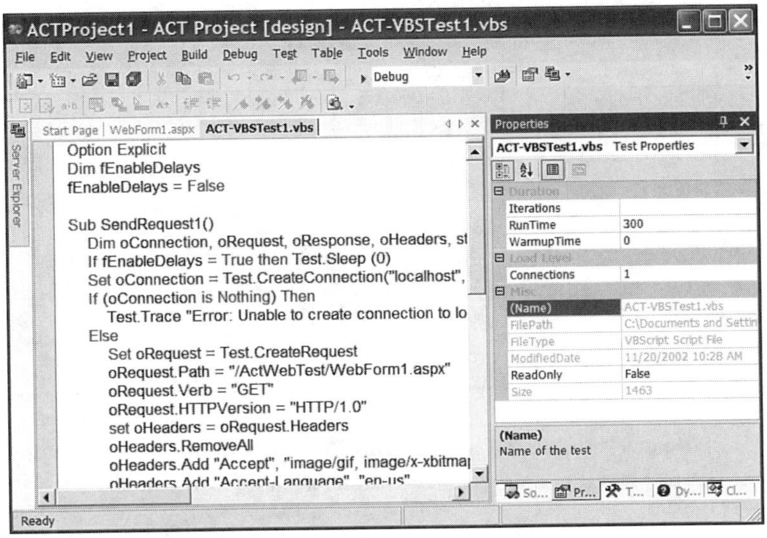

There are two basic methods of controlling how long a test runs: either by specifying the `RunTime` property (in this case, 300 seconds by default) or by the number of iterations.

If testing is based on time, a warm-up period can be set. The warm-up time could eliminate caching and other variables to allow a steady state to be achieved before performance measurements are started.

To allow quicker testing and demonstration, set Iterations to 200, which clears the 300 seconds.

The other important property is Connections. By default, this is set to 1. The Connections property controls how many simultaneous browser connections are made. The 1 corresponds to what you did when recording the browser session—only one browser was open.

Depending on the power of your client, you can set this to a higher value. With multiple connections, the number of requests per second will be higher until your test computer runs out of processor, memory, or network capacity.

To run the test, right-click on the `ACT-VBSTest1.vbs` test in the Solution Explorer and select Start Test, as shown in Figure 19.11.

FIGURE 19.11
Starting the ACT test.

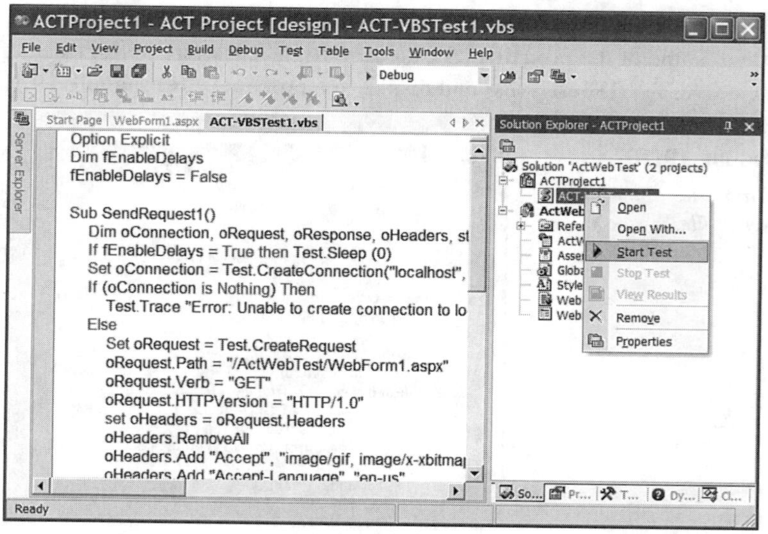

You can monitor the progress of the testing in the Output window. The output for my test is displayed in an expanded Output window in Figure 19.12.

The results include the total runtime, one second in this example. There were 200 iterations and, because there was only one request per iteration, 200 requests as well. The Avg. Requests/sec is 200.

FIGURE 19.12

The Output window results from running the ACT test.

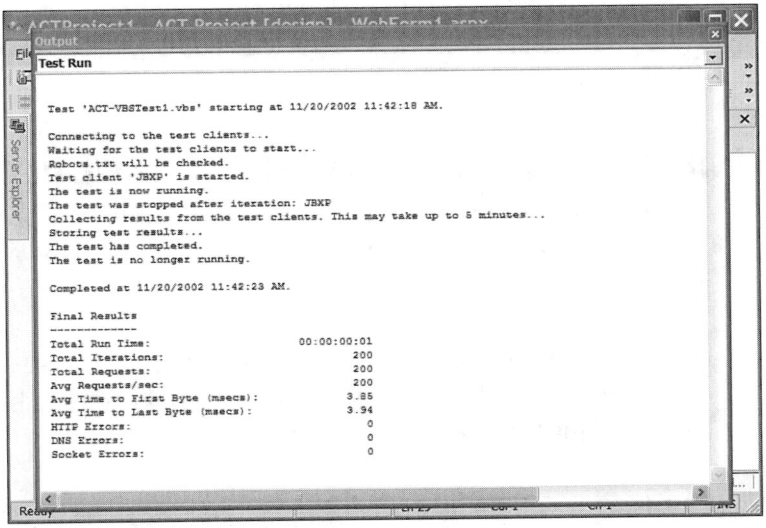

Avg Time to First Byte (msec) is the time between the request and when data starts arriving back from the Web server, averaged over all the requests. This includes any compilations the Web server needed to execute the page and communication delays; for instance, a satellite link might have a high data rate but long initial delay.

Avg Time to Last Byte (msec) is the time to the final response from the Web server. The difference between these is the time the Web server took to actually execute the entire page and actual transmission time (data rate related) on the intervening network. All HTTP, DNS, and Socket errors are also displayed.

You can view the final results by right-clicking on the test in the Solution Explorer and choosing View Results. The final results are shown as a row of data in the View Results window. If you run more than once, the multiple runs are displayed and saved until you delete them. Figure 19.13 shows the Application Test Center Results window with two tests listed.

FIGURE 19.13

Viewing the test results in the Results window.

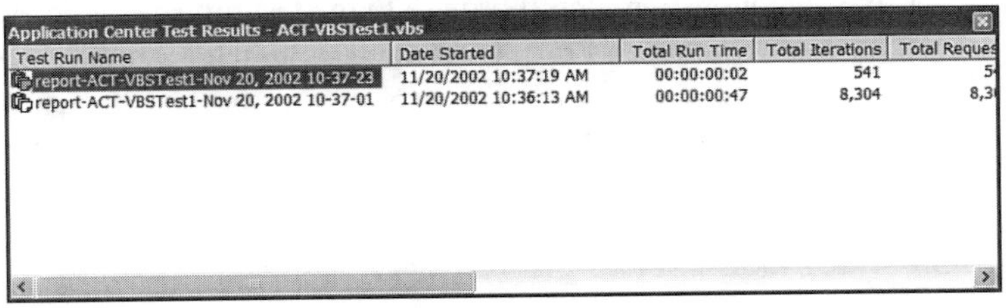

Now that you've seen how to create ACT tests in the Visual Studio .NET IDE, you can close Visual Studio .NET. Next, you'll learn how to use the standalone ACT application to run tests.

Using the ACT Standalone Application

To test the standalone application and the parameters that can be set in the Application Center Test environment, start with the standalone program, which can be found under the Visual Studio .NET Enterprise Features in the Visual Studio .NET folder on the Start menu.

When the ACT IDE is open, you're brought to the ACT Samples list that's installed when you installed Visual Studio .NET for the first time. Figure 19.14 shows the ACT standalone IDE when opened for the first time.

FIGURE 19.14

The ACT standalone application.

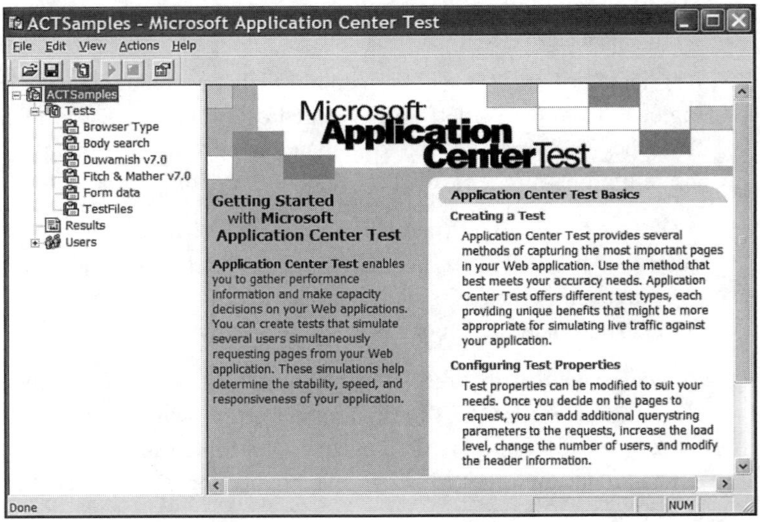

For this demonstration, you'll browse to the test project we created in Visual Studio .NET. Select File, Open Project and navigate to the location of the saved ActProject1 you created earlier. On my system, this project was saved to its default location under the ActWebTest solution in the Visual Studio Projects folder, which is at the path `C:\Documents and Settings\Administrator\My Documents\Visual Studio Projects\ACTWebTest\ACTProject1` as Figure 19.15 demonstrates.

FIGURE 19.15

Finding an ACT test.

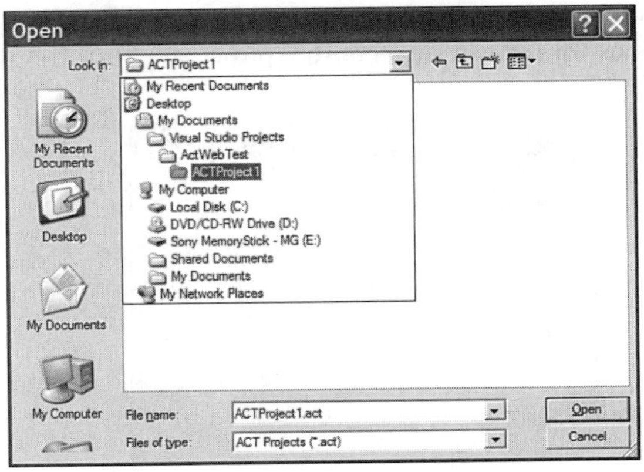

When the project is open and you click on the ACT-VBSTest1, the VBScript is displayed. On top is an area in which you can make notes about the test and the procedures that you took for future reference.

Next, right-click the ACT-VBSTest1 project in the left pane and select Properties to view the properties for this ACT project. The Properties dialog box is shown in Figure 19.16.

FIGURE 19.16

The ACT Properties dialog box.

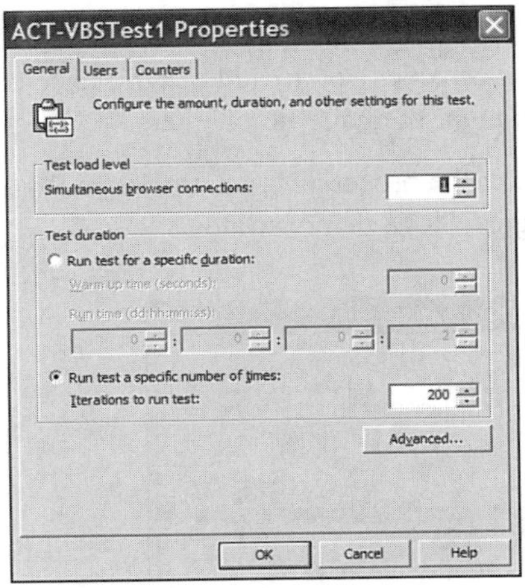

The General tab is where you set the number of simultaneous browser connections allowed and whether the test should be based on time or iterations. This is similar information to the property page displayed in the Visual Studio .NET IDE. Notice that the properties you set in the Visual Studio .NET IDE, such as the iteration setting of 2, are kept with the project.

If you click the Users tab on the Properties dialog, as Figure 19.17 demonstrates, you're shown the options for the users of the ACT project.

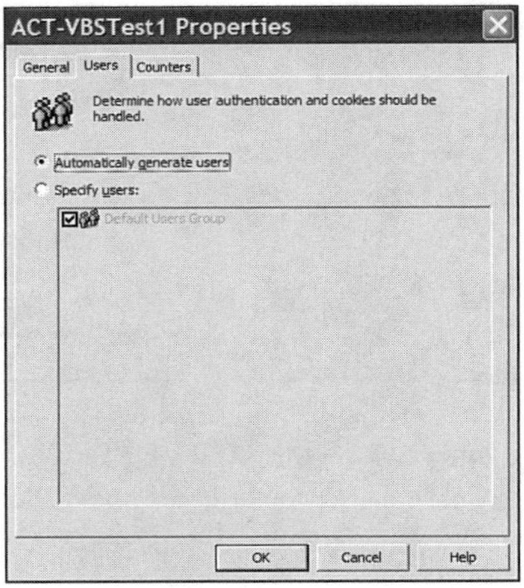

FIGURE 19.17
Navigating to the Users tab in ACT.

ACT automatically generates 20 default users. You can create your own users and group them. In this screen, you can only specify previously created groups of users, not specific users.

The final tab is Counters. This enables you to add performance counters for any computer in your network. By default, there are no counters.

I've added three counters here: the processor time, the server bytes/second, and the available bytes of memory as Figure 19.18 demonstrates.

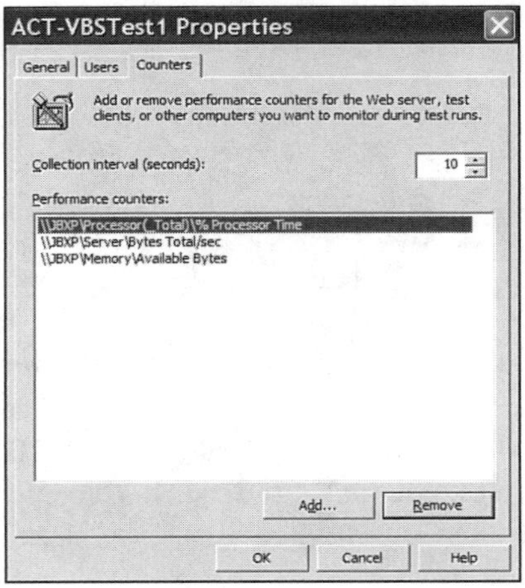

FIGURE 19.18
The Performance Counters list after adding to the ACT project.

Depending on the environment you're working in, the client computer (which drives the test) and the target Web computer may be separate machines.

As you add load, you can use the results of these counters to see whether either the client or the server has reached a peak load.

Close the Properties windows. Now right-click the ACT-VBSTest1 test in the left pane and select Start Test.

Real-time results are displayed as shown in Figure 19.19. Note that HTTP, domain name server (DNS), and socket errors are displayed as well as the number of iterations and the requests per second (RPS). If you click the Show Details button, a graphical representation of the test is displayed in the real-time results dialog. I also ran this with five connections. The RPS went up to 80 and the test time was three seconds. Because the test was very short, the differences weren't as dramatic as you would see with more iterations and/or a heavier test load.

FIGURE 19.19

Real-time results of the ACT test.

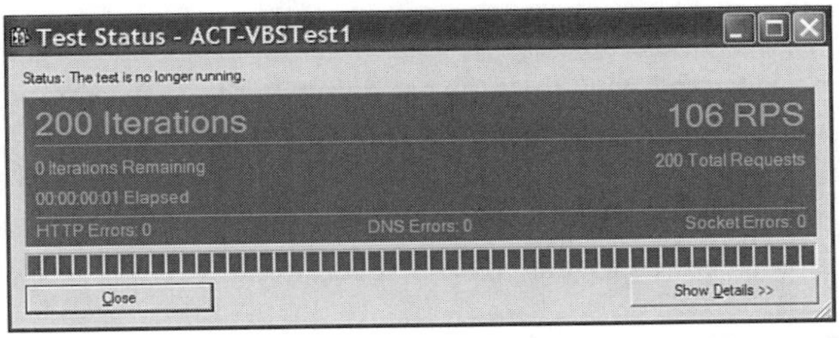

If you select Results from the left pane in the ACT IDE, you'll see a list of the different tests that have run, along with the Performance Counters used for each test. On my machine, I ran the test several times to test various output. You can see the extremely useful reports in Figure 19.20 if you select any of the tests listed in the Test Runs window.

In the Report window, you can select one of three report options: Overview, Graph, or Summary. Based on the type of information you're looking for from the test, each report gives you different data based on the test results.

Customizing the ACT Tests

As you saw earlier when adding a new ACT test in Visual Studio .NET, either JScript or VBScript can be used to create a test. Both allow access to the ACT object model. However, only VBScript is created by the browser-recording tool.

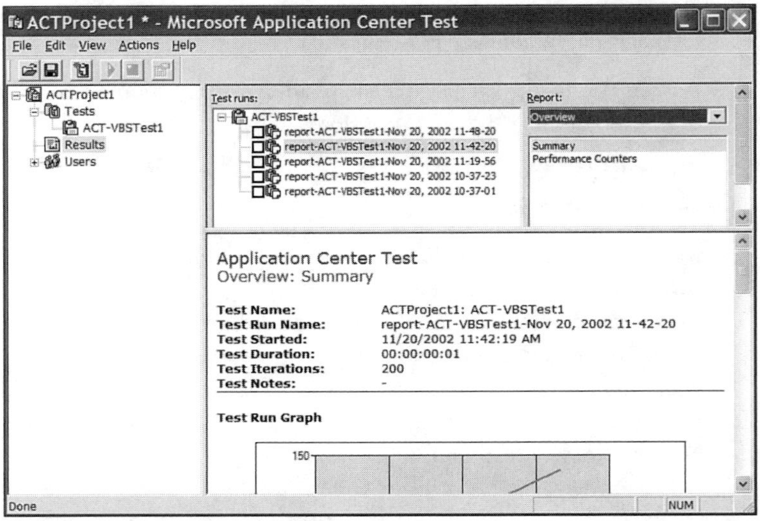

FIGURE 19.20
Viewing the results of ACT tests and the expanded reports.

To better understand what the tests are doing, we'll go over some of the more important objects in the ACT object model. As with any other object model, you can programmatically interact with any facet of the ACT tests that you're running by simply modifying the script that's running the test. After reviewing the major objects, we take a closer look at the script generated by the browser-recording tool.

The ACT Object Model

A number of objects are contained in the ACT object model. The core of it all is the `Test` object, which defines each test, its script, and other parameters.

The other objects not contained in the `Test` object are used to set up an environment, control the tests, and report the results. This is referred to in the documentation as the *Application Object Model.*

`Application` Object Model Level

The `Application` object contains objects that enable you to manipulate the test, such as `Project`, `Controller`, `Report`, and `User`. Each object is defined further in the following bullet points:

- `Project`: With the `Project` object, you can create a new project or open an existing project and modify and save changes. It also allows access to the collections of `Tests` and `UserGroups` contained within the project.

- `Controller`: The `Controller` object allows starting and stopping of tests in projects. This object can be thought of as the client computer running the test.
- `Report`: The `Report` object contained in the `Reports` collection stores information collected during the running of a test. This includes information about the computer the test ran on (the client), any performance counter information, requests used, and response codes received. It also contains basic information such as the requests per second, start time, duration, and report name.
- `User`: The `User` object is the entity running the test or the person doing the browsing if the testing isn't automated. The `User` object has a name, password, and a collection of cookies. The `User` objects are contained in a `UserGroup` collection, which in turn is contained in the `UserGroups` collection at the application level.

`Test` Object Level

The `Test` object level is the interface to the requests and responses being made from the client application to the Web server. Each of the core Test objects is further defined in the following bullet points:

- `Test`: The `Test` object is the main piece of running a test. The `Test` object creates connections and requests, and controls tracing users and the test environment. The `Test` object is also used to start and stop tests.
- `Connection`: The `Connection` object is created with the test object and manages the connection to the target Web page. With the `Connection`, you can specify the server, port, and whether an SSL connection is in use.
- `Request`: The `Request` object allows creation of a Web request, in a way very similar to what a Web browser does. The path, headers, verb (`get` and `post`, for example), encoding, and body are important properties. When the request is sent by a test, it results in a response that can be analyzed.
- `Response`: The `Response` object is returned by the Web server being tested. In addition to the headers and body returned, a number of other useful properties are returned such as result code, time to first byte, and time to last byte.
- `Header`: A `Header` is a name/value pair used for both requests and responses. Multiple headers may be included to store information about the HTTP request or response.
- `User`: `User` objects are used to log in to specific Web pages or services. They allow cookies, usernames, and passwords to be used when sending HTTP requests.

Walking Through the ACT Script

In this section, we walk through the script generated by the test wizard earlier today. A request routine is generated for each item on the page being browsed. These requests include the main page and each image, for example. In the simple example you created, you browsed only the main page, which did not contain any other objects and is the first `SendRequest1()` for the main page.

The first thing to note is that this is VBScript and all variables are declared without a data type and re-created as variants, which is the only data type in VBScript.

```
Option Explicit
Dim fEnableDelays
fEnableDelays = False

Sub SendRequest1()
```

The `Dim` also highlights the main objects of interest in ACT, the `Connection`, `Request`, `Response`, and `Header` objects:

```
Dim oConnection, oRequest, oResponse, oHeaders, strStatusCode
```

It's possible to set up delays between each request. Call it "think time" on the part of the client for a more realistic load:

```
If fEnableDelays = True then Test.Sleep (0)
```

Connections can fail for various reasons. Before proceeding, always make sure that the connection is created:

```
Set oConnection = Test.CreateConnection("localhost", 80, false)
If (oConnection is Nothing) Then
  Test.Trace "Error: Unable to create connection to www localhost "
Else
```

This and all the other requests in this example are `GET`. Other request verbs are `OPTIONS`, `HEAD`, `POST`, `PUT`, `DELETE`, `TRACE`, and `CONNECT`:

```
Set oRequest = Test.CreateRequest
oRequest.Path = "/"
oRequest.Verb = "GET"
oRequest.HTTPVersion = "HTTP/1.0"
```

This section resets the header to accept a list of types, some explicitly and some generic (`*/*`):

```
set oHeaders = oRequest.Headers
oHeaders.RemoveAll
oHeaders.Add "Accept", "image/gif, image/x-xbitmap,
   image/jpeg, image/pjpeg, application/vnd.ms-excel,
   application/vnd.ms-powerpoint, application/msword, */*"
oHeaders.Add "Accept-Language", "en-us"
```

Cookies that are supported and are under the control of code can be edited and manipulated using the test object. This shows a cookie has been detected but not explicitly manipulated:

```
'oHeaders.Add "Cookie", "ASP.NET_SessionId=ivzrqjj5vmua2v55foswsti1"
oHeaders.Add "Cookie", "(automatic)"
oHeaders.Add "User-Agent", "Mozilla/4.0 (compatible;
    MSIE 6.0; Windows NT 5.0; Q312461;
    .NET CLR 1.0.3705; .NET CLR 1.0.2914)"
'oHeaders.Add "Host", "localhost"
oHeaders.Add "Host", "(automatic)"
oHeaders.Add "Cookie", "(automatic)"
```

A response is expected by executing the Send request of the connection. It's possible that the connection has died or that there's some other reason the target server can't be contacted.

```
Set oResponse = oConnection.Send(oRequest)
If (oResponse is Nothing) Then
  Test.Trace "Error: Failed to receive response for URL to "
    + "/ActWebTest/WebForm1.aspx"
Else
```

The response codes returned are standard. Table 19.1 lists the return codes and their descriptions.

TABLE 19.1 Return Codes from ACT Test Responses

Return Code Range	*Description*
100 to 199	Informational messages
200 to 299	Successful request
300 to 399	Redirection occurred
400 to 499	Client error
500 to 599	Server error

19

Note that status codes can be more than three characters in length. Microsoft Internet Information Server (IIS) uses additional digits for a subcode. For example, 401.1 means Unauthorized – Login Failed.

```
      strStatusCode = oResponse.ResultCode
    End If
    oConnection.Close
  End If
End Sub

Sub Main()
  call SendRequest1()
End Sub
```

As you can see, the results in the script are very useful in determining what the macro has recorded and what steps the application is running.

Understanding the Test Environment

For simple regression testing of the functionality of your Web project on a development machine, the test environment isn't critical. But if you want to get repeatable performance results you can build on and compare with future testing, you must carefully set up a testing environment.

Some issues you might face are

- Providing enough load
- Isolating test machines
- Identifying bottlenecks in test environment

Here are some general rules for a test environment that will give you consistent results:

- The test environment must be isolated and contain only development or test Web servers. No production servers should be used unless other traffic has been shut off.
- A separate network should be set up so that broadcasts, probes, inadvertent file transfers, and any other unanticipated network traffic don't take place.
- The recommendation for stress testing is that the Web server's processor utilization be driven to at least 80%. This might not be possible using a single client computer.
- You can remove or minimize network bottlenecks by using the fastest possible components and avoiding the use of proxy servers or other protocols that require unnecessary overhead.
- To fully stress a Web application, you must increase the load until the Web server becomes the bottleneck and prevents further increases. If any part of the system is slower than the Web server or Web applications, it's impossible to measure the maximum.

Load Created by an ACT Client

The amount of load created by an ACT client varies and depends on many factors. As an example, the following test environment from the documentation shown in Table 19.2 might provide some guidance for setting up your own system.

TABLE 19.2 ACT Client Configuration

Configured Item	*Details*
Software	Windows 2000 Server
Processor	600MHz Pentium III
Memory	128MB

Based on the configuration in Table 19.2, the test details can be summarized: There were five requests. No delays were used between the requests. For the dynamic test, a single connection was used to request all five pages. The pages were all small (15 byte) HTML documents. The number of simultaneous browser connections was set to 10.

Table 19.3 lists the Web server configuration for a sample test.

TABLE 19.3 ACT Server Configuration

Configured Item	*Details*
Software	Windows 2000 Advanced Server running IIS 5.0
Processor	650MHz Pentium III
Memory	256MB

For this configuration, the average number of requests per second for a five-minute test run was about 445 RPS. The Web server CPU was at about 40% use, whereas the ACT client CPU was at 100% use.

A second, more realistic, test scenario used the Load URLs From File sample from the Dynamic Test Samples.

With both the Application Center Test client and the Web server running on the 650MHz machine mentioned earlier, Application Center Test created load levels of about 225 RPS. Other sample tests produced load levels similar to that on the same computer.

Scheduling Tests

Scheduling of tests can be done so that heaving loading can be done off hours and unattended. This is done by writing a Windows Scripting Host (WSH) script and then running it with the `AT` command.

Here's a sample script to run the test you've been working on:

```
Dim oProject, oController
'
' Create a project based on the existing project we have been working on
'
```

```
Set oProject =
  OpenMyProject("C:\Inetpub\wwwroot\ACTProject1", "ACTProject1.act")
Set oController = CreateObject("ACT.Controller")
'
' This is the "main" script routine
'
Call RunMyTest(oProject, "ACT-VBSTest1", oController)

Set oController = nothing
Set oProject = nothing

'
' End of main script
'
''''''''''''''''''''''''''''''''''''''''''''''''''''''''''
'
' Open ACT project.
'
''''''''''''''''''''''''''''''''''''''''''''''''''''''''''
Function OpenMyProject(strProjectPath, strProjectFileName)
  '
  Dim oProject
  '
  ' Ignore all errors
  '
  On Error Resume Next
  '
  ' Create a new project object
  '
  Set oProject = CreateObject("ACT.Project")
  '
  ' If it did not get created, report an error (should log this!)
  '
  If (Not(IsObject(oProject))) Then
   WScript.Echo("Error creating project object")
   Call WScript.Quit()
  Else
   '
   ' Open the our project
   '
   Call oProject.Open(strProjectPath, strProjectFileName, False)
   '
   ' Check for errors, exit if there are any
   '
   If (Err.Number > 0) Then
     WScript.Echo("Error opening project
     Path=" & strProjectPath & ", File=" & strProjectFileName)
     Call WScript.Quit()
   End If
  End If
  '
```

```
  ' Return the opened project
  '
  Set OpenMyProject = oProject
  '
End Function


''''''''''''''''''''''''''''''''''''''''''''''''''''''''''
'
' Run Act Test
'
''''''''''''''''''''''''''''''''''''''''''''''''''''''''''
Sub RunMyTest(oProject, strTestName, oController)
  Dim oTest, bIsRunning
  '
  ' Make sure that a test is not already running
  '
  bIsRunning = oController.TestIsRunning
  '
  If bIsRunning Then
   WScript.Echo("ACT is already running a test.")
  Else
   '
   ' Get the test out of the tests collection of the project
   '
   Set oTest = oProject.Tests.Item(strTestName)

   WScript.Echo("Test Start")
   Call oController.StartTest(oProject, oTest, False)
   WScript.Echo("Test End")
  End If
End Sub
```

Now you can use the AT command to schedule the task, as the following code demonstrates:

```
AT 19:30 /interactive /every:M,T,W,Th,F
  cscript.exe "c:\Tests\WeekdayStressTest.vbs"
```

Understanding the ACT Test Results

There are several pieces of information that help you figure out what the results of the ACT tests actually mean. The reports and performance counters are the most important tools you have to determine how your site will perform.

The two primary items you can determine from the reports are errors and page timings.

The errors are returned as response codes. All response codes in the 200s indicate normal operations. 100s are informational messages, 300s indicate redirection, 400s indicate a client error, and 500s indicate a server error. You saw the response codes earlier today in Table 19.1.

Page timings can be useful in determining the effect of either page coding or underlying database operations and caching. In the reports, this is primarily determined by looking at the TTFB (Time To First Byte) and TTLB (Time To Last Byte).

Noting these times and making changes to the logic or database access gives you a good way to track the resulting changes and make sure that you haven't introduced a delay you didn't mean to!

The performance counters for this testing, and many system problems as well, provide a wealth of information. The performance counters enable you to find when your clients and/or servers have reached their peaks in terms of processor, memory, disk I/O, and network throughput.

The idea is that you should make sure that the testing isn't bottlenecked by the client computer that's driving the testing. If the client computer CPU usage is above 90%, it's probably the limiting factor in being able to produce a load on the Web server.

By looking at various counters on the Web server, you should be able to determine performance issues. A rule of thumb is that the Web server CPU usage should be at least 80%. At that point, you'll see the maximum limit of the Web server and not the limitations of the client test computer.

Comparing RPS on various test runs will help you tune the Web server and the Web application.

Summary

Application Center Test gives you an extremely useful tool to determine requirements for your Web sites. By using the macro recording in Visual Studio .NET to record mouse and keyboard strokes to the browser, you can set up a test script that the ACT can run based on different performance parameters that you modify. Using tools such as ACT and Visual Studio Analyzer will answer the performance questions you might have.

Q&A

Q I don't like to use scripting. How can I do this in .NET?

A You can use interopt, wrap the ActiveX objects with .NET classes, and then use them within managed code.

Q What file types are generated by an ACT project, and what is each type used for?

A An ACT project uses `.act`, `.vbs` (or `.js`), and `.xml` files. The `.act` file is the ACT project file and ties together all the other files into a project that can be opened from either the Visual Studio .NET IDE or the standalone ACT program. `.vbs` or `.js` files contain scripting code used to run tests. A number of `.xml` files are used for test definitions, reports, and other output and settings.

Q What is the Connections property in the Visual Studio .NET IDE of an ACT project used to control?

A The Connections property determines how many simultaneous Web connections are made by the client controller to the Web site under test. Up to the limits of the client computer, communication channel, and Web server, increasing the connections increases the load placed on the Web server.

Q I need more info. What's next?

A There are some articles and resources on the Web that will get you going. These articles cover Web server tuning and more details on ACT:

`http://www.microsoft.com/applicationcenter/techinfo/productdoc/default.asp`

`http://www.microsoft.com/technet/treeview/default.asp?url=/technet/prodtechnol/acs/proddocs/ac2k/acjmwe_welcome.asp`

`http://www.microsoft.com/windows2000/techinfo/administration/web/tuning.asp`

Quiz

1. Using the Visual Studio .NET–integrated ACT test environment does not contain features such as _________, ___________, and _________ that can be found in the standalone version of ACT.
2. When you're using the ACT standalone application, setting the individual users and groups rather than letting ACT automatically generate users for your test gives you the benefit of ________________________________.
3. True or False: You should always figure that the ASP.NET worker process will take anywhere from 5 to 20 seconds to start when viewing test results.

Quiz Answers

1. Adding users and groups, setting performance counters, viewing graphical reports
2. Testing security through roles and viewing user-generated cookies for each test
3. False. You should change the `WarmupTime` property to let ACT give you the most accurate possible results.

Exercises

1. Add some more controls to the simple Web page used in today's lesson. Try different controls, text boxes, submit buttons, and images. Now generate a new test using the wizard and examine the resulting script—what is different?
2. Create an ASP.NET page that uses authentication and cookies. Create custom users and set the cookies to both succeed and fail. Use the wizard to generate a test, and make sure that you generate both valid login attempts and failing login attempts. What codes are returned?
3. Create a new Visual Basic .NET project (or your favorite .NET language) and convert the sample script for a scheduled test discussed in the chapter to .NET. (Hint: You must add a reference to the Microsoft ACT Application Object Model 1.0 Type Library on the COM tab.) This is also a good example of using the capability to use the interopt features of Visual Studio to gain access to an ActiveX object library.

DAY 20

Using Visual SourceSafe

Keeping your code safe is always a top priority. Using Microsoft Visual SourceSafe, you have a complete source code management solution. Because SourceSafe is hooked into the Visual Studio .NET integrated development environment (IDE), you have complete control over projects stored in SourceSafe without ever leaving your development environment. Today, you learn

- What SourceSafe is
- SourceSafe installation options
- How to use the SourceSafe Admin tool
- How to create SourceSafe projects in Visual Studio .NET
- How to access projects in SourceSafe from Visual Studio .NET
- How to check files in and out of SourceSafe
- How to merge and roll back source files that have changed

Introducing Visual SourceSafe

Microsoft Visual SourceSafe version 6.0c, or simply VSS, is the latest revision of Microsoft's source code control environment. Using VSS, you can manage your Visual Studio .NET solutions through a centralized database that keeps a history of changes made to files in a solution. Using a check-in/check-out metaphor, you selectively determine what files in a solution you need to work on, and then get the latest version of those files from the central VSS database. After you complete a file, or the work you need to do on it is finished, you check the file back in to VSS, which makes it available to other developers.

Every time a file is checked out of VSS, a copy of the actual file is given to you. The original file is retained in the VSS database. Every time you check a file back into the VSS database, a new copy of the file is made, reflecting the changes you made since the last checkout. By allowing VSS to manage your projects and solutions, you always have a complete history of every change made to any of the files under source code control. This makes it possible to revert to a previous version of a file or even a previous version of an entire solution.

Because VSS keeps the files in a database, in the unfortunate circumstance of a hard drive crash on your development machine, you can completely re-create a solution from the files that exist inside VSS. The nice thing about VSS is that it can store any type of file, not just the standard project files that you use in a Visual Studio .NET solution. You can store binary files, text files, and Word documents. Literally any type of text-based or binary file can be managed in the VSS database.

Based on how you installed VSS, you'll work in a single-developer mode or a team mode. If you're working with many people on the same project, VSS won't let you work on a file that another developer has checked out. You can override these settings in the VSS Admin tool, but it isn't always the best thing to do because you'd then have to merge the changes together, which leaves room for error. If you're a single developer and just need a robust source control system, VSS works the same way that it does in a multiuser model.

Installing VSS

The installation for VSS isn't integrated into the normal Visual Studio .NET installation process, so you must find the additional CD labeled Visual SourceSafe 6.0c, which is included with the Visual Studio .NET CD-ROMs. After you find the CD and start the setup process, you can choose from the three installation types in the following list:

Note

> VSS comes with only the Enterprise Architect version of Visual Studio .NET.

- Shared Database Server Setup Option—This installation option installs the VSS database as a shared database and copies the appropriate client tools to the shared server. When this installation is complete, you must install the VSS client tools that give you access to the shared database. This option is normally used in any team development environment. The `NetSetup.exe` file that's installed with a shared database server installation is what you'd use to install the client tools on the other developers' desktops.
- Custom Setup Option—The custom setup installation option should be used only if you don't want VSS to integrate into the Visual Studio .NET IDE. By choosing the custom setup option, you can enable or disable this feature. This option should be used only if you don't want any of the VSS features available in Visual Studio .NET, which defeats the main purpose of using VSS as a developer!
- Stand-Alone Setup Option—The stand-alone setup option creates a private database on a single machine to be used for source code control. This installation option is useful if you're a developer who works alone, and you want to use source code control in your projects. You must make sure that you manually back up the VSS database if you choose this option because a catastrophic failure of your hard drive will kill the VSS database.

After you've installed VSS, a new Microsoft Visual VSS program group is created that contains all the external tools that you can use to manage your VSS databases.

Using the Visual SourceSafe Administrator

The VSS Administrator enables you to manage users that have access to the SourceSafe databases. Using this tool, you can

- Add, edit, and delete users who have access to the VSS databases
- Change user passwords
- Set user access to read-only
- Lock a VSS database
- Clean up a VSS database and remove temporary files
- Create new VSS databases

- Archive projects
- Restore projects
- Change default application-level defaults, such as multiple checkouts, default project folders, and file type extensions that are allowed to be stored in the VSS databases

Figure 20.1 shows the VSS Administrator open with the Options dialog in the foreground. When you install VSS, two users are added to the database by default: `Admin` and `Guest`. The `Admin` password is blank, and if you're working on a network with multiple developers, you'll most likely want to change this password. On single-developer installation, you can leave the `Admin` password blank for ease of use. Each time you open a VSS tool, you must enter the username and password.

FIGURE 20.1

The Visual SourceSafe Administrator.

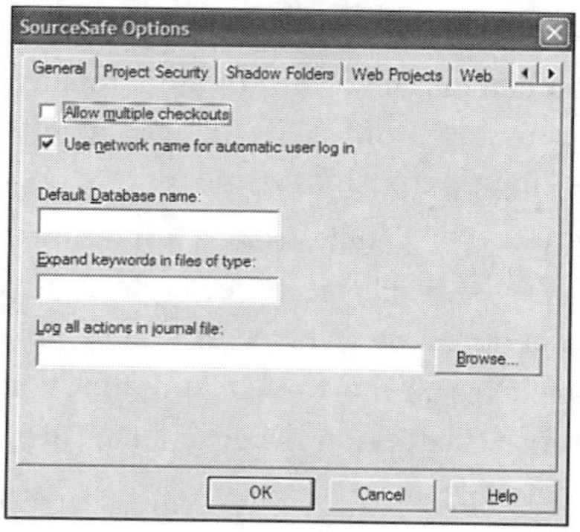

Depending on the environment you're working in, you might never use this tool. I've used SourceSafe for years in single-developer mode, and I've never opened the Admin tool.

Using the Visual SourceSafe Explorer

The Visual SourceSafe Explorer is the main application for managing projects under source code control. Using this tool, all the features of VSS are available to you. Figure 20.2 shows the VSS Explorer after a new installation of SourceSafe, with no projects under source control.

When you install VSS for Visual Studio .NET, most of the features available to you in the Explorer are integrated into the Visual Studio .NET IDE. This includes creating new projects, checking files in and out, and viewing file history. The reason to use the

Explorer is if you're in a multiuser environment and you need to determine which developers have items checked out, to get an overall view of the state of a project by running reports, or to perform tasks that aren't available in the Visual Studio .NET IDE.

FIGURE 20.2
The Visual SourceSafe Explorer.

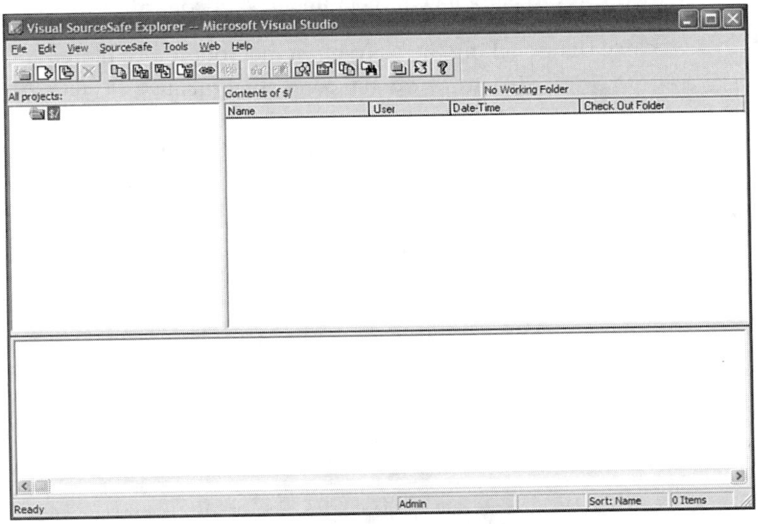

From the Explorer, you can also merge or branch projects and files. When you merge a file, the differences in two or more changed copies of a file are merged into a new version of the file. A merge involves at least two different files, which can be different versions of the same file or changes made to the same version of the file, and creates a new file made up of the results of the merge. Merging can occur when the user merges two branches or when the Check In or Get Latest Version command is used. *Branching* is the process of sharing a file with another project and then separating it into two or more branches. When you create a branch, the file in the project and its counterpart in other projects have a shared history up to the point of the branch, but they maintain separate history files after that point. Merging and branching are two of the more powerful file management features in VSS.

For today, you aren't going to use any of the external GUI features of VSS. Everything you do is from within the Visual Studio .NET IDE.

Creating Your First VSS Project

To learn how to use VSS and to become familiar with the menu options available to you in Visual Studio .NET for VSS, you must create a new Windows Forms application. You can name the project whatever you want, and the language doesn't matter because no code is written today.

When you create a new solution, you must create a new VSS project to manage it. There are two ways to get a new project under VSS control:

- By right-clicking the solution in the Solution Explorer and selecting Add Solution to Source Control from the contextual menu, as Figure 20.3 demonstrates

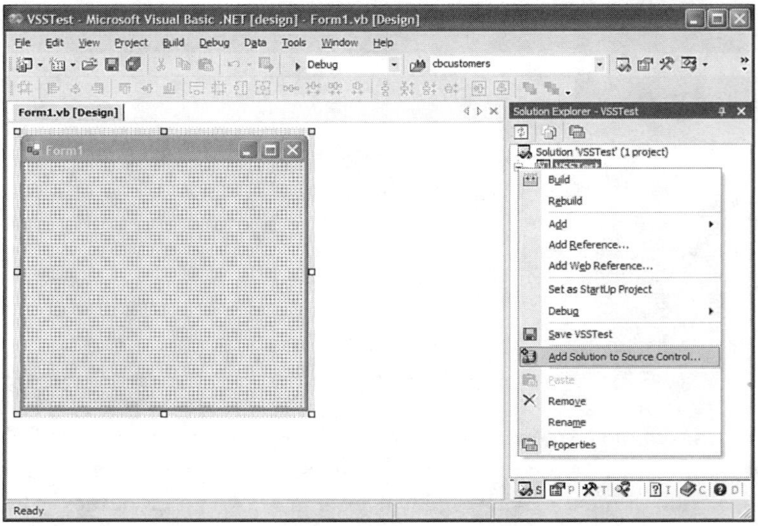

FIGURE 20.3
Adding a solution to VSS from the Solution Explorer.

- By selecting File, Source Control, Add Solution to Source Control

When you select the Add Solution to Source Control option, you're prompted with the login dialog for SourceSafe. After you enter **`Admin`** as the username, you're taken to the Add to SourceSafe Project dialog box shown in Figure 20.4.

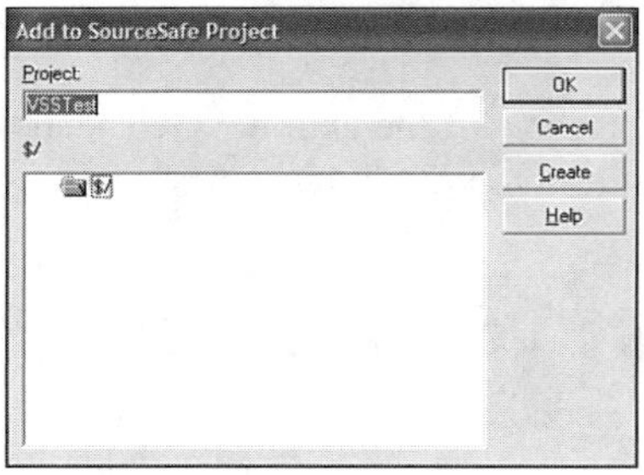

FIGURE 20.4
The Add to SourceSafe Project dialog box.

> **Note**
>
> In a multiuser environment, the SourceSafe administrator can set up the VSS server to use your network login information as the SourceSafe login information. When this is configured, you aren't prompted with the Login dialog each time you attempt to access a SourceSafe feature.

The VSS database manages projects in a folder hierarchy similar to the file system. There's a root folder, which is defaulted to `$/`, and each project you add to source control will have a unique folder under the root. When you create a new project in SourceSafe, a GUID is created that identifies the project within the VSS database. Because of this, you'll have problems when copying projects or renaming projects because the GUID travels with the project. SourceSafe has no idea how to differentiate between different projects with the same GUID.

In the Add to SourceSafe dialog, click the OK button to create the project in VSS with the default name of your solution. After the project is created, the files in your solution are created inside the VSS database and are checked in to SourceSafe. You know this because of the blue padlock icons that are attached to the files of your project in the Solution Explorer, as Figure 20.5 shows.

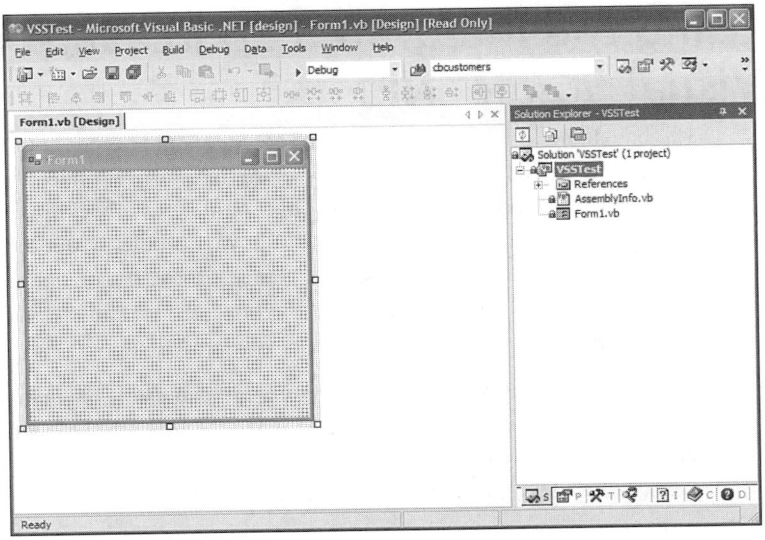

FIGURE 20.5
Solution Explorer files under source control after creating a new VSS project.

To see what SourceSafe actually did, go back to the SourceSafe Explorer. You'll see your project under the root folder and the files of the project in the Contents pane of the Explorer. Your SourceSafe Explorer should resemble Figure 20.6.

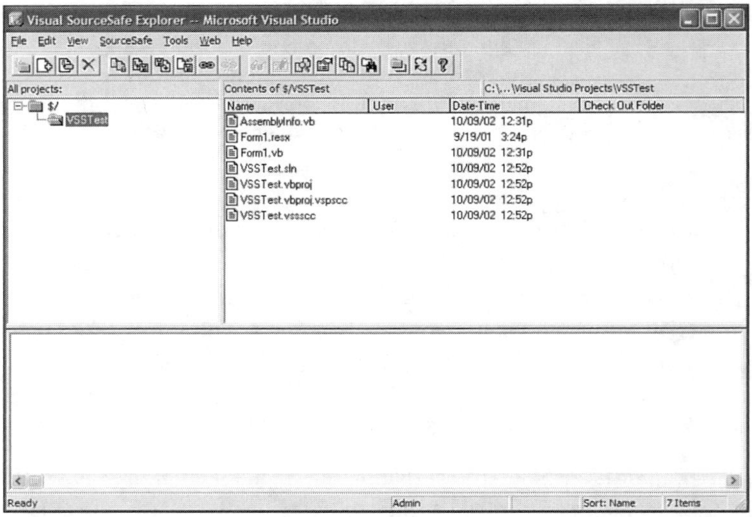

FIGURE 20.6

The SourceSafe Explorer after creating a new project in Visual Studio .NET.

Now that you've created a file in SourceSafe, you can start to use the integrated features of Visual Studio .NET to manage your projects.

Using the Integrated SourceSafe Tools in Visual Studio .NET

The backbone of what makes SourceSafe tick is the process of checking files in and out of the VSS database. When you're working in a project under source control, you're using it for any number of reasons. This could be as a backup to your solutions, as a way of keeping version history of files, or as a way to quickly undo changes to a file when something doesn't work as expected. None of these options is possible if you aren't maintaining a history of the changes to your files. For this reason, you must diligently check files in and out of SourceSafe as you need them.

To check a file out of SourceSafe so that you can use it, you can either right-click on the file in the Solution Explorer and select Check Out from the contextual menu, or you can simply attempt to modify the file and the automatic check-out process occurs. When you check out a file, you're prompted with the Check Out dialog shown in Figure 20.7.

In the Check Out dialog, you can select the files that you want to check out and enter notes as to why you're checking the file out. In this case, leave the defaults for this check out, which are the `Form1.vb` file and the solution files.

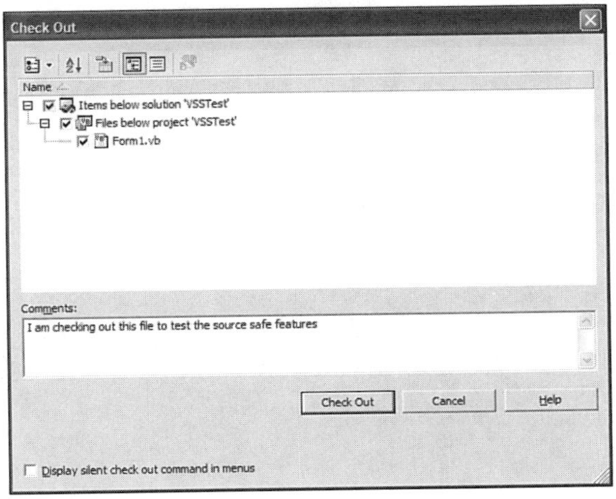

FIGURE 20.7
Checking out a file from Visual Studio .NET.

At this point, the file is available for you to modify. SourceSafe gives you access to a local copy of the file, and the original file remains in the SourceSafe database. A red check mark with an exclamation point is positioned next to the file name in the Solution Explorer, giving you an immediate indication that the file is checked out to you exclusively. Exclusively means that no one else can check out this file.

If you right-click on the `form1.vb` file in the Solution Explorer, you'll see the SourceSafe-specific options that are available to you. These include

- Check In
- Show Pending Checkins
- Undo Checkout
- Get Latest Version
- Compare Versions

We'll look at each of these options now, but not necessarily in the order of the menu options.

Showing Pending Checkins

If you select the Show Pending Checkins menu item, the Pending Checkins window opens. It's docked to the bottom of your IDE, as Figure 20.8 demonstrates.

From this window, you can view the files that you have checked out for this solution. You can check files back into the VSS database, add comments to the files, view the changes to the file since the last checkout, and undo the checkout all from the Pending Checkins window.

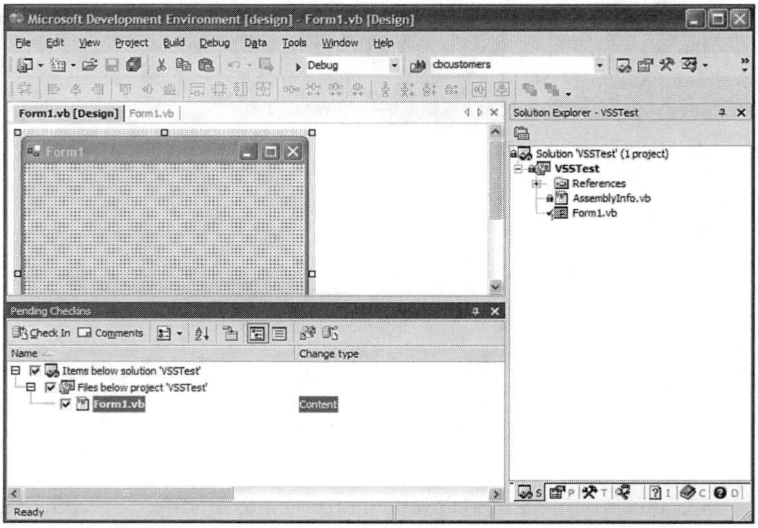

FIGURE 20.8
The Pending Checkins window.

Undoing a Checkout

The Undo Checkout option, which is accessible from the right-click contextual menu in the Solution Explorer from the Pending Checkins windows, enables you to revert to the original checked out version of the file you're working on. If you select this option, you're prompted with the Undo Checkout dialog box shown in Figure 20.9.

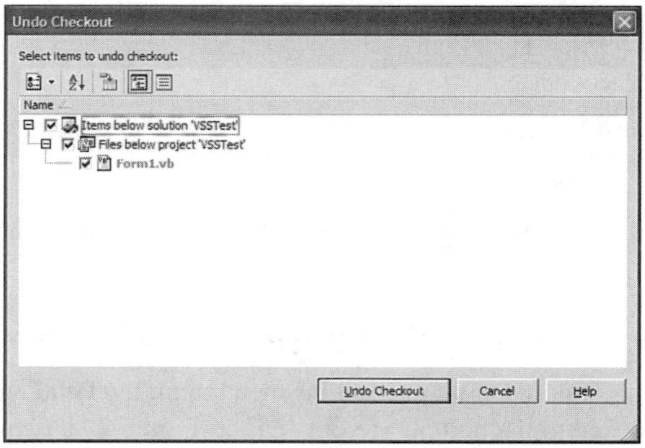

FIGURE 20.9
The Undo Checkout dialog box.

After you click the OK button, the file is sent back to the VSS database. If you modified the file since the last checkout, you are prompted with a dialog for each file that has changed, giving you the option to overwrite the files in the VSS database, cancel the undo checkout, or selectively leave dependent files checked out. Figure 20.10 shows the prompt after I made some changes to the `Form1.vb` class file and attempted to undo the checkout.

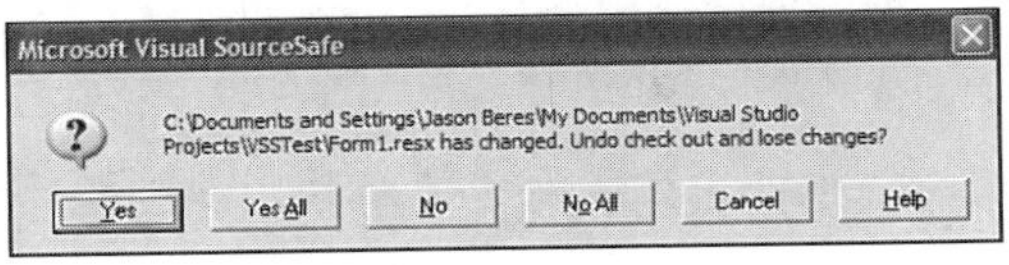

FIGURE 20.10
Warning dialogs when undoing a checkout.

The undo checkout option is very useful when you make a mistake. Because Visual Studio .NET saves all files before you can build an application, you're never working on unsaved files. If you've just checked out a file, made some changes, and realized that you screwed something up, you can revert to the good copy of the file in VSS by undoing the check out. This is a very good reason to be diligent about checking files back in when you have made changes to them.

Getting the Latest Version

After you've checked a file out or you still have a file checked in, you might want to retrieve the most current version of a file from the VSS database. The Get Latest Version menu option enables you to retrieve the most current version of checked-out and checked-in files from the current SourceSafe project.

One situation in which this would be useful is when you need to build an application that you've been working on. To make sure that you have the most current files, you should obtain the latest versions of the files from the VSS database before you build. Each time you open a project from SourceSafe, it retrieves the latest version, but most of us have projects open in Visual Studio .NET for hours or even days, so there might have been changes to files without your knowledge.

If the latest version of a file you're attempting to get is different in your solution from the version stored in VSS, you have the option of merging the files. At this point, VSS merges your changes with the file from the server. This might occur often in a team environment.

Comparing Versions of Files

The Compare Versions contextual menu item enables you to view the differences of your file compared to the last checked-in version in VSS. If you select the Compare Versions item, you're prompted with the Difference Options dialog box. This dialog enables you to choose the files to compare and the output format for the report. Figure 20.11 shows the Difference Options dialog box.

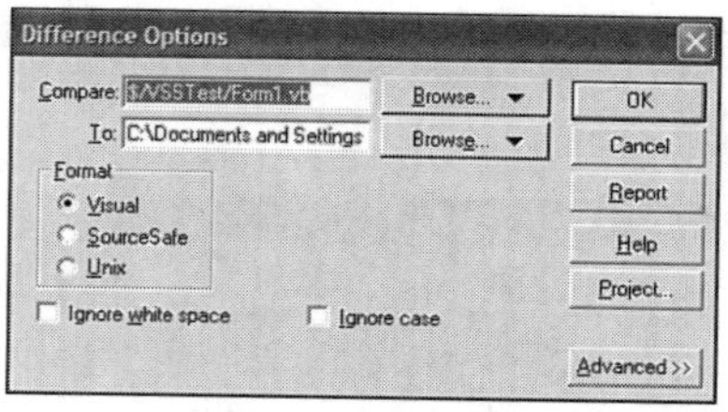

FIGURE 20.11

The Difference Option dialog box for comparing file changes.

Based on the format option you select—Visual, SourceSafe, or Unix—the output report shows different data. Figure 20.12 shows the Visual report option that's displayed after clicking the Report button.

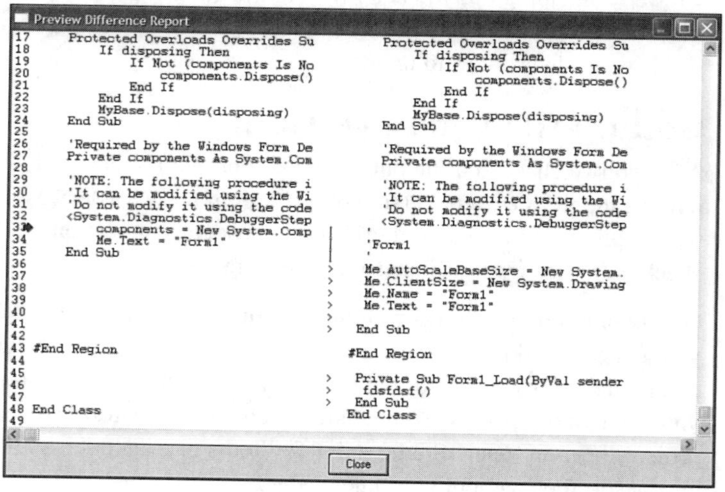

FIGURE 20.12

The visual differences report.

In Figure 20.12, the complete original file version and the checked-out version are displayed side by side. You can browse a line at a time to see the differences in the files. If you preview the SourceSafe or Unix Format options, only the lines that are different are displayed in the report.

Checking Files Back In

When you're done working with a file, you must check it back into SourceSafe so that the history is maintained and others have access to it. Selecting the Check In menu item prompts you with the Check In dialog shown in Figure 20.13.

After you check in a file, the local copy of your file is marked as read-only and the checked-in file is sent back to the SourceSafe database. In the database itself, only the changes from the last checked-out version, not the entire file, are stored.

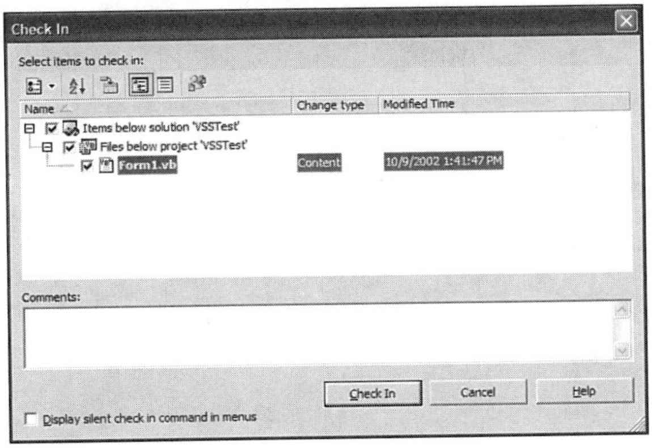

FIGURE 20.13
The Check In dialog box.

At this point, all the files in your solution are back in the SourceSafe database.

Note

> When checking files in, you must make a decision about what state a checked-in file should be left in. There are two scenarios when checking files in. The first scenario is that the file is completed, tested, and you're done with it. The second check-in option is that you want to maintain a strict history of the changes to your files in SourceSafe. When working as a single developer, that's okay; you pretty much know the state of your applications. If you're working with a team, other people might assume that because the file is checked in, it works and it will successfully compile in their application. If your company does a nightly build or a solution and your file isn't tested, the build will fail. So, use caution when checking files back into the VSS database.

Viewing the History of a File in SourceSafe

After you've started working with files in SourceSafe, you might need to view the history of a particular project or file. All the available SourceSafe commands are readily available by selecting the Source Control menu item from the File menu. The History menu item displays the history for the selected item in the Solution Explorer. In Figure 20.14, the `Form1.vb` file is selected in the Solution Explorer, and its history is shown in the History dialog box.

In this dialog, you can choose to roll back a version, get the latest version of a file, check out the file, get a report in the history, or view the SourceSafe version of the file.

FIGURE 20.14

Viewing a file's history with the History dialog box.

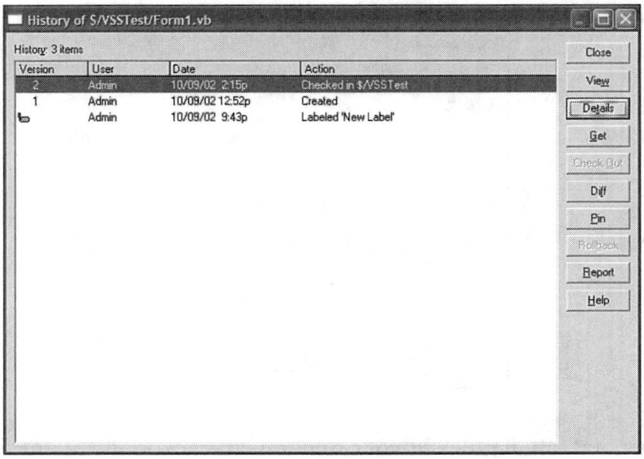

Because the `Form1.vb` file is checked in, the copy that's in the Solution Explorer is the same as the SourceSafe version. If you need to check the actual SourceSafe version of the file in the Visual Studio .NET IDE, you can click the View button. When you click View, you have the option of viewing the file in Notepad, the SourceSafe viewer, or Visual Studio .NET. Figure 20.15 shows the `Form1.vb` file being viewed in the IDE from the actual version stored in SourceSafe.

FIGURE 20.15

Viewing a SourceSafe file in the Visual Studio .NET IDE.

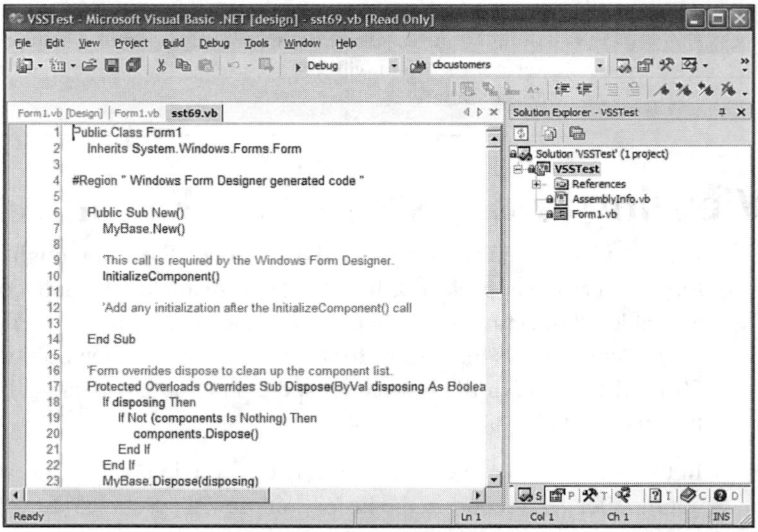

Notice that the tab for this file says sst69.vb. This is a temporary file that SourceSafe creates to allow the file to be viewed outside its database. To make the process of file comparisons and viewing faster, all the temporary files that are created by checking files in and out of the VSS database are stored in your solution's folder.

Opening an Existing SourceSafe Project

If you create a project for the first time using Visual Studio .NET, you're in control of creating the project in the SourceSafe database. Using the menu options you learned about so far today, you can easily create a new project in SourceSafe based on an existing Visual Studio .NET project.

If you didn't create the project and you need to create a local version of it to start developing with, you must open the version stored in SourceSafe. To do so:

1. Select the File, Source Control, Open From Source Control menu option. This dialog box lists the available projects in the VSS database.
2. You can select the project you want to open, and a local copy is then created for you.

As with the creation of a new SourceSafe project, the project and its files are read-only and are checked in by default when you open a project from source control.

Adding New Project Items or Projects

When working with projects in VSS, you're actually checking out only individual files, not the Visual Studio project file or the Visual Studio solution file. That means any time you add a new item to your projects or you rename an item in your project, you must check out the project file in the solution.

Adding an item is a straightforward task. When you add an item, the project file must be updated with the information about the new file. Because a project file in Visual Studio tracks each item in a project, the VSS database must be notified of your changes. After the normal Add Item dialog pops up and you select the type of item you're adding and give it a name, the Check Out For Edit dialog for the project pops up, as Figure 20.16 demonstrates.

At this point, the new item is added and the project file is updated. The problem is that the project file must be checked back in to VSS or no one can check it out to get your new changes. Therefore, as soon as you can, you must check the project file back into VSS so that other developers can access it. Because the default for a new item is checked in, when someone else grabs the latest version of the project, he'll see your newly added file.

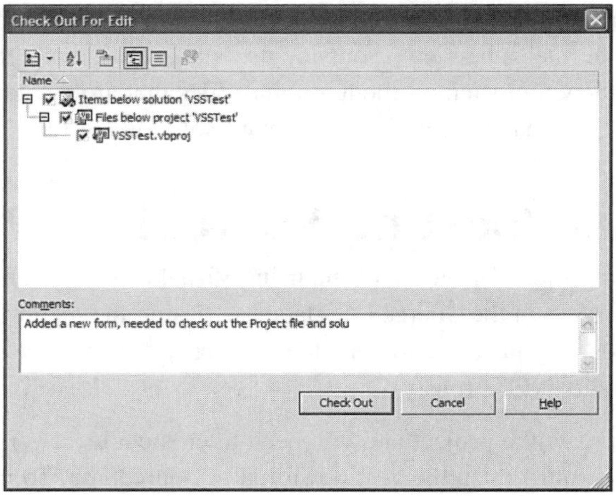

FIGURE 20.16
Checking out the project file when adding new items.

If you add a new project to a solution, the solution file is checked out and you're prompted with a warning similar to Figure 20.17.

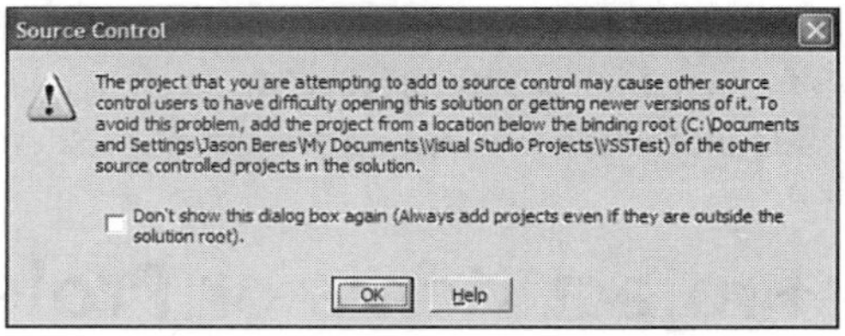

FIGURE 20.17
Warning dialog box when adding a new project to a solution.

Because both Visual Studio .NET and VSS maintain a hierarchy of the project and files in your solutions, the VSS database must associate a newly added project with the correct solution when adding a new project. That means you must create a new project folder underneath the existing root of the project in VSS. To get an idea of how this works logically, the Check In dialog shown in Figure 20.18 shows the hierarchy after adding a new project to a solution.

You can see that when VSS checks files back in, they're logically listed as File Below ProjectX or Items Below SolutionX. When you click the OK button on the Check In dialog after adding a new project to a solution, you're prompted to give the new project names in VSS. You can use the same project names that you use in the solution, and the correct hierarchy is maintained for others who attempt to access this solution.

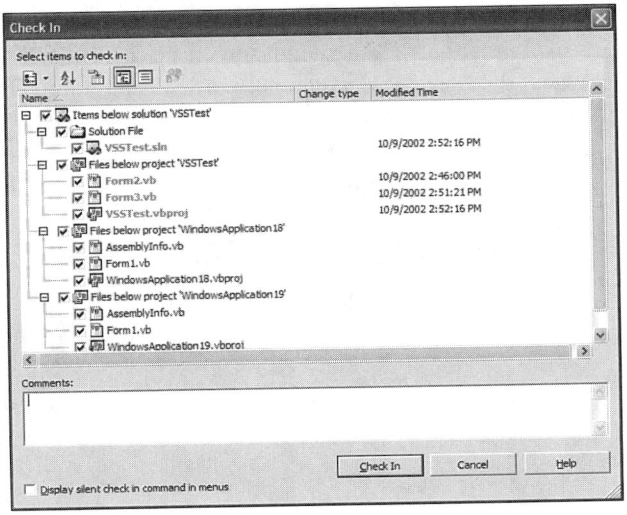

FIGURE 20.18
Solution hierarchy after adding a new project to a solution.

Renaming Projects or Project Items

Renaming items in a project under source control is not much more difficult than adding new items. Remember that you're always working with a local copy of the data, so any change you make on the local copy must be reflected in the VSS database. If you have an item in your solution and you need to rename it, the first step is to check the file back in. After the file is checked in, you can right-click the file and rename it as you normally would. At this point, you're prompted to check out the project file because it must be updated with the new filename. After you check out the project and rename the item, the renamed item appears as a checked-out file in the Solution Explorer. At this stage, the original file still exists with the original filename in VSS. After you check in the renamed file to VSS, a new item with new history is created. The original file remains intact. To see this in action, you can rename a file and then look at the SourceSafe Explorer. In Figure 20.19, I renamed `Form1.vb` to `FirstForm.vb` in the Visual Studio .NET IDE. This caused me to check the renamed file into SourceSafe, thus creating two versions of the file.

Because the project file was updated to reflect the name of the newly renamed file, it is the only one to show up in the project. The original file remains in SourceSafe forever or until you delete it.

The recommended way to rename a file is to first rename the file in the SourceSafe Explorer. After the file is renamed in SourceSafe, you can select Get Latest Version of the File from Visual Studio .NET. At this point, the file is read-only from SourceSafe using your local copy. You can now rename the file to the same name you used in the SourceSafe Explorer. SourceSafe attempts to check the file out. When prompted, you should check out the file as you would normally. Because the local file version detects that the file has been changed in SourceSafe, you're prompted on a course of action to take with this file. If you select Continue from the warning dialog, the renamed file will be read-only in the Solution Explorer and it will match the version stored in SourceSafe.

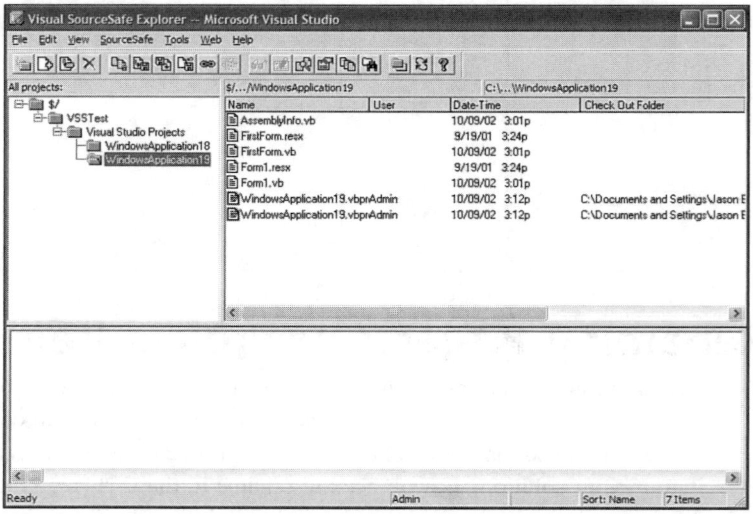

FIGURE 20.19
SourceSafe Explorer after renaming a file from Visual Studio .NET.

This can become a little confusing if you're working with a team of developers and people are always renaming files. The best way to make sure that you aren't losing any information or any of your work is not to allow multiple checkouts. As a result, the only person affected by a change is the person who actually renames the file. After you check in your files, you can get the latest versions of the files from the server and your project is up to date.

Summary

Today you learned how to use Visual SourceSafe and its tools in the Visual Studio .NET IDE. By putting your projects under source control, you have the benefit of knowing your source code is safe from accidental deletion of files and in a durable data store that can be backed up for archive purposes. By diligently checking in files after you've worked with them, you can build up a version history of your application's files. This enables you to roll back changes or even complete installations of applications with a few clicks of the mouse. In a team development environment, SourceSafe should be a requirement. If you're a single developer working alone on projects, you should always use SourceSafe to keep track of changes made to your code.

You've just about completed all 21 days of learning Visual Studio .NET. Tomorrow, on Day 21, you learn how to implement object role modeling using Visio.

Q&A

Q You didn't discuss working on ASP.NET applications. Why not?

A The SourceSafe process is the same for any type of application. The same capabilities you learned about today using a Windows Forms application work with ASP.NET applications, deployment projects, and add-in projects—basically all project types available in .NET are capable of being stored in SourceSafe.

Q I have deleted a file in my solution, but when I go back to the SourceSafe Explorer, it keeps showing back up. What am I doing wrong?

A You aren't doing anything wrong; you just skipped a step. Any time you delete a file from the Visual Studio .NET IDE, you must go to the SourceSafe Explorer and delete the file from there also.

Q I'm using Visual Studio .NET, but not the Architect version. Can I buy SourceSafe separately?

A Yes. SourceSafe is a regular retail product from Microsoft and can be purchased from `shop.microsoft.com` or any software reseller.

Q I like the Visual Studio .NET integration, but I actually need to manage SourceSafe from the SourceSafe Administrator and the SourceSafe Explorer. Can I get information about this stuff online?

A There are two good places to learn more about SourceSafe. The first is the .NET Framework SDK. Do a search for Source Control, and you'll find some documentation. In addition, there's an Architect Developer center on MSDN that has an article series about SourceSafe. The link is

`http://msdn.microsoft.com/library/default.asp?url=/library/en-us/dnbda/html/tdlg_rm.asp`

Quiz

1. Using the ____________________, you can add users to a SourceSafe database and archive existing databases.

2. To create another copy of a file that will maintain its own history, you should _____________ an existing file.
3. True or False: Even though I'm working with a local copy of the data, changes made to a file are reflected to other users as soon as I check a file in.
4. True or False: It's easier to manage individual projects in individual solutions in SourceSafe, so the recommended practice is to have single project solutions.

Quiz Answers

1. Visual SourceSafe Administrator
2. Branch
3. False. If a person is working offline, she might not get the newest version of a file unless she selects the Get Latest Version option when retrieving a file.
4. False. Because Visual SourceSafe manages projects in the same hierarchy in which they're managed in a solution, there's no difference in a single project solution or a multiproject solution.

Exercises

1. Create a new project in Visual Studio .NET and add it to SourceSafe. After the solution is added to SourceSafe and the project items are checked in, close Visual Studio .NET and delete the entire folder of the project you just created from the Visual Studio Projects folder. Next, reopen Visual Studio .NET. From the File menu, select Source Control, Open From Source Control. Your project should be restored to the state it was in before you deleted the project folder.
2. Create a new ASP.NET Web application. Use the various menu items in the IDE to add files and delete files after you've added the solution to SourceSafe. Notice how the capabilities you have in the ASP.NET application are the same as the Windows Forms application.
3. Open the Visual SourceSafe Administrator. From the Archive menu, familiarize yourself with the archiving capabilities of SourceSafe. Notice you can also delete files after they are archived, thus reclaiming space used for projects that are already rolled out.
4. From this day forward, use SourceSafe for every new project you create in Visual Studio .NET.

WEEK 3

DAY 21

Object Role Modeling with Visio

The final day of your 21-day journey to learning about Visual Studio .NET covers a seldom-used technology—seldom used until now, that is. Using Visio, which is part of the Visual Studio .NET Enterprise Architect version, you can create complex yet easy-to-understand data models. Data modeling has always been pushed to the side when it comes to writing applications—most of the time it's an afterthought. But using the tools provided by Visio and Visual Studio .NET, you can create very useful data models that represent your applications. Today, you learn

- What object role modeling is
- How to create data models using Visio
- How to create a database diagram from an ORM model
- How to create a SQL Server database from Visio

Introducing Object Role Modeling

Object role modeling (ORM) is a method of creating data models conceptually. Using English-like syntax, you can define a problem or a model that a process follows. Using the definitions that you determine make up the process, you can create a physical data model from the conceptual definitions.

In real life, everything is an object, and objects do things or play roles. Based on this conceptual way of looking at a problem, you can create sentences about the relationships between the objects and roles and how they interact with each other. After you figure out how the roles and objects are related, you can determine what a physical data model should look like.

To look at an everyday process in a conceptual manner, you could create a data model of what you do when you go grocery shopping. Thinking in terms of objects and roles, you would be a *Shopper* object. Your role as a *Shopper* is to *Buy Products* at a *Store*. A *Store* is also an object and its role is as a *Seller* of things. At the *Store* there are products, which are brought to the store by *Shippers*. Those *Shippers* get their *Products* from *Manufacturers.*

Therefore, by breaking down what happens when you go to the store, you can start to create a data model that might be used in a purchasing system or e-commerce application. Your model has buyers, sellers, products, manufacturers, and a lot more if you keep going with the conceptual idea.

When creating a model, you use the notions of objects and roles, and then you state facts about those how those objects and roles interact. A fact in the shopping case would be "shoppers buy products." This is plain English that anyone can understand.

You might be thinking that creating a few tables for a purchasing system isn't such a difficult thing to do. That might be true if you've done it before. However, in many cases, you must understand what a user will be doing in a process to dictate what the data model should look like. But in all cases, having the model available to others can give them a quick insight into what the final application actually will be doing, all by starting out with a conceptual view of a process.

At the end of the modeling process, the ORM tools in Visio create a fully normalized data structure in a database using the objects, roles, and facts that you define. If the requirements change or the model is incorrect, you can both modify the data model in Visio and update the database, or you can update the database and reverse-engineer the database back down to a data model in Visio.

This is a hugely powerful function of Visio. Consider an application that's been around for years, and everyone in the company knows it needs to be rewritten. There's nothing worse than just going headfirst into SQL Server or Oracle and deciding how to change data structures. Using Visio, you can reverse-engineer the existing database into a data model. When the model is in Visio, you can modify the objects, roles, and facts to create a new, well-formed data model based on current requirements. This not only assists in the process of getting the database fixed, but it forces you to understand the business problem at hand in a nontechnical manner.

To understand how you can use this conceptual view of a process to create a data model, you'll go through the creation of an ORM data model using Visio and then build that model into a normalized database.

Using Visio to Create an ORM Model

The first step in creating your ORM model is to open Visio and select the correct drawing template for the model. After Visio opens, select the Database drawing type and you're presented with a list of the available database templates that Visio offers. Figure 21.1 is what you should see when you select the Database category.

FIGURE 21.1

Database template options in Visio.

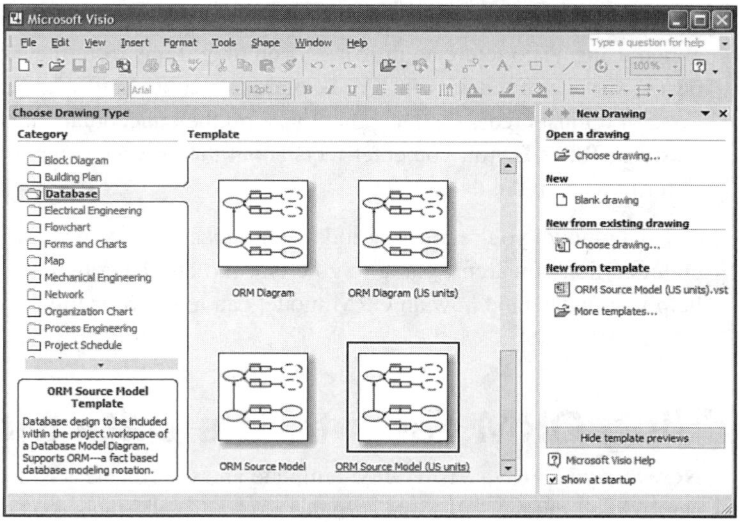

Selecting ORM Source Model (U.S. Units) takes you to the main Visio window for the model. Docked to the left of the IDE is the ORM stencil. Docked to the bottom of the IDE are the Database Rules, Business Rules, and Verbalizer tabs that you'll use to define the objects, roles, and facts that make up your model.

If you don't see the docked windows on the bottom of the screen, all the ORM-specific tools are located under the View option of the Database main menu. After the ORM template and the Business Rules window are open, your screen should resemble Figure 21.2.

FIGURE 21.2
The ORM Model template in Visio.

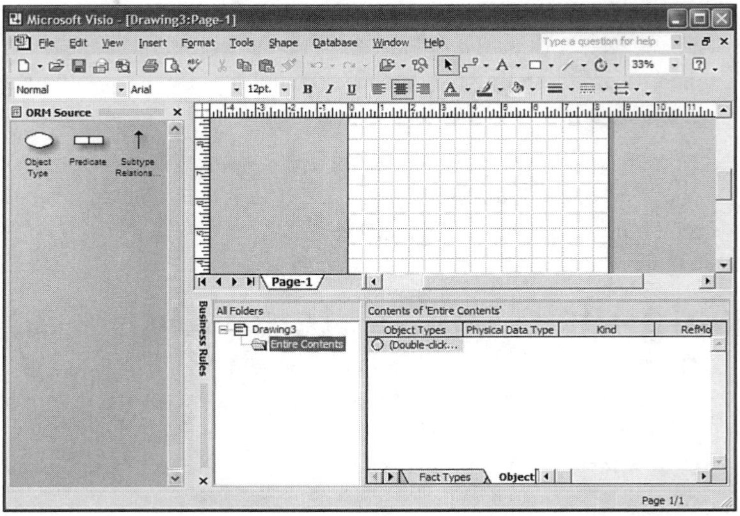

When using Visio to create drawings, you drag items from the stencil window onto the design surface of the drawing. You can do the same thing when creating ORM models. First, you must create the facts that make up the conceptual data model. Using the Business Rules Editor, you enter facts about the process you're creating, and those facts in turn make up the data model.

The data model you're creating today continues the e-commerce model that we talked about earlier. You aren't going to go crazy and build a complete system; the goal is to help you understand how an ORM model can make your life easier as your applications grow.

Adding ORM Facts to the Data Model

Now that you have a Visio ORM template and the Business Rules Editor open, you can start adding the facts that make up the model. To add facts, you can click the Edit button in the Facts list of the Business Rules window, you can just start typing on an empty row, or you can double-click on an empty row and the Fact Editor will pop up.

The facts you're going to add are for a customer and products. To start, click the Edit button on an empty row in the Facts list to bring up the Fact Editor, which is shown in Figure 21.3.

FIGURE 21.3

The Fact Editor.

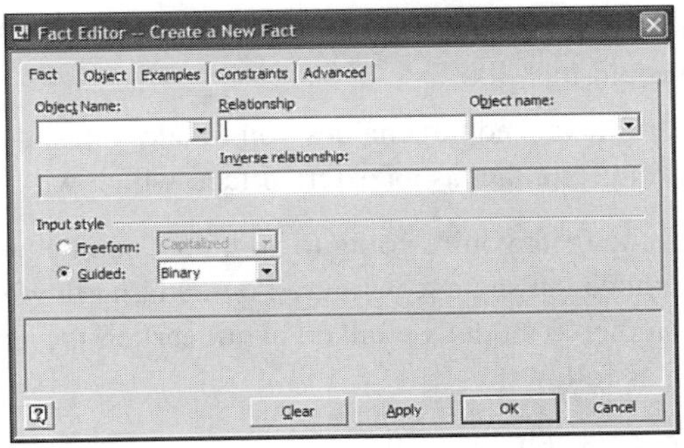

The Fact Editor is broken into five tabs. In each tab, you describe the fact that you are adding and how it relates to other facts. When you're done adding facts to the model, you take them into a database diagram and generate a table schema based on the facts. The following list describes each tab and its purpose when designing data models:

- Fact—You specify objects, how they relate to each other, and optionally specify their inverse relationship. These relationships make up the entities and values for the fact. For example, two objects might be Employee and Department. The relationship between the objects is "works for" or "is in," and the inverse relationship is "has." Therefore, an Employee works for a Department and a Department has Employees. You have two options for adding your fact input: Free Form or Guided. In the Free Form method, you simply type in relationships in an ORM-specific format. The Guided method breaks down the objects and relationships into logical parts, and it's the method you use today.
- Object—The Object tab enables you to define what the entity is, and what the values are for the objects you're adding. You can also specify entity attributes, such as a primary key.
- Examples—The Examples tab enables you to enter manual data based on the object relationships you're adding for the fact. Using this data, Visio can analyze the usage and determine the best constraints for the objects. You don't have to enter sample data, but doing so is a good idea if you aren't sure about the relationships you're defining.
- Constraints—The Constraints tab sets up the one-to-many, one-to-one, or many-to-one relationship between the objects. These constraints map directly to constraints in a database. For example, in a Customer and CustomerID relationship, you would say Each Customer has Exactly One CustomerID, and each CustomerID has Exactly One Customer. Your options for setting the relationships are Zero or One, Zero or More, One or More, and Exactly One. Based on how you added the fact,

you can rephrase the facts on this tab to better determine what Visio thinks the relationship should look like.

- Advanced—The Advanced tab enables you to add notes, define where a fact is derived from, and set a fact as an external fact, which will act as a proxy fact.

To better understand the facts you're going to add, they can be broken down into regular sentences. After you have the sentences figured out, adding the facts to the model is very easy. Using the e-commerce model we talked about earlier, the sentences for this model can be broken down as follows:

- Each Customer has a FirstName
- Each Customer has a LastName
- Each Customer has a CustomerID
- Customers purchase Products
- Products are purchased by Customers
- Products have a Name
- Products have a ProductID

The next step is to start adding the facts. The best way to get the model up and running is to just add the basic facts on the first tab of the Fact Editor. Then set up the entity/object relationships on the Object tab and the constraints on the Constraints tab.

For the first fact, add The Customer Has a FirstName fact. Your Fact Editor should look like Figure 21.4.

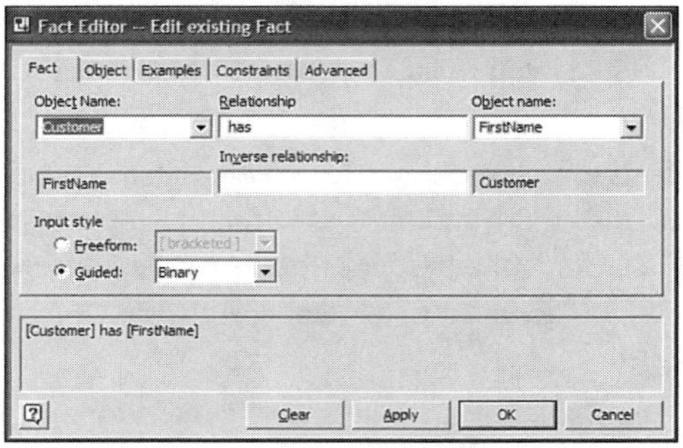

FIGURE 21.4
Adding the Customer has a FirstName fact.

Because there's no inverse relationship between a Customer and its FirstName, you don't need to do anything further to set up this first fact. After you click the Apply button, the Fact Editor clears and you can add further facts.

Using the same model as adding the Customer has a FirstName fact demonstrated in Figure 21.4, add three more facts with no inverse relationships as follows:

- Customer has LastName
- Customer has CustomerID
- Products have Name
- Products have ProductID

You are probably starting to see that by stating the facts in sentences, you can easily define the model. Until now, you've two main objects, Customer and Products, and you've defined attributes that they have, such as FirstName, LastName, and Name.

The next step is to add a fact that relates the Customer to the Products. For this new fact, you're going to add an inverse relationship. Because each Customer purchases Products, it means that Products are purchased by Customers, so the relationships between the object are set. Add the new fact to resemble Figure 21.5, which maps the Customer and Products together.

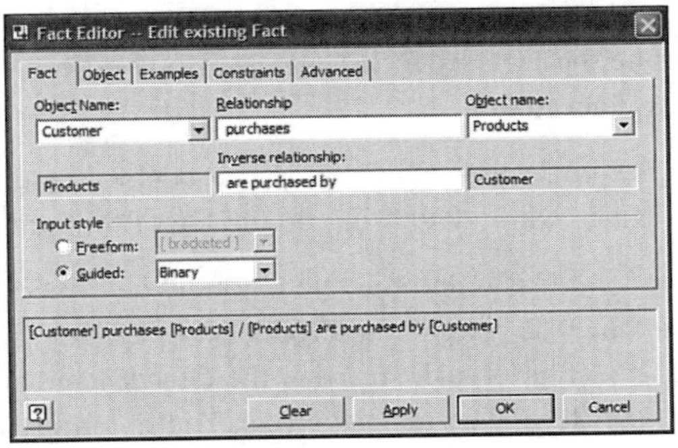

FIGURE 21.5

Creating the Customer/Products fact.

As you add each fact, you can see that the free-form text is displayed in the lower part of the Fact Editor. For the Customer/Products fact, the free-form text is

```
[Customer] purchases [Products] / [Products] are purchased by [Customer]
```

When you get to be an ORM wizard, you can modify the default view for adding facts to the Free Form view and add facts simply by typing the sentence.

If you click the OK button on the Fact Editor, you should see the Facts list in the Business Rules pane is filled with your facts. Your screen should look exactly like Figure 21.6.

FIGURE 21.6

The Facts list in the Business Rules window after you add your facts.

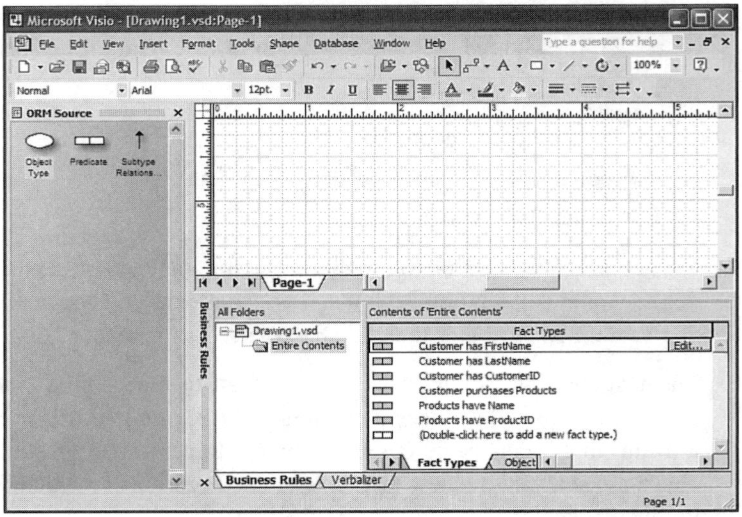

Now that all the facts are added, the basic structure of the model is in place. The next step is to further define the facts by modifying their properties in the Object tab and Constraints tab in the Fact Editor.

The first fact to modify is Customer purchases Products. Click the Edit button on this fact in the Business Rules window to bring up the Fact Editor, and click the Object tab.

Because each Product and Customer must be uniquely identified, you need to add an identifier for the Customer object and the Products object. To do so, select the Customer object in the Select Object list. Make sure that the Object Kind is set to Entity, not Value. Type **`CustomerID`** In the Reference/Identifier box. You're telling the Fact Editor that the Customer object is an entity with an identifier of CustomerID. In a database, an entity would be the row of data, and the value would be an attribute of that row. Your Fact Editor should look like Figure 21.7 after adding the reference/identifier entity attribute.

After you type in CustomerID for the Customer object, select the Products object from the Select Objects list, and type in **`ProductID`** for its reference/identifier. You've now defined the identifiers for the Customer and Product, so the two main tables in this conceptual model are starting to take shape.

Next, you must add some constraints for the Customer and Products objects. If you click the Constraints tab, you can see that the following two constraint questions must be answered:

- Each Customer purchases how many products?
- Each Products are purchased by how many Customers?

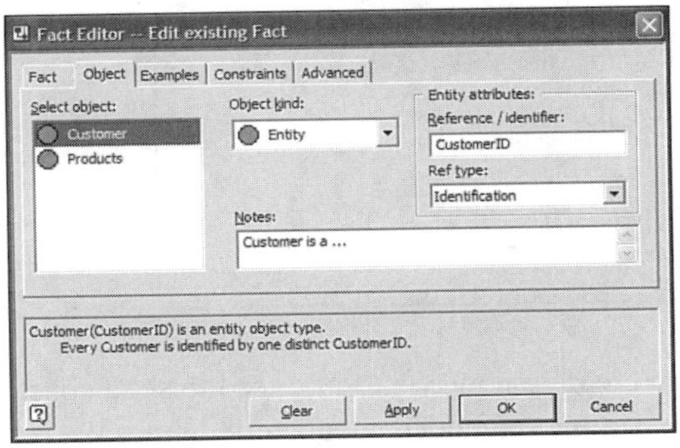

FIGURE 21.7

Fact Editor after adding an entity attribute for Customer.

For each question, you can select the relationship between the tables and the primary uniqueness of the objects between each other. For both constraint questions, the Zero or More constraint must be selected because each Customer can purchase Zero or More Products, and each Product can be purchased by Zero or More Customers.

The ORM text pane after setting up the Constraints should look like this:

```
[Customer] purchases [Products] / [Products] are purchased by [Customer]
        It is possible that some Customer purchases more than one Products
                and that some Products are purchased by more than one Customer.
```

In addition, your Fact Editor should look like Figure 21.8.

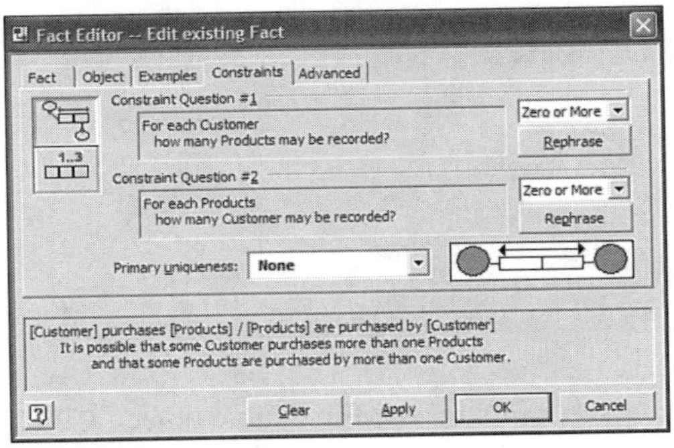

FIGURE 21.8

Fact Editor after adding Customer and Products constraints.

If the constraint must be defined further, you can click the Constraint Frequency button on the upper left of the Constraints tab to set maximum and minimum values for the constraints. Using this dialog box, it might be easier to set unique values for each object. Figure 21.9 shows what the Frequency Editor looks like, and how you might use it to define a One to Many relationship.

FIGURE 21.9

Using the Frequency Editor to define constraints.

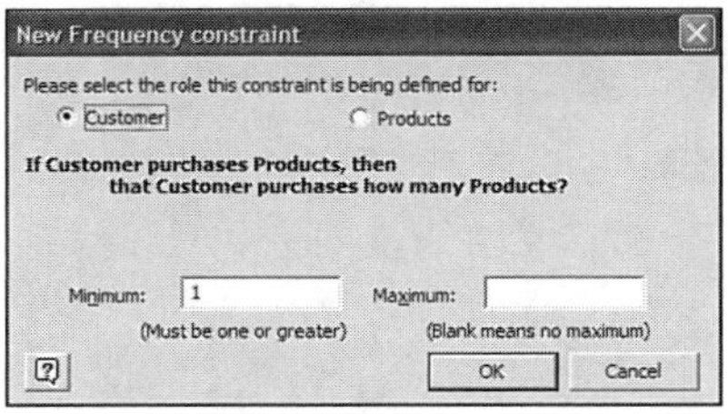

For the model you're creating now, you don't need to set a constraint frequency because the Zero or More constraint you added adequately defines the relationship between the Customer and Products roles.

At this point, you can click the OK button to close the Fact Editor and return to the Facts list in the Business Rules window. The next step is to define the properties for the remaining facts. To do so, select the Customer has FirstName fact, and click the Edit button in the Facts list to bring up the Fact Editor. When the Fact Editor is open, click the Object tab, and select FirstName from the Select Object list. Because the FirstName is a value of the entity Customer, you must set the Object Kind to Value, as Figure 21.10 shows.

FIGURE 21.10

Setting the Object Kind for the FirstName object.

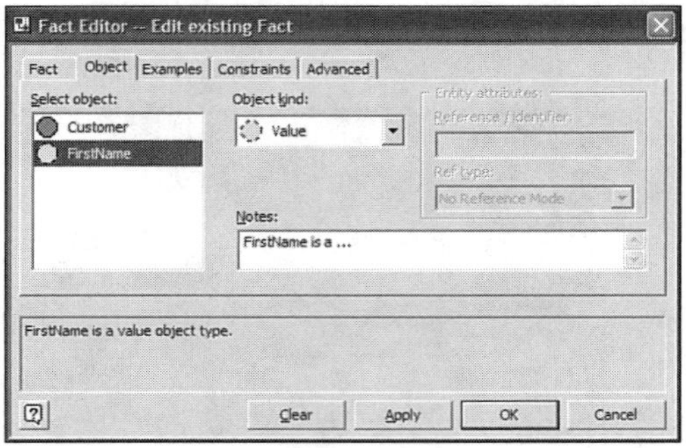

Next, you can set the constraints for the FirstName object. Click the Constraints tab; you'll see that Constraint Question #1 is "Each Customer has how many FirstName?". Set the value to Exactly Once because there can only be one FirstName for each customer. Set Constraint Question #2, "How many Customer has each FirstName?" to Zero or More. The phrase you have just built is

```
[Customer] has [FirstName]
        Each Customer has some FirstName.
        Each Customer has at most one FirstName.
```

This makes perfect sense when you think about designing database tables, and you can see that the conceptual design can be easily turned into a physical data model by setting properties and constraints on the objects in the ORM model.

The next step is to set the remaining properties on the facts. The following list is what you must do to set the remaining object properties and constraints. You're repeating the same steps you did for the FirstName fact.

- Customer has LastName: On the Object tab of the Fact Editor, set the LastName object as a value of the Customer object, and set the relationships on the Constraints tab to the following:

```
[Customer] has [LastName]
        Each Customer has some LastName.
        Each Customer has at most one LastName.
```

- Customer has CustomerID: On the Object tab of the Fact Editor, set the CustomerID object as a value of the Customer object, and set the relationships on the Constraints tab to the following:

```
[Customer] has [CustomerID]
        Each Customer has some CustomerID.
        For each CustomerID c, some Customer has CustomerID c.
        For each CustomerID y, at most one Customer has CustomerID y.
        Each Customer has at most one CustomerID.
```

- Products have Name: On the Object tab of the Fact Editor, set the Name object as a value of the Products object, and set the relationships on the Constraints tab to the following:

```
[Products] have [Name]
        Each Products have some Name.
        For each Name n, some Products have Name n.
        For each Name n, at most one Products have Name n.
        Each Products have at most one Name.
```

- Products have ProductID: On the Object tab of the Fact Editor, set the ProductID object as a value of the Products object, and set the relationships on the Constraints tab to the following:

```
[Products] have [ProductID]
        Each Products have some ProductID.
        For each ProductID p, some Products have ProductID p.
        For each ProductID y, at most one Products have ProductID y.
        Each Products have at most one ProductID.
```

You've now successfully set up the ORM model for the conceptual design of your new data model. Because you created all the facts not actually knowing whether they're correct, the best thing to do is to check the ORM model for errors.

Validating the Data Model

To validate the data model, select the Model Error Check item from the Database main menu. The model is checked for consistency errors in your facts, and you get a list of errors and warnings that make up the validation of the model in Visio's Output window.

For the model you just created, there'll be three warnings and no errors when the validation is complete. The Output window will have something similar to the following message:

```
Drawing1.vsd : Starting Conceptual Validation...
Drawing1.vsd : warning C1007: 'CustomerID'  :
  ➥Value object type playing mandatory role not recommended.
Drawing1.vsd : warning C1007: 'Name'  :
  ➥Value object type playing mandatory role not recommended.
Drawing1.vsd : warning C1007: 'ProductID'  :
  ➥Value object type playing mandatory role not recommended.
Drawing1.vsd : Conceptual Validation complete - 0 error(s) 3 warning(s)
```

Based on the constraints that were set up, the validation detected that although the model makes sense, there might be some problems with certain objects playing a mandatory role. In other words, the constraints were set to Exactly One or One or More. The CustomerID and ProductID facts are at fault because they were added as individual facts and as an identity reference for the Customer and Products facts. To fix these warnings, you can change the Constraint to Zero or More for the offending facts, but that isn't necessary to complete this exercise.

The next step is to move this conceptual model to a physical database. At this point, make sure that the drawing is saved, and remember its location; you'll need it in the next step.

Note

When working with ORM models and database models, Visio seems to churn and burn when opening and saving documents for the first time. This occurs only on the initial save, and subsequent saves are very fast. Don't end the Visio application prematurely if saving your model is taking a long time. It could take up to several minutes. Also, make sure that you've installed Visio Service Release 1 for Visio Enterprise Architects; it fixes many bugs in the ORM modeling feature.

Creating a Database Diagram from the Conceptual Model

To create a physical database from the conceptual model you just created, you must open a new Visio document database model diagram. From this new diagram, you add the ORM model. Follow these steps to get started:

1. From the File menu, select New, Database, Database Model Diagram (US Units).

   You're now at an empty Database Diagram model, with the Entity Relationships stencil docked to the left of the Visio IDE.

2. To add the ORM model, select Project, Add Existing Document from the Database menu.

   You're prompted with the Add Document to Project dialog box. Navigate to the saved ORM model, which in my case is `Drawing1.vsd` in the My Documents folder.

After the drawing is added, the Project pane is docked to the bottom of the IDE as shown in Figure 21.11.

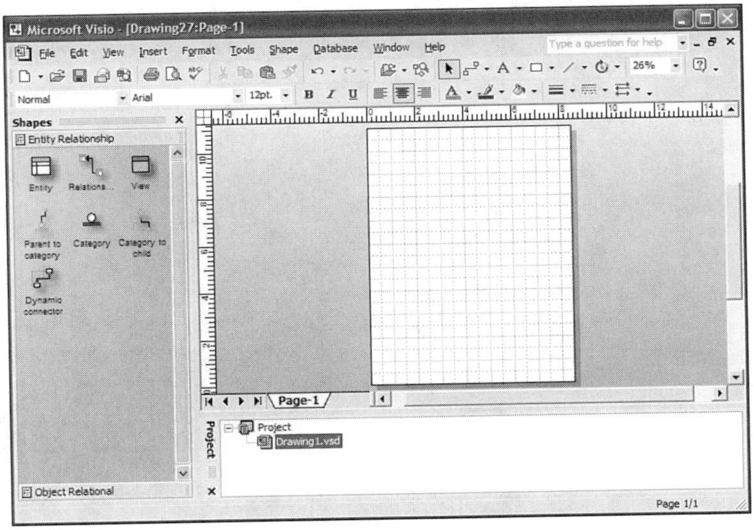

FIGURE 21.11

Database diagram drawing after adding the ORM model project.

The next step is to generate the physical database from the imported model. Using Visio, you can generate SQL scripts that can execute against a database to create the database, or you can use Visio to create the database and tables for you.

In this case, you're going to let Visio do all the work. The first step is to build the ORM model within the database diagram. To do so, select Build from the Database, Project menu. This step analyzes the facts of the ORM model and turns those facts into physical tables and views. When the build process is complete, your database diagram will have the Tables and Views pane open on the left of the screen (as Figure 21.12 shows) and the Output window will show the results of the build process. The Output window should list something similar to the following:

```
Starting Build...
C:\DOCUMENTS AND SETTINGS\JASON BERES\MY DOCUMENTS\DRAWING28.VSD :
     Updating existing database model project.
Drawing1.vsd : Merging Source Model.
Drawing1.vsd : warning C1007: 'CustomerID'  :
     Value object type playing mandatory role not recommended.
Drawing1.vsd : warning C1007: 'Name'  :
     Value object type playing mandatory role not recommended.
Drawing1.vsd : warning C1007: 'ProductID'  :
     Value object type playing mandatory role not recommended.
C:\DOCUMENTS AND SETTINGS\JASON BERES\MY DOCUMENTS\DRAWING28.VSD :
     Starting Mapping ...
C:\DOCUMENTS AND SETTINGS\JASON BERES\MY DOCUMENTS\DRAWING28.VSD :
     Tables(3) Columns(9) Logical Keys(9) Foreign Keys(2)
0 error(s), and 3 warning(s).
```

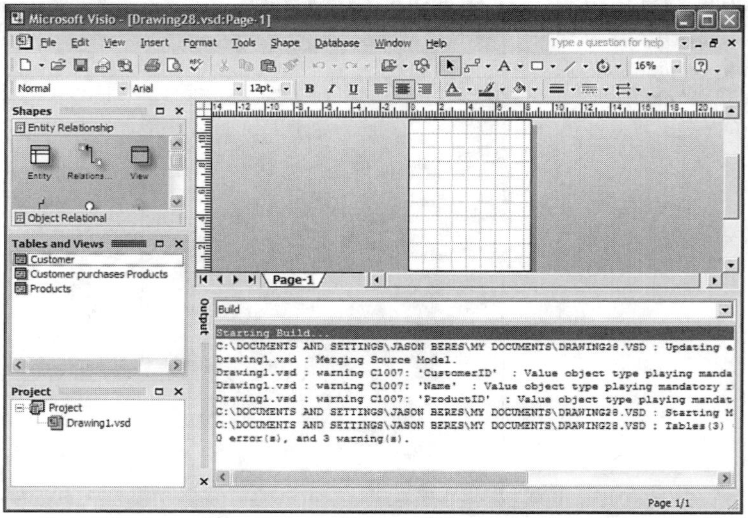

FIGURE 21.12
The Tables and Views window shown after you build the ORM model.

From the output, you can see that the build process created three tables, nine columns, and two foreign keys. The tables created are

- Customers
- Customer Purchases Products
- Products

From the Tables and Views window, drag the Customers table onto the drawing surface. When the table is added, right-click it and select Show Related Tables from the contextual menu. At this point, the Customer Purchases Products table is added to the diagram. To add the Products table, you can show the related tables from the Customer Purchases

Products table or just drag the table from the Table and Views window onto the drawing surface. You drawing should look something like Figure 21.13.

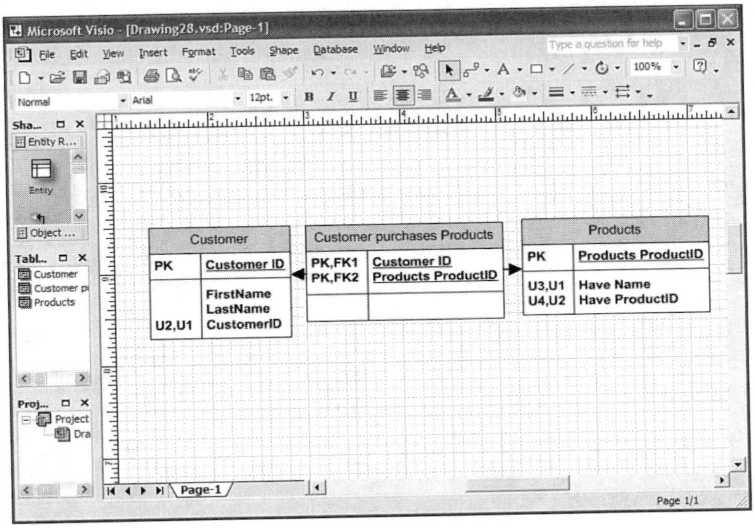

FIGURE 21.13
Database diagram after adding tables and views from the ORM model.

You can see that the table relationships are set up and the physical data model is starting to take shape. From what you learned earlier by adding facts to the table, you should be able to ascertain the following concepts:

- The CustomerID fact and ProductID fact aren't necessary because adding the entity reference takes care of setting the Primary Key information for the model.
- Adding mode value object types for each entity object further populates the database tables with the attributes that make up the entity object.
- Creating inverse relationships sets up the foreign key constraints between tables. The Customer Purchases Products table serves as the relationship link between the Customer and Products tables.

Now you can take the next logical step in the process and create the tables in SQL Server for the newly created database diagram.

Creating the Physical Database from the ORM Model

Using Visio, you can create the physical database from the conceptual model in any database that has an ODBC driver on your machine. The easiest way to accomplish this using the tools you have is to create an empty database in SQL Server using Visual Studio .NET, and then use Visio to create the tables using the information from the database diagram.

To do so, open Visual Studio .NET and make the Server Explorer visible. You aren't creating a project, you're just using the tools in the Server Explorer to create a database. After Visual Studio .NET is open, drill into your SQL Servers node. Right-click the NetSDK SQL instance and select New Database from the contextual menu, as Figure 21.14 demonstrates.

FIGURE 21.14

Getting to the SQL Servers node in Server Explorer.

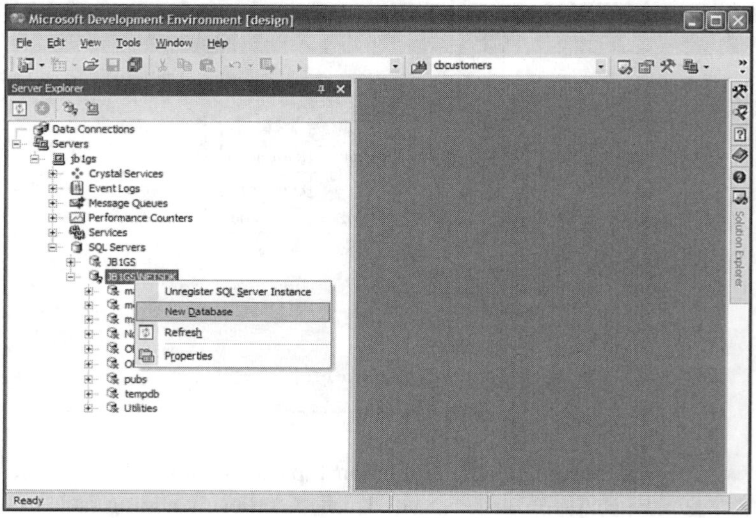

When you select New Database, the Create Database dialog box pops up. Enter **`ORM_Test`** as Figure 21.15 demonstrates and click the OK button to create the new database in SQL Server.

FIGURE 21.15

Creating a new database using the Create Database dialog box.

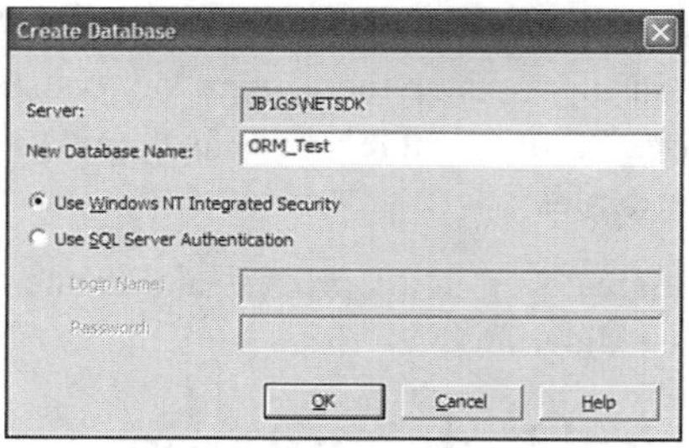

Return to Visio, and select Generate from the Database menu. The Generate Wizard dialog now pops up. The Generate Wizard guides you through moving the diagram into an actual database.

In the Generate Wizard dialog box, you have the options of generating the Data Definition Language (DDL) script, generating a new database, and storing the existing model in the database that you create. In this exercise, you're going to select all three options on the first step of the wizard. The dialog box should look like Figure 21.16.

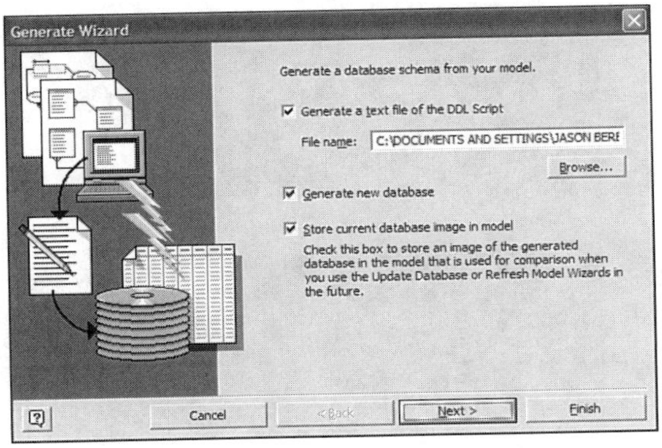

FIGURE 21.16
The first step of the Generate Wizard in Visio.

After you click the Next button, you're prompted to establish the database connection. Because you already created a database using Visual Studio .NET, select the Database Already Exists option (as Figure 21.17 demonstrates) and click Next.

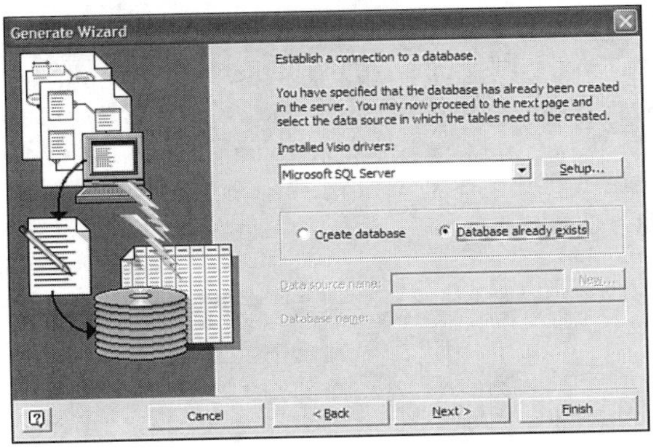

FIGURE 21.17
Establishing a connection to the database.

The next screen in the wizard lists the available ODBC connections on your machine. No ODBC connection is set up yet for the ORM_Test database, so click the New button to get the Create New Data Source dialog box as Figure 21.18 shows.

On the first screen of the Create Data Source Wizard, you must enter the friendly name and the server for the database you're connecting. In this case, you can name the data source **`ORM_Test`**, and set the server name to ***`your machine name`*****`\NetSDK`**, as you see in Figure 21.19.

FIGURE 21.18

Create New Data Source dialog box.

FIGURE 21.19

Setting the name and server for the new data source.

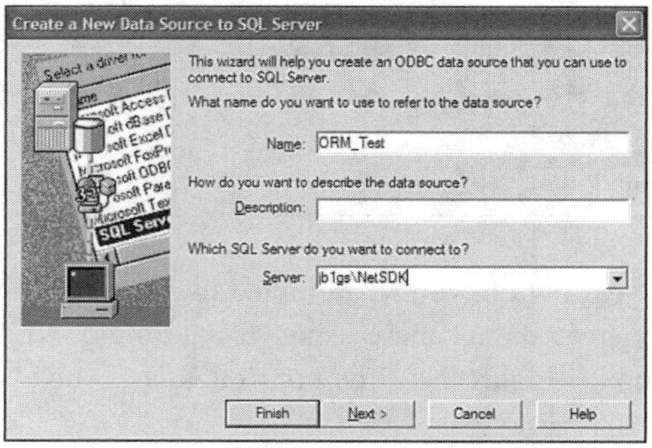

After you click Next, you're taken to the authentication setup for this server. Make sure that Windows Authentication is selected, and click the Next button. At this point, you must change the default database to which you'll be connecting. Click the Change the Default Database To check box and find the ORM_Test database you created earlier in the list, as Figure 21.20 shows.

FIGURE 21.20

Setting the default database for the ORM_Test database.

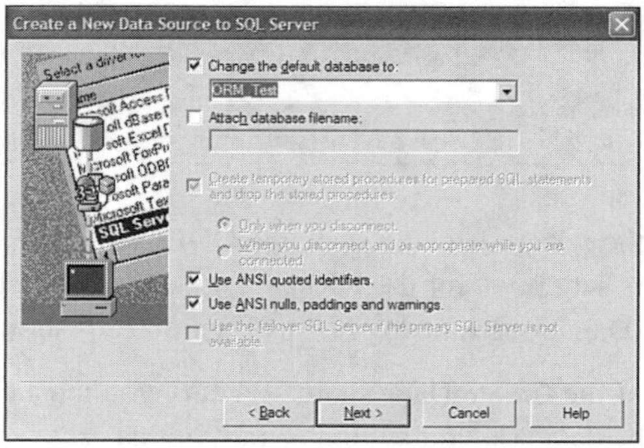

Now you can click Next, Next, and Finish to finalize the creation of the new data source. The data source is created and you're taken back to the Generate Wizard, which lists all the available data sources on your machine. Select the ORM_Test data source, as Figure 21.21 demonstrates, and click the Next button.

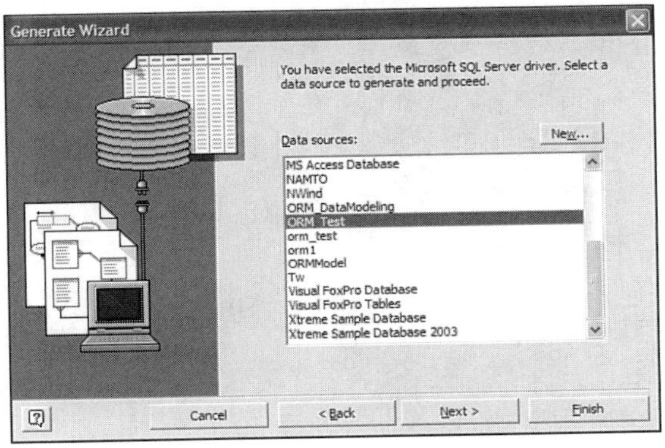

FIGURE 21.21
Selecting the ORM_Test data source in the Generate Wizard.

You're now prompted for the authentication information that Figure 21.22 shows. You can click the OK button at this dialog because the data source is set up to use Windows Authentication.

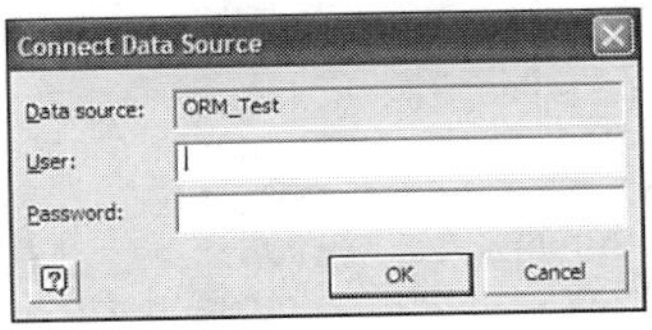

FIGURE 21.22
Setting the authentication on the data source.

You're given the review list of tables that will be created in the database. Figure 21.23 is what you should see now.

At this point, you can click Finish and the process of Visio connecting to the data source and creating the databases occurs. As the database is being created, your Output window shows the progress of the tables being created and any errors or warnings that occur in the Generate Wizard.

When the generation completes, the Code Editor pops up inside Visio and shows you the DDL scripts that were used to create the physical database. Listing 21.1 is the DDL script that Visio generated to build the ORM_Test database tables.

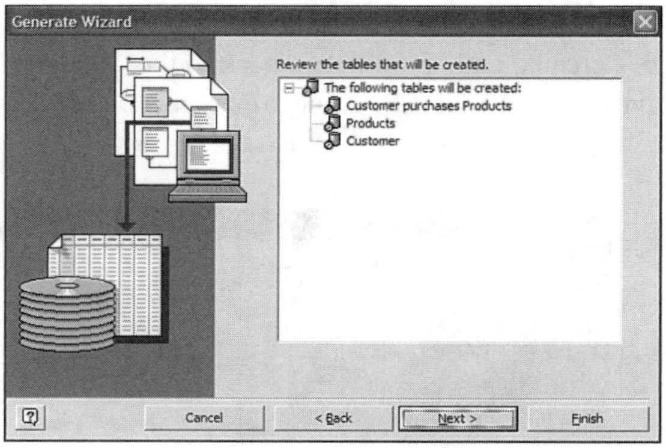

FIGURE 21.23
Reviewing the tables for the database.

LISTING 21.1 DDL Script Generated by Visio for the ORM_Test Database

```
/*    This SQL DDL script was generated by */
/*    Microsoft Visual Studio (Release Date: LOCAL BUILD).*/
/*    Driver Used :
/*    Microsoft Visual Studio - Microsoft SQL Server Driver.*/
/*    Document    :
/*    C:\DOCUMENTS AND SETTINGS\JASON BERES\MY DOCUMENTS\DRAWING28.VSD.*/
/*    Operation   :  From Visio Generate Wizard.*/
/*    Connected data source : ORM_Test          */
/*    Connected server      : JB1GS\NETSDK      */
/*    Connected database    : orm_test          */

/* Create new table "Customer purchases Products".    */
/* "Customer purchases Products" : Customer purchases Products
/*    / Products are purchased by Customer */
/*      "Customer ID" : Customer purchases Products     */
/*      "Products ProductID" : Products are purchased by Customer   */
create table "Customer purchases Products" (
        "Customer ID" char(10) not null,
        "Products ProductID" char(10) not null) ON 'PRIMARY'
go

alter table "Customer purchases Products"
        add constraint "Customer purchases Products_PK"
        primary key clustered ("Customer ID", "Products ProductID")
go

/* Create new table "Products".                              */
/* "Products" : Table of Products                            */
/*      "Products ProductID" : ProductID identifies Products   */
/*      "Have Name" : Products have Name                       */
/*      "Have ProductID" : Products have ProductID             */
create table "Products" (
        "Products ProductID" char(10) not null,
```

LISTING 21.1 continued

```
        "Have Name" char(10) not null,
        "Have ProductID" char(10) not null) ON 'PRIMARY'
go

alter table "Products"
   add constraint "Products_PK" primary key clustered
   ("Products ProductID")
go

/* Create new table "Customer".                              */
/* "Customer" : Table of Customer                            */
/*       "Customer ID" : CustomerID identifies Customer      */
/*       "FirstName" : Customer has FirstName                */
/*       "LastName" : Customer has LastName                  */
/*       "CustomerID" : Customer has CustomerID              */
create table "Customer" (
        "Customer ID" char(10) not null,
        "FirstName" char(10) not null,
        "LastName" char(10) not null,
        "CustomerID" char(10) not null) ON 'PRIMARY'
go

alter table "Customer"
       add constraint "Customer_PK" primary key
       clustered ("Customer ID")
go

/* Add the remaining keys, constraints and indexes
           for the table "Products".                        */
create unique index "Products_AK1" on "Products" (
        "Have Name") ON 'PRIMARY'
go

create unique index "Products_AK2" on "Products" (
        "Have ProductID") ON 'PRIMARY'
go

alter table "Products" add constraint "Products_AK1_UC1" unique (
        "Have Name")
go

alter table "Products" add constraint "Products_AK2_UC1" unique (
        "Have ProductID")
go

/* Add the remaining keys, constraints and indexes */
/* for the table "Customer". */
create unique index "Customer_AK1" on "Customer" (
        "CustomerID") ON 'PRIMARY'
go
```

LISTING 21.1 continued

```
alter table "Customer" add constraint "Customer_AK1_UC1"
        unique ("CustomerID")
go

/* Add foreign key constraints to table "Customer purchases Products". */
alter table "Customer purchases Products"
        add constraint "Customer_Customer purchases Products_
          FK1" foreign key (
          "Customer ID")
           references "Customer" (
           "Customer ID") on update no action on delete no action
go

alter table "Customer purchases Products"
        add constraint "Products_Customer purchases
        Products_FK1" foreign key (
        "Products ProductID")
        references "Products" (
        "Products ProductID") on update no action on delete no action
go

/* This is the end of the Microsoft Visual Studio */
/* generated SQL DDL script.*/
```

If you go back to Visual Studio .NET, you'll see the tables that have been created from Visio. Figure 21.24 shows the Customer table in design mode in SQL Server.

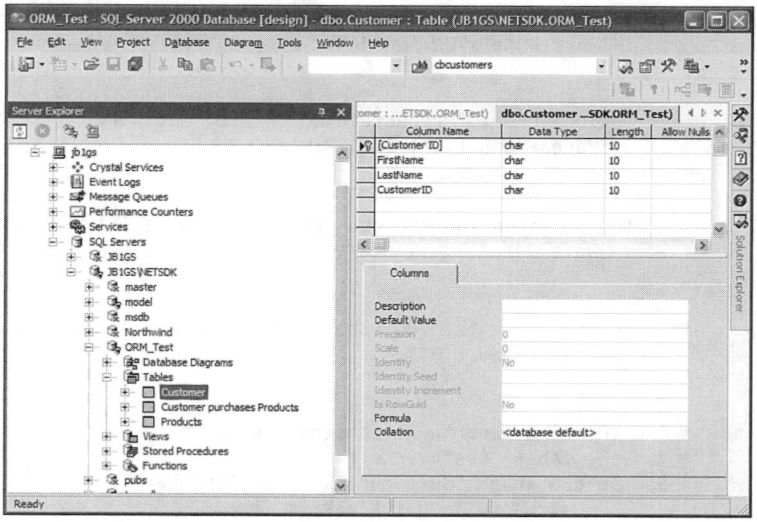

FIGURE 21.24

Customer table created by Visio in the Server Explorer.

Notice that each of the fields is `varchar(10)`, which isn't desirable in real life. In Visio, you can use the Object Types tab in the Business Rules window to modify data types and the lengths of fields.

Now that the database diagram in Visio has created the physical SQL Server database, you can modify either the model or the database and keep them both in sync using the tools in Visio. That's the two-way street that Visio has with either a database or an ORM diagram: You can manage each project from Visio and update them all from a central location.

Summary

Today you created a new ORM model, used it to create a database diagram, and used the diagram to create a physical database in SQL Server. You learned that by adding facts to the ORM model and setting roles and constraints on those facts, you can easily create a useful conceptual database model. After you've broken down the conceptual process into logical plain-English sentences, you can use Visio and Visual Studio .NET to manage your conceptual data models and physical databases using database diagram projects along with the ORM models that you create. The next step in understanding ORM is to use the tools in Visio to reverse-engineer a good example of a normalized database, such as the Pubs or Northwind databases that ship with MSDE and Visual Studio .NET. Doing so will help you understand how those facts make up the model that in turn creates the database.

Q&A

Q ORM is cool, but it seems like overkill. I'm a consultant, and this is a lot of work to go through each time I start a new project. Is it really necessary?

A That's a good point. Using ORM models to define a conceptual data model before you create a physical model is completely up to you. The nice thing about doing a conceptual model first is that it can help you really understand what needs to happen with the project. By interviewing the users of the system you're building and taking the information they give you and plugging it into a data model, you're actually building the physical database at the same time. Also, after the model is in the database, you can update Visio and then update the database using Visio, so you're actually creating a nice audit of everything you're doing. It isn't a bad practice to get into, but I think you must be disciplined if you decide to do it.

Q I'm trying to reverse-engineer a database in Visio as you suggested. But I keep running into problems after I create the data source and try to run the reverse-engineering process. Why?

A When reverse-engineering a database, make sure that you set up the correct Visio database drivers by selecting the Drivers menu item from the Tools, Options menu. This must be set up in conjunction with the OBDC data source you're reverse-engineering.

Quiz

1. Using the ___________, you can set an entity reference field for an object.
2. When you're done with the ORM model, you create a new _________ drawing and import the ORM model into it.
3. True or False: When you run the Generate Wizard to create the physical database, you must use the DDL script along with the tables created in SQL Server to finish creating the database.
4. When you add an _________________, you're really just setting up the primary and foreign key values between two tables.

Quiz Answers

1. Fact Editor
2. Database diagram
3. False. The DDL scripts are the scripts that generate the database, so they don't need to be used after the database has been created.
4. Inverse relationship

Exercises

1. Using the original ORM model that you created, add a Manufacturer role that has an inverse relationship with the Products role.

   The question you should use is

   ```
   Manufacturers create Products
   ```

   The inverse relationship is

   ```
   Products are created by Manufacturers
   ```

Add a few value references for the Manufacturer role, such as ManufacturerName, ManufacturerCity, and so on. You should also add an entity reference called ManufacturerID for the Manufacturer object.

After you've done that, re-create the database diagram and re-create the ORM_Test database in SQL Server.

2. In Visio, use the Reverse Engineer option from the Database menu in a new Database Diagram project. Reverse-engineer the Northwind database in your MSDE database, and study how the database was created based on the conceptual model that was reverse-engineered.

WEEK 3

In Review

Week 3 covered a broad range of interesting topics. You learned how to write internationally aware applications, how to automate your Visual Studio .NET environment, how to build reports, and how to keep your code safe with Microsoft Visual SourceSafe. You also learned how to stress test your applications, and you got insight in conceptual data design using object role modeling with Visio.

On Day 15, you learned how to use the globalization namespaces in .NET to write applications that are culturally aware. You learned how easy it is to correctly format controls on forms, currency data, and date/time data for different culture locales using the tools in Visual Studio .NET.

On Day 16, you were introduced to automation in Visual Studio .NET with macros. By writing your own macros, you learned that it's simple to automate repetitive tasks in the IDE. You learned how to use the macro recorder, and how to customize the code that the macro recorder generates to write automation code.

Day 17 took the knowledge you gained on Day 16 and applied it to writing add-ins. Add-ins are separate applications that you write in your .NET language of choice that can hook into the Visual Studio .NET IDE to give you more control than macros can. Writing applications with the Add-ins project templates enables you to develop compelling applications that interact and control the Visual Studio .NET IDE.

On Day 18, you were introduced to Crystal Reports for Visual Studio .NET. You learned how easy it is to write data-driven reports using either the push model or the pull model that

Crystal can use when working with data. You also learned how easy it is to use the Report Viewer control for both Windows Forms and Web Forms.

Day 20 ran you through the ins and outs of using Visual SourceSafe to control and manage your source code from Visual Studio .NET. You learned that by using SourceSafe's check-in and check-out functions, you have a complete history of changes made to your source code. You also saw how to roll back changes made to your code by using the tools in Visual Studio .NET and how to compare your code to the checked-in version of the code that SourceSafe is controlling.

Day 21 introduced you to conceptual data design using object role modeling templates in Visio. You learned that by breaking down a process into plain-English sentences, you can use the tools in Visio to create conceptual data models. Finally, you learned how to take the conceptual model written in Visio to a database diagram template to create a fully normalized SQL Server database.

INDEX

A

B

C

D

E

F

G

H

I

J–K

L

M

N

O

P

Q–R

S

T

U – V

W

X–Y–Z

Other Related Titles

Sams Teach Yourself VB .NET in 24 Hours
James Foxall
ISBN: 0-672-32080-0
$29.99US/$44.95CAN

ASP.NET Unleashed
Stephen Walther
ISBN: 0-672-32068-1
$54.99US/$85.99CAN

STY Crystal Reports 9 in 24 Hours
Joe Estes, et. al.
ISBN: 0-672-32090-8
$24.99US/$38.99CAN

Sams Teach Yourself SQL in 21 Days, Fourth Edition
Ryan Stephens and Ronald Plew
ISBN: 0-672-32451-2
$39.99US/$62.99CAN

ASP.NET Kick Start
Stephen Walther
ISBN: 0-672-32476-8
$34.99US/$54.99CAN

Sams Teach Yourself Windows.NET Forms in 21 Days
Chris Payne
ISBN: 0-672-32320-6
$39.99US/$62.99CAN

Sams Teach Yourself C# in 24 Hours
James D. Foxall, et. al.
ISBN: 0-672-32067-0
$29.99US/$44.95CAN

SAMS
www.samspublishing.com

All prices are subject to change.